John Stuart Mill

Richard Reeves is a leading social and political commentator, writing regularly for the *Observer*, *New Statesman*, *Guardian* and *Prospect*. He is a former Columnist of the Year and Young Financial Journalist of the Year and has held research fellowships at the Institute for Public Policy Research and the University of London. He lives in Buckinghamshire with his partner and three sons.

'Mill's work, especially *On Liberty* and *The Subjection of Women* – seems more resonant and provocative than ever these days... Richard Reeves is a first time biographer and a first-rate writer.' Susannah Herbert, *Sunday Times*

'In this lucid study, Reeves offers a timely re-evaluation of the father of British Liberalism.' Marc Lambert, *Scotland on Sunday*

'It is a brave biographer who tackles a subject as complex and controversial as J. S. Mill. Richard Reeves has succeeded in doing this with enviable style. I blush to say it so bluntly, but this is the best book I have read for a long time... Reeves is a good reader of Mill. He interrogates the texts, teasing out consistent lines of thought from adolescence to old age and highlighting Mill's changes of tack and intellectual evasions. He is no starry-eyed Millite, as modern liberals can be: he does not let his subject off the hook easily or present him as someone who can give us easy answers... Richard Reeves reminds us that in Mill's life and thought we do not find ways of solving specific problems but values that enrich democracy and personal life.' Ben Wilson, *Literary Review*

'Reeves' examination of Mill's thought is meticulously explored in parallel with his life... Reeves' account of Mill's strange childhood is tremendously moving. His sympathy for his subject becomes even more apparent as we move through the rest of Mill's life. The epilogue is a poignant farewell, reminding us that Mill was in large part responsible for shaping the world we live in today... Speaking of Mill's lasting influence, Reeves says: "The world he left was unquestionably better for his efforts. It still is." And we are better off for this book. Though it is a tragedy that a man whose life was dedicated to the pursuit of truth and liberty for all should spend his own in periodic misery, we are fortunate in at last having a biography that does justice to this sacrifice.' Milo Andreas Wagner, *Catholic Herald*

'Timely and readable... Reeves tells his stories well, and if he is right we should be looking to Mill for inspiration and enlightenment in our perplexing political times.' Jonathan Ree, *Prospect*

'Beautifully done... Reeves is right to devote a lot of space to Mill the activist; by doing so he puts Mill the thinker into context and converts him from a piece of uplifting statuary into a creature of flesh and blood.' David Marquand, *New Statesman*

'A fine new biography... A brave and very successful attempt to fit together the biographical details of Mill's life – his extraordinary childhood and education, his enduring love for Harriet – with the aspects of his philosophical writing which might have relevance today.' Laurie Taylor, 'Thinking Allowed', BBC Radio 4

'This lucid biography intermingling Mill's life and an account of his ideas could not have come at a more timely moment – when both socialism and liberalism have lost their way. Any reconstruction of British liberalism will surely need to incorporate Mill's ideas. This book represents their best contemporary compass.' Will Hutton

John Stuart Mill

VICTORIAN FIREBRAND

Richard Reeves

ATLANTIC BOOKS

LONDON

For Beth

First published in Great Britain in 2007 by Atlantic Books, an imprint of Grove Atlantic Ltd.

This paperback edition published in Great Britain in 2008 by Atlantic Books.

Copyright © Richard Reeves 2007

The moral right of Richard Reeves to be identified as the author of this work has been asserted in accordance with the Copyright, Designs and Patents Act of 1988.

1 3 5 7 9 8 6 4 2

A CIP catalogue record for this book is available from the British Library.

ISBN 978 1 84354 644 3

Designed by Nicky Barneby @ Barneby Ltd
Set in 11.75/14.75pt Adobe Caslon
Printed in Great Britain

Atlantic Books
An imprint of Grove Atlantic Ltd
Ormond House
26–27 Boswell Street
London WC1N 3JZ

Contents

><

List of Illustrations   vii

   Prologue   1
1. An Unusual and Remarkable Education (1806–20)   11
2. A Man Among Men (1820–6)   28
3. Strange Confusion (1826–30)   62
4. This Imperfect Companionship (1830–6)   80
5. Laid Hold of by Wolves: Conservative Influences   106
6. Independence (1836–42)   129
7. Eminence (1843–7)   161
8. French Revolutionary (1848)   185
9. A Dismal Science? (1848–52)   204
10. A Seven-Year Blessing (1852–8)   238
11. *On Liberty* (1859)   262
12. To Hell I Will Go (1859–65)   307
13. A Short, Bad Parliament (1865–8)   354
14. The Father of Feminism   413
15. Final Years (1868–73)   449
   Epilogue   481

Notes   489
Bibliography   582
Index   594
Acknowledgements   615

List of Illustrations

1. James Mill. Getty Images, 2757773.
2. Jeremy Bentham. Mary Evans Picture Library, 10002734.
3. Forde Abbey, 1817. Thomas Moore, *The History of Devonshire from the earliest period to the present . . . Illustrated by a series of Views, drawn & engraved under the direction of William Deeble*, vol. 1, London, 1829–30.
4. David Ricardo. Mary Evans Picture Library, 10037449.
5. John Arthur Roebuck. Getty Images, 3207249.
6. John Sterling. Courtesy of the author.
7. William Wordsworth. Mary Evans Picture Library, 10022170.
8. John Stuart Mill. Box 10, Mill-Taylor papers, LSE Archives.
9. Harriet Taylor. Courtesy of the State Library of South Australia, PRG 101/13.
10. John Taylor. Box 4, Mill-Taylor papers, LSE Archives.
11. Paris Revolution, 1830. Mary Evans Picture Library, 10197861.
12. Samuel Taylor Coleridge. Time & Life Pictures/Getty Images, 50683387.
13. Alexis de Tocqueville. Mary Evans Picture Library, 10038006.
14. Thomas Carlyle. Getty Images, 3276158.
15. Thomas Babington Macaulay. Mary Evans Picture Library, 10079857.
16. East India House, *c.*1850. Guildhall Library, q4025244.

17. William Molesworth. Mary Evans Picture Library, 10043224.
18. Francois Guizot. Mary Evans Picture Library, 10197452.
19. Auguste Comte. Mary Evans Picture Library, 10073295.
20. Harriet Taylor Mill. National Portrait Gallery, 5489.
21. Charles Kingsley. Mary Evans Picture Library, 10035367.
22. Thomas Hare. National Portrait Gallery, 1819.
23. Henry Fawcett and Millicent Fawcett, née Garrett. National Portrait Gallery, 1603.
24. 'Westminster Election: The Nomination in Covent Garden'. *Illustrated London News*, 22 July 1865.
25. Westminster Parliamentary Constituency. *Parliamentary Papers*, vol. 10, 1867–8.
26. Benjamin Disraeli addressing the Commons. Mary Evans Picture Library, 10047340.
27. Reform League Demonstration, July 1866. Mary Evans Picture Library, 10131860.
28. 'Miss Mill Joins the Ladies'. *Judy*, 2 November 1868.
29. 'The Westminster Guy', 1868. Public domain.
30. John Stuart Mill in *Vanity Fair*, 1873. Mary Evans Picture Library, 10039769.
31. John Stuart Mill and Helen Taylor. Hulton Archive/Getty Images, 2628338.
32. Charles Wentworth Dilke and Emilia Frances Dilke, née Strong. Mary Evans Picture Library, 10024509.
33. John Morley. Mary Evans Picture Library, 10076125.
34. Mill's grave in Avignon, France. Archives Municipales d'Avignon.
35. Millicent Fawcett's delegation to Mill's statue. Hulton Archive/Getty Images, 3335072.
36. John Stuart Mill. Hulton Archive/Getty Images, 3321219.

Dates of images have been omitted as in many cases it has proven impossible to establish these accurately.

Prologue

> ⤐ ⤏

Striding across St James's Park on his way to work, John Stuart Mill noticed a bundle lying beneath a tree. He carefully unpeeled layers of dirty blankets. Within them lay a newborn, newly killed baby. The previous summer's night had been warm, so those responsible had taken no chances, strangling the infant before discarding it.

Mill reported his find to a watchman, who would not have been surprised: London in 1823 was full of poor families who could not afford another child. Mill, however, was moved to action. With a friend, he toured a working-class district of London distributing a pamphlet which described and advocated contraception. The handbill, written by the campaigner Richard Carlile, contained the following advice: 'A piece of soft sponge is tied by a bobbin or penny ribbon, and inserted just before the sexual intercourse takes place, and is withdrawn again as soon as it has taken place. Many tie a piece of sponge to each end of the ribbon, and they take care not to use the same sponge again until it has been washed. If the sponge be large enough – that is, as large as a green walnut, or small apple it will prevent conception ...'[1] The pamphleteers were arrested for the promotion of obscenity and duly appeared before the magistrate at Bow Street. Once he realized who was in the dock, the magistrate lost his nerve, and referred the case to the Lord

Mayor of London. Despite an eloquent self-defence, John Stuart Mill lost his liberty for a couple of days.[2]

The youthful criminal – Mill was just seventeen – would subsequently become the highest-ranking philosopher of his century and the foremost public intellectual in British history. To this day he retains his status as the authentic voice of modern liberty. Already by that summer of 1823 he had embarked on a successful career in the East India Company, impressed the members of the Cambridge Union and completed a prodigious course of home schooling which is famous to this day – at the age of eight he had devoured Demosthenes in the original Greek.

Mill's family and friends, fearing irrevocable damage to his future prospects, worked hard to brush the incident under the carpet. Mill himself worried about the loss of some correspondence which detailed it. The damage limitation exercise was mostly successful: there was no public discussion of these events during Mill's lifetime, even when his past was raked over during two turbulent election campaigns. But the story was transmitted through the salons and clubs of London by means of doggerel verse, an important Victorian broadcasting device:

> There are two Mr M . . ls, too, whom those who like reading
> What's vastly unreadable, call very clever;
> And whereas M . . l senior makes war on *good* breeding
> M . . l junior makes war on all *breeding* whatever.

This stanza was reprinted in the obituary of Mill published by *The Times* fifty years after the incident, as evidence of his foolishness.[3] But this adolescent adventure by the 'boy-philosopher', as his friend Willliam Christie described him, speaks volumes about the true character of John Stuart Mill.[4] Far from being a 'Saint of Rationalism', as Gladstone affectionately dubbed him, he was a passionate man of action. John Morley, a Liberal politician and writer, often seen as 'Mill's representative on earth', described him as 'a man of extreme sensibility and vital heat in things worth waxing hot about'.[5] He was a philosopher, but he was a firebrand too.

Mill became an accomplished polemicist, firing off an article a week on Irish land reform throughout 1846, as the people of that nation starved under the inequities of the system he railed against. He was a humane administrator of Indian affairs, coming to hold one of the highest official posts in the East India Company by the time the Indian Mutiny boiled over. Mill was also a passionately engaged politician, fighting to preserve the rights of free speech and demonstration in public parks, ensuring that to this day, a corner of Hyde Park still represents this precious freedom, and attracting almost universal opprobrium for his legal pursuit of a murderous colonial governor. His political activism was lifelong: his last public speech just two months before his death, arguing for a redistribution of land rights, led to his ejection from the free-trade Cobden Club on the grounds of dangerous radicalism. As an enthusiastic botanical collector, Mill was observed, in his later years, with 'his trousers turned up out of the mud, and armed with the tin insignia of his craft, busily occupied in the search for a marsh-loving rarity in a typical spongy wood on the clay to the north of London'.[6] He was similarly unafraid to get his hands dirty in the political arena.

In his own day, Mill was accused of being 'an acrimonious partisan' and of 'descending too easily from the judgement-seat to the arena', but this was precisely the source of his greatness.[7] As an intellectual, Mill was constantly engaging with the problems of the real world. 'His life was not stimulated by mere intellectual curiosity,' wrote Morley, 'but by the resolute purpose of furthering human improvement'.[8] Mill was not the kind of philosopher who sat in a silent study, engaged in the painstaking construction of theoretical systems, according to which society should be remoulded; he was not in this sense a 'systematic' thinker. Whether this makes him a lesser one is another question: the systems generated by purer philosophers have often been of little use in dealing with the practical issues of real life – or worse, have been the inspiration for some of the most oppressive societies in modern history. Mill himself was dismissive of anyone who was a 'mere thinker'[9] and said that 'few of the systems of these systematic writers have any value as systems; their value is the value of some of their fragments'.[10] Mill's claim to our attention is not principally based on his treatises on Logic or Political Economy, canonical though they are in the history of Western thought (Thomas Carlyle's attack on Mill's economics as 'a dismal science' has unfortunately stuck to the discipline ever since). His greatest works are his taut *cris de cœur*, particularly *The Subjection of Women* and *On Liberty*.

In any case, Mill never acquired the necessary restraint of an elevated soothsayer. In political battles he would use all the polemic tools at his disposal; the Tories, for example, were 'the stupid party', though he later clarified his view in Parliament: 'I never meant to say that the Conservatives are generally stupid. I meant to say that stupid people are generally Conservative.'[11] Even those who influenced Mill were not immune. The poet-philosopher Samuel Taylor Coleridge, whose work Mill admired, was nevertheless an 'arrant driveller' on matters of political economy;[12] the Scottish writer Thomas Carlyle a 'true voice for the Devil' when addressing the issue of race.[13] Thomas Babington Macaulay, the eminent Whig historian, was, according to Mill, 'an intellectual dwarf, rounded off and stunted, full grown broad and short, without a germ or principle of further growth in his entire being'.[14]

The received picture of Mill as a bone-dry, formal, humourless Victorian is, then, a gross distortion. But the misrepresentation is partly his fault: his *Autobiography* presented an aloof portrait, a life, as one reviewer suggested, of 'monotonous joylessness'.[15] Mill's tone was one of observation, rather than confession, and the *Autobiography* certainly contained no startling revelations about Mill's eighteen-year relationship with the married Harriet Taylor, one of the most discussed affairs of the nineteenth century. Indeed, one of the explicit purposes of the book was to present an image of their partnership as a platonic one of intellect and spirit, rather than of a sexual nature. Mill did, in the end, marry Harriet, but he had to wait two decades.

In the course of his extraordinary life of action and reflection, Mill engaged with many of the great thinkers, politicians and writers of his day. William Gladstone was heavily influenced by Mill's economics; and Alexis de Tocqueville bound Mill's review of his landmark book *De la démocratie en Amerique* (*Democracy in America*) into his own working copy, on the grounds that the two had to be read together for his own work to be fully appreciated.[16] Mill made Alfred Tennyson's reputation, but almost stopped Robert Browning from writing. George Grote, the great Greek historian, was a lifelong friend. Mill duelled with Benjamin Disraeli in Parliament, and drew the young Millicent Fawcett, one of the most successful campaigners for women's rights in British history, to the hustings in the pursuit of women's rights – and helped to persuade Florence Nightingale of the same cause. Mill's much-tested friendship with Thomas Carlyle survived the accidental burning by Mill's maid of the only copy of the first volume of Carlyle's monumental history of the French revolution.

While Carlyle railed against almost all the changes of the modern world – for him, the 1867 Reform Act, which gave some of the working class the vote, represented 'the end of our poor old England'[17] – Mill assisted in the triumph of the idea of progress. Despite his many concerns about the future, he retained a progressive conviction that people, nations, cities and institutions could all, by the application of sound moral principles and robust social science, be made better. It was the self-declared duty of 'public moralists', such as Matthew Arnold, Walter Bagehot, John Morley and Henry Fawcett, to work tirelessly for the betterment of humankind.[18] But Mill stood above them all, with his unique combination of intellectual muscularity, forensic prose and personal passion.

Mill was raised by his father, James Mill, the historian of India – who was actively assisted in the task by the philosopher Jeremy Bentham – to be an apostle for utilitarianism, the rationalist philosophy founded on the scientific promotion of 'the greatest happiness to the greatest number'. For a few years, the utilitarian torch burned brightly in the young Mill's hands. After a self-described 'mental crisis', effectively a mid-life crisis at the age of twenty, Mill fell under the spell of poetry – famously dismissed by Bentham as merely lines that fell short of the margin – and began his journey away from the starker versions of utilitarianism towards a profound belief in the inalienable value of individual liberty. Mill was raised to promote 'happiness for the greatest number', but came to see that freedom was both necessary for and superior to happiness.

The animating idea at the heart of Mill's life and work is individual liberty. His image of a good society was one in which every man (and, he would add, every woman) can shape the course of their own life. This is not to say that Mill's liberalism was of the anything-goes, morally neutral, laissez-faire variety. He certainly considered that people should be free to live as they saw fit, as long as they did not harm others. But at the heart of his liberalism was a clearly and repeatedly articulated vision of a flourishing human life – self-improving, passionate, truth-seeking, engaged and colourful – which it was the job of individuals to cultivate, and the duty of society to promote. Mill wanted our lives to be free, but he also wanted them to be good.

For Mill, the principal enemy of individual freedom was not the law, but the attitudes of society. He argued presciently that the 'despotism of custom' could be as threatening to liberty as the tyranny of the state. Mill feared the stifling effects of public opinion, and heaped praise on eccentricity, individualism and 'experiments in living'. For Mill, to take a course of action simply because it was 'the thing to do' was to make no choice at all. His liberalism similarly fuelled his support for freedom of speech. He had a lifelong thirst for dissent, heterodoxy, and for the collision of opposing views. It was in the competition between and subsequent fusing together of opposing arguments, each usually containing a 'half-truth', that Mill believed the whole truth was to be found.

His liberalism was also at the heart of his support for gender equality. With typical pungency Mill wrote that in England 'there remain no legal slaves except the mistress of every house'.[19] In Mill's time, married women had no formal legal status regarding their property or their own children; and of course women had no vote. Mill was the first MP to put down legislation to give women the vote, winning seventy-four votes to his side, and was the moving spirit in the National Society for Women's Suffrage. Millicent Fawcett described him as the 'principal originator of the women's movement'.[20] In fact his support for women's rights provoked more hostility than any other position; but his liberalism could have led him nowhere else. For Mill, every individual, black or white, Christian or Hindu, male or female, must have the necessary liberties and resources to lead lives of their own construction. British feminism has many mothers, but only one father.

Mill, like Tocqueville, had deep reservations about democracy, however, stemming from a fear of the tyranny of the majority, especially an uneducated, easily-led majority. In the end, he was persuaded by experience that a broader franchise posed little threat; and consistently supported reform. Nevertheless it is quite clear that universal suffrage was very much less important to Mill than universal liberty. Even while supporting electoral reform, he opposed the secret ballot – seen as essential by all 'true' democrats – on the grounds that everybody should be willing to stand up publicly for their views. In this he was undoubtedly being idealistic; but it was a thoroughly liberal ideal.

It was Mill's liberalism which shaped his response to socialism, too. He was vehemently opposed to centralized state control of the economy, but was a strong supporter of socialism in the form of collective ownership of individual enterprises, competing in a market economy. In the final analysis, the best system was the one which provided for the 'greatest amount of human liberty and spontaneity'. For him, the value of economic, social and political arrangements was always to be measured by their liberating qualities. Mill was a liberal, a democrat and a socialist – in that order.

During the twentieth century Mill's importance was somewhat obscured by the bitter ideological struggle between Western capitalism and state socialism. Given the choice between the two it is quite clear which side Mill would have been on – but also, of course, quite irrelevant. Now that the clouds are clearing, Mill's true value can be seen once again. For one thing, in countless topical areas of policy, he remains instructive: the regulation of gambling, smoking, drinking and prostitution; modes of education provision; House of Lords reform; the grounds for foreign intervention by liberal states; women's rights; and models of capitalism, among others. But Mill demands our attention for a deeper reason too. The challenges facing affluent societies now are how to balance individual freedom with collective action; how to build democratic and civic institutions which 'empower' – in other words, build the characters of – citizens; how to cultivate national cohesion alongside diversity; how to honour authority while encouraging dissent. These were also the issues with which Mill grappled. His life's work was a sustained effort to make liberal democracy better, to infuse it with more truth, energy and freedom.

To understand Mill and his contribution, not only to his own century but to ours, his life and work must be viewed together. Mill was an intensely autobiographical thinker: for him the political and personal were inseparable. While his ideas still retain much of their original resonance, his legacy is also found in the example of his own life. In what follows, then, Mill's thought and life are essentially treated as one, each reflecting the other. Four of Mill's major intellectual engagements – with conservative philosophies, French thought and politics, liberalism, and feminism – are also given a more direct treatment.

Politically, Mill has been claimed, and continues to be claimed, by pretty much everyone, from the ethical socialist left to the laissez-faire, libertarian right – and at various points by every major political party. Today, two centuries after his birth, Mill's stamp of approval is still sought. It is difficult, however, to size up Mill using the measuring tools of twentieth-century thought. Was he left-wing or right-wing? A progressive or a conservative? For or against state action? An imperialist or anti-colonialist? Elitist or democrat?

Free marketer or socialist? Take your pick – there is evidence to support every answer. The point is that they are the wrong questions. If Mill sometimes looks inconsistent to modern eyes, it is usually because we use the wrong lenses. He wanted a society in which individuals had the freedom and strength to pursue their own goals, along with the virtue and character necessary to sustain collective life. 'The worth of a State, in the long run, is the worth of the individuals composing it,' wrote Mill in the final paragraph of the 'gospel' of freedom, *On Liberty*. 'A State which dwarfs its men, in order that they may be more docile instruments in its hands even for beneficial purposes – will find that with small men no great thing can really be accomplished.'[21]

CHAPTER ONE

An Unusual and Remarkable Education
(1806–20)

➤✦⬱

John Stuart Mill was born on 20 May 1806, the first child of James Mill, a struggling writer, and his wife Harriet, the daughter of a widowed lunatic asylum owner. Their home, 12 Rodney Terrace, Pentonville, London, was a wedding gift from Harriet's mother. Writing to another new father, James Mill proposed 'to run a fair race with you in the education of a son. Let us have a well-disputed trial which of us twenty years hence can exhibit the most accomplished and virtuous young man.'[1] It would be a trial for young John, too.

A couple of years after John's birth, James Mill befriended and formed a lifelong alliance with the radical philosopher Jeremy Bentham, who was also to have a considerable influence on the young John Stuart's future. When James Mill fell ill four years later, Bentham even offered to take care of his son if the illness became fatal, to ensure that the boy was properly raised to 'make Codes and Encyclopedias'.[2] James Mill reassured his mentor that he was 'not going to die, notwithstanding your zeal to come in for a legacy'. But he agreed to the legal guardianship, explaining that in the event of his early death, one of his greatest regrets would be to have 'left his [John's] mind unmade to the degree of excellence to which I hope to make it'.[3] Considerable hopes were already riding on a six-year-old pair of shoulders.

John Stuart Mill was a test case for his father's and Bentham's theory that every person is born as a *tabula rasa* – a clean slate – whose mind is shaped entirely by life experiences, especially those of childhood. Mill was raised in an intellectual Petri dish, explicitly designed to produce an ideal standard-bearer for radicalism, rationalism and reform. Raised to be a 'worthy successor' to both his father and his potential guardian, Mill was given a home education which has been a source of wonderment and condemnation ever since. The experiment was, as the twentieth-century philosopher Isaiah Berlin wrote, 'an appalling success'.[4] By the age of six Mill had written a history of Rome; by seven he was reading Plato in Greek; at eight soaking up Sophocles, Thucydides and Demosthenes; at nine enjoying Pope's translation of *The Iliad*, reading it 'twenty or thirty times'.[5] By the age of eleven he was devouring Aristotle's works on logic, before being moved on at twelve to political economy. Nor were these labours reluctantly undertaken: Mill recalled later that 'I never remember being so wrapt up in any book as I was in Joyce's *Scientific Dialogues*'.[6]

This extraordinary emphasis on education was also a reflection of James Mill's life story. He had read his way out of the poverty of Logie Pert, a Scottish town of mud-shacks, at the insistence of a mother sufficiently motivated by the prospect of advancement to change the name of the family from 'Milne' to the less common, and more anglophone, 'Mill'.[7] James had also received vital assistance from a wealthy patron, Sir John Stuart – after whom his first son would be named. As a young man, James tutored the beautiful Stuart daughter, Wilhelmina, and fell hopelessly in love with her. (He was in good company: Sir Walter Scott later fell hard for her, too.) Edinburgh University and a short-lived preaching career followed, before he decided to live by his pen in London. He never talked about his childhood, at least not in front of his family.[8]

As he had assured Bentham, James Mill survived his 1812 attack of gout. But Bentham would none the less be a significant figure for the Mill family in general, and John Stuart in particular. In 1815, Bentham helped to keep the growing Mill family out of poverty by installing them in the house next door to his own, in Queen's Square, Westminster, and charging them less than the market rent for the first five years of their occupancy. This was vital assistance at a time when James was earning next to nothing from journalism, breeding at an alarming rate for a professed Malthusian – by 1814 there were five children, including one somewhat tactlessly named Wilhelmina – and spending most of his energies on the colossal work that would make his name, *The History of British India* (1826).

Bentham decided that everyone would benefit from some time in the countryside, and successively leased two country houses for the Mill-Bentham clan. The grandest of these, Forde Abbey in Somerset, was the family home for six months of the year until John was twelve. In his famous *Autobiography*, completed towards the end of his life and published after his death, Mill described his time in the Abbey as 'an important circumstance' in his education:

Nothing contributes more to nourish elevation of sentiments in a people than the large and free character of their habitations. The middle-age architecture, the baronial hall, and the spacious and lofty rooms, of this fine old place, so unlike the mean and cramped externals of English middle class life, gave the sentiment of a larger and freer existence, and were to me a sort of poetic cultivation.[9]

Although Mill would spend much of his life railing against the aristocracy, he always appreciated the grandeur, space and beauty of their homes.

James Mill was understandably proud of his experiment. In a letter to the self-made tailor and political radical, Francis Place, he wrote: 'John is now an adept in the first six books of Euclid and in Algebra ... while in Greek he has read ... the last half of Thucydides, one play of Euripedes [sic] and one of Sophocles, two of Aristophanes and the treatise of Plutarch on education ... His historical and other reading never stands still, he is at it whenever he has any time to spare. This looks like bragging ...'[10] It certainly does. But there was plenty to brag about. Mill was not the only example of youthful achievement; by the age of twelve, Macaulay had produced a sizeable and serious compendium of history and Tennyson had written an epic 6,000-line poem. But for the sheer range and depth of his reading and learning, from the classics through logic to political economy, the first fourteen years of Mill's life surely stand alone.

Mill paid a heavy price for his education, not least in acute loneliness. He was aloof from his siblings, he had no friends, no toys, and few childish diversions. Again, he was not the only one: John Ruskin was only allowed to play with keys and bricks and ate only cold food on Sundays.[11] Mill did enjoy *Robinson Crusoe*, and his father procured *Arabian Nights* and *Don Quixote* for his amusement. He was especially keen on stories of brave, fiercely independent adventurers and, passing through the patriotic phase typical of most boys, supported the British against the American colonists: his father, of course, soon put him right. 'As I had no boy companions, my amusements,' he recalled, 'which were mostly solitary, were in general of a quiet, if not a bookish turn.'[12] His greatest loneliness stemmed from the absence of a confidante; he could talk to his father about cerebral matters, but never emotional ones. Mill's mother does not feature in the final version of his *Autobiography* at all; but in earlier, discarded drafts, he ponders how different life might have been if he had been blessed with 'that rarity in England, a really warm-hearted mother'. He believed it would have made 'his father a totally different being ... and would have made the children grow up loving and being loved'.[13]

There is no question here that Mill is being unfair. By the time he was writing these passages, he had turned away from his family because of a perceived slight against his new wife. A visitor recorded that in his early twenties, Mill 'was evidently very fond of his mother and sisters, and they of him'.[14] John, though, was close to neither parent: 'I had no one to whom I desired to express everything which I felt; and the only person I was in communication with, to whom I looked up, I had too much fear of ...'[15] As Mill's sister Harriet later wrote, their parents were 'living as far apart, under the same roof, as the north pole from the south'.[16] One contemporary said that James Mill treated his wife as a '*squah*' [*sic*].[17] Perhaps John enjoyed his summers at his guardian's Somerset estate as a partial escape from the loveless, ascetic atmosphere at home. The ageing Bentham – he was sixty when John was born – was a colourful character, with long golden locks, a walking stick named 'Dapple' and a chaotic working style, pinning notes all over his curtains. Every day, between twelve and one he would play the organ. At Forde Abbey there were games of 'battledore' and shuttlecock, walks, fishing for eels – and even occasional dances.

For a supposed ultra-rationalist, Bentham held some eccentric views. He did not believe in ghosts on the grounds that it was impossible to imagine spectral clothes, and yet no one ever saw a naked ghost. He did, however, retain a sufficient fear of goblins, acquired as a child, to be unable to sleep alone. His assistants were made to sleep in the same room as their master – a noisy duty, for as one of them remarked 'if Jeremy Bentham does not snore, he is not legitimate'.[18] Bentham also suggested that people should make memorial ornaments, or 'auto-icons', out of the corpses of their dead relatives. His own auto-icon, along with Dapple, is in the foyer of University College, London.

Visitors to the Bentham-Mill household were variously struck by the children's precociousness and otherworldliness. Francis Place, who spent a month at Forde Abbey in 1817, was impressed by James Mill's commitment to his children's education: he spent at least three or four hours a day with them as well as completing his own work 'without a moment's relaxation'. The days were organized with a military precision: James and eleven-year-old John were up at 5 a.m. to work on the proofs of the Indian history. Place also thought James Mill 'excessively severe' for depriving the children of their lunch because of a mistake of just one word in their translations. John, by now undertaking much of the education of his younger siblings, would go hungry for their mistakes, too. Of John, Place wrote that he was 'truly a prodigy, a most wonderful fellow; and when his Logic, his Languages, his Mathematics, his Philosophy will be combined with a general knowledge of mankind and the affairs of the world, he will be a truly astonishing man'.[19] Place saw the benefits of the regime, but it greatly unsettled Anne Romilly, wife of Sir Samuel Romilly, a legal reformer: 'They are all nice well-behaved children, but they are literally cram'd with knowledge, and I should fear that much of it may turn to indigestion rather than healthy nourishment.'[20]

This fear was unfounded, at least in the case of the eldest son. While the prodigious reading lists do give the impression that information was being swallowed at an alarming rate, John emphatically denied, later, that his education had been one of 'cram' and insisted that his father 'never permitted anything to degenerate ... into a mere exercise of memory'. He was taught to discover answers for himself, rather than being provided with them. Skills, rather than knowledge, were the most important fruits of his education. Mill learnt to interrogate every point of view and how to form and test his own ideas. 'My father,' he wrote later, 'strove to make the understanding not only go along with every step of the teaching, but if possible, precede it. Anything which could be found out by thinking, I was never told, until I had exhausted my efforts to find it for myself'.[21]

Like his father, the young Mill was greatly influenced by the Socratic method of constant questioning, which, he said, 'became part of [his] own mind ... The close, searching *elenchus* by which a man of vague generalities is constrained either to express his meaning to himself in definite terms, or to confess that he does not know what he is talking about ...'[22] He was taught to dissect bad arguments forensically, as well as to generate and defend his own views, recounting that 'the first intellectual operation in which I arrived at any proficiency, was dissecting a bad argument, and finding in what part the fallacy lay'.[23] His contemporary Leslie Stephen described John's education as a 'course of strenuous mental gymnastics ... he had been trained to argue closely; to test conclusions rather than receive them passively ...'[24] What James Mill could not foresee is that these talents would later be turned against his own work, and that he was in fact equipping his son for a journey away from him.

James Mill recorded an incident that illuminates the child prodigy as a true thinker, rather than a walking encyclopaedia. In 1818 a professor from the Royal Military College in Bagshot called on the Mill household. Finding James Mill out, he fell into conversation with the twelve-year-old John and asked him to describe his studies. Hearing the answer, the professor suspected John of being either a 'folly or a cheat', and thought James Mill 'was either fool enough to let the boy pass over a multitude of things without knowing them, or ... making the semblance of knowledge in him pass for the reality'. The sceptical professor returned with some colleagues and subjected John to what they considered a 'rigid examination', but which was almost certainly no more unnerving than his daily encounters with his own father. Convinced of the boy's genius, the College issued an unprecedented invitation to John to attend a series of chemistry lectures. The Governor of the College begged John to visit his home as much as possible and spend time with his own sons, in the hope that some of his learning might magically rub off. However, James Mill rushed his son back to London the moment the lectures finished, 'unwilling to leave him to the spoiling of the notice he is receiving'.[25]

John reported that his father's Socratic moral inculcations were 'justice, temperance (to which he gave a very extended application), veracity, perseverance, readiness to encounter pain and especially labour, regard for the public good; estimation of persons according to their merits, and of things according to their intrinsic usefulness; a life of exertion, in contradiction to one of self-indulgent sloth'.[26] James Mill expected the same virtues from his children – especially John – and was constantly on the lookout for any 'spoiling' or 'corrupting' influences, either of a moral or educational nature. He wanted to keep the intellectual air as pure as possible, to ensure that his tender plant did not grow awry.

Along with a formidable intellectual confidence, James Mill instilled in his eldest son a blend of Aristotelian virtue and protestant work ethic, largely by example. John worked at the same table as his father throughout his childhood; and when they were at Forde Abbey, both of the Mills and Bentham worked in the same room, even though they could have taken a room each.[27] John was directly provided with a very specific notion of what men did: they worked hard, with that work consisting of reading and writing. One of Mill's sisters said that John, uniquely among the children, had benefited from 'teaching by companionship', and there was certainly a strongly collegiate feel to John's working environment, one which he would replicate in adult life around a different table with the only woman he ever loved, Harriet Taylor.[28]

While the indoctrination into what would today probably be called workaholism was absorbed across the table, the lessons in virtue were more direct. Mill would later recollect the force with which his father impressed the message of the 'Choice of Hercules', a story in which the hero is forced to choose between two beautiful women, one flashing her cleavage and promising pleasure, the other demure and offering lifelong virtuous nobility.[29] It is not surprising that Mill's conscience always spoke to him 'in his father's voice'.[30] (Goethe, who Mill came to admire, had his Hercules solve the problem by grabbing one under each arm.)[31]

In the Mill household, then, discipline was tight, learning was given priority over play, and love was rationed. 'They are unlike other children. They do not know what a game of Play is,' lamented Mrs Romilly. For James Mill, pleasure was at best a distraction from the more important tasks of the mind, and at worst a positive evil. No holidays were ever allowed, as John recorded, 'lest the habit of work should be broken, and a taste for idleness acquired'.[32] One of the very few non-intellectual activities prescribed for the Mill boys was marching drill and sword practice under the tutelage of a sergeant from a nearby barracks.[33] But Mill would never be a swordsman: his pen was mightier.

John himself confessed that whatever the elegance and rigour of his mind, his body was ill-coordinated and clumsy. He was grateful that his father had 'saved' him from 'the demoralizing effects of school life', but was disappointed that 'he made no effort to provide me with any sufficient substitute for its practicalizing influences'. To his dying day John struggled to tie a cravat. And while he would become a dedicated long-distance walker – including multiple ascents of Mont Ventoux in his final years – games and sport were never part of his life. 'I never was a boy,' he told a friend decades later, 'never played at cricket: it is better to let Nature have her way'.[34]

If play was scorned by James Mill, so too was passion. Mill recorded that his father 'professed the greatest contempt . . . for passionate emotions of all sorts, and for everything which has been said or written in exaltation of them . . . the greatest number of miscarriages in life, he considered to be attributable to the overvaluing of pleasures'.[35] Stuck in a loveless marriage, James Mill chose to seal up his emotional side – and expected the same of his children. Harriet Grote, wife of George Grote, the historian of Greece and a friend of the adult Mill, described James Mill as 'the prototype of the Utilitarian character, almost to the point of caricature: self-made, manly, independent, rationally controlled (especially in the areas of sex and work), not giving way to feelings of any kind (especially of love)'.[36] Her analysis of the result on his eldest son was sharp. 'If anything could make intellectual culture odious and terrible, it is the ensample of that overstrained infant,' she wrote. 'One set of faculties is wrought up by artificial processes to preternatural acuity, leaving the physical side to shift for itself, all with the minimum of guidance from his guardians – the emotions being regarded as of no account, or noticed only with reprobation.'[37]

From a modern perspective, James Mill's anti-emotional regime seems cruel. Because he was his father's project, John also appears to have formed a weak attachment to his mother, who might otherwise have filled some of the void. As it was, John would have to learn for himself – the hard way – that feelings were as valuable as thoughts. In his notes for an 1829 debate on the relative merits of Wordsworth and Byron, Mill wrote: 'Education is 1. the education of the intellect. 2. that of the feelings. Folly of supposing that the first suffices without the last.'[38]

One of the main casualties of the elder Mill's aversion to pleasure was, according to his son, poetry, and particularly contemporary verse. Poetry held a special place in utilitarian demonology. For Bentham, 'all poetry was misrepresentation', on the grounds that it exaggerated for effect and used feelings to persuade. Mill would later point out, in a parricidal essay on Bentham, that poetry was far from alone in this respect – all good oratory does the same thing – and that in any case the quality of argument was improved as a result. While reading poetry was clearly not high on James Mill's list, his son was not entirely starved of verse. He read most of the ancient Greek and Roman poets, in original and translation. Milton's old damp cottage in Bentham's garden was briefly, and disastrously, home to the Mill family in 1810 and the poet remained a firm favourite of his father's. Mill, by contrast, would later come to accuse Milton of having 'the soul of a fanatic a despot & a tyrant'.[39]

He was also introduced by his father to the poems of Goldsmith, Burns, Gray, Cowper, James Beattie, Scott and Dryden. James Mill read the first book of Edmund Spenser's *The Faerie Queene* out loud to his son, showing at least that his austerity could relent now and again. It is true, however, that contemporary poetry never made it on to the Mill bookshelves: John would have to discover Coleridge, Wordsworth and Tennyson for himself. Before his later crisis opened his eyes to the potential of poetry, 'the correct statement would be not that I disliked poetry,' he said, 'but that I was theoretically indifferent to it.'[40]

Nevertheless John was made to write poetry, which he described as 'one of the most disagreeable of my tasks'.[41] His friend, and first biographer, Alexander Bain would write that Mill 'was born to read, not to write, poetry'.[42] It seems odd that James Mill, archutilitarian, would make his son write verse. But he did so for the precise reasons that Bentham attacked it: poetry was a better medium for communicating some messages, James Mill believed, because 'people in general attached more value to verse than it deserved'. There was perhaps no better illustration of the fact that James Mill was consciously preparing his son for a life of persuasion and activism, rather than for the ivory tower of pure philosophical thought. In an ideal utilitarian world, poetry would not be so valued, but given that it currently was, John should be equipped to use it in the interest of reform. As it turned out, almost certainly to the benefit of his reputation, Mill made no further attempts at poetry, at least in formal terms. A poetic spirit does however breathe through much of his writing, giving some of his prose the impact which his father and Bentham attributed to poetry. And poets and poetry – especially Wordsworth and Coleridge – would come to play a significant role in his life, intellectually as well as emotionally.

In discarded drafts of his *Autobiography*, John aired his childhood grievances against his father, reporting that 'both as a boy and as a youth I was incessantly smarting under his severe admonitions', and recounted that he was 'perpetually losing his temper' over mistakes, and described him as 'one of the most impatient of men'. James Mill clearly often expected far too much. His son recalled using the word 'idea' in a discussion and was asked to define the term, not to his stern father's satisfaction: Mill was thirteen. He recalled that he had been educated 'in the absence of love and in the presence of fear'.[43] But perhaps the level of fear should not be overstated. It was the absences in John's childhood that were most damaging, especially in the long run. When he complained of having been left 'morally stunted' as a result of his upbringing, Mill was referring to his emotional underdevelopment. Intimate relationships would never come easily to him. By the time he left home for the first time, at the age of fourteen, Mill had the education and intellect of a mature man, but his emotional vocabulary was that of a young child.

James Mill must bear much of the responsibility for his son's lack of emotional cultivation – and for the 'crisis' it would subsequently precipitate. But to be fair, he was in some ways an enlightened father for the age. While the Mill children certainly missed lunch, and were occasionally cuffed, 'flogger' John Keate, headmaster of Eton, was beating his charges black and blue. While most middle-class Victorian children were expected to be seen and not heard, the

Mill children often had the audacity to argue with adult guests, seemingly encouraged in this by their 'schoolmaster'. Many children of their time barely knew their father, but the Mill children spent hours each day with theirs. Mill himself reported that his siblings loved their father 'tenderly', before adding the melancholy qualification that, 'if I cannot say so much of myself, I was always loyally devoted to him'.[44]

Mill's moral sense, however, was well developed. When, as a sixteen-year-old, he lost his watch during a holiday with family friends, he wrote to his father to confess, pointing out that 'it was lost while I was out of doors, but it is impossible that it should have been stolen from my pocket. It must therefore be my own fault.'[45] It seems his father was forgiving on this occasion. If the young philosopher had been tempted to lie – and few sixteen-year-olds would not have been – he was clearly able to resist. Mill was to remain a more honest man than most, even on those occasions, especially during his years as a politician, when his candour made life more difficult for him.

By the age of twelve, Mill had acquired much of the intellectual equipment required for his extraordinary career as a political thinker and activist, through a deep immersion in classical history and philosophy and the example of his father's working habits. He assisted in the production of James Mill's *History of British India*, reading proofs out loud while his father checked them against his original drafts. The working knowledge of Indian affairs he thereby acquired would be useful to him during his own lifelong career with the East India Company. Mill also delved into Roman history, writing for his own 'amusement' a history of Roman government up to the introduction of the Licinian laws, drawing mostly on Livy and Dionysius. 'It was, in fact,' he said, 'an account of the struggles between the patricians and the plebeians', a struggle which he saw as continuing in nineteenth-century England, and in which he would play a significant part. James Mill encouraged his son in these 'useful amusements' but never asked to see the results, for which John was grateful, because it allowed him to write without the 'chilling sensation of being under a critical eye'.[46]

Current affairs, however, was one blind spot in Mill's education – he learned nothing, for example, about the French Revolution – even though Europe was in a period of turmoil and transition throughout John's childhood. Mill was born in war-time, but came of age in peace. While he read Homer's *Odyssey* and Ovid's *Metamorphoses*, the European powers were carving up the continent at the 1815 Congress of Vienna, to the soundtrack of Beethoven's specially written cantata, *Der glorreiche Augenblick* ('The Glorious Moment').[47] According to the historian Paul Johnson, the period 1815 to 1830 – the years in which Mill went from boy to man – were 'the birth of the modern ... In 1815 reaction seemed triumphant everywhere; by 1830 the *demos* was plainly on its way'.[48] Mill himself would go on to become one of democracy's most important analysts.

As he approached his teenage years, Mill's education changed direction. Logic, argument and political economy dominated the curriculum, starting with Aristotle's *Organon*. The focus was now on developing reasoning ability: 'From about the age of twelve,' he recalled later, 'I entered into another and more advanced stage in my course of instruction; in which the main object was no longer the aids and appliances of thought, but the thoughts themselves.'[49]

At the same time, John was being schooled in the persuasive arts, predictably enough using the classical orators as case studies. The adolescent Mill was especially interested in the way in which 'everything important to his [the orator's] purpose was said at the exact moment when he had brought the minds of his audience into the state most fitted to receive it; how he made steal into their minds, gradually and by insinuation, thoughts which if expressed in a more direct manner would have roused their opposition.'[50] It was none the less a largely silent exercise. While the young William Pitt had been taught by reading out loud in a number of languages, with an emphasis on melodious delivery, John Stuart Mill's education was almost always focused on the written word; the only exception being that he was made to read Plato and Demosthenes out loud, a task he described as 'painful'.[51] John would never be a great orator, having never learnt to vary his tone and pitch to good effect, and he struggled to pronounce the letter 'r' correctly until the age of six-teen.[52] Only when he lost his temper – as he would, for example, over Ireland in 1868 – could he raise the roof. The written word remained his most effective weapon.

Yet the lesson about both the tone and timing in argument would stay with the adult Mill. His writing always reflected the politics and interests of the reading audience. There was a palpable difference, for example, between his articles for the *Westminster Review*, a partisan radical journal, which for a while he both edited and owned, and the *Edinburgh*, a moderate Whig publication. Mill frequently held his fire on a subject until he judged that the time was ripe – examples include his support for the North in the American Civil War and for the emancipation of women. A shrewd tactician, Mill understood from an early age that in public debate, timing is often everything.

The year 1819 was an important one for the family, as James Mill secured his first regular salary as an examiner at the East India Company, cutting a path which his son would soon follow. It was also the year in which the thirteen-year-old John Stuart Mill undertook 'a complete course in political economy' and the point at which he emerged as a thinker in his own right.[53] James Mill had befriended the economist David Ricardo, and played a significant role in cajoling him into publishing his famous *Principles of Political Economy and Taxation* (1817), one of the founding works of classical economics. Ricardo's ideas on economics were similar to those of Adam Smith. He agreed that three principal forms of income – rent, interest and wages – accrued to three groups: landlords, capitalists and workers. But Ricardo added a strongly political twist. The chief obstacle to economic harmony and growth, he argued, was the protectionism of the landlords, which drove up the cost of living, and in turn was made possible by the political domination of the landowning classes. The prospects for economic progress were therefore contingent on some radical reallocation of political power.

It was an appropriate time for Mill to be learning about the connections between economic theory and social consequences: in August 1819, economic distress had driven thousands of Lancashire weavers on to the streets of Manchester, where they were cut down by the army in the 'Peterloo massacre': eleven dead and more than a hundred injured. The protectionist Corn Laws, which secured landowners' profits but made bread expensive, had been causing hardship and provoking riots – especially in 1812 and 1815 – for years before the Manchester eruption.[54] The years 1819 and 1820 would also demonstrate to Mill the essentially non-revolutionary nature of the English: an economic upturn and a royal scandal were enough to snuff out any further trouble in the following year. None the less, Mill would spend his life battling against the landlords and their 'unearned' incomes and insisting that the 'science' of economics was not a set of abstract laws, but was profoundly shaped by human institutions and interventions. Poverty was never, for Mill, a necessary price for progress.

James Mill had already seen the political implications of Ricardo's analysis, and was determined to publish his own treatise, intended to popularize Ricardo's insights. John did most of the groundwork for this book, published as *Elements of Political Economy* in 1826, and, he says, 'thought for myself almost from the first'.[55] He disagreed with his father on some points, and reported that on a few occasions his own view prevailed, which he rightly said was to his father's credit. The young Mill, probably fairly desperate for some affection, was also very taken by Ricardo on a personal level, writing later that 'by his benevolent countenance, and kindliness of manner, [he] was very attractive to young persons' and records his pleasure at being invited to Ricardo's house or to walk with him.[56] His death in 1823 was a blow to both father and son, but when James Mill bequeathed to his son a watch that Ricardo had left to him, John – perhaps remembering the traumatic watch loss of fourteen years earlier – insisted it went to his brother Henry.[57] Political economy would remain one of Mill's lifelong preoccupations and his own *Principles* would eclipse those of both his father and Ricardo, with Walter Bagehot later describing his position with regard to economics in the mid-century as 'monarchical'.

As an adult, Mill was acutely aware of the influence of what he described as an 'unusual and remarkable' education on his subsequent life. In his *Autobiography* (rightly regarded as a classic and still in print), he devoted as many pages to his first seventeen years as he did to his last thirty-three – the period in which all his major works were published, he married and became a widower, moved to France and served as an MP. His education was in fact one of the two motivations for writing the *Autobiography*; the other being the posthumous elevation and defence of his wife, Harriet. Mill's characteristically balanced assessment of his education included the recognition that it was an essential foundation for his subsequent success: 'If I have achieved anything, I owe it, among other fortunate circumstances, to the fact that through the early training bestowed on me by my father, I started, I may fairly say, with an advantage of a quarter of a century over my contemporaries.'[58]

Mill also believed that his education was proof of the capacity of very young children to learn much more than was typically believed at the time. He insisted that his achievements were no reflection on his abilities: 'If I had been by nature extremely quick of apprehension, or had possessed a very accurate and retentive memory, or were of a remarkably active and energetic character, the trial would not be conclusive; but in all these natural gifts I am rather below than above par.'[59] There is more than a touch of false modesty here; he did not believe for a moment that he was actually 'below par' in these areas, but his conviction that other children, similarly raised, would have reaped similar rewards, was genuine.

Mill would eventually rebel against his father's world-view, but he was the first to recognize that his achievements were possible because of the habits, skills and knowledge acquired across the table from his father. His childhood and education imbued him with a sense of the possibilities for human betterment and the urgent need for reforms to realize them. Mill's upbringing also gave him a strong work ethic. To label Mill prolific only hints at his productivity: his collected works occupy four feet of bookshelf. William Wordsworth, the poet who wrote in 1802 that the 'child is father of the man', and would later greatly influence Mill, produced the most sustained poetic treatment of child prodigies in his posthumous, autobiographical work, *The Prelude*. Much of this must have resonated with Mill when it was published in 1850, including a description of a lifelong trait of hot-housed children:

> All things are put to question; he must live
> Knowing that he grows wiser every day,
> Or else not live at all . . .'[60]

For the moment, Mill was enthusiastically putting 'all things to question' and was ready to strike out on his own. In 1820, at fourteen years of age, he was ready to take his first step towards independence. It turned out to be a significant one, and not merely because he was away from home for almost a year. He went to the country whose history and politics would inspire so much of his work, the country which he would come to love more than his own – where he would bury his wife, spend his last years, and be buried himself. He went to France.

CHAPTER TWO

A Man Among Men (1820–6)

➤✦

'Well, I must draw back one pet-boy from you,' wrote Jeremy Bentham to his brother Samuel. 'What say you to my sending you another? ... What other? Why John Mill, who you may shew for 6*d.* a piece and get rich.'[1]

So began Mill's year in France. Once the first 'pet boy', Bentham's research assistant Richard Doane, had returned from his sojourn – and managed to pass on a bit of French to his successor – Mill was off, five days before his fourteenth birthday. A boy then, he would return after the 'best months' of his youth as a young man, and as an ardent Francophile.

First his father had to break some news. The pair walked around Hyde Park on a May morning in 1820. London was peaceful again, after the excitement which had accompanied the trial and execution, a few weeks earlier, of Arthur Thistlewood, the radical who had conspired to assassinate the Cabinet. James Mill told his son that 'he had been taught many things which youths of [his] age did not commonly know', and warned him that people might pass comment on this fact – or, worse, compliment him on his prodigiousness. As Mill recalled, his father then made it clear that any such achievements resulted solely from 'the very unusual advantage which had fallen to my lot, of having a father who was able to teach me, and willing to give the necessary trouble and time, that it was no matter of praise to me'.[2]

In his *Autobiography*, Mill claimed to have been surprised by the revelation of his exceptional learning, and to have accepted his father's explanation unquestioningly. But it seems unlikely that he was as ignorant as all that: it cannot have escaped his attention that he was the only child attending the lectures at Bagshot. At least some of this modesty must have been fashioned for later public consumption; after all, in the year he left for France, Bentham described Mill as 'having the pride of Lucifer'.[3]

Mill set off on 15 May 1820. On his way south, he stopped in Paris, where he stayed for a week with Jean-Baptiste Say, the Ricardian political economist and correspondent of many British radicals. It was an engaging time to be in the French capital. The constitutional monarch Louis XVIII and his Prime Minister, the Duc de Richelieu, were attempting to rule with a degree of public involvement and consent and there was a 'lively murmur in Parisian society', according to the poet Lamartine. The fourteen-year-old Mill was already managing some conversations in French and was in some demand in the salons of Parisian radicals.

During the next leg of the journey, from Paris to Orleans, Mill was engaged in a squabble over who had the right to sit inside the horse-drawn coach, and had to endure a stretch between Orleans and Massay riding outside the diligence with a fat, chain-smoking butcher. The prissy young Mill recorded in his personal notebook that he was 'not a little incommoded by his smoking'.[4] (As an MP almost half a century later, he would support the introduction of no-smoking carriages on trains.) Even when the butcher got off after two days' travelling, there was little to celebrate: he was replaced by a 'dirty fille' with an 'eruption on her face, which made [the] place none of the pleasantest, particularly on account of the smell'.[5] Mill would be a lifelong supporter of the rights of the workers, but he would never travel 'coach' class again.

It was with some relief that he joined the other Bentham household in the early hours of 2 June, at the Chateau de Pompignan, near Toulouse, rented from Jean-Louis Lefranc de Pompignan, the son of one of Voltaire's great enemies. They were quite a family, even by Benthamite standards. Sir Samuel – who Mill had met once before, six years earlier – was a naval officer, engineer and mineralogist and had served in Russia, once crossing the entire Siberian plain to the Chinese border.[6] While Jeremy Bentham had been awarded honorary citizenship of France, Samuel had won the more glamorous prize of a gold-hilted sword and the rank of Brigadier General from Catherine the Great. The honour was given in thanks for repulsing a Turkish attack on the Black Sea port of Kherson – where Samuel Bentham had been sent as an engineer by Potemkin – using 'self-recoiling' cannon of his own invention to repel the enemy.

The Bentham children were almost as precocious as Mill, and twenty-year-old George took responsibility for organizing his education. It quickly became clear that in some areas, especially mathematics, the teaching would in fact be in the other direction; nevertheless it was from 'Mr George' that Mill would acquire his lifelong love of botany. It was Lady Bentham, though, who made the greatest impression. She was, Mill recalled in the *Autobiography*, 'a woman of strong will and decided character, with much general knowledge, and great practical good sense ... she was the ruling spirit of the household, as she deserved, and was well-qualified, to be'.[7] He could have been describing his own future wife, or drawing a contrast with his own mother, of whom he wrote that 'to make herself loved, looked up to, or even obeyed, required qualities which she unfortunately did not possess'.[8]

After two weeks at the Chateau, the family moved to an apartment in Toulouse for six weeks. The move kept being delayed for a variety of reasons – the Benthams were an appealingly disorganized family. John, however, was not happy. 'The confusion in the house is very great' he wrote in his journal, regular dispatches from which were sent to his father: 'There can be no regularity in anything at present ... the stay here begins now to be very tiresome to me, on account of the confusion of my being obliged to pack up my books so early, thinking that we were setting off the very next day, etc.

especially now, when I am excluded from the library.'[9] (In Mill's parlance, 'tiresome' indicates an even higher level of annoyance than 'incommoded'.) He was delighted when one day the Comte dropped by, took pity on him, and opened the library up again.

This was the only occasion that Mill's homesickness showed through. He begged his father for a letter, since 'it is now more than a month since I left England, and I dare say something must have happened worthy of notice'. He even hints at a topic, adding that 'we hear a great deal here of the Queen of England'.[10] Following the accession of George IV, news of the arrival of his estranged wife, Queen Caroline, at Dover (shortly after Mill left England) was indeed sweeping England and, according to one historian, was 'opening the age of public opinion politics'.[11] William Cobbett said that it had stirred 'every pen in England'.[12] It seems James Mill had little interest, however. Or at least, not enough to pass on to his son.

The French sojourn showed that Mill's study habits were well ingrained. At both the Chateau and in town, the Benthams tried to draw him away from his books, with regular excursions, dawn bathing trips to the river (which Mill hated), riding, fencing lessons and even – disastrously – dancing lessons. However, Mill greatly enjoyed Franconi's famous horse circus.[13] Lady Bentham passed some gentle judgement on her charge's prior educational experience in a letter to James Mill, in which she hoped 'that you will have satisfaction from that part of his education we are giving him to fit him for commerce with the world at large'. She was more frank when she asked if John could extend his stay by six months, by which time the family would be in Montpellier, mentioning that he still struggled to brush his hair.[14] Mill, too, was loving his time in France and was hoping to be able to stay.

His bibliophilia, however, was even greater than his francophilia. The gift he most appreciated during his stay was a set of portable bookshelves from the eldest Bentham daughter, and by any standards, but especially those of a fourteen-year-old away from his parents in the south of France, Mill's regime was spartan.[15] On 22 June he recorded waking after nine o'clock – 'I do not know for what reason, for I usually wake very early'.[16] He certainly did. His journal often states that he 'rose early', and at other times he was more specific: during the five days from 4 July to 9 July, he reported his hours of rising as 'five o'clock . . . five o'clock . . . six o'clock . . . 5¾ . . . five o'clock'.[17] On 8 July he gave a sample of his morning's occupation:

Rose at five o'clock; read five chapters of Voltaire; at 6¾, began to read another portion of the Treatise on the Use of Adverbs; Mr G. went to call on M. Sauvage and engaged him to give me lessons in French. At 7¾ commenced reading the 'Prometheus' of Lucian: from 8½ till 9, took my first lesson of *solfeges*, with the *principes de musique*; continued the 'Prometheus' till 9½, when we breakfasted. From 10½ to 10¾ was employed miscellaneously; went then to Madame Boulet's to practice my music; she had brought me some pieces of music. Returned at 12½, read 10 propositions of Legendre.[18]

At the same time, he was excited by rumours that as a result of widespread Italian revolutions 'the Pope's temporal powers are done away with (a most fortunate circumstance)'.[19] These hopes of revolution were soon dashed – the rumours were just that – but none the less the direct knowledge acquired by Mill during his time in France would serve his own radicalism well. His lessons and wide reading in French – especially of Voltaire, Racine and Molière – and immersion in French life quickly gave him the precious gift of fluency in the language, although he never lost his strong English accent.[20] His musicianship also improved significantly, causing him to write to his mother asking her to suspend his sisters' music lessons until his return because 'the bad habits I had acquired previously to coming here are the chief obstacle I am faced with'.[21] Music would become an important form of relaxation for Mill in later life, but he would only ever play the piano for his wife and stepdaughter.

In August, the family were on the move again, this time for a tour of the Pyrenees. These weeks strongly affected Mill: 'This first introduction to the highest order of mountain scenery made the deepest impression on me, and gave a colour to my tastes throughout life'.[22] Walking, especially in mountains, become a fixed feature of Mill's life. The Pyrenean trip was also the point when he began botanizing seriously with 'Mr George', a hobby which also would become a lifelong one. After returning briefly to Toulouse, the Bentham tribe settled in Montpellier. Mill, granted leave by his father to remain, attended lectures in logic and chemistry, perfected his French and made his first friend, Antoine Jérôme Balard, the future inventor of bromine. As he explained it years later to Auguste Comte, 'that is to say, a friend of my own choice, as opposed to those given to me by family ties'.[23]

In retrospect, Mill believed that 'the greatest, perhaps, of the many advantages which I owed to this episode in my education, was that of having breathed for a whole year, the free and genial atmosphere of Continental life.'[24] In the *Autobiography* he contrasted this with the insularity and pettiness of English discourse:

The chief fruit which I carried away from the society I saw was a strong and permanent interest in Continental liberalism ... keeping me free from the error always prevalent in England, and from which even my father with all his superiority to prejudice was not exempt, of judging universal questions by a merely English standard.[25]

Mill would shortly become one of England's leading – and, for a while, foremost – commentators on French affairs. Politically, France would be his benchmark and inspiration, the main laboratory for the great 'democratic experiment', until the 1850s when the United States attracted more of his attention. Mill never lost his conviction that an understanding of another nation – which was only really possible with fluency in its tongue – was a vital antidote to intellectual parochialism. 'Without knowing the language of a people, we never really know their thoughts, and their type of character', he told the students of St Andrews four a half decades later, 'and unless we do possess this knowledge, of some other people than ourselves, we remain, to the hour of our death, with our intellects only half expanded.'[26]

For now, though, it was time to head home, where he was soon to immerse himself in the public affairs of his own country. 'John [is] very much grown; looking almost a man; ... has got the French language – but almost forgot his own – and is nearly as shy and awkward as before,' reported James Mill to Ricardo. 'His love of study, however, remains; and he shews tractability and good sense. If he does not make what the French call an *aimable* man, I have no doubt he will make what the English call an amiable and a useful one.'[27]

James Mill judged that his son was ready for baptism into the Benthamite faith. Mill had not yet been introduced to his guardian's writings, and one of the very first books his father commanded him to read on his return from France in June 1821 was Pierre Dumont's French edition of Bentham's *Traité de Législation Civile et Penale*. The results must have been gratifying; according to Mill's own recollection, when he put down the last volume, he had 'become a different being. The feeling rushed upon me, that all previous moralists were superseded, and that here indeed was the commencement of a new era in thought.'[28]

The Benthamite creed, later to become known as 'utilitarianism', is the best-known moral theory of all time. Its expression in the 'greatest happiness principle' is more familiar than any Kantian, Aristotelian or Rawlsian formulation and the moral and political questions raised by Bentham are alive and well today. Contained in the Dumont edition of the *Traité* which so captivated Mill were key extracts from Bentham's *Introduction to the Principles of Morals and Legislation*. The opening sentences are perhaps the clearest in all of moral philosophy: 'Nature has placed mankind under the governance of two sovereign masters: pain and pleasure. It is for them alone to determine what we ought to do, as well as to determine what we shall do.'[29]

This was the foundation stone of utilitarianism. Attaining pleasure and avoiding pain were all that counted. We ought, morally, to do what will maximize pleasure and minimize pain. Fortuitously, these goals were precisely what drove human behaviour anyway. At a stroke, then, most of the painful questions of morality, ethics, psychology, philosophy, and even theology were dispensed with. Bentham simply dismissed the competing grounds given by other philosophers for human morality, such as an innate moral 'sense', individual 'rights', natural justice or natural law. His audacity was breathtaking.

Having established that pleasure was what we would – and should – seek, Bentham could state that 'utility' was simply defined as 'that property in any object, whereby it tends to produce benefit, advantage, pleasure, good or happiness (all this in the present case comes to the same thing) . . .' Of course not all pleasures were equal. So Bentham devised a 'felicific calculus' to assist in weighing competing claims. The value of a pleasure or pain to an individual depended on six factors: '1. Its intensity 2. Its duration. 3. Its certainty or uncertainty. 4. Its propinquity or remoteness 5. Its fecundity. 6. Its purity.' To which, considering a community of people, a seventh had to be added: '7. Its extent, that is, the number of persons . . . who are affected by it.'[30]

The value of any action was clear: the extent to which it promoted 'the greatest happiness of the greatest number' – a formulation originally arrived at by the Glaswegian philosopher Francis Hutcheson in 1725 but popularized by Bentham.[31] In a famous 'thought experiment' set by the utilitarian William Godwin, the reader was asked whether they should, in the event of a fire, save Archbishop Fenelon or Archbishop Fenelon's chambermaid – supposing, additionally, that the chambermaid was the reader's wife or mother.[32] The utilitarian answer was clear: Fenelon had the greater capacity to increase happiness, and so should be saved. The test vividly demonstrates the Benthamite model, as well as indicating that there might be something more than slightly wrong with it. Indeed, Godwin himself later retreated from this impossibly doctrinaire position.[33] As the twentieth-century philosopher Bernard Williams suggested, if we have to throw one person over the side of the lifeboat, our wife or a stranger, and we have to think about it, that's just one thought too many.[34]

Mill himself would later depart from much of Bentham's philosophy, at first stealthily and then explicitly. His own *Utilitarianism*, published forty years later, would present a radically different version. But at fifteen he was utterly convinced. For the young Mill, the 'principle of utility' underpinning Bentham's work made sense of his world, falling 'exactly into place as the keystone which held together the detached and fragmentary component parts of my knowledge and beliefs. It gave unity to my conception of things.'[35] This unifying power of the principle of utility for the teenage Mill was hardly surprising. After all, his knowledge and beliefs were the result of an education designed by perhaps the most ardent Benthamite of all, for the express purpose of producing a utilitarian disciple. But Bentham's work had given the young, 'tractable' Mill even more than a piece of intellectual architecture. It provided him with him a mission:

... the vista of improvement which he [Bentham] did open was sufficiently large and brilliant to light up my life, as well as to give a definite shape to my aspirations ... I now had opinions; a creed; a doctrine; a philosophy; in one among the best sense of the word, a religion; the inculcation and diffusion of which could be made the principal outward purpose of a life.[36]

Bentham did not shy away from the applications of his philosophy. In the *Traité*, for example, he applied his principles to issues of crime and punishment. The results, to modern eyes, were a curious mixture of the liberal and illiberal. On the one hand, Bentham believed that homosexuality should not be punished, since it harmed no one. On the other hand, if punishment was meted out it should be effective. What this meant in practice was that prison had to be 'a mill to grind rogues honest' an idea most fully realized in his plan for a 'hub and spoke' Panopticon prison, in which prisoners would be under the eye of warders twenty-four hours a day, and for which Parliament eventually paid him £23,000.

The following year, Mill read the manuscript of a book by 'Philip Beauchamp', the pen name of Mill's new friend and later pre-eminent Greek historian, George Grote, which was 'not on the truth, but on the usefulness of religious belief'.[37] Here was a striking example of the utilitarian approach. The important question about God was not whether He existed, but whether belief in His existence added to human happiness.

With his intellect and learning now put at the service of a clear creed, Mill was ready to evangelize. It was a good time to be a young man with a reforming mission. The 1820s were a period of relative economic and political stability, but there was at least a whiff of reform in the air: Robert Peel, Home Secretary for most of the decade, was introducing some legislation to protect factory workers and liberalizing the laws on trade union association. During the economic downturn of 1826, he even suspended the tariffs on corn, to bring prices more closely in line with depressed wages, an early warning of the shock to the body politic he was to administer two decades later, with the repeal of the Corn Laws.[38]

Mill embarked on a recruitment drive, indulging what one biographer has called his 'adolescent passion for founding societies'.[39] The first one was, predictably enough, a 'Utilitarian Society'. Mill says that he found the term 'utilitarian' in John Galt's novel, the *Annals of the Parish* (1821), in which the priest urges his parishioners not to leave the Gospel and become utilitarians. Unknown to Mill, Bentham had in fact used the term in a letter to Dumont decades earlier: 'I dreamt t'other night that I was a founder of a sect, of course a person of great sanctity and importance: it was called the sect of the Utilitarians.'[40]

The other original members of the correctly prophesized 'sect' were Richard Doane, Bentham's other 'pet boy'; William Eyton Tooke, whose father Thomas Tooke had started a Political Economy Club with James Mill; William Prescott, Grote's banking partner; William Ellis, an economist and later founder of the Birkbeck Schools in London; and George John Graham, a civil servant and future Registrar General. But it was the later members – John Arthur Roebuck, the Canadian radical and future MP, and Charles Austin, a lawyer – who proved to be the ones to watch. The group met fortnightly in Bentham's mothballed downstairs dining room for the next three years.

Thomas Babington Macaulay, perhaps the greatest English historian of the nineteenth century, was exposed to the group via his friendship with his Cambridge contemporary Austin and in 1829 wrote a critique of a 'society . . . composed of young men agreeing in fundamental principles, acknowledging Utility as their standard in ethics and politics ... expecting the regeneration of mankind, not from any direct action on the sentiments of unselfish benevolence, but from the effect of educated intellect enlightening the selfish feelings'. Macaulay also dismissed the disciples of James Mill and Jeremy Bentham as 'persons who, having read little or nothing, are delighted to be rescued from the sense of their own inferiority by a teacher who assures them that the studies they have neglected are of no value, puts five or six phrases in their mouths, lends them an odd number of the *Westminster Review*, and in a month transforms them into philosophers'.[41] He later apologized publicly for his tone of 'unbecoming acrimony', and the elder Mill forgave him, even supporting Macaulay's candidacy for a senior job in India, a gesture which Macaulay said demonstrated his 'generosity'.[42] Mill junior, however, would be a harsh critic of Macaulay throughout his life.

A second cluster of about a dozen earnest young men, dubbed the 'Society of Students of Mental Philosophy', met twice a week from 8.30 until 10 a.m. at Grote's house on Threadneedle Street. The members included five of the utilitarians – Mill, Graham, Ellis, Roebuck and Prescott – as well as Grote himself. Despite their name, the group began by addressing political economy, using the writings of Ricardo and Samuel Bailey, author of the influential *Critical Dissertation on the Nature, Measure and Causes of Value*, as their set texts. Their approach was predictably thorough. First, one of them would read a chunk of the text out loud. 'Our rule,' Mill wrote later, 'was to discuss thoroughly every point raised, whether great or small, prolonging the discussion until all who took part were satisfied with the conclusion they had individually arrived at ... never leaving it until we had untied every knot we found.'[43]

Satisfied with their progress in political economy, the group moved on to logic and then psychology, beginning with David Hartley's *Theory of the Human Mind*. After a well-deserved two-year break, the group reconvened to round off their work as they had begun – with James Mill – this time examining his *Analysis of the Phenomena of the Human Mind*, published in 1829. Hartley and James Mill were adherents to the 'associationist' school of psychology, based on the view that external stimuli shaped the human psyche by connecting certain activities with pleasure and others with pain. Mill followed Locke, Hartley and James Mill in seeing 'no ground for believing that anything can be the object of our knowledge except our experience'.

Mill was similarly already convinced that laissez-faire economics promoted the common good, that logic had to be based on demonstrable proof of hypotheses and that humans were motivated by the self-interested seeking of pleasure and avoidance of pain. But these conversations gave him the opportunity to develop his thoughts away from the brooding presence of his father, in the company of like-minded peers. He believed they marked his 'real inauguration as an original and independent thinker'.[44] The exhaustive, exhausting approach to discussion taken by the Threadneedle Street set certainly had a long-term influence. Mill said later that through these twice-weekly conversations:

I acquired ... a mental habit to which I attribute all that I have ever done, or ever shall do, in speculation; that of never accepting half-solutions of difficulties as complete ... never allowing obscure corners of a subject to remain unexplored, because they did not appear important; never thinking that I perfectly understood any part of a subject until I understood the whole.[45]

Mill's work would be marked consistently by a determination to gain all perspectives on an issue before pronouncing upon it, and an impatience with those – friend or foe alike – who failed to do so. When Mill was asked to review a book on logic by 'Mr George', his friend and tutor from France, he replied that the author's 'mistake was ... that of supposing that he was qualified to write on such a subject as Logic after two or three month's study'.[46] The review was never written.

These intellectual activities were also important to Mill for the companionship they offered. Following his return from France, he began to form the first English friendships of his life. One new friend, Charles Austin, paraded Mill around Cambridge and persuaded him to speak at the Cambridge Union, where he appears to have made a favourable impression. Mill recounted of Austin that 'it was through him that I first felt myself, not a pupil under teachers, but a man among men'. Mill thought that the radicalizing effect this brilliant young man had on his Cambridge contemporaries deserved to be 'counted a historical event'.[47] Indeed, Macaulay's nephew and biographer, George Trevelyan, reported that Austin 'effectually cured the young undergraduate [Macaulay] of his Tory opinions', to the distress of many of his friends. Trevelyan, writing in 1908, claimed that 'to this hour men may be found in remote parsonages who mildly resent the fascination which Austin of Jesus exercised over Macaulay of Trinity.'[48]

As Mill later moved away from the narrow form of utilitarianism advocated by his father and Bentham, however, so he became more distant from those who stuck to the creed, including Austin, who in any case was to become more motivated by the wealth that could be accumulated by brilliance at the bar than by the less tangible rewards of scholarship. Grote, an unbending utilitarian, would be dismayed by Mill's later heresies.

Mill's two closest friends after his eighteenth year were John Roebuck and George 'John' Graham. The three Johns – nicknamed the 'Trijackia' – spent a good deal of time together.[49] Mill and Graham began work on a treatise on political economy: Mill completed it alone, but did not publish it in full until 1844. On country walks with his two friends, Mill would fill his pockets with wild violet seed, and scatter them in the hedgerows to help them flourish. For the young utilitarian radical, even hedges could be improved.[50]

James Mill disapproved of these new friends, for reasons that are unclear: certainly his displeasure cannot have had political grounds. In the summer of 1824, during a weekend at the Mills' new weekend house in Mickleham, Surrey, Mill senior and Roebuck had a bitter quarrel. Roebuck and Graham left, and Harriet Mill senior fretted tearfully that 'John was going to leave the house, all on account of Graham and Roebuck'. Mill did not leave home, but he strongly defended his friends to his father. When the Trijackia reformed, Mill told the others that he had 'vindicated his position'.[51]

The row almost certainly made for a frosty Monday morning for both father and son, since by this time Mill junior was working for Mill senior in the Examiner's Department of the East India Company. His tutor was now his boss. This department, acting effectively as a civil service to the three Presidencies of the remote colony, was to become virtually a Mill monopoly: James Mill rose to the rank of Chief Examiner in 1830, a post he held until his death in 1836. John, having started in 1823, the day after his seventeenth birthday – the minimum age for Company jobs – also rose quickly through the ranks and inherited the top job twenty years later, months before the Indian Mutiny.

University had been dismissed virtually out of hand, despite a bequest from James Mill's old patron John Stuart expressly for that purpose, and the entreaties of Professor Townshend at Trinity.[52] Neither of the Mills, or Bentham, could see any value in John sitting in tutorials with the crusty, establishment dons of Oxford or Cambridge. Although James Mill had benefited greatly from Edinburgh University, the cases were hardly comparable. Bentham considered his own time at Oxford to have been a waste and this was not an unusual view: Edward Gibbon, the Roman historian, described his nine terms at Oxford as 'the fourteen months . . . most idle and unprofitable of my whole life'. [53]

The alternative career possibilities under consideration were politics, journalism and the law. Politics, given that MPs were unpaid, was difficult for anyone but the independently wealthy. The income from journalism was too unpredictable, especially for those writers who stuck to their principles. 'Writing for the press cannot be recommended as a permanent resource to any one qualified to accomplish anything in the higher departments of literature and thought' was Mill's later assessment. While there were those, such as Macaulay, who lived by their pen, writing under pressure to earn was no way to produce the work which both Mill and his father envisaged for his future: 'The writings by which one can live, are not the writings which themselves live, and are never those in which the writer does his best . . . those who support themselves by their pen must depend on literary drudgery.'[54]

That left the law. There does not seem to have been much enthusiasm on the part of either Mill for this option – according to John, his father simply saw the law as 'on the whole less ineligible for me than any other profession'.[55] None the less he began studying some law under John Austin, Charles's elder brother and a neighbour in Queen's Square. In the end, however, the East India Company seemed a safer berth. Mill does not seem to have minded missing out on a legal career. Indeed, he joined in the radicals' continual bombardment of the profession with some relish, declaring just a few years later that 'if our standard of morality includes any of the more exalted virtues, it appears to me as difficult for a lawyer to practice them as it is for a rich man to enter the kingdom of heaven'.[56] But he was 'not indifferent to exclusion from Parliament'.[57] This partly reflected the culture of the time: a parliamentary career was an important facet of the nineteenth-century gentleman's portfolio. David Ricardo was an economist, but also an MP. Macaulay was a historian and an MP. The Duke of Wellington won the battle of Waterloo; but he was also an MP and of course Prime Minister. Anthony Trollope and William Thackeray stood for Parliament; Walter Bagehot tried four times, without success.[58]

With his growing love of the countryside and botany, the other immediate disadvantage of Mill's new job was the 'unpleasantness of confinement to London', which he alleviated by walking for up to twenty miles on Sundays and spending as much time as possible in Mickleham. He also walked briskly to work, or to Grote's house for discussion, each morning. In later years, Mill established a fixed routine, arriving in his third-floor, triple-windowed office in Leadenhall Street at 10 a.m., where he would have a breakfast of tea, bread and butter and a boiled egg. His India work, piled on a high desk at which he stood or perched on a high stool, would typically be done by 1 p.m., leaving him free to converse with visiting friends – Grote 'announcing his advent by a peculiar and rat-tat with his walking stick' on Mill's office door – or turn to his writings.[59] One of his colleagues recorded Mill's working habits in the office:

The son [John], even when in conversation with others, seemed to be pre-occupied with his own thoughts, all the time moving restlessly to and fro, 'like a hyena,' as described to me. When particularly inspired, he used, before sitting down at his desk, not only to strip himself of his coat and waistcoat, but of his trousers; and so set to work, alternately striding up and down the room and writing at great speed.[60]

The job gave Mill financial security. After jumping from £30 to £100 in May 1825, his annual salary rose steadily to eventually reach £2,000 – equivalent to at least £125,000 today – in return for less than his full attention.[61] In a passage removed at his wife's suggestion from the *Autobiography*, Mill wrote that his career at India House 'precluded all uneasiness about the means of subsistence [and] occupied fewer hours of the day than almost any business or profession'.[62] He told one of his brother's friends that his literary output was only possible because he could 'get through my India work so quickly'.[63] Like his father, he showed not the slightest inclination to visit the country he was administering. But among the other gifts for which we should be grateful to the East India Company – and there are some – is the financial support given to these two outspoken radicals.

Mill's administrative work on India also directly influenced the nature of his colonialism. He would later argue that the non-political administration provided by the Company for India was superior to the more direct forms of colonial rule attempted in Ireland and America.[64] His views on the power of custom, the role of women, the economics of land and the demands of democracy were also informed, at least in part, by Indian affairs. Mill's work, which involved churning out thousands of instructions, decisions and memoranda, may also have had some less obvious consequences. One of the benefits, which he came to see only later, was that of seeing how 'public measures ... did not produce the effects which had been expected of them, and from what causes'. The daily experience of dealing with the often mundane details of Indian administration reinforced Mill's pragmatism and helped to inoculate him against the wild utopian schemes of so many of his contemporary thinkers, including, of course, Bentham himself. By Mill's own reckoning, the India House work was a defence against debilitating perfectionism: 'I became practically conversant with the difficulties of moving bodies of men, the necessities of compromise, the art of sacrificing the non-essential to preserve the essential. I learnt how to obtain the best I could, when I could not obtain everything.'[65]

By his late teens, then, Mill had a creed, comrades and a career. But he was not yet a 'public man' and he was ambitious to take his place among the reformers of the age. The discussion groups were useful for deepening understanding and cultivating friendships, but Mill did not simply want to analyse contemporary society: he wanted to improve it. Outside Parliament, there were two principal means of exerting some influence: the many debating and intellectual societies springing up across the nation, and the columns of the more serious publications. As a young man in a hurry, Mill threw himself at both.

London in the 1820s shared some of the 'lively murmur' of Paris. Mill's own debating debut occurred at a little-documented 'Mutual Improvement Society', meeting at Bentham's house, in a debate on the benefits of knowledge. But he soon had the chance of a larger hearing. In 1825, Roebuck attended a meeting of the followers of Robert Owen, founder of the cooperative movement, and suggested a debating duel between the Owenites and the utilitarian radicals. Both were on the side of reform, but while the Mill-Bentham tribe were committed to the free-market principles of Smith and Ricardo, the Owenites wanted to abolish private property altogether: it was an argument to which Mill would return repeatedly in later life. Battle was joined that November in what Mill described as a '*lutte corps-à-corps*' between Owenites and political economists'.[66] These appear to have been well-attended: at one point Mill estimated there were at least fifty bachelors in the audience.[67] In the course of the debate, Mill came up against twenty-eight-year-old Connop Thirlwall, who like Mill had been a child prodigy, reading Greek fluently at four, and later became a controversial Bishop of St Davids. Mill reckoned him the 'best speaker [he] had ever heard'.[68] At this point, his own debating style was a little wooden. His voice was frequently referred to by contemporaries as 'thin', and by his own admission, 'dry argument' was the only thing he could manage.[69] He apologized frequently for his inadequacy, fearing publicly 'that even my thoughts, feeble as they may be, will appear still more feeble by my manner of expressing them'. He clearly thought this admission struck the right self-deprecating note: he used precisely the same phrase at both the Mutual Improvement Society and in the debate against the Owenites.[70] In the debate itself, Mill took an unadulterated Ricardian stance on economics, praising the benefits of competition, the fixed nature of human self-interest and the sanctity of private property – views he would come to alter, though not abandon, as the years passed. On population, he stuck equally fast to the Malthusian view that population growth had to be curbed – voluntarily, of course – if progress were to be secured.

The popularity and quality of these debates led Mill and his cohort to establish a standing society, along the lines of 'The Spec' (the Edinburgh Speculative Society) and the Oxford and Cambridge Unions. Mill undertook the onerous duties of society Treasurer, as well as speaking regularly, and the London Debating

Society became a modest fixture of the capital's intellectual scene. For Roebuck, the exposure gained from the Society excited the interest of some of the voters of Bath and aided in his election to that parliamentary seat.[71] For Mill, the Society gave him an opportunity to practice some of the rhetorical skills he had so long admired in the classical orators. He continued to lament his poor speaking, but while he was clearly no Demosthenes he cannot have been too awful. One acquaintance described him as a 'great speaker', although later qualified his praise with the observation that 'the smallest ornament is a sin with this school, and they draw their conclusions from their narrow premises with logical dryness and precision'.[72]

Although the historian Stefan Collini suggests that a compendium of Mill's wit would be 'a slim one indeed',[73] there is some evidence in the debates of Mill's capacity for a droll put-down: 'Assertion without proof takes up little time; misrepresentation is always beautifully brief';[74] 'The honourable opener may learn that even when he is in the wrong, a little logic will do him no harm'; and 'If to have been to University be the end of education there is no doubt that by going to University that end may be most effectually attained.'[75] In one debate he reassured listeners that contrary to the fears of his opponent, the 'beauty of our women', 'good dinners' and 'turtle soup' would all survive parliamentary reform.[76] While Mill sneeringly dismissed 'frippery . . . pomp, and glare, and tinsel' in an opponent's speaking style, his own capacity for constructing resonant phrases was growing.[77] In August 1824, arguing for parliamentary reform, he said that 'a time is approaching when the enquiry, What has been, shall no longer supersede the enquiry, What ought to be, and when the rust of antiquity shall no longer be permitted to sanctify institutions which reason and public interest condemn'.[78]

Even at his best, however, Mill could never be called a great orator. As an MP in the 1860s he was not one who could easily 'hold' the house and his debating strength came from his careful preparation, unrelenting dissection of his opponents' arguments and fearlessness in attack. As well as winning new admirers, he therefore inevitably collected a clutch of enemies. Having successfully recruited a couple of Tories to the Society – the lawyers William Shee and Abraham Hayward – Mill proceeded to demolish them on a regular basis. He went over Hayward, it was said, 'as a ploughshare goes over a mouse'.[79] Abraham would – much later – serve his vengeance cold, as the author of a vicious obituary of Mill in *The Times*.

Any weaknesses as a speaker were amply compensated for by his virtuosity on the printed page. He was already wielding the weapon with which he would always be most formidable: his pen. Following his return from France, his 'intellectual cultivation', he said, came as much from writing as from reading.[80] Of course, he was still digesting a small library's worth of books each year, including Condillac, Helvetius, Hartley, Brown, Stewart, Berkeley, Reid, Condorcet, Goldsmith, Voltaire, Pascal and Courier, as well as the 'set texts' from his discussion groups. Early in the 1820s he also read a history of the French Revolution, almost certainly by François-Emmanuel Toulongeon,[81] in which he learned, 'to his astonishment, that the principles of democracy, then apparently in so insignificant and hopeless a minority everywhere in Europe, had borne all before them in France thirty years earlier, and had been the creed of the nation'.[82]

What is really astonishing, however, is Mill's ignorance of recent European history. Here was a young man who had just spent a year in France, who had undertaken possibly the most demanding education in history, who probably knew the details of the policy disagreements between Pericles and Cimon for each year between 457 and 450 BC, but was ignorant of the most important event in the history of the eighteenth and nineteenth centuries.[83] The lacuna clearly demonstrates that, voluminous though Mill's learning was, it was highly selective. His father's suspicion of things continental may have been a factor. Henceforth, Mill would remain absolutely *au fait* with political and intellectual developments in France, and for much of his life, France would act as a source of intellectual and political inspiration. He immediately imagined a similar rupturing of English society, and his own role in such an uprising. At this moment, he later recalled, 'the most transcendent glory I was capable of conceiving was that of figuring, successful or unsuccessful, as a Girondist in an English Convention'.[84]

Some of Mill's other reading was specifically intended to improve his own writing. The authors he admired were the ones who managed to combine 'ease with force', and he placed Goldsmith, Pascal and Voltaire in this category. As a result of their infusions, 'the bones and cartilage' of his own writing began in his estimation 'to clothe themselves in flesh, and the style became, at times, lively and almost light'.[85]

His first published work was a letter to the *Traveller* newspaper in December 1822, which took issue with an interpretation of Ricardian economics by the paper's owner Colonel Robert Torrens – who happened to be a friend of James Mill.[86] From here Mill moved steadily upmarket, via the *Morning Chronicle* in 1823 to the newly founded *Westminster Review* in 1824.[87] The editor of the *Chronicle*, John Black, had transformed it from a Whig publication to a radical, Benthamite mouthpiece after falling under James Mill's spell: George Grote claimed to be able to tell from Monday's editorial whether Black had eaten Sunday lunch in the Mill household.

One of the difficulties facing the budding, reform-minded writer in the first half of the 1820s was a shortage of outlets. The only two major reviews at the time were the *Quarterly*, which was Tory, and its Whig counterpart, the *Edinburgh*, and as one historian has put it, they, 'like their respective parties, [had] soon settled into a kind of convenient enmity'.[88] There was also a clutch of radical papers: Cobbett's *Political Register*, Leigh and John Hunt's *Examiner* and Henry White's *Independent Whig*, as well as the *Morning Chronicle*. But by and large their columns were filled with shallow invective rather than sustained argument – and as often as not aimed at each other, rather than the establishment. Cobbett and Henry 'orator' Hunt shared a particular dislike.[89] A dinner party attended by supporters of both men ended in a mêlée in which walking sticks were the principal weapons, and resulted in the loss of 'part of' Cobbett's waistcoat.[90]

The radical movement had in fact lost its way. There appeared little appetite for a repeat of Peterloo, and George IV's survival of the Queen Caroline affair, which began while Mill was in France, disheartened those who had – with some grounds – seen his throne tottering. The radicals and even, for a while, the Whigs had supported Caroline's claim to be Queen and she was loudly acclaimed in the streets. The Duke of Wellington worried that some of his junior officers were feeling divided in their loyalties. In response, the Tory government, under pressure from the king, introduced a 'Pain and Penalties' Bill to strip her of her titles should her widely suspected infidelity be proven. The nation was gripped. When the Lords debate – effectively a trial – began in August 1820, William Wilberforce bought nineteen Sunday newspapers so as not to miss a single titbit. Popular songs about the affair were sung in every alehouse and an exhibition of pro-Caroline artefacts was held, including a huge painting by Carloni showing her triumphantly entering Jerusalem.[91]

Although the evidence against the Queen was close to conclusive, in the end the Bill was dropped, as the pro-Queen faction, led by the radical MP Henry Brougham, threatened to produce cast-iron evidence that the king had – illegally – married again. As the year drew to a close, public interest in the affair disappeared as rapidly as it had arisen. The Whigs quickly accommodated themselves to George IV's coronation the following year, 1821; the militancy of the previous decade faded along with the Queen Caroline affair, and most of the nation got on with their lives. As Paul Johnson puts it in his monumental history of the period: 'The economy had been recovering throughout 1820, almost unnoticed. By summer 1821 it was booming – the opening of the first modern trade cycle. The nightmare conjured up by Peterloo thus dispersed, the country woke up prosperous, and the Radicals found themselves yesterday's men, rebels without a cause or a following.'[92]

The 1820s would thus be a decade for thoughtful reformers, such as Mill, rather than the populist orators. As the social historian Roy Porter puts it, 'swords were beaten into teaspoons'.[93] The coffee-houses – always centres of literary debate – were gaining in political importance, helped by a sharp reduction in coffee duties. But reformers still needed a vehicle for reforming ideas and campaigns. Parliament remained too much of a closed shop, and one of their great political hopes, Ricardo, was dead by 1823.

So Bentham decided to launch his own publication, called the *Westminster Review*, a journal which was to play a significant role in Mill's life. His father was surly about the choice of editor – John Bowring, a rival for Bentham's ear – and fearful that the whole enterprise was doomed. He none the less wrote the main piece for the first number, published in January 1824.[94] James Mill's opening was a sustained attack on the Whig aristocracy in general and the *Edinburgh Review* in particular. Mill junior did most of the research, re-reading all the old issues of the enemy publication. According to him, 'so formidable an attack on the Whig party and policy had never before been made; nor had so great a blow been struck, in this country, for radicalism . . .'[95] Certainly it was polemical enough for the publisher, Longman's, which had a stake in the *Edinburgh*, to back out of the enterprise. At this point, Robert Baldwin, James Mill's publisher, stepped in.

To almost everyone's surprise, including both Mills, the first issue was a commercial success and 'excited much attention'. All shoulders were now put to the wheel: 'There could be no room for hesitation,' wrote Mill, 'and we all became eager in doing everything we could to strengthen and improve it'.[96] Charles Austin wrote against primogeniture and George Grote tore into William Mitford's history of Greece. But Mill himself was the most prolific, writing thirteen articles between the second and eighteenth numbers. The *Westminster*, and Mill specifically, carried out a series of attacks not only on the competing reviews and their respective political parties, but on the aristocracy, the Church, the monarchy and the legal profession. Plans for parliamentary reform, greater freedom of speech, and an overhaul of the penal system were pursued in successive issues.

The group around the *Westminster* were bound together by their adherence to the reforming agenda. In economics this meant laissez-faire policies, especially free trade; in psychology, it implied adherence to 'associationism', the theory that we are all formed by our experiences; in politics, it was linked with support for a wider suffrage and opposition to the influence of the clergy; and in social affairs, voluntary birth control to halt the rise in population. They shared above all an unshakeable conviction in the power of liberated, enlightened human reason, and by extension the force of knowledge. Their motto could have been Immanuel Kant's imperative *sapere aude*, 'dare to know'.[97] Theirs was a modernized, anglicized version of the eighteenth-century Enlightenment project, a parallel the young Mill made explicit and relished. 'The French philosophes of the eighteenth century were the example we sought to emulate,' he said, 'and we hoped to accomplish no less results'.[98]

Mill thought the success of the review reflected the tone of the times: 'When the fears and animosities accompanying the war with France had been brought to an end, and people had once more a place in their thoughts for home politics, the tide began to set towards reform.'[99] For three years the *Westminster* rode the rising tide of political change and in the process, estimated Mill, 'made the Bentham school in philosophy and politics fill a greater place in the public mind than it had held before, or has ever held since.'[100] But although Bentham was the primary intellectual inspiration for the review's contributors, it was James Mill, and increasingly his son, who were its animating forces, cajoling friends into writing and finding new contributors as well as producing plentiful amounts of copy themselves. John said that while Bentham's was certainly 'a much greater name in history . . . my father exercised a far greater personal ascendancy'.[101]

Mill also helped to launch, and wrote for, the short-lived *Parliamentary History and Review* (1825–28), an annual publication which offered sharp, reformist commentaries on parliamentary debates, more often than not from the pen of a Mill or an Austin. Mill suggested in his *Autobiography* that his pieces for this *Review* marked the beginning of his editorial independence. They were 'no longer mere reproductions and applications of the doctrines I had been taught; they were original thinking ... there was a maturity about them ... which there had not been in any of my previous performances'.[102] With the exception of a strong piece on religious tolerance, Mill was overstating this claim to early independence. Although elegantly turned, these articles are in fact as doctrinaire as most of his other material from this period. He remained a loyal adjutant to his father and Bentham. Intellectually, almost all of the arguments made by Mill in print, or indeed in debate, could be traced back to his father, Bentham or to other members of the radical school. On political economy, the aristocracy, constitutional theory, the Church, population, institutional reform and psychology, all his moves were straight from the Bentham-Mill rulebook. John Roebuck's first impressions of Mill in 1824 were unequivocal: 'Although possessed of much learning, and thoroughly acquainted with the state of the political world, [he] was, as might have been expected, a mere exponent of other men's ideas, these men being his father and Bentham.'[103] Henry Taylor, another admirer, described him as 'the Apostle of the Benthamites'.[104] Thomas Carlyle's later jibe against Mill – that he was a 'made man' – would have been fair if it had referred to the years 1820 to 1825.

With the benefit of hindsight, it is possible however to discern three areas in which Mill was just beginning to fashion his own ideas: feminism, France and free speech. As he was beginning his entry into public life, a woman named Mary Anning was quietly digging in a field near Lyme Regis, Dorset, the reward for her labours being a fossilized ichthyosaurus, one of the most important palaeontological finds of the century. Her gender gave the find an added significance; it was a rare example of the slow infiltration of a handful of talented women into traditionally masculine domains. By his late teens, Mill began to write and speak on behalf of women. On 20 August 1823, a letter by a 'Lover of Justice' (Mill) was published in the *Morning Chronicle*, taking issue with the behaviour of a Queen's Square magistrate. The magistrate, hearing a complaint from a woman servant, had banished any journalist covering her side of the story from the court and accepted without interrogation the denial of the employer, whose name was William Lamb, the future Lord Melbourne and Prime Minister. Since Mill lived on the square it cannot have been difficult to determine authorship of the piece.[105] It was the start of a lifelong campaign by Mill to win for women the same legal protection enjoyed by men.

Even when writing or speaking on other subjects, Mill would make a point about women *en passant*. During one of debates with the Co-operative Society, in the middle of a passage about rhetorical style, he praises speakers who treat the audience 'like men, and I may add, like women, of judgement and sense', the parenthetical statement being designed to raise the male eyebrows of the attendees.[106]

His support for women marked an important breach with James Mill, who was decidedly conservative on this issue. Mill considered his father's *Essay on Government* to be a 'masterpiece' but 'most positively dissented [from] . . . the paragraph, in which he maintains that women may consistently with good government, be excluded from the suffrage, because their interest is the same as men'. Nor was the disagreement trifling: for the young Mill, the falseness of this claim was 'as great an error as any of those against which the Essay was directed'.[107]

Mill also began to escape from the parochialism of the British radicals by deepening his understanding of and expertise in French history and politics, and by the late 1820s would be considered an expert on France. His francophilia also indirectly caused a breach with the utilitarian tribe. Reading the biography of Baron Jacques Turgot, the French statesman and intellectual, Mill was struck by the fact that he had 'always kept himself perfectly distinct from the Encyclopedists'.[108] Turgot's example led Mill to 'leave off designating myself and others as Utilitarians, and by the pronoun "we" of any other collective designation, I ceased to *afficher* sectarianism.

My real inward sectarianism I did not get rid of till later, and much more gradually'.[109]

Most significant, from the perspective of his later concerns, were Mill's youthful forays into the issues of free speech and toleration. It was not a liberal era, especially with regard to religious and sexual differences: Catholics were excluded from public life, the suppression of anti-Christian literature was common and 'deviancy' was frowned upon.

Mill's principal concern was with freedom of opinion and belief. Prompted by the trial of Richard Carlile, the atheist publisher, for sedition and blasphemy in 1823, Mill issued three passionate pleas for free speech in the *Chronicle*, under the pseudonym 'Wickcliffe'. Some of Mill's articles were too strident for even the *Chronicle* but the published ones prefigure some of Mill's later themes, especially in *On Liberty*.[110] His abiding concern was not with the freedom of the press simply for its own sake, but with the dangers of allowing mainstream opinion to go unchallenged. For Mill, even a single voice should not be silenced, however erroneous, strident or profane it might appear. Dissent was a necessary ingredient of intellectual and social progress. To silence any view, he wrote in 1823, was 'to say that the people are better qualified to judge before discussion than after it: which is absurd, since before discussion, if their opinions are true it is only by accident, whereas after it they hold them with a complete conviction, and perfect knowledge of the proofs on which they are grounded'.[111]

While atheists were entitled to hold and publish their views, Christians of different denominations should likewise be free from discrimination: Mill's lead article for the first number of the *Parliamentary Review* of 1825 argued for the removal of all 'disabilities' faced by Roman Catholics.[112] The tide was already moving Mill's way, and four years later a Catholic Relief Act was finally passed under the Tory Government of the Duke of Wellington. Asked by Macaulay how the Prime Minister would propose the Bill to the sceptical peers, Lord Clarendon replied: 'Oh, it will be easy enough. He'll say: "My Lords! Attention! Right about face! March!"'[113]

Although Mill was fairly prolific during his late teens and early twenties, the most significant influence on his literary development during the period was a long, tiring wrestle with the work of the doctrine-maker himself, Jeremy Bentham. In 1825, Mill edited a chaotic, repetitious, gigantic pile of paper in Bentham's study into a five-volume classic of English legal theory, the *Rationale of Judicial Evidence*, published in 1827. Bentham was not easy to edit – Hazlitt had already quipped that having been published in French, Bentham should now be translated into English[114] – and the task 'occupied nearly all [Mill's] leisure for about a year'.[115] Given his work-rate, this provides a good indication of the scale of the challenge facing Mill – as well as of his loose definition of 'leisure'.

Mill was coy about being named as the editor of Bentham's *Evidence*, a work which would be hugely influential in the promotion of judicial reform, not from false modesty but because of his fierce pride. He told Bentham that he 'should be very sorry to be suspected of wishing to obtain a reputation at a cheap rate by appearing before the public under the shelter of your name'.[116] 'Amen,' replied Bentham, adding, 'If you know not what that means send to the Booksellers for a Hebrew Dictionary.'[117] In the end, Mill gave way and his name appeared.

The process of sifting through various drafts of Bentham's work, combining the best of each, influenced Mill's own writing methods. Throughout his life, he always made at least two drafts of his writings, and was a heavy editor of his own work. 'Everything which I wrote subsequently to this editorial employment,' Mill said, 'was markedly superior to anything that I had written before it.'[118] By the time Mill turned twenty, in 1826, it was becoming clear that his literary gift was going to provide more than adequate compensation for any lack of oratorical skill. A few years later, he noted that 'only when I have a pen in my hand can I make language and manner the true image of my thoughts'.[119]

In his own writing and debating during the period 1822 to 1826, Mill's principal form of engagement was attack. He was frustrated and angry at what he saw as the stupidity and conservatism of

English society, and especially its ruling classes. Even for a polemical age his forays were vituperative, and not all of them reflect well on him. A savage assault on David Hume's magisterial *History of England* – by way of a review of George Brodie's history – included the claim that 'regard for truth formed no part of his [Hume's] character ... it would be a vain attempt to describe the systematic suppression of the truth which is exemplified in this portion of his history'.[120] Mill would aim his fire across the political spectrum: the Duke of Wellington was predictably blasted – but so too, in 1825 in the course of the debate with the Owenites, was the radical hero William Cobbett, who was so revered that the essayist William Hazlitt had described him as a 'kind of *fourth estate* in the politics of the country'.[121] 'It does not follow that a man's opinion is good for anything because he has abilities,' said Mill, '– it is also necessary that he should have a little knowledge, and a little principle ... It is one of his [Cobbett's] peculiar characteristics that he pronounces with equal confidence upon the things which he knows, and upon the things which he does not know ...'[122]

The British constitution was a favoured target, and Mill especially took issue with English worship of the idea of 'constitutional balance'. As early as 1824, in front of the Mutual Improvement Society, Mill declared: 'There seems to be something singularly captivating in the word balance: as if, because anything is called a *balance*, it must, for that reason, be necessarily good.' Even if the metaphor were allowed, Mill pointed out that equilibrium between the 'balancing forces' of the constitution meant, logically, that 'the machine must stand still'.[123] Mill's pessimism was not entirely justified: the Great Reform Act of 1832 was less than a decade away.

The aristocracy – and its influence on politics – was of course a *bête noire* of all the radicals. Indeed, for Mill, the difference between Whigs and Tory was a 'petty question': all were landowners or nominees of landowners.[124] After all, he declaimed, 'Did they not almost all support the Six Acts? Do they not all support the Corn Laws?' The House of Commons was seen by Mill as an echo-chamber for the views of a tiny minority. Charles Grey, later Earl

Grey, had estimated in 1793 that the House of Commons was effectively controlled by two hundred aristocratic families, and although his figures were hotly disputed, 'Two Hundred Families' remained a staple of radical rhetoric into the nineteenth century and was often cited by Mill.[125] It was, as he said, 'a Constitution of the rich'.[126] Popular opinion, he argued, had little influence on the parliamentary process. So long as enough was done to avoid outright revolution, there was little to fear from the general population. 'The people may cry,' he said, 'but if they only cry, who will attend to their cries?'[127] While he privately opposed fox-hunting, he used the sport as the basis for a heavily satirical attack on the landed classes. Fox-hunting, he suggested, was 'an employment ... admirably fitted to keep their constitutions in repair – and themselves out of mischief ... it is much better that they should torment foxes, than men; and ... foxhunting is a far more proper pastime for such persons than judging or legislating'.[128]

It followed that Mill favoured a much wider suffrage, although he was not specific at this point about where the line should be drawn: he was more interested in proving the weakness of existing arrangements than in detailing their replacement. While Mill dismissed the idea of a permanent 'balance' in the constitution, he accepted the case for 'checks' on the power of any particular group or individual. In 1824, he ingeniously turned the argument that Parliament was a necessary check on the monarch against the aristocratically dominated chamber itself:

The theory ... of the British Constitution, is, that unchecked power is always abused: and it is because the King would be a tyrant, if he could, that a House of Commons is given to control him. How absurd then to say that the same check which is required by a king, is not required by a House of Commons! Have a hundred despots ever been found to be less evil than one?[129]

This argument merits some attention, because while it is used here to justify greater democratic participation it also contains the germ of Mill's later anxieties about working-class suffrage. His concern was always that one group should not hold sway over another. For him, liberty meant protection from 'despotism' of any kind. But if a hundred tyrants could be as evil as one, so could a million. Mill would later fear that 'the people', i.e. the majority working class, might wield the same despotic power over other classes, especially the professional middle class, of which he was a member, as the aristocracy currently did over them. In his greatest works he would warn of the 'tyranny of the majority' – words which echo the sentiments he was directing at this time at the Whig-Tory aristocratic establishment. It is also possible to detect the first stirrings of Mill's fear that 'the people' were not yet ready for democracy, although he did not, in this early, idealistic phase, take his argument to this conclusion. He admitted that the people were 'bigoted and prejudiced and stupid and ignorant enough', but blamed the ruling class for not providing them with an education: universal elementary education was still half a century away. In any case, he still preferred 'stupid, ignorant persons who have not a sinister interest to stupid, ignorant persons who have', in other words, the block-headed landowners.[130]

During this demanding period of writing, editing, and debating, Mill's energy was unquenchable. Walking to work from Westminster to the City, he would often be joined by one of his friends, and they would talk all the way. Otherwise he would use the time to think through a problem of logic, or prepare some phrases for an upcoming debate or review: it was on one such morning, crossing St James's Park, that he found the horrific bundle which was to lead to his brief imprisonment. With the exception of his rural excursions, every waking moment was filled with reading, writing, debating, editing, organizing and discussing. The London he traversed between home, Grote's house, the Freemason's Tavern – where the London Debating Society met – and his own office in Leadenhall Street was changing around him. The population of the city was soaring, and even as the country prospered, it did so as the 'two nations' that would come to dominate political life throughout the century. As the nation became richer, so its poor became more visible and Mill's economic egalitarianism – which he never abandoned – was on display in his early polemical works:

Everybody knows that the same sum of money is of much greater value to a poor man than to a rich one . . . The richer a man is the less he is benefited by any further addition to his income. The man of £4,000 a year has four times the income of the man who has £1,000 a year; but does anybody suppose that he has four times the happiness?[131]

Mill was already arguing in a speech made in 1826 that having secured the production of wealth through the defence of property rights and promotion of competition, the next concern of the legislator was 'what *distribution* conduces most to human happiness', to which his answer was: 'that which approximates the nearest to equality'.[132] These issues were not simply for the textbooks and debating societies: the economy was entering a new phase. Between 1821 and 1848, 5,000 miles of railway track were laid in the UK. In 1823, a revolutionary technique for road-building, the innovation of John Loudon ('tarmac') McAdam, was given parliamentary approval, and within two decades the UK had the best road system the world had seen for two millennia. After 1820, Britain was set on a century-long course of mobilization, industrialization and secularization – in short, modernization – which would last for a century.

This new world would need new thinkers, and Mill was determined to be one of the foremost among them. His goal was to put his ideas to work, influencing the course of events. He would be as much an activist as an analyst. Until 1826, none the less, he appeared as a distinctly bookish kind of radical. The young, dry Mill appeared to personify almost perfectly the general tendency of the utilitarians to downgrade feelings, or 'sentimentality' in favour of rationality – as he said in the *Autobiography*, to present 'utility as cold calculation; political economy as hard-hearted' – a weakness he later saw clearly. Among the group as a whole, 'cultivation of feeling (except the feelings of public and private duty) was not in much esteem ... What we principally thought of, was to change people's opinions.'[133]

Mill's prodigious learning, ascetic upbringing and formidable work ethic had indeed made him a very serious young man. 'I conceive that the description so often given of Benthamite, as a mere reasoning machine', he wrote in the *Autobiography*, 'was, during two or three years of my life not altogether untrue of me.'[134] He would in time, slowly and painfully, throw off some of the debilitating legacy of his earliest years. But he would always be a serious figure. A century after his death, the Monty Python philosophers' drinking song played on this aspect of his image: 'John Stuart Mill, of his own free will / after half a pint of shandy was particularly ill.'[135]

During the 1825 debates, one of the Owenites directly accused Mill of failing to displaying sufficient feeling, prompting him to reply that 'feeling [should] be kept strictly to its proper function, that of stimulating our exertions in that course which reason points out'. But his opponent had clearly hit a sore spot, because Mill went on, more than slightly defensively:

I must beg gentlemen not to suppose that I am destitute of feeling for no reason perhaps but because my feelings are under better regulation than theirs. No, Sir: if I am to be condemned for want of feeling, I will have a fair trial – I will be tried in the proper province of feeling – I will be tried in *action* ...[136]

While he could not refer to it, Mill had of course been tried in action just two years earlier, when he was arrested and imprisoned. On that day in the summer of 1823, Mill's opinions about population and poverty had not changed: it was the passionate feelings aroused by the finding of the dead baby that called him to act. So while the image of Mill's earnestness and dryness is clear and accurate, it is also only half the picture. In six years, Mill had become a Francophile, a zealously committed Benthamite and a radical, serious journalist, debater and civil servant. His productivity was extraordinary; even if he was not, as critics claimed, a 'machine', he certainly worked like one. The project of his father and Bentham to create a 'worthy successor' had, it seemed, been more successful than they ever imagined. From the blank slate of an infant boy's mind, they had fashioned a formidable disciple.

But in the autumn of 1826, at the age of twenty, Mill suddenly faltered. Doubt washed over him, and then depression claimed him. He was forced to make himself anew, an act which was to influence everything that followed – his philosophy, friendships, politics and even his love life – and which would also be the source of his immortal legacy: the most articulate plea for human liberty of the modern era.

CHAPTER THREE

Strange Confusion (1826–30)

>‹

At the age of twenty, Mill lost his faith. In his case, the religion was Benthamism, rather than Christianity, and he had been a true believer for just five years. But Mill's trauma was acute, none the less. During his feverish teenage years, Bentham's utilitarianism had become the 'keystone' of his beliefs.[1] Without it, he was lost. Mill's intellectual recovery from what he described as a 'mental crisis' – correctly labelled by Stefan Collini 'one of the best-known identity-crises in history' – would not be complete for decades, if ever.[2]

It began philosophically enough. In a 'dull state of nerves', Mill decided to conduct a thought experiment. 'Suppose', he suggested to himself, 'that all your objects in life were realized; that all the changes in institutions and opinions which you are looking forward to could be effected at this very instant: would this be a great joy and happiness to you? And an irrepressible self-consciouness answered, "No!" At this my heart sank within me: the whole foundation on which my life was constructed fell down.'[3] The psychology of this 'crisis' has been attributed by modern commentators variously to a yearning for God; a reaction to the overwork of the previous few years; an inevitable consequence of a Spartan childhood; and an unconscious rebellion against a tyrannical father.[4] The truth is almost certainly more prosaic. It was a miserable winter, he was desperately lonely, and he suddenly saw the hollowness of the philosophical religion to which he had subscribed. Mill was, as he described it, 'left stranded at the commencement of my voyage, with a well-equipped ship and a rudder, but no sail; without any real desire for the ends which I had been so carefully fitted out to work for'.[5] Mill became maudlin about the fact that an octave contained 'only five tones and two semitones', which severely limited a composer's options. 'I was', he said, 'seriously tormented by the thought of the exhaustion of musical combinations.'[6]

Mill's anguish was not visible to those around him, however; he continued to perform his duties at India House, as well as to attend and speak at the Debating Society. None of his friends, not even the other two members of the 'Trijackia', was aware there was anything wrong with him – an indication, perhaps, of a lack of intimacy in even his closest relationships. As he recalled, 'I sought no comfort by speaking to others of what I felt. If I had loved anyone sufficiently to make confiding my griefs a necessity, I should not have been in the condition I was.'[7] Mill was reminded of Macbeth's plea to his doctor to 'administer to his mind diseased', only to receive the reply: 'Therein the patient/Must minister to himself.'[8]

Mill's self-ministry began with tears and ended in poetry. Reading a passage of Jean-François Marmontel's *Mémoires*, which described the death of the writer's father, Mill found himself weeping. He was delighted. 'From this moment my burthen grew lighter,' he recalled. 'I was no longer hopeless: I was not a stock or a stone. I had still, it seemed, some of the material out of which all worth of character, and all capacity for happiness, are made.'[9] The 'material' underpinning Mill's recovery was emotion. After a childhood in which feelings had been largely scorned, Mill now came to believe that emotions were as important as thoughts. William Wordsworth, the conservative Lakeland poet, spoke directly to his new mood. In the famous 'Ode: Intimations of Immortality from Recollections of Early Childhood', Wordsworth described a similar bout of ennui, from which he also recovered:

A timely utterance gave that thought relief,
     And I again am strong.
The Cataracts blow their trumpets from the steep,
No more shall grief of mine the season wrong.[10]

When Mill reached the following lines, he must have felt that he was being addressed in person:

Thou, whose exterior semblance doth belie
     Thy Soul's immensity;
Thou best Philosopher, who yet dost keep
Thy heritage, thou Eye among the blind . . .[11]

Wordsworth, Mill insisted, captured 'thought coloured by feeling, under the excitement of beauty'.[12] Mill became evangelical about the poet, much to the dismay of his radical friends who, John Morley reported, 'used to get very angry with him for loving Wordsworth'.[13] The poet was certainly on the other side of the political spectrum: in 1818, he had campaigned vigorously against the radical Henry Brougham, who was trying to prise one of the two Westmorland parliamentary seats out of the grip of the principal local landowner, Lord Lonsdale, who had installed two of his sons in them. Some of Wordsworth's fellow poets were as dismayed as the radicals: Byron used the preface of his masterpiece, *Don Juan*, to savage Wordsworth for his hypocrisy and treachery and Shelley addressed a sonnet to him on the matter, concluding sadly that 'thou leavest me to grieve, / Thus having been, that thou shouldst cease to be'.[14] Weeks before his death, Mill recalled to a friend how he had responded to the anger of his friends during this period. '"Wordsworth," I used to say, "is against you, no doubt, in the battle which you are now waging, but after you have won, the world will need more than ever those qualities which Wordsworth is keeping alive and nourishing"'.[15]

Above all, Mill came to believe that poets could powerfully describe the vital, emotional dimension of human life. On a personal level, poetry fuelled his own journey away from the ascetic rationalism of his own upbringing. Almost a century earlier David Hume had passed through a similar phase, described by his physician as 'the Disease of the Learned', and for which he sensibly prescribed claret and riding. Hume's experience clearly influenced his later philosophy, especially in his distrust of pure reason and emphasis on human affinity. 'Be a philosopher,' Hume concluded, 'but amidst all your philosophy be still a man.'[16]

John Bowring told Caroline Fox in 1840 that Mill 'was most emphatically a philosopher, but then he read Wordsworth, and that muddled him, and he has been in strange confusion ever since, endeavouring to unite poetry and philosophy'.[17] But Bowring had accurately foreseen the impact of Mill's new interests on his long-term intellectual preoccupations: he became convinced that technocratic reform of social, educational and political arrangements – the principal focus of the 'philosophic radicals' – was an insufficient basis for progress. The character of individuals became as important to Mill as the design of institutions or legislation. What he described as the 'internal culture of the individual' was henceforth a crucial theme in Mill's thought, and the emotional ingredients of that culture were placed on a par with the intellectual ones. 'The cultivation of the feelings' he said, 'became one of the cardinal points in my ethical and philosophical creed.'[8]

During an 1828 debate in which he spoke on the subject of 'Perfectability', Mill suggested that 'the passions are the spring, the moral principle only the regulator of human life'.[19] As the Mill scholar John Robson has pointed out, the 'only' in this sentence was indicative of Mill's new outlook.[20] From a philosophical standpoint, Mill's views reflected the work of earlier writers such as Hume and Rousseau, and anticipated the work of later philosophers who have attempted to integrate an understanding of the role of feelings into a discipline dominated by a narrow rationalism.[21]

Mill's shifting views were put to the test in January 1829, when he and Roebuck found themselves, for the first time, on opposite sides in the Debating Society, arguing respectively for the merits of

Wordsworth and Byron. The subject was not treated light-heartedly, at least by Mill. Having said in a previous session that he did not have the stamina to speak for two hours, he proceeded to spend at least that much time defending his poetic saviour.[22] Mill lamented the 'contemptuous laugh' with which Roebuck had introduced certain Wordsworth passages – including 'I wandered lonely as a cloud' – and set three tests for the greatness of poets: their capacity to describe objects, feelings and thoughts.[23] Mill declared Wordsworth as pre-eminent in the first and third categories and at least a match for Byron in the second. Indeed, he was, Mill claimed, the only contemporary English poet with a claim to the first rank.[24] There was also an autobiographical dimension to Mill's argument. In the only confessional passage in all of his debating speeches, he explained that Wordsworth had helped him to emerge from a period when he 'thought life a perpetual struggle'.[25]

In later years, Mill would relegate Wordsworth below Shelley, Tennyson and especially Coleridge, who would in time have a profound influence on Mill, as much for the depth of his philosophy as for the beauty of his poetry. It was Coleridge who Mill retrospectively recruited in his own *Autobiography* to describe his 1826–7 depression:

> A grief without a pang, void, dark, and drear,
> A stifled, drowsy, unimpassioned grief,
> Which finds no natural outlet, no relief,
> In word, or sigh, or tear . . .[26]

What Mill may not have known was that this poem, 'Dejection: An Ode', was itself inspired by the first four stanzas of Wordsworth's 'Immortality'.[27]

Mill's engagement with poetry marked a significant step away from his philosophical roots and his first group of friends. His relationship with Roebuck was weakened by the Wordsworth v. Byron bout and Mill left the Debating Society shortly afterwards. In his *Autobiography*, he said the departure was the result of having had 'enough of speech making'.[28] But at the time, and in private, Mill gave a more personal explanation: 'I am resolved hereafter to avoid all occasions for debate, for they cannot now strengthen my sympathies with those who agree with me, & are sure to weaken them with those who differ.'[29]

Mill's crisis, and embrace of Wordsworth, also led him to re-evaluate the *modus operandi* and motivation of reformers. Theory was no longer enough. It was not sufficient to rely, in Macaulay's phrase, on 'the effect of educated intellect, enlightening the selfish feelings' – rather, a desire for human betterment had to be based on a love of humankind.[30] Mill clearly did not try too hard to disguise himself, or his own feelings, in one debate, ostensibly on 'The Use of History':

He who is just starting in his worldly career, and before whose enraptured sight visions of earthly grandeur and the applause of men are now for the first time floating, he may think that these things are sufficient for happiness. But it is he who has obtained these things, or he who even without having obtained them (and there are such men) has sickened of the pursuit, it is for him to feel that it is all hollow, and that it is necessary to the happiness of human beings to love human beings, and therefore necessary to think them deserving of love.[31]

So ashamed was Mill now of an earlier essay attacking emotion and sentiment, that he retrieved it from Harriet Grote, to whom he had lent it, and burned it.[32] In the full flood of his newly discovered love of poetry, Mill even suggested that it could capture 'intuitive' truths about human existence, endorsing Wordsworth's view of poetry as the most philosophical writing, 'not standing upon external testimony, but carried alive into the heart by passion; truth which is its own testimony'.[33] Writing in 1833 to Carlyle, Mill declared:

I conceive that most of the highest truths are, to persons endowed by nature in certain ways which I think I could state, intuitive; that is, they need neither explanation nor proof, but if not known before are assented to as soon as stated ... Now one thing not useless to do would be to ... make those who are not poets understand that poetry is higher than logic, and that the union of the two is philosophy.[34]

Just a few years later, Mill would have moved away from this extreme position, castigating the 'intuitionist' school as a brake on necessary reform, and arguing strenuously that any philosophy that saw certain truths, whether about mathematics or morality, as being discovered '*a priori*' – in other words as simply 'innate' rather than being externally learned or tested – was the very foundation of political conservatism.

In his early twenties, however, Mill was convinced not only that poetry was a vital element in human flourishing, but that poets, or 'artists', should play a key reforming role. 'Although a philosopher cannot, by culture, make himself, in the peculiar sense in which we now use the term, a poet,' he wrote in 1833, 'a poet may always, by culture, make himself a philosopher.'[35] The Benthamite school, by contrast, were staunchly rational in their approach: utilitarian science would both diagnose and prescribe for society's ills. Poets were at best a distraction: in the first edition of the *Westminster Review*, Peregrine Bingham, a Benthamite barrister, wrote disparagingly that 'Mr Moore [the one who lampooned Mill over his arrest in 1823] *is* a poet, and therefore is *not* a reasoner'.[36] Reason held the key to progress, not rhyme. Wordsworth ironically described the rationalist mindset in *The Prelude*:

> ... What Delight!
> How glorious! in self-knowledge and self-rule,
> To look through all the frailties of the world,
> And, with resolute mastery shaking off
> The accidents of nature, time, and place,
> That make up the weak being of the past ...[37]

It was Shelley – Mill's wife's favourite poet – who argued in 1821 that because of their appreciation and production of 'intellectual beauty', poets were the 'unacknowledged legislators of the world'. But Mill did acknowledge them.[38] He became a voracious consumer of contemporary poetry and, by way of two essays in the *Monthly Repository* in 1833, added poetry criticism to his portfolio of activities.[39] Yet it was not the area in which he displayed his greatest originality. Although there are moments of insight to be found in these appraisals – one of the best known is that 'eloquence is heard, poetry is overheard' – Mill's theory of poetry was almost as derivative of Coleridge as his teenage outpourings had been of Bentham.[40] He suffered sporadically from 'gloom and morbid despondency' throughout his life, but except during the darkest moments of his first, and worst, depression, Mill was more concerned with the ideas expressed by a poem than with its simple beauty.[41] 'Mr Mill was not', a contemporary recounted shortly after his death, 'a cultivator of Art for Art's sake.'[42] He was especially interested in the way poetry could connect feelings with thoughts: poets were 'so constituted that emotions are the links of association by which their ideas, both sensuous and spiritual, are connected together'.[43]

While Mill is not, then, a significant figure in the history of literary criticism, he could claim at least one important critical success, bringing Alfred Tennyson – later the poet laureate – to wider notice, via a glowing review in 1835. Mill praised the young poet's ability to create scenes 'in keeping with some state of human feeling' as well as his 'advancing ... intellectual culture'.[44] Robert Browning, on the other hand, felt Mill's critical lash. Asked by a mutual friend, William Johnson Fox, to review 'Pauline', Mill penned a lukewarm welcome for which, highly unusually, he could find no publisher. At the same time, Mill pencilled his private, deeper misgivings about the poem on the flyleaf of his copy. He especially disliked the 'flummery' of the closing sections, which failed to mask the amorality of the 'hero' in accepting Pauline's love without true reciprocation. This was surely, Mill scribbled, a reflection of the author, who 'seems ... possessed with a more intense and morbid self-consciousness than I ever knew in any sane human being'. Fox ignored Mill's request to keep these comments from Browning – and they caused the poet greater distress than his failure to sell a single copy. To complicate matters, the model for Pauline, Eliza 'Lizzie' Flower, was Browning's youthful *amour*, the object of a recent flirtation with Mill, and now Fox's mistress. The poem was only reissued at the end of Browning's life, and even then, he said, with 'extreme repugnance'.[45]

Mill's 'crisis' had a further, deeper impact on his mature thought. It marked the beginning of his journey away from the narrow version of utilitarianism of his father and Bentham. After his own struggle to re-create himself, Mill would place thereafter human autonomy – his version of 'liberty' – at the heart of his philosophy, economics and politics. He described to Carlyle how it was his extraordinary education that had paradoxically given him the resources to move away from Benthamite views: 'None however of them all has become so unlike what he once was as myself, who originally was the narrowest of them all … fortunately however I was not *crammed*; my own thinking faculties were called into strong though partial play; & by their means I have been able to *remake* all my opinions.'[46]

This concept of 'remaking' – what Goethe and the German romantics called *Bildung* – was by the late 1820s beginning to affect Mill. His mature philosophy would be founded on a conviction that the range of opportunities for self-creation and autonomy – defined properly as 'self-rule' – were the standard against which cultures, political systems, economic institutions and philosophical ideas should be judged.

Mill's most heretical thoughts were kept to himself, but the new Mill gradually became known to his friends. His friendship with Roebuck diluted into a sometimes wary acquaintanceship, before ending abruptly a few years later as a result of Mill's relationship with his future wife, Harriet Taylor. But as one John was lost, another was found. In 1828, the Debating Society had gained two new members – Frederick Denison Maurice and John Sterling – who were politically radical but 'vehemently opposed' to

Benthamism and who introduced into discussion, recalled Mill, 'the general doctrines and modes of thought of the European reaction against the philosophy of the eighteenth century'.[47] Their hero was Coleridge. Mill said that the pair injected into the Society a 'third intellectual party or nuance, opposed both to the Benthamite and to the Tory sections which used to fight their battles there'.[48]

Maurice was destined to be a great public figure, the first principal of the Working Men's College and a professor of moral philosophy at Cambridge. Mill already knew him a little via mutual friends and ranked him above Coleridge in terms of sheer intellect, but was disappointed to see him frittering it away on an ill-fated, lifelong attempt to rehabilitate the Anglican Church along radical lines – a project which culminated in the formation of the Christian Socialist Movement. There was 'more intellectual power wasted in Maurice than in any other of my contemporaries', Mill estimated. 'Few of them certainly have had so much to waste.'[49]

It was Sterling who was to become the closest friend of Mill's life, Harriet excepted. After offering his own 'long and rambling' contribution to the poetry debate, Sterling was delighted – and, along with plenty of other members, slightly startled – by Mill's eloquent defence of Wordsworth.[50] The two men quickly became close and in his later poem, 'The Election', Sterling reminisced 'how youths at clubs, while sipping coffee, solve / The questions pedants through long life revolve'.[51]

Although the same age, in temperament, they were a stark contrast. Sterling was chaotic, itinerant, exuberant and reckless – and no intellectual. In 1830 he was deeply involved in a wild scheme to help General Torrijos and a rag-tag bunch of rebels overthrow the repressive Ferdinand VII of Spain, using a boat commissioned by Sterling's cousin Robert Boyd and a group of lightly armed Cambridge Apostles, including Tennyson. Mill appears to have done nothing to dissuade his friend from this madness; nor, however, did he show the slightest sign of reaching for a musket himself. At the eleventh hour, and entirely typically, Sterling fell madly in love with Susan Barton – his wife-to-be – and the seaborne plot collapsed. Boyd and Torrijos went anyway, and were summarily shot by the fully informed Spanish secret police. If Sterling was fortunate on this occasion, it was the exception to a general rule of misfortune. He lost his wife and mother within an hour of each other, and died himself at the age of thirty-eight. From his deathbed, Sterling described Mill as:

> a friend of many years, and one of the truest and worthiest, uniting a warm, upright and really lofty soul with a still and even cold appearance and a head that reasons as a great Steam Engine works ... my intimacy with him has been one of the two great fortunes of my life – though hardly I suppose were ever two creatures more unlike than he and I. I have often wondered that he put up with me at all. Yet I am sure he would cut off his right hand tomorrow if he could see me recover from this illness.[52]

For Mill, the personality differences between them were part of the attraction; he told Sterling that he knew of 'no person who possesses more, of what I have not, than yourself'.[53] In full flight from his ascetic upbringing, Mill was likely to have been just as delighted that someone like Sterling – an openly and deeply emotional man – would want to be friends with him, as vice versa. The friendship validated his new identity. Sterling confessed to Mill how his preconceptions of him as a 'manufactured' man were shattered during the Wordsworth debate – surely music to Mill's ears. Mill missed his friend hugely when he departed, in 1831, for seven years in the West Indies.

By then, however, he had met Harriet and had also befriended the inventor William Bridges Adams, later the creator of the 'Adam's Axle' for trains.[54] Again it was a case of opposites attracting. Mill told Adams that 'while I require to be warmed, *you* perhaps occasionally to be calmed'. He also told Adams:

> We two possess, what, next to community of purpose is the greatest source of friendship between minds of any capacity; this is, not *equality*, for nothing can be so little interesting to a man as his own double; but,

reciprocal superiority. Each of us knows many things which the other knows not, & can do many things which the other values but cannot himself do, or not so well.[55]

This ideal of a friendship based on a 'reciprocal superiority' would later be placed at the heart of Mill's feminist reinvention of marriage.

During his early twenties, Mill continued to widen his social circle. His beloved summer walking tours were always group outings. John Graham and a colleague from India House, Horace Grant, accompanied him along the Sussex coast in 1827. The four-man party for the 1828 excursion – this time across Berkshire and Buckinghamshire – included Edwin Chadwick, a stern Benthamite and the architect of both the Poor Law Amendment Act of 1834, which established the hated workhouses (the 'Poor Law Bastilles'), and a raft of public health measures intended to reduce the spread of cholera. To many, Chadwick was not an attractive personality: *The Times* acidly suggested that a visit from Chadwick was as unwelcome as one from cholera itself and his work on the poor laws led Disraeli to dub his guiding philosophy 'Brutilitarianism'.[56] Wordsworth had men like Chadwick in mind in this passage from 'The Old Cumberland Beggar':

> ... Statesman! Ye
> Who are so restless in your wisdom, ye
> Who have a broom still ready in your hands
> To rid the world of nuisances ...[57]

Mill took detailed notes on all his walking trips, thankfully for his own amusement only: if he was an indifferent literary critic, he was a dreadful travel writer. In the course of his 1828 tour he describes both the wood, Penley Hangings, and High Wycombe as being 'embosemed' in hills, Windsor as 'very striking', Mapledurham as 'a neat little village with a church' and a property near Hurley as 'an extremely old and old-looking manor house'.[58] Nevertheless, Mill's enjoyment of the countryside and the exercise is clear throughout. When the quartet reached the perimeter of the Cliveden estate, two of the party, including Mill, bunked over the fence in order to trespass across the grounds, rejoining the less adventurous pair on the other side.[59]

For his 1831 tour of the Lake District, Mill was joined by another young man with a 'broom in his hands', Henry Cole. The driving force behind the Great Exhibition of 1851, Cole would also become the founder of the South Kensington Estate, home to the Science, Natural History and Victoria and Albert Museums as well as the Royal College of Art and Royal Albert Hall. Dickens, who satirized him in *Hard Times* as the 'school inspector . . . always with a system to force down the general throat like a bolus', disliked his Utilitarian view of the role of art in society.[60] But neither his public-spiritedness nor his Englishness were in question: his 1845 winning design for the Royal Society of Arts, Manufactures and Commerce (RSA) was for a teacup and saucer.

Of course, the two men were in Wordsworth country. Indeed, the choice of destination was almost certainly inspired by the poet – Mill's journal indicates that almost everywhere he looked he recalled Wordsworth's description of the scene.[61] Mill had met him briefly at a London breakfast, but now seized the opportunity to spend almost four days roaming and conversing with Wordsworth at Rydal Mount. The more prosaic Cole stayed away. Delighted by his conversations with the poet, Mill told Sterling that 'all my differences with him, or with any other philosophic Tory, would be differences of matter-of-fact or detail, while my differences with the radicals and utilitarians are differences of principle'.[62] While he was in the area, Mill also dropped in for tea with the future poet laureate Robert Southey, a man he had dismissed just a few years earlier as the leading apologist for the establishment, 'advocating strenuously . . . the reigning opinions . . . to heap insult and opprobrium on all who dissent from those opinions'.[63] Bentham had been more direct, describing him as 'an ultra-servile sack-guzzler'.[64] By the time he supped with Southey, Mill's breach with the strict utilitarians was almost complete.

One of the 'differences of principle' between Mill and the purer utilitarians was over the role of history in progressive thought. Jeremy Bentham and his school paid little attention to the past, a shortcoming which Macaulay highlighted in his 1829 assault on James Mill's theory of government. 'We have here an elaborate treatise on Government,' Macaulay wrote, 'from which but for two or three passing allusions, it would not appear that the author was aware that any government actually existed among men. Certain propensities of human nature are assumed; and from these premises the whole science of politics is synthetically deduced!'[65] For the Benthamites, of course, this was praise. 'Happy is the nation without history', declared Cesare Beccaria, one of Bentham's inspirations.[66] Macaulay argued, in stark contrast, that all the raw materials of contemporary politics could be found by carefully sifting through the past.

Brooding over Macaulay's article, Mill saw that his father's view was indeed inadequate. Society was not a blank sheet of paper. The history of institutions and cultures was a necessary component of their future. But Mill also saw the conservative implications of Macaulay's reliance on history as the only reliable guide to the future, with theory and ideology cast aside. What Mill was searching for was a philosophy of history which could combine the best of both sides of the Macaulay–James Mill debate. He found one in French. At the Debating Society, Mill had befriended Gustave d'Eichthal, who introduced him to the work of Claude Henri de Rouvary, Comte de Saint-Simon, his recently deceased master and the father of French socialism. Saint-Simon argued that history passed through alternating eras of stability and change – 'organic' and 'critical' periods; that conflict of opposites led to a resolution different to either; that societies were continually breeding the seeds of their own destruction; and that both ideas and institutions appropriate for one age would become redundant in the next and need replacing.[67] Karl Marx was one nineteenth-century thinker strongly influenced by this view of history – Mill was another.

'The very idea of a "spirit of the age"', Mill wrote in an essay of the same title, published in seven parts in the *Examiner* during the first half of 1831, is one 'essentially belonging to an age of change'. Mill believed that during such a 'critical' transforming phase there was a struggle between old and new ideas, out of which a new synthesis would be forged. 'Mankind have outgrown old institutions and old doctrines,' Mill wrote, 'and have not yet acquired new ones ... the times are pregnant with change.'[68] These were plausible enough claims, as cholera spread across London and rioters under 'Captain Swing' swept across the south of England, smashing threshing machines and 'liberating' workhouses: 101 capital sentences were passed against the agitators, of which nine were carried out, and more than eight hundred were either imprisoned or deported.[69] Lord Grey's Whig government was panicky, favouring reform but fearing revolution, and Mill, in London, was personally witnessing an economic, social and industrial revolution which was changing the face of the capital with every passing year. As he wrote in 1831, a man 'may learn in a morning's walk through London more of the history of England during the nineteenth century, than all the professed histories in existence will tell him concerning the other eighteen'.[70]

In this fevered atmosphere, Mill offered the cool Saint-Simonian analysis that while the aristocracy and Church had been forces for good in the past – during the last 'organic' period of stability – they had become obstacles to progress as the world changed around them. The value of any specific law or institution was necessarily contingent upon the social, political and economic context of the time. Today's progressive institution might have been yesterday's roadblock to reform – and vice versa. 'To find fault with our ancestors for not having annual parliaments, universal suffrage, and vote by ballot,' he wrote, 'would be like quarrelling with the Greeks and Romans for not using steam navigation.' In other words, his father was wrong. But so was Macaulay. 'I differ', added Mill, 'from those who ridiculously invoke the wisdom of our ancestors as authority for institutions which in substance are now totally different, howsoever they may be the same in form.'[71]

None the less it is easy to see why Mill's friends were unhappy. Historical sensitivity and 'spirits' of ages were not part of the radical lexicon. Mill even threw in some quotes from Goethe, recalling later that at this point 'the influences of European, that is to say, Continental thought, and especially those of the reaction of the nineteenth century against the eighteenth century were streaming in on me'.[72] Carlyle's delighted proclamation on reading the essay was: 'Here is a new Mystic!'[73] Henry Cole recorded a conversation in 1831 with Mill in which he 'talked about his own personal character which he bore with other people. With utilitarians, said he, he was a mystic – with mystics a utilitarian – with Logicians a sentimentalist and with the latter a Logician.'[74]

But while Mill's intellectual explorations were unsettling to his fellow radicals, they had not dented his own political radicalism. If anything he had become more revolutionary. He was plotting the launch of a radical newspaper with Chadwick,[75] and even as his article 'The Spirit of the Age' (1831) was circulating, Mill was writing to Sterling that he 'should not care though a revolution were to exterminate every person in Great Britain and Ireland who has £500 a year. Many very amiable persons would perish, but what is the world better for such amiable persons?'[76] (Mill may have forgotten that his own salary had risen to £600 a year a couple of years previously.)

It was across the Channel, though, that radicalism really erupted. In 1830, in the face of Parisian uprisings, the regime of Charles X collapsed under the weight of its own incompetence. Mill recounted that it 'raised my utmost enthusiasm, and gave me, as it were, a new existence'.[77] The 'Trijackia', brought together again by their shared radical enthusiasm, sped to Paris and shook hands with Lafayette, a hero reborn. At the opera, they called excitedly for the 'Marseillaise', shouting 'Debout! Debout!' (Stand up!) when Louis Philippe, the 'Citizen King', stepped into the royal box.[78] But Mill's excitement was short-lived. He saw quickly that the new government was riddled with 'cowardice, imbecility' and corruption, and much more interested in power than democracy.[79] His retrospective assessment was that by contrast to the heroism and restraint of the workers, 'the bourgeois oligarchy, who have enthroned themselves in the yet warm seats of the feudal aristocracy, have that very common taste which makes men desire to level down to themselves, but not an inch lower'.[80]

Mill's views during the years following his crisis do not fit easily into a coherent intellectual model. 'If I am asked what system of political philosophy I substituted for that which, as a philosophy, I had abandoned,' he wrote in his *Autobiography*, 'I answer, no system: only a conviction that the true system was something much more complex and many sided than I had previously had any idea of.'[81] Mill deliberately sought out an eclectic range of people and views and came to despise minds which he saw as closed. In debate, he tore into Prime Minster George Canning's statement that he would always oppose widening the franchise – a pledge Lord John Russell would repeat a decade later, earning himself the label 'Finality John'. Of course, there were serious, sensible arguments against reform:

But to hear a man gravely pledge himself to be always of the same opinion – bind himself by a solemn promise that the arguments which convince him now, upon his honour shall convince him to his dying day – that what he thinks advisable now he will think advisable always howsoever circumstances may change ... is utterly ludicrous.[82]

Mill, like the economist John Maynard Keynes a century later, would judge the greatness of a person's intellect by their capacity to change their mind, rather than by their fixed attachment to a particular view. Indeed, Mill even welcomed passionate disagreement within government, on the grounds that people of 'talent and knowledge' will differ, and so a ministry must 'either be composed of persons who differ, or it cannot be composed of such men'.[83]

Mill began to realize that his period of intellectual exploration had misled some people about his true views, not least Carlyle, to whom he explained in October 1833 that he was in a state of '*recovery* after the petrification of a narrow philosophy'.[84] He went on, three months later, to describe how he had become

> catholic and tolerant in an extreme degree, and thought one-sidedness almost the one great evil in human affairs . . . I scarcely felt called upon to *deny* anything but denial itself . . . I never, or rarely, felt myself called upon to come into *collision* with any one . . . there has been on my part something like a want of courage in avoiding, or touching only perfunctorily, with you, points on which I thought it likely we should differ.[85]

For these few years of his life Mill could sometimes epitomize the liberal of stock jokes, unable to take even his own side in an argument. His openness to ideas from any source, and willingness to see both sides of a dispute, meant he was, as one modern scholar has put it, 'continually being hit by the boomerang of his own ideas'.[86] At twenty-five, having abandoned his early, pure faith, Mill had accumulated something of a rag-bag of opinions. He remained, for the most part, a Ricardian in economics, and still thirsted after institutional and political reform. But he had absorbed a Saint-Simonian view of history, a German Romantic concept of *Bildung* or 'self-creation', and a Wordsworthian theory of the role of the imagination. The kaleidoscope had been shaken, and the pieces were still moving.

It was in this confused, newly liberated state that Mill fell in love. In many ways it was not a surprising match. Harriet Taylor was intelligent, pretty, vivacious, progressive, open-minded and poetic. But his admiration was shared by others – not least by her two children, and her husband.

CHAPTER FOUR

This Imperfect Companionship (1830–6)

＞＜

In the summer of 1830, Mill was filled with restless energy. He was about to depart for Paris and had recently been elected a member of the Athenaeum, a new, intellectually orientated gentleman's club. He was also caught up in the excitement of the general election, which was to put the radical reformer Henry Brougham into Parliament and cost the Duke of Wellington the premiership.[1] The loss of his friend Eyton Tooke, who had killed himself earlier in the year in the tragically mistaken belief that his love for another friend's sister was unrequited, strengthened Mill's zeal: 'The more affectionately I cherish his memory, the more ardently shall I pursue those great objects in which he took so deep an interest.'[2]

Mill was also taking an active part in the numerous *salons* springing up across London, at which some of the most brilliant minds of the nation were to be heard. He was a regular at those hosted by Harriet Grote, Sarah Austin and Mrs Charles Buller. A new generation of conversationalists was on the rise: Sydney Smith's appraisal of one performance by Macaulay was that he had 'occasional flashes of silence, that make his conversation perfectly delightful . . .'[3]

An invitation, then, to join Mr and Mrs John Taylor of Finsbury, London, for dinner would have been unremarkable. Mr Taylor was a prosperous pharmacist and supporter of radical causes, and a particular patron of political refugees. Also at the dining table was Harriet Martineau, arguably Britain's first successful female journalist, William Johnson Fox, the pastor of the South Place Unitarian Chapel where the Taylors worshipped, the other two members of the Trijackia, Roebuck and Graham, and Harriet's friend Lizzie Flower, with whom Fox was falling in love under the nose of his wife.

The evening appears to have gone well. Roebuck, many years later, recalled that 'Mrs Taylor was much taken with Mill', but it is hard to know how much weight to give this memory: a few months after the dinner, Harriet and her husband conceived their third child.[4] Mill was reported to have been more interested in Lizzie, for whom he might have been a better catch than Fox.[5] For one thing, he was not bad looking. According to Carlyle, he was 'a slender, rather tall and elegant youth, with a small clear Roman-nosed face, two small earnestly-smiling eyes; modest, remarkably gifted with precision of utterance, enthusiastic, yet lucid, calm . . .'[6] Caroline Fox, a later friend, described his 'exquisitely chiselled countenance, more resembling a portrait of Lavater than any other that I remember'.[7] If Roebuck's recollection was correct, it was, however, most likely John's intellect rather than countenance that caught Mrs Taylor's attention. The idea to invite Mill had in fact come from Fox, in response to a request from Harriet for more cerebral stimulation. While the early years of her marriage had been happy, her husband, described by Carlyle as 'an innocent dull good man', was not a man of ideas, and the relationship began to suffer.[8] Harriet Grote, decades later, recalled Harriet Taylor's attitude to her spouse: 'she was tired of him & cared for clever people – Mill met her . . . & she fascinated him & entangled him . . . she was a very pretty woman . . .'[9] According to Carlyle, writing a couple of years after the fateful dinner, she was 'vivid' and 'iridescent . . . a living romance heroine, of the clearest insight, of the royalest volition, very interesting, of questionable destiny'.[10] One of Fox's daughters later recalled Harriet being 'possessed of a beauty and a grace quite unique of their kind . . . A small head, a swan-like throat and a complexion like a pearl. Large dark eyes, not soft or sleepy, but with a look of quiet command about them.'[11]

Fox may also have hoped to persuade Mill to write for the *Monthly Repository*, a Unitarian journal which he edited, and from the following year also owned. Fox was an engaging character, a colourful conversationalist as well as a theologically liberal, politically radical pastor, and would go on to become one of the most powerful orators of the Anti-Corn Law League. Even without the attractions of Harriet, an association between Mill and the Unitarian circle would not have been surprising. Religious dissenters of all stripes were among the leading radicals and reformers of the time, and the Unitarians were more advanced in their views than most. Plenty of Unitarians were also utilitarians and the two groups had been allies in the establishment in 1828 of the non-denominational University College, on Gower Street in London. Disraeli even suggested that Unitarianism was a religious version of utilitarianism, and shared its defects. 'Both omit imagination in their system,' he said, 'and Imagination governs mankind.'[12]

Lack of imagination was not an accusation that could be levelled at Fox's crowd, nor, by the 1830s, Mill: art, music and poetry were important ingredients in their lives. Lizzie Flower was a composer, and her sister Sarah was a writer, who would later write the hymn 'Nearer My God to Thee'. The reforming earnestness and high-spirited feminism of the circle was encapsulated in Leigh Hunt's 1837 poem, 'Bluestocking Revels', which depicted Apollo savouring 'blue-stocking blisses' as he 'sits / Conversing till morning with beauties and wits'.[13] Hunt was editing the *Monthly Repository* at the time. Mill was certainly keen on the group. 'Among the persons whom Mr Fox frequents,' he told Carlyle, 'I have met with several men and women who are decidedly characters, realizing an idea of their own & free from halfness of all sorts.'[14]

The picture of the love affair that was to develop between Mill and Harriet is cloudy, for obvious reasons. Several of the early letters are hard to date with certainty, while Mill claimed in the *Autobiography* that it was 'years' before their relationship 'became at all intimate or confidential'.[15] Their surviving correspondence casts no light on the first three years of their relationship, but there are nevertheless at least two pieces of evidence which suggest that the relationship moved beyond that of mere friendship rather more quickly.

First, there is a note from Lizzie Flower to Harriet, dated June 1831, which enquires of a recently published review of Byron: 'Did you or Mill do it?'[16] Second, in a letter to John Taylor almost certainly dating from earlier the same year, the London-based French writer B. E. Desainteville, expressed his pleasure at witnessing a 'reconciliation' between his correspondent and Mill.[17] Within a year of meeting in 1830, then, Harriet's closest friend already saw her and Mill as intellectual collaborators or soulmates; and something had happened requiring 'reconciliation' between the two men in Harriet's life.

If they were not in love by the summer of 1831, they certainly were by the following year. Harriet decided to tell her husband, who forbade her to see Mill again. Initially she attempted to heed the command and Mill received the devastating news in a note delivered by the loyal Lizzie, on his return from a summer walking holiday with Henry Cole in the New Forest and on the Isle of Wight. He wrote back dutifully, promising not to write or call and thereby add 'one extra drop into her cup of sorrows'. Mill also slipped some forest flowers he had picked for her into the envelope and held out the hope that their paths would cross again: 'At whatever time, in whatever place that may be so, she will find me always the same as I have been, as I am still.'[18]

He did not have to wait long; by the autumn of 1832, contact had been re-established. An awkward modus vivendi evolved. Mill was now living with his family in Vicarage Place, Church Street, Kensington, where he would remain until he finally married Harriet twenty years later. However, he was permitted to dine with Harriet at the Taylor's home at least two or three times a week – although only in the company of others – and on these evenings John Taylor would go out to his club. John Taylor bought a country house for Harriet at Keston Heath, Kent, where she spent most of her time; a few years later she relocated to Walton-upon-Thames. Taylor visited her in Kent for the occasional weekend; Mill was there for the majority of the others.

Whether Mill and Harriet were having a sexual relationship during these visits is a question which historical scholarship has so far been unable to determine. Harriet's own version of events suggested that she was sexually 'faithful' to both men by having sex with neither; Theodor Gomperz reported a conversation with her decades later in which she led him to believe she had been a *Seelenfreundin* to both men.[19] Carlyle quickly dubbed Harriet 'platonica', and some of Mill's friends would ascribe his later bouts of illness to sexual frustration.[20] If the relationship was platonic, however, it was often conducted with the breathlessness of a secret sexual liaison: 'Yes dear, I will meet you, in the chaise, somewhere between this and Southend,' scrawls Harriet breathlessly in one note, '. . . tomorrow will be delightful and I am looking forward to it as the very greatest *treat* . . .'[21] We do not know whether this assignation took place.

With Harriet back in his life, Mill picked up his pen with renewed vigour, publishing a series of articles on art and music in the *Examiner* – at one point rashly hailing Lizzie Flower's setting of Goethe's 'Mignon' as superior to Beethoven's – and giving Fox an essay 'On Genius' for the *Repository*.[22] Some of Mill's arguments in these articles from the early 1830s prefigured later concerns with the maintenance of individuality in a democratic age, and the role of education in promoting autonomy. In 'On Genius', Mill looked back reverently to the intellectual culture of ancient Athens: 'Her philosophers were not formed, nor did they form their scholars, by placing a set of ready-made truths before them, and helping them to put them on.' By contrast, he wrote, contemporary education was all 'cram'. The danger, then, was that the 'mental light' of the nation had 'lost in intensity at least a part of what it has gained in diffusion; whether our 'march of intellect' be not rather a march towards doing without intellect, and supplying a deficiency of giants by the united efforts of a constantly increasing multitude of dwarfs'.[23] Mill would be a lifelong, passionate supporter of universal, compulsory education, but at the same time he would always fret that curricula were being designed to encourage conformity rather than individuality. There is also more than a hint of elitism in his views at this point – his concerns about the nature of the curricula seem premature, given that for the 'multitude' the only education available in the first half of the century was at church or in the 'ragged schools'.

Most importantly, Mill insisted that a 'genius' was not someone who displayed a dazzling intellect or made amazing discoveries, but a person who was fully self-determining and autonomous. Deciding our views for ourselves, imaginatively shaping our own destinies – these were the ingredients of real genius: 'Whosoever, to the extent of his opportunity, gets at his convictions by his own faculties, and not by reliance on any other person whatever – that man, in proportion as his conclusions have truth in them, is an *original thinker*, and is, as much as anybody ever was, a *man* of *genius*.'[24] The definition of genius here is virtually synonymous with Mill's later articulations of individual autonomy in his 1859 masterwork, *On Liberty*, and is opposed to the views of Wordsworth, who had declared in an 1815 essay that genius was 'the introduction of a new element into the intellectual universe'.[25]

In the article, Mill also strongly prefigured one of the principal arguments of *Utilitarianism*, declaring that a life of passive contentment was not a worthy one:

If the multifarious labours of the *durum genus hominum* were performed by us for a supernatural agency, and there were no demand for either wisdom or virtue, but barely for stretching out our hands and enjoying, small would be our enjoyment, for there would be nothing which man could any longer prize in man ... Whether, according to the ethical theory we adopt, wisdom and virtue be precious in themselves, or there be nothing precious save happiness, it matters little; while we know that where these higher endowments are not, happiness can never be ...[26]

Mill's insistence in this early essay that a good life could not be provided by an external agency echoed Harriet's concern with individuality. An unpublished essay of hers from around the same time – it is not dated but the paper is watermarked 1832 – described the 'spirit of conformity' as 'the root of all intolerance ... what is called the opinion of society is a phantom power, yet as is often the case with phantoms, of more force over the minds of the unthinking than all the flesh and blood arguments which can be brought to bear against it. It is a combination of the many weak, against the few strong...' Harriet also stressed the importance of strong individual characters: 'The remedy is, to make all strong enough to stand alone; and whoever has once known the pleasure of self-dependance [sic], will be in no danger of lapsing into subserviency.'[27]

By this point, Mill and Harriet were beginning to have some intellectual influence on each other. It is of course difficult to disentangle the effects of Harriet on Mill from those of Mill on Harriet. A review by Harriet of Bernard Sarrans' *Lafayette, Louis Philippe, and the Revolution of 1830* bears the hallmarks of Mill's style.[28] Equally, the quotes from Harriet's essay lamenting the 'phantom power' of the 'opinion of society' and the centrality of 'self-dependence' could be dropped unnoticed into almost any paragraph of 'On Genius' or indeed *On Liberty*. But while Harriet was clearly influencing Mill's thought, the extent of the influence should not be overstated. There is no reason to think that Mill's views would have been substantially different had he ended up with, say, Lizzie Flower – although his life certainly would have been. And it quickly became clear which of the two had a future as a writer: after a flurry of indifferent reviews and poems in 1832 – one containing the arresting assertion that 'flowers are Utilitarians' – Harriet did not publish again for almost twenty years.[29]

While Mill and Harriet were emotionally and intellectually absorbed in each other, the nation around them was being transformed. The Industrial Revolution was gathering steam: since 1815 iron output had quadrupled to a million tons, and Britain was also entering the age of the train.[30] Fifty-four Railway Acts were passed between 1825 and 1835, and in the following two years, another thirty-nine bills for more lines went through Parliament. William Huskisson, MP, had become, in September 1830, the first victim of the railways, his death under the wheels of the Rocket and the opening of the Liverpool–Manchester railway marking the beginning of a decade of reform.[31] The greater freedom of movement of both people and ideas resulting from the expansion of the rail and road networks made political change unstoppable. Palmerston correctly declared in 1828 that 'when people saw such populous places as Leeds or Manchester unrepresented, whilst a green mound of earth returned two members, it naturally gave rise to complaint'.[32] He was specifically thinking of Penryn and East Retford – but there were similar mounds all over the nation: the new Liverpool–Manchester line passed close to the tiny village of Newton, with two MPs. Even if people did not see these glaring democratic inequalities, they could read about them: newspaper circulation had passed the thirty million mark by the 1830s, double the level at the turn of the century, and well above today's figure.[33]

The election of MPs before 1832 was a rotten, haphazard affair: Robert Southey, for example, the poet with whom Mill had taken tea, had been 'elected' to represent the seat of Downton, without his knowledge, while he was abroad on holiday.[34] The 1832 Act expanded the electorate from 366,000 to 642,000, but the real 'greatness' of the Great Reform Act lay in the abolition of fifty-six 'rotten boroughs' and the halving of the representation of another thirty, with their parliamentary seats being redistributed to growing industrial towns such as Manchester, Birmingham and Sheffield.

Jeremy Bentham had been a lifelong advocate for parliamentary reform and witnessed the new era ushered in by the 1832 Act just two weeks before his death. According to the essayist William Hazlitt, in his own *Spirit of the Age*, the immodest master utilitarian had wanted to live each of the remaining years of his life at the end of each of the next few centuries, in order to see the growing impact of his ideas on the world.[35] He would not have needed to wait so long. The 1830s witnessed the rise of a more rationalist, Benthamite approach to government. The state was increasingly seen as having a responsibility to investigate and act on social problems, and economists, scientists and policy-orientated intellectuals were growing in importance. 'These are the days of advance,' wrote Tennyson in his 1855 work, *Maud*, 'the works of the men of mind.'[36] The nation was deemed to be something of a mess, and an alliance of the experts – the 'men of mind' – and reformers, Wordsworth's 'men with brooms', were going to tidy it up.

The 1830s, indeed, was the decade in which the foundation stones of the modern state were laid. The construction would take over a century to be complete, but the main trends – investigating, rationalizing, regulating, inspecting, democratizing and secularizing – had been firmly established before the decade was out. The principal legislative fruits of the new mood were the Factory Act (1833), which began to regulate working hours for children; the Poor Law Amendment Act (1834), which established a nationally regulated workhouse system; the Prisons Act (1835), which founded a national prisons inspectorate; and the Municipal Reform Act (1835), which created borough councils elected by ratepayers and which marked, according to G. M. Trevelyan, the 'high-water mark of Benthamite Radicalism acting through the Whig machine'.[37]

Mill entered into intellectual and political combat with relish. He had high hopes of the fresh crop of radicals entering the new Parliament, elected under the new franchise even after Brougham fell into the vanity trap of accepting the Lord Chancellorship – Grey's ruse to keep him out of the Commons – thereby 'dropping onto the Woolsack as his political deathbed'.[38] But while the reformers were in a celebratory mood, conservatives across Europe looked aghast at the changing political scene. Rossini almost stopped composing. When the Houses of Parliament caught fire in 1834, the emperor of Russia thought it divine retribution for the Reform Act. Charles Lamb, the essayist, shortly after hearing Hazlitt's deathbed hopes 'that things will go back again', wrote: 'Can we ring the bells backwards? Can we unlearn the arts that pretend to civilise and then burn the world? There is a march of science. But who shall beat the drums for its retreat?'[39]

Mill was, of course, one of the most enthusiastic marchers. But by the spring of 1833, at least half his mind was on other, homelier matters. He explained a slackening in his schedule of publications in veiled terms. 'I am not working much,' he told Carlyle, 'but much is working within me'.[40] The truth was that the strain of the unusual set-up with the Taylors was beginning to show. Depression, which would stalk Mill for much of his life, hung over him. 'I will not if I can help it give way to gloom and morbid despondency,' he wrote to Carlyle, without admitting the proximate cause.[41]

A letter to Fox – who had by now embarked on his own affair with Lizzie Flower – reveals both the increasing frequency of Mill's visits to the Taylor household in Kent Terrace, near Regent's Park, and the rising stress for all concerned. 'I seldom go there without special reasons on that day of the week,' he explained to his friend, who had asked if Mill would be there the following Wednesday, 'for ... it cannot be right in the present circumstances to be there *every* evening.'[42] In the late summer of 1833, Mill made a declaration to Harriet, in a note which is sadly lost to history. Quite possibly, she destroyed it. Whatever he said, he made quite an impression, as her response reveals:

I am glad that you have said it – I am *happy* that you have . . . I have always yearned to have your confidence . . . It is but that the only being who has ever called forth all my faculties of affection is the only one in whose presence I felt restraint . . . You can scarcely conceive dearest what *satisfaction* this note of yours is to me . . . *Yes* – these circumstances *do* require greater strength than any other – the greatest – that which you have, & which if you had not I should never have loved you and would not love you now.[43]

Mill's anguish was deeply private. There is no mention of Harriet in any of the surviving letters to his friends, even to John Sterling. Indeed, she is never mentioned by name; she is described even to Fox and Lizzie Flower only as '*her*'. Mill's father apparently disapproved of the relationship, but Mill himself refused to discuss it with any member of his family. Meanwhile, though, London buzzed with innuendo. On arriving back in London in 1834 after a two-year sojourn in Scotland, the Carlyles were quickly brought up to speed. Jane Carlyle relayed the hottest gossip to her brother-in-law, 'that a young Mrs. Taylor, tho' encumbered with a husband and children, had ogled John Mill so successfully that he was desperately in love'.[44]

Although it is clear that the rumours circulating were upsetting to all parties, Mill and Harriet rather boldly attended a soirée together at Mrs Buller's and, according to Roebuck, as they entered, 'a suppressed titter went around the room'. The next day, Roebuck walked through the stinking, packed streets of an overcrowded London to warn his friend that he was in danger of bringing ridicule on himself. He was received coldly by Mill, and recalled that when he dropped in again the following day, 'the moment I entered the room I saw that, as far as he was concerned, our friendship was at an end'.[45] Over the next few decades, the two men would launch a review together, campaign for many of the same reforms, debate with Alexis deTocqueville, and serve alongside each other in the House of Commons. They corresponded politely; in one letter to a third party, Mill even refers to 'our friend Roebuck'.[46] But to all intents and purposes the friendship was over.

Mill, however, admitted to William Fox that: 'she [Harriet] sees that what ought to be so much easier to me than to her is in reality more difficult − costs harder struggle − to part company with the opinion of the world, and with my former modes of doing good ...'[47] Harriet Martineau, who was one of the most eager transmitters of the rumours, had, according to a wounded Mill, the 'faculty of making herself personally disliked, by means it would seem of inattention to Christ's precept "judge not, that ye be not judged"'.[48]

Suffering at the hands of the gossips, and with their marriage at breaking point, the Taylors decided on a trial separation. Harriet decamped to Paris, but only after spending an agreeable evening with Mill. 'Far from being unhappy or even low this morning, I feel as tho' you had never loved me as well as last night,' she wrote the next day. 'Adieu darling. How nice next month will be. I am quite impatient for it.'[49] The 'next month' saw Mill join her in Paris for a period of six weeks. The Parisian experiment raised hopes in both men: John Taylor was convinced that a spell apart would heal the wounds in their marriage; Mill was equally certain that the separation was merely the first step toward a permanent breach. For Harriet, it meant 'so much more pain than I thought I was capable of, but also O how much more happiness'.[50] Writing to Fox from Paris, Mill was full of excitement at this new chapter in the relationship:

I am astonished when I think how much has been restrained, how much untold, unshewn and uncommunicated till now ... almost all which has ever caused her misgivings with regard to our fitness for each other was mistaken in point of fact – that the mistakes no longer exist – & that she is now quite convinced that we are perfectly suited to pass our lives together – better suited indeed for that perfect than for this imperfect companionship.[51]

But in the same letter to Fox, Mill also made it clear that Harriet was far from settled on her course of action: 'I am happy, but not *so* happy as when the future appeared surer.' Harriet barely had time to regain her composure following Mill's departure when John Taylor arrived for his own, unsuccessful attempt to win her over. There was a degree of gentlemanliness in the contest, at least from Mill, who noted the 'really admirable generosity & nobleness which he [Taylor] has shewn under so severe a trial'.[52] Taylor's feelings about Mill are not extant. In his post-Parisian flush, Mill told Fox that if Harriet wrote a literary sketch of the French capital for the *Repository* it would be 'the most beautiful thing ever written'.[53] The piece never appeared, so Mill's optimistic prediction cannot be tested. But it marked the beginning of a lifelong habit of Mill's to put Harriet on a literary pedestal.

Harriet clearly admired and loved Mill greatly, too. But there were no easy options for her. Divorce from Taylor would require an Act of Parliament, and separated or divorced women had no rights whatsoever over their children, who remained the 'property' of their father under all circumstances. Few women were yet in a position to earn their own living, and while in her immediate circle progressive views about gender and marriage were common currency, in the world as a whole opinion was still generally conservative.

Mill and Harriet decided to exchange private letters discussing the position of women and the institution of marriage.[54] They were in almost complete agreement on both issues – and considerably in advance of the general views of their time. Mill wrote:

The question is not what marriage ought to be, but a far wider question, what woman ought to be. Settle that first, and the other will settle itself. Determine whether marriage is to be a relation between two equal beings, or between a superior & an inferior, between a protector and a dependent; & all other doubts will easily be solved.[55]

Mill's principal argument in the letter was that marriage had worked for women when they could not fend for themselves, and had needed some way to hold on to men once 'the passing gust' of passion had gone. But in a world where physical strength was of lessening importance, these arguments for marriage were redundant: 'in the progress of civilisation, the time has now come when women can aspire to something more than merely to find a protector ... Woman ... is now ripe for equality.'[56] For Harriet, legal and educational equality would mean that women would no longer have to 'barter [their] person for bread'.[57]

Mill and Harriet also agreed that the most important move towards the 'enfranchisement of woman' was the provision of education, so that marriage would cease to be an economic necessity, and become, in Mill's words, an 'affection of equality which alone deserves to be called love'.[58] Both thought that marriages should be dissolvable at the wish of either party, although Harriet suggested a minimum two-year period between separation and the finalization of divorce, as well as rebranding divorce as 'Proof of affection', on the grounds that once a relationship became loveless, divorce was an act of mutual kindness.[59]

The couple competed to pour the greatest quantity of vitriol on the existing state of marriage, in terms that suggest their own circumstances were understandably adding a personal dimension to their views. For Mill,

of all the more serious acts of the life of a human being, there is not one which is commonly performed with so little of forethought and consideration, as that which is irrevocable, & which is fuller of evil than any other acts of the being's whole life if it turns out ill ... Marriage is really ... a lottery: & whoever is in a state of mind to calculate the chances calmly and value them correctly, is not at all likely to purchase a ticket.[60]

Harriet, who married John Taylor at the age of eighteen, wrote a thinly veiled autobiography: 'In the present system of habits & opinions,' she wrote, 'girls enter into what is called a contract perfectly ignorant of the conditions of it, and that they should be so is considered absolutely essential to their fitness for it!'[61]

It is difficult, from a modern perspective, to grasp the degree of radicalism of these views in the 1830s. While Wordsworth and William IV were free to squire several illegitimate children across the country, women essentially had only the choice of being a wife, a virgin or a trollop. Mill may have thought women 'ripe for equality' – but not many of his contempories, even women, would have agreed with him. Sarah Ellis, in her popular 1843 manual, *The Wives of England, Their Relative Duties, Domestic Influence and Social Obligations,* warned that 'in the case of a highly gifted woman, even when there is an equal or superior degree of talent than that of her husband, nothing can be more injudicious or fatal to her happiness than an exhibition even of the least disposition to presume upon such gifts'.[62] Even men who supported women's education and votes were often bemused by them: Henry Brougham famously did not know how to talk to clever women.[63] While Mill engaged in various campaigns for equality, he felt able to go public with the full extent of his feminism only in 1869.

The band of radicals who had entered the Commons in the early 1830s were at best lukewarm on women's rights. Harriet wrote to Roebuck in 1832, asking him to propose an amendment to the 1832 Reform Act admitting women to the electorate, but to no avail.[64] Not that much could have been expected even if he had been an enthusiast: the Whig ministry, while dependent on the votes of the Radicals, offered them little more than crumbs from the table. Roebuck's early attempt to win support for universal free education resulted in an annuity of just £20,000 to be distributed among schools – which, as Mill's biographer Michael Packe points out, was less than a third of the spending of the state of Massachusetts for the same purpose. In any case, the radicals were, as so often, more interested in fighting each other than the Whigs and Tories: Roebuck and the *Morning Chronicle* editor John Black even fought a duel, thankfully victimless. Individual radical leaders tended to pursue their own hobby-horses: for Joseph Hume this was government waste; for Cobbett, currency reform; for Daniel O'Connell, Irish land reform; for Grote, the introduction of a secret ballot; and for Bowring, the sound of his own voice.

While there was a cacophony of radical voices in Parliament throughout the 1830s, their impact was negligible, and political energy passed back quickly to the Tories, led from 1834 by Robert Peel. Although Mill described a pre-election speech given by Peel at Tamworth in 1834 – seen by most historians as the first party manifesto – as 'empty mouthing', it would be the Tories who made most of the political running over the subsequent decades, until the ascent of Gladstonian liberalism, in which Mill would play his own part.[65]

With the radicals leaderless and rudderless, Mill once again attempted to provide leadership from outside Parliament through the vehicle of a serious, radical journal. The old *Westminster Review* had become a pale shadow of its *Edinburgh*-slaying days: Colonel Thomas Perronet Thompson, a former governer of Sierra Leone, had become editor, proprietor and principal contributor in 1829. Sadly his financial commitment, which amounted to a massive £30,000 in total, was not matched by his political or literary skills. An increasing number of pages had to be filled with information on his two obsessions: the Corn Laws, and the workings of the innovative Enharmonic Organ.

The idea for a new journal had been mooted among Mill and his friends since the passing of the Reform Act, but they were hobbled by a lack of money. In June 1834, Mill found a backer: the aristocratic, radical MP Sir William Molesworth, who was friendly with Thackeray, hated the Whigs and hugely admired Mill. Molesworth underwrote a new *London Review* and offered Mill complete editorial control, although the nominal editorship had to lie elsewhere because of Mill's employment at India House. Mill successfully tested Molesworth's promise of a free hand by rejecting a piece he had written about Brougham; the only result was that the proprietor was temporarily 'rather out of humour with John'.[66]

The review would break some ground. First, articles were to be articles, rather than being dressed up as 'reviews'. Second, contributors would write under their own names or fixed *noms de plume*, rather than sheltering behind the fiction of a collective editorial voice: for the first time in serious journalism, 'we' would be replaced by 'I', allowing the *London* to carry dissenting pieces on the same issue. It would not be a sectarian journal, but a forum for all the best ideas in the land, regardless of their origin; Mill wooed Carlyle as a contributor more assiduously than anyone else. From the outset, it was clear that the *London Review* would be an almost exact facsimile of Mill's own philosophical position:

The review ought to represent not radicalism but neoradicalism, a radicalism which is not democracy, not a bigoted adherence to any forms of government or to one kind of institutions, & which is only to be called radicalism inasmuch as it does not palter nor compromise with evils but cuts at their roots – & a utilitarianism which takes into account the whole of human nature not the ratiocinative faculty only ... which holds

Feeling at least as valuable at Thought, & Poetry not only a par with, but the necessary condition of, any true & comprehensive Philosophy.[67]

Mill was excited. 'John', wrote Molesworth, 'is in such spirits that he says he would make it succeed single-handed. Old Mill will write, consequently we shall be 'spectable'.[68] The first issue of the *London Review* rolled off the presses in April 1835. It was an auspicious time for a launch; the market for reviews and periodicals was expanding rapidly, and the publishing industry received a fiscal fillip the following year, when the fourpenny tax on newspapers was reduced to a penny.[69]

The elder Mill opened the edition with a 'state of the nation' piece – essentially a rehash of all his earlier opinions on politics and economics – while his son made his first serious foray into moral philosophy: a diluted version of his reformulated utilitarianism. Mill's piece was a response to an attack on utilitarian philosophy and experimental science by Adam Sedgwick, who was a considerable geologist as well as a devout Christian: he once announced to a meeting of the British Association that if he ever found his science interfering with his faith, he would 'dash it to the ground'. He was certainly no philosopher, and Mill easily dismissed most of his arguments. Yet while Mill's article certainly reads as a strong attack on an enemy of utilitarianism, it also offered some glimpses of his own growing disillusionment with the theory. Mill was frequently defending a different version of utilitarianism from the one Bentham laid out. Sedgwick, Mill complained, 'lumps up the theory of utility – which is a theory of right and wrong – with the theory, if there be such a theory, of the universal selfishness of mankind'.[70] But of course Bentham had argued precisely that individuals *did* act out self-interest, seeking to maximize their own pleasure and minimize their own pain.

Mill was still a long way from revealing the full extent of the alteration in his views, however, for fear of his father's reaction. In his *Autobiography* he admits that 'my relation to my father would have made it painful to me in any case, and impossible in a review for which he wrote, to speak out my whole mind on the subject at this time'.[71] In private correspondence or under the cloak of anonymity, he was prepared to go much further. He had already written a much sharper piece on the limitations of Bentham's philosophy for Edward Lytton Bulwer's *England and the English*, published in 1833. Bulwer wanted to trumpet the piece but Mill insisted it be buried as an Appendix, where it was safely ignored. Late in 1834 he flagged the article to John Nichol, shortly to be Professor of Astronomy at Glasgow, but added: 'It is not, and must not, be known to be mine.'[72] It is one of the great ironies of Mill's life that even in 1834, approaching thirty and declaiming in favour of free speech, argument and dissent, he was muzzling himself for fear of his father. He was much more candid to Carlyle. In a letter in 1834 he rehearsed his later attempts to provide a richer definition of happiness, gained only through autonomous self-development:

I am still, & am likely to remain, a utilitarian; though not one of 'the people called utilitarians' . . . nor a utilitarian at all, unless in quite another sense from what perhaps any one except myself understands by the word . . . You will see, partly, with what an immense number & variety of explanations my utilitarianism must be taken . . . Though I hold the good of the species . . . to be the ultimate end (which is the alpha and omega of my utilitarianism) I believe with the fullest belief that this end can in no other way be forwarded but by the means you speak of, namely by each taking for his exclusive aim the developement [sic] of what is best in himself.[73]

James Mill, of course, had no such concerns. And far from being ''spectable', his elderly hands were penning lines more inflammatory than ever. While John used the second issue of the *London* to launch Tennyson's career, his father now opened fire on the Church of England – not only on its outrageous constitutional position, Jurassic theology and blinkered education methods, but also on the character of the clergy and the content of their sermons. The attack was unhelpful to the young *London*, damaging circulation among those with more moderate opinions on religion and the Church, and giving the journal precisely the labels – atheist, sectarian, radical, oppositional – which Mill wanted to avoid. Molesworth suffered personally, too: the article caused the woman he was courting to refuse him.[74] As it happened, this was James Mill's last salvo, and his son would go on to build a journal which would last well into the twentieth century and be an important part of the movement to place national life on a scientific, enquiring basis. If, as Roy Porter writes, 'progress was the opium of enlightenment' in the Britain of the early nineteenth century, journals like the *London* were where you turned for a dose.[75]

The work required by the *London* was a useful distraction for Mill from the turbulence of his relationship with Harriet, who had returned from Paris only to disappoint both her husband and Mill: the arrangement was to continue as before. It shows the attraction that Harriet held for both Mill and Taylor that she was able to get them both to agree to such an unorthodox and unsatisfactory setup. Both of them, it seems, preferred to have half of Harriet than none at all. On the surface it seems to have worked; very occasionally they would even all dine together with other guests.[76] Mill's status in the house was ambiguous, being sometimes the guest, sometimes the host. He certainly felt it necessary to pay for restocking the wine cellar.[77]

The arrangement did not, however, permit Mill and Harriet to socialize as a couple, except with Fox and Lizzie Flower. 'I do not, half enough, see *anybody* along with her', Mill complained to Fox, '*that* I think is chiefly what is wanting now – that, and other things like it'.[78] He also stated, somewhat opaquely, that their 'affairs have been gradually getting into a more & more unsatisfactory state'.[79] For her part, Harriet lamented that 'happiness has become to me a word without meaning'.[80] She fretted that Mill loved her less than she loved him; he worried whether he would be able to be happy without having her all to himself, and he was still troubled by potential damage to their respective reputations.

At the same time, there were effusive declarations of love. At the end of one letter in 1834 Mill scribbled 'o you dear one', to which she added 'my *own adored* one!'[81] Harriet described Mill as 'the light of my life'.[82] Both took huge pleasure in their weekends together in Keston Heath, an oasis in which they could escape the chilly disapproval of her husband and the 'clacking tongues' of the society gossips. When Harriet was in London, a favoured meeting place was the new Zoological Gardens in Regent's Park – another symbol of the dawning age of knowledge, science and control. Harriet and Mill usually chose to rendezvous by their 'old friend Rhino'.[83] In short, they were at the second stage of their love affair, when doubt competes with delight.

The strain was not eased by an eruption of controversy at the South Place Chapel, where in the spring of 1834 Mrs Fox made an official complaint to the congregation about her husband's infidelity. He survived the uproar – which became a debate about the inflexibility of marriage – made a financial settlement, and went off to live with Lizzie Flower in Bayswater. Observing these events, Carlyle offered a typically waspish analysis:

Most of these people are very indignant at marriage and the like; and frequently indeed are obliged to divorce their own wives, or be divorced: for although the world is already blooming (or is one day to do it) in everlasting 'happiness of the greatest number', these people's houses (I always find) are little Hells of improvidence, discord, unreason.[84]

In 1835, the couple had their first serious row. Mill became so frustrated that he criticized Harriet for not having the courage to leave her husband, accusing her of having a character marked by 'the extreme of anxiety and uneasiness' as well as creating 'chimeras about nothing'. He contrasted her timidity with the courageous elopement of George Sand and Alfred de Musset, an unfortunate example, as it turned out, given that they broke up within a year. Mill was afraid, in some way as a result of the situation, of having an 'obscure, insignificant and useless life' – perhaps not an uncommon fear among men turning thirty.

Harriet replied not once, but twice – and with increasing indignation. She explained, presumably not for the first time, the reasons for her decisions, and demonstrated both her strength of will and candour in criticism, characteristics which would serve Mill well over the next quarter-century. Referring to the possibility of leaving her husband to be with Mill, she wrote:

I do not hesitate about the certainty of happiness – but I do hesitate about the rightfulness of, for my own pleasure, giving up *my* only earthly opportunity of 'usefulness'. *You* hesitate about your usefulness & that however greater in amount it may be, is certainly not like mine *marked out* as duty. I should spoil four lives & injure others. This is the only hesitation . . . Now I give pleasure around me, I make no one unhappy, & I am happy tho' not happiest myself.[85]

Harriet, in fact, was taking a strictly utilitarian line: the current situation was the one which collectively maximized the happiness of all the people involved, even at the cost of less happiness for herself and Mill. He, the supposed heir of utilitarianism, was urging the path of selfish romance. As for his fears about his own success, Harriet was suitably caustic:

Good heaven have you at last arrived at fearing to be '*obscure & insignificant*'! What *can* I say to that but 'by all means pursue your brilliant and important career'! Am *I* to choose to be the cause that the person I love feels himself reduced to 'obscure and insignificant'!. . .There seems a touch of Common Place vanity in that dread . . .'[86]

There is certainly no evidence that he was drifting into obscurity in these years. During 1834 and 1835, as well as managing and editing the *London Review*, Mill produced a substantial and glowing review of the first volume of Tocqueville's *De la démocratie en Amerique*, published some translations of Plato's dialogues in Fox's *Repository* (along with his own notes on the vital importance of imagination to platonic thought) and ploughed through his work at India

House. His day job was briefly the location for the next round of hostilities with Macaulay, who in his capacity as a member of the Supreme Council of India, was leading a charge in 1835 to abolish subsidies for colleges teaching the classical Indian languages of Sanskrit and Arabic, and to make English the official language of instruction. Mill, by contrast, believed that supporting elite Indian education was the key to winning the loyalty of the upper classes, who he hoped would then 'act extensively upon the native character and to produce elementary books and translations.'[87] Mill was here demonstrating his growing interest in the cultural role of elites, and his support for locally sensitive education but he was overruled, and felt 'the annoyance of one having for years (contrary to the instincts of his nature which are all for *rapid* change) assisted in nurturing & raising up a system of cautious & deliberate measures for a great public end ... finds them upset in a week by a coxcombical dilettante litterateur who never did a thing for a practical object in his life'.[88]

At the beginning of 1836, Mill was busier than ever: he received a promotion and a salary increase to £800 a year at India House, and his father was taken seriously ill, leaving Mill to pick up much of his work. James Mill, suffering from 'consumption' (tuberculosis), had retreated to the family country house in Mickleham, demanding marmalade and milk, which the household, to his consternation, could not instantly provide.[89] Meanwhile Mill's relationship with Harriet continued to be bittersweet. 'John continues to be in a rather pining way,' his father wrote to his second son James, who was en route for service in India, 'though as he does not choose to tell the cause of his pining, he leaves other people to their conjectures'.

Molesworth, equally bustling, opened the new Reform Club the same year and it was the non-sectarian Mill who persuaded him to allow Whigs to join. The busy Baronet had also snapped up the *Westminster* from Colonel Thompson, who had lost his market to the fresher *London Review* and was happy to be free of his burden for £1,000. The two journals were merged, giving Mill a near-monopoly of the serious end of the radical journal market. He was determined to make the newly merged review a 'striking one', but the incompetence of the nominal editor, Thomas Falconer, meant that almost all the editorial work was falling on Mill's shoulders.[90]

His health collapsed under the strain. His lungs became too weak for him to undertake his sanity-restoring weekend walks and his digestive system was also in spasm. Yet Mill was determined upon the excellence of the first issue of the newly merged review, due in April 1836, and soldiered on. He opened the issue with an essay of his own: 'Civilization – Signs of the Times'. For Mill, the signs were decidedly mixed: on the one hand, 'civilisation', narrowly defined as wealth creation and population, was clearly advancing, especially in Britain; on the other, the social and moral corollaries of economic growth augured less well. 'The age', he wrote, was not 'equally advanced or equally progressive' in all areas, with some 'stationary, or even retrograde'. He pointed in particular to the loss of individual character, the lack of heroic leaders from the 'more opulent' classes, and the difficulty of exerting moral and cultural leadership as symptoms of malaise.[91]

Mill was influenced here by the French historian-politician François Guizot – his review of the latter's *Histoire de la civilisation en Europe* had been published three months earlier – as well as the Romantic poets. Guizot, according to Mill, made a vital distinction between 'the improvement of society and outward life, and that of the inward nature of man'.[92] In his article on Sedgwick, Mill similarly worried that England was prospering in terms of 'her docks, her canals, her railroads', but not in the character of her people: 'Things, in England, are greater than the men who accomplished them.'[93]

Mill co-authored a review of Guizot's lectures for the January 1836 issue of the *London Review* with Joseph Blanco White, a writer and liberal theologian.

When we say a country advances in civilisation, we may mean that external life is becoming more secure and more agreeable ... Or we may mean that the mental faculties of mankind are unfolding themselves – that a higher spiritual culture is introducing itself – that the individuals of whom society is made up, are advancing more and more towards the perfection of their nature – that the national mind is becoming wiser, nobler, more humane, or more refined, and that more numerous or more admirable individual examples of genius, talent, or heroism are manifesting themselves.[94]

A sign of the latter, richer, version of civilization would be a shift towards employee ownership of firms, Mill wrote in 'Civilization', prefiguring one the most important of his later economic policy preoccupations: 'There is not a more accurate test of the progress of civilization than the progress of the power of co-operation.'[95] Mill's wider conception of 'civilization' was almost identical to of Coleridge's 'cultivation', which the poet-philosopher defined as becoming 'more eminent in the best characteristics of Man and Society; farther advanced in the road to perfection; happier, nobler, wiser'.[96]

'Civilization' was one of Mill's most philosophically conservative offerings. Coming on the heels of his public praise of Wordsworth, it confirmed his steady departure from the narrow tenets of Benthamite utilitarianism. Mill was therefore surprised by his ailing father's warm reception for the piece, which was argued 'on grounds and in a manner which I certainly had not learnt from him'. This was a sign, as Mill admitted in his later years, that his father was perhaps more open-minded than he had thought.[97] As it turned out, 'Civilization' was the last of his son's work that James Mill was to see. His health improved sufficiently for him to be moved back to London, only to deteriorate again. On his deathbed, though, James Mill could feel some satisfaction. He was surrounded by evidence of his influence: Parliament had been reformed, the modern, technocratic state was being born and the dispassionate 'expert' – on issues such as health, economics, justice and trade – was becoming a new national hero.

On 23 June 1836, James Mill died. His eldest son was not with him, as he was still terribly ill himself and had been sent to recuperate in Brighton. At the burial service in the graveyard of Kensington Church, the emotional Molesworth wept. Of course his eldest son grieved too, but for Mill the loss of his father evoked complex, contradictory emotions. Watching the coffin of the man who had been both his mentor and tormentor being lowered into the ground, John Stuart Mill felt a great loss, but also a flicker of freedom. To Bulwer he wrote: 'As good may be drawn out of evil – the event which has deprived the world of the man of greatest philosophical genius it possessed . . . that same event has made it far easier to . . . soften the harder & sterner features of [the review's] radicalism and utilitarianism.'[98] The impact of his father's death was nevertheless profound: from this day onwards, Mill suffered with 'an almost ceaseless twitching over one eye'.[99]

The depleted family retreated to Mickleham, where Mill asked both Horace Grant, an India House colleague, and Thomas Carlyle to join him; Harriet, of course, could not. As usual, Carlyle spared nothing in his description of the scene to his wife Jane, who was in Scotland:

There was little sorrow visible in the house, or rather none, nor any human feeling at all; but the strangest *unheimlich* kind of composure and acquiescence, as if all human spontaneity had taken refuge in invisible corners . . . his [Mill's] eyes go twinkling and jerking with wild lights and twitches; his head is bald, his face brown and dry – poor fellow after all. It seemed to me the strangest thing what this man could want with me.[100]

Many of Mill's friends, family and admirers had of course been asking themselves the same question for some years. What did he want with a man whose work he had once judged such 'consummate nonsense'?[101] The rot had started with Wordsworth, of course. But since then Mill had fallen under the influence, so it seemed, of Carlyle, Saint-Simon, Tocqueville and Coleridge – all more or less unacceptable to radical orthodoxy. Mill knew that by

1834 he was considered 'a lost sheep who has strayed from the flock and been laid hold of by the wolves'.[102] The truth is that after his 'crisis', nobody ever took hold of Mill's mind again. Some schools of conservative thought, nevertheless, had a deep influence upon his thinking. To understand Mill, we have to hear the wolves howl.

CHAPTER FIVE

Laid Hold of by Wolves:
Conservative Influences

'Of all the cants that ever were canting in this canting world,' fumed William Hazlitt of Coleridge's *Lay Sermon*, 'this is the worst!' Even before it was published, Coleridge's former protégé had predicted that it would be an apologia for 'despotism, superstition and oppression'.[1] Hazlitt's level of vituperation was unusual, but his view of Coleridge was not. Carlyle attacked Coleridge's teachings as a 'mass of richest spices putrefied into a dunghill' and 'transcendental moonshine'.[2] In liberal and radical circles, Coleridge was generally treated with contempt: he was opium-addled, lazy, erratic and deeply conservative on almost all the important economic, social and political issues of the day. James Mill and Coleridge lived within a few miles of each other, and were almost exact contemporaries, being born and buried within a couple of years of each other, but there was no overlap at all in their views of the world.[3]

Coleridge, as one of the greatest English Romantics, railed against the rise of cities, industry, democracy and clocks and lamented the loss of religious faith, worship of nature and proper acknowledgement of the value of the human spirit. He hated utilitarianism, a 'mechanico-corpuscular' philosophy, and its central aim of universal hedonism: 'But *what* happiness?' he asked. Your mode of happiness would make *me* miserable.'[4] By Millian standards, Coleridge was scandalously unproductive. All of his important writings would fit comfortably into one of the thirty-two volumes of John Stuart Mill's collected works. His opium addiction and its impact upon his health were partly to blame; during his maritime Mediterranean adventures in 1804, the constipation resulting from his habit became so bad that at one point his ship had to be brought alongside a navy ship and a doctor summoned. Coleridge detailed this sweat-drenched 'day of Horror' in his journal:

The Surgeon instantly came, went back for Pipe & Syringe & returned & with extreme difficulty & exertion of the utmost strength injected the latter. Good God! – What a sensation when the obstruction suddenly shot up!. . .O what a time! – equal in pain to any before. Anguish took away all disgust, & I picked out the hardened matter & after awhile was completely relieved. The poor mate who stood by me all this while had the tears running completely down his face.[5]

It is difficult to imagine a more unlikely source of inspiration for the cerebral Mill. But the intended disciple of the 'mechanico-corpuscular' creed made the same pilgrimage as so many of his generation, to Highgate, to hear Coleridge speak. Through John Sterling and Frederick Maurice he became more familiar with the contours of the poet's thought and in his *Autobiography* describes Coleridge as the most important of the voices leading him away from the narrow sectarianism in which he had been raised, and in a letter of 1834 the debt is weighed even more heavily.[6] 'Few persons have exercised more influence over my thoughts and character than Coleridge has,' he told John Nichol, 'not much by personal knowledge of him, though I have seen and conversed with him several times, but by his works, and by the fact that several persons with whom I have been very intimate were completely trained in his school'.[7]

Mill was unusual in being more affected by Coleridge's written words than by his talk, which was as legendary for its ceaselessness as its brilliance. 'Coleridge', wrote one Highgate pilgrim, was like 'a barrel to which every other man's tongue acted as a spigot, for no sooner did the latter move, than it set his own contents in a flow'.[8] When Coleridge gave a series of lectures at the Royal Institution in London, the resulting traffic jams were so great that Albemarle Street became the nation's first official one-way thoroughfare, a perverse legacy for a man so opposed to state control and urbanization.

Coleridge was certainly the leader of the pack of conservative 'wolves' influencing Mill, especially during the 1830s – but Carlyle continued to shape his thinking too. The German poet Johann Wolfgang von Goethe, and two Frenchman, Alexis de Tocqueville and Auguste Comte – a brilliant but eccentric philosopher – were persuasive voices too. While neither of them could be straightforwardly classified as conservatives, there were elements of their thinking which pulled Mill away from his rationalist Benthamite roots. By the end of the decade, the five main strands of Mill's brand of 'conservatism' were clear. On public display in his essays on 'Civilization' (1836) and 'Coleridge' (1840) and in his reviews of Tocqueville's two-part De la démocratie en Amerique (1835 and 1840) were commitments to: intellectual eclecticism and open-mindedness; robust institutional and cultural defences against the dangers of 'mob rule' inherent in democracy; a guiding, intellectual elite as a safeguard of liberal culture; a strong sense of 'nationalism' as a necessary societal glue; and, finally, the need for moral education to ensure the survival of robust individualism, virtue and heroism.[9]

These would all remain important facets of Mill's mature work. From his conservative sources, he learned that a liberal society requires not only a liberal set of rules and laws, but also a liberal culture at both an individual and national level. But Mill was not – and was never in danger of becoming – a political conservative. During the late 1830s, his calls for parliamentary reform, national education, and his commitment to the success of the new radical party were at their strongest, and he was highly selective about the messages he took from the enemy camp. Coleridge was wise on national institutions, education and the role of imagination in self-culture, but on political economy he was an 'arrant driveller'.[10]

Nevertheless, in Mill's new frame of mind, every view, regardless of its source, was to be treated seriously. Coleridge was a direct influence here: 'Great minds,' he wrote, 'are never wrong, but in consequence of being in the right, but imperfectly.'[11] Elsewhere he suggested that 'the Nominalists and Realists ... were both right, and both wrong' and that 'the Conservative party sees but one half of the truth'.[12] Mill would frequently return to the idea of opinions as 'half-truths' in his mature writing. It was in this spirit that he could describe Bentham and Coleridge as 'completing counter-parts' rather than, as most saw them, diametrically opposed rivals. He strove to avoid, in Carlyle's words, 'the completeness of limited men'.[13]

Mill was also persuaded of the value of open-mindedness by the writings of the German Romantics, especially Goethe, mostly transmitted to him second-hand via Henry Crabb Robinson's land-mark essays in the *Monthly Repository*, Carlyle's translation of *Wilhelm Meister* and Sarah Austin's translation of Johann Daniel Falk's *Characteristics of Goethe*.[14] In his *Autobiography*, Mill said that 'Goethe's device, "many-sidedness", was one which I would most willingly, at this period, have taken for mine,'[15] and described Goethe in 1832 as 'one of the wisest men, and men of greatest genius, whom the world has yet produced'.[16] But Mill did not adopt precisely the same view as Goethe. For the German, the truth was diffused throughout an ocean of ideas and thoughts – a *Vielseitigkeit* – and could not be simply fished out.[17] For Mill, the truth was real and solid – it was just that under typical circumstances, dif-ferent individuals or factions captured a portion of it, with each one showing an 'invincible propensity to split the truth, and take half, or less than half of it'.[18]

During the course of the 1830s, Mill became a fierce opponent of sectarianism in intellectual endeavour. He 'marvelled at the blind rage with which the combatants rushed at one another'[19] in the debates of the age and confessed to Sterling: 'I sometimes think that if there is anything which I am under a special obligation to preach, it is the meaning and necessity of a catholic spirit in philo-sophy.'[20] Indeed, his essays on Bentham and Coleridge were expressly intended to be blows struck against the 'rootedly sectarian ... spirit of philosophy'.[21] For Mill, there was also a personal dynamic at work here. Having been raised in what he considered to be a sect, he had found the resources to strike out on his own and was contemptuous of those who were unwilling to make the same journey, 'to face, even with the nation at their back, the coldness of some little coterie that surrounds them'.[22]

It was not possible, Mill now believed, to arrive at a single, perfect solution to any of mankind's problems. The role of philosophy 'was to supply, not a set of model institutions, but principles from which the institutions suitable to any given circumstances might be deduced'.[23] Mill was left with a lifelong suspicion of any philosophical 'systems', especially those which conjured vast, synthetic social structures from a single analytical blueprint. For Mill, unlike utopians like Karl Marx, there was 'no necessity for a universal synthesis'.[24]

It was in this catholic frame of mind that Mill began to reconsider his views on democracy, especially during the late 1830s. By this point, according to the *Autobiography*, Mill had 'ceased to consider parliamentary democracy as an absolute principle, and regarded it as a question of time, place and circumstance.'[25] He continued to believe that a wider involvement in politics was likely to produce the best government and, by involving people in political action, better citizens.[26] But he increasingly saw dangers in democracy too, fearing that in the hands of an ill-educated, ill-informed electorate, democracy could prove to be dangerous. This concern deepened over the next two decades, so that by the 1850s Mill was writing that he and Harriet were 'much less democrats than I had been, because so long as education continues to be so wretchedly imperfect, we dreaded the ignorance and especially the selfishness and brutality of the mass'.[27]

There were two foreign nations in which Mill saw the democratic experiment under way, and the attendant dangers were most forcefully demonstrated to him by an aristocratic citizen of one country commenting on the other. Alexis de Tocqueville's classic, prescient study of the American democratic experience strongly influenced Mill. Even from the distance of the twenty-first century, Tocqueville's acuity is evident. Chapter headings in his work include: 'Of the taste for physical wellbeing in America', 'Why some Americans manifest a sort of fanatical spiritualism' and 'Why the Americans are so restless in the midst of their prosperity'. In his 1835 and 1840 reviews of Tocqueville's two volumes, Mill poured praise on his open-minded and balanced assessment of democracy in action; it is telling that Tocqueville was quoted on both sides of the debate on the 1867 Reform Act. While Tocqueville praised the equality, dynamism and freedoms of American society, he also warned that in a 'democratic' society there was a danger of individualism and atomization, a tendency which was checked in America by vigorous local, voluntary organizations, but which could well be more dangerous in Europe with weaker forms of community association.

Mill believed, like Tocqueille, that democracy was to be welcomed only once the citizens of a nation were ready for it. 'There is much to be said about Ireland,' Mill wrote privately in 1837. 'I myself have always been for a good stout Despotism – for governing Ireland like India. But it cannot be done. The spirit of democracy has got too much head there, too prematurely.'[28] This was why Mill, while supporting parliamentary reform and significant extensions of the franchise, did not, in the 1830s and 1840s, lend his weight to campaigns for universal suffrage. He thought the Chartists, campaigning for the vote for all men, as well as payment for MPs, the secret ballot and annual elections, provided a useful corrective to the complacency of the ruling classes, and he personally contributed to their library and to a testimonial fund for their leader William Lovett.[29] 'I have never met with any associated body of men whom I respect so much as I do your Association,' he enthused to Lovett in 1842. 'I am really anxious to come among you, & to know you better, & to find out what means I have of aiding you'[30] Mill even offered him and any of his colleagues the rare honour of dinner at his house – an invitation which the Chartists, by this point heartily sick of the faint hearts of middle-class radicals, appear to have declined. But Mill also insisted that he could not join the movement: 'The same horror which you yourself entertain of class legislation, makes me object, in the present state of civilization at least, if not on principle, to a legislature absolutely controlled by one class.'

Mill's concerns about democracy were widely shared at the time. Right across the political spectrum, up to and including the anarchist Proudhon, democracy was generally greeted with scepticism at best. As the historian John Dunn explains, 'until almost the end of the nineteenth century, democracy, under that name, remained the political goal of small groups of extreme dissidents or movements . . . which sought to challenge the existing order frontally and fundamentally.'[31]

Mill saw, however, that democratization was an inescapable movement of the age. 'The machine is in the people's hands,' he said, 'but how to work it skilfully is the question.'[32] For him, problems occurred when mass democracy ran ahead of the acquisition of the skills necessary to both sustain and restrain it. 'Man cannot turn back the rivers to their source,' wrote Mill, 'but it rests with himself whether they shall fertilize or lay waste his field.'[33]

Mill was, as he put it, 'a shade or two more favourable to democracy' than Tocqueville.[34] This was for two reasons. First, Mill thought that Tocqueville had conflated democracy and free-market economics and that the less favourable trends he had observed in America resulted as much from the obsessive pursuit of wealth as from the right to vote. 'The most serious danger to the future prospects of mankind,' he wrote, 'is in the unbalanced influence of the commercial spirit.'[35] Second, Mill put more faith in the potential of social progress to improve conditions for democracy. As things stood, Britain faced 'the anomaly of a democratic institution in a plutocratically constituted society', but Mill believed that more education, greater civic participation and a stronger 'moral culture' could prepare the ground for a more democratic political system.[36] In the short run, an educational qualification for voting was necessary – a view which he supported all his life. But over time, democratic participation could itself help to infuse the public-spiritedness with which democracy could be made safe. Mill thought that political institutions were, or ought to be, 'an agency of national education'.[37]

Tocqueville was so impressed with Mill's review that he bound a copy into his own edition of *De la démocratie en Amerique*. 'Of all the articles written on my book,' he wrote to Mill, 'yours is the only one whose author has made himself completely master of my thought, and has known how to exhibit it to the public.'[38] The two men, who met in London in May 1835, along with Roebuck, formed a mutual admiration society.[39] 'I would rather have a monthly letter from you than read any monthly publication I ever knew,' Mill gushed.[40] He dubbed the Frenchman 'the Montesquieu of our own times'.[41] Two decades later, after a long lull in their correspondence, Mill wrote to Tocqueville and praised the 'noble love of liberty' pervading his new work *Ancien Régime*. Tocqueville replied that 'there is no one whose opinion matters to me so much as yours … Until I had your approval, I could not feel certain that I had done well.'[42]

As well as their similar views on democracy, Mill and Tocqueville were drawn together by their shared liberalism. 'I love liberty by taste,' Tocqueville explained to Mill, 'equality by instinct and reason'.[43] They also found common ground in a love of classical history, which informed their analyses of politics and society. In his famous Funeral Oration, the Athenian general, Pericles, had argued for democracy in terms which Mill and Tocqueville would have equally endorsed:

For we alone regard the man who takes no part in public affairs, not as one who minds his own business, but as good for nothing; and we Athenians decide public questions for ourselves or at least endeavour to arrive at a sound understanding of them, in the belief that it is not debate which is a hindrance to action, but rather not to be instructed by debate when the time comes for action.[44]

Mill had a Periclean view of democracy, which could not be reduced to a set of constitutional arrangements or rules on suffrage but had to be an ongoing, active process in which citizens enhanced their own autonomy by shaping the conditions of their own existence. At the same time, the fate of the Athenians proved a stark warning of the need for continuous growth and adaptation: Mill cited with approval Guizot's assessment of ancient Athens that 'never did any people unfold itself so brilliantly in so short a time', only to be quickly 'exhausted ... It seemed as though the creative force of Greek civilisation had spent itself, and no other principle came to its assistance.'[45]

Mill worried a good deal in his mature work about the tyrannical tendencies of prevailing views, but in the 1830s his primary concern was to ensure that the opinions of the learned were ascendant. He opposed a radical demand, advocated by Roebuck and others during the debates on the 1832 Reform bill, that MPs be legally obliged to stand by 'pledges' made to their electors. Mill insisted that elected members, hopefully 'the wisest and best men in the nation'[46] should be able to act as they saw fit, rather than as their electors prescribed: 'the test of what is right in politics is not the will of the people, but the good of the people, and our object is, not to compel, but to persuade the people to impose, for the sake of their own good, some restraints on the immediate and unlimited exercise of their will'.[47]

But Mill was certainly not content to leave leadership to Members of Parliament. Drawing particularly on Coleridge and Comte, Mill came to believe that one of the most important bulwarks against the dangers of democracy was a non-political intellectual class with the status and resources to offer wise guidance to the nation.

Coleridge's *On the Constitution of the Church and State* made a strong impression on Mill. 'If you have [read *Church and State*],' he wrote to John Nichol, his Glaswegian correspondent, in 1834, 'tell me whether you agree with it in the main (I mean the Church part of it) as I do.'[48] In 'the Church part', Coleridge argued for a financially endowed 'national church' on the grounds that it should provide a 'clerisy', an intellectual elite, including but not restricted to clergy, comprised of 'the learned of all denominations ... all the so-called liberal arts and sciences, the possession and application of which constitute the civilisation of a country, as well as the theological.'[49] Coleridge contemptuously dismissed the idea that academic institutions – except Oxford and Cambridge – could provide this role, dubbing the new universities 'lecture bazaars under the absurd title of universities'.[50] Coleridge had provided, in Mill's eyes, a new and radically different argument for giving a 'national church' an endowment of land or revenue: 'For what purpose?' he asked in his 1840 essay on Coleridge. 'For the worship of God? For the performance of religious ceremonies? No; for the advancement of knowledge, and the civilization and cultivation of the community.'[51]

'We honour Coleridge', wrote Mill, 'for having vindicated against Bentham and Adam Smith and the whole eighteenth century, the principle of an endowed class, for the cultivation of learning, and for diffusing its results among the community ... the definitive establishment of this fundamental principle [is] one of the permanent benefits which political science owes to the Conservative philosophers.'[52] In a more obscure article, 'Corporation and Church Property', published seven years earlier, in 1833, Mill had made his support even clearer, in terms that vividly demonstrate the extent to which his inherited utilitarianism had been transformed by the infusion of conservatism:

The endowments of an established church should continue to bear that character ... and under any circumstances, as much of these endowments as is required should be sacredly preserved for the purposes of spiritual culture; using that expression in its primitive meaning, to denote the culture of the inward man – his moral and intellectual well-being, as distinguished from the mere supply of his bodily wants.[53]

For Mill, the Coleridgean clerisy was an antidote to Tocqueville's fears: an endowed class provided a 'security, far greater than has even existed in America, against the tyranny of public opinion over the individual mind'.[54] In 'Civilization', Mill highlighted the need for both an improvement in the character of the masses and the maintenance of an intellectually superior force as a counterweight to them:

> With regard to the advance of democracy, there are two different positions which it is possible for a rational person to take up, according as he thinks the masses prepared, or unprepared, to exercise the control ... If he thinks them prepared, he will aid the democratic movement ... If, on the contrary, he thinks the masses unprepared for complete control over their government – seeing at the same time, that, prepared or not, they cannot 'long' be prevented from acquiring it – he will exert his utmost efforts in contributing to prepare them, using all means, on the one hand, for making the masses wiser and better; on the other, for so rousing the slumbering energy of the opulent and lettered classes ... so calling forth whatever of individual greatness exists or can be raised up in the country, as to create a power which might partially rival the mere power of the masses.[55]

The role of the clerisy, then, was not to hold back the tide of progress, but to guide it. Mill knew that the forces of modernity could not be stopped, even if that were desirable. Democratization, secularization and industrialization were simply facts of life. Stupid conservatives denied this fact, Mill declared to Sterling, 'chain[ing] themselves to the inanimate corpses of dead political and religious systems'. The challenge for the elite was to 'cut a safe channel for the flow of events'.[56] For similar reasons Mill was initially attracted to Comte's concept of a *pouvoir spirituel* (an intellectual and spiritual authority) as a necessary alternative to 'the ascendancy of mere wealth'.[57] Mill even coined a name for the cadre, the 'pedantocracy' which Comte used with alacrity.[58] It subsequently became clear, however, that Comte saw the *pouvoir spirituel* not as a group of philosophical advisers and persuaders, but as authoritarian leaders – a vision with which, needless to say, Mill was in emphatic disagreement. For Mill, the clerisy could only influence the majority through the free exchange of ideas – which were themselves 'a power in history' – rather than through holding executive power.[59] Mill did not believe that people should defer to wealth, social position or title, but to learning and wisdom. He wanted 'not the blind submission of dunces to men of knowledge, but the intelligent deference of those who know much to those who know still more'.[60] Mill wanted philosophers, not philosopher-kings. By 1847, he had in fact moved away from his support for a clerisy, abandoning the idea that 'a leisured class, in the ordinary sense of the term, is an essential constituent of the best form of society'.[61]

While Mill gradually cast off this element of his early conservatism, he never gave up his support for a Coleridgean form of nationalism, for a 'strong and active principle of cohesion among the members of the same community or state'.[62] In his criticism of Bentham, Mill wrote that 'a philosophy of laws and institutions, not founded on a philosophy of national character is an absurdity'.[63] Unless people had a strong sense of the nation being greater than the sum of its parts, Mill believed that it would be impossible for them to put the general good before their own, narrowly defined, interests. In *A System of Logic: Ratiocinative and Inductive*, published in 1843, Mill was the first English writer to use the word 'consensus' in relation to societies.[64] His views were a long way, however, from the jingoism of the Victorian Tories and their blind adulation of military heroes: he was, for example, consistent in his attacks on Wellington, a national hero. And his eloquent distinction between progressive and 'vulgar' nationalism has lost little of its force in the subsequent century and a half:

We need hardly say that we do not mean nationalism in the vulgar sense of the term; a senseless antipathy to foreigners; an indifference to the general welfare of the human race, or an unjust preference of the supposed interests of our own country; a cherishing of bad peculiarities because they are national; or a refusal to adopt what has been found good by other countries. We mean a principle of sympathy, not of hostility; of union, not of separation. We mean a feeling of common interest among those who live under the same government ... We mean, that one part of the community do not consider themselves as foreigners with regard to another part ... that they ... feel that they are one people, that their lot is cast together.[65]

In his 1840 essay on Coleridge, Mill wrote: 'In all political societies which have had a durable existence, there has been some fixed point; something which men agreed in holding sacred; which it might or might not be lawful to contest in theory, but which no one could either fear or hope to see shaken in practice.'[66] Mill was evidently pleased with this line of thought and reprinted this chunk of the essay in his *System of Logic*.[67] But his modern critics, especially the American schloar Gertrude Himmelfarb, have had a field day with this strand of his conservatism, and the way it seems to undermine the later, starker liberalism of *On Liberty*.[68] They argue that the notion of something which is 'sacred' cannot be squared with Mill's later endorsement of the necessary collision of opinions, and wonder how he could have allowed even the possibility that it might be illegal to challenge such a belief.

Mill himself saw the tension between his views on the value of a 'fixed point' to hold societies together and the need for robust, open dissent. In 1851, when the seed of *On Liberty* was starting to germinate, he published the third edition of the *System of Logic*, and the text of the passage cited above was changed from 'which it might or might not be lawful to contest in theory' to 'which, wherever, freedom of discussion was a recognized principle, it was of course lawful to contest in theory'.[69] The original essay was similarly altered when he published it in his *Dissertations and Discussions* in 1859.

This minor editorial retreat does not, however, get Mill off the hook and the charge of inconsistency remains strong. The Mill of 'Coleridge', as Himmelfarb suggests, could in places be read as an acute critic of the Mill of *On Liberty*. There is however a good case for the defence too. First, it has to be borne in mind that, much to the consternation of some of his admirers, Mill rarely wrote merely for the sake of philosophical exactness. He wrote, especially in his essays, to persuade. He criticized Bentham's style, which he said was undermined by the fact that 'he could not bear, for the sake of clearness and the reader's ease, to say, as ordinary men are content to do, a little more than the truth in one sentence, and correct it in the next.'[70] Mill himself often deliberately overstated his case, and the correction would sometimes only appear in a separate article altogether. Here Mill can be seen acting as his own 'completing counterpart'.

Second, Mill's revisions to the *System of Logic* do show that he later saw that any shared national convictions could not be placed beyond the reach of legal, robust dissent. His settled opinion was that a liberal society would be better for the presence of some broadly shared symbols or values which promoted 'allegiance and loyalty', but that these should be open to question and scrutiny and available for substitution over time.

Third, even in 'Coleridge', Mill made a connection between loyalty and liberalism. Just before the section cited by Himmelfarb as contrary to *On Liberty*, he discussed what the 'feeling of allegiance' might focus upon in different societies at various stages of development:

This feeling . . . 'may attach itself to a common God or gods . . . to certain persons . . . to laws; to ancient liberties, or ordinances. Or finally (and this is the only shape in which the feeling is likely to exist hereafter) it may attach itself to the principles of individual freedom and political and social equality, as realized in institutions which as yet exist nowhere, or exist only in a rudimentary state.[71]

The lesson that Mill had received rather reluctantly from Macaulay – that societies co-evolve with their institutions – he accepted readily from Coleridge. For Coleridge, an institution could only be understood by grasping 'the Idea of it', or the principle behind it.[72] Institutions which embodied an idea could not be summarily abolished. For Mill, the French *philosophes* had failed to recognize that a 'year zero' approach to human history, concerned with simply sweeping away existing institutions and systems of belief, was doomed to failure, as the history of the French Revolution demonstrated: 'They [the revolutionaries] threw away the shell without preserving the kernel; and attempting to new-model society without the binding forces which hold society together, met with such success as might have been anticipated.'[73] While Mill disagreed with Wordsworth's politics, he publicly endorsed his vision of the twin foundations of progress:

> *Past* and *future* are the wings
> On whose support, harmoniously conjoined,
> Moves the great spirit of human knowledge;[74]

What both Wordsworth and Coleridge saw, according to Mill, was that institutions, even ones which could be seen on purely rational grounds to have outlived their usefulness 'had rendered essential services to civilization, and still filled a place in the human mind, and in the arrangements of society, which could not without great peril be left vacant'.[75] This did not mean, of course, that the existence of an institution was sufficient proof of its current value, or its claim of certain powers. Mill was as zealous for reform as ever, especially in education, parliament and the law. But his reforming philosophy was now one which paid considerable respect to history, to existing institutional structures and to evolved value-systems. He had travelled a long way from his 1824 demand that 'the rust of antiquity ... no longer be permitted to sanctify institutions which reason and public interest condemn'.[76]

A decade later, Mill had a little more respect for the rust. His embrace of certain conservative insights made him no less of a radical, but it did make him a more pragmatic one. In a short piece in the *Globe and Traveller* from 1835 – in which he discussed the Tory labelling of the radicals as 'Destructives' – Mill made the case for nationally specific, historically sensitive reform:

If it means people who are for the abolition of the monarchy and the House of Lords, and the establishment of an American republic, very good and wise men have thought that this would be desirable; but even of these we never saw or heard of one who wished the experiment tried in this country in defiance of the old and deep-rooted national attachments to those institutions ... The only change which they [the people of England] desire, or even tolerate, is the reform or removal of something which is doing them positive or visible harm. They make no alterations for the sake of symmetry; when an institution is working well, that contents them.[77]

If Coleridge focused Mill's mind on the role of institutions and the value of national sentiment, and confirmed his historicism, it fell to another conservative, Carlyle, to convince him of the importance of robust, moral individuals in the shaping of society. While Mill's personal relationship with Coleridge was minimal, Carlyle was a close friend for many years, despite their differences in style. The Scotsman was tempestuous, egotistical and bitchy, and the sizeable chip on his shoulder remained despite his success. For all his barbs at the Foxes and their circle for their marital shortcomings, Carlyle's own marriage to Jane Welsh was famously awful, with little love lost or gained on either side. When a friend of Tennyson's wondered why the pair did not simply separate, the poet defended the marriage on the wise grounds that 'any other arrangement would have made four people miserable'.[78]

Carlyle was also one of the staunchest enemies of utilitarianism, parliamentary reform and political economy. For Carlyle, the 'Statistical Inquiry' of economists was contemptible. In *Sartor Resartus*, written before he met Mill, although not published until five years later, Carlyle warned that

the progress of Science ... is to destroy Wonder, and in its stead substitute Mensuration and Numeration ... Shall your Science ... proceed in the small chink-lighted, or even oil-lighted, underground workshop of Logic alone; and man's mind become an Arithmetical Mill, whereof

Memory is the Hopper, and mere Tables of Sines and Tangents, Codifications and Treatises of what you call Political Economy, are the Meal?[79]

The Mills, or at least James Mill, were a regular target for his punning jabs: as well as the Arithmetic Mill, Carlyle conjured a 'Mill of Death', and some 'Motive-Millwrights', all in the service of 'the monster UTILITARIA'.[80]

Before his embrace of conservative influences during the 1830s, Mill had thought little of Carlyle's work, but Carlyle's romanticism appealed to his later, agnostic mood. When Carlyle wrote that 'thought without Reverence is barren, perhaps poisonous; at best, dies like cookery with the day that called it forth', he articulated Mill's new concern with a historical, moral approach to reform and his shift away from the antiseptic approach of the purer utilitarians.[81] In 1831, at the outset of their friendship, Mill wrote with some enthusiasm to Sterling:

Another acquaintance which I have recently made is that of Mr Carlyle, whom I believe you are acquainted with. I have long had a very keen relish for his articles in the Edinburgh and Foreign Reviews, which I formerly thought such consummate nonsense; and I think he improves upon a nearer acquaintance ... He seems to me as a man who has had his eyes unsealed, and who now looks around him & sees the aspects of things with his own eye.[82]

Sterling was wary of Carlyle, however, and at one point Mill even berated his ultra-romantic friend for 'not estimating [Carlyle] highly enough'.[83] Carlyle would later write a brilliant biography of Sterling's life, marred only by its contention that its subject was lost and hopeless, worshipping false gods such as Coleridge, until falling under the correcting influence of Carlyle himself.

In 1832, after the death of his father, Carlyle moved back to Scotland for two years, but his friendship with Mill had been sufficiently well established to produce a voluminous and fascinating correspondence: Carlyle had the reporter's knack for drawing people out of themselves. 'You I look upon as an artist, and perhaps the only genuine one now living in this country,' Mill effused in an early letter, contrasting his own role as being 'in a humbler sphere; I am rather fitted to be a logical expounder rather than an artist.'[84]

For Carlyle, democracy, radicalism, Chartism, political economy and social science were all at best distractions from the key task at hand: improving the inner lives and strength of character of individuals. The need was for moral, not parliamentary, reform. He believed that history was born of the actions of people, not economic or social forces. 'Social Life is the aggregate of all the individual men's Lives who constitute society,' he wrote, 'history is the essence of innumerable biographies.'[85] While the bulk of humanity was in such a depraved, semi-bestial state, and enslaved to the 'Police called Public Opinion' (a theme Mill would develop), Carlyle insisted that it was essential that the strong and wise rule over them.[86] An indication of the depth of this obsession is the title of his 1841 book: *On Heroes, Hero-Worship and the Heroic in History*. The looming presence of these authoritarian supermen in Carlyle's writing, along with his racism – most eloquently voiced in 'An Occasional Discourse on the Nigger Question' – made him a forerunner of fascism: Hitler greatly enjoyed his *Frederick the Great*. Carlyle's muscular individualism and romanticism also found an admirer in the poet and essayist Ralph Waldo Emerson, who acted as an successful cheerleader and agent for him in America. While Carlyle may have struck a chord with the Führer in his bunker, he also inspired the literary woodsman in his cabin, Henry Thoreau, who wrote an adulatory essay on his works in 1847.[87] In the 1830s, however, Carlyle was exerting a more direct influence on the man who would become the world's most eloquent liberal. Carlyle would certainly have approved of Mill's concern, voiced in his 1836 essay 'Civilization', that 'there is ... much more of the amiable and humane, and much less of the heroic. There has crept over the refined classes ... a moral effeminacy ... One of the effects of a high state of civilisation upon character, is a relaxation of individual energy ... Heroism is an active, not a passive quality.'[88] Carlyle would have been similarly pleased with Mill's opinions on freedom of discussion, expressed in a letter of 1833, which bring a blush to the cheek of any admirer of *On Liberty*. 'I have not any great notion of the advantage of what the "free discussion" men call the "collision of opinions",' Mill said, 'it being my creed that Truth is sown and germinates in the mind itself, and is not to be struck out suddenly like fire from a flint by knocking another hard body against it.'[89]

Such sentiments were of course entirely at odds with Mill's mature work, and can only be understood as representing both the outer limits of his wanderings into conservative territory, and his desire to please the audience he was addressing. Mill would become the foremost 'free discussion' man in modern history, but not all of the conservatism had rubbed off by the time he came to write *On Liberty*. He continued to share with Carlyle and other conservatives an enduring concern with individual character, and for moral and educational transformation. Nevertheless, even from the start it was clear that while Carlyle's focus was on the necessary virtues of a tiny, heroic class, Mill was concerned with the character of all people: unlike Carlyle, Mill wanted not just a handful of heroes, but a whole society of them.[90] One of his main worries about democracy concerned the prospects for individual character, not just among the elite, but in the population in general. 'The individual,' he wrote in 'Civilization', 'becomes so lost in the crowd that ... an established character becomes at once more difficult to gain, and more easily to be dispensed with.'[91] For Mill, an autocratic hero was an oxymoron. Even in 1833, he disagreed profoundly with Carlyle about Napoleon. 'I ... cannot, with you, allow the one excellence strength of will, to outweigh the entire want of any virtuous purpose.'[92]

After initially imagining that Mill would become his disciple, Carlyle gradually came to see that Mill's intellectual agenda was very different to his own. Their friendship was already cooling by 1835, when it faced a stiff test. Carlyle had completed the mammoth first volume of his masterpiece, *The French Revolution*, which contained such immortal phrases as 'the whiff of grapeshot' and 'sea-green incorruptible'.[93] He gave it to Mill, asking for his views. Mill's housemaid seems to have mistaken the manuscript for scrap paper, which was then used as splendid kindling for the kitchen fire. The entire manuscript was lost, save for a single, singed fragment. After a frantic, hopeless search – his 'extreme distress' was vividly recollected by his sister years later – Mill realized the awful truth.[94] He had to confess, but he would not do it alone. Clutching the surviving scrap, he clattered across the dark London streets in a cab to Kent Terrace; he needed Harriet at such a moment of despair. Outside the Carlyle's home at No. 5 Cheyne Row, Harriet waited in the cab. At the doorway, an ashen-faced Mill asked Jane to join her. Both Carlyles thought, reasonably enough, that the elopement was finally under way.[95] When the confession came, Carlyle was extraordinarily forgiving, considering that he did not work from notes and so had to begin again. He even suggested that Mill's agony was probably worse than his own, but did allow Mill to compensate him financially for some of the lost time – although not to the extent that Mill wished. Needless to say, when *The French Revolution* was published in 1837, the *London and Westminster* reviewer, Mill, gave it a hero's welcome.[96]

After surviving the book-burning incident, Mill's friendship with Carlyle began to falter from the mid-1830s onwards, as the profound differences between their philosophies became clearer and as Mill came to suspect the Carlyles of peddling rumours about himself and Harriet. Carlyle himself recognized that the relationship was changing, reporting in 1835 that to love Mill would be 'like loving the 47th of Euclid' (the famous geometric proposition stating that the square of the length of a right-angled triangle is equal to the sum of the squares of the other two sides).[97] In 1836, Jane Carlyle lamented to her husband that Mill's intellect 'seemed to be failing him in its strongest point: his implicit devotion and subjection to you'.[98] The following year Carlyle wrote of Mill: 'I love him much, but as a friend frozen within ice for me.'[99]

In May 1840, Carlyle – now feted in London society, no small thanks to the endeavours of his young friend – gave a lecture on 'The Hero as Prophet'. He taunted 'Benthamee Utility, virtue by Profit and Loss' before going on, 'If you ask me which gives, Mahomet or they, the beggarlier and falser view of Man and his Destinies . . .' at which Mill, preventing him from completing the sentence and with Harriet at his side, stood up and shouted 'No!'[100] The couple attended no more of his lectures, and within a few years the breach was almost complete. Mill and Carlyle would end up as public opponents over both slavery and the controversial case of Governor Edward John Eyre, who was violently to repress a Jamaican uprising a quarter of a century later. Mill's considered view on Carlyle, expressed in 1869, was that 'it is only at a particular stage in one's mental development that one benefits much by him'.[101]

While Mill was clearly heavily influenced by Carlyle and the other conservative 'wolves', he was never in danger of becoming a slavering disciple. He drew deeply on Coleridge but did not share his intuitionist ideas, declaring in his 1840 essay on the poet that he was 'at issue with Coleridge on the central idea of his philosophy'.[102] His letters to Carlyle were almost always prefaced with an apology for not having written sooner, or at greater length.[103] Carlyle sought Mill out, precipitated their correspondence and derived a great deal of benefit from his relationship with him, not least from an entrée into literary London and Mill's vitally important 1837 review of *The French Revolution*, which made Carlyle's reputation. In 1834, Carlyle had hoped for the editorship of the *London Review*, a role which would have effectively made Mill his boss.[104] In other cases, too Mill was as much donor as beneficiary: his essay on Coleridge played an important role in the poet's posthumous rehabilitation, and he likewise burnished Tocqueville's reputation in Britain with his review of *De la démocratie en Amerique*.

While Mill absorbed some important lessons from conservatives, he remained largely optimistic about the great changes taking place around him. He never enrolled into the 'Jeremiah School', unlike many nineteenth-century conservatives, who saw little that was positive in the dirt, noise and agnosticism of the industrial era. As a young man, Mill had seen and lamented the fact that pessimists were taken more seriously, and had made a plea on behalf of optimists and progressives which remained part of his lifelong credo:

I know that it is thought essential to a man who has any knowledge of the world to have an extremely bad opinion of it ... I have observed that not the man who hopes when others despair, but the man who despairs when others hope, is admired by a large class of persons as a sage, and wisdom is supposed to consist not in seeing further than other people, but in not seeing so far.[105]

Mill's fears about the future were real enough, but they were outweighed by his hopes. A democratic, liberal and egalitarian age was being born. Of course there were attendant dangers, but the potential for human advancement was also great.

Mill knew, however, that some of his evolving views would not find universal favour. Of his 'Coleridge' essay he said that 'perhaps not one person who reads it will like it'.[106] Mill's old utilitarian cadre were certainly in despair about his openness to conservative thinking. Bowring dismissed him as 'a renegade from philosophy, Anglicè − a renouncer of Bentham's creed and an expounder of Coleridge's'.[107] But the conservatives themselves were acutely − if not always immediately − aware that he was not a member of their pack. After years of friendship, Carlyle commented ruefully that 'if John Mill were to get up to heaven, he would be hardly content till he had made out how it all was. For my part, I don't much trouble myself about the machinery of the place, whether there is an operative set of angels, or an industrial class.'[108] At the end of 1836, in the aftermath of his father's death and the political upheavals of the early 1830s, Mill's mind was in any case on more worldly matters: his own health, for one thing; Harriet, of course; the struggling *London and Westminster Review*, and his deepening thoughts on logic. Above all, he was focused intently on British politics, where the parliamentary radicals were making their last, doomed, throw of the dice.

CHAPTER SIX

Independence (1836–42)

>+<

London celebrated Christmas in 1836 with the heaviest snowfall on record and an influenza epidemic. Mill, his health in any case far from recovered, was suffering along with everyone else.[1] Nevertheless his spirits were high. At the beginning of 1837, the inaugural year of the Victorian age, he saw a revolution ahead, writing excitedly to Tocqueville: 'The approaching [parliamentary] session will be next to that of 1830/1831, the most important since 1688 – & parties will stand quite differently at the commencement & at the close of it.'[2]

Mill was right about a shuffling of the political deck, but his hopes of a renewed radical surge were to be repeatedly dashed. It was the Tories, under Robert Peel's brilliant leadership, who emerged victorious. By the end of the decade Mill would turn away from active engagement in politics, exhausted by the failed effort to rally progressive forces, disenchanted with the parliamentary radicals and disillusioned by the innate conservatism of the English people.

For now, though, there was all to play for. With the Whigs, under the urbane, plodding Lord Melbourne, reliant on radical and Irish parliamentary votes to stay in office, the few dozen men loosely clustered around Joseph Hume – as well as Roebuck and Grote, who entered the Commons in 1832 representing, respectively, Bath and the City of London – held considerable power. 'A broken pitcher kept together by a string is no bad representation of the present ministry and the rads,' said Roebuck. 'The ministry are the broken pitcher, the rads the string.'[3] The great hope of the radicals, including Mill, was a split in the Whig party between those who opposed further reform and the more progressive wing. They believed that the time had come for Parliament to represent the real divides in the country, and for a smashing of the cosy two-party system. 'Why bother the poor?' asked Melbourne, when the Queen asked about extending education provision, 'Leave them alone!'.[4] Political representation now had to be reshaped, Mill said, to allow for a 'contest . . . between the two principles which divide the world, the aristocratic and the democratic . . . The problem will then be reduced to its simplest terms: Who is for the aristocracy and who for the people, will be the plain question.'[5]

For most of the radicals, the single most necessary reform was the introduction of the secret ballot. It was 'the key', according to Henry George Ward, a radical MP, that would 'unlock . . . the portals of the constitution'.[6] Once the act of voting was protected from intimidation and bribery, the radicals were sure that the forces of democracy would tend naturally towards a liberal, reforming direction. The number of MPs supporting this measure – dubbed the 'ballot men' – was seen by the radicals, entirely wrongly as it turned out, as a measure of radical strength in Parliament; and the motion, traditionally moved by Grote, was gaining ground. It won 106 votes in 1833, 146 in 1835, 155 in 1837, 200 in 1838, and 216 in 1839. 'You will soon see the ballot a cabinet measure,' Mill assured Tocqueville at the start of 1837, '& then reform will have finally triumphed: the aristocratical principle will be completely annihilated.'[7] Mill was wrong on both counts. The momentum towards the secret ballot was lost with the accession of Peel to the premiership in 1841, and would not be passed until 1872 (by which point Mill himself had changed sides on the issue): and it was the radicals who were annihilated.

As so often, lack of direction, leadership and focus were the hallmarks of the political radicals, 'a motley confused jarring miscellany of irreconcilable theorists' according to one of their number.[8] Mill was frustrated by their squabbling and lack of strategic direction. He longed, privately, to lead them himself. 'I often wish that I were among them,' he wrote in 1837. 'Now would be the time for knitting together a powerful party, and nobody holds the scattered threads of it in his hands except me. But that cannot be while I am in the India House. I should not at all mind leaving it if I had £300 a year free from anxiety and literary labour, but I have at most £100. *Sed tempus veniet.*'[9]

The *London and Westminster Review* would have to suffice as a political weapon. Once again, Mill would try to control parliamentary events from the outside, using the force of his written argument to bludgeon the radicals into order and set out a vision for political change. He found a role model in Armand Carrel, who, Mill said, had used his editorship of the French *National* to make himself 'without a seat in the legislature or any public station beyond the editorship of his journal, the most powerful political leader of his age and country'.[10] For Mill, 'the true idea of Carrel is not that of a literary man, but of a man of action, using the press as his instrument'.[11] (It is difficult, however, to imagine Mill meeting his end as Carrel did, fighting a duel to defend his reputation.) While Mill was disdainful of 'hack journalists', who were less honourable than prostitutes and 'slaves of the day', he now envisaged a lofty, democratic role for learned journals.[12] 'It is now beginning to be felt,' he wrote in October 1837, 'that journalism is to modern Europe what political oratory was to Athens and Rome, and that, to become what it ought, it should be wielded by the same sort of men.'[13]

For the moment, though, Mill himself was immersed in daily political manoeuvres. His hopes of a sundering of the Whigs were unrealistic, but not wild. The king had suggested a coalition government between the Tories and conservative Whigs just three years earlier. The Whigs were a loose grouping, and were divided on issues ranging from parliamentary reform to the Corn Laws.

The radicals also saw the world around them being transformed by the Industrial Revolution, heightening their hopes for a similar political reconfiguring. 'Liberal opinions are gaining,' exclaimed the radical Joseph Parkes 'as indeed must be the case with such a vast increase in locomotion and such a rapidly progressing diffusion of knowledge.'[14]

The shift of people to cities, and capital to machinery, even convinced romantics like Tennyson, after his first train ride, that the nation was in the process of a profound process of uplift: 'Let the great world spin for ever down the ringing grooves of change' he declared in his poem 'Locksley Hall'.[15] (Tennyson later explained that he thought the train had run inside grooves rather than upon rails.) Martin Tupper's *Proverbial Philosophy*, a perfect specimen of middle-brow Victorian verse, captured the national mood of progress in 1838:

> This double decade of the world's short span
> Is richer than two centuries of old;
> Richer in helps, advantages and pleasures,
> In all things richer – even down to gold.[16]

Still, not everyone embraced the rush to modernity; the new queen would complain a few years later about the unnecessary hustle of a forty-four miles-per-hour train journey, and John Ruskin cautioned that 'it does a man, if he be truly a man, no harm to go slow: for his glory is not at all in going, but in being'.[17] Few, however, could deny the evidence of their eyes, or in some case their nostrils: malodour was the necessary accompaniment to nineteenth-century material progress. The Thames was already 'soiled and darkened with livid, false tints', although it would be two decades before the stink became sufficiently bad to force MPs to vacate their perches at Westminster and sign some serious public health regulations into the statute book.[18]

Certain that social and economic changes would bring political radicalism in their wake, Mill insisted that any support by radical

MPs of the Melbourne administration should be 'qualified and dis-trustful'.[19] A *London and Westminster Review* article by William Molesworth, edited, of course, by Mill, argued that the radicals should 'assume an independent attitude, and pursue their ends without reference to the existence or non-existence of the Whig ministry'.[20] Understandably, the Whig attitude towards the radicals was hostile and Melbourne was privately pleased when the Tory Francis Burdett beat the radical John Temple Leader, a close friend of Molesworth, in a by-election.[21]

Alongside Molesworth, George Grote was one of the parlia-mentary figureheads of the group who dubbed themselves 'Philo-sophic Radicals'. Although no leader himself, Grote and his wife were seen by many as a political force to be reckoned with. Cobden reported that he had met 'Mrs. and Mr. Grote . . . I use the words Mrs. and Mr. because she is the greater politician of the two.' Syd-ney Smith said she was 'the queen of the radicals', and claimed – in jest – that she was the origin of the word 'grotesque'. For Francis Place, she simply '*was* the philosophic radicals'.[22]

The Grote household in Eccleston Street was the epicentre of a unique political party, one with no ties to a class, or a special interest group, but determined to act in accordance with clear philosophical principles: utilitarianism, laissez-faire economics and democratiza-tion. 'Those whom . . . we call philosophic radicals,' explained Mill in an article in the April 1837 issue of the *London and Westminster*, 'are those who in politics observe the practice of philosophers – that is, who, when they are discussing means, beginning by considering the end, and when they desire to produce effects, think of causes.'[23] This avowedly intellectual stance was not always politically advantageous: Joseph Parkes, on the centrist side of the radical group, wished his allies 'had more sense and less Logic'.[24]

Mill was not a member of the Grote grouping and was still viewed sceptically by his supposed allies. Mrs Grote saw him as a 'wayward intellectual deity'.[25] None the less, he was more focused on political machinations than at any other time in his career, including his three years as an MP. As much as any of the parliamentarians, he genuinely believed that the party system was about to be recast. To Francis Place he wrote: 'Pray do not think of hibernating. Radicalism seem to me to have a better chance just now than it has ever had before.'[26] He was consistently bracketed with the 'Ultras', as Melbourne dubbed them. When *The Spectator* (then a progressive publication) constructed a fantasy radical cabinet, Mill's name was on the list – even though he was not in Parliament.[27]

But the spring hopes of the radicals were royally crushed in the summer of 1837. William IV finally dropped dead on 20 June at the age of seventy-two and his eighteen-year-old successor, Queen Victoria, rapidly won over not only her Privy Council but the whole nation. Joseph Parkes complained of a 'bellyache' as he lamented the 'epidemic of loyalty' and 'Queen mania' that seized the nation.[28] The new queen would give her name to an extraordinary period of creativity, change and progress, and Mill would become its voice and conscience. As a twentieth-century commentator put it: 'If ever one man ever represented an epoch, Mill represents Victorianism.'[29] For the moment, however, Queen Victoria was bad news for the radicals. In the summer elections of 1837 they were almost destroyed as a parliamentary force. Roebuck lost his seat (though he returned in 1841) and Grote scraped by six votes into the fourth of four seats for the City of London, having led the poll in 1832. Melbourne hung on, much to the relief of the young queen, who was already reliant on the fifty-seven-year-old patrician. In the autumn, Lord John Russell uttered his famous 'finality' speech on parliamentary reform. In the debate on the Queen's Speech, Thomas Wakley, a radical MP, moved an amendment that the House consider an extension of the suffrage: it received 20 ayes, against 509 noes.

Undaunted by the election results and sanguine about a the likelihood of a Conservative government, Mill continued to urge the radicals onwards, by putting, as he said, 'ideas in their heads and purpose in their hearts' and instructed them to sit on the opposition benches rather than prop up the Whig administration.[30] Given the perilous parliamentary situation, Mill's position was seen by moderate reformers such as Albany Fonblanque, the editor of the *Examiner*, as utopian and irresponsible in roughly equal measures. Fonblanque was hardly a Tory – one of his sons was even called Bentham – but throughout 1838 the *Examiner* poured scorn on the radicals and on the *London and Westminster*. Fonblanque tore into the group's pretensions, especially their self-appointed label of 'philosophical radicals', suggesting: 'To us it appeared better ... that the world should find out that they were philosophical, than that they should declare it of themselves.'[31] Mill responded, in private and contrary to his published definition of the grouping, that in fact no such label had been adopted for fear of a '*coterie* air which it was felt to be objectionable'.[32] Fonblanque also poked fun at the radicals' diminutive parliamentary representation, describing them as 'certainly the smallest minority that ever gave itself party airs ... Two such parties would be necessary to make a whist party ... Party cannot in this instance be called the "madness of many" but it may justly be termed the eccentricity of two.'[33] Finally, Fonblanque named and shamed the *London and Wesminster* for representing the opinions of the philosophical radicals, provoking a furious response from Mill:

What is the meaning of *your* insisting on identifying me with Grote or Roebuck or the rest?... Have you forgotten ... that my radicalism is of a school the most remote from theirs, at all points, which exists? *They* knew this as long ago as 1829, since which time the variance has been growing wider & wider.[34]

To drive the point home, Mill insisted that not only was he philosophically distant from the radicals, but apart socially too: 'With regard to 'the Grote conclave' there may be such a conclave, but I know nothing of it, for I have not been within the doors of Grote's house in Eccleston Street & have been for the last few years completely estranged from that household.'[35]

These angry exchanges with Fonblanque highlight a fatal weakness in Mill's position during the latter half of the 1830s. On the one hand, he wanted to use the *London and Westminster* to introduce a wider range of voices – including those of Carlyle, Sterling and Tocqueville – than had been possible while his father was alive. On the other, it was the instrument through which he was trying to lead the radicals, and these twin objectives were incompatible. Not only did the *London and Westminster* carry articles by Thomas Carlyle and by John Sterling in 1838, it carried a glowing portrait of Carlyle *by* Sterling.[36] Commissioning a clerk in holy orders, as Sterling then was, to eulogize a ferocious opponent of democracy and utilitarianism was certain to arouse suspicion among the radicals. Mill's review of Carlyle's *French Revolution* – 'no work of greater genius, either historical or poetical, has been produced in this country for many years' – and the anxiety about democracy in his Tocqueville review were unsettling to the very people he was trying to influence.[37] Mrs Grote was sceptical, of course, but even the Austins, reading in Malta, were concerned – 'clamorous against the article by Carlyle' and warning the editor that he 'would ruin the review' if he published any more.[38] Sterling had seen the problem from the outset, noting that if the review was 'to be a Radical Organ it must show a bad carping sneering partisan newspaper kind of spirit'.[39] In fact, Mill managed to make the *London and Westminster Review* sufficiently carping to alienate moderates like Fonblanque without making it sufficiently partisan to exert the necessary authority over the parliamentary radicals.

For many, Mill's final betrayal came in his essay on Bentham, published in the *London and Westminster* in 1838. Setting his old mentor alongside Coleridge as one of 'the two great seminal minds of England in their age', Mill praised Bentham's work on legal philosophy and reform: 'He found the philosphy of law a chaos, he left it a science: he found the practice of law an Augean stable, he turned the river into it which is mining and sweeping away mound after mound of its rubbish.'[40] But the bulk of the essay amounted to a devastating critique. Bentham had fallen short on a number of fronts, failing, above all, to 'derive light from other minds'. Mill wrote: 'His contempt of all other schools of thinkers; his determination to create a philosophy wholly out of the materials furnished by his own mind was his first disqualification as a philosopher.'[41]

He also attacked Bentham's utilitarianism for analysing human behaviour purely in terms of self-interest: 'Man is never recognized by him [Bentham] as being capable of pursuing spiritual perfection as an end; of desiring, for its own sake, the conformity of his own character to his standard of excellence, without hope of good or fear of evil from other source than his own inward consciousness.'[42] For Bentham, complained Mill, 'man, that most complex being, is a very simple one.' The traditional Benthamite approach saw individuals as containers of happiness or misery. 'Call them men, call them monks, call them soldiers, call them machines,' Bentham had declared, 'I care not so long as they be happy ones.'[43] Mill, however, now insisted that moral excellance and self-cultivation had intrinsic value, which could not be boiled down to simple 'utility'.

Mill was also doubtful about the practical value of Bentham's 'principle of utility' on the grounds that 'utility, or happiness, is much too complex and indefinite an end to be sought except through the medium of various secondary ends, concerning which there may be, and often is, agreement among persons who differ in their ultimate standard'.[44] Mill was here extending the argument he had first made in his 1833 review of Robert Blakey's *History of Moral Science*:

The real character of any man's ethical system depends not on his first and fundamental principle, which is of necessity so general as to be rarely susceptible of an immediate application to practice; but upon the nature of those secondary and intermediate maxims, *vera illa et media axiomata*, in which, as Bacon observes, real wisdom resides.[45]

Mill also distanced himself from Bentham's insistent neutrality about the ethical value of different activities, encapsulated in his famous claim that poetry was no better than push-pin,[46] a childish game in which players balance pins on the brim of a hat:

If he [Bentham] thought at all about any of the deeper feelings of human nature, it was but as idiosyncrasies of taste, with which the moralist no more than the legislator had any concern ... To say either that man should, or that he should not, take pleasure in one thing, displeasure in another appeared to him as much an act of despotism in the moralist as in the political ruler.[47]

In his own *Utilitarianism*, published in 1861 Mill would take a further step away from Bentham, by making an explicit distinction between 'higher' and 'lower' pleasures. Mill later doubted the wisdom of launching his earlier heretical attack, or at least of its timing. 'I have often felt', he wrote in the *Autobiography*, 'that Bentham's philosophy, as an instrument of progress, has been to some extent discredited before it had done its work, and that to lend a hand towards lowering its reputation was doing more harm than service to improvement.'[48]

Unsurprisingly, the 1838 article angered many of the radicals. Francis Place wryly suggested that 'Mill has made great progress in becoming a German Metaphysical Mystic' and that 'excentricity [sic] and absurdity must sometimes be the result'.[49] Even William Molesworth's patience seems to have run out and Mill was obliged to take over the *London and Westminster* as sole proprietor, a move which he subsequently described as 'very imprudent' from a financial standpoint, but which did give him total editorial freedom.[50] There could be no question now whose voice was being relayed through its pages. Drafting a letter to Edward Lytton Bulwer, the novelist-politician, Mill explained that he was delaying the publication of a political article until it was clear 'what my relations are likely to be to parties in parliament', before amending the sentence to read 'what the relations of the review are likely to be'.[51] It is surprising, given that the world knew that the *Review* was Mill's mouthpiece, that he bothered to remove the 'my' at all.

Mill's position with the radicals was further weakened by persistent rumours about the role played by Harriet. Just as Aspasia was supposed by many to be responsible for her husband Pericles'

Funeral Oration, so Harriet, with even less evidence, was alleged to be feeding Mill his lines.[52] Godefroy Cavaignac, a French refugee and leading light in the *Société des Droits de l'Homme*, dubbed her 'the Armida of the London and Westminster'.[53] He may have been suffering from sour grapes, however, as there is some evidence that Mill rejected his literary offerings.[54] In any case, while Harriet undoubtedly had a great interest in the conduct of the journal, there is no indication of any direct editorial influence.

By this stage, the couple had settled into their 'imperfect companionship'. Both had serious health concerns, which were alleviated by extended continental rest-cures. After his father's death in 1836, Mill had been granted three months leave by India House and headed to Paris with his brothers, sixteen-year-old Henry, who was also seriously unwell, and twelve-year-old George. Harriet was already there, with her three children and a nursemaid. The whole party travelled to Lausanne, where Mill and Harriet left at least the older children with the nurse, and travelled on together to Nice; whether Harriet's youngest daughter Helen, then five years old, went with them or stayed in Switzerland is not known.[55] Carlyle, writing to Sterling, reported that Mill was in France, and that 'Mrs Taylor, it is whispered, is with him, or near him. Is it not very strange, this pining away into dessication [*sic*] and nonentity, of our poor Mill, if it be so, as his friends all say, that this charmer is the cause of it?'[56]

Mill and Harriet spent almost two months in Piedmont and on the bay of Genoa, before returning to Switzerland to collect the children and getting back to London in time for the flu season. Although Mill's health was still fragile – he was suffering from headaches, stomach ache and eyestrain – he had no choice but to throw himself into his work. The spasmodic twitching over his eye worsened. On his father's death, Mill had been promoted again, to third Examiner, and had a pile of India House tasks awaiting him. As the head of the household, he now also had to deal with the family's financial and domestic affairs, as well as editing and writing for the review. Apologizing to Sarah Austin in January 1837 for the tardiness of a reply to her letter, he complained of 'the endless drudgery I have had upon my hands, with arrears of India House business and private affairs, without counting review matters or any other writing'.[57] This is one of the very few instances when Mill complained about his workload.

Mill was too busy to take a long holiday in 1837, but squeezed in an autumn walking tour through the Cotswolds and the Brecon Beacons, almost certainly with Harriet.[58] Carlyle continued to look upon the couple with pity: 'His *Platonica* and he are as constant as ever: innocent I do believe as sucking doves, and yet suffering the clack of tongues, worst penalty of guilt. It is very hard; and for Mill especially as unlucky as ever.'[59] They do not appear to have been suffering too badly, however, and their relationship, nurtured during weekends at her country home, continued to ripen. 'I do not think I shall see you before Tuesday – that is a terrible long time,' she wrote to him in 1837. 'When I think I shall not hold your hand until Tuesday the time is so long & my hand so useless. Adieu my delight. je baise tes jolis pattes. *cher cher cher*.'[60] Plenty of couples would wish for such unluckiness.

Mill's financial fortunes were also on the upturn: his new £1,200 annual salary, equivalent to at least £100,000 today, put him in the very top of the earnings league, giving him an income three times that of the Governor of the Bank of England and comfortably in the top 0.5 per cent of the income distribution.[61] Mill did not possess the independent wealth necessary to support both a parliamentary career and a high standard of living, but his high income was completely secure. Mill was a leading member of the growing professional class, who were largely immunized from commercial concerns and therefore able to comment in a fairly disinterested fashion on political economy. 'To a certain extent,' writes the social historian Harold Perkin, the professional man 'was above the economic battle, with the same freedom to take sides, to turn his thumbs up or down, as a spectator in the Roman Colosseum.'[62]

For Mill, this freedom was exercised through the *London and Westminster Review*, which, as well as covering economics, carried articles on politics, literature, poetry, the politics of France, music, and philosophy. He had his fair share of editorial frustrations and trials, though. In April 1839, he was 'very much annoyed' when the latest nominal editor of the *Review*, the Scottish journalist John Robertson, ignored an instruction from Mill to spike an article defending women writers against 'Crokerisms' anonymous critical attacks named after John Wilson Croker, who was proud of his editorial record for 'savaging' women.[63] The piece upset Abraham Hayward, Mill's old enemy from the London Debating Society, who was prone to a little Crokerism himself. On another occasion, Mill assured Bulwer that an article from him on the social influence of the royal court 'would be a great treasure' to the *Review*. Sadly it was not. Three months later, Mill wrote to Robertson: 'I cannot bestow upon Bulwer's article any milder name than despicable ... God grant that nobody may read it, or that whoever does, will instantaneously forget every word of it.'[64] Few editors have escaped such moments.

More happily, Charles Buller contributed a glowing review of Charles Dickens's *Pickwick Papers*, which was taking the English-speaking world by storm in 1836 and 1837. Mill himself continued to deliver his course of education on French history and politics, with a special mission to 'din ... into people's ears that Guizot [the French statesman and historian] is a great thinker & writer'.[65] He also used his new editorial freedom to continue hammering away at the political scene and urge the radicals to separate from the Whigs. But even he was becoming frustrated and despondent about the prospects offered by the current crop of parliamentarians. 'I have been trying ever since the reform bill to stimulate, so far as I had an opportunity, all sections of the parliamentary radicals to organize ... a union, & system of policy,' he wrote to Bulwer in March 1838, 'not saying to them: Adopt my views, do as I bid you – but Adopt *some* views, do *something*.'[66] He subsequently recognized that his attempts to lead from an editor's chair had been doomed from the outset: 'It was a task only for one who, being himself in Parliament, could have mixed with the radical members in daily consultation, could himself have taken the initiative, and instead of urging others to lead, could have summoned them to follow.'[67]

But as radical hopes were fading, Mill saw on the horizon a knight, or more precisely an earl, who could rescue the cause. Lord 'Radical Jack' Durham, an arrogant, independent, populist politician, had been seen by Mill since 1834 as a possible 'great prize' for the radicals.[68] Melbourne, the Prime Minister, fearing exactly what Mill hoped for, had sent Durham on a diplomatic mission to St Petersburg in 1835. By the summer of 1837 he was back and the Whig patriarch had to think of some new distraction, which fortuitously presented itself. The two Canadian provinces – Upper and Lower – were in turmoil, in part because increasing numbers of settlers were from America, and uncomfortable with British rule. The consensus among the political classes was that war and/or independence were imminent. Melbourne, while privately believing the loss of the two colonies 'might not be of material detriment', decided to dispatch Durham to the scene.[69] Durham agreed, but on stiff terms: Buller, a man whose radical credentials had been impeccable since he voted for the abolition of his own rotten-borough seat, was to be his secretary and he insisted on full plenipotentiary powers. Mill gave Durham a fulsome send-off in the *London and Westminster*, hoping that following a Canadian triumph, presumably involving a degree of self-government, he would return ready to lead a radical party, and ultimately a radical government: 'A Durham ministry within the year' was the radical objective, Mill decreed.[70] With his moderate brand of radicalism, encompassing the secret ballot, triennial parliaments and household suffrage, Durham was, for Mill, the man who could finally unite all the 'natural' radicals in the country and Parliament.

On his arrival in Quebec, Durham released most of the 160 rebels but banished the leader, Louis Papineau, and a score of others. He then immersed himself in the economic and social problems of both provinces and established a special council to oversee Lower Canada. The turbulence abated. Back in London, however,

Durham's actions were criticized by the Tories for being too lenient, by the radicals for being too harsh, and by the Whigs for threatening the constitutional fabric of the Empire. Melbourne, with some relish, bowed to parliamentary pressure: Durham learned from a New York newspaper that his powers had been rescinded, and set off for home.

Once again, where others saw only disaster, Mill found hope. 'The present turn in Canadian affairs brings Lord Durham home, incensed to the utmost (as Buller writes to me) with both Whigs and Tories,' he wrote to Molesworth in October 1838. 'the formation of an efficient party of moderate Radicals, of which our review will be the organ, is certain – the Whigs will be kicked out never more to rise, and Lord D. will be head of the Liberal Party and ultimately Prime Minister ... he is the man for us ... This has awakened me out of a period of torpor about politics ...'[71]

Buller used the month-long voyage home to draft much of the report on the expedition as well as trying to persuade Durham to see himself as a radical party leader. Molesworth and others arranged an enthusiastic welcome at Devonport. But Durham was ill, and his only thought was to finish the report on the future of Canada. Shortly after his return, he rebuffed a delegation from the Westminster Reform Association. Moderate Whigs, worried about his intentions, warned him away from the radicals, confirming Mill's fears that 'the damned pseudo-radicals [will] get round him and talk him over'.[72] Edward Ellice, precisely the sort of reforming Whig the radicals wanted Durham to capture, characterized Mill, for Durham's benefit, as being a man 'with considerable learning, and critical talent – but also a "denisen of Utopia"'.[73]

Durham's reputation, and the status of his report, hung in the balance. Mill tipped it. In a strongly argued defence of Durham's conduct in the December 1838 issue of the *Review*, Mill successfully set the tone for subsequent debate. Listing Durham's achievements in quelling the disturbances, deterring the United States, examining the causes of the original disenchantment, and considering the future governance of the colonies, Mill wrote: 'If this is failure,

failure is but the second degree of success; the first and highest degree may be yet to come.'[74] The article cost the *Review* a third of its sales, and provoked the furious response from Roebuck, who was Canadian, that Mill's argument could equally be used to justify the repressive policies of Castlereagh, Peter the Great or Napoleon. Mill 'having the faculty of finding irrefragable arguments for every side of every question,' Roebuck fumed, 'it was not difficult to trump up a defence for Lord Durham'.[75] Mill knew that his intervention had been decisive: 'I saved Lord Durham – as he himself, with much feeling, acknowledged to me.'[76] It was an example of the importance of timing. In his *Autobiography*, Mill described the Durham article as 'the word in season, which at a critical moment does much to determine the result; the touch which determines whether a stone, set in motion at the top of an eminence, shall roll down on one side or on the other'.[77]

Durham's report became, as Mill correctly said, the blueprint for 'a new era', in which colonies could move towards self-government within the Empire.[78] In retrospect, then, Mill's defence of Durham had lasting liberal value, but at the time, the Durham saga demonstrated how far he was willing to bend his principles to the exigencies of the moment. The defence was undertaken for the express purpose of 'acting at once upon him and upon the country', and there is no question that in different circumstances Mill would have been sharply critical of some of Durham's more dictatorial moves.[79] This was Mill the political partisan, not Mill the even-handed philosopher. In the end, his hopes of a radical revival came to nothing as Durham, a broken man, died a few months later. His legacy, however, thanks greatly to Mill, was secure and the Whig government enacted many of his proposals for a reunification of the two Canadian provinces under a degree of self-rule. Mill would have the satisfaction, thirty years later, of walking into the 'aye' lobby for the British North America Bill, which created a new, federal, virtually self-governing Dominion of Canada passed through the Commons 'as if it were a private Bill uniting two or three English parishes'.[80]

Durham's refusal to lead the radical charge confirmed all Francis Place's anti-aristocratic prejudices. 'He had a chance such as few men have had,' he complained to Mrs Grote, 'but he was all a Lord and none a man.'[81] The antipathy was mutual; Durham complained that Place always wore a 'coat of bristles' in the company of the luckier born.[82] For Mill, it signalled the end to his hope that the parliamentary radicals could be anything more than 'a mere appendage of the Whigs'. He told Robertson that, 'if there is to be no radical party there need be no Westminster Review . . . it is one thing to support Lord Durham in *forming* a party; another to follow him when he is only joining one'.[83] Mill subsequently detached himself from politics, made plans to divest himself of the *Review*, began to make his peace with the moderates, and turned his mind to his new work on logic. Even Mrs Grote was out of heart, and began her own journey back to Whig acceptability; and a miserable Molesworth, appropriately enough, started editing the work of Thomas Hobbes.

Mill was initially inclined to blame the parliamentary radicals for failing to seize their historical moment. Their tactical incoherence, ill-discipline and 'spineless imbecility' were certainly all factors in their defeat and his own attempts to direct events from outside Westminster had been unsuccessful.[84] 'A considerable expenditure of head & heart' had been made, he wrote to his new friend Robert Barclay Fox in Falmouth, in an attempt 'to breathe a living soul into the Radical party – but in vain – there was no making those dry bones live'.[85] Mill later approved John Austin's view that 'the country did not contain the men'.[86] His heaping of the blame for the disappointments of the late 1830s on to the radical MPs reflected Mill's conviction that within the general population there was widespread desire for more serious change. Mill insisted, without evidence, that 'there was a great deal of passive radicalism in the electoral body' and that 'England is moderate Radical'.[87] As late as the early 1850s, when he was drafting his *Autobiography*, he was still castigating the radical MPs, especially Grote, for having had 'no enterprise, no activity'.[88] Later he tacitly admitted his miscalculation of the national mood and by the time he rewrote the *Autobiography* in the 1860s, the failure of the radicals was attributed to impersonal historical forces, rather than personal inadequacies: 'Their lot was cast in the ten years of inevitable reaction, when the Reform excitement being over ... power gravitated back in its natural direction, to those who were for keeping things as they were; when the public mind desired rest.'[89]

Mill had also failed to see how the established 'aristocratic' political parties were adapting to the changing social and economic circumstances. The Whigs had already embarked upon what Asa Briggs has called 'reform by instalments' and even the laid-back Melbourne had been persuaded, after reading an article by James Mill, of the case for the secret ballot. It was the Tories under Robert Peel's leadership, however, who most clearly recognized the case for pragmatic reform, and government for, if not yet by, the middle classes. By 1843, Peel, who saw true Conservatism in the enactment of 'judicious reforms', would be establishing the Health of Towns Commission, the first significant step towards improved public health, heavily influenced by the magisterial report of the arch-Benthamite, Edwin Chadwick.[90] A Tory reformer did not fit into Mill's picture of the political ecology of the period, however. He publicly denounced Peel as a 'third-rate man', 'perhaps the least gifted man that ever headed a powerful party in this country', one who 'does not know his age; he has always blundered in his estimate of it'.[91] By 1841, as Peel settled in for a five-year term of office before splitting his own party on a point of principle, an act that should have elicited Mill's admiration, it was painfully clear that it was Mill who had blundered in both his assessment of politics and his estimate of politicians. Mill never lost his blind spot on Peel, however: as late as 1861, he was still using Peel to make an unfavourable comparison between the character of British politicians and those of Washington and Jefferson.[92]

Having declared in 1838 that 'radicalism has done enough in speculation; its business now is to make itself practical', by 1841 Mill had reversed course and was forced to conclude that 'the progress of liberal opinions will again, as formerly, depend upon what is *said* and *written*, and no longer upon what is *done*'.[93] A pattern had by now been established: Mill would spend the rest of his life oscillating between two poles – a belief that immediate political change was both possible and necessary; and a conviction that politics was a sideshow and only the cultivation of new ideas and culture could usher in change. Periods of intense partisan interest and involvement in political matters by Mill – as in the early 1820s, the late 1830s, 1846, 1848–9, 1862 and 1865–8 – were typically followed by an abrupt disengagement, accompanied by bitter denunciations of politics, politicians and sometimes the general population, and a recommitment to a life of the mind.

Serious-minded students of Mill's life sometimes appear to lament the waste of energy of his partisan periods, especially during the 1830s. 'For four years he struggled hopefully, and for two more years valiantly,' write modern scholars Bruce Kinzer, John Robson and Ann Robson of the second half of the 1830s. 'He lost both time and money, and temporarily at least some of his mental peace and some of his friends, in an attempt through the editorship of the *London and Westminster Review* to concentrate radical opinion.'[94] Mill's 'political' periods, however, vitally informed his scholarly efforts: works whose purpose was almost always to clear the ground for social, economic and political reform. Without his forays into political territory, Mill might well have written less on other matters, not more. Even his failures seemed to provoke a renewed commitment to the development of ideas, so his partisan periods were in one sense refueling stops along his radical, intellectual journey.[95] The scholar Joseph Hamburger points out that during the 1830s Mill played 'two philosophic roles ... the Coleridgean philosopher who was broadly concerned with human culture ... and "moral regeneration" [and] a more narrowly conceived philosophic role, when he emphasized change in political institutions ... In this role he sought to be a spokesman and intellectual guide for the parliamentary radicals.'[96]

An important difference between these two Mills was the time-frame within which they worked. The 'narrow', political Mill was concerned to bring about certain changes in the immediate future, including a wider suffrage, greater freedom of speech, the rationalization of welfare and government, and freer trade and exchange. The 'broad', Coleridgean Mill was more concerned with the longer term, and very often with the potential consequences of the very measures his 'narrow' alter ego was advocating – collective mediocrity, a tyranny of public opinion, an overweaning central state and wasteful economic competitiveness. This dual time-frame explains what sometimes appear to be contradictory positions taken by Mill. He supported the highly centralizing Poor Law Amendments, while writing about the dangers of state centralization; he advocated a much larger electorate but worried that mass democracy might drive down standards in public life; he wanted the widest possible dissemination of ideas, but was also concerned about the way public opinion might hamper freedom just as effectively as despotic governments. A recurrent and attractive feature of Mill's work is his recognition that today's solutions create tomorrow's problems, and that both need to be addressed.

Mill had watched the last chapters of the Durham saga from abroad, having fled, ostensibly for the sake of his health, from the London winter of 1838–9 to the south of France and then Italy. Harriet was also unwell, according to her husband, and headed for the sun.[97] It is not clear, though, how ill Mill actually was at this point. Just before the continental trip he had managed a bracing walking tour from Devon to Dorset, and his colleagues were impressed that a man so ill could have pursued the Durham case with such vigour.[98] Mill's doctor was none the less persuaded that six months away from India House was required. On the evidence available, it seems as if the greatest British philosopher of the nineteenth century overstated his physical symptoms in order to get a sicknote and slip off to Italy with his mistress: if so, surely only the most hard-hearted could think less of him for it.

After a nauseous eighteen-hour crossing of the Channel, Mill met Harriet in Paris in time to celebrate the 1839 New Year. Their only chaperone was Harriet's daughter Helen, now seven years old and generally called 'Lily'. The trio proceeded south, variously by post, steamship and French warship, to Naples, via Chalon, Lyons, Marseilles, Leghorn and Rome. Nobody, except Lily, knew that the couple were together. In sleepy Sorrento, across the bay from Naples, they stayed at a hotel called La Sirena. Visiting the area sixteen years later, Mill wrote to Harriet (by then his wife): 'Here I am darling & at the same inn, La Sirena which looks as pretty as possible; only I think we were not on the ground floor which I am now.'[99] After a few restful weeks on the Bay of Naples, the couple returned to Rome in time for spring, where Mill ran into John Sterling and the pair spent many happy hours admiring the Sistine Chapel and other historical sites. Recounting the trip years later, Sterling described an afternoon at the baths of Caracalla:

We sat there with the city behind us, and in front the Campagna, or open plains, with the ruins of the brown aqueducts, and high and bright beyond the whole range of Alban Hills, rising up to the Monte Cava where stood of old the temple of the Latin Jupiter. Mr. Mill is a man to feel the nobleness of such a prospect, and we were very happy sitting there in the air as if we had been a thousand leagues from all the world but that of Antiquity.[100]

Either Mill did not tell Sterling that Harriet was also in the city, or his friend managed a heroic feat of discretion, never breathing or writing a word to that effect.[101] In any case, the continental trips of both 1836 and 1838–9 inevitably invite questions about Mill's level of physical intimacy with Harriet. The topic was certainly a lively one at the time, with London society apparently divided between those who condemned them because they were lovers and those who pitied them because they were not. Carlyle was a one-man gossip exchange, delighting in passing on Cavaignac's stories of the couple 'eatin' grapes together off o' one bunch, like two love-birds' in Paris and countless other rumours and innuendoes.[102] Carlyle seized on news that Harriet was moving into temporary accommodation in 1839 as evidence that matters had come to a head, writing to Sterling: 'Mrs. Taylor ... is living not at the old abode in Regent's Park, but in Wilton Place, a street where as I conjecture there are mainly wont to be *Lodgings*. Can it be possible? Or if so what does it betoken?'[103]

What it betokened, in fact, was that John Taylor was in the process of renovating the house at Kent Terrace and had secured a short-term home for the family in the meantime. Sterling's reply, which contains one of very few mentions in his correspondence of the matter, is perhaps as close to the truth as we shall get. 'I think it is a good sign of a man that he feels strongly that kind of temptation,' he wrote, 'but a far better one that he both feels it and conquers it, which I shall trust that Mill has done and will do.'[104]

In a more emancipated age, it is harder to take on trust that this couple, who were clearly deeply in love and who spent so much time together, including long unchaperoned sojourns by the balmy Mediterranean, refrained from acting on their evidently strong physical desire for each other. Mill certainly had the eye and desires of a heterosexual man. He told Harriet of a dream about the ideal combination, in a woman, of 'sincere friend' as well as a 'sincere Magdalen'; in 1855, four years after their marriage, he would complain of having 'not seen a single handsome woman at Athens'.[105] Mill and Harriet would scarcely have been curiosities if they had been adulterous. In any list of nineteenth-century luminaries, the minority is very often formed by the group who did not engage in an extramarital liaison: even George Grote celebrated the completion of his mammoth history of Greece with a fling.

If Mill and Harriet are simply taken at their word, the debate is closed; their own statements on the matter are unequivocal. The question is whether they are true. During the drafting of the *Autobiography* in the 1850s – after their marriage – Mill wrote to Harriet: 'We have to consider, which we can only do together, how much of our story it is advisable to tell, in order to make head against the representations of enemies when we shall not be alive to add anything to it. If it was not to be published for 100 years I should say, tell all, simply & without reserve. As it is there must be care taken not to put arms in the hands of the enemy.'[106]

Harriet agreed that discretion was the better part of valour and suggested that the *Autobiography* contain:

a summary of our relationship from its commencement in 1830 – I mean given in a dozen lines – so as to preclude other and different versions of our lives at KisN and WalN [her country houses] – our summer excursions, etc. This ought to be done in its genuine truth and simplicity – strong affection, intimacy of friendship, and no impropriety. It seems to me an edifying picture for those poor wretches who cannot conceive friendship except in sex – nor believe that expediency and the consideration of feelings of others can conquer sensuality. But of course this is not my reason for wishing it done. It is that every ground should be occupied by ourselves on our own subject.[107]

Mill agreed, but asked Harriet to draft the requisite paragraph: if she did, the letter has not survived. Undoubtedly the *Autobiography* was intentionally crafted to counter 'false interpretations' of their relationship and show that it was 'one of strong affection and confidential intimacy only'.[108] The couple were determined to 'occupy the ground' of their posthumous reputations, which means that the letters which survive are those they wished to survive, and which they knew were almost certain to be published. An example of their attempts to manage their posthumous reputations came when they eventually married in 1851. The nervous groom signed the marriage certificate 'J. S. Mill', before being told that he had to write out his name in full, at which point he somewhat awkwardly appended the remainder of the names above the initials. Mill fretted about this lapse, even suggesting that they marry again, 'and this time in a church', so that he could have another crack at writing his name. His concern was how the signature might look to others, as he explained in a letter to Harriet:

The reason must be at once apparent to any one who sees it, as it is obvi-ous that J. S. Mill was written first, and the remainder filled in afterwards. It is almost superfluous to say that this is not stated for your information – you being as well aware of it as myself, but in order that there may be a statement in existence of the manner in which the signature came to present this unusual appearance.[109]

Mill was here explicitly using a letter to Harriet – a 'statement in existence' – to send a message to the wider world. Given this sensi-tivity to the broader audience for whom they were often writing, it is necessary to take much of what they said on the issue of their relationship with at least a pinch of salt.[110]

If they were indeed as restrained as they said, it was not because of a moral bar to extramarital sex. In the *Autobiography* Mill insist-ed that they 'did not consider the ordinances of society binding on a subject so entirely personal' and elsewhere predicted that 'to have held any human being responsible for the fact [of sexual relations] itself . . . will one day be thought one of the superstitions and bar-barisms of the infancy of the human race'.[111] A proposed article entitled 'Enlightened Infidelity' would have raised a few eyebrows, but in fact it was a forgettable argument about the value of religious criticism.[112]

The rationale for sexual restraint given in the *Autobiography* was the avoidance of any conduct which might 'bring discredit on her husband, or therefore on herself'.[113] This is pretty risible, given the damage to poor John Taylor from unending public gossip and humiliation, regardless of his wife's protested fidelity. The justifica-tion raises questions, in turn, about the two-year period between John Taylor's death and Harriet's second marriage to Mill; if they only abstained for his sake, and saw being unmarried as no obstacle to sex, why did they wait until their own marriage for their 'com-plete union', the 'partnership of their entire existence', as Mill stat-ed?[114] Possibly they thought a suitable period of grieving was required or perhaps they were more conservative about sex and marriage than they liked to suggest. Alexander Bain recorded that 'in the so-called sensual feelings he was below average' and that ' he made light of the difficulty of controlling the sexual appetite' – which, if true, would have helped.[115] Or maybe they merely covered their tracks, both contemporaneously and historically, and lied in the *Autobiography*. One of the two surviving letters from Mill to Harriet in this period certainly suggests no lessening of ardour. 'While you can love me as you so sweetly & beautifully shewed in that hour yesterday, I have all I care for or desire for myself,' he wrote. 'The influence of that dear little hour has kept me in spirits ever since – thanks to my one only source of good.'[116]

Their sex life, or sexless life, remains a source of inspiration to some up to recent times: a 'Lonely Hearts' advert in the *New York Review of Books*, dated 17 March 1983, read: 'Female seeks male intellectual for Platonic correspondence in a similar vein to Mill and Taylor. Box 10544.'[117] But it is a source of scholarly contention too. While the first modern Mill biographer, Michael Packe, was 'quite certain they never went to bed together' before their marriage, a contemporary biographer of Harriet, Jo Ellen Jacobs, suggests they never had sex at all, because Harriet had been infected with syphilis by her husband. Jacobs states that 'Harriet and John would happily have had intercourse had it been safe to do so. Unfortunately, it was not.'[118] Nicholas Capaldi, another Mill biographer, discounts both the idea of sex before marriage or abstinence after it. 'Not a scrap of evidence exists for either one of these extreme speculations,' he declares.[119] A century and a half on, the question of Mill's sex life still gets people hot under the collar.

Jacobs' evidence is only circumstantial: Harriet's symptoms, which could possibly be explained by syphilis; the otherwise inexplicable understanding of her husband; her visits to Dr Edward William Tuson, who had a specialist interest in venereal diseases; and an apparent request to Roebuck for some mercury, then a common treatment for the disease.[120] It is also a fact that Mill and Harriet did remain childless after their own marriage, but Harriet was forty-three by then. If true, the syphilis theory leads to a likely conclusion that Mill died a virgin. However, it can be countered on circumstantial grounds, too. The hint – and it is no more – that Harriet was seeking mercury from Roebuck makes no sense at all. After all, John Taylor himself was a pharmacist and had access to the whole range of medications. If he had indeed infected Harriet, and was as a result willing to countenance her relationship with Mill, it seems likely that he would have brought home a bottle or two of medicine. In any case, mercury was taken for any number of ailments; Mill himself was taking it years later for his digestive system.[121]

Mill's sex life is important in terms of understanding him as a man, of course, but there are some philosophical implications too. Mill was his century's pre-eminent thinker on the content of a good life – of which sex must surely form a part. More specifically, in his version of utilitarianism, Mill insisted that it was not only the quantity of pleasure that counted but its intrinsic quality. He distinguished between lower pleasures, defined as 'animal appetites' consisting of 'mere sensation' and 'higher' pleasures 'of the intellect, of the feelings and imagination, and of the moral sentiments'. Mill suggested sampling, to see which was preferable: 'Of two pleasures, if there be one to which all or almost all who have experience of both give a decided preference, irrespective of any feeling of moral obligation to prefer it, that is the more desirable pleasure.'[122] Mill's view was that the majority of people who had experienced the pleasure of, say, having sex and reading poetry, would find the latter a more intrinsically valuable pleasure; but according to his own philosophical rules he would have been prohibited from making any such judgement unless he had himself experienced both.[123]

Whatever the exact physical nature and history of Mill and Harriet's intimacy, his adoration for her was lifelong and total. Next to her, he said, the Romantic poet Percy Shelley was nothing 'but a child'. Harriet was a 'consummate artist' and 'great orator', combining a 'passion for justice' with both a 'genuine modesty' and the 'loftiest pride'.[124] She was now the principal focus for Mill's romanticism. As far as she was concerned, his hyperbole knew no bounds. 'Thanks dearest dearest angel for the note,' he wrote to her the year before their marriage:

What a perfect orator you would make – & what changes might be made in the world by such a one, with such opportunities as thousands of male dunces have ... you can both think, & impress the thought on others – can both judge what ought to be done, & do it. As for me, nothing but the division of labour could make me useful ... a real majestic intellect like yours I can only look up to & admire.[125]

During his lifetime and since, Mill has been accused of having a false view of Harriet's talents, and of overstating her influence on his intellectual life. It is certainly fair to say that when it came to Harriet, Mill lost his fabled powers of objective judgement. Which is, perhaps, just another way of saying that he was in love with her.

By the 1840s the couple had clearly found an acceptable way of living, conducting their relationship in semi-seclusion, mostly in Walton-on-Thames, where Harriet had found a new rural refuge. As the new decade opened, Mill was in retreat, from a social environment which was unconducive to his relationship with Harriet, and a political one which augured ill for his radical hopes. Mill asked George Henry Lewes to thank Mrs Lewes (a title George Eliot would later assume) for a social invitation in 1841, 'the *spirit* of which I most cordially accept (I never go to evening parties in the *flesh*)'.[126] His private life was almost exclusively devoted to quiet weekends with Harriet, and his intellectual focus was on the production of ideas rather than noisy parliamentary stratagems.

Along with most of the other radicals, Mill had backed away from direct involvement in political affairs, following the foundering of the hopes heaped on Durham's shoulders. 'Even I', he wrote to Macvey Napier, editor of the once-hated *Edinburgh Review*, 'am compelled to acknowledge that there is not room for a fourth political party in this country – reckoning the Conservatives, the Whig-Radicals, and the Chartists as the other three.'[127] He also received a lesson in mortality from his brother Henry, who was dying of consumption, which may have strengthened his desire to complete his own intellectual labours. Stuck for the winter at Falmouth after missing the boat to Madeira – where Mill's mother had hoped the warmth would help Henry's worsening condition – the Mill clan had fortunately run into John Sterling and his close friend Dr Calvert, who decided to stay too. Sterling introduced the Mills to a local Quaker family, the Foxes, and a number of firm friendships were formed, especially between the daughters, Clara Mill and Caroline Fox. Caroline, the diarist in the family, heard tales of the great John Stuart Mill from Sterling – with whom she seems to have been in love – and viewed his imminent arrival in March 1841, when Henry's days were visibly numbered, with a mixture of trepidation and excitement.

Despite the sorrowful context for the trip, Mill appears to have been in high spirits. Delighted to be with Sterling for a second successive spring, he interrupted a picnic at Penjerrick to comment 'on the elation of spirits he always experienced in the country, and illustrated it, with an apology, by jumping'.[128] After exploring Pendennis cavern, the supposed 'saint of rationalism' proposed leaving behind their candles as an offering to the gnomes. He was kind to Caroline: detaching a bramble from her clothes during a country walk, he mused on the 'power of turning annoyances into pleasures by undertaking them for your friends – a genuine alchemy'.[129] Some of his lightheartedness was also on display. He told her he had been bald since the age of twenty-two, and caused great delight by informing her that her observation that 'you can't ask a book questions' had been anticipated by Plato.[130]

Mill's happiness, as his little brother lay dying, might appear callous, but death was much more a fact of everyday life in the days before twentieth-century medicine and public health. By modern standards, the lives of most Victorians were wracked by tragedy. Harriet had already lost three of her brothers: one, William, just a few months previously. When Henry, surrounded by his family, died on 4 April 1841, Caroline reported that Calvert said to Mill: 'This sort of scene puts an end to Reason, and Faith begins', to which he reportedly replied: 'Yes'.[131] Twelve days later, Mill wrote to Robert Barclay Fox, the head of the family that had taken the

Mills to its bosom. Reflecting on mortality, he gave a clear enunciation of his own faith: 'There is only one plain rule of life eternally binding, & independent of all variations in creeds & in the interpretations of creeds & embracing equally the greatest moralities & the smallest – it is this – try thyself unweariedly till thou findest the highest thing thou are capable of doing, faculties and outward circumstances being both duly considered – and then DO IT –.'[132]

After a period of procrastination and prevarication, Mill, finally, a week after Henry's death, signed the *London and Westminster Review* (thereafter to be published without the 'London' in the title) over to his friend Henry Cole and the wealthy William Hickson, who was 'the first disciple I ever had', according to Mill.[133] Mill had sunk more than a year's salary and several years of labour into the publication, against which he balanced its three principal achievements.[134] First, the launching of Carlyle's literary career with the review of his *History of the French Revolution*. This is a fair claim; Mill's review undoubtedly spiked the guns of those lined up to attack Caryle, and made the *History* what would today be dubbed a 'must-read' book. (Dickens carried a copy in his pocket.) It was only after the success of the first volume of the *History* that Carlyle was able to find an English publisher for *Sartor Resartus*, written seven years earlier. The second achievement was the salvaging of Durham's report, and the third, the seminal essay on 'Coleridge', of which Mill remained justifiably proud throughout his life. A kinder, or less modest assessment would also list Mill's 1835 review of Tocqueville's work, which first brought the Frenchman to English attention.

While the *Review* had enjoyed some undoubted intellectual and literary successes, it had failed as a political weapon, just as the radicals had failed as a political grouping. Unable to alter the political landscape, Mill was forced to accommodate himself to it. A fortnight after divesting himself of his own *Review*, Mill wrote to Napier to offer his services to the journal he had spent his early twenties savaging as a bastion of conservatism. 'I myself,' Mill wrote, 'am under the impression that there is very little of what I should now be inclined to say to the public in a review, which would be at all in contradiction to the established character & purposes of the Edinburgh.'[135]

Napier responded enthusiastically, much to Mill's satisfaction.[136] Between October 1840, when he gave the *Edinburgh* his review of the second part of Tocqueville's book, and 1863, when he switched his literary loyalties to the new *Fortnightly Review*, Mill published eleven substantial articles on its Whiggish pages. While he sometimes smarted at Napier's editorial excisions and privately described him as 'timid' and beholden to an 'octogenarian clique' of backers, he was careful to remain on good enough terms to ensure regular commissions.[137] Having requested and received a complimentary opinion from Napier on an article which he had just published in the *Westminster*, Mill assured him that 'I should never send anything there which you would take, if I were not under a sort of personal obligation to the present proprietor.'[138]

Having secured the *Edinburgh* as an outlet, Mill turned next to Fonblanque and his *Examiner*. By the summer of 1841 his political stance had apparently undergone a significant shift since the late 1830s, when he had been urging a strategy of non-cooperation between the radicals and the Whig administration. 'I am quite as warm a supporter of the present government as you are,' he insisted to Fonblanque. 'Except Lord Palmerston's Syrian folly, I have seen nothing in their conduct since the last remodelling of the ministry two years ago, but what is highly meritorious ... they have come up to my terms, so it is no wonder that I am heart & soul with them.'[139] Perhaps Mill had forgotten just how exacting his terms had been, just a few years earlier; more likely, he was indulging a small 'half-truth' of his own. In any case, Peel defeated Melbourne in the elections later that year.

Even though Mill was determined to keep up a presence in the reviews, his freedom from the grind of editorial duties from 1841 onwards allowed him to work on his *System of Logic* and attend meetings of the Political Economy club, where he proposed a number of debates, on issues ranging from the definition of 'demand', through to short-termism in capital investment and the mutual benefits of international trade – this last a dress rehearsal for one of the finest chapters of his later *Principles of Political Economy*.[140] Mill could see that the theory of economics was falling behind the development of the economy itself. While the policy-oriented intellectuals in the Club speculated about the financing of new plants, iron output was doubling every decade. While they wondered about how to capitalize railways, the railway companies went on building, creating unprecedented economic and social opportunities. The industrialization and consequent growth of English cities was accelerating, but there was a human price being paid. The average life expectancy for a child born to a working-class family in Manchester in 1837 was only seventeen years, compared to thirty-eight in rural Rutland.[141] Joseph Fletcher, a school inspector and 'moral statistician', lamented the onset of industrialization for 'its smoke, its dirt, its bustle, its deformation of the face of nature, and the independent rudeness of its millions' as well as its 'lost bonds of neighbourhood'.[142]

England might have been politically conservative, but it was in the very vanguard of economic change. Alongside the grinding poverty of early industrialization, an age of opportunity was being born – and there were plenty ready to seize it. In the summer of 1841 Thomas Cook was struck by a thought: 'What a glorious thing it would be if the newly-developed powers of railways and locomotion could be made subservient to the promotion of temperance!'[143] A series of increasingly ambitious Cook's Tours took groups of teetotallers, numbering in their hundreds, on trips to Liverpool, Scotland and North Wales. Of the millions who visited the Great Exhibition a decade later, 150,000 were customers of Thomas Cook, including a party of 3,000 day-tripping Sunday School children. Newspapers and magazines attracted growing, and increasingly national audiences. While Cook brought trains and teetotalism into profitable partnership, in 1841 a new magazine, *Punch*, began its 160-year campaign to puncture the egos of the British establishment; as a controversial parliamentarian a quarter of a century later, Mill would be a regular object of praise and ridicule on the magazine's pages.

For the moment, however, he was focused on the drier labours of his *System of Logic*. After his political disappointments, he convinced himself that this was the correct use of his energies. 'It is becoming more & more clearly evident to me that the mental regeneration of Europe must precede its social regeneration,' he told Robert Barclay Fox. 'There never was a time when ideas went for more in human affairs than they do now.'[144] Mill was about to test his own theory. Five days before Christmas 1841, his 'big book' was ready.[145] He sent a sample to the publisher John Murray, in the expectation that it could be published 'in the approaching season'.[146] He told Sterling that it would allow a proper estimate to be made of his philosophical abilities, but to Fox he played down any hopes of significant impact: 'I don't suppose many people will read anything so scholastic.'[147] Mill's expectations were pleasantly confounded. It was another two years before *A System of Logic* rolled off the presses, but when it did, Mill estimated that it was read by everybody who could ever be expected to digest such a formidable tome.

Although Mill burned with a desire to influence the world, he had no interest in the power offered by the Church or a university, and did not feel he had the financial resources to seek power in Parliament. He had failed to exercise much influence as an editor. But in March 1843, almost overnight, he came into possession of the opaque, formidable power which stems from a reputation for intellectual greatness. Having acquired this power, the question was what to do with it.

CHAPTER SEVEN

Eminence (1843–7)

'They keep me here yet – indeed I could not stand when I tried to get up,' Harriet wrote shakily to Mill in the middle of 1841. 'I am nervous and feverish ...'[1] Mill was nervous too. His beloved Harriet had entirely lost the use of her right leg, and was extremely weak in her left. Mill cancelled his summer travel plans and stayed as close to her as possible throughout the summer and autumn. Although the symptoms eased over a period of many months, Harriet would never be able to walk any distance again.

Mill's own health was also patchy throughout the year, culminating in a typical winter bronchial complaint. By the following spring, however, the couple were both in better shape. Caroline Fox reported that by May 1842 Mill was 'in glorious spirits':

He is greatly relieved at having finished his 'Logic' and is going to mark out the best passages for me . . . He said 'My family have no idea how great a man I am!' He is now saving up his holidays for a third journey to Italy; he had serious hopes of an illness in the winter, but was conscientious enough not to encourage it.[2]

Mill could only have been 'hoping' for illness in order to grab another extended continental break with Harriet. Unfortunately, in the same year the American States reneged on their bond debts, a move which hit the wallets of wealthy England hard. It took Mill some years to repair first his family's bank balance, and then his own. He was even obliged to chase Henry Cole for £100 owed for his articles in the *Westminster Review*.[3] Mill and Harriet would have to wait until 1844 before their next extended escape.

Mill was not hopeful that the *Logic* would do much to lessen his financial worries, but was anxious to see the fruits of more than a decade's labour in print and was deeply frustrated when his excerpts sat on the desk of the publisher John Murray for three months – despite increasingly irate pleas from Mill for a response.[4] Unknown to Mill, Murray was ill, and it was this which led to the irritating delay. In the end, a negative answer was 'extorted' from him, allowing Mill to offer the work to another publisher, William Parker, who accepted enthusiastically.[5] Mill was still annoyed decades later, noting in his *Autobiography* that 'Murray . . . kept it until too late for publication that season, and then refused it, for reasons which could just as well have been given at first'.[6]

In fact the book was better for the hiatus, thanks to the services of Alexander Bain, a young admirer of Mill's. Bain would go on to be a formidable intellectual force himself, the first biographer of both James and John Stuart Mill, and founder of the journal *Mind*. He was introduced to his hero at India House in the summer of 1841. Bain recalled:

His tall slim figure, his youthful face and bald head, fair hair and ruddy complexion, and the twitching of his eyebrow when he spoke, first arrested the attention. The vivacity of his manner, his thin voice approaching to sharpness, but with nothing shrill or painful about it, his comely features and sweet expression – would have remained in my memory though I had never seen him again.[7]

Bain became a close collaborator and a good friend. Twice a week for the next few years, he would join Mill for the walk home from the City to Kensington. During his illness of 1841, Mill resorted to public transport, but by 1842 reported to his new protégé that he was walking to work again, 'without the self-indulgence of omni*bi*'.[8] Bain was asked to read and comment on the draft of the *System of Logic*, and was able to strengthen the argument in a number of places, especially by adding examples of the scientific method Mill was advocating.

When the six-book treatise, under the full title *A System of Logic, Ratiocinative and Inductive, Being a Connected View of the Principles of Evidence and the Methods of Scientific Investigaton*, appeared in March 1843, Mill was under no illusions about its popular appeal. The competition that season included John Ruskin's *Modern Painters*, Thomas Carlyle's *Past and Present*, and Charles Dickens's *A Christmas Carol*. He initially forbade his young friend Caroline Fox from reading it, on the grounds that 'it would be like me reading a book on mining because you live in Cornwall – it would be making Friendship a burden'.[9]

Although the *Logic* was reviewed in neither the *Edinburgh* nor the *Quarterly Review*, and was launched overenthusiastically in the *Westminster* by a more than slightly partial reviewer – Alexander Bain – the book was an immediate commercial and academic success. 'It will last as long as England,' exclaimed Sterling.[10] Within a few years, the book had achieved canonical status in the universities. By the beginning of the next century, the Conservative Prime Minister Arthur Balfour – no friend to Mill's thought – would rank his authority stamped by the *Logic* as 'comparable to that wielded forty years earlier by Hegel in Germany and in the Middle Ages by Aristotle'.[11] Mill was surprised by the level of demand for the work, which sold steadily throughout his life and for which he was preparing an eighth edition in the year before his death in 1873. 'How the book came to have, for a work of the kind, so much success, and what persons compose the bulk of those who have bought, I will not venture to say read, it,' he recalled, 'I have never thoroughly understood.'[12] Mill was almost certainly correct in his assumption that, unlike Dickens, not all his buyers were readers. Even the adoring Harriet described it as 'so very dry a book'.[13] Rather, the *Logic* was one of those works which became a vital addition to the bookshelves of all self-respecting educated households.

A System of Logic was a search-and-destroy mission against 'intuitionism', the philosophy constructed around the belief that there are certain truths which exist in the world, and that the job of science is to discover them. For intuitionists, including most of the German Romantics, these truths, described by Immanuel Kant as '*a priori*', were not open to rational proof; they were 'innate'. Most intuitionists insisted they had been pre-inserted by God, and were known to be true because their falsehood was simply inconceivable. In mathematics, for example, it was not possible to imagine that two plus two could equal anything other than four.

Mill, in the deepest moments of his romantic period in the 1830s, steered dangerously close to such views.[14] But for the remainder of his life he battled against a philosophy which for him was 'an instrument for consecrating all deep-seated prejudices'.[15] He did not care deeply about the basis of mathematics, but he knew that intuitionist thinking provided an important foundation for conservative political philosophy. 'Whatever may be the practical value of a true philosophy of these matters,' he wrote in the *Autobiography*, 'it is hardly possible to exaggerate the mischiefs of a false one.'[16] 'You have very rightly judged that, to give to the cultivators of a physical science the theory of their own operations was but a small part of the object of the book,' Mill wrote to Theodor Gomperz, one of his few German admirers in 1854. 'That attempt was chiefly valued by me as a necessary means towards placing metaphysical & moral science on a basis of analysed experience, in opposition to the theory of innate principles ... the regeneration so urgently required, of man and society ... can never be effected under the influence of a philosophy which makes opinions their own proof, and feelings their own justification.'[17] The divine right of monarchs to rule, the superior status of the aristocracy and the power of the church could all be seen as part of a 'natural', intuitive state of affairs. Mill had spent much of his youth engaged in tactical battles against conservative politics; in the *Logic* he set about attacking this branch of conservatism at its root, convinced that 'prejudice can only be successfully combated by philosophy'.[18]

His principal task was to outline a non-intuitionist version of what modern philosophers call 'epistemology' – a theory of knowledge, or how we know what we know. 'You call Logic the art of telling others what you believe,' he wrote to Carlyle. 'I call it, the art, not certainly of knowing things, but of deciding whether you know them or not: not of finding out the truth, but in deciding whether it is the truth that you have found out'.[19] John Skorupski, a leading contemporary analyst of Mill, has suggested that the *System of Logic* would be better regarded among modern scholars if it was retitled *A System of Epistemology*.[20]

Mill opened his argument by setting out one of the ways a conclusion can be drawn from a general principle, dubbed a 'syllogism' by Aristotle. Mill gave the following example: 'All men are mortal. The Duke of Wellington is a man. Therefore, the Duke of Wellington is mortal.' How, though, he asked, do we produce the starting position – the claim that all men are mortal? Is it simply known intuitively? Mill thought not. His argument – and it was a strong one – was that the initial proposition was itself based on an accumulated store of examples. He believed that we correctly infer that the Duke of Wellington will die, because lots of other men – indeed, all men – have shown themselves to be mortal. 'All inference is from particulars to particulars,' insisted Mill. 'General propositions are merely registers of such inferences already made, and short formulae for making more … the conclusion is not an inference drawn *from* the formula, but an inference drawn *according* to the formula.'[21]

Disproof of any opinion, by way of a new experience, had to be a constant possibility, according to Mill. He cited John Locke's example of the King of Siam, who believed the tales of his European visitors until they told him that an elephant could sit on water if it were cold enough. The Siamese king knew as a general proposition that water cannot support an elephant's weight. This might even have seemed 'intuitively' true, given that for him, ice was inconceivable. For Mill, all human knowledge was based on human experience, and alterable through experience. The truths and concepts of the world were not 'out there' waiting for us to discover them; rather, we *construct* truths and concepts which help us to explain the world, in the knowledge that they could at some point be disproved. For all his romantic leanings, Mill's epistemology was austerely empirical. For him, there was simply no such thing as a self-evident truth.[22]

Mill's stalking horse in the *Logic* was William Whewell, the leading philosopher of science of his day, coiner of the word 'scientist', and the Master of Trinity College, Cambridge. Sydney Smith said of him that 'science is his forte; omniscience is his foible'.[23] He was a formidable opponent, which was one of the reasons Mill decided to attack him. Mill hoped that Whewell would reply, thus generating some helpful controversy.[24] In fact it took the Trinity eminence six years to counter-attack, by which time the *Logic* had overrun the university libraries. Mill could have taken aim at Whewell's weak efforts in moral philosophy, but he deliberately used the *Logic* to assault him on his own turf – the methods of mathematics and physical science – in order, as he said later, 'to drive it [intuitionism] from its stronghold'.[25] Mill's war against intuitionism, however, was to have no end. In the 1860s, he would return to the field, this time to demolish a less worthy but more famous opponent, Sir William Hamilton, in *An Examination of Sir William Hamilton's Philosophy*.

One of Mill's pet hates was the tendency of intuitionists, including Carlyle, to use upper case letters to highlight the innateness of certain truths: The Infinite, The True, The Absolute and The Beautiful were particular favourites. As soon as he saw capital letters, Mill saw red and in *Hamilton* he had some witty fun at the intuitionists' expense:

When we are told of an 'Absolute' in the abstract, or of an Absolute Being ... we are entitled to ask ... absolute in *what*? Do you mean, for example, absolute in goodness, or absolute in knowledge? or do you, perchance, mean absolute in ignorance, or absolute in wickedness? for any one of these is as much an Absolute as any other.

Mill could not resist sticking the knife in a little further, pointing out that 'when (descending to a less lofty height of abstraction) we speak of The Horse, we mean to include every object of which the name horse can be predicated'.[26] He would later warn Hickson that 'italics are bad enough but Capitals make anything look weak'.[27]

From a twenty-first-century perspective, Mill's philosophy of knowledge creation looks dated, even conservative. Many of the phenomena which scientists work with today – relativity, lasers, quarks and black holes – are concepts which could not have been arrived at by inferring from 'particular to particular', given that they are not observable at all. Einstein would have given Mill quite a bit of difficulty. But in the mid-nineteenth century, his empiricism was a powerful battering ram against conservative ideologies, and quack science. At the time Mill was publishing, doctors at University College London were being convinced that the world was suffused with an invisible, superfine magnetic liquid. Mesmerism, named after Franz Anton Mesmer, who worked in 'lilac taffeta robes' and prescribed wind pipes and harmonicas to help shift the mesmeric fluid around a patient, enjoyed a brief vogue. More dangerously, the view that cholera was caused by bad air, or 'miasma', persisted despite the efforts of Dr John Snow, who had observed the characteristics of different outbreaks, and inferred in good Millian fashion from each particular case to the general proposition that cholera was borne by water.[28]

Although Mill steered clear of theology in the *Logic*, formally leaving open the question of supernatural power, it was clear to careful readers that his assault on intuitive truth left God on pretty shaky ground. Privately Mill was aware of this, telling the 'two young Cornish women', Caroline Fox and her sister Anna Maria, of his pleasure at a review in the *British Critic* which concluded that if the principles of the *Logic* were 'adopted as a full statement of the truth, the whole fabric of Christian Theology must totter and fall'.[29] He suggested to the Fox women that if they insisted on reading some of the *Logic* it should be the chapter on Liberty and Necessity, which he said was 'short & in my judgement the best chapter in the two volumes'.[30] The Foxes did as he suggested, and replied with what Mill described as a 'flaming panegyric'. But this was still not enough for him 'to take off my injunction against reading the remainder of the book (which however is, I assure you, quite as clever) so whoever does read any of it must know that she does it at her own risk & responsibility'.[31]

In the recommended chapter, Mill attempted to rescue his growing insistence on freedom of choice and autonomous character-formation from his continued belief that psychology was a science, subject to necessary laws of cause and effect, just like physics or chemistry. It is one of his most striking attempts at circle-squaring. His first move was an assault on 'fatalism' or 'irresistibleness'.[32] A fatalist, Mill said, 'believes ... not only that whatever is about to happen will be the infallible result of the causes which produce it (which is the true necessitarian doctrine), but moreover that there is no use struggling against it; that it will happen however we may strive against it'.[33]

The fatalist doctrine, Mill believed, had damaging implications for public policy. The Owenites, for example, against whom he had debated in the 1820s, argued against the punishment of crime on the grounds that the character of the criminal, which causes the act, was itself caused by the surrounding social and economic environment. If an individual's character had been shaped for them, especially by the 'associations' made in their childhood, the Owenites reasoned, how could they now be held responsible for the consequence of that character? Mill agreed that character was the spring of action, but also insisted that characters could be reshaped, both by external factors and by the individuals themselves. It was true that people shaped the character of others, but that did not mean people could not shape their own character too. 'If [others] could place us under the influence of certain circumstances, we, in like manner, can place ourselves under the influence of other circumstances,' he wrote, 'We are exactly as capable of making our own character, *if we will*, as others are of making it for us ... the work is not so irrevocably done as to be incapable of being altered.'[34] This also meant that individuals were responsible for their own actions: 'to call anything a sin & yet say that the sinner is not accountable for it', he told one Christian critic, 'seems to me if the word sin means anything, a direct contradiction.'[35] Mill saw punishment as an appropriate mechanism for the reformation of a criminal's character, or as he put it, for 'restor[ing] the mind ... to that normal preponderance of the love of right, which many moralists and theologians consider to constitute the true definition of our freedom'.[36] What was now required, Mill concluded, was the creation of a science delineating the processes by which characters were formed. While 'mankind have not one universal character', there were, he suggested, 'universal laws of the Formation of Character': 'And since it is by these laws, combined with the facts of each particular case, that the whole of the phenomena of human action and feeling are produced, it is on these that every rational attempt to construct the science of human nature in the concrete, and for practical purposes, must proceed.'[37]

This science, which would be 'An Exact Science of Human Nature', was dubbed by Mill 'ethology'. It would draw, he said, on the findings of psychology in order to gauge the influence of the moral and physical environment on individual as well as 'national or collective' character. This was not a technical exercise, but a deeply political one:

The subject to be studied, is the origin and sources of all those qualities in human beings which are interesting to us, either as facts to be produced, or to be avoided ... and the object is to determine ... what actual or possible combinations of circumstances are capable of promoting or of preventing the production of those qualities.[38]

For Mill, these questions were of course deeply personal, too. Given his own upbringing, and the accusations he faced of being a 'made man' – a creature entirely of his father's creation – he had to believe that he had broken free, that the path of his life had not been set by forces outside his control. Indeed, for him, 'this feeling, of our being able to modify our character if we wish, is itself the feeling of moral freedom which we are conscious of'.[39]

Mill thus attempted to steer a middle course between the extremes of free will and fatalism. Of course our characters were shaped by our circumstances, he said: this is why social science could fuel human improvement, by changing the environment appropriately. But at the same time he maintained that our desire to shape our own characters was itself one of those circumstances. What fatalist philosophies missed was 'the power of the mind to co-operate in the formation of its own character'. And so, in a shining application of his conviction that opposing doctrines each contain a 'half-truth', Mill's triumphant conclusion was that while the fatalist doctrine had a 'stronger sense of the importance of what human beings can do to shape the characters of one another . . . the free-will doctrine has . . . fostered in its supporters a much stronger degree of self-culture'.[40]

Mill was pleased with his solution, bolstering as it did his own need to feel free, as well as reconciling the competing claims of two opposing doctrines in a way which left social planners with opportunities to improve people, without denying the capacity of individuals to improve themselves, and retaining the notion of individual responsibility. Leaving the construction of the ethology to another day – a day which in fact never came – he moved swiftly on to other matters. Nevertheless Mill's argument does not stand up to close scrutiny, which may be why he never scrutinized it too closely. It is certainly true that people can desire to, and perhaps succeed in, altering their own characters. But where does the desire to change our character come from in the first place? Only, surely, from the same sources as our character. As the Mill scholar Alan Ryan forensically puts it: 'Either there is already in the agent some element which will lead to his wanting to change and thus being able to change, or else there is nothing *he* can do about it. And in either case, the picture we get is of the agent sitting watching his character's behaviour – not the picture Mill intended to give us.'[41]

Free will is not, in the end, compatible with strict laws of psychology or an 'exact science' of character-formation, and Mill himself shelved any plans to construct such a science. In his later works, especially *The Subjection of Women*, he continued to insist that characters were shaped by circumstances, not nature – and that a science of character-formation was urgently needed – but he also issued, in *On Liberty*, a manifesto for freedom. Mill remained convinced that individual character, and the processes by which it was formed – 'the Art of education, in its widest sense' – were vital political and social issues.[42] But he moved away from the idea that an 'exact' or complete 'science' could be constructed.

Mill's conviction that individuals were responsible and free also lay behind his contempt for the 'intolerable mass of pseudo-philanthropy' and 'wild notions about the mode of being good to the poor', which he thought were blighting the decade.[43] He was dismissive of many of the social reforms which, in the light of social history, are typically seen as steps, albeit small ones, in a progressive direction. In 1844, the year that Robert Peel's government tightened the regulation of working hours, Mill complained of a 'prodigious current setting in every day more strongly, of superficial philanthropy . . . everybody is all agog to do something for the poor . . . whom it greatly strengthens in the faith that it is other people's business to take care of them.'[44] He made the same point to Macvey Napier: 'The general tendency [of the speculations now afloat] is to rivet firmly in the minds of the labouring people the persuasion that it is the business of others to take care of their condition.'[45]

Mill's continued dislike of Peel may have heightened his disdain: the best he could say of the man who had embarked on a series of public health initiatives, as well as factory and mining legislation, was that 'his hinges are well oiled and he yields to pressure'.[46] His real gripe, however, was with the paternalistic motivation of the reformers, exemplified by the leading reformer, a Christian Tory aristocrat, Lord Ashley. Describing a visit to his ancestral seat, in rural Dorset, Ashley wrote: 'What a picture contrasted with a factory district – a people known and cared for, a people born and trained on the estate, exhibiting towards its hereditary possessors both deference and sympathy, affectionate respect and a species of allegiance demanding protection and repaying it in duty.'[47] Unsurprisingly, Ashley 's zeal for improvements in the conditions of the poor was matched by an implacable opposition to democracy.

'Mine is that masculine species of charity which would lead me to inculcate in the minds of the labouring classes the love of independence, the privilege of self respect, the disdain of being patronised or petted, the desire to accumulate and the ambition to rise': the lines are from the free-trader and radical Richard Cobden, but could be from Mill.[48] He was virtually silent, for example, on one of the great social demands of the mid-century, a maximum ten-hour working day, which was signed into law in 1847, and in private was disdainful: 'The doctrine of averting revolutions by wise concessions does not need to be preached to the English aristocracy. They have long acted on it to the best of their capacity, & the fruits it produces are soup-kitchen and ten hours bills.'[49] Macaulay, by contrast, lambasted the factory owners for suggesting that 'what makes a population stronger and healthier and wiser and better can ultimately make it poorer'.[50]

Mill's left-of-centre admirers tend to gloss over the anti-philanthropic dimension of his views and pay little attention to an important article, 'The Claims of Labour', which he persuaded the 'timid' Napier to carry in the *Edinburgh Review* in 1845. Mill opened by conceding that there was much that was 'salutary and promising' in the growing conviction that 'the labouring classes shall earn more, work less, or have their lot in some other manner alleviated.' The bulk of the article, meanwhile, was devoted to the dangers of the 'philanthropic spirit'. The mood had shifted, he suggested, for a number of reasons: the legacy of Malthusian concerns about population; the rise of Chartism; the greater publicity given to the conditions of the destitute as a result of the Poor Laws; the publication of powerful books on the subject, such as Carlyle's *Past and Present* of 1843, in which the 'Condition of England' question was central; and the reverberations of the 1832 Reform Act, which had been 'to politics what the Reformation was to religion – it made reason the recognized authority, not authority'.[51]

Out of this ferment a renewed paternalism had emerged, Mill wrote, with the piecemeal social reforms 'celebrated as a new moral order, or an old order revived, in which the possessors of property' were to 'resume their place as the paternal guardians of those less fortunate'. He deployed all his polemic weaponry against this trend, pointing out that there were already workers being provided with all their food, lodging and clothing. 'Who were these?' he asked: 'The slaves on a West Indian estate.' For Mill, the danger with Victorian philanthropy was that it would breed a slave mentality, by undermining independence of spirit and self-reliance: 'With paternal care is connected paternal authority . . . it is one thing to tell the rich that they ought to take care of the poor, another thing to tell the poor that the rich ought to take care of them . . . All classes are ready enough, without prompting, to believe that whatever ails them is not their fault, but the crime of somebody else.'[52]

Rather than insulating the poor from the vagaries of life, Mill believed they should be equipped and encouraged to make the best of them, on their own terms. This meant universal education, 'not to improve people as workmen merely, but as human beings'. He wanted 'schools in which the children of the poor should learn to use not only their hands but their heads'. Similarly, workers should not be seeking protection from their employers, but forming new enterprises in which they themselves had a stake, so that they could 'become their own employers'. He quoted with approval the motto of an experimental factory owner: '*Aide-toi, le ciel t'aidera.*' Mill was here prefiguring a lifelong interest in the formation of co-operatives, and other methods by which workers could 'make themselves capitalists'.[53] Rather than placing themselves in a paternal posture towards the poor, he wrote to Napier, the government and upper classes had to recognize that 'the greater part of the good they can do is indirect, & consists in stimulating & guiding the energy & prudence of the people themselves.'[54]

Two decades later, campaigning for his seat in Parliament in 1865, Mill had not retreated from his earlier views. 'The rich had sympathies enough for the poor when they came before them as objects of pity,' he told an apparently supportive crowd, 'they had almost universally a kind of patronizing and protective sympathy for the poor, such as shepherds had for their flocks (*laughter and cheers*) – only that was conditional upon the flock always behaving like sheep (*renewed laughter, and hear, hear*).'[55]

It must be said that Mill was wrong, or rather premature in his concerns. The working classes in the 1840s were a very long way from the personal economic circumstances necessary for any reasonable conception of individual choice and agency. But these views demonstrate that for Mill, the litmus test of any social reform, economic system, school curriculum or political arrangement was the degree to which they would enhance or erode autonomy. The social reformers of the age worried about how to get workers more food, money, leisure and health. Mill worried about how to get them more freedom.

The acclaim which had greeted the *Logic* meant that Mill's views on these topical subjects were taken more seriously: he was now a public figure. As such, he was even more concerned to gather the widest possible range of views, and modify his own positions accordingly. He successfully begged the astronomer Sir John Herschel to criticize the *Logic*, reporting honestly that he 'valued the pointing out of an error more highly than any amount of praise'.[56] Indeed, Mill was as open with his own critical comments as he hoped people would be with theirs. Commenting in 1842 on the first draft of Edwin Chadwick's report on the *Sanitary Condition of the Labouring Population of Great Britain*, Mill wrote that the content was strong, but that it was 'utterly ineffective from the want of unity and of an apparent thread running through it and holding it together'.[57] Chadwick drafted to Mill's satisfaction, and the final report was highly effective indeed, leading to the establishment of the Royal Commission on the Health of Towns and the General Board of Health. Mill duly gave a warm welcome to Chadwick's report in the *Examiner*, helping to launch a decades-long 'sanitary movement': as Disraeli would later lament, '*Sanitas sanitatum, omnia sanitas*'.[58]

Basking in the success of the *Logic*, and with his finances mostly repaired, Mill was able to use some of the holiday time he had accumulated. In 1844, he and Harriet, accompanied by Helen, were able to escape to France. For two months the trio explored the Normandy countryside by steamboat and diligence, greatly admiring Rouen cathedral. They were clearly in good spirits: Helen, who turned thirteen during the trip, recorded in her diary, 'I think I have enjoyed my birthday this year as much as I ever have.'[59]

The meandering joys of the French summer were followed, for Mill, by a mortal loss. John Sterling, following the deaths of both his wife and mother, was dying. The last major book he read was the *Logic* and his praise was unconstrained. It was, he said, 'the labour of many years of a singularly subtle, patient, and comprehensive mind. It will be our chief speculative monument of this age.'[60] As Sterling weakened under the onslaught of the disease which stalked Victorian Britain, tuberculosis (it had already killed James and Henry Mill and Harriet's closest friend, Eliza Flower), Mill urged his friend to live: 'Even by your mere existence you do more good than many by their laborious exertions ... None of us could hope to meet with your like again – & if we did, it would be no compensation.'[61] When it was clear that the battle was lost, Mill sent a moving farewell. 'I have never so much wished for another life as I do for the sake of meeting you in it', he wrote. 'I shall never think of you but as one of the noblest, & quite the most loveable of all men I have ever known or ever look to know.'[62]

With their closest friends dead and Mill's public status secure, Harriet and Mill withdrew even further from social life. 'My own life goes on just as it did,' Mill told the radical writer and doctor Henry Chapman at the end of 1844, 'and I see very few people.'[63]

As well as avoiding gossip, the high-minded pair were also anxious to be free of the grubby influences of lesser mortals. While Mill was a master of public modesty, in his correspondence with Harriet he often revealed a strong sense of his own importance and wisdom, and described English society as 'so insipid an affair' that people 'of any really high class of intellect, make their contact with it so slight, as to be considered as retiring from it'.[64]

Out of the public gaze, Mill and Harriet deepened both their emotional and intellectual relationship. In the *Autobiography*, Mill said that Harriet's cerebral strengths lay in two main areas: in the description of 'ultimate aims; the constituent elements of the highest realizable ideal of human life', and also in the delineation of 'immediately useful and practically attainable' social changes. By contrast, his own strength 'lay wholly in the uncertain and slippery intermediate region, that of theory, or moral and political science'.[65]

This description of the division of labour between the two can be mapped almost precisely on to one of the most important sections of the *Logic*, in which Mill outlined the respective roles of social science and art in promoting change. He argued that science could help to generate plausible strategies for achieving certain social ends. But it could not define the ends – that was a job for an 'artist'. 'The art proposes to itself an end to be attained, defines the end, and hands it over to the science,' he wrote. 'The science receives it, considers it as a phenomenon or effect to be studied, and having investigated its causes and conditions, sends it back to art with a theorem of the combinations of circumstances by which it could be produced.'[66] Goals such as the 'preservation of health' and the 'cure of disease' were not 'statements of science' but were assumed by the 'hygienic and medical arts' to be 'fitting and desirable ends'. The general premises of art – of what 'should be' – formed a 'body of doctrine which is properly the Art of Life, in its three departments, Morality, Prudence or Policy, and Aesthetics; the Right, the Expedient, and the Beautiful or Noble, in human conduct and works'.[67]

In 1844, there was sufficient demand for Mill's work – 'one of the effects of the Logic' – for him to repackage and publish some old essays in a book format: standard practice, then and now, for the newly arrived public intellectual.[68] In one of these pieces, 'On the Definition of Political Economy', written in 1831, Mill had outlined his theory about art and science in almost identical terms: 'The language of science is This is, or This is not; This does, or does not, happen. The language of art is, Do this; Avoid that. Science takes cognizance of a *phenomenon*, and endeavours to discover its *law*; art proposes to itself an *end*, and looks out for *means* to effect it.'[69] Harriet, then, was a true artist, and Mill a mere jobbing scientist. This is rubbish, of course: it was falsely-modest nonsense for Mill to suggest that he was unskilled in the consideration of ultimate ends. The more important point is that Mill was fitting Harriet and himself into a model which he had already built, rather than being inspired by her into its creation.

Mill was evidently a fierce loyalist when it came to those he loved, and not just Harriet: he eased his younger brother George into a job at India House (by now effectively a second residence for the Mill family) and lobbied William Hickson (new co-owner of the *Westminster*) on behalf of his baby sister, Mary Elizabeth Mill, who was trying to place an article on political economy.[70] Despite his growing philosophical and social distance from George Grote, Mill also gave a warm and thoughtful welcome to the first two instalments of his mammoth, and still unsurpassed, history of ancient Greece in the *Edinburgh* in October 1846. His response to Grote's work, which continued with a review of three more volumes of the work, also in the *Edinburgh*, in 1853, are Mill's most important writings on classical history, throwing some new light on Mill's attitudes to democracy, liberty and civic life, all of which were powerfully shaped by his own perception of the great Athenian experiment.

Mill thought that conservative historians such as William Mitford had uncritically used Thucydides, Plato and Aristotle to turn the history of Athens, especially after the death of Pericles, into a stark warning against democracy; Connop Thirlwall took the same view, dismissing Mitford's work, published between 1784 and 1810, as 'a Tory party pamphlet in five volumes'.[71] Mill's reviews heaped praise on Grote for counter-balancing these 'Tory perverters of Grecian history' as well as for showing persuasively that the anti-democratic judgements made by Thucydides – his condemnation of Cleon, for example – were not in fact supported by Thucydides' own historical narrative.[72] Mill was not simply cheerleading for Grote, though, and showed some historical virtuosity of his own: to limber up for the first review, he reread all of Homer, and correctly disputed Grote's assessment that Books 2–7 of the *Iliad* had been added to the original story at a later date.[73] He also used Grote's volumes as a springboard to draw his own picture of Athens as a nation which had managed to be democratic without a 'tyranny of the majority' overwhelming the freedom of action and thought necessary for genius to flourish and knowledge to advance. The Athenian embrace of both liberty and democracy was only possible because the very nature of public participation promoted civic, liberal sentiment. 'The daily workings of Athenian institutions ... [with] every sort of question ... discussed by the ablest men of the time, with earnestness of purpose and fullness of preparation,' argued Mill, 'formed a course of political education, the equivalent of which modern nations have not known how to give even to those whom they educate for statesmen.'[74] This 'education' of the ancient Athenians cultivated the solidaristic feelings which the Mill of 'Coleridge' thought necessary for the flourishing of all nations at all times, in combination with the freedom of thought and action so vital to the Mill of *On Liberty*. Indeed, much of his political philosophy can be seen as an attempt to recapture what he saw as the best features of Athenian democracy, for an industrial world.

By the mid 1840s, Mill's hopes for progressive reform were rising again. He pointed to 1846 – the year Lord John Russell succeeded Robert Peel, who had just abolished the Corn Laws – as the year concluding a fourteen-year battle between 'Improvement' and 'Stationary forces' and the 'inauguration of improvement as the general law of public affairs'.[75] Mill saw himself as an agent of improvement, and had by now shrugged off any lingering inferiority about his lack of poetic ability, having realized that 'prose is after all the language of business, & therefore is the language to do good by in an age when men's minds are forcibly drawn to external effort.'[76] The *Edinburgh Review* was now established as the preferred medium for his own prose, but his relationship with Napier remained prickly. In private, Mill berated 'the Edinburgh review & the Holland-house set who preside over it' as 'the last refuge of the ideas & tastes of a generation ago', and was unhappy about some substantial restrictions placed on the territory he was able to cover in 'The Claims of Labour', as well as some editorial excisions of his review in 1845 of Guizot's *Essais sur l'histoire de France*.[77]

Mill also had a scuffle with Napier about the word 'idea', which the editor thought he was deploying incorrectly. 'It is used in the ordinary sense in which we speak of 'men of ideas',' Mill responded. 'If that were altered the whole of the first part of the paragraph must be recast.'[78] His vehemence over such an apparently trivial point must have surprised Napier, who let it go. What he could not have known, of course, was that an inadequate definition of exactly the same word had earned Mill the starchy disapproval of his father twenty-six years earlier.[79] It was in defence of his father's honour, however, that Mill was most aroused against the *Edinburgh*. In a review of the *Memoirs of Jeremy Bentham*, John Bowring, his father's old rival, had reprinted a snide remark by Bentham about James Mill, who he said had argued 'against oppression, less because he loves the oppressed many, than because he hates the oppressing few'.[80] Mill complained heartily of the thoughtless circulation of 'idle words which one man may say of another in a moment of ill humour', which were in any case 'very probably misreported by Bowring'.[81] Napier allowed Mill a short letter of defence, which enlarged on his central, contentious complaint: 'It is surely very blameable in a biographer to publish every casual expression which such a man, or indeed any man, may have let fall to the disparagement of others.'[82]

As the decade wore on, Mill seemed to become more sceptical

about the importance of review journalism, to which he had attached such great importance ten years earlier. 'It seems to me that reviews have had their day,' he wrote to his old tutor John Austin in 1847, '& that nothing is now worth much except the two extremes, newspapers for diffusion & books for accurate thought.'[83] Three years after the publication of his own first attempt at 'accurate thought' in book form, the *Logic*, Mill was preparing a second edition and was already at work on his second 'big book', which would be published as the *Principles of Political Economy* in 1848. Throughout 1846 he was also, however, heavily engaged in newspaper 'diffusion'. His subject was the unfolding tragedy in Ireland, where the fungal disease *Phytophthora infestans* had destroyed the crop of potato on which the bulk of the population depended. He used his new status as the brain of liberal Britain to batter away at the complacency of the ruling class, churning out thirty-nine *Morning Chronicle* articles titled 'The Condition of Ireland' – which was he said, 'the most unqualified instance of signal failure which the practical genius of the English people has exhibited.'[84] The remedies on offer were inadequate, according to Mill, and he tore into schemes to promote emigration, compensate landlords, and even those offering some degree of 'outdoor' poor relief to starving peasants. For Mill, the solution was to instil in the Irish peasantry a sense of responsibility, not dependency. What was needed was a reform which 'must be something operating upon the minds of the people, and not merely upon their stomachs ... They must have something to strive for, some rational ambition'.[85] As so often, he was concerned with the improvement of character: 'You will never change the people but by changing the external motives which act on them, and shape their way of life from the cradle to the grave.'[86] When Queen Victoria, inspired by an idea of John Pemberton Plumptre, MP, ordered her subjects to fast for a day in an attempt to persuade God to relieve the forced fast of an entire nation, Mill boiled over at a 'piece of empty mummery ... on the occasion of a public calamity ... belonging to an entirely gone-by order of religious ideas'.[87]

Mill was convinced that the only long-term solution to Ireland's deep-rooted problems was the recovery and redistribution of the uncultivated waste lands. The government should provide tools to those who needed them, and initiate drainage projects. This, he argued, would 'stir the minds of the peasantry from one end of Ireland to the other ... We want something which may be regarded as a great act of national justice – healing the wounds of centuries by *giving*, not *selling*, to the worthiest and most aspiring sons of the soil, the unused portion of the inheritance of their conquered ancestors.'[88] He provoked the ire of *The Times*, and many parliamentarians, as much by the tone as the content of his radicalism. Even some of his friends dubbed the articles Mill's 'Clinical Lectures'.[89]

At around the same time, Mill wrote an article titled 'What Is to be Done with Ireland?' which described the condition of the country as 'an abomination in the sight of mankind', 'the work of England's ignorance, of England's prejudice, of England's indifference', and specifically the result of 'a radically wrong state of the most important social relation which exists in the country, that between the cultivators of the soil and the owners of it; that vicious state having been protected and perpetuated by a wrong and superstitious English notion of property in land'.[90] It was not published, of course: Mill had good instincts about how far he could push an argument at any particular moment. But it laid the ground for his final public detonation on the subject, *England and Ireland*, twenty years later.[91]

For now he contented himself with finding a hundred different ways of describing his central proposition, relentlessly counterattacking his opponents, and celebrating any sign that events were moving in the right direction. By the end of 1846, he had reduced his rate of fire, on the optimistic grounds that he had 'in great measure, as far as may be judged by appearances, carried my point, viz. to have the waste land reclaimed and parcelled out in small properties among the best of the peasantry'.[92] Mill's torrent of words and argument sparked debate, but made not the slightest difference to policy towards Ireland. Seventeen years later he privately admitted that his attempts to force the issue of smallholdings had been 'without the slightest success', and in the posthumous *Autobiography* recognized that his endeavours were 'an entire failure'.[93]

Nevertheless, Mill's grasp of the inequities in the distribution of land underlying the crisis was unequalled: 'The whole fruits of centuries of oppression and neglect are coming home to us in a single year,' he wrote.[94] His solution was also an imaginative, progressive one which would have altered the course of Irish economic history, had it been implemented. But he was as guilty as most of the political class in his underestimation of the immediate pressing needs of the Irish nation, and guiltier than most in his overestimation of the danger of dependency – certainly compared, at any rate, to the danger of death. The cultivation of public land would have done little to save the one million Irish who could not wait until the next season for food. Reacting to news of the harvest failure, Robert Peel had ordered a public works programme – creating 140,000 jobs – and bought £100,000 of American maize to be sold at low prices to the poorest.[95] Of course this was pitiful, but at least the Conservative Prime Minister recognized the need for action, which his successor Lord John Russell certainly did not. 'Now financially, my course is easy,' wrote Charles Wood, Russell's Chancellor, to the Irish viceroy. 'I have no money and therefore I cannot give it ... Where the people refused to work or sow, they must starve.'[96]

Mill's stance was not as removed from this viewpoint as modern admirers might wish. While some City merchants, including Thomas Baring and Baron Lionel de Rothschild, set up a fund to try to help the Irish, Mill's public pronouncements were hardly calculated to put pressure on the rich or on the government to dig deeper into their pockets. 'We must give over telling the Irish that it is our business to find food for them,' he wrote. 'We must tell them, now and for ever, that it is *their* business ... They have a right, not to support at public cost, but to aid and furtherance in finding support for themselves.'[97]

At the same time, he was opposed to the one realistic alternative to starvation open to many Irish: emigration. This was an odd stance, given his general enthusiasm for colonization. Mill argued, first, that it was an ineffective response to the crisis, compared to his own solution of opening up and cultivating the waste lands: 'Why offer them landed property on the other side of the globe, when there is landed property vacant at their very door, capable of being made fit for their use ... at a mere fraction of the expense?' His second objection was that the Irish were not made of the right colonizing stuff: 'Ireland must be an altered country at home before we can wish to create an Ireland in every corner of the globe, and it is not well to select as missionaries of civilization a people who, in so great a degree, yet remain to be civilized.'[98] Heedless of the concerns of England's newly-crowned king of letters, at least one and a half million Irish fled for their lives, mostly to North America. As to the quality of the 'ingredients', Mill would surely have been reassured by some of the results – two descendants of the emigrants were John Fitzgerald Kennedy and Robert Kennedy.

In the end, for all his eloquence and reputation, Mill was ignored on both sides of the Irish Sea. After a period of engagement with political life, by 1847 he was in his usual state of reaction, declaring the reactionary *Times* to be 'the substantial ruler of the country' and describing himself as 'never ... so thoroughly disgusted with the state of public affairs.'[99] Discussions with William Hickson about taking back the *Westminster* also led nowhere.[100] So Mill turned away again from the political arena, and back to his *Political Economy* – which was to cement his position as the leading British thinker of his day. As 1847 closed, a quietly successful new year beckoned.

In the event, of course, 1848 was far from quiet. Alexis de Tocqueville sensed the change in the wind. He rose in the French Chamber of Deputies to issue a warning. 'We are sleeping on a volcano,' he declared. 'Do you not see that the earth trembles anew? A wind of revolution blows, the storm is on the horizon.'[101] When a series of political volcanoes erupted across the European Continent, the English ruling classes – liberal Whigs and Tories alike – masked their fear with pride in their own nation's anti-revolutionary soul. But not Mill. Once again, French revolutionary fervour flowed straight into his veins. His deep love of France, and his deep desire for a better world, overwhelmed both his Coleridgean conservatism and Benthamite pragmatism. His youthful Girondist dreams were reinvigorated. He would be, for the last time, a French revolutionary.

James Mill (1773–1836), 'the prototype', according to a contemporary, 'of the Utilitarian character, almost to the point of caricature: self-made, manly, independent, rationally controlled'.

Jeremy Bentham (1748–1832), Mill's secular 'godfather'. His utilitarianism provided to the young Mill 'a creed; a doctrine; a philosophy; in one among the best sense of the word, a religion'.

Forde Abbey, Bentham's summer residence, sketched by Lady Romilly, who visited in 1817 when the Mills were also present.

David Ricardo (1772–1823), the 'kindly' and radical economist.

John Arthur Roebuck (1801–79), a leading parliamentary radical and a close friend Mill in his early adulthood.

John Sterling (1806–44): passionate, romantic and unlucky – and Mill's closest male friend.

William Wordsworth (1770–1850). The beauty of his poetry helped Mill out of h 'mental crisis'.

A cameo of Mill in his mid-30s. His friend, Caroline Fox, described his exquisitely chiselled countenance, more resembling a portrait of Lavater than any other that I remember'.

Harriet Taylor (1807–58). The only woman Mill ever loved, but with whom he had to settle for an 'imperfect companionship' while she was married to John Taylor (1796–1849), who was 'an innocent dull good man', according to Thomas Carlyle.

Paris Revolution, 1830. French revolutions were a constant source of inspiration and disappointment for Mill. He wrote that the 1830 uprising 'raised my utmost enthusiasm, and gave me, as it were, a new existence'.

Samuel Taylor Coleridge (1772–1834) was the most significant of the conservative intellectual influences on Mill in the 1830s and 1840s.

Alexis de Tocqueville (1805–59). The liberal French aristocrat was 'the Montesquieu of our own times' according to Mill.

Thomas Carlyle (1795–1881). Mill's friendship with the Scottish sage survived the accidental burning by Mill's maid of the first draft of his history of the French Revolution, but not Carlyle's views on the 'nigger question'.

Thomas Babington Macaulay (1800–59). The brilliant Whig historian was a rival for the title of England's leading man of letters; in private Mill described him as a 'coxcombical dilettante litterateur who never did a thing for a practical object in his life'.

East India House, London, *c.*1850. Mill worked for the
East India Company from 1823 to 1858, making him 'practically conversant
with the difficulties of moving bodies of men'.

EDITOR OF 'LONDON & WESTMINSTER REVIEW.'

William Molesworth (1810–55), owner of the *London and Westminster Review*,
and an indulgent proprietor: when Mill rejected one of his articles, he was merely
'rather out of humour with John'.

Francois Guizot (1787–1874), the French historian and politician. If history did not yet have its Newton, declared Mill, Guizot was 'its Kepler, and something more'.

Auguste Comte (1798–1857). Mill described his *Cours de philosophie positive* as 'very nearly the grandest work of the age', but was embarrassed by the Frenchman's totalitarian politics, a form of 'liberticide'.

Harriet Taylor Mill (1807–58). The couple were married in 1851 and were able, finally, to enjoy a 'partnership of our entire existence. For seven and a half years that blessing was mine', declared Mill. 'For seven and a half only!'

CHAPTER EIGHT

French Revolutionary (1848)

>‹

'I am hardly yet out of breath from reading and thinking about it,' exulted Mill to his journalist friend Henry Chapman. 'Nothing can possibly exceed the importance of it to the world or the immensity of the interests which are at stake on its success.'[1] The event injecting such excitement into the middle-aged Mill in February 1848 was the revolution which had just swept a provisional government into power in France. The romantic revolutionary who had imagined himself an English Girondist in his teens, who had rushed to Paris in his twenties to shake Lafayette's hand, once again saw a new world being born across the Channel.

Mill believed, correctly, that the 1848 French Revolution would have an international impact. As before, however, he was initially wildly over-optimistic about the nature of the changes which would be wrought. 'If France succeeds in establishing a republic and reasonable republican government, all the rest of Europe, except England and Russia, will be republicanized in ten years, and England itself probably before we die,' he predicted. 'There never was a time when so great a drama was being played out in one generation.'[2]

But Mill would not be dashing to Paris this time: while revolutionaries across Europe were toppling governments and heads of state, Mill tripped over a loose brick next to the Kensington Grove entrance in Hyde Park and sustained a nasty injury to his hip. He was prescribed a belladonna plaster, which resulted in an infection and for several weeks, according to Bain, 'he was both lame and unable to use his eyes'.[3] He managed to produce a letter for the *Spectator* and a leader comment for the *Daily News*, both of which accused the British media of misrepresenting the actions of the provisional government and 'discrediting reform' by 'blackening France'.[4] Once Mill was sufficiently recovered he issued a lengthy and positive assessment of the Revolution, in part by means of a savage assault on the published views of the old, and former radical, Lord Brougham. It was a piece that the *Edinburgh Review* would not have carried. On occasions such as this, Mill fell back on the reliable radicalism of the *Westminster*.

Defence of France came naturally to Mill. Even before 1848, he had already taken up the self-appointed post of advocate for French revolutionaries to a domestic audience of 'stupid, incurious' English.[5] His strongest article for the earlier incarnation of the *Westminster Review*, published in April 1828, had been a defence of the French Revolution against 'the Tory misrepresentations' offered by Sir Walter Scott in the introduction to his *Life of Napoleon*, and specifically against the view, then prevailing, that the Revolution had led ineluctably to the Terror.[6] France was also a nation 'to which by tastes and predilections I am more attached than to my own'.[7] Whenever possible he travelled there, usually with Harriet, who appears to have shared his francophilia. To her he wrote that 'any place in France if it be ever so far off seems so much a home to us'.[8] Ever since his teenage year in France, he had contrasted the tone of social life in the two countries: in his *Autobiography* he compared the 'frank amiability of French personal intercourse, and the English mode of existence in which everybody acts as if everybody else (with few, or no exceptions) was either an enemy or a bore'.[9] In contrast to conservative England, Mill saw France as a laboratory for social experimentation and the ferment of ideas. 'In England I often think that a violent revolution is very much needed, in order to give that general shake-up to the torpid mind of the nation which the French Revolution gave to Continental Europe,' he wrote to John Austin. 'England has never had any general break-up of old associations & hence the extreme difficulty of getting any ideas into its stupid head.'[10] In truth, however, Mill was anti-revolutionary at home.

Mill's deep knowledge of French history and politics also gave him an opportunity to set himself apart from his peers, to stand as a lofty critic of his own society. He was constantly, and usually legitimately, berating the English for their insularity and smugness and failure to understand even their nearest neighbour. If this made him 'un-English', so be it. 'I do not know how a writer can be more usefully employed than in telling his countrymen their faults,' he told Napier, who had cut some passages lamenting English inwardness from his 1845 article on Guizot, '& if that is considered anti-national I am not desirous to avoid the charge'.[11] In the turbulence of 1848, when much of English society was worried about a French revolutionary invasion, Mill was almost a sole voice supporting the provisional government in Paris.

The ageing Lord Brougham had suggested in his reactionary pamphlet that the Revolution was unpopular throughout France and had been undertaken by, alternately, the 'dregs of the populace' and a 'handful of armed ruffians'. He also opposed the Revolution on the grounds that 'the like of it was never before witnessed by men'.[12] In his 'Vindication of the French Revolution of February 1848', Mill sarcastically summarized Brougham's argument: 'Half-a-dozen obscure men overthrew a government which nobody disliked, and established one which nobody desired. A singular incident, of a government which, so to speak, falls down of itself.' He pointed out that the regime of Louis Philippe, after a brief reforming flourish in the 1830s, had become increasingly corrupt and repressive, encouraging the worship only of the 'cash-box and ledger'. More importantly, Louis Philippe, the 'Citizen King', and his ministers, including Guizot, had lost their standing by virtue of their conservatism: in the present condition of the world, 'No government can now expect to be permanent unless it guarantees progress as well as order; nor can it continue really to secure order, unless it promotes progress.'[13]

Mill scorned fears of imminent war, pointing out that although the new French government had torn up the 1815 treaties, it had also made pacific noises. He heaped praise on the new first minister Alphonse de Lamartine, pointing to his 'beautiful *Histoire des Girondins*' as evidence of his astute moderation.[14] He mistakenly defended the administration against charges of brutality when putting down a working-class insurrection in June and, of course, he heartily approved of the abolition of slavery in French colonies. Parting company with French liberals such as Tocqueville, Mill also supported the pledge by the new government, enshrined in the *droit au travail*, to create full employment. 'Whosoever works at any useful thing, ought to be properly fed and clothed before any one able to work is allowed to receive the bread of idleness,' he wrote. 'Every one of the living brotherhood of humankind has a moral claim to a place at the table provided by the collective exertions of the race.'[15] Mill added, however, that such a right to work would be a 'fatal gift' unless it was made conditional on the beneficiaries refraining from having children.

The attempt by the Provisional Government to create a system of workshops – *ateliers nationaux* – providing work for all, was, however, doomed to almost instant financial failure against a background of high unemployment and plunging tax revenues. Macaulay waspishly, but accurately, said the Parisian government was 'refuting the doctrines of political economy in the way a man would refute the doctrines of gravitation by jumping off the Monument'.[16] Mill agreed that the economics of the national plan were weak, but he also insisted that experiments with various forms of 'co-operative production' would prove one of the most important legacies of the Revolution. 'There will doubtless be a great deal of experimental legislation, some of it not very prudent,' Mill wrote to the Austins, who were watching events with trepidation from Germany. For him, though, France was the social testing bench of Europe: 'there cannot be a better place to try such experiments in than France. I suppose that regulation of industry in [*sic*] behalf of the labourers must go through its various phases of abortive experiment, just as regulation of industry in behalf of the capitalist had done.'[17] The Austins were concerned about the Revolution, not least because of the potential impact on their own wallets, but Mill was scathing about his old friends' selfishness. 'I do not attach all the importance which ... he [John Austin] seems to attach to the effect of the Revolution on individual interests,' he wrote to Sarah. 'The monetary crisis in London last October produced quite as much suffering to in-dividuals as has arisen, or, as far as I can see, is likely to arise, from an event which has broken the fetters of Europe.' [18]

Mill's various defences of the 1789, 1830 and 1848 French Revolu-tions rested on the justice of the actions of the Parisian crowds in 'breaking the fetters' of oppressive government. In contrast to Edmund Burke, who lamented the ascendancy of the 'swinish mul-titude', Mill always relished the breaking up of the power of the stubborn, regressive French ruling classes.[19] This was not to say, however, that he would have supported the same revolutionary activity in England. With his strong sense of historical and nation-al context, Mill saw that what was right for one nation was unlikely to be appropriate in another with a different culture, history and institutional geology. 'We are the ballast of Europe,' he said, 'France its sail.'[20]

Britain's 'ballast' was certainly in evidence in 1848. As revolutions swept across Europe, the British Chartists managed only a petition and a final desultory march. A nervous Wellington filled London with troops and special constables, one of whom, Prince Louis Napoleon, was shortly to play a much more significant role in the history of democracy. But the crowds on Kennington Common on 10 April were actually smaller than during previous Chartist events, and the speeches were shortened by a sustained downpour. The dejected Chartist leader Feargus O'Connor quickly agreed to a request from the Metropolitan Police that the plan to carry the petition across the river en masse be abandoned: in England, it seemed, revolutions could be rained off. Mill wryly recorded the 'glorious tenth of April, when the demon revolution, or at least a noisy braggart that attempted to look like him, sneaked away at the sight of a special constable's staff'.[21]

In fact, the Chartists were more peaceful than demonic, the middle classes had no interest in radical change, and Russell's Whig government was resolute. 'Our little riots are mere nothing,' wrote a smug Queen Victoria to her uncle Leopold, King of the Belgians, 'and the feeling here is good'.[22] The contrasting fortunes of the European nations gave a new resonance to Tennyson's lines in *The Princess*, published in the year before the eruptions:

> God bless the narrow sea which ...
> And keeps our Britain, whole within herself,
> ... God bless the narrow seas!
> I wish they were a whole Atlantic broad.[23]

In Dickens's *Our Mutual Friend*, Mr Podsnap lectured a visiting Frenchman in similar, if ironic, vein:

'We Englishmen are Very Proud of our Constitution, Sir. It Was Bestowed Upon Us By Providence. No Other Country is so Favoured as This Country.'

'And *other* countries,' said the foreign gentleman. 'They do how?'

'They do, Sir,' returned Mr. Podsnap, gravely shaking his head; 'they do – I am sorry to be obliged to say it – *as* they do.' [24]

Mill criticized the insular Podsnappery of English minds in his inaugural lecture at St Andrews University two decades later. 'Improvement consists in bringing our opinions into nearer agreement with the facts; and we shall not be likely to do this while we look at facts only through glasses coloured by those very opinions,' he warned. 'But since we cannot divest ourselves of preconceived notions, there is no known means of eliminating their influence but by frequently using the differently coloured glasses of other people: and those of other nations, as the most different, are the best.'[25]

Few were willing to look at politics through French glasses in 1848, but there was at least a phalanx of MPs pushing reform on to the agenda. Despite – or perhaps because of – the fading away of Chartism, MPs spent July seriously debating a substantial package of democratic improvements. In a move reminiscent of the political mood of the 1830s, a group of about sixty radicals, led by the veteran radical Joseph Hume, broke away from the Whigs to form their own party and introduced a 'little charter', which demanded household suffrage, the secret ballot, triennial parliaments and further moves to equalize the size of parliamentary districts.

Radicalized by the eruptions in France, Mill plunged once again into the domestic political debate. This time his role was heavyweight commentator rather than party organizer, and in a series of articles for the *Daily News* he encouraged both the radicals and Parliament more generally in a reforming direction. Despite the continental revolutions, Mill was more realistic than he had been a decade earlier about the prospects for a dramatic domestic political realignment. None the less, the proposed reforms offered him another opportunity to stress what he saw as the real political division between 'those who are for no change at all, or for such changes only as would make no difference in the spirit of government' and those who 'think that a large reform of parliament, in a democratic direction, but short of actual democracy, is desirable in itself, and suitable to the circumstances of the present time'.[26]

Mill was delighted that a real argument about the merits of reform had been forced, and not by the Chartists but by middle-class radicals. In contrast to the oppositionist stance he adopted in the 1830s, he now urged principled compromise on the radicals in words which every parliamentarian, to this day, should be made to read before taking their seat: 'Their practical conduct as politicians necessarily partakes of compromise. Their demands and systematic aims must often fall short of their principles. But let them not therefore cut down their principles to the measure of their demands.'[27]

Mill himself shared the concern of conservatives that the 'crude opinions and unguided instincts of the working class' must not become 'the directing power in the state', but the lesson of France was that the working classes would not have more than their just influence, even in a legislature chosen by universal suffrage: 'After a revolution made by workmen, not twenty members in an assembly of nine hundred are working men.'[28] Mill's tone here was however markedly more democratic than a decade previously, when he had fretted about the destructive impact of working-class suffrage. He now saw three powerful reasons why the working class should gain at least some representation. First, it would force political leaders to pay attention to the concerns and needs of the whole population, and to debate the 'vital question with which all Europe rings, and which fills every thinking mind, both in England and on the continent, with anxiety – the question how to make the rights of property acceptable to the unpropertied'.[29] Second, the granting of political power to the working class would act as powerful motivation for wider education, both because 'the discussions of parliament and of the press would be ... a continued course of political instruction for the working class' and because the fear of an ill-informed electorate would force Parliament to introduce universal education. Third, the voicing of working-class interests in Parliament would make it 'the place of discussion for adverse interests and principles, the arena where opposing forces should meet and fight out their battles, that they may not find themselves reduced to fight in a less pacific field.'[30] These were all themes that Mill would flesh out later in the *Principles of Political Economy* and *Representative Government*. Despite his efforts, though, the little charter was thrown out by a vote of 351 to 84. Almost two decades would pass before the next instalment of parliamentary reform – the 1867 Reform Act – by which time Mill would be able to cast his own vote.

Repeating his analysis of the previous decade's disappointments, Mill lamented the absence of radical leadership and the innate conservatism of the English. In May 1849 he issued his standard post-match report: 'As for England, it is dead, vapid, left quite behind by all the questions now rising,' he told Henry Chapman. 'From the Dukes to the Chartists, including all intermediate stages, people have neither heads nor hearts.'[31] Changes in ideas would, once again, have to precede changes in politics. His contempt for his English contemporaries, politicians and intellectuals alike, meant that he had to look across the Channel for inspirational individuals. In Mill's mental universe, almost all the heroes were French. He idolized Armand Carrel, the radical journalist, and hugely admired Tocqueville, of course, and heaped praise on Lamartine. There were also two other Frenchmen who influenced his intellectual development: Auguste Comte and François Guizot. Mill's admiration was perhaps the only thing the two men shared. Comte was a detached, narcissistic, eccentric philosopher; Guizot was an accomplished historian, Machiavellian politician and big-league power player. He was a casualty of the 1848 revolution, being dismissed from his position as French prime minister by Louis Philippe the day before his own abdication. Guizot arrived as an exile in London in dramatic style, penniless and disguised as a footman.

As a politician, Guizot was the subject of Mill's alternating scorn and worship. 'I have for many years [this was in 1845] been oscillating in Guizot's case between great esteem and considerable misgivings,' he said.[32] In 1830 he had dismissed him as a backwards-looking defender of aristocracy, but by 1840, Guizot was held up as 'as immeasurably the greatest public man living', and contrasted, inevitably, with Robert Peel. By 1847, Guizot was again full of 'low tricks and equivocations'.[33] Macaulay was more direct, and more consistent in his opinion: although he also admired Guizot the historian, his conduct as a politician had always been, in his view, 'at home all corruption, and abroad all treachery'.[34]

Fortunately, Guizot was not a political influence on Mill – or at least, not directly. In 1840, during his tenure as French ambassador in London, he had invited Mill to dinner on the same evening as a young Tory who would later embody many of Mill's political hopes: William Ewart Gladstone.[35] It was Guizot's assessment of the history of Europe that made an impact on Mill. At the birth of the scholarly discipline of history – Britain had only just started to catalogue and officially care for its national archives – he was attracted to Guizot's more scientific approach to the course of events than the one offered by Whig historians such as Macaulay. Of course the 'science' was in its infancy, but if history did not yet have its Newton, declared Mill, Guizot was 'its Kepler, and something more'.[36]

Mill had already embraced the Saint-Simonian distinction between periods of stability and transition; Guizot added a further, dynamic dimension. The engine of progress, he suggested, was the 'systematic antagonism' between rival sources of power such as religion, knowledge, military strength, numbers and force, and wealth. The contradictions in any society provided the energy for its advancement, according to Guizot; the competing forms of power are like runners in a pack, jostling for and sharing the leading position, and as a result urging the whole field onwards.[37] For Mill, this 'systematic antagonism' had the additional benefit of ensuring humane politics: 'There is not one of these powers which, if it could make itself absolute, and deprive the others of all influence ... would not show itself the enemy of some of the essential constituents of human well-being.'[38] Fresh influences added to the constructive 'chaos of progressing nations. Even the 'Germanic ... barbarian invaders', of the fifth and sixth centuries, Mill agreed, had brought something vital into the European mix – 'the spirit of liberty'. While the liberties of the ancient Greeks and Romans had been primarily political:

the modern spirit of liberty, on the contrary, is the love of individual independence; the claim for freedom of action, with as little interference as is compatible with the necessities of society, from any authority other than the conscience of the individual. It is in fact the self-will of the savage, moderated and limited by the demands of civilized life; and M. Guizot is not mistaken in believing that it came to us, not from ancient civilization, but from the savage element infused into that enervated civilization by its barbarous conquerors.[39]

Auguste Comte was engaged in a similar project to construct a theory of history, and had already played an even more important role in Mill's intellectual life. For Comte, history offered the raw materials from which 'positive' laws of progress could be identified.[40] Mill especially admired Comte's gigantic multi-volume *Cours de philosophie positive*, published between 1832 and 1840. Having read the work 'with avidity', Mill declared it 'very nearly the grandest work of the age' and 'one of the most profound books ever written on the philosophy of the sciences'.[41]

The attempts by Guizot and Comte, along with other French historians such as Jules Michelet and Louis Thiers, to delineate the norms driving history were ultimately doomed. A science of history was no more possible than a science of human character. Their ideas nevertheless gave Mill theoretical grounds for believing in the inevitable forward march of liberal society, distanced him still further from 'end state' theories of politics or philosophy in which history would grind to a halt, and gave him a historical perspective from which to attack the Whiggish tendencies of English historians, from Burke to Macaulay. These Whig historians gloried in the gradualism of British progress, by contrast to the chaotic convulsions suffered by France. Armed with his French historicism, Mill railed against the Whig treatment of history as a storehouse of sensibly acquired glories, and condemned their lack of idealism regarding the future trajectory of society.

Predictably enough, Mill was caustic about Macaulay's great *History of England*, the publication of which brought a fitting close to a year of foreign revolution and domestic placidity. 'I have no doubt like all his writings it will be & continue popular,' Mill complained to Harriet, 'it is exactly au niveau of the idea of shallow people with a touch of the new ideas – & it is not sufficiently bad to induce anyone who knows better to take pains to lower people's estimate of it.'[42] Mill himself certainly made no public attempt to undermine the work, and his assessment here was almost certainly tinged by professional jealousy. Macaulay was a successful competitor in the mid-Victorian intellectual marketplace: Napier praised

Mill's piece on Guizot in the *Edinburgh Review* by pointing to 'passages worthy of Macaulay', but was wise enough not to convey this particular form of praise to Mill directly. Bain wrote of Mill's writing style: 'nothing could have made him a Macaulay'.[43] There was more to Mill's distaste for Whig history than personal animus, however. For a start, along with most schoolchildren to this day, he simply found English history unexciting compared to the flamboyance of France: 'I think English one of the least instructive of all histories – (French perhaps the most & certainly the most instructive in so far as history is ever so).' He also detected in much English historical writing an absence of national self-criticism. The biggest danger of Macaulay's history, for Mill, was that it would encourage the natural 'conceit' of the English.[44]

Macaulay certainly flattered England by means of comparisons to France, pointing especially to the French habit of violently removing existing institutions and replacing them with an abstractly conceived apparatus, which led inevitably to anarchy and then despotism – a pattern which was in fact about to repeat itself between 1849 and 1851. As Macaulay put it, 'I would not take the trouble of lifting up my hand to get rid of an anomaly which was not also a grievance.'[45] Lord Brougham put the same Whig historical case well: 'Laws are made; codes and constitutions grow. Those that grow have roots; they bear, they ripen, they endure. Those that are fashioned are like painted sticks planted in the ground, as I have seen trees of liberty: they strike no root, bear no fruit, and decay swiftly.'[46] The Whig interpretation of history permitted a relaxed, organic stance with regard to the messiness, contradictions and idiosyncracies of British constitutional and political life. This approach was anathema to both the broom-wielding Benthamites, intent on tidying up the mess, and the purist French ideologues. As Louis Thiers disparagingly described the British situation, *'le roi règné et ne gouverne pas'* (the King reigns but does not govern) – a perfect description of the constitutional settlement to this day.[47]

As Stefan Collini has pointed out, there was a self-congratulatory smugness about much of the English historical writing of the period and Mill justifiably berated his countrymen for their tendency to 'hug themselves & think they are the only people who are good for anything'.[48] While Macaulay held up France as a salutary warning, Mill used the example of French radicalism as a battering ram against the complacency of the English, whom he believed to be 'more in need of monitors than adulators'.[49] One of Mill's most acute critics, James Fitzjames Stephen, lamented his 'profound settled disapprobation' of England, but was more perceptive than most about Mill's motivation: 'Possibly much of this may arise from the fact that Englishmen are the audience who are to be addressed,' he suggested. 'If Mr. Mill had been writing for French readers, and had cared enough for their welfare, he would probably have said as many unpleasant things about them as he has said about us.'[50] In his private correspondence and journals, Mill was indeed quite as scathing about the French as the English, and his public indulgence towards France, at least in intellectual matters, was more apparent than real; it was hyperbole rather than bias. The modern scholar Georgios Varouxakis suggests that Mill used France to provide the 'other half of the truth' to the received English one. Mill certainly believed that just as individuals could learn from one another, so could nations: 'I am ... deeply convinced,' he told Comte, 'that the combination of the French spirit with the English spirit is one of the most essential requirements of intellectual reorganization.'[51] His own role, at least until the 1850s, was to bottle the France spirit for export to England.

Even if Mill's pro-French pronouncements can be seen, in part, as a deliberate promotion of free trade in ideas, his hostile attitude to English schools of historical thought was none the less a blind spot in his thinking. Collini has suggested that his 'unrelenting, self-defining, antagonism to a stereotype of English complacency obscured any more appreciative view of the cogency of the Whig case in general or of the intellectual strengths of this style of thought in general'.[52] Mill, who saw the appreciation of another culture as a protection against bias ('using the differently coloured glasses of other people') was unable to derive much value from the history and progress of his own.[53]

Mill's public engagement with French affairs came to an end after his 1848 and 1849 interventions, but the legacy of his immersion in French politics and ideas, and in particular his long wrestle with the philosophy of Comte, was visible in much of his later work. The two men never met, but exchanged eighty-nine letters between November 1841 and May 1847. It is hard to imagine two men with a starker difference in outlook. While Mill elevated open-mindedness to the status of a moral virtue, Comte refused on principle to properly engage with criticism. He regularly entered cleansing periods of 'cerebral hygiene' in which he read only his own writings; it was a great honour to Mill that Comte interrupted one of these disinfectant sessions to read the *System of Logic*. Comte's contemptuous attitude to poetry also touched a nerve for Mill. When he accused Schiller of 'silly metaphysical sentimentality', Mill insisted on the German's 'truly poetic gift'.[54] Mill was, however, attracted not only the Frenchman's scientific methodology for history but also to his vision of a new humanist religion, which could bind societies together without the need for faith in supernaturalism. In 1848 Mill was convinced that Comte's *culte de l'humanité* – effectively a secular faith – was 'capable of fully supplying the place of religion, or rather (to say the truth) of *being* a religion'.[55]

There were also two areas of profound intellectual disagreement, however, which would eventually lead to an abrupt end to their correspondence. Comte's 'positivism' prescribed the whole of society as the unit of analysis and agency rather than the individual – and he coined the term 'sociology' to describe this new field. For him, the individual would be subsumed into the fabric of society as a whole, and display a flawless concern for the greater good, which he dubbed 'altruism'. For Comte, 'man ... as an individual, cannot properly be said to exist, except in the too abstract brain of modern metaphysicians'.[56] At this stage in his own development, Mill certainly believed that it was possible to link sociology with psychology via his proposed science of 'ethology', but he also insisted that individuals could not be dissolved into society. 'Men, however, in a state of society are still men; their actions and passions are obedient to the laws of individual human nature,' he wrote in the *Logic*: 'Men are not, when brought together, converted into another kind of substance, with different properties.'[57]

Comte was also a leading proponent of the new 'science' of phrenology and firmly believed that because women's brains were smaller than men's, they were naturally less intelligent. Mill, typically, read widely on phrenology before gently pointing out the inherent weaknesses in Comte's approach.[58] In good experimental style, he noted that while he had been told by a phrenologist that he had a 'very pronounced ... organ of constructivity', he was in fact 'completely deficient in this faculty. I lack mechanical aptitude, and my incapacity in all operations that require manual dexterity is really prodigious.'[59] (Mill's fencing teacher could have confirmed this two decades earlier.) Harriet was more direct, pointing out that small-headed men must, then, also be assumed to be inferior to those born with larger skulls. It may be that Comte was a less than objective judge of women's qualities: his wife of seventeen years had just left him; a result, he subsequently decided, of having been 'brought up under blameworthy principles, and with a false notion of the essential function that her sex must play in the human economy'.[60] For Comte, progress for humanity meant regress for women: 'the modern regeneration [of society] will increasingly return them completely to their essentially domestic life.'[61]

Comte's application of these principles in his *Système de Politique Positive* to the construction of a political system confirmed Mill's fears.[62] A new world order was to be established, in which the middle class would be eradicated, divorce prohibited and the world broken up into republics under the rule of single governors appointed by the Grand Pontiff of Humanity, who was of course to be based in Paris – the new capital of the world and centre of religion. All books were to be burnt, except a hundred of the Grand Pontiff's choosing. The identity of the Pontiff was not made explicit, but few were in any doubt who Comte had in mind for the role. The religious order was described in loving detail: the positivists would not cross themselves, but tap their head on the three points relating to love, orderliness and progress, and pray for two hours a day at the Temple of Humanity. While supporting the philosophical basis of a humanist religion, Mill admitted to 'the ridiculousness which everybody must feel in his [Comte's] premature attempts to define in detail the *practices* of this *culte*'. Thomas Henry Huxley, Darwin's promoter, satirized the scheme as 'Catholicism minus Christianity'. 'Others may laugh,' Mill wrote much later, 'but we could far rather weep at this melancholy decadence of a great intellect.' For Mill the precision of these rules demonstrated the 'mania for regulation for which Frenchman are distinguished among Europeans, and Comte among Frenchmen'.[63]

Mill came to be embarrassed by the enthusiastic tone of his correspondence with Comte and showed his letters only with great reluctance to Bain. Harriet was also allowed to view them, with predictable results, especially on the issue of women's equality. 'These have greatly surprised and disappointed me,' she told Mill.

Comte's is what I expected – the usual partial and prejudiced view of a subject which he has little considered . . . I am surprised in your letters to find your opinion undetermined where I had thought it made it up – I am disappointed at a tone more than half-apologetic with which you state your opinions . . . This dry sort of man is not a worthy coadjutor & scarcely a worthy opponent.[64]

Any lingering loyalty Mill might have towards his former correspondent evaporated when Comte heaped praise on the man who, in 1851, starred in the traditional sequel to a French Revolution, a *coup d'état*, and bestowed on himself the title Napoleon III. Comte described the death of the infant republic as 'a fortunate crisis which has set aside the parliamentary system and instituted a dictatorial republic'.[65] Needless to say, Mill took a very different view.

It was small comfort to Mill that in his article on the 1848 French

Revolution he had correctly identified the two factors which would lead to dictatorship: the direct election of a head of state, and the character of Louis Napoleon himself. While there was much in the French constitution signed on 4 November 1848 to praise – universal (male) suffrage, a free press, free speech, freedom of assembly and opinion – Mill worried about the Provisional Government's decision to allow the electorate to vote for the President. He suggested that this would 'prove to be the most serious mistake which the framers of the French Constitution have made'. Mill pointed to the other great democracy, the United States of America, where direct presidential elections – rather than, as Mill preferred, election by legislators – had resulted in a string of presidents who were 'either an unknown mediocrity or a man whose reputation has been acquired in some other field than that of politics'.[66]

In France, the risk was less mediocrity than megalomania. In the election of December 1848, Louis Napoleon, after his stint moonlighting as a British constable, swept aside Lamartine and Cavaignac and claimed the Presidency. Tocqueville told the British ambassador, Lord Normanby, that 'there only remains now one question, whether it is the Republicans or the Republic itself which the country cannot abide'. Mill tore into the new President as 'a stupid, ignorant adventurer who has thrown himself entirely into the hands of the reactionary party & but that he is too great a fool, would have some chance by these means of making himself emperor'.[67]

Unfortunately, Napoleon was not as great a fool as Mill hoped. After patiently packing the government with supporters for two years, in 1851 Napoleon seized absolute power for himself, tearing up the Constitution. Not only did his rise create the immediate threat of war with Britain – until the two nations were drawn into an uncomfortable alliance by events in the Crimea – but it snuffed out hopes of French democracy and, perhaps most painfully of all for Mill, suggested that Macaulay's assessment that revolution led inexorably to dictatorship was accurate. It is small wonder that following Napoleon's coup, Mill was 'downhearted about French affairs'. He abandoned his 1849 view that 'the whole problem of modern society will be worked out in France & nowhere else' and never wrote about France again.[68] After this, Mill would look west, to the more robust democracy of America, for glimpses of the future. The United States, especially after the victory of the north in the Civil War, would demonstrate for Mill the virtues of the 'self-help characteristic of the energetic people' and of 'constitutions made by the people'.[69]

While Mill's intellectual relationship with France died with the republic, his personal affection for the country remained. Mill loved the country like a brilliant wayward son – a stark contrast to his sober, sensible, unexciting sibling, England. 'It is impossible not to love the French people & at the same time not to admit that they are children,' he wrote, '– whereas with us even children are care-hardened men of fifty. It is as I have long thought a clear case for the *croisement des races*.'[70] Like an indulgent paterfamilias, Mill was far from objective in his opinion of Britain's neighbour. Bain concluded that as far as France was concerned, Mill 'dealt gently with her faults, and liberally with her virtues'.[71] There was a part of Mill which would remain forever French; the hot-blooded, ill-fated revolutionary impatience of the French radicals inspired as well as disappointed him. Usually he was a common-sense, English kind of radical – though he would have died on a barricade before admitting it. But there were times when he was ignited with a fervour for justice – over the American Civil War, the Governor Eyre pursuit, or the right to speak freely in London's parks – which was distinctly French.

'If you went to sleep in 1846 and woke in 1850,' wrote Mark Pattison, Rector of Lincoln College, Oxford, in his 1885 *Memoirs*, 'you would wake into a different world.'[72] This was an overstatement. In Britain, the long era of free trade had been inaugurated, but otherwise the Victorian pattern of rapid industrialization and modest modernization had continued much as before. Revolutions had set Europe aflame, but by 1850 most of the democratic experiments had been snuffed out. Mill's own world, though, had been profoundly reshaped. For almost two decades he had been in love with another man's wife. But on the 18 July 1849, Harriet became a widow.

CHAPTER NINE

A Dismal Science? (1848–52)

>‹<

'You must remember,' Harriet scolded her husband after he visited the doctor, 'that the number of *glasses* he allows means of the *ordinary* size.' She also warned John Taylor against mixing his drinks – 'the mixture of beer and wine is always so unwholesome' – and suggested French rather than Spanish wine, on the grounds that it 'acts more on the stomach than on the bowels'.[1]

Harriet's advice on alcohol was dispensed from the southern French town of Pau, to which she had retreated for the first few months of 1849. If John Taylor took any notice, it was to no avail. In March he reported a worsening in his health – he knew, in fact, that he was dying – and asked her to come home. Harriet, however, was due to meet Mill in Bagnères, a Pyrenean town of which he had fond memories from his adolescent year in France. 'The reason I cannot [come back to England immediately] is that I have arranged to meet Mr. Mill,' she explained to her husband. 'He is to have three weeks holiday on account of his health which has been the whole winter in a very precarious state . . . I feel it as a duty to do all in my power for his health.'[2]

Mill was certainly not at the peak of fitness, but was perhaps not quite as ill as Harriet suggested. By this point he described his 'dimness of sight' from the belladonna incident in 1848 as 'slight', and the idea of him joining her had been under discussion for some time. In February, he had reassured Harriet that he had 'taken care to let my ailments be generally known at the I H [India House]' and so had 'no doubt it will be easy to get a two or three months holiday in spring if we like'.[3] He was obviously well enough to make the journey south, where he and Harriet strolled around Bagnères and Toulouse before making an unhurried journey home. When Harriet finally arrived in London on 14 May 1849 she discovered that John Taylor's bowel problems were not caused by injudicious boozing, but by cancer. She immediately gave her entire attention to her husband, and for two months nursed him fretfully and almost continuously. It is hard to imagine that there was no guilt mixed in with her other emotions.

Mill's role was to act as a stress-release valve for the carer and provide reading material for the patient. In June, he was at the receiving end of Harriet's frustration. 'You talk of my writing to you "at some odd time when a change of subject of thought may be rather a relief than otherwise"!' she wrote. '*Odd time!* Indeed you must be ignorant profoundly of all that *friendship* or *anxiety* means when you can use such pitiful narrow-hearted expressions ... It is the puerility of thought and feeling of any utterly headless and heartless propriety old maid.' In July, as the end neared, Harriet asked Mill for 'any Mags. or Revs. you have, for him ... Especially I want the Edinburgh *at the earliest* possible. Don't call again.'[4]

John Taylor died on 18 July 1849. Harriet worried now over where to bury him, which clergyman to use for the service and – above all – whether to invite Mill to attend:

My *first* impression about your coming was a feeling of 'better not' grounded on some sort of distance which of late existed. But now on much consideration it seems to me in the first place that coming is certainly thought a mark of respect? Is it not? And that therefore your not doing so will be a *manque* of that. Then again the public in some degree & *his* public too have heard or are sure to hear of the Dedication – of our intimacy – & on the side of his relations, nor that I know of on mine, there does not appear to be any medisance [gossip].[5]

Mill's reply has not survived, but there is no evidence that he attended the funeral. Loyal to the end to his estranged, determined wife, Taylor had made her the sole beneficiary of his estate. He had endured a great deal: the transformation of his marriage into a distant practical partnership, with Harriet a wife in name only; the knowledge that her love was directed elsewhere; the indignity of dining at his club while Mill dined in his home; and the endless whispering and gossip. Since the early turbulent years of the triangular arrangement, he had acquiesced in all his wife's wishes – except one. In 1848, Mill had wanted to dedicate his *Principles of Political Economy* to Harriet. She herself thought it 'desirable'. John Taylor, by contrast, was so upset by the idea that he made himself walk up and down Pall Mall before replying to the letter in which she had floated the idea. He did not calm down very much, though. 'Under our circumstances,' he declared, 'the dedication would evince on both author's part, as well as the lady to whom the book is to be dedicated, a want of taste & tact which I could not have believed possible ... The dedication will revive recollections now forgotten & will create observations and talk that cannot but be extremely unpleasant to me.'[6]

The book was printed without the dedication, though Mill and Harriet insisted on pasting it into a few gift copies circulated to friends, news of which almost certainly percolated back to John Taylor.[7] Mill and Harriet then explained their decision to confine the dedication to a select group of readers in terms which, to put it kindly, were at some distance from the truth. Harriet told their old Unitarian, adulterous friend William Fox that she herself had decided to limit the dedication to a few copies, 'my reason being that opinions carry more weight with the authority of his name alone'.[8] In the *Autobiography*, Mill declared that Harriet's 'dislike of publicity alone prevented their insertion in other copies of the work'.[9] In itself these modest rewritings of history are trifling, of course, but they do serve as a warning not to accept on trust their statements on other matters.

The samizdat dedication demonstrated of Mill's lifelong mission to deify Harriet: 'To Mrs John Taylor/As the most eminently qualified of all persons known to the author either to originate or to appreciate speculations on social improvement, this attempt to explain and diffuse ideas many of which were first learned from herself, is with the highest respect and regard dedicated.'[10] This description of Harriet's influence on the *Principles* is hugely over-stated, especially with regard to the first edition. If there was an-other voice alongside Mill's, it was surely that of David Ricardo, the economist inspired and cajoled by Mill senior and described by Mill junior as the 'greatest political economist' of his generation. Mill told John Austin, just before publication, that he was 'sticking pretty closely to Ricardo on the points which he touched. I doubt if there will be a single opinion (on pure political economy) in the book which may not be exhibited as a corollary from his doctrines.'[11]

The *Principles* did indeed draw substantially on Ricardo, but it also established Mill as the highest-profile economist of the Victo-rian era. The success of the book in 1848 gave him, according to the Victorian writer Walter Bagehot, a 'monarchical' status in political economy for decades. The *Principles* ran to seven editions in Mill's lifetime, each of no less than a thousand copies. In 1865, a cheap 'people's' edition was issued, and sold more than 10,000 within three years.[12] With the *System of Logic* already in its second edition in 1846, and selling steadily, Mill now stood astride the British intellectual stage. 'At Oxford we swallowed Mill, rather undigest-ed', recalled the legal scholar and historian Albert V. Dicey. 'He was our chief intellectual food until 1860'.[13]

As Mill had promised Austin, the theoretical chapters of the *Principles* were essentially an exposition of laissez-faire economics, helping to establish the classical school in its near-hegemonic posi-tion for the whole of the nineteenth century. Three key Ricardian features stood out. First, the presumption that prices were the result of an interaction of supply and demand in the marketplace. 'Hap-pily,' wrote Mill, 'there is nothing in the laws of value which remains for the present or any future writer to clear up; the theory of the subject is complete.'[14] Mill's only qualification to the then accepted wisdom on the way prices were set (made in the *Logic* rather than the *Principles)* was that this process was always ongoing, so that prices could never be seen as fixed. 'It is a principle of political economy that prices, profits, wages, &c. "always find their level"; he wrote, 'but this is often interpreted as if it meant that they are always, or generally, *at* their level; while the truth is, as Coleridge epigrammatically expresses it, that they are always *finding* their level.'[15]

The second Ricardian feature concerned international exchange, and to this day the relevant chapter remains one of the finest arguments for free trade between nations. Mill insisted that cross-border trade was driven by cost advantages – 'when it is cheaper to import than to produce' goods – and not, as Adam Smith suggested, by over-supply. Mill made the standard economic argument that international competition drives up global productivity: 'Whatever causes a greater quantity of anything to be produced in the same place, tends to the general increase of the productive powers of the world.'[16] It was the 'intellectual and moral' advantages of global trade, though, which most animated him:

It is hardly possible to overrate the value, in the present low state of human improvement, of placing human beings in contact with persons dissimilar to themselves, and with modes of thought and action unlike those with which they are familiar. Commerce is now what war once was, the principal source of this contact ... It is commerce which is rapidly rendering war obsolete, by strengthening and multiplying the personal interests which are in natural opposition to it.[17]

Third, Mill echoed Ricardo's belief that since there was a fixed amount of money available for pay – a 'wage fund' that had to be shared between all workers – in the long run families would be condemned to live on subsistence wages if they continued to have too many children. Mill's moral Malthusianism is explained at least in part by these views of economic laws. So while most reformers, for example, opposed the inhumane separation of spouses in work-houses, Mill saw it as an 'essential part of . . . moral training'.[18] One of the many advantages of co-operatively owned companies, he later told a correspondent, was that it would make 'the necessity of regulating population . . . palpable to everyone'.[19]

Mill's ambitions for the *Principles* were not however confined to the speculative sphere. His principal aim was not to advance the theories of exchange and value, trade, investment and wages, but to apply them to the social problems of the day. Just before the third edition of the *Principles* was published in 1852, he wrote to a German correspondent:

I confess that I regard the purely abstract investigations of pol. economy . . . as of very minor importance compared with the great practical questions which the progress of democracy & the spread of Socialist opinions are pressing on, & for which both the governing and governed classes are very far from being in a fit state of mental preparation.[20]

The second half of the work's title indicated the areas where Mill did his most original work: *Principles of Political Economy: with Some of Their Applications to Social Philosophy.* Mill had a lifelong conviction that economics was more than a scientific exercise, and that it had a vital role to play in human progress. Twenty-three years earlier, arguing with the Owenites in the London Debating Society, Mill had defended political economy, concluding one of his speeches with the 'pleasurable thought' that he might have 'in some small degree . . . contributed to set right in your estimation a science which does not deserve the obloquy which you have too readily cast upon it: and to prove that in the bosoms even of political economists there may burn as pure a flame of benevolence as even the torch of Mr. Owen can have kindled in yours'.[21]

The *Principles* was Mill's sustained attempt to show 'Political Economy, not as a thing by itself, but as a fragment of a greater whole'.[22] His role model here was not the technically minded Ricardo, but a more famous predecessor, mentioned four times in the short preface. Even before he set about writing the book, Mill told Henry Chapman that he was hoping to produce something 'not in the abstract manner of Ricardo but in the popular manner of Adam Smith ... such a book if one were able to do it well would at once supersede all the existing treatises, which are, one and all, effete and useless except as a matter of history.'[23]

To this end, Mill distinguished clearly between the laws of production, whose elucidation was indeed a scientific matter, and distribution, which was 'partly of human institution: since the manner in which wealth is distributed in any given society, depends on the statutes or usages therein prevalent'.[24] The economics of production represented the discipline in its 'abstract sense', and had 'nothing to do with the comparative estimation of different uses in the judgment of a philosopher or moralist', but distribution was a different matter: Mill argued that the 'human institutions' shaping the flow of income and wealth were open to constant challenge, and should differ according to both historical time and place.[25] Property rights, for example, were products of social and political choice, not economic laws. 'The distribution of wealth, therefore, depends on the laws and customs of society,' he insisted. 'The rules by which it is determined, are what the opinions and feelings of the community make them, and are very different in different ages and countries: and might be made still more different, if mankind so chose.'[26] By 1867 Mill would be calling for an 'emancipation' of the science of economics from the 'doctrines of the old school (now taken up by well to do people) which treat what they call economical laws ... as if they were laws of inanimate matter, not amenable to the will of the human beings from whose feelings, interests, & principles of action they proceed. This is one of those queer mental confusions which will be wondered at by and by.' [27]

Karl Marx denounced Mill's separation of the means of production from the nature of distribution as 'a shallow syncretism', and Mill certainly drew the distinction too sharply.[28] But if his analysis was unforgivably bourgeois from a Marxist perspective – and by modern standards, he clearly had 'right-wing', free-market views on the dynamics of production – his applied economics had a radical edge. He attacked the landlord class, for example, who through their ability to charge rent on land which they had simply inherited, 'grow richer, as it were, in their sleep, without working, risking or economizing'.[29]

His central economic policy concern was to distinguish between 'earned' and 'unearned' income (or 'life incomes' and 'permanent incomes') and to use the tax system as a wrecking ball against the latter.[30] To facilitate a much greater spread of wealth, Mill proposed a financial cap on the amount any individual could receive in the form of inheritance. 'I see nothing objectionable,' he explained, 'in fixing a limit to what any one may acquire by mere favour of others, without any exercise of his faculties, and in requiring that if he desires any further accession of fortune, he shall work for it.' He accepted that such a law would be unenforceable until public opinion was behind it, but insisted that great social and economic advantages would result from a reduction in the number of 'enormous fortunes which no one needs for any personal purpose but ostentation or improper power'.[31]

Tax, for Mill, was an important mechanism for generating equality, rewarding merit and promoting prudence. He would have liked to have abolished income tax, given that it was a tax on effort and ability, but recognized that fiscal demands made this a distant prospect. In the meantime, while income tax was still in existence, he supported a substantial tax-free allowance, sufficient for 'life, health, and immunity from bodily pain'.[32] Once a person's income rose above this tax-free level, it should be taxed at a flat rate. To 'tax the larger incomes at a higher percentage than the smaller is to lay a tax on industry and economy,' he wrote, 'and to impose a penalty on people for having worked harder and saved more than their neighbours'.[33] For the same reasons, Mill opposed the taxation of savings – at least while income tax was also being levied – but favoured consumption taxes. 'You are aware', he told a fellow economist, 'that I would, if I could, exempt savings from income tax, & make the tax on income virtually a tax on expenditure. By this rule, any portion of income should be taxed only if spent on private uses, but should be free from taxation (at least at its origin) when devoted to public ends.'[34] Mill also believed that 'the luxuries of all classes' were 'fit objects of taxation', giving as examples 'male servants or . . . horses & carriages', and was open-minded about taxing alcohol on revenue-raising, rather than moral, grounds.[35]

Mill expected such views to cause fireworks, but was determined to use his post-*Logic* status to try and effect some changes. 'I fully expect to offend and scandalize ten times as many people as I shall please, but that is "all in a day's work",' he told Henry Chapman. 'I always intended to make that use of any standing I might get among publicists. I have got a certain level of that sort by the *Logic*, and I now cannot too soon use it up in useful investments.'[36] But even though the *Principles* was published in the year of European revolution, it dropped placidly into the studies of the contented British reading classes. Carlyle seized the opportunity presented by its publication to denounce the whole enterprise of political economy as a 'dismal science', and Ruskin, in 1860, took some swipes not only at Mill but at economists in general in his *Unto This Last*.[37] Otherwise the book was well received, with Mill's balanced arguments giving most readers something substantial to agree with.

George Jacob Holyoake, founder of the co-operative movement and a famous atheist, enthusiastically published long extracts from the *Principles* in his journal *The Reasoner, A Weekly Journal, Utilitarian, Republican and Communist*. On the other hand, Mill had to issue a riposte to an American reviewer who had turned him into 'a participant in the derision with which he speaks of Socialists of all kinds and degrees'.[38] Mill's intellectual eclecticism and open-mindedness, which were on fine display in the *Principles*, helped to secure the book's status as the standard economics work of the century, but also reduced its polemical impact.

By the publication of the third edition in 1852, Mill had revised the *Principles* in a more radical and socialist direction. 'I have entirely recast several important chapters; in particular the two most important, those on Property & on the Futurity of the

Labouring Classes' he wrote to Dr Adolf Soetbeer, who may have received the news with mixed feelings, given that he had just finished his translation of the first edition.

The progress of discussion & of European events has entirely altered the aspect of the questions treated in those chapters; the present time admits of a much more free and full enunciation of my opinions on those subjects than would have had any chance of an impartial hearing when the book was first written; & some change has also taken place in the opinions themselves.[39]

Mill did not mention the other radicalizing factor: Harriet. Now that she was a widow, he was working even more closely with her, and she unquestionably sharpened Mill's socialism between 1849 and 1852. At the same time, John Taylor's death appears to have made them even more aware of the potential for gossip. In the twenty-one months between Harriet being widowed and marrying Mill, they were discreet about their movements and tried hard to avoid compromising situations: Mill does not appear to have spent the night at her Walton house unless a suitable chaperone was present.[40] It is not known when the couple first discussed marriage, or whether there was any 'proposal' – and indeed, if there was, who made it. In their exchange of views eighteen years earlier they had competed to issue the strongest denunciation of the existing institution of marriage as both sexist and illiberal. Nor had there been any reason to plan seriously for such an eventuality: John Taylor was only ten years older than Mill and, until his last few months, in considerably better health.

Congratulating his French friend Gustave d'Eichthal on his forthcoming marriage in 1841, Mill had written that similar sentiments were difficult to offer in England, where 'in nine times cases out of ten [marriage] changes a man of superiority for the worse without making him happy'.[41] But he was clearly confident that he and Harriet would be the exception to this rule. On 21 April 1851, in Melcombe Regis, Dorset, the couple were married by the registrar.

Their witnesses, and only audience, were Helen and Algernon Taylor. 'No one ever was to be more congratulated than I am,' Mill wrote to his little sister Anna.[42]

Mill did not of course see himself as a newly installed patriarch. Back in 1832, Mill had visited St Michael's Mount and considered sitting in the window of an old tower, an act which – so local folklore insisted – would grant the sitter all power in a marriage. 'At the hazard of passing for cowards,' Mill recorded in his journal, 'and at the sacrifice of our prospect of conjugal preeminence, we unanimously forbore to fill St. Michael's Chair.'[43] Now, though, Mill was serious about his desire to eschew the traditional powers attached to Victorian husbands and drew up a disclaimer. 'The whole character of the marriage relation as constituted by law being such as both she and I entirely and conscientiously disapprove,' he wrote, 'I, having no means of legally divesting myself of these odious powers ... feel it my duty to put on record a formal protest against the existing law of marriage, in so far as conferring such powers; and a solemn promise never in any case or under any circumstances to use them.'[44]

Their marriage meant that from the 'great evil' of John Taylor's death, Mill was able to derive his 'greatest good ... adding to the partnership of thought, feeling and writing which had long existed, a partnership of our entire existence'.[45] However, the union with Harriet caused a deep rupture between Mill and the rest of his family. The Mill womenfolk – his mother, and sisters Clara and Harriet – still lived at home in Kensington and were apparently uncertain how best to respond to the abrupt announcement that Mill was now married to the woman they had been forbidden from discussing in his presence for two decades. They did not, as he thought they should, bustle around to Kent Terrace to present their congratulations to their new relative. Mill interpreted this as a snub to his new wife and cut off all familial relations with the perpetrators. Harriet persuaded him that they should make a formal call to Kensington, but such was his coldness that it was a disaster.

The Mill women tried to make amends: one of the sisters,

Harriet, attempted to call on her new sister-in-law, but was turned away by her brother; Mrs Mill senior crossed the choking London streets to see her son at India House, but it was all to no avail. In response to a sad note from Clara, denying any intentional 'incivility', Mill responded: 'You are certainly mistaken if you suppose that I said you had been uncivil to my wife. I said you had been wanting in all good feeling and even common civility to us. My wife and I are one.'[46] There is some uncertainty about whether Mill actually sent this letter, but after his mother's peace mission to Leadenhall Street, he definitely sent her this missile: 'I received today two most silly notes from Clara & Harriet filled with vague accusations . . . I hope you were not the worse for your journey to the I.H.'[47] It is hard to imagine that Mrs Mill was not.

George Mill, slowing dying of tuberculosis in Madeira, wrote an ill-advised letter to Harriet questioning how the marriage squared with the feminist principles of the couple, expressing regret that he had only learned of the marriage 'second hand', and signing off, 'Believe me/dear Mrs Taylor (I can't forget the old name), Yours affectionately, Geo G. Mill'.[48] Harriet sent a sharp enough response, but Mill gathered all his invective and flung it at his young brother. 'I have long ceased to be surprised at any want of good sense or good manners in what proceeds from you – you appear to be too thoughtless or too ignorant to be capable of either', was the opening sentence of the last letter he wrote to his only surviving brother. 'What imaginary principles are they which should prevent people who have known each other the greater part of their lives, during which her and Mr Taylor's house has been more a home to me than any other, and who agree perfectly in all their opinions, from marrying?'[49] George's pique-filled letter was certainly foolish, ill-timed and rude, but it seems likely he had also hit a sore spot when he pointed out the apparent hypocrisy of the couple given their views on marriage. He also had some grounds for being upset that his brother had not bothered to mention the impending nuptials, in a letter written just thirteen days before the ceremony.[50] None the less, for the last two years of his life, before he died in 1853, George would be without the comfort of his older brother's correspondence.

Mill's other sister, Mary, who had four years earlier married Charles Colman, kept up a long letter-writing campaign to win her brother back. In 1854 Mill complained to his mother that Mary had sent 'another of [her] vulgar and insolent' letters.[51] Three years later she tried and failed again (it did not help that she stated her desire for him to become a Christian). 'I do not know why you write to me after such a long interval if you cannot shew more good sense or good feeling than are shown in this note,' he replied. 'There is certainly nothing in your note to make me desire that there should be any more communication between us than there has been for many years past.'[52]

Mill's behaviour towards his family after his marriage was indefensible. On an essentially trumped-up charge, he declared his blood relatives guilty of the crime of paying insufficient respect to Harriet and then acted in a manner which can only be seen as cruel. It has been described justly as the 'greatest blot on his character'.[53] When his mother was dying, in June 1854, Mill – his own health admittedly weak – departed for a tour of Normandy and Brittany. He wrote to her, requesting – not for the first time – that she appoint a different executor to her will 'either instead of me, which I should prefer, or as well as myself'.[54] She reluctantly agreed, and when he received news of her death, Mill immediately gave all authority to his new co-executor, Mary's husband. 'I am glad I was not in England when it happened,' he confided to Harriet, 'since what I must have done & gone through would have been very painful & wearing & would have done no good to anyone.'[55]

Mill was entitled to a share of his mother's modest estate, which he was strongly inclined to refuse. Harriet felt differently, though, and her authority on such financial and household matters was confirmed by his response: 'About that matter of my mother's inheritance, of course as your feeling is so directly contradictory, mine is wrong, & I give it up entirely.' He did however refuse to take a plate which his mother had specifically earmarked for him, telling Harriet that 'to us it would be only worth its value as old silver'.[56]

There are doubtless a dozen competing psychological explanations for Mill's rejection of his blood family, but it is clear that his feelings for Harriet were at the bottom of it. Now that he had Harriet to himself, Mill felt that he needed nobody else. She was, as the editors of his later letters, Francis E. Mineka and Dwight N. Lindley put it, 'the all-sufficient centre of his existence'.[57] He wanted nobody else intruding into their sacred space, and put most of his friendships into suspended animation. But while Mill was increasingly ill-disposed to his family, and ambivalent about his friends, his ardour for Harriet deepened. In the two years following John Taylor's death, Mill's letters to Harriet overflowed with love. She was his 'dearest dearest angel', and his 'dearest dearest love'.[58] In a description which supported Bain's assessment of Harriet's deistic status, Mill wrote that a letter from her was 'like something dropt from heaven', 'I had been literally pining for it'. Having seen her, Mill wrote that he was 'fresh from the immediate influence of your blessed presence'.[59]

As well as their passion, Mill and Harriet shared an enduring concern with the status of women, and after John Taylor's death Harriet was able to shape more directly Mill's feminism, while he was able to persuade her to go public with hers. As Stefan Collini put it, 'any complete account of Mill's thinking on the subject of women would have to come to terms with the role of this very clever, imaginative, passionate, intense, imperious, paranoid, unpleasant woman'.[60] For what it is worth, the evidence on Harriet's unpleasantness is inconclusive.

On a minor level, it seems unlikely that without Harriet at his side, Mill would have spent so many hours making the language of the third edition of the *Principles* more gender-neutral, replacing hundreds of occurrences of 'his' with 'their'.[61] More actively, in 1852, Mill also lodged with the Home Secretary, Sir George Grey, a violent protest against a Bill to restrict the sale of arsenic to adult males, following a couple of high-profile cases in which women had used the poison. It was, Mill insisted, a 'gross insult to every woman in the country', putting upon them 'the stamp of the most degrading inferiority'. He lambasted the tendency of the Commons to react in knee-jerk fashion to the latest public scare: 'Is it the part of a legislature to shape its laws to the accidental peculiarities of the latest crime reported in the newspapers? If the last two or three murderers had been men with red hair, as well might Parliament have rushed to pass an Act restricting all red haired men from buying or possessing deadly weapons.'[62] Using hair colour as a means for attacking stereotypes based on physical characteristics was one of Mill's favourite rhetorical devices.

His protest nevertheless remained within the confines of a private letter and he did not, as he did on other occasions or for other issues, fire off a newspaper piece. The Bill was passed. Mill was acutely aware of the heretical nature of his feminism and – for the moment – was still acting fairly cautiously. He had not moved very far from his position in 1835, when he had stated that the issue of women's suffrage was 'not one which, in the present state of the public mind, could be made a topic of popular discussion with any prospect of practical advantage'.[63] In a series of working notes, mostly in Mill's hand but clearly the result of joint work, the couple were more explicit about the way women's subordination shaped their character and sexual strategies for gaining status. 'The woman's whole talent goes into the inducing, persuading, coaxing, caressing, in reality the seducing, capacity,' they wrote. 'In whatever class of life, the woman gains her object by seducing the man. This makes her character quite unconsciously to herself, petty and paltry.'[64] These observations were not published.

In 1850, Mill told Hickson that his 'opinions on the whole subject [of . . . the entire position which present laws & customs have made for women . . .] are so totally opposed to the reigning notions, that it would probably be inexpedient to express all of them'.[65] Instead, Mill gave the *Westminster Review* an article of Harriet's, which he and Harriet referred to as 'Emancipation of Women', but was published in 1851 under the less ambitious title 'The

Enfranchisement of Women'. In the article, Harriet drew a parallel between the position of women and negro slaves, and criticized the 'unjust ... prejudice of custom' which permitted one group of society the right to decide for another 'what is and is not their "proper sphere"'.[66] The article foreshadows many of the arguments Mill would make nineteen years later in *The Subjection of Women*. But Harriet was much stronger in her opinions than Mill would ever be, at least publicly, in one section of 'Emancipation': the impact of motherhood on women's lives. In words which should resonate in boardrooms to this day, she insisted that 'it is neither necessary nor just to make imperative on women that they shall be either mothers or nothing, or that if they have been mothers once, they shall be nothing else during the whole remainder of their lives.'[67] The impact of maternity on the opportunities for public and labour market participation was acknowledged by Mill, but only in passing, and in *Subjection*, he would take a fairly conservative view of women's domestic labour.

Mill seemed content to let William Hickson believe that Harriet's article was written by him, although he was honest about its true authorship in subsequent correspondence.[68] Six years later, George Jacob Holyoake, the 'secularist' publisher, reprinted thousands of copies of the article, without a named author, under the title 'Are Women Fit for Politics? Are Politics Fit for Women?'. Mill and Harret were annoyed that Holyoake had not sought permission for the reprint, and furious about the 'vulgarity' of some of the editing, in particular the frequent replacement of 'women' with 'woman', a usage they both found hugely patronizing. Otherwise, the couple did not mind too much that the article had ended up in more hands. For Mill, placing Harriet's article was a shrewd way of getting some of these dangerous opinions into the public domain without too much risk to his own reputation – a risk which, as he would discover with *Subjection*, was all too real.

If Mill was unorthodox in his views on women, he was similarly against the mood of the times on the issue of race. Theories of racially determined superiority – supported by the likes of Charles

Kingsley, Anthony Trollope and Charles Dickens – were in the ascendancy. In 1850 Mill was prodded into publication by a racist rant from Carlyle, in which Mill's former friend derided the 'negro' as a 'Black Quashee' who was 'up to the ears in pumpkins' and 'working about half an hour a day'. Carlyle's message to the 'negro' was: 'You will have to be servants to those that are born *wiser* than you, that are born lords of you – servants to the whites.'[69] Mill's repudiation of this 'true work of the devil' was published in *Fraser's Magazine*. He denied that any person was born 'more capable of wisdom' than any other, and used a rather tortured analogy of trees growing in different soil and climates to argue that it was circumstances that determined differences in human characteristics. It was rare for any race to develop spontaneously beyond a 'very low grade', he insisted, so that 'no argument against the capacity of negroes, could be drawn from their not being one of these rare exceptions'. On the contrary, Mill argued, 'negroes' could be seen as the founders of civilization, since the 'original Egyptians are inferred, from the evidence of their sculptures, to have been a negro race: it was from negroes, therefore, that the Greeks learnt their first lessons in civilization'.[70] The piece was coherent and clear, but it lacked Mill's usual rapier-thrust phraseology. Carlyle dismissed it as 'shrill, thin, poor, and insignificant'.[71]

In his correspondence and journals, Mill himself made a number of comments on the capacities of various races, including the Indians, Irish and Greeks, which to modern ears sound straightforwardly racist. He was not fan of modern Greeks, for instance, who he believed showed the 'same brainless stupidity, & incapacity of adapting means to ends, in the acts of their government [as] ... I had observed in the common people'. He told Harriet: 'Still, if they get education they may improve.'[72] But Mill never deviated from his conviction that any observed differences in racial or national character were wholly the result of variations in historical and social context, and he was scathing, too, about the qualities of the supposedly superior races, noting in his 1854 journal that 'the characteristic of Germany is knowledge without thought: of France, thought without knowledge: of England, neither knowledge nor thought'.[73] From today's perspective, Mill's egalitarian stance on race is unexceptional, but it was bordering on eccentric in the mid-nineteenth century. Alexander Bain spoke for many when he said that Mill's insistence on 'the Helvetius doctrine of the natural equality of human beings in regard of capacity' was 'the first of his greatest theoretical errors as a thinker', and an area in which 'Mill never accommodated his views . . . to the facts'.[74]

The doctrine of natural equality underpinned Mill's feminism as well as his anti-racism, and he explicitly linked the two. In the *Subjection of Women* he would write that it was profoundly wrong 'to ordain that to be born a girl instead of a boy, any more than to be born black or white, or a commoner or a nobleman, shall decide the person's position through all life'.[75] Bain complained incredulously of Mill that 'he grants that women are physically inferior, but seems to think that this does not affect their mental powers', but Mill refused to link physical attributes to intellectual stature.[76] Being in love with a physically diminutive but fiercely intelligent woman – Harriet was 5ft 1in – may have indirectly influenced his views on natural equality, but by 1851, as a fully engaged intellectual partner, she was having a more direct impact too, especially on the heated issue of socialism: the scholar William Stafford writes that 'Mill was the first of the orthodox economists to take socialism seriously.'[77]

In the *Autobiography* Mill reflected that in the first edition of his *Principles*, the 'difficulties of Socialism were so strongly stated, that the tone was on the whole that of opposition to it'.[78] With Harriet acting as adviser, he set about shifting the balance. Given his status as Britain's premier intellectual, Mill's views on socialism were of considerable public interest in the mid-nineteenth century, but given subsequent history they have become highly charged – with Mill claimed as both friend and enemy to socialist thinking and practice. There is good evidence that Mill saw himself as having moved into the socialist camp. He insisted in 1850 that he was 'far more a Socialist' than Charles Kingsley, objecting principally to Kingsley's prefixing of 'Christian' to the movement, and in 1849 he reassured Harriet that 'progress of the right kind seems to me quite safe now that Socialism has become *inextinguishable*'.[79]

When Mill wrote about 'socialism', or even 'communism', he did not of course have in mind the vast state-run economies which emerged in twentieth-century Eastern Europe and China. In moral terms, Mill was counter-posing 'socialism' to selfish 'individualism', and in economics he was thinking about co-operative associations, constructed on a community scale, competing with each other in a market economy – a typically Millian blend of the best of capitalism with the best of socialism. He pinned considerable hopes on communal forms of ownership, citing as examples not only Robert Owen's New Lanark and the various French schemes, but also the Leeds Flour Mill and Rochdale Society of Equitable Pioneers. 'We may, through the co-operative principle, see our way to a change in society,' he suggested, 'which would combine the freedom and independence of the individual, with the moral, intellectual and economical advantages of aggregate production.' The productivity of workers would be given a 'vast stimulus' because it would be their 'principle and their interest – at present it is neither – to do the utmost, instead of the least possible, in exchange for their remuneration'.[80] Mill wanted, as Stafford writes, a world in which 'labour would be hiring capital', rather than the other way around, and he strongly supported the 1852 Industrial and Provident Societies Partnership Act, which removed some of the legal obstacles to forming co-operative associations.

By this point, Mill was convinced that one of the main objections to worker-owned companies – that they encouraged laziness – had been overstated. He admitted that 'communistic labour might be less vigorous than that of a peasant proprietor, or a workman working on his own account,', but insisted that 'it would probably be more energetic than that of a labourer for hire, who has no personal interest in the matter at all'.[81] Mill thought that a surge in community *esprit* might in any case prevent any reduction of effort caused by a more equal distribution of resources. 'History bears witness to the success with which large bodies of human beings may be trained to feel the public interest their own,' he suggested – sadly without identifying these utopias – 'and no soil could be more favourable to the growth of such feeling, than a Communist association.'[82] He also praised those socialists who gave equal rights and responsibilities to women.

While he was open to socialist ideas, Mill thought the working classes, especially those in England, were far from ready for their application. One of the principal obstacles to socialism, he wrote, was 'the unprepared state of the labouring classes & their extreme moral unfitness at present for the rights which Socialism would confer & the duties it would impose'.[83] The resistance of English workers to 'piece work' – in which pay was related to output – was seen by Mill as evidence of their 'low moral condition',[84] and even in the later, more socialist-friendly editions of the *Principles*, Mill was damning: 'We look in vain among the working classes in general for the just pride which will choose to give good work for good wages; for the most part, their sole endeavour is to receive as much, and return as little in the shape of service, as possible.'[85] In correspondence with a curate, he added a further moralistic twist, lamenting that the working class 'idea of social reform appears to be simply higher wages, and less work, for the sake of mere sensual indulgence'.[86] Hardly workshy himself, Mill saw purposeful labour as a vital part of human flourishing, not for its own sake, but for what it produced. 'Work, I imagine, is not a good in itself,' he wrote during the course of his attack on Carlyle over black slavery. 'Even in the case of the most sublime service to humanity, it is not because it is work that it is worthy; the worth lies in the service itself ... While we talk only of work, and not of its object, we are far from the root of the matter; or if it may be called the root, it is a root without flower or fruit.'[87]

Mill's enthusiasm for cooperation in economic activity was based on an optimistic appraisal of the benefits, which included:

the healing of the standing feud between capital and labour; the transformation of human life, from a conflict of classes struggling for opposite interests, to a friendly rivalry in the pursuit of a common good to all; the elevation of the dignity of labour; a new sense of security and independence in the labouring classes; and the conversion of each human being's daily occupation into a school of the social sympathies and practical intelligence.[88]

He also believed that 'moral education' in general would help to prepare the ground for greater cooperation: indeed, he predicted that workers themselves would begin to refuse to accept mere wages, so that even 'private capitalists ... will gradually find it necessary to make the entire body of labourers participants in profits.' Like Marx, he wanted to free work from the wage relationship. Unlike Marx, he believed that liberation lay not in changing the laws of economic exchange, but in reforming the moral stature of the worker. He praised *De la liberté du travail* (1845), by French economist Charles Dunoyer, which stressed the role of social custom and moral character in the promotion and creation of good work.[90]

'The great end of social improvement,' Mill wrote, 'should be to fit ['the labouring classes'] by cultivation for a state of society combining the greatest personal freedom with that just distribution of fruits of labour which the present laws of property do not even profess to aim at.'[91] Underlying Mill's views on socialism, cooperation and work was a growing concern that the increasingly competitive economy was improving material wealth, but also generating a set of cultural values which threatened to coarsen and cheapen social life.

I confess I am not charmed with the ideal of life held out by those who think that the normal state of human beings is that of struggling to get on, that the trampling, crushing, elbowing, and treading on each other's heels, which form the existing type of social life, are the most desirable lot of human kind, or anything but the disagreeable symptoms of one of the phases of industrial progress.[92]

It was easy for Mill to say this, of course. His comfortable, highly paid job at the East India Company, obtained through his father, exempted him from the need for any trampling or elbowing. But his concerns about the influence of economic competition were long-standing, and went to the very heart of his idea of progress. In his early twenties, Mill had fretted to his French correspondent Gustave d'Eichthal that 'the commercial spirit, amidst all its good effects, is almost sure to bring with it wherever it prevails, a certain amount of this evil'. Already he thought that the 'very worst point in our national character [was] the disposition to sacrifice every- thing to accumulation' and by 1844 he was lamenting the tendency to 'measure the merit of all things by their tendency to increase the number of steam engines, & to make human beings as good machines & therefore as mere machines as those'.[93]

Compared to the existing arrangement of society, then, 'with all its suffering and injustices', socialism or communism would be a clear step forward. For some advocates of socialism, this would be enough, but not for Mill. 'To make the comparison applicable, we must compare Communism at its best, with the régime of individ- ual property, not as it is, but as it might be made. The principle of private property has never yet had a fair trial in any country; and less so, perhaps, in this country than in some others.'[94] In the third edition of the *Principles*, Mill envisaged and advocated a reformed free-market economic system, based on a proper definition of pri- vate property (ie. not including land or inherited wealth), aggressive wealth redistribution and universal education. 'Private property,' he wrote, 'in every defence made of it, is supposed to mean, the guarantee to individuals of the fruits of their own labour and abstinence.' The actual laws of property, however, had 'never yet conformed to the principles on which the justification of private property rests'.[95] Mill recognized that inequality was a necessary consequence of property rights, but made a passionate plea for a more egalitarian economic philosophy:

That all should indeed start on perfectly equal terms, is inconsistent with any law of private property: but if as much pains as has been taken to aggravate the inequality of chances arising from the natural working of the principle, had been taken to temper that inequality by every means not subversive of the principle itself; if the tendency of legislation had been to favour the diffusion, instead of the concentration of wealth ... the principle of private property would have been found to have no necessary connexion with the physical and social evils which almost all Socialist writers assume to be inseparable from it.[96]

Even in his most socialist phases, Mill took a pragmatic view, insisting that 'the question of Socialism is not ... a question of flying to the sole refuge against the evils which bear down humanity; but a mere question of comparative advantages.'[97] This agnosticism was a very long way from the famous opening sentence of a socialist tract published within weeks of the first edition of Mill's work: 'The history of hitherto existing society is the history of class struggle.'[98]

Although Mill, along with most of the intellectuals of his generation, never engaged with Karl Marx's work, there were some arguments in his *Communist Manifesto* to which he would have been open, including the state appropriation of all land. By 1857, he told a correspondent that 'in principle I am quite in favour of considering all land as the property of the State, and its rent as a fund for defraying the public expenses'.[99] Likewise, Mill would have heartily endorsed Marx's goal of a society in which 'the free development of each is the condition of the free development of all'.[100] He also appreciated the political potential of the movement towards collectivism. 'Socialism', Mill declared in his vindication of the 1848 revolution in France, 'is the modern form of protest, which has been raised, more or less, in all ages of any mental activity, against the unjust distribution of social advantages.'[101] He was sceptical, however, about the ability of communism to provide the conditions for free and individual development. As well as adding the more upbeat sections on socialism for his third edition of the *Principles*, Mill included warnings about its potentially stifling social effects which can only now be read as prophetic. 'The question', Mill asked of communism, 'is, whether there would be any asylum left for individuality of character; whether public opinion would not be a tyrannical yoke; whether the absolute dependence of each on all, and surveillance of each by all, would not grind all down into a tame uniformity of thoughts, feelings and actions.'[102]

The result of these alterations and additions to the *Principles* was to position Mill as agnostic on the benefits of capitalism versus socialism. It was another, related set of revisions which revealed most about the development of his thinking. Considering the relative benefits of different economic systems forced Mill to clarify in his own mind which benchmarks should be used to make the judgement. 'The decision [between 'individual agency' and 'Socialism'],' he declared, 'will probably depend mainly on one decision, viz. which of the two systems is consistent with the greatest amount of human liberty and spontaneity.'[103] His doubts about socialism and communism sprang from his liberalism.

No society in which eccentricity is a matter of reproach, can be in a wholesome state . . . It is yet to be ascertained whether the Communistic scheme would be consistent with that multiform development of human nature, those manifold unlikenesses, that diversity of tastes and talents, and variety of intellectual points of view, which not only form a great part of the interest of human life, but by bringing intellects into stimulating collision, and by presenting to each innumerable notions that he would not have conceived of himself, are the mainspring of mental and moral progression.[104]

So although Mill did become more enthusiastic about socialism in the years following the first publication of the *Principles*, the main story of these years was the deepening of his liberalism. The process of evaluating the merits of competing economic systems stoked Mill's concern for individual freedom, which would find its fullest expression in *On Liberty*, but was prefigured in much of his earlier work. In the middle of a fairly technical discussion about the role of government in the *Principles*, Mill stated his case in terms which anticipate his later fears about the 'despotism of custom':

In this country, however, the effective restraints on mental freedom pro-ceed much less from the law or the government, than from the intolerant temper of the national mind; arising no longer from even as respectable a source as bigotry or fanaticism, but rather from the general habit, both in opinion and conduct, or making adherence to custom the rule of life, and enforcing it, by social penalties, against all persons who, without a party to back them, assert their individual independence.[105]

Mill outlined a test which could be applied to help set the limits of external interference in an individual's activities. 'There is a circle around every individual human being, which no government, be it that of one, of a few, or of the many, ought to be permitted to over-step,' he wrote. 'The point to be determined is, where the limit should be placed; how large a province of human life this reserved territory should include. I apprehend that it ought to include all that part which concerns only the life, whether inward or outward, of the individual, and does not affect the interests of others, or affects them only through the moral influence of example.'[106] Here, in a nutshell, is the 'harm principle' made famous by *On Liberty*.

The deep connections between Mill's socialism and liberalism demonstrates that the revisions made for the third edition of *Principles* were not undertaken in blind obedience to Harriet, an impression given by many biographers and scholars. The role of Harriet is in fact one of the most contested themes in Mill's life. For some commentators, everything from the *Principles* onwards is read as at the very least a joint production, and quite possibly as Harriet's thoughts flowing through Mill's pen. Nicholas Capaldi suggests that Harriet was a 'great influence' on Mill's life and thought; for Jo Ellen Jacobs, their work, 'beginning with the *Principles of Political Economy*, tended more and more to co-authorship'; according to Michael Packe, Harriet wielded an 'astounding, almost hypnotic control of Mill's mind'.[107] Packe also claimed for her a good deal of the credit for Mill's subsequent essays, especial-ly *On Liberty* and *The Subjection of Women*: 'In so far as Mill's influ-ence, theoretic or applied, has been of advantage to the progress of the western world, or indeed of humanity at large, the credit should rest upon his wife at least as much as himself.'[108] Packe is overstating the case, but in doing so follows faithfully in Mill's footsteps. In private and in public, Mill was at pains to emphasize Harriet's unique brilliance, eclipsing his own merely workmanlike abilities. Sometimes he did explicitly position himself as a translator of her thoughts, as her amanuensis, at one point likening her to Bentham, 'the originating mind', and himself to Pierre Dumont, the French translator of Bentham's *Traité de Legislation*.[109] Mill exceeded even these heights with the praise heaped on Harriet in the *Autobiography* (in passages which she saw and approved), where she is described as a 'consummate artist', who, were it not for the restrictions on women, would have been 'eminent among the rulers of mankind'. When she died in 1858, he lamented to Louis Blanc, 'this country lost the greatest mind it contained'.[110]

These public protestations of Harriet's genius did her a disservice, and have continued to do so ever since. 'Unfortunately for both,' recounted Bain, 'he outraged all reasonable credulity in describing her matchless genius, without being able to supply corroborating evidence.'[111] As a result, Harriet's real contribution has been too easily devalued. She provided Mill with the intellectual partnership which his father failed to do; forced him to engage more fully with the issues arising from socialism; managed his literary, household and business affairs with skill and tenacity (significantly improving his publishing deal for the *Principles*, for example); deepened his commitment to the rights of women; and throughout their life together provided him with constant reassurance and inspiration.[112]

Seeing Harriet as a hypnotizer or bewitcher of Mill diminishes the mutual intellectual respect each had for the other. The substantial changes made for the third edition of the *Principles* had to wait until the couple had enough time together to work on the necessary changes. Harriet suggested the chapter on the 'Futurity of the Labouring Classes', the one which dealt more directly with socialism, and, according to Mill, heavily influenced its content. Not that they always agreed, of course. During an exchange on how tough a line to take on the anti-liberal tendencies of socialism, Mill declared to Harriet that while he thought 'the objections as now stated to Communism to be valid ... if you do not think so, I certainly will not print it, even if there were no other reason than the certainty I feel that I never should long continue of an opinion different from yours on a subject which you have fully considered'.[113] Importantly, however, the passage stayed in. There was also a lively exchange between them on the time it would take for a society to acquire the altruistic instincts necessary for socialism to work. Harriet thought it could be a matter of years, while Mill believed at least a generation would be needed, telling her: 'I cannot persuade myself that you do not greatly overrate the ease of making people unselfish.'[114] Mill always believed that progress towards a cooperative economy would be gradual.

There was also a clear difference of opinion between the two on the regulation of labour: 'among other trash did you observe Hume said – "To interfere with the labour of others ... is a direct violation of the fundamental laws of society",' wrote an indignant Harriet in 1849. 'What a text this would be for an article which however no newspaper would publish. Is not the Ten Hours' Bill an "interference &c &c"?' The reason Mill did not attempt an article along these lines was not the reluctance of a newspaper editor, but the fact that he himself was ambivalent about the Ten Hours Bill, which he saw as part of the wrong-headed philanthropy of the ruling classes.[115] Whatever Mill said, Harriet never directly dictated his views, but as two intelligent, passionate people, they certainly debated them.

Mill's attitude to socialism was in any case shaped as much by the state of the national accounts as by the state of Harriet's mind. Although he was critical of many features of the industrial economy, he was also alive to its potential for raising living standards and widening opportunities. It was harder to argue for socialism when capitalism was, by and large, delivering more money, more choice and more freedom. In 1851, Britain celebrated its commercial prowess in style with the Great Exhibition, the result of the energy of Mill's walking partner, Henry Cole, twice chairman of the Society for the Encouragement of Arts, Manufactures and Commerce (now the Royal Society of Arts or RSA), and the vision of Prince Albert. The success of the Exhibition is hard to judge from this historical distance, although it is often seen as proof of Britain's economic and cultural dominance. Thirteen thousand exhibitors displayed their wares to six million visitors, and the resulting profit of £186,000 was used by Cole to purchase the land upon which the great museums of London stand today.

However, it was the structure within which the Exhibition took place which provided the most powerful emblem of England at the mid-point of the Victorian century. Designed by Joseph Paxton in four weeks, and erected in just over four months, the 2,000-foot-long Crystal Palace soared to over 100 feet in height, comfortably accommodating some of Hyde Park's most magnificent elms. John Ruskin was dismissive of the 'glittering roof', but Charles Kingsley is reported to have burst into tears on entry, declaring the experience to be 'like entering a sacred place', which in a way it was: a celebration of the holy trinity of trade, science and prosperity. Along with Dickens, Thackeray, Place and Lovett, Mill lent his name to a committee charged with promoting the Exhibition to the 'Working Classes'.[116]

This temple of commerce and progress was encased in more than a million square feet of glass, a substance which had just been freed of taxation, a true enlightenment measure. The fact that not a single pane was broken in anger says everything about the peacefulness of English life then, given what a tempting target it must have presented to anyone with a brick and a grievance. We do not know if Mill visited the Exhibition – if he did there is no mention in any surviving correspondence – but as he was in London, it seems likely. He was certain of its significance: sixteen years later he would optimistically describe it as an event which was to 'unite all nations, and inaugurate the universal substitution of commerce for war'.[117]

Of course this hope was not fully realized: the Crimean War was soon to pit the European powers into a bloody, pointless loss of life, India was a few years from revolt, and Napoleon III was already looking east. For Britain, though, the period between 1851 and 1873 was one which the historian W. L. Burn aptly dubbed 'the age of equipoise'. Economic growth was almost uninterrupted, social and political reforms advanced at a Whiggish pace, and confidence in English institutions, ideas, character and naval power was at an all-time high. The flames of socialism were barely flickering. This period, between the economic and political turbulence of the 1830s and 1840s, and the financial crisis of 1873, was, according to Asa Briggs, 'a great plateau bounded on each side by deep ravines and dangerous precipices.' The economic historian Walt Whitman Rostow similarly labelled it the 'great Victorian boom'.

This prosperous plateau was the domestic economic backdrop against which Mill wrote the works for which he would be remembered: he died just two days before the May 1873 stock market collapse in Vienna, the 'Victorian equivalent of the Wall Street crash', according to the historian Eric Hobsbawm.[118] Mill's interest was therefore in the impact of broad, inevitable movements in society – especially economic growth, democracy and mass communication – on the long-term prospects for liberty, imagination and intellect. The possibilities and challenges of deep financial ruptures, bitter class conflict and profound ideological struggle did not appear in his mature thought, in part at least because there was so little sign of them around him. In this sense, Mill was a peacetime philosopher.

He shared with most of his contemporaries the view that the freeing of trade, diffusion of knowledge, raising of educational standards and creation of wealth would create a brighter future. As Eric Hobsbawm has pointed out, the drama of Victorian Britain was not of revolution, upheaval or crisis, 'it was the drama of *progress*, that key word of the age: massive, enlightened, sure of itself, self-satisfied but above all inevitable'.[119] Mill gave a conditional welcome to this spirit of progress sweeping the nation as the 1850s advanced, endorsing the moves of friends such as Chadwick and Cole to improve public health and the quality of administration, which were being generally lauded in general society and in the artistic community. In 1852, Ford Madox Brown started painting the large canvas which famously celebrated the progress of the era, *Work*. It depicts men digging a ditch for new sewage works – although Brown had thought it was for a water pipe – posters for various kinds of improvement, perhaps for the Working Men's College, and both Frederick Maurice and Thomas Carlyle. Brown explained his desire to capture the 'British excavator, or navvy in the full swing of his activity (with his manly and picturesque costume, and with the rich glow of colour which exercise under a hot sun will impart) ... it appeared to me that he was at least as worthy of the powers of an English painter as the fisherman of the Adriatic, the peasant of the Campagna, or the Neapolitan *lazzarone*.'[120]

Unlike Ruskin, Wordsworth and Carlyle – whose contempt is visible in Madox Brown's painting – Mill was not instinctively opposed to the outward signs of progress. Railways, on the whole, were seen by him as a positive development. There was a welcome, no-nonsense directness about the age which was being felt in politics too. In an 1848 article calling for more equal electoral districts, Mill pointed out that 'we are living in an age of railroads ... Now-a-days, rather than not go straight to our object, instead of winding around the hill we even tunnel through it. The spirit of the time requires that its machinery, whether for physical or political purposes, shall be efficient ... Electoral districts are mechanical. And why not?'[121]

Mill was not then a knee-jerk critic of what Ruskin dismissed as the 'steam-whistle society', but nor was he a blind advocate of industrialization for its own sake. As an avid botanist and walker, he was acutely sensitive to what would today be called environmental concerns. Indeed, Mill has a very good claim to the title of the first 'green' economist. He was concerned that the growth of population and increase in production might create a world 'from which solitude is extirpated' and in which 'every rood of land [is] brought under cultivation ... every flowery waste or pasture ploughed up, all quadrupeds or birds which are not domesticated for man's use exterminated as his rivals for food'.[122]

While most economists, then as well as now, view a stalling in economic growth as a calamity, Mill on the contrary urged a new sensitivity to the environmental costs of continued expansion and extraction:

If the earth must lose that great portion of its pleasantness which it owes to things that the unlimited increase of wealth and population would extirpate from it, for the mere purpose of enabling it to support a larger, but not necessarily a better or a happier population, I sincerely hope, for the sake of posterity, that they will be content to be stationary, long before necessity compels them to it.[123]

Later in life, influenced no doubt by his own burgeoning collection of plants, Mill also anticipated arguments for environmental protection based on biodiversity. Just as intellectual progress relied upon a free range of ideas, so advancement in science and medicine required a wide diversity of species. 'As if anyone could presume to assert that the smallest weed may not, as knowledge advances, be found to have some property serviceable to man,' he wrote. 'The united power of the whole human race cannot reproduce a species once eradicated ... what is once done, in the extirpation of races, can never be repaired.'[124]

Mill's reverence for nature was democratic. He fought a successful letter-writing campaign to save the elm trees of Piccadilly when the road was widened, and unlike Wordsworth, who fiercely opposed the building of a railway line into the Lake District, and the 'working-class day-trippers' who would surely follow, was a fierce and lifelong advocate of access to the woods and dales on the countryside.[125] When the Archbishop of Canterbury fenced in the area around Addington Hills and 'stopped' a public road leading to them, Mill looked forward to the day when the land would revert to the state, and the 'people of Croydon sally out with axe in hand, and level the fences which have been set up to exclude them from what was morally as much their birthright as any man's estate is his'.[126] He was also optimistic that people would prove capable of making sacrifices in their own lives for the sake of generations to follow, arguing that 'the supposition, that human beings in general are not capable of feeling deep and even the deepest interest in things which they will never live to see, is a view of human nature as false as it is abject'.[127]

Mill saw economic growth as a means of providing the resources for a better, happier life for all; but also feared that, by becoming an end in itself, it threatened to remove material poverty at the price of corroding the planet and impoverishing the soul. He thought that if existing wealth was more evenly distributed, and the brake applied to population growth, sufficient material resources were already available. 'It is only in the backward countries of the world that increased production is still an important object. In those most advanced, what is economically needed is a better distribution, of which one indispensable means is a stricter restraint on population.'[128] His youthful concerns about moral and cultural 'civilization' had not abated.

Eighty-two years after the publication of the *Principles*, the economist John Maynard Keynes, who had read Mill closely, wrote: 'It will be those peoples who can keep alive, and cultivate into a fuller perfection, the art of life itself and do not sell themselves for the means of life, who will be able to enjoy the abundance when it comes.'[129] These words could have been lifted from Mill, and perhaps they were: in the *Principles*, he favourably contemplated an economic state which Ricardo and others feared, in which profits, wages and growth became stagnant. 'A stationary condition of capital and population implies no stationary state of human improvement,' he insisted. 'There would be as much scope as ever for all kinds of mental culture, and moral and social progress; as much room for improving the Art of Living and much more likelihood of its being improved, when minds cease to be engrossed by the art of getting on.'[130]

Mill had an Aristotelian ideal of a society in which learning, imagination, self-cultivation and public spirit were dominant. Such a culture would, he forecast, 'exhibit these leading features: a well-paid and affluent body of labourers; no enormous fortunes, except what were earned and accumulated during a single lifetime; but a much larger body of persons than at present, not only exempt from the coarser toils, but with sufficient leisure, both physical and mental, to cultivate freely the graces of life'. In this nirvana, 'while no one is poor, no one desires to be richer, nor has any reason to fear being thrust back, by the efforts of others to push themselves forward'.[131]

Unlike many of his fellow economists, Mill placed political economy firmly in a human context. Economics was our servant, not our master, and he painted an attractive picture of what a 'post-materialist' society might look and feel like. But he lacked an account of how his sketchy version of progress was to be promoted. Education, very broadly defined, played a large part in Mill's thinking, with 'better minds' educating the mass into 'better things', and new forms of economic organization fuelling the growth of 'social sympathies'. In the end, the vital ingredient in the transition to a better society seemed to be 'character'; a better society could only be built with better people.

However, because Mill never finished – indeed, never started – his proposed 'Science of the Formation of Character' (the 'Ethology'), his account of social change is incomplete.[132] He was a penetrating critic of contemporary trends, and an inspiring sketcher of the future, but had less to say on how to get from here to there. This was because he was, in the end, more liberal than progressive. Mill wanted people to be different – and better – but he shuddered at systems designed to force them to be so. Explaining to Harriet the importance of an essay on the subject of 'liberty', he complained in 1855 that 'opinion tends to encroach more & more on liberty, & almost all the projects of social reformers of these days are really *liberticide* – Comte, particularly so'.[133] Mill hoped that people would use their growing liberty to cultivate the arts of life and support each other, and he believed they could be encouraged to do so. In the end, however, it was up to them. Presented with the choice between freely chosen selfishness and coerced cooperation, Mill unhesitatingly backed freedom.

Individual character, moral cultivation and freedom of action were all more important to Mill than material accumulation. The most powerful sections of his *Principles* are not those outlining the laws of economics, but those describing their limitations. Reading Montaigne's *Essays*, he underlined a single sentence: 'The poverty of material goods is easily cured; for poverty of the soul there is no cure.'[134] Mill agreed with the first half of the sentence, but not the second. Curing the 'poverty of the soul' was, for him, the real definition of progress – and the animating impulse for the remainder of his life's work.

CHAPTER TEN

A Seven-Year Blessing (1852–8)

➤<

'At present I expect very little from any plans which aim at improving even the economical state of the people by purely economical or political means,' Mill wrote at the opening of the 1850s. 'We have come, I think, to a period, when progress, even of a political kind, is coming to a halt, by reason of the low intellectual & moral state of all classes. Great improvements in education ... are the only thing to which I should look for permanent good.'[1]

Following his interventions over France, the success of his *Principles* and his marriage to Harriet, Mill spent most of the 1850s in retreat from public and social life. Chartism was dead, reform was off the agenda, and the moderate Whigs were ascendant in Parliament: politics, according to Eric Hobsbawm, was in a state of 'hibernation'. The economy, meanwhile, was putting on yet another growth spurt: exports grew more rapidly in the first seven years of the 1850s than in any other period of British history. According to one contemporary observer, a proposed bill against Sunday trading 'created five times more popular agitation than all the reform measures united'. The great Californian and Australian gold discoveries – an 'electric impulse to the entire business world', according to *The Times* – were stimulating an explosion of capital investment and trade. What Adam Smith's mentor, Francis Hutcheson, lauded as the 'calm desire of wealth' was the principal animating force of society.[2]

The prospect of further parliamentary reform was rekindled, albeit briefly, in 1853, the year after Lord Aberdeen's government had restored the Whigs to power after Lord Derby's short Conservative administration, made famous for its anonymity by the Duke of Wellington's response to the list of ministers: 'Who? Who?' Mill's reaction, however, was tepid. His fears of mass democracy were at their peak: in private correspondence he worried repeatedly about the dangers of minority viewpoints being 'swamped' by an influx of MPs from the working classes, and he did not bother to publish his three suggestions for reform: extending the existing electoral franchise to women; further redistribution of parliamentary seats towards more equally sized electorates, and the introduction of an educational qualification requiring all voters to possess basic abilities in 'reading, writing and arithmetic'.[3]

His worries about giving the working classes the vote would only begin to lessen on his discovery, in 1858, of proportional representation. For the moment he confided to Harriet that 'it is very doubtful if lowering the franchise will not do more harm than good'. It was also at this point that Mill also began to share, among selected correspondents, his views on the dangers of the secret ballot, a proposition he believed had 'sunk to far inferior men' and which 'would now be a step backward instead of forward'.[4]

In any case, the outbreak of war in the Crimea killed off any prospect of immediate parliamentary reform and allowed Mill to focus his attention on his various works in progress, including the *Autobiography*, in which he wrote: 'I am now convinced that no great improvements in the lot of mankind are possible until a great change takes place in the fundamental constitutions of their modes of thought.'[5] He was also publicly silent on the war, but in private was an enthusiast for the enterprise, mostly because of his disapproval of Russia in general and the expansionist Tsar Nicholas in particular. 'There is perfect unanimity among all parties here & the war feeling seems to pervade everybody in a manner which nobody thought would ever happen again,' he told Harriet. 'I am glad of it.' There was an almost jingoistic tone to another marital missive:

'The English have shown pluck in spite of all the Times could do.' (*The Times* opposed the war.) However, Mill did regret the consequent rehabilitation of the new ally, Napoleon III, who was feted during his visit to London in April 1855 with Empress Eugenie. To Mill he remained a 'crafty French despot', and his red-carpet treatment 'exhibited the whole people of all ranks in England in the most contemptible and disgusting light'.[6]

With his reputation as the nation's leading public intellectual now firmly established on the twin pillars of the *Logic* and the *Principles*, Mill was able to eschew topical journalism and focus on more durable concerns. In the last twenty-five years of his life he published just fifty-eight newspaper pieces, compared to 368 in the previous quarter-century.[7] The peripatetic *Westminster Review* had passed out of William Hickson's hands to John Chapman in 1851, after Mill once again declined to take on his old publication. Chapman was to be a competent and committed editor for the next forty-three years, and launched the career of Marian Evans (aka George Eliot), his co-editor, lodger and mistress. It was Marian who persuaded him to keep trying for Mill's engagement and endorsement, though Mill was uncertain. He was supportive in principle, given that the review was the 'only organ through which really advanced opinions can get access to the public', and offered some constructive criticism of Chapman's new prospectus, including the advice to avoid the term 'Philosophic Reformers' which was 'a worn-out & gone-by expression; it had a meaning twenty years ago'. He also sent a warning about his own desire to contribute to the *Westminster* under the 'new management', which would 'entirely depend on the opinion I form of it after seeing it in operation'. To make Chapman even more nervous, he then sent another note just as his first edition was going to press: 'The first number will show what meaning the writers attach to the word Progress, & how far the review will be an organ of it.'[8] In the end, Mill supplied just one article to the *Westminster* during the 1850s, although he would become more supportive, both editorially and financially, in his later years.[9]

The 1850s were thus outwardly a decade of relative quiet for Mill.

He skirmished with the intuitionists again in a review of Whewell's lectures on *The Elements of Morality* – which contained 'an apparatus for converting ... prevailing opinions, on matters of morality, into reasons for themselves', and welcomed a new tranche of volumes of Grote's *History of Greece* in the *Edinburgh Review* in 1853, admiring the tone as much as the content of the work. In private he rated Grote as significantly superior to the intellectual 'dwarf' Macaulay because 'instead of striving to astonish he strives to comprehend & explain'.[10] He penned a brief article of support for civil service reform in 1854 but published nothing in 1855. Across the following two years, 1856 and 1857, Mill published just five articles – and four of these were on botany, running cumulatively to just ten pages in the *Phytologist*. A changing of the guard at the *Edinburgh* in 1855 also made him disinclined to continue publishing on its Whiggish pages. The editor's chair had been taken by Henry Reeve, formerly of the hated *Times*. 'Reeve is editor of the Edinburgh! It is indeed fallen,' Mill lamented to Harriet. 'For us it is again a complete exclusion.'[11] In fact Mill would write again for the *Edinburgh*, but long after Harriet's death.

But Mill was hardly inactive – his was a productive hibernation. On top of his India House labours, he was beginning to draft a series of works which would be published only years later – including *On Liberty*, *Utilitarianism*, the *Autobiography*, and two of the *Three Essays on Religion*. Much of this work was undertaken in the new marital home, which Mill and Harriet had deliberately chosen for its distance from the London social scene. It was in 'a quiet corner' overlooking Blackheath, seven miles from the city centre. Helen, now twenty years old, and her older brother Algernon, or 'Haji', completed the household. With the exception of their old friend William Fox, now a widower, their rule for invitations seems to have been 'English need not apply': the only other known visitors were the Italian historian and statesman Pasquale Villiari, Theodor Gomperz, Mill's German admirer, and Louis Blanc, the French socialist. They also extended an invitation to Giuseppe Mazzini, the erstwhile *London and Westminster* contributor and now Italian revolutionary leader, as 'among the few persons to whom we can sincerely say that they may feel sure of being welcome'.[12]

Marriage had apparently done little to subdue Mill's feelings for Harriet. At home with her, he would always make the early evening tea and improvise on the piano, for her ears only. The atmosphere was of almost unnatural calm. Haji later recalled of Mill that he 'never knew him to utter a cross word or show impatience in her regard, not to demur to any expressed wish on her part; and, it must be added,' – indeed it must, given Harriet's posthumous reputation – 'she no less considered his wishes in all things'. When they were apart, Mill's letters crackled with love and longing. She was more than ever 'my own dearest one! ... dearest dearest angel', 'my own precious darling wife' and 'my perfect one'.[13] If Mill was travelling without Harriet, his first stop was always the post office. 'How I long for the first sight of that dear handwriting,' he wrote; to him it was '*the* pleasure of absence'. For Mill, 'words of love in absence are as they always were, what keeps the blood going in the veins'. From Montpellier, in 1854, he made a request more usually associated with adolescent crushes: 'Will my darling kiss her next letter just in the middle of the first line of writing – the kiss will come safe & I shall savour it. Adieu *darling*.' The middle-aged, supposedly dry, rationalist philosopher signed off his letters like the lovestruck youngster he remained throughout the marriage: 'adieu with a thousand loves', or 'a thousand loves & blessings & kisses' or 'kisses to my own divine treasure'.[14] Depending on his location, other languages were sometimes deployed: 'Adieu again mio bene', 'Mille mille baci' and 'Addio con tutti I baci possibili – ah dearest how I do love you'.[15]

With Mill's infatuation for Harriet came, necessarily, insecurity too. Even when she became his wife, he worried that he might lose his appeal for her. Four years after their marriage, he reported 'a horrible dream ... I had come back to her & she was sweet & loving like herself at first, but presently she took a complete dislike to me saying that I was changed much for the worse – I am terribly afraid sometimes lest she should think so, not that I see any cause for it, but because I know how deficient I am in self consciousness & self observation.'[16] There is more than a touch of naivety in the way Mill expressed his attachment to Harriet, and it is very easy to react cynically to his exuberance, but at the same time, the romantic, semi-tragic love he felt for her, sustained over quarter of a century, is inspiring. What is beyond dispute is that Mill was one of the most passionate of all the great Victorians.

Now that he had Harriet, Mill broke off or dramatically reduced contact with many of his friends and colleagues, including Grote, Chadwick and Bain – who greatly missed his walks to work with Mill. Between 1849 and 1857, Mill appears not to have written to either of the Grotes, and in the same period Chadwick received just seven letters, compared to almost a hundred in the fourteen years after Harriet's death. Mill wrote to Harriet in southern France, where she had retreated from the English winter in early 1854, that he had 'seen nobody this long while, enjoying a happy immunity from calls'.[17]

While few personal letters were being written, Mill's correspondence had 'swelled to a considerable bulk', as organizations and individuals around the world sought his opinion, endorsement or advice. The new Poor Law Reform Association wanted his backing so badly that they were willing to change their statement of aims to meet some of his objections, but to no avail. The Neophyte Writers' Society invited him to sit as a member of its Honorary Council, and was rebuffed in terms which show that even as a maturing liberal, Mill had partisan bones: 'Now I set no value whatever on writing for its own sake & have much less respect for the literary craftsman than for the manual labourer except so far as he uses his powers in promoting what I consider true & just.'[18]

Nevertheless Mill's growing fame did not go to his head. He refused to be photographed for an 1858 volume, the National Gallery of Photographic Portraits: 'I do not think,' he told the compiler, Herbert Fry, 'my personal appearance can be a matter of any interest to the general public'.[19] He had already turned down the offer of an Irish parliamentary seat, made to him by Frederick Lucas, leader of the Tenant League and founder of *The Tablet*, citing the incompatibility of a political career and his work with the East India Company.[20] It does not seem that he was very seriously tempted: his episodic disgruntlement with politics was at its peak in the 1850s.

With Britain torpid and France tyrannical, Mill found his attention drawn increasingly across the Atlantic. America had been mostly out of his thoughts since the Tocqueville essays of the 1830s and when he had considered the former colony, it was usually as a standing warning against avarice. In the *Principles*, he suggested that in America, one sex was 'devoted to dollar-hunting' and the other to 'breeding dollar-hunters', a jibe which was taken out, but only for the sixth edition, of 1865. He had also given short shrift in 1848 to a reviewer in the *North American Review*, who took issue with his advocacy of equality for women. The tone of the piece, Mill wrote, was 'really below contempt. But I fear that a country where institutions profess to be founded on equality, and which yet maintains the slavery of black men and of all women, will be one of the last to relinquish that other servitude.'[21] Now, after the Napoleonic counter-revolution in his beloved France, Mill began to see the 'great democratic experiment' of America in a more favourable light. A convention of women held in Massachussetts, calling for women's rights, greatly pleased him, he told Harriet, not least because it was 'outspoken like America, not frightened and servile like England'. As the decade progressed, his enthusiasm for America grew. By 1854, echoing the view of *The Economist* that the eventual global superiority of the US was 'as certain as next eclipse', he told an (admittedly American) correspondent that he was 'one of those who believe that America is destined to give instruction to the world, not only practically, as she has long done, but in speculation also'. It probably helped that Mill's works were selling well stateside, with his *Principles*, published by Little Brown, proving particularly successful. In 1857, he was elected a Foreign Honorary Member of the American Academy of Arts and Sciences, filling the place left vacant on the death of Sir William Hamilton, upon whose work he would later launch a book-length attack. 'There is in America a public for ... speculations,' Mill wrote back, accepting the honour, 'at least as thoughtful and more earnest than that of England'.[22] Four years later, America would play much more than a speculative role: for Mill, the Civil War would be a pivotal moment in world history, and in the struggle for liberty.

For the moment, though, Mill was concerned to get as many of his own thoughts and as much of Harriet's wisdom down on paper before one or both of them died. This was not paranoia or pessimism; for much of the decade, one or the other of them was seriously ill. They were constantly travelling to the Continent, very often separately, in search of health cures. In the autumn of 1853 they were in Nice when Harriet suffered a severe haemorrhage of her lung. A local doctor, Dr Cecil Gurney, treated and – Mill believed – saved her. In 1860, in a strange intertwining of fates, Haji would marry Ellen Gurney, the physician's sister, only for her to die four years later.[23] Once Harriet had recovered, she and Mill moved on to Hyères, from where Mill, having run out of sick leave, had to head north. On the way home, he missed a coach connection and spent the day hiding from the bitter cold at the Hotel de l'Europe in Avignon. 'This inn (l'Europe) seems good,' he told Harriet, 'plenty of rooms au premier & an easy staircase ... good coffee & excellent butter which was the only thing bad at Marseilles.'[24] Mill would bring Harriet to the hotel five years later, in their darkest hour.

Soon it was Mill's turn to feel the brush of death. While Harriet steadily gained strength on the Mediterranean, Mill arrived back in London at the beginning of January 1854 in a weakened state. He told Harriet that his colleagues at India House were delighted to see him, 'there being a general impression that I was so ill that there was no knowing when I might come back (or perhaps if I should ever come back at all)'. In fact he was seriously unwell, coughing blood, sweating copiously at night and with an intermittently racing pulse. Like his father and two brothers before him, Mill had tuberculosis. Eventually the doctor Mill shared with Queen Victoria, Sir James Clark, confirmed the diagnosis. It was not a shock: fourteen years earlier, as his brother James lay dying, Mill had confided quietly to Caroline Fox: 'I expect to die of consumption.' In his diary entry for 3 April 1854, Mill wrote: 'I look upon it as a piece of excellent good fortune to have the whole summer before one to die in.'[25]

From this point on, even though he would in fact live another two decades, Mill felt himself to be in a race with death. While Harriet was away, he began a diary in which he attempted to record one useful thought each day. One was deeply personal: 'I feel bitterly how I have procrastinated in the sacred duty of fixing in writing, so that it may not die with me, everything that I have in my mind which is capable of assisting the destruction of error and prejudice and the growth of just feelings and opinions.' At the same time, he was dismissive of his efforts to date: 'I seem to have frittered away the working years of life in mere preparatory trifles' – an accusation from which, of all people, Mill was surely immune. The previous year he had urged Harriet, 'We have got to finish the best we have to say, and not only that, but publish it while we are alive.'[26] Now publication was a secondary issue. Capturing his thoughts was the priority.

Mill, typically, ignored any advice to rest, believing, as Bentham had, that exercise was the cure for most ills. Whenever possible, he continued his long Sunday walks and he embarked on a course of treatment recommended by Dr Francis Ramadge, author of *Consumption Curable*, which involved blowing into a metal trumpet-like device for half an hour three times a day, in order to keep the lungs expanded for longer and prevent the growth of new tubercules. Mill considered Ramadge's theories as good as any other. 'I certainly think,' he told Harriet, 'any person would be very foolish to let themselves die of consumption without having tried him & his treatment.' In the meantime, he struggled to maintain order on the domestic front, relying on Harriet to direct affairs from afar. It was she who instructed him how to handle a dispute with a neighbour involving the brief colonization of an outhouse by rats. The need for constant reordering of candles, soap and meat was another source of anxiety; Mill wondered at one point if Kate, the housekeeper, was cheating him. Harriet's status as head of household matters was made clear in one letter: 'Should the bills now be paid?', asked the nation's premier economist.[27]

At any event, the walking or blowing seems to have worked and Mill made a remarkable recovery. In April, he was not strong enough to cross to Paris to meet Harriet and accompany her home, but by June he was touring Normandy and Brittany. While he would suffer the usual complaints of age, consumption never threatened him again as it had in 1853 and 1854. With his health renewed, Mill made the only serious foray into public policy of his married years. In March 1854 he had been asked by Sir Charles Trevelyan to support the plan he and Sir Stafford Northcote had devised for the introduction of competitive entrance examinations for the civil service – a reform which was to change the character of British government: while the Northcote–Trevelyan plan was being examined, Charles Dickens was drafting his description of the pointless 'Circumlocution Office', an unsurpassed parody of the civil service, that would feature in *Little Dorrit*. Overlooking the dubious family connection – Trevelyan was Macaulay's brother-in-law – Mill was sufficiently enthusiastic about a change which could 'raise the character not only of the public service but of Society itself' that at Trevelyan's request he even removed from his supporting letter a criticism of the proposal that candidates be required to produce a certificate of baptism. With this exception, the proposal for an examination was a straight piece of Benthamism – the great man himself had described exams as the perfect devices for 'maximising aptitude' and 'minimising expense'.[28]

By this point, Mill had got the *Autobiography* – referred to as 'The Life' by himself and Harriet – into a 'perfectly publishable state'. The next priority was a series of essays on the themes which most animated them. In February 1854, Mill reminded Harriet of the list that they had compiled together: 'Differences of character (nation, race, age, sex, temperament). Love. Education of tastes. Religion de l'Avenir. Plato. Slander. Foundation of morals. Utility of religion. Socialism. Liberty. Doctrine that causation is will. To these I have now added from your letter: Family, & Conventional.' Harriet's influence extended to the setting of work priorities: 'I want my angel to tell me what should be the next essay written. I have done all I can on the subject she last gave me.'[29] Almost all of the listed subjects would be tackled. The only one entirely missing from Mill's publication record is 'Love', which is a shame. It would have been better to have heard from him on love than on free will, a subject which Mill had already addressed in the *Logic* and went on to tackle at book-length in *An Examination of Sir William Hamilton's Philosophy*.

The other essays drafted in the mid-1850s, especially *On Liberty*, *Utilitarianism* and *Thoughts on Parliamentary Reform*, an overture to *Representative Government*, were deliberately written as titrations of thought rather than treatises. As Mill told Harriet, they would be published, 'if not in the best form for popular effect, yet in the state of concentrated thought – a sort of mental pemican [*sic*], which thinkers, when there are any after us, may nourish themselves with & then dilute for other people'. In his 1854 diary, he tested one pemmican:

Quality as well as quantity of happiness is to be considered; less of a higher kind is preferable to more of a lower. The test of quality is the preference given by those who are acquainted with both. Socrates would rather choose to be Socrates dissatisfied than to be a pig satisfied. The pig probably would not, but then the pig knows only one side of the question: Socrates knows both.[30]

This metaphor, slightly adapted, would find its way into *Utilitarianism*. It is a playful image and another piece of counter-evidence to the wisdom received by too many commentators – Isaiah Berlin, who perhaps should have known better, lamented Mill's 'total lack of humour.' Mill had a genuine appreciation of the value of amusement; indeed, he thought it 'a great defect in a character to be without lightness ... A certain infusion of the laughing philosopher ... is a prodigious help towards bearing the evils of life, and I should think has saved many a person from going mad.'[31] But it is true that his own writing does not provoke spontaneous laughter in the reader; he was a very long way from the comic brilliance of Bagehot, Lamb or Hazlitt. Nor could anyone claim Mill as a raconteur – he was not a natural at the art of 'table talk', so highly regarded among the Victorian chattering classes. But he was not incapable of banter. Caroline Fox described a dinner conversation about Christian names, in which Mill said: 'Now, you see, I should have the protection of St. John the Evangelist, and the Baptist, and many others; but as they have so much to do, it is well to court the favour of some more obscure saints'. He was also perfectly capable of enjoying the wit of others. According to Bain, Mill made 'numerous sallies that amused the moment, as well as amateur wit usually does', and added that 'his enjoyment of a good joke was intense'. Bain specifically recounted him bursting into laughter at a poster of 'General Tom Thumb' dressed as Romulus, naked except for a spear and shield.[32] Mill, then, was not a prime example of the 'laughing philosopher', but neither was he a sourpuss. Nevertheless the false image of Mill as a dry, forbidding individual remains to this day.

Unfortunately, Mill had little to smile about in 1854. Throughout the year, the couple's pattern of alternating illness continued and a planned joint trip to northern France was undertaken by Mill alone. The East India Company had raised his salary by £200 a year, perhaps fearing, and if so correctly, that he was considering retirement. During the French trip he scouted for possible retirement locations, on top of his usual activities of botanizing and appraising butter quality: Brittany boasted 'very good butter even in the smallest places', but in Normandy, he sadly reported, 'it is seldom good & I have never yet found it very good'. All the butter consumption helped him to regain some of the weight lost earlier in the year: by 5 July he weighed 67 kilos, two more than when he left home; a week later another kilo had been added to his lanky frame: 'It shews how much weight I must have lost before, as these six pounds make not the smallest perceptible difference to the eye.'[33]

On his return, he plunged into his India House work, so that there could be no obstacle to a planned winter escape to Italy and Greece. His only published article, in November 1854, was a two-paragraph letter in the *Morning Post* on the patchy application of new laws intended to protect women from domestic violence. As the departure date approached, however, it became clear that Harriet was not up to the rigours of such a tour and she established herself instead in Torquay, with Helen for company. Mill managed to get a sick leave certificate for eight months' absence signed by Dr Clark.[34] There is no doubt that Mill was far from well, but the length of the leave – as well as his ability to undertake some fairly gruelling expeditions during his absence – suggests that the Directors of the East India Company were being unusually lenient in order to keep Mill in their employ. In any case, he worked with such awesome efficiency that if necessary he could do a year's work in a few months.

Mill left Harriet on 7 December 1854 and set out for the Continent the following morning. His solo adventures began badly; on arriving in Boulogne in December 1854, after a rough crossing, he immediately vomited. Once recovered, he headed quickly to the relative warmth of Bordeaux and then meandered across the south of France. He passed through Avignon, which he now saw was a 'splendidly beautiful place', and reported to Harriet that 'the people were going about everywhere so cheerful & gay this fine fête day'.[35] His route then took him through Bordeaux, Toulouse, Montpellier and Marseilles – where he sailed for Genoa. By mid-January he was in Rome and chanced upon Frederick Lucas, the friend who had tried to persuade him to enter Parliament a few years earlier, and who now served as an agreeable companion for touring the city's monuments and artistic glories.

For Mill, as for many of the Victorians – Gladstone, Browning, Dickens and especially Ruskin – Italy was inspirational territory.

During his Roman sojourn, his enthusiasm for a liberal polemic intensified. 'The more I think of the plan of a volume on Liberty,' he told Harriet, 'the more likely it seems to me that it will be read and will make a sensation. The title itself with any known name to it would sell into an edition. We must cram into it as much as possible of what we wish not to leave unsaid.' In his *Autobiography*, Mill recalled that it was 'in mounting the steps of the Capitol, in January 1855, that the thought first arose of converting it into a volume'. His recollection was faulty, however. At the time he told Harriet that the thought solidified in his mind as he returned to his hotel after a day during which he visited the Vatican; his first recorded visit to the Capitol was in fact some days later.[36] Perhaps it suited Mill's self-image better to suppose that *On Liberty*, his greatest work, was inspired by the democratic symbolism of the Capitol rather than the sacred incense of Catholicism.

Mill spent a total of two and a half months in Italy, including both the outbound and return legs of his travels, and spent most of his time on aesthetic pleasures, especially art and church architecture. From Naples he diagnosed himself as being 'in a complete nervous state from the sensation of the beauty I am living among'. He was appalled that the King of Naples and the Pope had locked away various Venuses from public view on the grounds of decency, asking: 'If these things are done in Italy what shall we come to next?' Later he reported that there were 'so many fine statues & pictures all over Florence that I could soon get into the kind of feeling I had at Rome of being bathed in art.' His favourite Titian was an *Assumption* in Milan and he described the painter as 'of the earth earthy'. He admired Mantegna's frescoes, and the later Raphael's 'peculiar glow of colour'. He visited churches and cathedrals with the zeal of a pilgrim – although for him the pleasures were aesthetic and anthropological – and he much preferred to view paintings in churches than in private galleries. He especially enjoyed services for the blessing of lambs at the basilica of St Agnes outside Porta Pia and for the blessing of horses in St Antony's church, Rome. Vespers at Santa Maria del Popole were overshadowed by the organist 'trilling away like a comic opera', but it must have been better than the music played during the Palm Sunday service at Messina cathedral, which a disgruntled Mill left part way through.[37]

At La Scala, Milan, Mill 'admired exceedingly' a performance of Meyerbeer's *Le Prophète* which was 'got up in the most splendid style ... is a very shewy opera, full of pomp and spectacle'. The artistic delights of Italy, and a nostalgic return to La Sirena, the inn in Sorrento which Mill and Harriet had discreetly visited sixteen years earlier, were followed by more testing travel. The next leg of Mill's tour, through Sicily and Greece, gave him the chance to see for himself the sites of the battles and orations he had studied in his youth. He stood on the Pnyx, the hill where Demosthenes and Pericles spoke, and the frogs in Attica reminded him of Aristophanes' play in which a chorus of the creatures serenades Bacchus. 'What light it throws on Greek history to know', he enthused to Harriet, 'that Acro Corinth is seen as a great object from all these heights [around Athens]'. The journeys around the coast of Sicily and across the Peloponnese, however, were demanding. Mules were required for much of the travelling and Mill's determined botanizing in Sicily resulted in an infection in his thumb, which had been jabbed by a thorn. Near the Turkish border, Mill and Mr Dawson, a travelling companion he had met in Athens, needed the protection of ten soldiers against bandits, and for much of the journey Mill's accommodation was a hayloft or basic inn. Undaunted, he continued his search for decent butter, and was perturbed to discover that there was none available at all in Catania: 'I note as a curious fact, that when I asked for butter I was told none was to be had'. Fortunately, 'the butter at Syracuse was excellent'.[38]

In Corfu, Mill was welcomed by the Chief Secretary of the government of the Ionian Islands, George Bowen, who was a former fellow of Brasenose College and, according to Mill, had 'much of the Logic almost by heart'. The Residentship of Cefalonia [*sic*] was likely to become available, and both Bowen and the Lord High Commissioner of the Ionian Islands, Sir John Young, tried to persuade Mill to accept the post. He and Harriet seriously considered the offer. 'I do not believe there is a more beautiful place in the world & few more agreeable,' he wrote, 'the burthen of it to us would be that we could not ... have the perfectly quiet life, with ourselves & our own thoughts, which we prefer to any other.' It seems that climate was at least as big a factor as privacy, though. Harriet told her brother that though 'much tempted' by the offer, 'I do not think we shall accept it, we both dread the heat which is said to be excessive in the summer.'[39]

For the moment, though, the heat in the Ionian islands was manageable, and Mill's stamina allowed him to cover many more miles than most healthy men a decade younger could have managed. 'It is curious', he wrote, 'that when I am too tired or weak to do anything else I can climb mountains'. In fact his greatest enemies, throughout Sicily and rural Greece, were small, industrious insects and for most of the journey the middle-aged philosopher was flea-ridden. From Andritzena he reported that 'during the night they danced a saraband on my face ... In the morning while I was sponging myself nearly a dozen of the enemy gathered on my legs & feet ... One little rascal had the impudence to bite my hand to my very face ... I feel like a horse tormented by flies'. The Greek fleas were more formidable than their Sicilian allies, being both more numerous and aggressive. Mill counter-attacked 'early in the morning before they are awake'.[40]

Mill was glad to escape his tiny adversaries and return to Italy, where he dawdled in Florence, meeting a new correspondent Pasquale Villari, the historian and politician who, although 'a little dark man', greatly impressed him with his learning and curiosity. Mill crossed the Alps in a covered, horse-drawn two-person sledge, with bright sunshine glaring off the snowfields, and then hastened from Lucerne to Paris, where he met Harriet in the third week of June. He was back at his desk in Leadenhall Street a couple of weeks later. As a health cure, the trip could not be counted a success: at various points his digestive system was in a parlous state, and he was often coughing blood. At the end of the trip he weighed ten stone – exactly the same as when he departed.[41] The fact that Mill was able to undertake such a strenuous tour at all, however, shows the overall robustness of his health.

Mill and Harriet had been apart for seven months, a long period of voluntary separation given that they had been forced by circumstances to live apart for so many years. In fact, of the eighteen months from January 1854 to June 1855, the couple were together for just six. Mill also took a walking holiday, without Harriet, in each of the following three summers. Illness was the principal reason for the separations, but not the only one. There was no obvious reason why Mill could not have spent his long 1854–5 sick leave with Harriet on the south coast of England and he was often conscious of the loss of their time together: he nearly turned around a day into his trip and a month later he urged Harriet: 'let us make what we can of what human life we have got', before adding, 'which I am hardly doing by being away from you'.[42] One of the caricatures of the couple – then and today – is of a man helplessly twisting under a woman's spell, but Mill's willingness to disappear for months at a time is hard to fit into this picture.

Retirement from India House would of course have given them much more time together, and was constantly on their mind. They wanted to live abroad – probably in France – but were worried about access to decent bookshops.[43] They also decided that they needed a guaranteed income of £500 a year, and could only be sure of £420 on the basis of their existing savings. If Mill was forced into retirement on grounds of ill-health, the company would be obliged to pay him £800 a year, two-thirds of his current salary. If he left of his own accord, however, the level of his pension was at the discretion of the Directors. So Mill continued his commute to Leadenhall Street.

Mill and Harriet were being hugely conservative in their financial planning. For one thing, there could have been little doubt that the East India Company would give Mill some sort of pension, given his long and loyal service: certainly enough to make up the £80 shortfall from their target retirement income. He was also receiving reasonable royalties from the continued sales of the *Logic* and the *Principles*: his book earnings for 1853 were £375, 'pretty well to have come in', he remarked to Harriet, 'from writings of which money was not at all the object'. Even the political economy essays, published a decade earlier, continued to sell: 'this is encouraging', he wrote, 'since, if that sells, I should think anything we put our name to would sell.'[44] With hindsight, he must have regretted the decision not to retire early as Harriet would live just a few months past his eventual departure in 1858. But Mill was hardly the first, or last, to make such a mistake.

Following his Italian and Greek adventures, Mill was even more determined to present his and Harriet's ideas in a form which would have the most practical impact. After all his months in the cradles of two ancient civilizations, Mill was now in workmanlike mode. He had read and enjoyed Goethe's *Italienische Reise* (*Italian Journey*), but thought the poet had made the mistake of idolizing the past. It was 'impossible', he wrote,

for a modern, with all the good will in the world, to tightlace himself into the dimensions of an ancient. Every modern thinker has so much wider a horizon, & there is so much deeper a soil accumulated on the surface of human nature by the ploughings it has undergone ... We all need to be blacksmiths or ballet dancers with good stout arms or legs, useful to do what we have got to do, useful to fight with at times – we cannot be Apollos & Venuses just yet.[45]

In her husband's absence, Harriet had followed his example and fallen out with her own family – although in her case with some cause. The trustees of John Taylor's estate were Harriet's brother-in-law Arthur Ley and Mill's colleague and friend William Thornton. In early 1855 neither seemed fit for the task: Thornton was very ill, possibly mortally so, and Ley, Harriet knew, was a wife-beating drunk. Harriet wanted Ley to resign as a trustee, but Caroline, his wife, remained loyal. Fortunately Thornton recovered, and the immediate crisis abated, but Harriet's relationships with her mother and Caroline remained distant. Mrs Hardy nevertheless seems to have remained fond of Mill, even if relations with Harriet were strained, writing to her in concerned tones on reading of his ill-health on retirement: 'If change of air were needful to him, I hope I need not say how glad I should be to see him as my guest. Pray give my love to him and tell him so. I know it would be in vain to ask you – you have not enough interest in me to visit me.'[46]

With Mill and Harriet now both estranged from their families, they lived a quiet life when they were at home, working throughout 1855 and 1856 on their manuscripts and entertaining the very select group of friends who were given passes to Blackheath. Theodor Gomperz, Mill's German disciple, described his master's mode of life in adulatory terms:

Mill was always the same – in his office at India House, buried under maps and files, at dinner with his friends, on top of a mountain, at the Political Economy Club, or in the wilds with this botanical box – his mind effortlessly drawn to the highest flight of ideas. At all times willing to enter in an interchange of question and answer, he yet was modest, and as unselfish as he was unaffected.[47]

At the end of 1856, the Mills' home became their own for the first time since their marriage. Haji had already left and now Helen broke out of her mother's orbit, pursuing a career as an actress, unfortunately with more enthusiasm than success. Harriet was deeply unsure about the move, not least because of the social opprobrium attached to the profession. Helen worked as 'Miss Trevor' and her identity was a well-kept secret. The separation between the two previously inseparable women was far from easy and there was a good deal of tetchiness on both sides. 'I wish you to be wholly uninfluenced by me in all your future proceedings,' Harriet wrote. 'I would rather die than go through again your reproaches for spoiling your life. Whatever happens let your mode of life be your own choice henceforth.'[48] Helen joined a theatre group in Scotland, but after a promising start, struggled to secure decent parts, at one point being reduced to the role of a singing pantomime fairy. In 1857, Harriet braved a Scottish February to visit her daughter, and was rewarded with another bout of ill-health. Mill caught the mail train to Edinburgh, brought her home and then installed her in Brighton where she slowly regained some strength.

By this time, Mill had been promoted at the India House to his father's old position of Chief Examiner, pushing his salary up to £2,000 a year in March 1856. His elevation ought to have signalled a reduction in his writing duties, as he had moved to a strictly supervisory role: in each of the previous twenty years, Mill's political dispatches on behalf of the Company had filled two huge volumes, each 'five or six inches thick'.[49] But any hopes of a gentle end to his career were extinguished on 10 May 1857, in the Indian town of Meerut, forty miles to the north-east of Delhi. The Indian 'Mutiny', sparked by the refusal of sepoys to use the cartridges for the new Enfield rifle – the grease for which contained forbidden animal fats – spread across northern India, until the British managed to regain control at the end of the year. Massacres took place on both sides, although of course at home it was the Indian siege of Lucknow, and the slaughter of women and children at Kanpur, rather than the British decimation of the population of Allahabad or the 'peppering away at niggers', which was 'enjoyed amazingly' by British officers in Delhi, that made the news.[50]

The loyalty of the majority of Indian troops to the East India Company was arguably the single most important factor in the suppression of the uprising. But the eruption of violence, which only finally petered out in 1859, was seen by the political classes as final proof that the country now had to be controlled directly from Westminster. Although it was doomed, the Company did not go without a fight, however, and Mill was in the last ditch. The defence he drafted at the request of the Directors has surely the sharpest introduction of any state paper in British history, contrasting the record of the Company in India with the lamentable record of the British government in America, and submitting:

That your Petitioners, at their own expense, and by the agency of their own civil and military servants, originally acquired its magnificent empire in the East. That the foundations of this empire were laid by your Petitioners, at that time neither aided nor controlled by Parliament, at the same period at which a succession of administrations under the control of Parliament were losing to the Crown of Great Britain another great empire on the opposite side of the Atlantic.[51]

The Board of Directors and other officials were delighted with Mill's efforts, sufficiently so that at least one of their number took credit for them, much to Thornton's annoyance, and Mill's wry amusement. Thornton recalled:

I could scarcely believe my ears when one of the Directors, alluding to the petition, spoke of it as having been written by a certain other official who was sitting by his side, adding, after a moment's pause, 'with the assistance, as he understood, of Mr. Mill', likewise present. As soon as the Court broke up, I burst into Mill's room, boiling over with indignation, and exclaiming, 'What an infamous shame !' and no doubt adding a good deal more that followed in natural sequence on such an exordium. 'What's the matter?' replied Mill, as soon as he could get a word in, 'M— (the Director) was quite right. The petition was the joint work of — and myself.' 'How can you be so perverse?' I retorted. 'You know that you wrote every word of it.' 'No,' rejoined Mill, 'you are mistaken: one whole line on the second page was put in by M—.'[52]

Even Mill's eloquence could not prevent the Company's extinction, although the Derby government, which replaced Lord Palmerston's administration before the Bill dissolving the Company became law, did adopt some of Mill's subsequent suggestions, including the creation of an arms'-length advisory council. India House, the imposing HQ in Leadenhall Street in which two generations of Mills had toiled, was unceremoniously pulled down in 1860. Mill's petition was written as an employee of the Company, of course, but it also reflected his own deeply held opposition to the conversion of the administration of India 'into a thing to be scrambled for by the second and third class of English parliamentary politicians' – a pretty accurate summary of the ninety years which would elapse before India was finally free. For all its terrible faults, the East India Company was also born of the Enlightenment, and was interested in the pursuit of knowledge and reason. Dozens of menageries, research stations and botanical expeditions – all funded by the Company – provided, as Paul Johnson points out, 'the basic knowledge of the natural history of south Asia'.[53]

For Mill, the Company's abolition meant that he was finally able to retire, having 'given enough of [his] life to India', on a handsome annual pension of £1,500. Thornton and Mill's other colleagues rallied to buy a leaving gift, raising enough to commission a silver inkstand, designed by the architect Digby Wyatt, best known for his work with Brunel on Paddington Station. On the lid of the box containing the stand was a bas-relief copy of Raphael's fresco of the *School of Athens*, in which the greatest thinkers of ancient Greece are depicted, a work that Mill had admired in the Vatican three and a half years earlier.[54] However Mill got wind of the plan, which caused the only argument he ever had with Thornton. 'I had never before seen him quite so angry,' wrote the guilty party. 'He hated all such demonstrations ... He was sure they were never altogether genuine or spontaneous. There were always several persons who took part in them, merely because they did not like to refuse' – a down-to-earth example, in Mill's mind, of the tyranny of public opinion – 'and, in short, whatever we might do, he would have none of it.'[55] Thornton none the less ordered the manufacturers, Messrs. Elkington, to deliver the inkstand to Mill's house in Blackheath, with orders for the delivery boy to leave it with a servant and hurry away before anyone could protest. Apparently the ruse worked: the inkstand and case were thereafter visible on the mantelpiece of Mill's drawing room.

Mill did manage, however, to fend off the suggestion of a seat on the new advisory council on Indian affairs, using his stock excuse of ill health, and he and Harriet were able, at last, to settle into early

retirement. He was fifty-two, she fifty. In October 1858, they headed off to enjoy some French sun and hunt for a retirement location.
By the time they reached Lyons, Harriet had developed a bad
cough, so they halted. Mill was unconcerned: she had had many
similar episodes before. 'Mama is decidedly better today,' he reassured Helen on 21 October, 'and has no doubt that she shall be quite
well with two or three more days more rest.' After a few days, they
moved on to Avignon, where Harriet's condition deteriorated
sharply. She was unable to sleep or even lie down. Her coughing
became incessant. Mill dashed off a letter to Dr Gurney in Nice,
who had treated Harriet five years earlier: 'My wife is lying at the
Hotel de l'Europe, so very ill that neither she nor I have any hope
but in you to save her ... I implore you to come immediately. I
need hardly say that any expense whatever will not count for a
feather in the balance.' Three days later he made use of the new
telegraph to cable his step-daughter: 'She is not better or perhaps
worse have written to beg Dr G to come.'[56] Mill's appeals were in
vain. Harriet died in their hotel room on 3 November, 1858.

For a whole day, Mill sat alone with her corpse. Then he rallied
himself to lock up her papers, and write formally to the Mayor of
Avignon informing him of the death and enclosing 1,000 francs for
the poor. Gurney and then Helen arrived, and offered what consolation they could. 'For seven and a half years that blessing was
mine,' he lamented. 'For seven and a half years only!' Mill asked
Thornton to place the obligatory notices in the papers. 'It is doubtful', he told his friend, 'if I shall ever be fit for anything public or
private, again. The spring of my life is broken.' In the formal notice,
Mill described Harriet's demise as being to the 'inexpressible grief
& irreparable loss of those who survive her'. He would, in fact,
express his grief repeatedly, and would spend the remaining fifteen
years of his life attempting to repair the loss by promoting the opinions and ideas which he saw as their joint legacy. In the same month
that Harriet died, Mill sent his publisher the manuscript of a work
dedicated to the memory 'of the friend and wife whose exalted
sense of truth and right was my strongest incitement, and whose

approbation was my chief reward'.[57] It was a fine memorial. *On Liberty* is the greatest celebration of the value of human freedom ever written. With it, Mill secured a permanent place in the history of progress – and opened a new chapter in his life.

CHAPTER ELEVEN

On Liberty (1859)

><

'Would you read aloud what it says on the first page? I should explain that the object is to make sure you're turned off after each stimulus.' The command is directed to the eponymous hero of Kingsley Amis's novel *Jake's Thing*, who has been sent to a clinic in an attempt to restore his interest in sex. Obediently, Jake recites: 'Apart from the peculiar tenets of individual thinkers, there is also in the world at large an increasing inclination to stretch unduly the powers of society over the individual, both by the force of opinion and even by that of legislation.' After being shown a picture of a naked woman – with his physiological reaction carefully monitored – Jake reads another passage: 'If all mankind plus one were of one opinion, and only one person were of the contrary opinion, mankind would be no more justified in silencing that one opinion than he, if he had the power, would be justified in silencing mankind.'[1]

The source of the anaphrodisiac passages is not identified, but they are, alas, familiar as excerpts from *On Liberty*, published in February 1859. For readers who recognize the phrases, the conjured image of Mill, the dry, forbidding, black-coated Victorian prude, provides a perfect counterfoil to the soft-porn interventions of the clinicians. Amis, in line with popular prejudice, casts Mill as not merely unsexy – but as the antithesis of sex. It is a tribute of sorts, although it is disconcerting to ponder what Mill would have made of it. There is no difficulty, though, in imagining his delight at finding *On Liberty* in another modern context, ranked as the fourteenth 'most harmful book of the 19th and 20th centuries' by the conservative American magazine *Human Events* in 2005; Mill's short, great book was just two places below Lenin's *What is to be Done?* and above both Darwin's *Origin of Species* and Gramsci's *Prison Notebooks*.[2]

On Liberty is Mill's best-known work: everybody who has read Mill has read it. Readers of quality newspapers will stumble across a mention of the essay on a weekly basis. Quotations from it are scattered across public conversation, so that in places, the essay now reads like a collection of aphorisms. Few doubt its status as a masterpiece; as a panegyric for individual liberty and the nobility of a self-governed life it remains unsurpassed. But the very success of *On Liberty* makes it a dangerous book, too. Despite Mill's intention to 'cram into it as much as possible', it skates over his considered views on a range of subjects, not least the role of government, the position of women and the nature of happiness. John Rawls's *A Theory of Justice* comprehensively summarizes the author's liberalism – likewise, Friedrich Hayek's *Road to Surfdom*. But *On Liberty*, a short polemical essay, is a different species of philosophical writing. Read in isolation today it is often misunderstood and misappropriated, especially by those on the political right.

Mill's target in *On Liberty* was not the state, but any social conditions which militated against the 'education or development of ... the qualities that are the distinctive endowment of a human being'. To his German admirer Theodor Gomperz, Mill summarized the subject of his 'small volume' as 'moral, social, & intellectual liberty, asserted against the despotism of society'.[3] The central tenets of *On Liberty* are that: 'individuality' is the very essence of a good life; freedom of speech and action are necessary conditions of human progress; and each person should be free to think and live as they wish, so long as they do no harm to others.

The volume had a dramatic impact on Mill's contemporaries, elevating him still further in the intellectual pantheon of the age. Charles Kingsley recorded that it made him 'a clearer headed & braver-minded man on the spot', correctly grasping that its' principal value was as 'an unequalled plea ... for the self-determining power of the individual, and for his right to use that power'. Thomas Hardy recalled the volume as one which 'we students of that date knew almost by heart'; Hardy's own copy of *On Liberty* is more heavily annotated, underlined and underscored than any other surviving book from his library. The essay was celebrated, reviewed and attacked across the world. Within two years even a Russian edition was available. 'It has been read by hundreds of thousands', wrote Frederic Harrison three decades later, 'and, to some of the most vigorous and conscientious spirits amongst us, it became a sort of gospel'. An American admirer urged his countrymen to read the book: 'Many, many verses of Mill's are more full of life than some of the worshipped Hebrew hallucinations.'[4] *On Liberty* has never been out of print and each generation fights new battles, or re-fights old ones, across the churned-over battlefield of the text, seeking in the process to find answers to the inescapable questions of the modern era: how to blend and balance freedom and duty in the pursuit of a good life. Love or loathe it, *On Liberty* is the New Testament of liberalism.

On Liberty's most famous lesson was what subsequent scholars have dubbed the 'harm principle'. No passage from a philosophical work is as widely quoted as this one: 'The only purpose for which power can rightfully be exercised over any member of a civilized community, against his will, is to prevent harm to others. His own good, either physical or moral, is not a sufficient warrant.'[5] The muscular simplicity of Mill's concept has given it an unequalled position and permanence in intellectual and political life. Few contemporary debates about the regulation of personal behaviour are complete without Mill's principle being invoked: it has featured, for example, in almost all the arguments across the world regarding smoking bans in public places – often on both sides, which would have pleased him. The principle is common currency in scholarly circles. Upon Mill's slender foundation – his description of the principle takes up just three pages of the essay – vast edifices of thought and argument have been built. The legal scholar Joel Feinberg's *Harm to Others*, published in 1984, restricted its scope to the application of the principle to the criminal law – but none the less ran to four substantial volumes.[6]

The harm principle had been trailed in Mill's *Principles*, but almost as an aside and without provoking any comment; from the moment of its publication in *On Liberty*, however, it was under attack. Mill rashly described it as 'one very simple principle as entitled to govern absolutely the dealings of society with the individual'.[7] In practice, the principle is far from straightforward and immediately prompts a series of questions. Can 'harm' be satisfactorily defined? Are there actually any actions at all which can be said to *only* hurt the individual, given that whatever happens to them will have knock-on effects on friends and family? Can society run without its members meeting obligations to one another which go beyond not harming each other? What if certain kinds of coercion can be shown to raise levels of happiness? The weight of scholarship addressing these questions since 1859 would test the sturdiest bookcase. A great deal of attention has been paid, for example, to Mill's definition of 'harm'. Academics have pointed out that during the course of his argument Mill appeared to define his concept of harmful conduct as any which would 'affect prejudicially the interests of others'.[8] If any action which impacts upon the interests of others is counted as harmful, it becomes very difficult to see where to draw the line. One person's interests are affected prejudicially when another refuses to eat fruit, because that increases their chance of getting ill, raising the costs of the NHS and therefore everyone's tax bill. It is quite clear, however, where Mill would stand on compulsory fruit-eating orders.

The truth is that Mill used many words and phrases at least as often as 'harm', including not only adverse influence on 'interests', but also 'injury' or 'injurious; 'hurt' or 'hurtful'; 'evil' or 'evils';

'mischief'; 'wrong' and even 'security'. It is hard to imagine that he was deliberately signalling something different each time; he was just, like any good writer, finding different ways to make the same point. Modern professional philosophers are very careful to define their terms exactly, and use words with great precision. But Mill was not a professional philosopher, and in any case *On Liberty* – unlike the *Logic* – was not a theoretical work. It was more of a tract than a treatise.

Mill himself accepted that 'no person is an entirely isolated being', and that harming oneself would therefore mean 'mischief to ... near connexions, and often far beyond them'. If a person, through their behaviour, was failing in a 'direct and assignable obligation' to others, the case was 'taken out of the self-regarding class and becomes amenable to moral disapprobation in the proper sense of the term'. Society could – and should – frown upon the father who spends all his wages in the pub. Mill insisted, however, that it was the 'breach of duty' which triggered the involvement of society, not the particular nature of the activity. A man should be just as much shunned for spending his money on books as on booze, if his family went hungry as a result. There was also no suggestion that the state should get involved in this instance. Only if there was a 'definite duty' to the 'public' did a privately harmful action become a publicly harmful one. 'No person ought to be punished simply for being drunk,' said Mill; 'but a soldier or a policeman should be punished for being drunk on duty.'9

Similarly, but more controversially, Mill stretched the definition of harm to include an otherwise innocent action which, for that particular individual, was known to lead to a harmful one. Somebody who had committed a violent crime while drunk should thenceforth, Mill said, 'be placed under a special legal restriction, personal to himself; that if he were afterwards found drunk, he should be liable to a penalty'. This apparently highly illiberal measure was permissible, Mill argued, because 'the making himself drunk, in a person whom drunkenness excites to do harm to others, is a crime against others.'10

Mill also accepted the occasional need for the state to act to prevent possible future harm, although he also warned that this justification was 'more liable to be abused, to the prejudice of liberty' than 'punitory' action after the event. Poison, for example, could be purchased for the purpose of murder, but Mill insisted that it should not therefore be banned, because it also had 'innocent' and 'useful' purposes; perhaps he had in mind the rats which inconvenienced him during the spring of 1854. Mill's compromise was to permit sales of poison, but to insist that the seller recorded the details of the sale and the purchaser, including a given purpose for which the poison had been bought – particulars which were in fact already required by law. In addition Mill proposed that a third party signatory might also be present. 'Such regulations,' he wrote, 'would in general be no material impediment to obtaining the article, but a very considerable one to making an improper use of it without detection.' So it seemed in practice: when a certain John Tavell used some 'Scheele's Prussic Acid' to kill his mistress in 1845 instead of, as he had claimed, to treat his varicose veins, the chemist in Bishopsgate was able to provide the necessary evidence for his conviction and hanging.[11]

Beyond such modest restrictions, Mill believed that people should be left to their own devices, even if they were self-destructive ones. Drunkenness may not have been good for society as a whole, but if no duty was being breached, this was the kind of 'inconvenience ... which society can afford to bear, for the sake of the greater good of human freedom'. He also accepted that certain forms of behaviour – 'gambling, or drunkenness, or incontinence, or idleness, or uncleanliness' – may be generally known to be 'injurious to happiness', but it would still be wrong to ban or 'repress' them, for three reasons.[12] First, if the activity in question were truly self-destructive, the visible example of individuals engaging in it would be 'more salutary than hurtful' by highlighting its 'painful or degrading circumstances'. Second, it was more effective to educate and train humans from birth in better habits than to ban them later. 'Society', after all, 'has had the whole period of childhood and nonage in which to try whether it could make them capable of rational conduct in life.' Third, legal sanctions against bad behaviour were likely to backfire, because of inherent human bloody-mindedness, which Mill rather admired:

If there be among those whom it is attempted to coerce into prudence or temperance, any of the material of which independent and vigorous characters are made, they will infallibly rebel against the yoke ... it easily comes to be considered a mark of spirit and courage to fly in the face of such usurped authority, and to do with ostentation the exact opposite of what it enjoins.[13]

Mill never returned to any of the questions raised by the harm principle, however, or spent any time developing or defending the concept, which, for him, was essentially a side-show. His principal goal in *On Liberty*, and in all his subsequent works, was the elucidation and advocacy of a particular view of a good life, based on the free and energetic development of individual character. In his *Autobiography*, Mill described *On Liberty* as 'a kind of philosophical text-book of a single truth'. Many writers, Gertrude Himmelfarb included, have wrongly assumed that he was here referring to the much-disputed 'simple principle', or harm principle, but here is how Mill actually went on to describe this single truth, which is the essence of his liberalism: 'the importance, to man and society, of a large variety in types of character, and of giving full freedom to human nature to expand itself in innumerable and conflicting directions'.[14]

A vital precondition for individual self-development was unrestricted freedom of opinion and expression, and *On Liberty* opened with a call for freedom of speech which resonates to this day. His advocacy of free discussion was based upon a particular conception – a very Victorian conception – of the role of knowledge in human advancement; at no point did he stray anywhere near 'human rights' grounds for free speech. Mill argued that progress depends on truth; that truth was most likely to emerge from a constant collision of opinions; and that freedom of speech was necessary to generate such collisions.

He insisted that allowing even apparently foolish, dangerous and false views to gain the public's ear would serve truth, for three reasons. First, any opinion may be true, no matter how eccentric it seems at first. Suppressing it, in this case, would slow the march of knowledge. Although Mill did not give specific examples of suppression in *On Liberty*, in his essay on Coleridge he had highlighted the 'superstition' which lay behind the persecution of Galileo, as well as the reluctance to publish of some contemporary geologists, one of whom, Charles Darwin, would issue his book *On the Origin of Species by Means of Natural Selection* in the same year as *On Liberty*. Mill insisted that 'ages are no more infallible than individuals; every age having held opinions which subsequent ages have deemed not only false but absurd; and it is as certain that many opinions, now general, will be rejected by future ages'.[15]

Second, even if the currently received doctrine happened to be true, it was beneficial to allow counter-arguments which would generate a 'clearer perception and livelier impression of truth, produced by its collision with error'. Even the Roman Catholic Church, he pointed out, appointed a Devil's advocate to argue against the canonization of a saint. Mill even suggested that, in the absence of genuine intellectual opponents, it was 'indispensable to imagine them, and supply them with the strongest arguments which the most skilful devil's advocate can conjure up'. This was because 'both teachers and learners go to sleep at their post, as soon as there is no enemy in the field'. An unchallenged view, even if correct, became, said Mill, a 'dead dogma, not a living truth'. Erroneous views were to be valued for their service in keeping the truth alive and awake.[16]

Thirdly, Mill suggested that in an exchange of opinions, it was rare for one to be entirely right and the other entirely wrong. In another echo of Coleridge, he declared that typically, 'conflicting doctrines, instead of the one being true and the other false, share the truth between them'.[17] Only by bringing them into contact and conflict could any approximation of the whole truth be constructed. This was an argument not simply for freedom of expression, but for an ongoing, positive debate between those of opposing views – which is of course a much tougher demand.

It was vital, then, that people should be free to publicly criticize religious beliefs, which might after all be erroneous. Mill anticipated the position of those who might seek to ban only 'intemperate' expressions of religious criticism, pointing out that 'this offence is given whenever the attack is telling and powerful, and that every opponent who pushes them hard, and whom they find difficult to answer, appears to them, if he shows any feeling on the subject, an intemperate opponent'. For Mill, the fact that someone's views gave offence to others could never be a reason for their repression. The only ground for regulating speech was to prevent incitement to illegal actions:

Even opinions lose their immunity, when the circumstances in which they are expressed are such as to constitute their expression a positive instigation to some mischievous act. An opinion that corn-dealers are starvers of the poor ... ought to be unmolested when simply circulated through the press, but may justly incur punishment when delivered orally to an excited mob assembled before the house of a corn-dealer.[18]

Of course the point at which the expression of an opinion constitutes 'positive instigation' was not entirely clear in 1859, and is even less so in an age of amplification, television and the internet. Nevertheless, Mill set a pretty demanding test: in his example, the mob has not only to be excited, but actually in front of the corn-dealer's house. The incitement has to be clear and direct for any sanctions to be legitimately applied.

Openness to the views of others was also the path to wisdom and progress at an individual level, according to Mill. Any person worth listening to, he said, 'has kept his mind open to criticism of his opinions ... No wise man ever acquired his wisdom in any mode but this.' There is more than a touch of autobiography in this passage, which concludes: 'The steady habit of correcting and completing his opinion by collating it with those of others, so far from causing doubt and hesitation in carrying it into practice, is the only stable foundation for a just reliance on it.' He accepted that this could be a demanding way to live, and that our own lazy yearning for reassurance could work against us: in an 1837 article on Sir Arthur Helps's book, *Thoughts for the Cloister and Crowd*, he wrote that 'the motive which induces most people to wish for certainty is the uneasiness of doubt; that uneasiness removed, they turn on their pillow and go to sleep'. Once again, Mr Podsnap in *Our Mutual Friend* could be cast as Mill's anti-hero: 'I don't want to know about it; I don't choose to discuss it; I don't admit it.'[19]

Mill has been accused by some modern historians of both inconsistency and hypocrisy on the issue of free speech and colliding opinions. There is no denying that when he was 'seized by wolves' during the height of his admiration for Carlyle and Coleridge he significantly departed, in private correspondence, from the supportive line on free speech he had adopted in his youth and expressed in *On Liberty*. Even in later years, it can be argued that Mill did not always scrupulously practise what he preached. He rebuffed the Neophyte Writers' Society on the grounds that he only wanted to support writers who were 'promoting what I consider true & just', and in 1866 he told the Unitarian James Martineau that he was supporting his rival, George Croom Robertson, for the post of Professor of Logic and Mental Philosophy at University College London, because 'though I have no reason to think his claims superior to yours in any other respect, [he] would certainly teach doctrines much nearer than yours to those which I myself hold on the great philosophical questions.'

Mill also had a fierce row with Elizabeth Gaskell. In her biography of Charlotte Brontë, Gaskell had published a letter from the novelist which referred to Harriet's 'Enfranchisement of Women'. 'When I first read the paper,' Brontë had written, 'I thought it was the work of a powerful minded clear-headed woman, who had a hard, jealous heart, muscles of iron, and nerves of bent leather; of a woman who longed for power and had never felt affection.' When he read the published letter, a few months after Harriet's death, Mill was apoplectic. He told Gaskell she had 'neglected the usual and indispensable duties which custom (founded on reason) has imposed of omitting [*sic*] all that might be offensive to the feelings of individuals'. More chilling to any biographer, though, and especially to a biographer of Mill, was the next passage:

The notion you seem to entertain that everything said or written by any one, which could possible throw light on the character of the sayer or writer, may, justifiably, be published by a biographer, is one which the world, and those who are higher and better than the world, would, I believe, perfectly unite in condemning.[20]

Where, in these examples, is the tribune of free speech, the advocate of muscular dissent? In the first two incidents outlined above – the Neophyte Writers' Society and the UCL Professorship – Mill can be defended on the grounds that his concern was precisely to promote a diversity of opinions, by supporting those with views which might indeed be close to his own, but which also went against prevailing opinion. As far as the argument with Gaskell is concerned, Mill might have argued that freedom of opinion should not be confused with a free-for-all of published personal details, but this wouldn't really do, because it would simply beg the question of who was the judge of the difference between the two. In fact, what this episode showed was that when it came to a possible slur against his beloved, recently deceased, wife, Mill's personal feelings triumphed over the cool application of his philosophical principles. Set against a lifetime's worth of free-speech advocacy – from his backing, at the age of seventeen, of Richard Carlile's right to publish atheistic views, through to his campaign as an elderly MP to secure the right to public demonstrations – making too much of such incidents amounts to nit-picking.

Mill actually offered financial and intellectual support to friends and foes alike, so long as he believed them to be genuinely engaged in a search for the truth. When Alexander Bain was struggling to persuade his publisher to print the second volume of his psychology, *The Emotions and the Will*, because the first volume had lost money, Mill, just days after Harriet's death, fired off a letter to the publisher guaranteeing him against possible loss. The guarantee was not in the event required, in part because of an enthusiastic review by Mill in the *Edinburgh Review*. Mill offered to do the same for Herbert Spencer – coiner of the phrase 'survival of the fittest' – who was struggling to publish the later volumes of his *System of Synthetic Philosophy*. 'Such proposals would have been remarkable even if there had been entire agreement of opinion,' Spencer recalled after Mill's death. 'But they were the more remarkable as being made by him under the consciousness that there existed between us certain fundamental differences, openly avowed'. When Spencer was preparing an attack on *An Examination of Sir William Hamilton's Philosophy*, Mill wrote: 'Nothing can be more agreeable to me than to hear that you are going to answer me in the Fortnightly Review. I hope you will not spare me.'[21]

Even more telling is the recollection of William George Ward, a Roman Catholic theologian, and author of the review of the *Logic* in the *British Critic*, with whom Mill engaged in a spirited correspondence. In the preface to his 1860 work, *On Nature and Grace*, Ward wrote that 'of Mr Mill certainly, if of any man living, it may be truly said, that he aims at doing the fullest justice to every school of thought, however remote from his own; and that the one aim, which consciously influences his intellectual exertions, is the pursuit of truth.' Given these examples, and Mill's lifelong active engagement with thinkers and activists from a diverse spectrum, Gladstone's description of Mill as the 'most open-minded man in England' does not seem ridiculous; nor does Spencer's description of a 'generosity that might almost be called romantic'.[22] But if a life of constant debate and re-examination of ideas and beliefs was appealing to Mill, to some of his readers it sounded demanding. Mill's old friend Caroline Fox wrote to a friend:

I am reading that terrible book of John Mill's on Liberty, so clear, and calm, and cold: he lays in one as a tremendous duty to get oneself well contradicted, and admit always a devil's advocate into the presence of your dearest, most sacred Truths, as they are apt to grow windy and worthless without such tests, if indeed they can stand the shock of argument at all. He looks you through like a basilisk, relentless as Fate. We knew him well at one time, and owe him much; I fear his remorseless logic has led him far since then. He is in many senses isolated, and must sometimes shiver from the cold.[23]

Mill was not alone, however. Helen had stepped smartly into her mother's shoes, and from the moment she arrived in Avignon became Mill's organizer, housekeeper and assistant. 'Surely no one ever before was so fortunate, as after such a loss as mine, to draw another such prize in the lottery of life,' Mill wrote in the *Auto-biography*, 'another companion, adviser, and instructor of the rarest quality'. Mill's praise was, once again, excessive, but there can be little doubt of the debt that he owed to his step-daughter; she gave him a new lease of life. His 'chère fille', he told a friend, was the 'one person beside myself who most loved her [Harriet] & whom she most loved, & we help each other to bear what is necessary'.[24] From now on, she was always 'his daughter', and he was always 'father', united by their love for the memory of Harriet.

Before returning to Blackheath in November 1858, Mill had bought a small house, the Hermitage de Monloisier, near the cemetery at St Veran, Avignon, where Harriet was buried. It was, according to a twentieth-century description, a 'little Provençal country house; simple but in good taste'. Sitting in three hectares of land, the house had previously belonged to a baker who had command-ed a national guard in 1848.[25] Mill would spend roughly half his time here for the remaining fifteen years of his life, writing, botanizing and trimming roses. Louis Rey, the Pastor of the Protestant Church in Avignon – to which Mill diligently paid his dues – became Mill's closest friend in the town. He said that Mill's love for Harriet reached the 'height of a religion ... a sort of Christianity with a female Christ ... he brought to her all that was best in his feelings and thoughts'. Mill himself said that 'her memory is to me a religion'.[26]

Needless to say, Mill spared no expense or convenience in creating an appropriate physical memorial for Harriet. The design was based on sketches from his own hand. Only marble from the quarry at Carrara, the same kind used for both Marble Arch and Michelangelo's *David*, would suffice. The first piece ordered was only big enough for the top slab, so more was requested. When they arrived, one was chipped, so Mill paid 3,000 francs for yet another. A long-planned trip to Greece was postponed in order to ensure that the memorial was finished correctly, Mill and Helen distracting themselves with ambitious planting schemes – roses, laurels elm, laburnum – for their garden. It was early in 1860, a year after the publication of *On Liberty*, before all the marble was ready. Three labourers set to work on the memorial, at five francs a day: Paul Liehiere (three days), Simon Roux (two days) and someone identified only as 'Poutes', for five days.[27]

There is no question that it was an expensive business. The bill from Pascal, the local architect, was 4,825.14 francs and the town got 3,000 francs for the permanent upkeep of the grave. The final price of the marble is not known, but cannot have been less than 10,000 francs. Packe's estimate of £1,500 for the total cost (about £100,000 in today's terms) looks, if anything, on the low side. Having delayed his retirement on financial grounds, Mill now turned his money into stone. Helen was certainly conscious of the cost. Imploring Haji (Algernon) to attend the unveiling ceremony, which she and Mill looked forward to as 'quite an epoch', she hoped he would not consider his train fare, in view of 'the immense expense that the whole thing has been and will be'.[28] The inscription on the tomb reads:

AS EARNEST FOR THE PUBLIC GOOD
AS SHE WAS GENEROUS AND DEVOTED
TO ALL WHO SURROUNDED HER
HER INFLUENCE HAS BEEN FELT
IN MANY OF THE GREATEST
IMPROVEMENTS OF THE AGE
AND WILL BE IN THOSE STILL TO COME
WERE THERE BUT A FEW HEARTS AND INTELLECTS
LIKE HERS
THE EARTH WOULD ALREADY BECOME
THE HOPED-FOR HEAVEN

In Pascal's files there is a French translation of the inscription, in Mill's hand, written on the black-edged stationery he used for years after Harriet's death. Perhaps the craftsman who etched the English words wanted to know what he was writing; perhaps Mill considered putting the tribute in French; perhaps Pascal was simply curious. Either way, Mill would continue to work for the hoped-for heaven – 'le ciel espère' – in which every man, and of course every woman, would have the freedom and resources for a rich, flourishing life. In Harriet's true memorial, *On Liberty*, he wrote: 'The only freedom which deserves the name ... is that of pursuing our own good in our own way.'[29] Individuality is the lodestar of the entire work, and if he had still been in Wordsworthian mood, Mill might have used as illustration the poet's praise in his *Prelude* for those with 'sovereignty within':

> Oh! who is he that hath his whole life long
> Preserved, enlarged this freedom in himself?
> For this alone is genuine Liberty.[30]

For Mill, a good life was one led on our own terms, which is why the idea of coercing people into happier or better states – with the important exceptions of children and 'barbarian' peoples – was a contradiction in terms. Carlyle hated Mill's restraint: 'As if it were a sin to control, or coerce into better methods, human swine in any way,' he ranted to his brother. 'Ach Gott in Himmel!' As Alan Ryan, one of the leading Mill scolars of the twentieth century, puts it, Mill 'wanted volunteers for virtue, not conscripts'. One of the things that made a person's life good was the fact that it was their own, that the freedom was 'in themself'. For Mill, it was vitally important that individuals not only be authors of their opinions, but also architects of their lives: 'he who lets the world, or his own portion of it, choose his plan of life for him, has no need of any other faculty than the ape-like one of imitation,' he wrote. 'He who chooses his plan for himself employs all his faculties.'[31]

This did not mean that each individual had to follow a different path to one another, but that their path should be positively chosen, rather than sheepishly followed. 'Originality does not consist solely in making great discoveries,' he wrote, strongly echoing his 1833 article 'On Genius': 'whoever thinks out a subject with his own mind, not accepting the phrases of his predecessors instead of facts, is original.' For Mill, a real 'genius' was someone more individual than others, and 'less capable, consequently, of fitting themselves . . . into any of the small number of moulds which society provides in order to save its members the trouble of forming their own character.' Liberty, then, was not simply the absence of coercion or restraint, but active 'self-creation'. The ugly term 'autonomy' – literally, self-governing – gets closer in some ways to what Mill meant than 'liberty', and it is striking that he used the phrase 'l'autononomie de l'individu' to describe the main theme of *On Liberty* to a French correspondent.[32]

Nor, for Mill, was liberty a static state of affairs; rather, it was manifested in each person progressing 'nearer to the best thing they can be'. He prefixed his essay with what he called a 'motto' from Wilhelm von Humboldt's *Sphere and Duties of Government*, published in 1854: 'The grand, leading principle, towards which every argument unfolded in these pages directly converges, is the absolute and essential importance of human development in its richest diversity.' The passage was not idly chosen: the theme of human development is the golden thread running through *On Liberty*, and indeed most of Mill's subsequent major works. Humboldt's name appears nine times in an essay in which Hume, Voltaire and Hobbes are absent, and Bentham, Locke and Kant each make a single appearance. Mill especially endorsed Humboldt's claim that 'the end of man . . . is the highest and most harmonious development of his powers to a complete and consistent whole'.[33]

Throughout the essay, Mill used organic metaphors for individuals. While the eighteenth-century philosopher Immanuel Kant had declared that 'out of the crooked timber of humanity no straight thing was ever made', for Mill people were not dead timber, but living trees – driven by their very nature to grow, stretch and seek the light. 'Human nature is not a machine to be built after a model, and set to do exactly the work prescribed for it,' he insisted, 'but a tree, which requires to grow and develop itself on all sides, according to the tendency of the inward forces which make it a living thing.'[34] When he argued against repression, Mill did not use spatial terms like 'invade' or 'interfere'; for him, repression inhibited natural growth, with people turned into 'pollards', or 'compressed', 'cramped', pinched', 'dwarfed', 'starved' or 'withered'. The reason he wanted people to be free was so that they could grow, and in his highly optimistic view of human nature, the tendency towards growth was immanent in each and every person. As Alan Ryan writes, 'Mill's concern with self-development and moral progress is a strand in his philosophy to which almost everything else is subordinate'.[35]

The consequence of individuals following their own lifeplans would be a kaleidoscope of different lifestyles, which Mill welcomed. 'As it is useful that while mankind are imperfect there should be different opinions,' he wrote, 'so is it that there should be different experiments in living; that free scope should be given to the varieties of character . . . and the worth of different modes of life should be proved practically, when any one thinks fit to try them.' The only way people could discover the best way to live was by trying out a variety of different modes, and comparing notes on the results. In his diary, the day before sending Harriet their planned list of essays in February 1854, Mill had railed against Goethe's ideal of a cultivated individual as 'rounded off and made symmetrical like a Greek temple or a Greek drama ... Not symmetry, but bold, free expansion in all directions is demanded by the needs of modern life and the instincts of the modern mind.' Mill wanted individuals to ask when planning their lives, 'what do I prefer? or, what would suit my character and disposition? or, what would allows the best and highest in me to have fair play, and enable it to grow and thrive?'.[36]

Some of Mill's critics assumed that he was in favour of diversity simply for its own sake: James Fitzjames Stephen, a powerful contemporary critic of Mill's work, retorted that 'although goodness is various, variety is not in itself good'.[37] But Stephen had missed Mill's point. Variety was not 'in itself' good, but was necessary and welcome precisely because 'goodness is various'. Mill valued diversity because it increased the raw materials available for each of us to fuel our personal development.

The real test of Mill's liberalism came when he considered activities which not only he, but the overwhelming body of opinion thought harmful and degrading – such as drunkenness, gambling and prostitution. True to his own harm principle, Mill's starting point was that these were areas best left to the individual. Though a moderate drinker himself, Mill was incensed by moralistic attempts to police people into sobriety, which had resulted in an early attempt at prohibition in the United States and the formation, in 1853, of an Alliance for the Legislative Suppression of the Traffic in all Intoxicating Liquors in Britain.[38] This was at a time of 'moral panic' about the gin palaces and penny gaffs being frequented by the poor. In *On Liberty*, Mill quoted from the manifesto of the Alliance: 'I claim, as a citizen, a right to legislate whenever my social rights are invaded by another ... If anything invades my social rights, certainly the traffic in strong drink does. It destroys my primary right of security, by constantly creating and sustaining social disorder ... and by weakening and demoralizing society, from which I have a right to claim mutual aid and intercourse.'

This 'social rights' argument roused Mill's ire to contemptuous heights. Such a 'monstrous principle', he declared, could justify absolutely any 'violation of liberty', being a 'doctrine [which] ascribes to all mankind a vested interest in each other's moral, intellectual, and even physical perfection, to be defined by each claimant according to his own standard'. Mill did support a system of licensing for pub landlords – persons of 'vouched-for respectability' – given that 'offences against society are especially apt to originate there'. Similarly, he advocated such regulation for opening hours 'as may be required for public surveillance'. Beyond this, he insisted that 'the choice of pleasures' for other people, and their 'mode of expending income' were 'their own concern and must rest with their own judgement'. Here he was continuing a campaign, begun twenty-five years earlier in the *Monthly Repository*, against the 'beer house purism' of temperance-inclined legislators.[39]

Mill was similarly scathing in *On Liberty* about Sabbatarian legislation, which banned certain kinds of 'amusements' such as the theatre, dancing and drinking on the Lord's Day. We should take our cue from Tacitus, Mill believed: '*Deorum injuriae Diis curae*' ('Leave offences against the Gods to the care of the Gods'.) However he did not single out Christian morality, and often used Islam as an example in his arguments against any religious codes being given the force of law, even in a community in which adherents were in the ascendancy. He cited the 'rather trivial' example of not eating pork (which was perhaps not so trivial, given that it was insensitivity to this prohibition that sparked the Indian eruptions of 1857): 'Suppose now, that in a people, of whom the majority were Mussulmans, the majority should insist upon not permitting pork to be eaten within the limits of the country.' This, in his view, would be an indefensible infringement of liberty, because even if eating pork was 'disgusting' to the majority, it did not harm them: 'with the personal tastes and self-regarding concerns of individuals the public has no business to interfere'.[40] For readers in 1859, the issue of Islamic law was one which applied only to far-flung countries and so could be viewed, as it was for Mill, as principally an intellectual exercise. His liberalism on this point perhaps reads more provocatively today.

Mill also tackled an issue which, by contrast, was of more immediate concern to most Londoners. In 1857, the Metropolitan Police estimated that the capital contained 2,825 brothels and 8,600 prostitutes. Evening visitors to the Haymarket were treated to what was popularly dubbed the 'Haymarket march past' and even Dostoevsky, in 1862, 'noticed mothers bringing their young daughters to do business'.[41] From paupers in Hoxton to bejewelled horse-riding courtesans in Hyde Park, prostitutes were as much part of mid-century London life as street markets, hansom cabs or hangings, and the question of the possible regulation of their activities was being actively discussed.

Mill began his argument by allowing that 'fornication ... must be tolerated'; surely a relief to all his readers. What this meant, more specifically, was that prostitution could not be made illegal. His dilemma concerned the legal position of the middlemen of the business: 'should a person be free to be a pimp?' The detached tone with which Mill tackled the issue was enough to inflame some readers, including James Fitzjames Stephen: 'I do not think that the State ought to stand bandying compliments with pimps,' he protested. 'My feeling is that if society gets its grip on the collar of such a fellow it should say to him, "you dirty rascal".'[42]

Actually what was most striking about this section of *On Liberty* was the rigour with which Mill tried to apply his own harm principle, given not merely the likely reaction from critics but his own personal distaste for prostitution. Whatever his own moral views, Mill could not countenance the state making a person – in this case, a pimp – culpable for inducing another into a legal act. If members of society were free to try to 'dissuade' people from engaging in a particular act, then liberty demanded that others should 'be free to persuade' too: 'Whatever it is permitted to do, it must be permitted to advise to do.' Of course, the pimp had a financial interest in the matter, and one which was 'opposed to what is considered as the public weal' but punishing him would result in the 'moral anomaly of punishing the accessory, when the principal is (and must be) allowed to go free; of fining and imprisoning the pro-curer, but not the fornicator'. Mill later suggested that the solution to the problem of prostitution would lie in any case on the demand-side, as an improvement in the condition of marriage and in the morals of men removed the artificial need for bought sex.[43]

It must be said that Mill never questioned the superiority of marriage, heterosexuality or monogamy, even though plenty of his countrymen were busy challenging them in their personal lives. In his world-view, sex was usually an 'animal appetite', often further relegated by the prefix 'mere', and one which, if anything, needed taming rather than being given freer expression. He was in no sense a philosopher of the flesh. The only 'properly human organ' for Mill was 'the reasoning and thinking brain'.[44] So while he supported 'experiments in living', there was no suggestion that his ideal tableau for society encompassed energetic sexual experimentation. Mill was in favour of love, and in favour of freedom, but was not in favour of 'free love'. He was completely silent, for example, publicly and privately, on homosexuality and on the laws making 'sodomy' punishable by death, while his mentor Bentham had written, at least seven decades earlier, a sixty-page argument for the de-criminalization of 'paederasty' on the grounds that it brought pleasure to the voluntary participants and 'produces no pain of any kind to any one'. Of course Bentham was too afraid to publish this first known call made for homosexual law reform in England (it was discovered and published in 1978) and it is not known if Mill ever read it. If he had, he would surely have remembered Bentham's caustic comment on the law: 'It is wonderful that nobody has ever yet fancied it to be sinful to scratch where it itches, and that it has never been determined that the only natural way of scratching is with such or such a finger and that it is unnatural to scratch with any other.'[45]

Mill's vision of a full, autonomous life – continuous self-renewal along with an openness to new ideas, experiments and opportuni-ties – required a great deal of personal energy. 'Vigour' was there-fore an essential ingredient in his idea of a good life and a good society. He had always believed that energy and liberty were close relations, pointing to the 'vigorous impulse which the awakening of liberty gives to the human faculties'. Mill was in tune with his times here, writing for an audience who still used 'earnestness' as a term of praise. Leslie Stephen, the brother of Fitzjames, in his appraisal of Henry Fawcett (an economist and politician with whom Mill would later become good friends) summarized both Fawcett and prevailing opinion when he lauded 'the old maxim ... that one virtue lies at the base of all others: call it force, energy, vitality, or manliness, or whatever you please.' Mill himself could not be accused of lack of energy, of course. Throughout his life he wrote, read, walked, climbed, argued, botanized and campaigned at a rate which is frankly humbling. 'Strong impulses are but another name for energy,' Mill wrote in *On Liberty*. 'Energy may be turned to bad uses; but more good may always be made of an energetic nature, than of an indolent and impassive one.'[46]

One of the more telling charges that Mill levelled at Christian morality, at least in its existing form, was that its ideal was 'passive rather than active', more concerned with 'Abstinence from Evil, rather than energetic Pursuit of the Good'. Florence Nightingale, whom Mill admired, connected passivity with convention and the oppression of women in her 1852 *Cassandra*: 'What else is conventional life? *Passivity* when we want [i.e. need] to be active. So many hours spent every day in passively doing what conventional life tells us, when we would so gladly be at work. And is it a wonder that all individual life is extinguished?'[47] The words 'energy', 'active' and 'vital' (or their derivatives) appear forty-four times in *On Liberty*, compared to thirty-one mentions of 'individuality' and forty-nine of 'freedom'. To many readers, it could all sound a bit exhausting. Certainly this was the view of the fictional Richard Phillotson, husband of Sue Bridehead in Thomas Hardy's 1895 novel, *Jude the Obscure*:

Sue continued: 'She, or he, 'who lets the world, or his own portion of it, choose his plan of life for him, has no need of any other faculty than the ape-like one of imitation.' J. S. Mill's words those are. I have been reading it up. Why can't you act upon them? I wish to, always.'

'What do I care about J. S. Mill!' moaned he. 'I only want to lead a quiet life!'[48]

But a quiet life was not what Mill had in mind for his readers. For him, the energetic pursuit of a self-defined, self-improving life was a vital component of individual character. 'One whose desires and impulses are not his own,' he insisted, 'has no character, no more than a steam-engine has a character.' The good news, for Mill, was that this meant there were 'as many possible independent centres of improvement as there are individuals'. In *Hamilton*, Mill would even insist that people 'are under a moral obligation to seek the improvement of our moral character'. A better world could be made only with better people or as he put it in *On Liberty*, 'it really is of importance, not only what men do, but also what manner of men they are that do it'.[49]

Mill himself lamented the existing state of the character of the masses, whom he described as 'starved specimens of what nature can and will produce'. But he was also tough on himself, and on those of his class who he felt were not performing at the required level. He was especially incensed by the failure of talented people to live up to their promise: Herbert Spencer was 'so good', he said, that 'he should have been better'. At the same time, Mill retained an optimistic view of the potential for human improvement – back in 1831 he had proclaimed the 'indefinite progressiveness of the human mind' – and this conviction ran through *On Liberty*. He assumed that under the right conditions – with wide access to education, and freedom of opinion and lifestyle – people would energetically develop original characters and lead virtuous lives. From a modern psychological perspective, this is clearly utopian; as Gertrude Himmelfarb has pointed out, Mill 'looked to liberty as a means of achieving the highest reaches of the human spirit; he did not take seriously enough the possibility that men would also be free to explore the depths of depravity'.[50]

In his conviction that good characters could be formed, Mill placed a heavy emphasis on the role of 'habit'. In the *Logic* Mill had contrasted 'habits of hurtful excess' with a 'habit of willing . . . commonly called a purpose'. Here he was echoing many of the leading psychologists and physiologists of the day, such as Bain, Spencer and Henry Maudsley, who even suggested that habits might leave physical traces in the nervous system. Mill's point was that if we wanted to change our character, we could do so by altering our habits. In his 1835 essay 'Civilization', he had broadened this approach to call for 'national systems of education, and forms of polity, calculated to invigorate the national character'.[51] For him, some of the most powerful sources of such development were participation in the economy (hence his support for cooperatives), in relationships, (hence his insistence on gender equality) and also in politics, where he argued for more participative flavour in national politics as well as for much stronger local democracy.

On Liberty was not, however, a political argument; Mill wrote that 'the Liberty it treats of is moral and intellectual rather than political'. *Representative Government*, published in 1861, would be his principal theoretical statement on government and politics. Yet the state still had an important role to play in cultivating the conditions for autonomy and for improving the moral fibre and intelligence of the nation. His criteria in *Representative Government* for assessing the quality of a governmental apparatus were two-fold: 'the quality of the machinery itself', but also 'the degree in which it tends to increase the sum of good qualities in the governed, collectively and individually'.[52]

Mill never produced a fully fledged theory of the state, although he tackled the question from various angles in a range of different works including *On Liberty*, the *Principles* – which contained a fairly technical discussion of areas in which the state should and should not intervene – and a number of essays and reviews, particularly an 1862 article with the misleadingly narrow title 'Centralisation'. The most that can be extracted from these various sources is a set of highly general, loosely applied principles. In a letter of 1847 to his old neighbour John Austin, discussing the 'province of government', he wrote: 'I doubt if much more can be done in a scientific treatment of the question than to point out a certain number of *pro*'s and a certain number of *con*'s of a more or less general application ... leaving the balance to be struck in each particular case as it arises.'[53] In the *Principles*, Mill was equally critical of those who had a blanket opposition to state intervention – a 'spirit of resistance *in limine* to the interference, merely as such' – and 'impatient reformers', who thought 'it easier and shorter to get possession of the government than of the intellects and dispositions of the public'. In *On Liberty* he stated that the 'interference of government is with equal frequency, improperly invoked and improperly condemned'.[54] Pragmatism, rather than ideology, was Mill's watchword when it came to state activity. It is appropriate then that this was one area in which he could engage in some uncharacteristic patriotism: 'The general tone of English feeling on these subjects is on the whole, we think, very much what it ought to be. There is no blind prejudice against having recourse to the State ... But there is a strong persuasion that what can be tolerably done in any other way, had better be done in that way than by the government.'[55]

It is therefore dangerous to draw conclusions about Mill's attitude to the role of the state from any single publication – and particularly from *On Liberty*. In this essay, Mill focused on the areas in which the state should not intervene, repeating, essentially, only half of the argument in the *Principles*. This gives the text a more laissez-faire tone than Mill's work considered as a whole, which has been endorsed enthusiastically by later free-marketeers. (A similar error may be made by those who read Adam Smith's *Wealth of Nations* without considering his *Theory of Moral Sentiments*.) One of their favourite passages is the one in which Mill suggested that 'if the roads, the railways, the banks, the insurance offices, the great joint-stock companies, the universities, and the public charities, were all of them branches of the government ... not all the freedom of the press and popular constitution of the legislature would make this or any other country free otherwise than in name.'[56]

Mill, then, was not in favour of wholesale nationalization and, true to his Ricardian upbringing in economic matters, he was consistently and robustly in favour of free-market operations with every departure from them, 'unless required by some great good', being a 'certain evil'. Market competition was essential for national prosperity, he believed, as well as for ensuring that the working population was striving towards excellence. But he was also aware that markets did not guarantee competition. In 1865 he personally gave some modest financial support to the Wolverhampton Co-operative Plate Lock Manufactory, which was being threatened by a predatory pricing campaign by its privately owned neighbours. This was, for Mill, intended to promote competition: 'Against fair competition I have no desire to shield them [the Co-operative],' he explained. 'Co-operative production carried on by people whose hearts are in the cause . . . ought to be able to hold its ground against private establishments.' He similarly recognized that there were some areas where a free market would act against the public interest, and at various points he argued that the water supply, city parks and postal service should be in state hands.[57]

Government had a more positive role, too, in raising 'the sum of good qualities in the governed'. Though the state should avoid coercion, it could still act to encourage people to be better. In essence, as Alan Ryan has pointed out, he treated the state as an 'individual writ large', with similar freedoms and restraints. The clearest expression of this came in his essay 'Coleridge':

Beyond suppressing force and fraud, governments can seldom, without doing more harm than good, attempt to chain up the free agency of individuals. But does it follow from this that government cannot exercise a free agency of its own? – that it cannot beneficially employ its powers, its means of communication, and its pecuniary resources . . . in promoting the public welfare by a thousand means which individuals would never think of, would have no sufficient motive to attempt, or no sufficient power to accomplish?[58]

He believed the state could do most for 'public welfare' by promoting education, supporting activities for which consumer demand was underdeveloped or necessarily insufficient, supporting the poor, and solving what modern economists call 'collective action' problems – in other words, those which require coordination.

The sub-heading of the section on state support for education in the *Principles* reads: 'Large exceptions to *laisser-faire*. Cases in which the consumer is an incompetent judge of the commodity. Education.' Mill believed that consumers were the best judges of their 'material wants', but that they were unlikely to demand education, lamenting that 'those who most need to be made wiser and better, usually desire it least'. He argued that schooling fell into the category of those goods in which 'the supply called forth by the demand of the market will be anything but what is really required. Education, therefore, is one of those things which it is admissible in principle that a government should provide for the people,' although he did not want to see the government having a monopoly or 'complete control' in the education field. Mill also believed that school should be compulsory, on the liberal grounds that education 'strengthens as well as enlarges the active faculties ... it is help towards doing without help'.[59]

A decade later, in *On Liberty*, Mill had shifted his stance somewhat. He still believed that demand for education was too low. But rather than advocating the direct provision of schools by the state, he argued for a legal obligation on parents to secure a satisfactory elementary education for their children, with the government subsidizing or paying the school fees of the poor. 'If the government could make up its mind to *require* for every child a good education,' he wrote, 'it might save itself the trouble of *providing* one.' He was now even more concerned to keep the government out of educational provision. 'That the whole or any large part of the education of the people should be in State hands I go as far as anyone in deprecating.' His views on a nationally fixed curriculum were similarly clear: 'All that has been said of the importance of individuality of character, and diversity in opinions and modes of conduct, involves, as of the same unspeakable importance, diversity of education. A general State education is a mere contrivance for moulding people to be exactly like one another.'[60]

Just as consumers were likely to demand too little education, so they might also fail – at least in the short-term – to appreciate

other things, of the worth of which the demand of the market is by no means a test; things of which the utility does not consist in ministering to inclinations, nor in serving the daily uses of life, and the want of which is least felt where the need is greatest. This is peculiarly true of those things which are chiefly useful as tending to raise the character of human beings. The uncultivated cannot be competent judges of cultivation.[61]

This was a topic which Mill intended to address in detail: among the list of essays he and Harriet were planning in the mid-1850s was one which he did not complete, on the 'Education of tastes'. But the topic recurred in a number of other publications too. In *Utilitarianism* he insisted that once a certain level of 'cultivation' had been reached, the demand for superior products and services communicated through the market would be sufficient:

A cultivated mind – I do not mean that of a philosopher, but any mind to which the fountains of knowledge have been opened – . . . finds sources of inexhaustible interest in all that surrounds it; in the objects of nature, the achievements of art, the imaginations of poetry, the incidents of history, the ways of mankind past and present, and their prospects for the future.[62]

The difficulty he saw was that many people were not yet in possession of such a 'cultivated mind', and that many of these finer tastes were acquired ones. 'Every one who takes pleasure in a simple tune has the capacity of fully enjoying Weber & Beethoven,' he insisted, 'but very often he derives little or no pleasure from a first hearing of them.' Even if people were aware of the long-term

benefits of a 'finer' activity, it might still lose out to a more immediate gratification. 'Men often, from infirmity of character,' he
noted in *Utilitarianism*, 'make their election for the nearer good,
though they know it to be the less valuable.'[63] In the meantime it
was necessary for the state to stand in, both in order to substitute
for and cultivate stronger demand for exercise, nature, good housing, or art. In a letter written to Herbert Spencer in 1859, Mill supported government subsidies for public baths 'in order to foster the
taste for them, and render them ultimately a profitable private speculation'. In his 1845 article on 'The Claims of Labour' he endorsed
the movement to give workers land in the form of allotments, not
to turn them into peasant farmers or depress wages, but in order to
'promote the taste for gardening', a well-tended garden being both
'comfort, and a badge of comfort'. Housing, too, required some
state investment: 'The taste for better house accommodation has
still to be created' he told a correspondent in 1866, '& until it is created, private speculation will not find its account in supplying that
improved accommodation.' In a posthumously published newspaper article, Mill also judged it perfectly legitimate for governments
to 'disburse considerable sums in order to foster high art and
encourage a taste for it among the public'.[64]

In all of these areas, Mill hoped that state subsidies would only
be required for a short period of time, after which 'cultivated' consumers would be demanding pools, gardens and paintings. There
were other activities, however, where even in the long run, government support might be required. Undertakings of public benefit
such as a 'voyage of geographical or scientific exploration', for
example, might be provided for by private subscription – indeed,
Mill sometimes used this as an example of 'public spirit' – but the
uncertainties involved made this 'rare and precious resource' one for
which the state might have to continue to provide funding.[65]

Mill also saw the case for government support of a 'learned class',
probably through the endowment of 'Professorships, with duties of
instruction attached'. Once again, he was in touch with the mood
of the times: the Victorian elevation of 'The Professor' into a sym-

bol of progress would shortly reach its zenith in the novels of Jules Verne, and tax-funded professorships were a watered-down version of Mill's earlier enthusiasm for a Coleridgean 'clerisy'. But in case anybody might think him guilty of special pleading, or of calling for an intellectuals' gravy-train, Mill sternly pointed out that 'the occupation of some hours every day in a routine employment, has often been found compatible with the most brilliant achievements in literature and philosophy.'[66] Of course, Mill had never attended or taught at a school or university, and he was far from being alone in combining a day-job with political and philosophical labours: Walter Bagehot and George Grote were both bankers, Matthew Arnold a school inspector, and Fitzjames Stephen a barrister.

There were areas, too, where people might be sure what they wanted, but could only get it by acting in concert – what is now known as a 'collective action' problem. In these circumstances, the state might have a role to play as orchestrator of diffuse demands into a particular good. Parks and public health measures fell under this heading, but in the *Principles* Mill highlighted shorter working hours to 'exemplify the manner in which classes of persons may need the assistance of law, to give effect to their deliberate collective opinion of their own interest'.

It was only an illustration, however, and Mill was profoundly and increasingly uneasy about legislation in this area. 'I am not expressing any opinion in favour of such an enactment,' he insisted in the *Principles*, and added to the 1862 edition, the first to appear after *On Liberty*, 'which has never in this country been demanded, and which I certainly should not, in present circumstances, recommend.' Mill thought that the best way to bring about a change was 'by a quiet change in the custom of the trade; short hours, becoming, by spontaneous choice, the general practice, but those who chose to deviate from it having the fullest liberty do so'.[67] Mill saw an argument in theory for the regulation of working hours, but as his liberalism deepened he became increasingly uncomfortable with the idea of forcing people to restrict their own working hours, and the issue was not mentioned at all in *On Liberty*.

Nor did *On Liberty* contain any of Mill's arguments in favour of state welfare payments to the poor, which were sketched in a number of other publications, and fleshed out most fully in the *Principles*. The case in favour hit all of Mill's key notes, emphasizing liberty, energy, self-reliance, as well as social sympathies, duty and fairness. Mill believed that four principles ought to lie at the heart of any system of financial support for the poor. First, society owed a degree of support to its poorest members: 'Human beings ... should help one another; and the more so, in proportion to the urgency of the need: and none needs help so urgently as one who is starving.' Nowadays this is of course an uncontroversial statement, but in making it Mill stood against the prevailing Malthusianism of many political economists of the day. Second, that responsibility must be shouldered by government – not because charitable alternatives were unavailable, but because they were erratic and unreliable: 'charity almost always does too much or too little: it lavishes its bounty in one place, and leaves people to starve in another'.[68] Third, the level and nature of the support should not create what Mill called 'demoralization' and today would be called welfare dependency. In 1834, Mill had hammered this argument home in a newspaper article on the reform of the Poor Laws. 'No person who is able to work, is entitled to be maintained in idleness, or to be put in a better condition, at the expense of the public than those who contrive to support themselves by their unaided exertions.'[69]

While Mill recognized that an over-generous system could reduce work effort, he also saw that the absence of help could have a similar effect. Once again, energy was the *summum bonum*. 'Energy and self-dependence are, however, liable to be impaired by the absence of help, as well as by its excess,' he warned. 'It is even more fatal to exertion to have no hope of succeeding by it, than to be assured of succeeding without it. When the condition of any one is so disastrous that his energies are paralysed by discouragement, assistance is a tonic, not a sedative: it braces instead of deadening the active faculties.'

Fourth, the state should make no distinction between the 'deserving' and 'undeserving poor'. 'The dispensers of public relief have no business to be inquisitors,' he wrote. 'Guardians and overseers are not fit to be trusted to give or withhold other people's money according to their verdict on the morality of the person soliciting it.'[70]

Mill's view of the role of the state, then, was a very long way from the minimalist one of right-wing, or even anarchist, fantasy, in which the government is tasked only with protecting individuals from each other. Indeed, he recognized that the nature of economic and social advance necessarily meant more legislation, agreeing with Charles Dupont-White, whose works *L'individu et l'état* and *La centralisation* he reviewed in his 1862 'Centralisation', that 'society and its interests become more complicated' and population growth and urbanization 'involves evils and dangers which on a smaller scale it was allowable to overlook'. As two examples 'among a thousand', Mill pointed out that 'when there were no railways, there needed no Railway Acts' and highlighted 'the vast trouble which society is now obliged to take in order to prevent its principal sources of water supply from being poisoned'.[71]

Mill had an activist vision for the state, which should create and sustain the conditions for individual and social progress, engender demand for beneficial goods and services, and help the poor. He was equally clear, however, that it was the energy, initiative and responsibility of individuals and communities that shaped the nation, writing in *On Liberty* that 'the worth of a State, in the long run, is the worth of the individuals composing it'. He suggested that even in cases where 'the individuals may not do the particular thing so well, on the average, as the officers of government, it is nevertheless desirable that it should be done by them'. Certain activities should be left to the populace 'as a means to their own mental education – a mode of strengthening their active faculties, exercising their judgement.' For Mill, this was 'a principal (though not the sole) recommendation of jury trial ... of free and popular local and municipal institutions; of the conduct of industrial and philanthropic enterprises by voluntary associations.' All these activities were part of the 'peculiar training of a citizen'. In addition, Mill wanted to keep the government out of as many activities as possible in order to promote the diversity and difference which he saw as vital ingredients for liberty: 'Government operations tend to be everywhere alike. With individuals and voluntary associations, on the contrary, there are varied experiments and diversity of experience. What the State can usefully do, is to make itself a central depository, and active circulator and diffuser, of the experience resulting from many trials.' The same argument applied, he argued, to the relationship between central and local government, where the 'practical principle' should be 'the greatest dissemination of power consistent with efficiency', with a 'special duty' on Whitehall officials to 'make knowledge acquired in one place available for others'.[72]

In terms of the potential threats to individual freedom, however, Mill was much more worried about what citizens, acting en masse, might do to each other, than the power of the state. The 'despotism of custom'; a 'social tyranny' of 'prevailing opinion'; a 'yoke of opinion': these were the evils against which *On Liberty* preached. The seventeenth-century philosopher Thomas Hobbes had argued that liberty existed wherever there was a 'Silence of the Law', but for Mill liberty could equally be threatened by the clamour of the masses. Borrowing heavily from Tocqueville, Mill warned of a potential 'tyranny of the majority', which was not 'restricted to the acts which it may do by the hands of its political functionaries'. Society could 'issue its own mandates' and when it did, it practised:

a social tyranny more formidable than many kinds of political oppression, since, though not usually upheld by such extreme penalties, it leaves fewer means of escape, penetrating much more deeply into the details of life, and enslaving the soul itself. Protection, therefore, against the tyranny of the magistrate is not enough: there needs also protection against the tyranny of the prevailing opinion and feeling.[73]

Mill singled out the suppression of unorthodox views on religious matters as an example of this social tyranny: 'so natural to mankind is intolerance in whatever they really care about, that religious freedom has hardly anywhere been practically realized.' He described the dangers of both Spanish anti-Protestantism and the apparent American aversion to Mormon polygamy. While admitting that the law in England was more liberal than in most countries, he did manage to find some lingering examples of legal religious oppression, citing the case of a Cornish man imprisoned in 1857 for uttering and writing on a gate some 'offensive words concerning Christianity'. But if the burden of English law was lighter, Mill believed that 'yoke of opinion was perhaps heavier' than in other European countries: 'Our merely social intolerance kills no one, roots out no opinions, but induces men to disguise them.' The problem this created, in his view, was an 'intellectual pacification': 'Who can compute what the world loses in the multitude of promising intellects combined with timid characters, who dare not follow out any bold, vigorous, independent train of thought, lest it should land them in something which would admit of being considered irreligious or immoral?'[74] Mill did not give any examples of these inhibited intellects, but it seems likely that this was partly autobiographical; he may also have known that Charles Darwin was delaying publication of his famous work in part because of 'some trepidation at the thought of exposing' himself as 'an atheist'. Bold individuals were thus needed to combat the deadening influence of opinion and custom:

Precisely because the tyranny of opinion is such as to make eccentricity a reproach, it is desirable, in order to break through that tyranny, that people are eccentric. Eccentricity has always abounded when and where strength of character has abounded; and the amount of eccentricity in a society has generally been proportional to the amount of genius, mental vigour, and moral courage which it contained. That so few dare to be eccentric marks the chief danger of the time.[75]

Mill's argument here is strained: it is highly doubtful, for example, that 'eccentricity' is in any way related to 'moral courage'. The

1940s were not perhaps an especially eccentric decade for Britain, but nor were British citizens lacking in courage or moral fibre. Yet Mill's fear is clear enough: he was terrified that mass communication and mass democracy would bring the mass production of people in their wake. This tendency would be reinforced, he had argued in 'Civilization', by the rise in circulation and geographical reach of the press: 'The newspaper carries home the voice of the many to every individual among them; by the newspaper each learns that others are feeling as he feels ... The newspaper is the telegraph which carries the signal throughout the country, and the flag around which it rallies'.[76] Eccentricity was seen by Mill as a kind of canary against these dangers, giving prior warning that the vital oxygen of individuality was being sucked away.

The identification of these new threats to eccentricity and individuality, like most of the arguments Mill posed, was the subject of fierce debate from almost the moment of publication. *On Liberty* was an intellectual hand-grenade rolled into the reading rooms of all the best clubs – his own, the Athenaeum, included. Three principal charges were levelled at Mill in the ensuing disputes: that he had undervalued the positive role of social custom; he had legitimized individualistic selfishness; and he had overstated the 'tyranny' being exercised by majority opinions.

Many critics accused him of underplaying the role of social conventions and moral codes in the sustaining of good life. James Fitzjames Stephen denounced *On Liberty* for promoting 'anarchic democracy', and the liberal cleric Richard Hutton – converted from Unitarianism to Anglicanism by F. D. Maurice – insisted that custom must be brought to bear on acts which 'extinguish that sense of the inviolable sanctity of social life which is its best and most distinctly religious bond'. In his advocacy of 'experiments in living', Mill prompts even modern critics to accuse him of 'bohemian nonsense'.[77]

Mill's argument was more subtle than many of his critics acknowledged, however. He recognized that while majority opinion could be used oppressively, it could also act as a non-coercive spur to desirable behaviour. In 1828, he had argued that such was the force of public opinion that it was vital it be 'well directed in respect of morality'. In his unpublished note to Harriet on marriage, he had suggested that legal restrictions on divorce might be lessened, in part because 'opinion', in place of law, could 'act as great efficacy to enforce the true rules of morality in these matters'. Social pressure was in fact one of the ways in which harmful actions could be sanctioned. 'Acts injurious to others' – in *On Liberty* Mill used deceit as an example – were 'fit objects of moral reprobation.' Similarly, those who failed in their duty to another were rightly open to 'moral disapproval in the proper sense of the term', although here the 'proper sense' qualification suggests that Mill was perhaps aware of some ambiguity in his argument.[78]

If public opinion was not necessarily tyrannical, nor was social custom inevitably despotic. Indeed, part of the purpose of 'experiments in living' was to allow others to learn from them, and a collective wisdom to be accumulated:

It would be absurd to pretend that people ought to live as if nothing whatever had been known in the world before they came into it; as if experience has as yet done nothing towards showing that one mode of existence, or of conduct, is preferable to another ... But it is the privilege and proper condition of a human being, arrived at the maturity of his faculties, to use and interpret experience in his own way.

For individuals to live according to the example of their society and peers was not proof of sheep-like conformity: the critical question was whether they had 'used and interpreted' it autonomously. 'He who does anything because it is the custom, makes no choice', Mill wrote. Collective experiences and customs could therefore provide people with valuable guidance but they could never produce a template for the perfect life – precisely because individuals are unique. 'Different persons', Mill insisted, 'require different conditions for their spiritual development; and can no more exist healthily in the same moral, than all the variety of plants can in the same physical, atmosphere and climate.' His point was not that people should never follow custom – indeed his hope was that customs could be a useful guide – but that in doing so they were 'using all their faculties' and making a conscious choice of their own 'plan of life'.[79]

What concerned him was the quality of the collective advice and ideas on offer; he was afraid that public opinion, if it simply took the form of the agglomerated views of the mass, would in fact provide fairly shoddy directions to the ordinary citizen. The danger was that 'the opinions of masses of merely average men are everywhere becoming the dominant power'. If everyone were cultivated, intelligent and thoughtful, their combined voice might be worth listening to, but as it was, 'the general average of mankind are not only moderate in intellect, but also moderate in inclinations'. 'The multitude are without a guide', Mill had lamented in his 1831 'Spirit of the Age', while in *On Liberty*, he suggested that 'the honour and glory of the average man is that he is capable of following ... that he can respond internally to wise and noble things, and be led to them with his eyes open'.[80]

Mill believed, then, that individuals should be free to follow their own path and could learn some lessons from the 'experiments in living' others, as well as themselves. These lessons should never be imposed, but should be inculcated through both education, and the force of customs and public opinion. But in the current state of society, only an elite of a 'highly gifted Few' could be trusted with the task of divining which customs were 'worthy of general adoption'.[81] An ill-educated mass, with little time or inclination for moral musing, would threaten its own advancement if it simply adopted its own collective views, gathered up by the mass media and played back to the originating audience.

Some of the sharpest attacks on Mill's essay focused on its supposed endorsement of individualism and selfishness. Herbert Cowell, a barrister moonlighting as an archly conservative reviewer, lamented Mill's 'ideal panorama of human society as a scene of one vast Jamaica revolt, in which all sense of duty and subordination is merged in the divine right of every man and woman to do as he pleases'. But in supporting individuality, Mill was far from endorsing individualism. His vision of the 'hoped-for heaven' was not an atomistic or egotistic one and he placed great weight on the 'social virtues', especially altruism. In *On Liberty* he urged that 'instead of any diminution there is need of a great increase of disinterested exertion to promote the good of others'.[82]

Mill's position on social relationships was demonstrated by his treatment of two thorny subjects: responsibilities towards children, and freedom to divorce. In a section of *On Liberty* which is often skipped over by modern liberals, Mill described the act of producing children without adequate resources to feed and educate them as a 'moral crime, both against the unfortunate offspring and against society'. Legal prohibitions in 'many counties on the Continent' which forbade marriage 'unless the parties can show that they have the means of supporting a family' were not, in Mill's view 'objectionable as violations of liberty'. Leaving aside the fact that Mill's grasp of international law was shaky – in fact only Bavaria had such a prohibition – and his assurance that such a marriage ban could only apply in a country 'over-peopled, or threatened with being so', it was still a startling proposal from the saint of liberalism. For Mill, though, it was a straightforward case of harm to others in which 'the consequence of their [the parents] indulgence is a life or lives of wretchedness and depravity to the offspring, with manifold evils to those sufficiently within reach to be in any way affected by their actions'.[83]

If Mill was not exactly laissez-faire about marriage, his views on divorce did not amount to undiluted individualism either. *On Liberty* contained his most thoughtful discussion of this issue, although somewhat awkwardly placed and, Mill insisted, purely 'for purposes of illustration'. Humboldt's ultra-liberal proposal that marriage be made instantly dissolvable merely on the 'declared will of either party', was, he believed, going too far. While each person should be free to construct their lives according to their own plans, they did not live in a vacuum, and so those plans would inevitably overlap with those of other people. He focused on the commitment that characterizes an intimate relationship:

When a person, either by express promise or by conduct, has encouraged another to rely upon his continuing to act in a certain way – to build expectations and calculations, and stake any part of his plan of life upon that supposition – a new series of moral obligations arises on his part towards that person, which may possibly be overruled, but cannot be ignored.[84]

This evocation of 'moral obligations' as a brake on individual freedom of action is a million miles away from the moral anarchy Mill was charged with wanting to unleash; he insisted that commitments carried responsibilities, that ties did bind us together. Such commitments did not, of course, make marriage contracts inviolable, but they were:

A necessary element in the question; and even if, as von Humboldt maintains, they ought to make no difference in the *legal* freedom of the parties to release themselves from the engagement (and I also hold that they should not make *much* difference), they necessarily make a great deal of difference in the *moral* freedom.[85]

Mill was also criticized for overstating in *On Liberty* the social constraints on religious criticism, eccentricity or 'experiments in living'. Macaulay captured the spirit of these disagreements. 'I went to the Athanaeum, and staid there two hours to read John Mill on Liberty and on Reform. Much that is good in both,' he wrote in his journal, but added:

What is meant by the complaint that there is no individuality now? Bolder invention was never known in science than in our time ... the clairvoyance, the spirit-rapping, the table-turning and all those other dotages and knaveries, indicate rather a restless impatience of the beaten paths than a stupid determination to plod on in those paths ... He is really crying 'Fire!' in Noah's flood.[86]

James Fitzjames Stephen stated bluntly that Mill was 'distinctly wrong in asserting that, as a matter of fact, originality of character is ceasing to exist'. Even the historian Henry Buckle, an admirer of Mill and author of perhaps the warmest review of *On Liberty*, suggested that 'on the whole, individuality is not diminishing, and that so far as we can estimate the future, it is not likely to diminish.'[87]

The views of Mill's critics are understandable: it certainly did not look as if the nation was in the grip of tyrannical anti-eccentric conformity. *On Liberty* was published in the same year that Charles Blondin tight-roped across Niagara Falls. The end of the decade had seen a craze for coded love letters on the pages of *The Times*: one adulterous pair saw their code cracked by Charles Wheatstone, who, as Professor of Experimental Philosophy at King's College London, was perhaps not as busy in professorial pursuits as Mill would have liked. The last message, sent on 15 January 1854, read: 'FLO. – 89545 6454401 214 739844 30 6307284446. 84314 51 2274 12 0214 943426 326352 08585, 9.2., 8177327853. 81770'. Or, as Wheatstone could have told readers: 'Flo. – I fear dearest our cipher is discovered. Write at once to your friend, 'Indian Shawl', P.O., Buckingham, Bucks.' Mill's strictures about eccentricity were being read by a public who recently would have seen, or at least read about, 'The Baboon Lady', supposedly a cross between a human and an ape, who danced the Highland Fling and sang arias. (When she died giving birth to her manager-husband's child, he demonstrated his entrepreneurial spirit by mummifying them both and putting them on show in London.)[88]

Nor was there much evidence for the dangerous suppression of opinion on religious matters. Mill was writing during a period of secularization: the religious census of 1851 found that fewer than half the population were not attending church or chapel – less than in the United States at the beginning of the twenty-first-century. One vicar in Oldham lamented that the nation was subsiding into 'semi-heathenism'. Contrary to Mill's suggestion for a heavy 'yoke of opinion' on matters of faith, Lord Shaftesbury had encapsulated back in the early eighteenth century the general trend towards English pragmatism: 'All wise men are of the same religion.' Asked by a woman what that religion was, he famously replied: 'Madam, wise men never tell.'[89] Since then the nation had calmly absorbed David Hume's scepticism in his *Philosophical Essays* of 1748 and the revisionist views on Christianity in Edward Gibbon's *Decline and Fall* in 1778.

It was true that Mill and a number of his peers, who he described as the 'brightest ornaments' in the national intellectual firmament – he might have had in mind Darwin, Huxley, Spencer or Macaulay – were less than completely open, in public, about their religious scepticism. But it is hard to think, considering their work, that these self-imposed ordnances had prevented the development of 'bold, vigorous, independent train of thought', as Mill suggested. When punishments were meted out for unorthodox views they were usually mild: James Anthony Froude, the biographer of Carlyle and a fellow of Exeter College, Oxford, saw a copy of his anti-religious novel *The Nemesis of Faith* being thrown in the fire by the sub-rector in front of the undergraduates; the other college Fellows also refused to converse with him in the Senior Common Room. This must have been disagreeable for Froude, but it hardly represented an English Inquisition.[90]

If Mill had treated *On Liberty* like all his other works, he would surely have responded to these wide-ranging criticisms in the second edition; but there was to be none. As a tribute to Harriet, 'consecrated to her memory', *On Liberty* had to remain untouched: 'I have made no alteration or addition to it, nor shall I ever,' he declared in his *Autobiography*. It was only in this latter work, published fourteen years later and after his death, that Mill would answer the critics. His first move, on the question of the need for greater variety in individual character, was to turn his opponents' fire on themselves: 'Nothing can better shew how deep are the foundations of this truth [of the need for variety in character] than the great impression made by the exposition of it at a time which, to superficial observation, did not seem to stand much in need of such a lesson.'[91] Here Mill appeared to be suggesting that his critics were blind to their own captivity in the trap of conformity:

a weak argument to make against the likes of Macaulay and Stephen.

Mill's next defence was more credible. He admitted that the essay's fears of 'an oppressive yoke of uniformity in opinion and practice, might easily have appeared chimerical to those who looked more at present facts than tendencies; for the gradual revolution that is taking place in society has this far been decidedly favourable to the development of new opinions'. These improvements, however, were characteristic of any 'age of transition' such as the one England was passing through: the real test, Mill insisted, would come later, when the new 'creeds' were settled and the risk of individuals being 'compressed' might re-emerge. Protection for individuals from the 'noxious power' of convention would then depend on whether 'mankind have by that time become aware that it cannot be exercised without stunting and dwarfing human nature. It is then that the teachings of *On Liberty* will have their greatest value. And it is to be feared that they will retain that value for a long time.'[92]

For some Mill fans, this settles the argument. Rather than focusing on the 'superficial' and 'chimerical' trends of the present, he was in fact sending a message in a book to the future.[93] It may indeed be the case that Mill's fears of a prevailing orthodoxy stifling individuality resonate more strongly today than they did in 1859 – but it is hard to credit Mill for this. In an attempt to meet the criticisms of *On Liberty*, without appearing to alter his arguments, Mill was engaged in this section of the *Autobiography* in some rather contorted post-hoc rationalization. In *On Liberty* itself, he could not have been clearer in his view that the risk to individuality was current. Recycling a phrase he had first used in 1836, he wrote: 'At *present* individuals are lost in the crowd.' Elsewhere, too, the tone was of topical description rather than forecast: 'There *is* also in the world an increasing inclination to stretch unduly the powers of society over the individual' and 'society *has* fairly got the better of individuality'. Attributing Europe's superiority over China to its greater diversity of 'character and culture', Mill warned that 'it *already begins* to possess this benefit in a considerably less degree'. Underlining the vital importance of multiplicity of lifestyles, he went even further, warning that variety was 'in this country *every day* diminishing' and that 'in *our times*, from the highest class of society down to the lowest, *every one lives* under the eye of a hostile and dreaded censorship'.[94] [All the italics in this paragraph have been added.]

By retrospectively recasting *On Liberty* as a social forecast rather than a contemporary analysis, Mill avoided having to cede any public ground to his critics. This was an uncharacteristically defensive strategy; on other occasions he was quite willing to change his mind, alter his works, change a particular emphasis or admit an earlier mistake. His hidebound approach to *On Liberty* was almost certainly related to the memorial status of the essay; revising the text would, to Mill, have been like chipping some marble off Harriet's grave. If she had lived another decade Harriet and Mill would surely have revised *On Liberty* together, and while a second edition would have been just as robust on freedom of speech, the centrality of individuality in well-being and the dangers of a tyranny of the majority, it might also have been more even-handed about the present and more open-minded about the future. It would perhaps have more clearly described individuality as a gift of progress, but one which progress could also destroy. Its tone could have been that of a physician warning a patient to stop smoking in order to avoid lung cancer, rather than an oncologist confirming the diagnosis.

On Liberty would also have made a stronger case if Mill had highlighted the most telling example in Victorian England of the 'despotism of custom': the virtually unchallenged assumptions about the status, role and nature of women. Temperance movements and Sunday trading laws were minor issues compared to entrenched gender inequality. It was patriarchy, rather than religion, that was the real enemy of liberty. It would be another decade before the publication of *The Subjection of Women*, with only a handful of hints in *On Liberty* of what was to come, including Mill's comment that 'the man, and still more the woman, who can be accused of ... not doing "what everybody does" is the subject of as much depreciatory remark as if he or she had committed some grave moral delinquency'. Pointing out that moral codes are usually set by the ascendant class, Mill also paired some examples in which one group was illegitimately dominant: 'Spartans and Helots, planters and negroes, princes and subjects, nobles and roturiers, men and women.' Then, tucked between the discussions of pub licensing laws and education, came a foretaste of the radical arguments of *Subjection*:

The almost despotic power of husbands over wives needs not be enlarged upon here, because nothing more is needed for the complete removal of the evil, than that wives should have the same rights, and should receive the same protection of law in the same manner, as all other persons; and because, on this subject, the defenders of established injustice do not avail themselves of the plea of liberty, but stand forth openly as champions of power.[95]

Of course, the 'nothing more' rather understates the scale of the challenge, which remains unmet in most nations in the world a century and a half later, and Mill himself would also spend much of *Subjection* arguing that sexist opinions, customs and habits were in fact at least as damaging as discriminatory laws – echoing precisely the analysis of *On Liberty*. Mill's feminism completed his liberalism. In *On Liberty*, however, he pursued the issue no further, aware that attitudes towards women were so deeply grounded that a premature attack risked simply undermining the proponent. Perhaps one source of the marvellous anger of *On Liberty* was Mill's knowledge that the very evil he was assailing was constraining him from making his best case.

His fears were justified: Mill's overt feminism would make him many enemies and disappoint many of his most ardent admirers. But when he did reveal the full extent of his views on gender equality, he also began an energetic campaign – conducted within and outside Parliament – for women's rights. By the late 1860s, he came to believe, wrongly as it turned out, that women were on the brink of winning the right to vote. Part of the reason for his optimism was that after the torpidity of the 1850s, the 1860s would witness the revival of a genuinely reforming spirit in political and intellectual circles. On 6 June 1859, in Willis's Rooms on St James Street, a new political party – the Liberal party – was born, and in November, after a prolonged gestation, Darwin's *Origin of Species* was published, inaugurating in Mill's view 'an era in thought in its particular subject'.[96]

Mill was naturally pleased that his own contribution had caused some ripples. 'I really had no idea of being so influential a person as my critics tell me I am,' he suggested, over-modestly, to Bain, in response to the wide-ranging debate sparked by *On Liberty*. 'But being thought to have influence is the surest way of obtaining it really'. For all its faults, the continued popularity of *On Liberty* demonstrates that Mill's influence is still being felt a century and a half on. Even allowing for the bias of John Morley, Mill's most steadfast disciple, few could disagree with his conclusion that *On Liberty* 'belongs to the rare books that after hostile criticism has done its best are still found to have somehow added a cubit to man's stature'.[97]

As the 1860s opened, Mill could legitimately claim some rest and relaxation. He was fifty-three years old, at a time when English male life expectancy was under forty, having narrowly escaped death from consumption. The only demand made of him by the rump of the East India Company was that he cash his generous pension cheques. He was a widower with a devoted companion and an agreeable house in the gorgeous French Vaucluse, a short stroll from his beloved wife's grave. His garden was full of nightingales. Mill had already produced his generation's definitive works in both logic and political economy, and crowned them with a stunning evocation of the liberal ideal. His career as a public intellectual could now taper off to a quiet, dignified finale. Mill was not finished, however. As England was to discover, he was just getting into his stride.

CHAPTER TWELVE

To Hell I Will Go (1859–65)

⇥⇤

'Life here is uneventful, and feels like a perpetual holiday,' Mill confessed to Thornton from Avignon. 'It is in truth too self-indulgent a life for any one to allow himself whose duties lie among his fellow-beings, unless, as is fortunately the case with me, they are mostly such as can be better fulfilled at a distance from society than in the midst of it.'[1] On the surface, Mill did indeed seem be settling into a leisurely regime of walking, botanizing, reading, writing, dining with friends and spending at least half of his time six hundred miles from dreary English weather and politics. In 1860, his publications ran to just two articles, both botanical. The first, 'Wallflower Growing on the Living Rock', can safely be quoted in full:

It seems to be noticed as remarkable (see Phytologist, vol. iv, p.6) that Mr. Sim found Cheiranthus Cheiri on the living rock. It grows profusely on the precipitous part of St. Vincent's Rock, at the end of Bristol.

In the other, only slightly longer piece, Mill displayed a rare burst of patriotism, albeit phytological, insisting that England was superior to southern Europe in both ferns and the 'flowery beauty of our spring'.[2]

But while Mill was outwardly serene, he was working just as hard as ever. Between Harriet's death at the end of 1858 and his election to Parliament in 1865, Mill published, in addition to *On Liberty*, his major work of political theory, *Considerations on Representative Government*; the final instalment of his lifelong wrestle with Bentham's moral philosophy, *Utilitarianism;* a settling of his accounts with his principal French correspondent in *Auguste Comte and Positivism*; two substantial essays on the American Civil War; and a door-stopping chunk of metaphysics in the form of *An Examination of Sir William Hamilton's Philosophy*. He also ramped up his political activities, vociferously supporting parliamentary reform, women's rights and the northern American states. It would be said of the pensioner in this period that he 'ceases to be a philosopher and becomes the partisan' and that he was 'chief of the Satanic School in England'. For his part, Mill told Helen in 1860 that it 'it is better for me to try to serve my opinions in other ways as well as with a pen in my hand'.[3] While other men in their late fifties reach for a pipe and pair of slippers, Mill dug out his political boxing gloves.

His political fervour was heightened by the rekindling of some old friendships – especially with George Grote and Alexander Bain – and also a widening circle of new ones. Mill did not write to either of the Grotes during his married years; in the following decade he wrote nineteen letters to George, and four to Harriet. The revival of the friendship was sufficient for Mill and Helen to join the Grotes for a summer weekend in 1861, and for Christmas in 1862. For Mill these were doubly nostalgic trips, since the Grotes were now owners of Barrow Green, one of Bentham's houses in which Mill had spent his youthful summers. In 1863 Mill and Helen happily dog-sat for their friends: 'We took Daisy to Savile Row and duly delivered him there on Monday,' he reported to Harriet Grote. 'It cost both Helen and me an effort not to make use of your kind permission to take him with us to Avignon, but prudence prevailed, on account of the absence of any fence capable of restraining his wandering propensities. He is most beautiful and amiable dog and his pleasant ways have been a great source of enjoyment to us.'[4]

At some point in 1861, Mill was tinkering with his *Autobiography* and substantially redrafted a section relating to Grote's performance as a parliamentarian in the 1830s. The original draft described him as 'almost inactive', his time in the House 'almost wasted' and speculated that 'if his courage and energy had been equal to the circumstances, or to his knowledge and abilities, the history of those ten years' relapse into Toryism might have been very different.' In the revised version, Grote was included in the group who had been 'honest, and faithful to their opinions' and 'braved any amount of hostility and prejudice rather than desert the right'. It seems likely that the change in Mill's relationship with Grote prompted the revisions and by 1865 he was describing him (to Grote, at any rate) as 'one whose good opinion and good feeling I value more than that of any other living man'.[5]

Mill was also busy organizing Saturday night dinner parties in Blackheath, as well as occasionally enticing guests to Avignon. Mill had once told his wife – contrary to both his feminism and associationism – that 'a man is by nature incapable of giving a dinner party'.[6] So Helen continued to play a vital role as hostess. In addition to the Grotes and the Bains, Mill and Helen's guests included Louis Blanc, Theodor Gomperz, William Thornton, John Morley, as well as half a dozen new friends. One of the most important of these new friends was the barrister-cum-political theorist Thomas Hare, who Mill met in 1859 and to whom he felt a considerable intellectual debt. Hare had come up with a plan for a new voting system that averted what, for Mill, was the most grievous danger of wider suffrage – a legislature commanded by the working classes. In 1835, reviewing Tocqueville, Mill had warned that the 'one and only danger of democracy' was the creation of legislators who were 'mere delegates for carrying into execution the preconceived judgment of the majority'.[7] He assumed that the working classes would vote for candidates from their own class, who were unlikely to be men of intelligence and wisdom, and would simply pursue class interests. While supporting universal suffrage as an 'ultimate aim', he feared the combination of universal suffrage, low levels of education and a first-past-the-post voting system, for reasons outlined in his major political work, *Representative Government,* which occupied much of his time during 1860 and was published in 1861:

The natural tendency of representative government, as of modern civilization, is towards collective mediocrity: and this tendency is increased by all reductions and extensions in the franchise, their effect being to place the principal power in the hands of classes more and more below the highest level of instruction in the community . . . the great majority of voters would be manual labourers; and the twofold danger, that of too low a standard of political intelligence, and that of class legislation, would exist in a very perilous degree.[8]

Mill's concerns were uncontroversial at the time. Macaulay went further and warned that universal suffrage would be 'fatal to the purposes for which government exists' and 'utterly incompatible with the existence of civilisation'. Harriet Grote warned Lord Amberley, son of Lord John Russell, in 1866 to 'avoid committing himself to sentimental democratic views . . . lest he should one day have to recede from positions taken up in the warmth of popular sympathies'. Walter Bagehot, whose famous *English Constitution* was published between 1865 and 1867, and to which *Representative Government* was often compared, similarly insisted that the best government was by the 'select few' and worried that modern democrats faced a new order of challenge compared to their ancient predecessors. The Greeks, he said, did not have to combine in their polity 'Somerset labourers and men like Mr Grote. *We have.*'[9]

Thomas Hare's scheme, a form of proportional representation (PR), allowed Mill to square his support for working-class votes with his insistence upon the need for 'superior minds' in Parliament. 'I have not been so delighted with any political treatise for many years,' declared Mill after digesting Hare's 1859 paper, *A Treatise on the Election of Representatives, Parliamentary and Municipal.* To Hare himself he wrote: 'You appear to me to have exactly, and for the first time, solved the difficulty of popular representation;

and by doing so, to have raised up the cloud of gloom and uncertainty which hung over the futurity of representative government and therefore of civilisation.' It was a scheme, Mill concluded, 'for which I shall henceforth be a zealous apostle'.[10]

He was as good as his word, and started by welcoming the plan in a long article in *Fraser's*, 'Recent Writers on Reform', in April 1859. The two struck up a spirited correspondence, exchanging ten letters in 1859 alone and matching in frequency the Mill–Comte correspondence of the early 1840s. Although the details of Hare's scheme were complex, the essential concept was simple: the number of voters should be divided by the number of MPs, and anybody receiving the resulting number of votes would sit in Parliament. Voters could also name second and third preferences – and so on *ad infinitum* – with the lower preferences being activated once candidates higher up the list had gained sufficient votes for election, or were knocked out.

For Mill, this blueprint was '*the* great discovery in representative government'. Hare, he said, had found 'an effectual and practicable mode of preventing numbers, in a popular constitution, from swamping and extinguishing the influence of education and knowledge.' The practicality of Hare's scheme was less obvious to most other observers, but it seems likely that any form of PR would have captured Mill's imagination. Mill wanted more working-class representation, so that the concerns of ordinary people could be aired and addressed in Parliament: radical MPs – the 'well-dressed friends' of the working class – were showing, to Mill's mind, little success in this regard. But he did not want working-class domination, and saw Hare's scheme as a way to 'ascendancy to none and justice to all'.[11]

Armed with Hare's plan, Mill henceforth took great pains to distinguish in his writings between 'false democracy', which he variously described as 'mere mob-government' or a 'despotism of the numerical majority', and 'true' democracy, which was a system in which 'every or any section would be represented, not disproportionately, but proportionately'. This 'fair representation of minorities' would ensure, he wrote in *Representative Government*, that 'a democratic people would ... be provided with what in any other way it would almost certainly miss – leaders of a higher grade of intellect and character than itself. Modern democracy would have its occasional Pericles, and its habitual group of superior and guiding minds'.[12]

Even under PR, 'superior and guiding minds' would still, of course, be outnumbered, but Mill was not concerned, because he thought their intellectual and moral advantages would allow their views to carry disproportionate weight, even in a proportionate Parliament:

Represented, as that minority would be likely to be, by the ablest heads and noblest hearts in the nation, their representatives would probably acquire considerable personal ascendancy over the other section of the House ... The cause of the minority would be likely to be supported with such consummate skill, and such a weight of moral authority, as might prove a sufficient balance to the superiority of numbers on the other side.[13]

Conservatives and liberals should equally favour PR, Mill told a new correspondent, the American Unitarian minister Moncure Conway: 'It is indeed at once a direct corollary from the first principles of democracy and a most powerful corrective to all evils liable to arise from the forms of democratic government hitherto in use'. Disraeli's refusal to consider even a mild degree of minority protection drew the rebuke from Mill in *Representative Government* that 'the Conservatives, as being by the law of their existence, [were] the stupidest party'.[14] The fact that the barb was in a footnote did nothing to dim his enemies' memory of it, as Mill would later discover.

Mill was also convinced that time was short. 'The numerical majority are not the strongest force yet,' he reminded Bain. 'The point to be decided is, how much power is to be yielded to them.' Universal suffrage was coming, at least for men, and it was vital to establish the right structures from the outset. 'If the American form of democracy overtakes us first,' he worried, 'the majority will no more relax their despotism than a single despot would.' The ability of charismatic leaders to woo the masses was also a cause for concern: Mill saw John Bright as a 'mere demagogue and courtier of the majority'.[15] France, of course, offered an even more brutal lesson on the dangers of democracy in the hands of a uncultivated population: 'The millions of voters who, in opposition to nearly every educated person in the country, made Louis Napoleon President,' Mill wrote, 'were chiefly peasants who could neither read nor write, and whose knowledge of public men, even by name, was limited to oral tradition'. Mill's dislike of Napoleon III was unquenchable: when he brought a gun from London to Avignon – for Helen's protection when she was alone in the house – he worried half-seriously whether he would be stopped at customs: 'I believe importation of arms is prohibited, not to mention that they may think I intend to fire at the Emperor.'[16] Mill's views about democracy were shaped by the fact that the people of nation he most loved had elected the man he most hated.

As well as some form of proportional representation, Mill urged in *Representative Government* a second defensive wall against the ignorant masses: an educational qualification for voters. 'I regard it as wholly inadmissible that any person should participate in the suffrage,' he wrote, 'without being able to read, write, and, I will add, perform the common operations of arithmetic.' Mill hoped and believed that, 'before long', rising educational standards would mean that an education test would 'exclude nobody', but never retreated from the view that 'universal teaching must precede universal enfranchisement'.[17] He also insisted that there should be no representation without taxation. Allowing non-taxpayers a vote, he said, amounted 'to allowing them to put their hands into other people's pockets for any purpose which they think fit to call a public one'.[18] Anybody who had received poor relief in the previous five years should also be disenfranchised, on the same grounds, and at one point he even toyed with the idea of a poll tax.

Mill also supported 'plural' votes, a mechanism for giving more electoral power to those with 'education and knowledge'. 'When all have votes,' he wrote in 1859, in *Thoughts on Parliamentary Reform*, 'it will be both just in principle and necessary in fact, that some mode be adopted . . . by which the more intrinsically valuable member of society . . . should, as far as practicable, be singled out, and allowed a superiority of influence proportioned to his higher qualifications.' He suggested a weighted voting system, in which lawyers and vicars, for example, would get six votes for every one granted to an 'unskilled labourer'.[19] Mill could not be faulted for lack of candour in his explanation, writing: 'It is the fact, that one person is *not* as good as another, and it is reversing all the rules of rational conduct, to attempt to raise a political fabric on a supposition which is at variance with fact.'[20] In Mill's mind, it seemed, while all were proportional, some were more proportional than others.

Mill initially thought that Hare's scheme – which he discovered only after publication of *Thoughts on Parliamentary Reform* in 1859 – might 'render ultimately unnecessary' these plans to give more votes to those with 'proved superiority of education'. But by 1861, his view had, if anything, hardened. Even 'if the best hopes which can be formed on this subject [of PR], were certainties,' he wrote in *Representative Government*, 'I should still contend for the principle of plural voting.' Nor was plural voting, like restrictions in the franchise, a temporary evil. 'I do not look upon equal voting as among the things which are good in themselves,' he said.[21] On this issue, Mill's views were more Tory than radical. There had already been an attempt in 1859 to give extra votes to university graduates, members of the learned professions and holders of £50 worth of savings, and the Conservative leader Benjamin Disraeli would resurrect these 'fancy franchises' in his 1867 Bill. In the end Disraeli withdrew these clauses, though Mill's correspondence suggests that he would have supported extra votes for the 'learned professions'.[22]

In the last years of his life, Mill realized that his fears about the impact of wider suffrage had been overstated, but during the 1860s he was constantly casting around for devices to control the flow of the majoritarian tide. In 1864, he wrote to the 3rd Earl Grey, the son of the tea-drinking reformer, with yet another democracy-diluting wheeze. His idea was to allow unenfranchised members of the working class who passed an educational test to 'be allowed to choose electors, say one in ten or one in five of their number, who should form, along with the direct electors, the parliamentary constituency'. This would give the working classes 'a substantial power in Parliament but not the complete control of it'. Even Grey, a supporter of indirect voting schemes, was unenthusiastic and the scheme never found its way into any of Mill's published works.[23]

From a radical perspective, Mill's real betrayal was his opposition to the introduction of a secret ballot – votes for MPs were at the time made in public, but many liberals and radicals urged privacy in order to reduce corruption and intimidation. 'If James Mill,' fumed the ageing Francis Place, 'could have anticipated that his son John Stuart should preach so abominable a heresy ... he would have cracked his skull.'[24] For Mill junior, however, the opportunity to vote in secret had never been an article of faith. In his youthful, radical days he had believed it would speed up other reforms; now he thought that circumstances had changed and, that on balance, secret voting would do more harm than good. The requirement to vote openly was clearly accompanied by dangers of coercion, intimidation and bribery, but the risk with secret voting was, in Mill's father's words, a 'base and mischievous' vote. 'Thirty years ago,' Mill wrote, 'the main evil to be guarded against was that which the ballot would exclude – coercion by landlords, employers, and customers. At present, I conceive, a much greater source of evil is the selfishness, or the selfish partialities of the voter himself.'[25]

Mill insisted that the vote was not a individual 'right' but a 'public trust'. 'There will never be honest or self-restraining government,' he told George Cornewall Lewis, the old *Edinburgh Review* editor in 1859, 'unless each individual participant feels himself a trustee for all his fellow citizens and for posterity. Certainly no Athenian voter thought otherwise'. The act of voting, he told a correspondent in 1867, was undertaken 'as a return to the civilization to which he owes not only all the security and peace, all the highest enjoyments of his life, but also the possibility of attaining refinement and moral elevation'.[26]

Growing freedom of opinion, and a steady reduction in the numbers of people tied directly to landowners made the risks of corruption and coercion much less. 'The progress of circumstances has done and is doing more and more, in this respect, the work of the ballot,' according to Mill. Nevertheless he remained alive to the possibility of an individual suffering in their marketplace for their views and saw that 'shopkeepers were more in need of [the ballot] than the working classes', because of the danger that they would be boycotted for their views.[27] At the time Mill was writing – let alone by today's standards – these views on secret voting were conservative; yet they reveal an important intersection between his views on liberty and democracy. A democracy was not, for him, simply a conglomeration of private interests, but a means of promoting and exercising the public duties necessary for the maintenance of civilized life. He would have endorsed the view of John Adams, one of America's founding fathers, that 'positive passion for the public good' was a foundation of 'real Liberty' and good government. This meant, for one thing, that people should be willing to experience some inconvenience to vote: opposing postal voting, Mill declared that 'a man who does not care whether he votes, is not likely to care much which way he votes and . . . has no moral right to vote at all.'[28]

It is difficult, however, to square Mill's position on the secret ballot with his polemic against the despotism of custom in *On Liberty*. If opinion was increasingly tyrannical, there was surely an even stronger case for secrecy to protect individuals. This was certainly the view of Henry Romilly, the younger son of the couple who visited Forde Abbey when Mill was a child, in his criticism of Mill's position. 'At periods of political excitement,' Romilly wrote, 'the practical sense to an elector of the phrase "Responsibility to public opinion" is too often . . . at your peril, vote for any candidate but the popular candidate.' In a review of Romilly's pamphlet, Mill admitted that the potentially despotic influence of opinion was a powerful argument for the secret ballot, but concluded none the less that he was 'for leaving the voter open to the penalties of opinion, but not to those of brute force', since public opinion was more likely to make 'the voter more careful to act up to his sincere opinion'.

There is some evidence that Mill's subconscious, at least, was unconvinced by his own arguments. In 1854 he had recounted a dream to Harriet: 'I was disputing about the ballot with Calhoun, the American, of whom in some strange way I had become the brother – & when I said that the ballot was no longer necessary, he answered "it will not be necessary in heaven, but it will always be necessary on earth".'[29] When Mill was writing, however, heaven was in the far distance and it is likely that the distorting effect of open voting was still considerable. He was also on the wrong side of history: in 1872, William Gladstone would pass the secret ballot into law.

If Mill placed exacting demands on voters, he was even tougher on their representatives. MPs should not canvass for votes or spend their own money on campaigns; they should be willing to vote against the wishes of those who had elected them; and they should receive no money from the public purse. Their deliberations had to enlighten, instruct and energize the nation: Mill wanted independent, courageous, thoughtful politicians, rather than party hacks. He had always regarded the practice of canvassing for votes as a 'degrading practice' – but his bigger concern was with the growing role of money in politics. The freedom to spend on electioneering, he warned, made for a new 'property qualification of the worst kind. The old property qualification ... only required that a member of Parliament should possess a fortune; this requires that he should have spent one'. The result of the rising cost of campaigning – which included plentiful bribery – was to 'limit access to Parliament to rich men' and prevent 'democratic persons from being elected'.[30]

If Mill was reassuring reformist ears on campaign funding, he opposed another core radical demand: the payment of MPs. For Mill, giving salaries to politicians would attract 'a low class of adventurers', chiefly concerned with their own 'pecuniary returns'. He did not pull any punches: 'It amounts to offering 658 prizes for the most successful flatterer, the most adroit misleader of a body of fellow-countrymen. Under no despotism has there been such an organized system of tillage for raising a rich crop of vicious courtiership.'[31] It was also vital that MPs were free to deliberate freely on the great questions before them, and he remained fiercely opposed to the tying of parliamentarians' hands in the form of binding 'pledges' to their constituents, which was a popular radical demand. The voter should no more expect their representative 'to act according to their judgment, any more than they require a physician to prescribe for them according to their own notions of medicine'. Electors 'should choose as their representatives wiser men than themselves, and should consent to be governed according to that superior wisdom'.[32]

Mill's view of the role of Parliament was as an agora for the modern age, a place which would act as the principal site of deliberation, argument and decision. It would be 'at once the nation's Committee of Grievances, and its Congress of Opinions'.[33] With his concern to promote constructive dissent and the collision of opinions, the deliberative function of Parliament was paramount. 'Representative assemblies are often taunted by their enemies with being places of mere talk and bavardage', he wrote, perhaps thinking either of Carlyle, who had berated any view of Parliament as a 'Talking-Apparatus' instead of an 'Acting-Apparatus', or Bentham, who had judged that it was 'as difficult to build politics on deliberation as to build military or medical science with one word for "front" and "back"'. 'There has seldom been more misplaced derision', wrote Mill. 'I know not how a Representative assembly can more usefully employ itself than in talk, when the subject of talk is the great public interests of the country.'[34] In Mill's political theory, debate was the vital means by which 'superior' minds could wield their necessary influence on events, as well as educate the nation at large.

The deliberative function of Parliament was one argument in favour of bicameralism, Mill thought, with the necessary 'give and take' between an upper and lower House acting as 'a perpetual school' and improving the quality of resulting legislation. The

House of Lords, if it was to play this role – and Mill was not always convinced it should – evidently needed reform. In the 1830s, during his most Coleridgean phase, he had urged that the goal should be to 'remodel the present House of Lords, without taking away its character as such'. It was important, for example, that the name not be changed, because in a revolutionary age the nation could not 'afford to lose any hold over the people's minds which existing names, historical reflections, traditional attachment, custom, and imagination give to the institutions' which 'act as barriers to ... restrain the unenlightened or incautious exercise of the people's will'. In the short term, then, he was willing to tolerate a rump of hereditary peers to help preserve the 'character' of the institution.

By 1848, however, flushed by the continental revolutions, he believed that 'howsoever composed', the House of Lords was 'a serious hindrance to improvement' and 'worse than superfluous – it is injurious'. By 1861, in *Representative Government*, he suggested that if there was to be an upper house, it ought to be a 'Chamber of Statesmen', modelled on the Roman Senate; eight years later, after first-hand experience of Parliament, he finally concluded that the peers were 'too stupid and too conservative to be moved' and doubted 'if a Second Chamber can ever again carry weight in English politics, unless popularly elected'.[35]

Mill was consistently opposed, however, to an elected head of state, pointing to the unfortunate examples, in his mind, of France and America. In his 1837 article on Armand Carrel, his French hero, Mill lamented the turning of 'the highest office in the State, the only place which carries with it the most tempting part (to common minds) of power, the show of it', into 'a prize to be scrambled for by every ambitious and turbulent spirit ... in the mean turmoil of a perpetual canvass'. By contrast to Bentham, who saw the monarch as the 'corrupter-general', Mill thought in 1848 that a constitutional monarchy was in fact 'suited to the tone of thought and feeling characteristic of England'.[36]

As an institution, the monarchy helped to define what Mill termed a 'feeling of nationality'. Shared religion, a common language and geographical boundaries also had a part to play in binding nations together; but the very strongest generators of nationality were 'identity of political antecedents; the possession of a national history, and consequent community of recollections; collective pride and humiliation, pleasure and regret, connected with the same incidents in the past'. At the same time, Mill saw nations as moral communities, in which the demands of public participation kindled patriotism: 'Let a person have nothing to do for his country,' he declared in *Representative Government* 'and he will not care for it.' For these reasons, Mill thought that governments should almost always be national, and that 'free institutions' were 'next to impossible in a country made up of different nations'.[37] But if Mill offered some succour here to nationalist parties, his exception to this rule would be less palatable to many. He suggested that smaller, 'inferior' nations may in fact do better as part of a bigger one:

Nobody can suppose that it is not more beneficial to a Breton, or a Basque of French Navarre, to be brought into the current of the ideas and feeling of a highly civilized and cultivated people ... than to sulk on his own rocks, the half-savage relic of past times, revolving in his own little mental orbit ... The same remark applies to the Welshman or the Scottish highlander, as members of the British nation.[38]

Not of course that all power should be sucked towards Westminster and Whitehall: in *Representative Government* Mill restated his commitment to robust, vital local government. At the time, Britain was the 'least centralized in Europe', which Mill saw as good news, especially by comparison to France. An over-excited member of the French Assembly had once called for 'One God, one France, one King, one Chamber' and Mill approved of Sir Walter Scott's withering response that such a philosophy of central control amounted to 'one mouth, one nose, one ear, and one eye'.[39]

The ability to adapt to local conditions was a huge advantage of locally based bodies, but the existing forms of local administration were not up to the task of managing modern problems: strong doses of rationalization and democratization were necessary. Mill insisted that elected county councils should replace the existing, unelected 'Quarter Sessions' of local gentry, which were now the 'most aristocratic institution ... in England', a 'jobbing and *borné* local oligarchy'. (This reform was finally achieved in 1888.) The division of London into half a dozen squabbling districts was ludicrous, according to Mill, preventing necessary cooperation and having 'no purpose but to keep up the fantastical trappings of that union of modern jobbing and antiquated foppery, the Corporation of the City of London'.[40] A few years later, Mill would introduce the first parliamentary bill to create a single London Corporation.

Mill presciently suggested that the 'noisy and exciting' argument about 'Forms of Government' for nation-states would soon end with agreement on some version of democratic, representative government, while the debate about the relationship between central and local government would be ongoing: 'The answer to the question between governmental and central, and private or local action is perpetually varying; depending not upon a single principle, but on a compromise between principles, the elements of which are not exactly the same in any two applications.'[41] Later he congratulated himself that he had 'steered carefully between the two errors' of the 'unreasoning prejudice' against central government on one hand, and the 'mischiefs' of concentrating too much power in London on the other: it was Tocqueville, Mill said, who had saved him from a utilitarian bias towards central government.[42]

But his principal political adviser now was Thomas Hare, and through him Mill formed another important friendship with Henry Fawcett, professor of political economy at Cambridge. After their first meeting in February 1860, Mill declared Fawcett to be a 'fine fellow' and the two become friends and political allies. On economics, Fawcett was essentially Mill's mouthpiece, knowing the *Principles*, according to Leslie Stephen, the way a Puritan knew the Bible. But it was Fawcett's personal qualities that most impressed Mill. When he had been blinded two years earlier (his father accidentally shot him in the face during a hunting trip, sending one pellet into each eye), Fawcett announced: 'It shan't make any difference in my plans of life.' He certainly lost none of his reforming zeal or zest for life, rowing in a dons' eight dubbed 'The Ancient Mariners', joining his wife, Millicent Garrett Fawcett, in a lifelong devotion to the cause of women's rights, and, from 1865, sitting in Parliament where he was one of the more effective radicals: 'If this fellow had eyes,' exclaimed Disraeli, 'how one should damn them.'[43] Later in his career, occupying the position of Postmaster-General under Gladstone, Fawcett introduced the penny post and postal orders.

While most of Mill's widening circle of friends were from the professional classes, his choices were not based on social standing, but on like-mindedness and commitment to change. One of his other new friends was John Plummer, a self-educated former factory worker whose writings on working hours and strike action Mill read closely from 1859 onwards. Mill lent Plummer books and support, and Mr and Mrs Plummer became regulars at the Blackheath dinner table.

Mill's re-engagement with the issues of the day, after the happy tranquillity of married life, coincided with another quickening in the pace of political, economic and social change. 'It is a privilege', wrote Disraeli in 1862, 'to live in this age of brilliant and rapid events. What an error to call it a utilitarian age! It is one of infinite romance!'[44] In this passage – which shows how early the misuse of the term 'utilitarian' began – Disraeli was poking fun at the earnestness of the time. But he was right. Swathes of cities were being cleared for new housing developments, a movement celebrated by Johann Strauss's popular 'Demolition Men's Polka'. Strauss's inspiration was the decision of Emperor Franz Josef to remove the city limits on development in Vienna – but the escalation from urbanization to suburbanization was even more advanced in London. Karl Marx dominated the communist First International almost from its inception in 1864, but his own relocation from a cramped apartment in Soho to a family house near Hampstead Heath was a better indication of the spirit of the age.[45] A rejuvenated movement for free trade – led by Richard Cobden – had found a powerful convert in the new Chancellor, William Gladstone, who incorporated dramatic cuts in tariffs and an Anglo-French trade treaty in his 1860 budget. In England, rapid economic progress was as always tempered by the countervailing forces of tradition and domesticity: 1861 saw the first publication of two of the great publishing successes of the century – *Hymns: Ancient and Modern* and *Mrs. Beeton's Book of Household Management*.

Mill diligently kept in touch with political and economic developments, even when he and Helen were in Avignon, 'gathering the health and spirits ... necessary to render life in England endurable to us', and had the major journals of the day redirected to him or asked friends to keep copies, which he would then assiduously plough through on his return. Mill ensured that his own voice was heard, too, especially since the success of *On Liberty*, and relinquished the royalties on 'people's editions' of his major works, which included the *Principles* and *Representative Government*, in order to keep the price down, and was rewarded with stronger sales.[46] By 1863, he could boast to an American correspondent, the Boston architect Charles Cummings, that having been 'regarded as a writer on social scientific subjects ... little heard of by the miscellaneous public', his burst of essays had given him 'what I had not before, popular influence'. His periodical writing picked up significantly during the first half of the 1860s, with pieces in *Fraser's*, the *Edinburgh Review* and the *Fortnightly Review*. He also gave three articles to Henry Chapman, who was still valiantly keeping the *Westminster Review* afloat. By 1868 he was providing direct financial assistance to the journal, turning a £100 loan into a gift and, along with Charles Darwin and George Grote, signing round-robin fundraising letters.[47]

Through the Political Economy Club – one of the few extra-marital activities which Mill had kept up during the Harriet years – he saw Gladstone in action, and also met one of his new and regular correspondents, the young Irish economist John Elliot

Cairnes. 'There was a discussion led off by J. S. Mill,' wrote an excited Cairnes to a friend in 1861, 'But my greatest triumph has to be recorded yet. On leaving, J. S. Mill happened to be going the same way, and actually took my arm and walked along Pall Mall with me! You would suppose from his manner that *I* was conferring the compliment on *him*.'[48] Mill and Cairnes subsequently became good friends, united by their similar views on economics and utilitarianism and their joint support for the north in the American Civil War. 'Whenever I read anything you write,' Mill wrote to him the following year, 'I feel growing up in me, what I seldom have, the agreeable feeling of a brotherhood in arms.' Cairnes and his wife became frequent visitors to Blackheath, sometimes accompanied by their housemate Moncure Conway, with whom Mill also struck up both a friendship and correspondence.

Mill's new levels of activity even led him, in 1865, shortly before becoming an MP, to his first meeting of the National Association for the Promotion of Social Science – of which he had been a council member since 1858 – to endorse Hare's paper on reforming metropolitan elections in order to reduce corruption. This was an issue Mill would pursue in Parliament three years later, with great energy but no success.[49]

Before he took up his place in the Commons, however, Mill had some other intellectual labours to complete, including a full-throated exposition of his own version of the Benthamite philosophy for which he was supposed to have been the apostle. His engagement with utilitarianism had thus far been conducted under the cover of reviews of the works of others: Bentham's in 1833 and 1838, Robert Blakey's in 1833, Adam Sedgwick's in 1835, Coleridge's in 1840 and Whewell's in 1852. Now, at the age of fifty-five, it was time for Mill to put all of his own cards on the table. *Utilitarianism*, drafted in 1854 and 'thoroughly revised' in 1860, was published in three parts in *Fraser's Magazine* at the end of 1861 and in book form two years later.

To this day, the 'little treatise' provides a training ground for would-be philosophers, most of whom are given the agreeable task of pointing out the deficiencies in its argument; Alan Ryan points out that the essay has 'become a classic through the efforts of its opponents rather than those of its friends'. Mill was certainly not at his best in the work: even Ryan admits that it 'represents Mill at his most exasperating'.[50] Although he was by now much more of a liberal than a utilitarian, Mill still wanted to prevent the philosophy of his mentor and father being tossed into an early intellectual grave, as what Carlyle dubbed a 'pig philosophy'. In 1858 he pointed out to Gomperz that 'there are not many defences extant of the ethics of utility' and to Charles Dupont-White in 1861 he explained that '*l'idée de l'Utile* est ... très impopulaire'.[51]At the same time, Mill wanted to add the last instalment of his own thinking on the subject.

He was fairly ambivalent about the work, however. Although it ran to four editions during his lifetime, he did not bother to revise it in the light of the considerable criticism it provoked. Between the first publication of the essay and his death twelve years later, *Utilitarianism* is mentioned by Mill just eleven times in his correspondence, compared to thirty-three references to *On Liberty*, and gets just five lines in his *Autobiography*. Mill never considered a cheap 'people's edition' of the essay – a fact which cannot be explained by fears about philosophical complexity because he did entertain the idea of one for the *Logic*. In 1866, he asked the publishers, Longman, to send some free copies of his most important works to the Durham Cooperative Institute: *Utilitarianism* was not on the list.[52] It is clear that the essay was not taken as seriously by Mill as it has been by everyone else.

Mill's aim in the work was to rehabilitate some of the essential ideas of utilitarianism in a form which would make them more acceptable to the chattering classes and more amenable to his own liberalism. For these purposes he employed – as he wrote of a work by another writer – 'only as much depth of philosophy as the purpose required'. He opened on familiar ground with an attack on intuitionist philosophies based on an innate 'moral instinct' beyond rational explanation. Next he argued for a philosophy which valued actions in terms of their consequences for a particular 'end' or what is now dubbed a 'consequentialist' philosophy. 'All action is for the sake of some end,' he wrote. 'When we engage in a pursuit, a clear and precise conception of what we are pursuing would seem to be what we need.'[53] One of Mill's long-standing criticisms of William Whewell was his failure to articulate a direction in which good lives ought to point. In his 1852 review of Whewell's writings, Mill used an analogy to make his case:

Let it be required to find the principles of the art of navigation. Bentham says, we must look to an 'external end;' getting from place to place on the water. No, says Dr. Whewell, there is a 'simpler and more satisfactory' mode, viz. to consider that there must be such an art; that it must be for a ship; for a ship at sea; and for all the parts of a ship. Would Dr. Whewell prevail on any one to suppose that these considerations made it unnecessary to consider, with Bentham, what a ship is intended to do?[54]

Mill was crystal clear about what the 'ship', or society, should be doing: 'The Utilitarian doctrine is, that happiness is desirable, and the only thing desirable, as an end.' He also did some linguistic housekeeping, attempting to rescue the term 'utilitarianism' from its 'perverted use' by the 'common herd, including the herd of writers' as meaning 'the rejection, or the neglect, of pleasure in some of its forms; of beauty, or ornament or amusement'. As Mill correctly protested, 'Bentham, who maintained the theory of utility, meant by it, not something to be contradistinguished from pleasure, but pleasure itself.'[55] It was too late, of course, and 'utilitarian' remains to this day a word with a divided personality, meaning one thing in common use and the opposite in formal philosophy.

So far Mill had been on fairly solid ground, but his argument quickly dereriorated. Even if the requirement for some ultimate 'end' is accepted, it is far from certain that this end should be happiness. It could just as well be learning, or virtue, or – and this is the obvious rejoinder to Mill – liberty. He added rather briskly that such ends 'are not amenable to direct proof', and that the only real evidence available for the ultimate desirability of something was that people did, in fact, seem to desire it:

The only proof capable of being given that an object is visible is that people actually see it. The only proof that a sound is audible, is that people hear it: and so of the other sources of our experience. In like manner, I apprehend, the sole evidence it is possible to produce that anything is desirable, is that people do actually desire it.[56]

This passage has been hammered to death ever since its publication, and rightly so. The fact that something is desired is at best circumstantial evidence for its desirability. A person might desire to rob a bank or blow up innocent people on a tube train. To take people's existing desires at face value was an especially strange strategy for Mill: he was, after all, the one who had said that society was in the grip of a 'tyranny' of public opinion. In some of his other writings, he adopted a much more sensible approach to the definition of ends. In an 1834 article on Plato's *Gorgias*, he argued that while virtue was a vital constituent of a happy life, it was impossible to prove it logically: 'No arguments which Plato urges have power to make those love or desire virtue who do not already: nor is this ever to be effected through the intellect, but through the imagination and the affections'. In the *Logic*, he suggested that the assumption that people act out of a self-interested desire to maximize their own happiness should be treated as only an 'approximation' of real life, rather than an infallible guide.[57] Either suggestion was an improvement on what appeared in *Utilitarianism*. Mill's casual editorial treatment made matters worse. When Theodor Gomperz, preparing to translate the essay, pointed out for the second time the vulnerability of the 'proof' as stated, Mill replied that 'it had escaped my mind that you thought that argument [in need of] ... further explanation and development', added that he had 'not had time regularly to rewrite the book', and gave Gomperz a free rein to alter the passage in the German version if he wished. (He did not.)[58]

Mill fared somewhat better in his attempt to show utilitarianism to be a solidaristic rather than selfish doctrine. He insisted that it was general, rather than individual, happiness which was the goal: 'happiness is a good: that each person's happiness is a good to that person, and the general happiness ... therefore a good to the aggregate of all persons'. Again, as a stand-alone statement this won't quite do. It is quite plausible that one person's happiness comes at the expense of another's, rather than in tandem with it. There is no automatic relationship between personal and collective happiness. In fact Mill was merely guilty of some sloppy writing here. In a letter to a confused reader in 1868, he clarified his position: 'I did not mean that every human being's happiness is a good to every other human being; though I think, in a good state of society & education it would be so. I merely meant in this particular sentence to argue that since A's happiness is a good, B's must be a good, C's a good, &c., the sum of these goods must be a good.'[59]

If Mill had only added a similar sentence to the fourth edition of *Utilitarianism*, published three years later, millions of hours of seminar-room angst could have been saved over the last century and a half. The question would have remained, however, whether individuals had any interest in collective happiness. Why should any individual, Mill asked rhetorically, be 'bound to promote the general happiness?' His answer was; by themselves being influenced in the right way: 'The whole force of external reward and punishment, whether physical or moral ... become available to enforce the utilitarian morality'. He suggested that 'the influences which form moral character' could be designed in such a way as to ensure that 'the feeling of unity with our fellow creatures shall be (what it cannot be doubted Christ intended it to be) as deeply rooted in our character ... as the horror of crime is in an ordinarily well brought-up young person'.[60] Mill gave no ground here to the intuitionists; conscience was still a wholly human creation. His point was simply that a conscience could be so instilled as to become second nature. Once again, however, in the absence of clear evidence on the way characters were shaped – the missing science of 'ethology' – it was hard to see what his conclusion meant in practice.

Mill was at his strongest in the last chapter of the book, 'On the Connexion between Justice and Utility', which was originally written as a separate essay, and before the other chapters. The idea of justice, he suggested, rested on the strongly developed personal sense of having certain 'rights', which meant having 'something which society ought to defend me in possession of'. Agreeing with Bentham that the idea of a 'natural' right was intuitionist nonsense, Mill said the reason why a particular right should be upheld was 'general utility'. The utilitarian argument for justice was that the right to 'security' – of person, property and contract – was 'to every one's feelings the most vital of all interests ... Nearly all earthly benefits are needed by one person, not needed by another; and many of them can, if necessary, be cheerfully foregone, or replaced by something else; but security no human being can do without'.[61]

He insisted that the chance to base our life plans on secure ground was necessary for both happiness and liberty: in a later letter he said that the 'very first and most essential' of 'the conditions which enable mankind to dwell together in nations and communities' was that individuals 'should be able to trust one another's engagements.'[62] Like altruism, the requirements of justice could be inculcated into individuals; the 'strengthening of social ties' and 'powerful agency of external sanctions' that occurred with the 'healthy growth of society' created characters who automatically acted in such a way as to promote not only their own good, but the good of others.

Having claimed that Jesus was a utilitarian and that loving your neighbour as yourself was 'the complete spirit of the ethics of utility', Mill went on to argue that such a morality could also be promoted without a supernatural faith – citing Comte's 'Religion of Humanity' as an example. Within the bounds of the essay, his argument here is perfectly sound. People can be morally moulded, as much in a utilitarian fashion as in any other. The difficulty comes when these passages are set alongside those from *On Liberty*, in which Mill attacked his fellows for squeezing 'into any of the small number of moulds which society provides in order to save its members the trouble of forming their own character'; pretty much what he appeared to be advocating in *Utilitarianism*.[63]

The question of whether the two essays can finally be reconciled is one which will keep scholars engaged for the foreseeable future. A large part of the answer might depend on some clarification of what Mill actually meant by 'happiness' in the first place. In *Utilitarianism* he saw a happy existence as 'not a life of rapture; but moments of such, in an existence made up of few and transitory pains, many and various pleasures, with a decided predominance of the active over the passive, and having as the foundation of the whole, not to expect more from life than it is capable of bestowing'.[64] His attempt to counter Carlyle's opinion of utilitarianism as a base, swinish system – one shared by many others, even if in less colourful language – also required, Mill believed, an appreciation of different qualities of pleasure:

It is quite compatible with the principle of utility to recognize the fact, that some *kinds* of pleasure are more desirable and more pleasurable than others. It would be absurd that while, in estimating all other things, quality is considered as well as quantity, the estimation of pleasures should be supposed to depend on quantity alone.[65]

This 'absurdity' is of course precisely what Bentham had insisted upon: pleasures were to be crunched through the 'felicific calculus' to see which was the greater in quantity. Mill, meanwhile, insisted that 'higher pleasures', i.e. those 'of the intellect, of the feelings and imagination, and of the moral sentiments', were intrinsically better than 'lower pleasures', those which, in his words, involved 'mere sensation' or the satisfying of 'animal appetites'.[66] Mill's claim to be a utilitarian was now in some peril. The whole point of Bentham's utilitarianism was that it provided a single benchmark for judging activities, whereas Mill had now introduced another, qualitative element into the equation, raising the difficult question of who was to say which pleasures are greater. Mill might have preferred reading Socratic dialogues to having sex, but it is hard to find grounds, especially any recognizably liberal ones, on which this preference be generalized to others. In an attempt to solve this problem, he introduced the idea of an experienced referee, whose qualitative judgments were based on experience of both:

If one of the two [pleasures] is, by those who are competently acquainted with both, placed so far above the other that they prefer it, even though knowing it to be attended with a greater amount of discontent, and would not resign it for any quantity of the other pleasure which their nature is capable of, we are justified in ascribing to the preferred enjoyment a superiority in quality, so far outweighing quantity as to render it, in comparison, of small account.[67]

Mill had obviously travelled a long way indeed from Bentham by this point, suggesting that a 'pleasure' which brings 'discontent' – itself a difficult idea to grasp – might be 'superior' to one which does not. What Mill was driving at here was a distinction between what he considered to be true 'happiness' on one hand, and mere 'content' or 'satisfaction' on the other. 'Superior' humans would, Mill insisted, choose out of a 'sense of dignity' to keep their cultivation, even at the price of losing some 'momentary object of desire'. To press the point home, he used a justly famous image: 'It is better to be a human being dissatisfied than a pig satisfied; better to be Socrates dissatisfied than a fool satisfied.'[68]

If this was utilitarianism, it was not in a form which Bentham would have recognized. Grote justifiably doubted Mill's 'persistence in the true faith'; although to his friend he was more circumspect, contenting himself with the hope that Mill would soon 'return to ... higher speculative and logical subjects.' William Stanley Jevons, the orthodox Manchester utilitarian, wrote of Mill's essay that 'the view which he professes to uphold is the direct opposite of what he really upholds'. Similarly, one of Mill's earliest biographers,

W. L. Courtney, observed that *Utilitarianism* was 'considerably embarrassed by the want of any clear conception of what happiness is'.[69] Mill certainly had an ideal of life, but while this included happiness, it was not reducible to it. Close readers of his works had in fact been exposed to it two decades earlier, in the *Logic*: 'I do not mean to assert that the promotion of happiness should be itself the end of all actions or even of all rules of actions ... the cultivation of an ideal of nobleness of will and conduct should be to individual human beings an end to which the specific pursuit of happiness ... should give way.'[70]

If, he wrote in *Utilitarianism*, 'it may be doubted whether a noble character is always the happier for its nobleness', there could be no doubt that 'it makes other people happier, and that the world in general is a gainer by it'.[71] This is an appealing thought, but may well be a false one. Indeed, it is quite likely that a noble character, say a campaigner against global warming, who is constantly measuring carbon footprints, will make others less happy without any lessening of their own nobility.

Mill was attempting to squeeze the ingredients of what he considered a worthwhile life, more fully fleshed out in *On Liberty*, into a nominally utilitarian framework. Into his definition of happiness, Mill had inserted nobility, virtue, dignity, selflessness, variety, activity and humility. He had 'enlarged Utilitarianism,' wrote the *Spectator* obituarist a dozen years later, 'till it was hardly recognizable as Utilitarianism'. In arguing for 'utility' as an end goal, he had insisted that this meant 'utility in the largest sense, grounded on the permanent interests of man, as a progressive being'. These 'interests' included liberty, of course, and Mill argued in *On Liberty* that 'where, not the person's own character, but the traditions or customs of other people are the rule of conduct, there is wanting one of the principal ingredients of human happiness'.[72] This was a line of argument which promised to ease the tension between liberalism and utilitarianism – if freedom made people happy, Mill could have his cake and eat it.

It was a logical extension of Mill's position that the way to secure happiness was not, as the US Constitution supposes, to pursue it. Instead, it would be the result of living a full, autonomous life, aiming at another object, some 'art or pursuit, followed not as a means, but as itself an ideal end'. 'Aiming thus at something else,' Mill concluded, people 'find happiness by the way.' In the *Autobiography* he wrote:

Ask yourself whether you are happy, and you cease to be so. The only chance is to treat, not happiness, but some end external to it, as the purpose of life. Let your self-consciousness, your scrutiny, your self-interrogation, exhaust themselves on that; and if otherwise fortunately circumstanced you will inhale happiness with the air that you breathe, without dwelling on it or thinking about it, without either forestalling it in imagination, or putting it to flight by fatal questioning.[73]

From Mill's perspective, *Utilitarianism* marked an end rather than a beginning. In it, he finally laid to rest the ghosts of his father and Bentham. The essay looked backwards, offering a final settling of his Benthamite accounts, and scarcely featured in his thoughts or actions in the remaining dozen years of his life, while the ideas contained in *On Liberty* underpinned his future actions as both a politician and public intellectual. *Utilitarianism* illustrated Mill's past; *On Liberty* illuminated his future.

Even if Mill had been inclined to guard and improve *Utilitarianism* after its publication, events across the Atlantic in any case stole his attention. The eruption of the American Civil War in 1861 galvanized and politicized Mill in the same way that the French Revolution had thirteen years earlier. He immediately saw 'the transcendant importance of the stake at issue [*sic*] in the present contest'. 'The English organs of opinion cry out for a recognition of the secession, for letting slavery alone', he complained to Cairnes, 'but slavery will not let freedom alone'.[74] By this point, America had replaced France in Mill's intellectual affections and he described himself as 'one who takes as deep and continuous an interest in the political, moral and social progress of the United

States as if he were himself an American citizen'.[75] For Mill, the contest was over a single issue: slavery. The war was not between north and south, it was between 'free and slaveholding America'. Allowing the Southern, slaveholding states to secede from the North would amount, he believed, to an acceptance of the institution of slavery and a triumph for slavery in America, the nation which was 'destined to give instruction to the world'.[76] He would have agreed with the claim of the modern historian Henry Commager that while Europe dreamed the Enlightenment, America had made that dream come true. If slavery won, the dream would become a nightmare and the 'whole futurity of mankind' would be darkened. This was why, for Mill, the 'present gigantic struggle' was 'full of the most important consequences to humanity, stretching into the remotest future.'[77] No American, Mill averred, could have read Abraham Lincoln's anti-slavery proclamation 'with more exultation' than he did.

Such views seem uncontroversial to modern readers, but they were far from mainstream at the time. For one thing, domestic economic considerations argued for support for the South, which provided most of the cotton required for the 'cotton counties' of Lancashire, Cheshire and Derbyshire.[78] A Northern blockade of Southern shipping was soon felt on the streets of Manchester, and of course plenty of conservatives supported the rights of the Southern landowners. Mill had no tolerance for these attitudes. People who believed England should have supported the South from the outset of the conflict were those, he said, who would have 'for the sake of cotton, made Satan victorious'. The reaction of England to the conflict was a moral test and one which, especially in the first year or so of the war, was being failed. In two articles published in 1862, 'The Contest in America' and 'The Slave Power', a review of a book by Cairnes, he lambasted the press in particular for a 'moral feeling which is philosophically indifferent between the apostles of slavery and its enemies'. These views were more favourably received in New England than in England: Boston reprints of both articles sold quickly.[79]

The American conflict turned friends into enemies and vice versa. Radicals like John Roebuck insisted that 'the first doctrine of Radicalism ... was the right of a people to take self-government', whereas for Mill it was not a war of independence but simply a 'slaveholders' rebellion'.[80] Gladstone – the man upon whom Mill would later pin great political hopes – told a cheering Newcastle crowd in October 1862: 'We may have our own opinions about slavery; we may be for or against the South; but there is no doubt that Jefferson Davis and other leaders have made an army; they are making, it appears, a navy; and they have made what is more than either, they have made a nation.'[81]

Gladstone would later perform one of his sharpest U-turns on the issue, and praise the 'magnificent moral spectacle' of the English working classes supporting the North against their own economic interests, but he can hardly have been surprised that his Tyneside speech was taken as tacit support for the South. To the Duchess of Sutherland the following month he insisted: 'But the South has not my sympathies, except in the sense that the North has them also. I wish them both cordially well.'[82]

Mill, by contrast, was not in a cordial frame of mind. As Gladstone was speaking, the presses of the *Westminster Review* were turning out Mill's review of Cairnes's book, in which he lamented the fact that the 'general sentiment of the people' was 'bitterly reproachful of the North, while for the South, the aggressors in the war, we have either mild apologies or direct and downright encouragement? and this not only from the Tory and anti-democratic camp, but from Liberals, or *soi-disant* such?'[83] The choice of the radical *Westminster* was not surprising; as Bain said, Mill usually turned to it 'when he wanted room for his elbow'. To his friends, Mill expressed his 'disgust' at the 'sad aberration of English feeling at this momentous crisis'. He felt 'ashamed and grieved' by the attitude of his countrymen, especially among so-called liberals, which he predictably contrasted with the more liberal sentiments on the Continent. His philosophical adversary William Whewell, on the other hand, was so incensed by the pro-Southern tendencies of *The*

Times that he refused to have the paper in his house. Hearing this, Mill wrote to him: 'No question of our time has been such a touchstone of men & so tested their sterling qualities of mind & heart – as this one – & I shall all my life feel united by a sort of special tie with those, whether personally known to me or not, who have been faithful when so many were faithless.'[84]

John Bright, the liberal politician and orator, was one of the few pro-Northerners – for him the eventual triumph of the North would be 'the event of our age' – and when he addressed a trade union meeting in St James's Hall in March 1863, Mill hurried along. Gomperz accompanied him:

I shall never forget the venerable man as he sat there like a youth, deeply agitated, applauding the speeches not only of John Bright and Professor Beesley, but also the simple words of an Irish workman. This had been, for some time at least, Mill's first appearance in a public meeting, and by those who knew him, he was warmly greeted.[85]

Mill thought his attempts to prick the conscience of England with his pen were 'likely to give great offence' and told Bain that they were 'the most hazardous thing for his influence he had yet done'. He was right. Even Grote thought that he was 'violent against the South ... embracing heartily the extreme Abolitionist views, and thinking about little else in regard to the general question'. *The Economist* said that in this kind of writing, Mill 'ceases to be a philosopher and becomes the partisan'. Mill seized on reports of a terrible attack on a man accused of helping slaves escape to give his case an extra polemical edge: 'The South are in rebellion not for simple slavery; they are in rebellion for the right to burn people alive.'[86]

With his liberal protagonists in mind, Mill pointed out that while he had supported most of the 'rebellions' which had taken place during his lifetime, he never supported rebellion for its own sake; the purpose of the uprising was paramount:

I certainly never conceived that there was a sufficient title to my sympathy in the mere fact of being a rebel; that the act of taking arms against one's fellow citizens was so meritorious in itself, was so completely its own justification, that no question need be asked concerning the motive ... Secession may be laudable; but it may also be an enormous crime.[87]

For Mill, the only acceptable outcome was a crushing of the Confederacy and all of the 'power of the slaveholding caste', along with the introduction of equal rights for all black Americans. Only with 'full equality of political rights to negroes', Mill insisted, would 'the opening words of the Declaration of Independence ... cease to be a reproach to the nation founded by its authors'. In the new world, he lamented, 'the aristocracy of skin, and the aristocracy of sex, retain their privileges'. Mill was even more isolated in these opinions; his ally Cairnes was willing to settle for peace based on containment of the existing slave states as an independent nation – until Mill changed his mind.[88] For Mill, nothing less than total victory for the North was required. 'I cannot join with those who cry Peace, peace', he wrote. 'War, in a good cause, is not the greatest evil a nation can suffer. War is an ugly thing, but not the ugliest of things: the decayed and degraded state of moral and patriotic feeling which think nothing is *worth* a war, is worse.' This was not a pose he struck simply for this particular cause: fifteen years earlier he had written that war was 'infinitely less evil than systematic submission to injustice'.[89] None the less, his interventions in the debate over the American war transformed his reputation. For the first time, he was seen as a fervent polemicist rather than a careful thinker. But far from shrinking back from this role into a more comfortable, speculative life, Mill would, over the next decade, occupy his frequently partisan role with growing relish.

Mill's attitude to the American Civil War reflected his analysis of the moral grounds for intervention in foreign affairs. Stung into editorial action by reports that Palmerston was opposing a Suez canal because of the potential damage to home-grown industry, in

1859 he had written 'A Few Words on Non-Intervention', an attempt to outline the 'true principles of international morality'. Mill's only formal statement on foreign policy, it began by attacking the idea that national self-interest should be the only guide to foreign policy. Nations, he insisted 'have duties . . . towards the weal of the human race'. Suppose the Suez canal was good for other nations but damaging to England, he speculated: attempting to stop the project on the basis of this 'wicked principle' would be 'to declare that its [England's] interest and that of mankind are incompatible – that thus far at least, it is the enemy of the human race.'[90]

Mill then turned to the grounds on which sovereign nations might interfere in the affairs of another. He dismissed the notion of waging 'war for an idea' as being 'as criminal as to go to war for territory or revenue . . . it is as little justifiable to force our ideas on other people, as to compel them to submit to our will in any other respect'.[91] Unsurprisingly, Mill focused on the argument for interventions in support of liberty, but made a sharp distinction between support for internal freedom movements, and for free nations under attack from a 'despotic' one. Intervention to support freedom movements within an individual nation was unwise:

If they have not sufficient love of liberty to be able to wrest it from merely domestic oppressors, the liberty which is bestowed upon them by other hands than their own, will have nothing real, nothing permanent. No people ever was and remained free, but because it was determined to be so . . . If a people . . . does not value freedom sufficiently to fight for it, and maintain it against any force which can be mustered within the country . . . it is only a question in how few years or months that people will be enslaved.[92]

If a free country was militarily threatened by another nation, however, Mill argued that the rest of the free world had a moral duty to defend them: intervention to maintain the balance of power between nations was not the same as intervention to upset it within a nation. 'The doctrine of non-intervention, to be a legitimate principle of morality,' he wrote, 'must be accepted by all governments.' This meant that 'intervention to enforce non-intervention is always rightful, always moral, if not always prudent.' On this basis, Mill thought that England should have supported Hungary in her efforts to throw off Russian-backed Austrian oppression in 1849.[93]

Not that all nations were ready for independence, of course. Mill's vision of world affairs clearly differentiated between 'barbarous' and 'civilized' nations, and he argued that it was likely to be in the interests of the former to be 'conquered and held in subjection' by foreigners: 'Independence and nationality, so essential to the due growth and development of a people further advanced in improvement, are generally impediments to theirs'.[94] He fleshed this point out further in *On Liberty*: 'Liberty, as a principle, has no application to any state of things anterior to the time when mankind have become capable of being improved by free and equal discussion. Until then, there is nothing for them but implicit obedience to an Akbar or a Charlemagne, if they are so fortunate as to find one.'[95] This view of development, heavily influenced by Mill's experience with the East India Company, underpinned his colonialism. He supported the Empire, not for the sake of England, whose 'direct benefit is extremely small', he assured Cairnes, but for the sake of the colonies, for whom the link was 'a great good'. Three years before his death, he was still 'entirely in favour of retaining our connexion with the colonies so long as they do not desire separation'.[96]

People, and nations, were 'civilizable', Mill insisted, and so a nation ought be granted independence once it was ready, as his view on Canada had demonstrated in the 1830s. In the meantime, the job of the superior nation was to prepare its charge for freedom. Benign colonialism, according to Mill, was a kind of 'government of leading-strings . . . the one required to carry such a people the most rapidly through the next necessary step in social progress.' He concluded: 'I need scarcely remark that leading-strings are only permissible as a means of gradually training the people to walk alone.' This approach has been labelled by Alan Ryan 'self-abolishing imperialism'.[97] Mill consistently denied that there were any inherent differences between races, with differences in characteristics being the result of circumstances and history, rather than innate attributes. This was not a common view at the time, even among liberals: Charles Kingsley wrote that 'It was this mistake which has led him [Mill] and others into that theory that the suffrage ought to be educational and formative'.[98]

One of the countries Mill may have felt needed some tighter reins was Greece, which he visited with Helen in the first half of 1862. 'The people are very backward', he complained, but he was hopeful that advances would follow the growth in 'material prosperity, which in modern civilization is usually the first step towards moral progress.'[99] In fact, the Greek people were leading themselves towards freedom: a military uprising at Nauplia during Mill's visit to the country was the first step in a revolutionary chain of events which would lead to the king's overthrow and the establishment of a representative democracy.

It was Mill's second tour of the country which, in its ancient incarnation, greatly influenced his thinking. He was, as Bain wrote, 'quite as much as Grote, a Greece-intoxicated man'. Mill actually asked the Grotes to join him and Helen for the trip, but they declined on health grounds. It was almost certainly a wise decision: the journey to Greece was marked by heavy snow in northern Italy, 'incessant rain' at Corfu and fog in Athens.[100] The excursions from Athens across the Peloponnese were not for the faint of heart. The group camped each night, 'sometimes in forests,' Helen wrote to a friend, 'where our men lit huge fires, throwing on the trunks of two or three whole trees, to keep the wolves from our horses. Sometimes we were in wild and desolate regions deserted even by the shepherds and their flocks, and where we heard the cry of jackals, the owls and the night hawks all night'.[101] Nevertheless, at the age of fifty-six, Mill thoroughly enjoyed himself, declaring the trip a 'complete success' and earnestly reporting the topography of crucial historical sites to Grote. After camping for two days at the foot of Parnassus, and another two on its plateau, he declared the beauty of

Greece to be 'incomparable'.[102] Mill and Helen then made a leisurely journey to their French home, stopping off to see Gomperz in Vienna, before arriving in Avignon at the end of August, in time for Mill to rattle off 'The Slave Power' for the October issue of the *Westminster*.

Theodor Gomperz had fallen madly in love with Helen, and begged permission to come to Avignon. Mill, presumably with Helen's knowledge, was less than sensitive in his handling of his friend's anguish. 'Come by all means if you like, though I should not for an instant have thought of proposing it to you', was the less than effusive opening line of Mill's reply. He went on: 'I do not invite my friends to this place, unless in very rare cases when I happen to have an interval of leisure'.[103] As a statement of fact, this was simply untrue: Hare, for example, visited for a week in the autumn of 1864 when Mill, by his own reckoning, had 'much work cut out' on the sixth edition of the *Political Economy*. This rebuff from the man who was Gomperz's intellectual hero as well as stepfather of his heart's desire plunged the sensitive Austrian into despair. He asked Mill what he should do. 'You seem to ask my opinion,' Mill replied, 'and if I gave it sincerely, I have no choice but to say – painful as it is to say it – that I do not think you have any chance.'[104]

Perhaps reconizing his earlier insensitivity, Mill offered, in a series of letters, his own recipe for recovery from heartbreak. 'I have always found that real intellectual work is to me all that Cicero in his oration pro Archia says of literature – when one wants healthy excitement, an outlet for energy, active pleasure, or consolation, nothing else affords it in the same degree . . . It would give me great comfort to see you reaping the same benefits from the same cause'. Perhaps unsure whether he had got his point across, Mill next told Gomperz that he and Helen were 'really anxious' about him, adding that 'it would be a great relief to us if we knew that you had exchanged a life of brooding over painful thoughts for a healthful exertion of the active faculties'.[105] Whether it would have been as much of a relief to Gomperz is hard to say, but he did bounce back in the end. Perhaps Mill was worrying about his protégé in July 1863 when he absentmindedly missed a train to Kent, where he was headed for a botanizing excursion. In any case, he filled the resulting two-hour wait in productive fashion, getting his hair cut and popping into his brokers, and once in Kent, found a satisfactorily 'boggy neighbourhood', rich in species missing from his herbarium.[106]

By this time, Mill had fired his twin bolts on the American Civil War, and was busy meeting an older and apparently less immediate challenge. During 1862 and 1863, his principal intellectual endeavour was the writing of a lengthy dismemberment of the philosophy of Sir William Hamilton and his followers. On the face of it, there was little similarity between the 500-page metaphysical monster that is *An Examination of Sir William Hamilton's Philosophy* and the vituperative interventions on the American Civil War. For Mill, however, the link was clear. Hamilton was still 'the great fortress of the intuitional philosophy' in England, and a 'hand-to-hand fight' with his legacy was necessary because of the way it influenced the politics of class, gender and race:

I have long felt that the prevailing tendency to regard all the marked distinctions of human character as innate, and in the main indelible, and to ignore the irresistible proofs that by far the greater part of those differences, whether between individuals, races, or sexes, are such as not only might but naturally would be produced by difference in circumstances, is ... one of the chief stumbling blocks to human improvement. This tendency has its source in the intuitional metaphysics which characterized the reaction of the nineteenth century against the eighteenth.[107]

Mill thought that regressive attitudes towards black people, whether in America or Jamaica – perfectly encapsulated by Tennyson's view that 'niggers are tigers, niggers are tigers' – were based on false notions of innate properties. This was a philosophy which therefore had to be attacked 'at the very root'.[108] *Hamilton* is now one of Mill's least-known works, and many of the philosophical issues it raises have been overtaken by subsequent intellectual events. But in 1865, when the book was published, it caused something of a sensation. For one thing, Mill and Hamilton were at that time the 'Big Two' in British philosophy, so the volume offered the prospect of a thinking person's joust. Many of the issues Mill raised, especially on the knowability of God, the nature of the mind, and the consciousness of an external world, were highly topical. Mill's attack on a particular branch of Christian theology also made headlines, because of his parliamentary candidacy. The first edition of 1,000 copies in April 1865 had to be followed by a second of the same print-run in July; a third edition, substantially revised, appeared the following year and a fourth was published in 1872.

Hamilton covered much of the same ground as the *Logic*. As Alan Ryan writes, there is an 'air of *déjà vu* about much of the argument'. Congratulating Mill on the volume, Grote said it was 'full of expansions of the doctrines more briefly adumbrated in your Logic'.[109] Of the sections in *Hamilton* which did tackle new subjects, the strongest was Mill's dissection of Hamiltonian theology, as fleshed out in *The Limits of Religious Thought* by Hamilton's main disciple, another Oxford professor, Henry L. Mansel. Mill thought this was 'a detestable . . . absolutely loathsome book' and, in return, Mansel thought that Mill's work was 'utterly mischievous'. Mansel argued that the nature of God was beyond the reach of human reasoning. 'A God understood' he said, 'would be no God at all': human concepts, words and feelings could not be attached to the unknowable deity.[110] Mill pushed Mansel's argument to the logical conclusion that humans could therefore have no way of knowing whether God was good, just, merciful or benevolent, in the sense of having the attributes which mortals attached to the words 'good', 'just', 'merciful' and 'benevolent'. And we really have no business, Mill argued, worshipping a being about whom we know nothing: 'Whatever power such a being may have over me, there is one thing which he shall not do: he shall not compel me to worship him. I will call no being good, who is not what I mean when I apply that epithet to my fellow-creatures; and if such a being can sentence me to hell for not so calling him, to hell I will go.'[111]

Even in this, the most 'sawdustish' of Mill's works (the term is inevitably Carlyle's), Mill could not resist the polemical force of a great phrase, and 'to hell I will go' certainly caused some ripples. Mansel dismissed it as 'an extraordinary outburst of rhetoric', but failed to adequately answer its challenge. The conservative *Record*, suggested that Mill might now be considered, like Shelley before him, the leader of 'the Satanic School' and went on to name and shame some of Mill's supporters in the upcoming election in Westminster, including 'the Rev. F. D. Maurice, the Rev. J. L. Davies, the Rev. Leslie Stephen, the Attorney-General ... with the appended sanction of the Dean of Westminster, and the *Right Hon. W. E. Gladstone*!' The leader writer of the *Morning Advertiser* was even more upset, declaring that 'we have never, in the whole course of our reading, met with ranker Atheism'.[112]

On the other side of the row, the *Spectator* suggested that the passage was 'the true language of prophets and apostles about God' and – in a later issue – that it 'expressed the faith of thousands, theologians, mystics, practical men, both in the past and present, who have deeply considered and passionately rejected Mr. Mansel's peculiar heresy.'[113] F. D. Maurice sent a copy to Charles Kingsley, exalting it as 'a grand and affecting theological statement'. The Bishop of St David's, Connop Thirlwall, Mill's sparring partner from the Owenite debates four decades earlier, said the phrase 'breathes the purest spirit of Christian morality'. Mill was 'much amused' by the reaction and told Grote: 'All this is pretty much as I expected, and wished.'[114]

Mill's theological arguments from *Hamilton* have stood the test of time; but the same cannot be said for his metaphysics – the area of philosophy concerned with essential first principles such as being, consciousness and knowledge of the external world. Metaphysical speculation tackles questions such as 'Who am I?', 'How do I know the world around me is real?', 'What is it made of?' and 'Who is this "I" person?' One of the most important elements in metaphysics is the perception of matter, and in line with the empirical psychology of his father and Bentham, Mill insisted that sensations were the building blocks of our understanding of the external world. 'Matter may be defined,' he decided, as 'a Permanent Possibility of Sensation'. In an example which prefigured twentieth-century Wittgensteinian debates, Mill summarized his view:

I see a piece of white paper on a table. I go into another room ... though I have ceased to see it, I am persuaded that the paper is still there. I no longer have the sensations which it gave me; but I believe that when I again place myself in the circumstances in which I had those sensations, that is, when I go again into the room, I shall again have them; and further, that there has been no intervening moment at which this would not have been the case. Owing to this property of my mind, my conception of the world at any given instant consists, in only a small proportion, of present sensations ... The conception I form of the world existing at any moment, comprises, along with the sensations I am feeling, a countless variety of possibilities of sensation.[115]

So far, so good: Mill's theory of matter was not perfect, but perfectly defensible. Where he got into difficulty was in applying his ideas to the way we perceive ourselves, and specifically, how we know our mind. If possibilities of sensation constituted the external world, this left the question of what constituted the internal one, or what Mill called 'the Ego'. He suggested that 'the belief I entertain that my mind exists, when it is not feeling, or thinking, or conscious of its own existence, resolves itself into the belief of a Permanent Possibility of these states'.[116] The problem with this argument, as Mill readily conceded, was its circularity. The mind knows itself by its thoughts and feelings; but the existence of those thoughts and feelings presupposes the existence of a mind to generate them. Faced with a potentially fatal blow to his theory, Mill ducked. 'The truth is,' he wrote, 'that we are here face to face with that final explicability, at which, as Sir W. Hamilton observes, we inevitably arrive when we reach ultimate facts.' After a bit more muttering about 'true incomprehensibility', Mill departed the field: 'I think, by far the wisest thing we can do, is to accept the inexplicable fact, without any theory of how it takes place; and when we are obliged to speak of it in terms which assume a theory, to use them with reservation as to their meaning.'[117]

Intuitionist opponents seized on this admission which, as Bain pointed out, made Mill 'appear, after all, to be a transcendalist like themselves, differing only in degree'. Although Mill made heavy revisions to the work for the third edition, this particular section was untouched, with just a note added, directing readers to Mansel's rejoinder. Perhaps Mill knew the argument was fragile to the touch. 'Metaphysics,' according to one distinguished practitioner, 'is the finding of bad reasons for what we believe upon instinct.'[118] Here, at least, Mill's metaphysics are a case in point.

The publication of *Hamilton* also caused another spat with Carlyle. At an Edinburgh banquet held in the Scottish prophet's honour, Lord Neaves, a judge and amateur balladeer, regaled the company with a new composition, of which verse 8 gives a good flavour:

> We banish hence Reid's Common Sense;
> We laugh at Dugald Stewart's blather;
> Sir William, too, and Mansel's crew,
> We've done for you and Mind and Matter.
> Speak no more of Mind and Matter:
> Mill with mud may else bespatter
> All your schools of silly fools,
> That dare believe in Mind and Matter.
>   Stuart Mill on Mind and Matter
>   Stuart Mill on Mind and Matter
>   Stuart Mill Exerts his skill
>   To make an end of Mind and Matter.[119]

Carlyle was delighted, using his cutlery to conduct the music and 'chanting laughingly ... every time the chorus came round, beating time in the air emphatically with his fist.'[120] Mill wrote him a short note, ostensibly a delayed reply to a query about German translators, which concluded: 'Please thank Mrs Carlyle for her remembrance of me. I have been sorry to hear a rather poor account of her health & to see by your Edinburgh address that your own is not quite satisfactory'.[121]

If Mill's friendship with Carlyle was on the rocks, there was no shortage of replacements. As well as the Plummers, Grotes, Cairnes, Hares, Bains, Spencers and Thornton, Mill and Helen struck up a friendship with Lord Amberley, son of Lord John Russell, and his wife Kate, the fourth daughter of Lord Stanley of Alderley. The four-way friendship was forged at a weekend party at the Grotes's new Surrey home, organised as part of a campaign by Harriet Grote to keep the familial show on the road following a recent social embarrassment.[122] On finishing his monumental Greek history, Grote had decided to seize some fleshier pleasures of the moment, in the form of an affair with a sculptress. He had, said his wife, 'made an old fool of himself'.[123]

Against this unpromising social backdrop, the other four guests became friends. Kate recalled her Sunday afternoon conversation with a 'congenial and sympathetic' Mill: 'He said the great thing was to consider one's opponents as one's allies; as people climbing the hill on the other side.' (It was evidently the Mill of On Liberty speaking, rather than the Mill of 'The Contest in America'.) Unaware that plans were afoot to entice him to stand in Westminster, Mill advised Amberley to try for the seat and, just a few days later, Mill wrote to Chapman on Amberley's behalf, saying that 'there is no young man coming forward in public life on whom I build so much hope'. Russell, demonstrating that the Victorian obsession with puns was not restricted to the comic press, asked his son if he had 'got nearer his Mill-enium by his visit'.[124] An indication of Mill's closeness to the couple is given by a couple of pages of Kate's journal, showing that after joining a dinner party in Blackheath one Sunday in June 1866, the Amberleys invited Mill to dinner the following day, and tea the day after that.[125]

Before his entry to Parliament, however, Mill's principal base was still Avignon. One of the many friends who made the trip south was William Thornton, who confirmed the idyllic nature of

Mill's Provençal life. With trips to local sights, including Petrarch's valley and the Pont du Gard, interspersed with days of reading and walking, 'you may imagine how much I am enjoying myself' he wrote to Fawcett,

and no small part of my pleasure consists in seeing how cheerfully and contentedly, if I may not say how happily, Mill is living. I feel convinced that he will never be persuaded permanently to abandon this retreat, for here, besides the seclusion . . . he has also close at hand the resting-place of his wife, which he visits daily, while in his stepdaughter he has a companion in all respects worthy of him.[126]

Thornton told Gomperz that he rated his relationship with Mill more highly than all his other friendships put together, and the three weeks he spent with him in Avignon as 'the happiest in his life'. Mill's social interactions do seem to have softened over the years. Earlier pen-portraits stressed his powers of analysis and his seriousness; in the 1860s it was his civility and wisdom that were most remarked upon. 'His manner is entirely that of a gentleman and man of the world, with a tender grace and sweetness about it rarely met with,' said Charles Eliot Norton, an American scholar and co-editor of the *North American Review*, to which Mill was a subscriber. Moncure Conway described Mill as 'a man of delicate sentiment, eloquent manners, and affectionate nature.'[127]

Mill's newly expansive social life did not, however, stretch to include his own family. To his sister Jane in Paris he wrote in 1865: 'The cause of my not having called on you is that it is many years since I have passed more than a few hours at Paris.' He certainly changed trains quickly in the French capital on most of his journeys to and from Avignon. Not always, though: he met Gustave d'Eichthal, and on at least one occasion he stayed at the Hotel Windsor on the Rue de Rivoli and tried to meet up with the Grotes for dinner.[128] Jane could have been forgiven for thinking her elder brother's excuse a poor one, but it seems that Mill preferred the company of Taylors to Mills, even years after Harriet's death. Her memory still burned brightly, too: during a weekend stay at the Amberleys in 1865, Kate recalled that Helen was lamenting that she was a bad interpreter of her mother; 'whereupon Mill stood up & said with tears in his eyes, "No, no one could interpret her, she was above everyone and inspired everyone."' Kate also reported that Mill was playing the piano again, but never 'before people'.[129]

Harriet would surely have approved of his last literary effort before the submersion in Westminster politics. Having finished off the intuitionists (in his own mind at least), Mill now wanted to settle his score with Auguste Comte. He had spurned an opportunity to do so a decade earlier via a review in the *Westminster* of Harriet Martineau's translation of the *Cours de philosophie positive*, on the grounds that he would be unable to be as critical of Comte in that journal as he wished to be. His deepening disquiet with Comte had therefore been demonstrated principally through editorial alterations to the *Logic*, from which he had removed dozens of laudatory comments and inserted some negative ones, especially in the second and third editions of 1846 and 1851. In the third edition of *Hamilton* he also used a footnote to downplay Comte's influence on the *Logic*.[130]

Nevertheless, given that his earlier praise of Comte had been a major contributory factor in the Frenchman's growing influence in England, Mill clearly felt the need to tackle the subject head-on. It was only fair to Chapman, the *Westminster*'s embattled editor, to give him the articles, which appeared in two parts in April and July 1865; *Auguste Comte and Positivism* was also published in book form before the year was out. Comte's rise to intellectual prominence gave Mill a cover-story for his earlier, warmer attitude towards the father of sociology. In the *Autobiography* he suggested that when the *Logic* was first produced, Comte's work was 'so unknown and unappreciated ... that to criticise his weak points might seem superfluous', but that once he had 'taken his place ... as one of the conspicuous figures in the thought of the age' it was desirable that 'some one should undertake the task of sifting what is good from bad in M. Comte's speculations'.[131] The implication was that while

Mill had always been doubtful about Comte, he had hidden his concerns for honourable intellectual reasons. Given Mill's willingness on other occasions to openly declare a change of mind or opinion, this convoluted and disingenuous explanation suggests that he was embarrassed about his earlier enthusiasm.

None the less he stuck to his initial view that Comte possessed a great intellect; in his 1854 diary, Mill had identified him as the only writer on the Continent who was more than a mere 'commentator', and one of the very few who could 'draw what they say from a source within themselves'. When Comte died, in 1857, Mill wrote to Harriet: 'It seems as if there would be no thinkers left in the world'. For the 1862 edition of the *Logic* he added a sentence praising Comte's 'great powers', and now, in his 1865 essays, he ranked Comte's philosophical abilities as greater than those of Descartes and Leibniz.[132] He also retained his admiration for Comte's philosophical foundation, which rested within the anti-intuitionist tradition and restated his support for Comte's theory of history, with societies driven by internal 'social dynamics' through the various stages of history: theological, metaphysical and positive. Mill also agreed with Comte – and disagreed with Anglo-Saxon writers like Henry Buckle – that knowledge was not the only basis and benchmark of progress: 'M. Comte shows ... a most acute sense of the causes which elevate or lower the general level of moral excellence; and deems intellectual progress in no other way so beneficial as by creating a standard to guide the moral sentiments of mankind, and a mode of bringing those sentiments effectively to bear on conduct.'[133]

At the same time he knew where Comte would end up taking his philosophy, so his praise was tempered: he admitted to feeling like 'the man in the story, who being asked whether he admitted that six and five make eleven, refused to give an answer until he knew what use was to be made of it'. When it came to Comte's applications of his philosophy, Mill warned his readers that 'the ludicrous side of the subject' was being approached. Indeed, the details of Comte's political and religious apparatus could not have been written by a man 'who had ever laughed'.[134] Mill denounced the repression of ideas and individual thought in the Comtean political system, dramatized by the proposed 'holocaust' of books. Comte had argued that while the free development of capacities was a necessary precursor to the positivist state, once that state had been arrived at, the primary goal was control: this was a doctrine from which, hardly surprisingly, Mill expressed his 'entire dissent'. He also departed from the French thinker's insistence that marriages be 'rigidly indissoluable', having some fun with the only exception he offered to this rule, which was when one of the spouses had received a criminal punishment. Mill pointed out that 'M. Comte could feel for the injustice in this special case, because it chanced to be the unfortunate situation of his Clotilde.' (After being abandoned by his wife, Comte had inconveniently fallen in love with Clotilde de Vaux, a prisoner's wife.[135])

Eventually, after describing Comte's diktat that people must imagine all words and numbers as being written in green letters on a white background, Mill ran out of patience. 'We cannot go on any longer with this trash', he wrote, and his very final published word Comte was, appropriately enough, 'ridiculous'.[136] Replying to a wounded letter from Richard Congreve, who had resigned his Oxford fellowship to devote himself to the positivist cause, Mill explained his robustness:

It is precisely because I consider M. Comte to have been a great thinker, that I regard it as a duty to balance the strong & deeply held admiration which I express for what I deem the fundamental parts of his philosophy by an equally emphatic expression of the opposite feeling I entertain towards other parts. It is M. Comte himself . . . who has thrown ridicule on his own philosophy by the extravagance of his later writings ... Any weaker terms would not put you in full possession of what I feel in the matter.[137]

Mill did, however, remove 'trash' – the word to which Congreve most objected – for the bound edition. Yet even as he was demolishing the specifics of Comte's system, Congreve and others – including Frederic Harrison, Harriet Martineau and George Eliot – were enthusiastically carrying them out in a Church of Humanity established just off Lamb's Conduit Street in Holborn, London. The positivist parishioners published a journal called *The Beehive*, a symbol of the perfect order which would prevail in a positivist community. For a while, Mill worried that these Comtists would lead the working-class leadership astray, but by the end of century, damaged by inevitable factional splits, the movement had petered out.[138]

Auguste Comte and Positivism – in both essay and book form – was of course only part of Mill's output for 1865. In the same year, he also published the first two editions of *Hamilton*, the third edition of *Representative Government*, the sixth editions of both the *Logic* and the *Principles*, as well as the first people's editions of *On Liberty*, the *Principles* and *Representative Government*. His recollection, understandably, was that 'I had now settled, as I believed for the remainder of my existence, into a purely literary life'. But as John Morley, the writer and Mill's protégé, would declare years later, 'nearly every Englishman with any ambition is a Parliamentary candidate, actual or potential', and Mill was no exception. He had 'a long slumbering idea of being in Parliament', according to Bain. Though he might have intellectually shaken off his adolescent wish to be a 'Girondist in an English Convention', the passion that fired his politics was still undiminished forty-five years later. He was as convinced in the 1860s as he had been in the 1830s that the House of Commons was the only place where 'a really advanced liberal party' could be created.[139] It also seemed, with Gladstone dominating the political scene, and reform in the air, that the time for rapid political advance might finally have arrived. In 1864 Gladstone made his famous declaration that 'every man ... not incapacitated by some consideration of personal unfitness or political danger, is morally entitled to come within the pale of the constitution'.[140]

In this hopeful climate, Mill agreed to stand as a Liberal

candidate in the parliamentary constituency of Westminster. He would insist constantly that he had no personal interest in becoming an MP – the word 'sacrifice' appears frequently in his speeches and articles from the period – but he was unable to disguise his appetite for the task at hand. The very fact of contesting a seat immediately raised his profile. 'Certainly this election affair is a better propaganda for all my political opinions than I might have obtained for many years,' he wrote to Hare, 'and it is selling my cheap editions, and indeed the dearer ones too, in a most splendid manner.' Even the possibility of his election, he told another correspondent, had 'greatly increased my influence: it has opened a communication between me & the general mind of the country: thousands will look to me now who knew nothing of me before: I am getting the ear of England.'[141] However, as Mill was to discover, English ears would not care for much of what they heard. During his single term in the Commons, Mill would offend mainstream opinion on many of the most pressing issues of the day. Anybody who had been expecting him to adopt a posture of lofty detachment was given a rude awakening between 1865 and 1868. On the surface, he was an internationally acclaimed, sixty-year-old philosopher and economist. But in his youthful heart, he was a Girondist still.

CHAPTER THIRTEEN

A Short, Bad Parliament (1865–8)

>‹<

On the dusty outskirts of Avignon, unseen by the tourists, runs the Avenue Stuart Mill. At the bottom edge of the blue street sign is an epitaph: 'John Stuart Mill. Philosophe Economiste et Homme Politique Anglais.' Mill's reputation as a philosopher has stood the test of time; in London, the blue English Heritage plaque outside his childhood home reads simply: 'John Stuart Mill, philosopher, lived here'. But by the end of Mill's life, his role as *un homme politique* was the dominant element in his public persona, and the most controversial. In the nineteenth century, Mill's overall standing was damaged by his years as a Member of Parliament. The prevailing judgement at the time was that he would have done better sticking to his books – a view which has only been challenged by Mill scholars in recent years. After his three years as an MP during the historic Parliament of 1865–8, *The Times* was lamenting Mill's 'vehement, narrow partisanship' and the 'impetuous eagerness' which had led him into the position of being 'the apostle of a small and not very select band of zealots.'[1] Of course *The Times* was no friend, but even a fairer observer like Alexander Bain thought that while he was in Parliament his 'idea of ventilating questions that had as yet scarcely any supporters' was 'carried to an extreme'.[2]

For Mill, however, his political activities were the natural extension of his work as an intellectual. Mid-Victorian mainstream opinion may have been shocked by his 'partisanship' on women, Ireland, rights to public demonstration and racism; Mill saw them as the natural political outcrops of his egalitarian, liberal philosophy. His election was an experiment with the potentially volatile mixture of intellectual and politician: with what happens when a leading scholar steps, in Leslie Stephen's phrase, from 'the judgement-seat to the open arena'.[3] Mill's political campaigns also acted as testing grounds for his theories. On a number of occasions he was forced, in rowdy public meetings, to justify his stance on issues such as the secret ballot, women's suffrage, restrictions in family size, Sunday trading, temperance and working-class representation. Apparently damning quotes from his books – including his claim that 'the working classes' were 'habitual liars' – were frequently shouted at him for explanation, and the press provided a running commentary on his performance. No other British intellectual of Mill's stature, before or since, has had this kind of exposure. One of the benefits for posterity is that it is possible to see the areas in which Mill was willing to compromise and those where he refused to move an inch: his years in the thick of political life thus illuminate his deepest convictions and his public character.

John Morley recalled that Mill 'sat in the House for a short and bad parliament, where old parties were at sea, new questions were insincerely handled, and the authority of leaders was dubious and disputable'.[4] It was a fair appraisal of the background, but Mill was clear about what he could achieve. He was certainly not in politics for the sake of ministerial advancement. 'I look upon the House of Commons not as a place where important practical improvements can be effected by anything I can do there,' he told one correspondent in 1867, 'but as an elevated Tribune or Chair from which to preach larger ideas than can at present be realized.' A parliamentary seat provided a 'vantage ground from which opinions can be promulgated to a larger audience & with a far greater probability of being listened to, than from any other position except perhaps that of the editor of a widely circulated daily paper.'[5]

Mill's near-iconic status as an intellectual helped to secure his election, as Walter Bagehot explained in his *English Constitution*: 'What did the Westminster electors know of Mr. Mill? What fraction of his mind could be imagined by any percentage of their minds? They meant to do homage to mental ability, but it was the worship of an unknown god – if ever there was such a thing in this world.'[6]

Mill's 1865 candidacy was indeed pretty Olympian, at least in its early stages. Replying to the initial request to stand, he accepted with a series of conditions which amounted to a declaration that he would only stand for Parliament if he was not obliged to behave like a politician. He would spend no money on his campaign; four years later he would be able to boast that 'neither of my contests had cost me one penny directly or indirectly'.[7] His refusal to dip into his own finances for his own campaign gave the comic papers some good copy. The topical magazine *Fun* commented:

> From Avignon to Westminster
> Journeyed omniscient Mill
> Whose lucky fate 'tis to be great –
> His friends, to pay the bill.[8]

Mill also refused to campaign, beyond writing down his opinions. 'I must ... decline to offer myself to the electors in any way,' he told the Westminster Liberal Electoral Committee, which had been formed to support his candidacy. He planned, in fact, to remain in France throughout the campaign. Like Burke almost a century earlier, Mill would give no pledges to his constituents beyond a promise to be true to his principles. 'My only object in Parliament,' he wrote, 'would be to promote my opinions'.[9] He also tried without success to get the Committee to consider other candidates, including his friend Edwin Chadwick.

In a subsequent letter to the committee for his election, Mill declared his support for women's suffrage, a widening of the franchise to 'give to the labouring classes a clear half of the national representation', taxation of 'luxuries', a legal right for working people to combine and strike, and an end to any legal disadvantages on the grounds of religion. He also spelled out his opposition to the secret ballot. Of course, none of this would have surprised anybody familiar with his published work, although his commitment to 50 per cent working-class representation, which he repeated during the campaign, was more specific than he had given in any of his writings.[10] Given that the letter was published in *The Times* and elsewhere in April 1865, nobody could accuse Mill of being elected under false pretences. Bagehot described it as 'one of the most remarkable' addresses 'ever delivered by any candidate to any constituency – especially in respect to the qualities of honesty, simplicity, and courage'.[11]

The committee, under the chairmanship of James Beal, took Mill's stringent demands in their stride. At the meeting to formally adopt him as candidate, Chadwick and Amberley spoke for the absent deity. But the most powerful endorsement – and the one which got the most column inches – came from John Roebuck, Mill's estranged friend, who said he had 'taught me pretty much all I know upon politics and philosophy ... and I owe him a greater debt of gratitude than I owe to any man living or dead'. Roebuck forecast that Mill would 'represent the thought, the philosophy, the great powers of the thinking people of England'. Although he regretted that Mill's 'private comfort' would be reduced by the 'disagreeable ... turmoil and trouble' of politics, he hoped for the sake of the nation that he would agree to run. 'If I consult the interests of my country,' he concluded to cheers, 'I would go down on my knees for Mill to stand.'[12]

As both Westminster seats were vacant, another Liberal candidate was also in the frame. Robert Wellesley Grosvenor, a thirty-year-old scion of the wealthy property-owning family, was already campaigning, having been embraced by the Whiggish tendency among Westminster Liberals as a suitably mainstream candidate. Before being approached himself, Mill had told Kate Amberley that the Liberal party 'could not have one [a candidate] worse than Mr. Grosvenor, for at a meeting he had been at he had been as illiberal as possible for a liberal to be – about America'.[13] Fourteen years earlier, Mill had openly criticized – albeit in a tucked-away footnote to his review of Newman's *Political Economy* – Grosvenor's grandfather, the 2nd Marquess of Westminster, for the accumulation of 'gigantic' wealth for which 'no one will pretend' he had 'given full value'.[14]

It seems unlikely that Grosvenor had read the comment, but none the less he attacked Mill, implying that he was out of touch and a hostage to radical interests. In his first address, Grosvenor reported with heavy irony 'there was a man of surpassing eloquence and superlative talent coming forward for the honour of representing them. He might be Garibaldi, the Pope, Count Bismarck, Jeff Davis or General Tom Thumb' – prompting cries of 'oh' from the crowd – but Grosvenor said of himself that he came 'forward independent of all parties or sections, and, if elected, would not be the delegate of any, but the representative of all.'[15] At his next meeting, Grosvenor said the American Civil War was the result of 'the failure of purely democratic institutions', and supported independence for the Southern states. When the audience responded negatively, crying 'slavery, slavery!', Grosvenor adopted the unusual tactic of turning his back on the audience and addressing his comments only to those on the platform – which apparently did little to quieten the crowd.[16] A landowning, pro-Southern, anti-democratic Liberal was hardly an attractive running mate for Mill. But then, Mill was not 'running' in any recognizable sense.

At this early stage, the press was decidedly pro-Mill. The *Telegraph*, then a progressive newspaper, compared him favourably to the usual 'titled nobodies and prosperous nonentities' that ran for Parliament. 'No political thinker of the present day', the editorial added, 'has exercised an influence like this man.' There would be 'new hope for the cause of Liberalism, if the historical centre of that high political creed' returned 'its foremost intellectual professor'. The *Morning Star* saw Mill as 'one of the greatest of living Englishmen'.[17] Even *The Times* was warm.

During most of the 1865 campaign, the two committees working to elect Mill and Grosvenor worked separately, with occasional sniping at each other. Eventually, however, they were forced into an uneasy alliance by what appeared to be a growing threat from the Conservative candidate, who also bore a household name: Mr W. H. Smith. Son of the successful bookseller, Smith was not expected even by his friends to win, but was energetic enough to worry the bickering Liberals.[18] He ran as a 'Liberal Conservative', and was in fact at least as liberal as Grosvenor. His biographer claimed that he had only been driven towards the Tories by the 'haughty Whigs' of the Reform Club, who had blackballed him because of his status as a 'tradesman'. In a clear dig at Mill, Smith said he would 'pledge' himself to local issues. He did not have a monopoly of support among his fellow retailers, however: Mill's campaign received donations from, among others, Fortnum and Mason and Debenhams.[19]

By May, Mill seemed uncertain about his prospects, at least in private. To Max Kyllmann, a German émigré and campaigner for the cooperative movement, Mill wrote: 'I think it hardly possible it [his candidacy] should succeed ... there is no *set* of political men who really wish to have me in Parliament: neither Whigs, not Tories, nor the Bright radicals (though I hear that B. himself speaks in my favour), nor any other set of radicals except perhaps the Cooperative section of the working classes.'[20]

By June, he was laying 'considerable odds on Grosvenor and Smith' and Helen was equally pessimistic. As the election neared, Mill's committee also became jittery. Their candidate's attitude towards family size was coming under scrutiny, with the *Standard* highlighting his 'dangerous and disgusting' theories on population and marriage.[21] Of course it could have been very much worse: Mill's youthful arrest was raised in neither of his election campaigns, which is surprising. Perhaps nobody thought of it; perhaps even his greatest enemies felt it to be beneath them.

The biggest firefight, however, was over his alleged attacks on religion in *Hamilton*, which continued even after the Dean of Westminster had declared his support for him. A couple of years earlier, Mill had found it 'quite amusing to see how speculations on religious and other subjects, which have for generations been familiar to instructed people here . . . are just now getting down to the inferior strata of cultivation.'[22] He was less amused now, though. His plan had been to spend the last weeks of the campaign making 'a tour in the Cevennes and Auvergne, beginning at Alais, and going round by Le Vigun [sic], the Lozère, the Cantal, and Mont Dore, to Claremont' – an election itinerary most politicians would envy.[23] In the end, after an exchange of increasingly heated letters with his committee members, Mill cut short the trip and returned to London to face his electorate. He was not happy about the departure from his own declared rules of engagement, but conceded that it was 'due to those who have taken so much trouble about me that I should not give them the impression that for my own convenience I expose them to the probable frustration of all their endeavours'.[24]

Mill arrived in London and delivered four election meetings in the first fortnight of July. By political standards, he was accorded a rock-star reception. At the first meeting in St James's Hall – officially just an open meeting with his committee – hundreds crowded into the room, with 'a brilliant array of beauty, in galleries set apart for the ladies' helping to swell the numbers until 'every foot of space was closely occupied. Mr Mill's formal entry was the signal for applause, again and again renewed, lasting several minutes.'[25] Speaking impromptu, apparently not warned by his committee of the potential turnout, a visibly nervous Mill confined his remarks to the nature of his candidacy and the basis of his politics. Having apologized for his lack of preparation, and recorded his honour at his selection, Mill went on, according to a newspaper report of the meeting: 'If there is a time when a person may be allowed to speak of himself, it is on such an occasion as this . . . I have sat by the cradle of all the great political reforms of this and the last generation; and I have not only sat by the cradle of these reforms, but before I was out of my teens I was up and stirring and writing about them.(*Hear.*)'[26]

It was an irrefutable claim. Although the nature and intensity of

Mill's engagement varied over the years, he was a lifelong political animal. Having established that he was no ingénue, Mill reached for a guaranteed cheer by mentioning his old alliance with Roebuck and then described his own philosophy of political activism: 'I have never been one of those who have left things alone when they have been an uphill fight, but I have left them when the fight was no longer difficult. When the thing was prosperous I have left it for a time, and have said 'This matter no longer requires me,' and have therefore transferred my services to those who did. (*Loud cheers*.)'[27] Conscious that some of his views were outside mainstream opinion, he then urged a longer-term view upon his listeners: 'I have been accustomed all my life – and all history confirms the same thing ... to see that the crotchet of today, the crotchet of one generation, becomes the truth of the next and the truism of the one after. (*Cheers*.)'[28]

Two nights later, Mill sat before a still larger crowd, with the same 'feature not common to election assemblies': large numbers of women. The chairman, Dr Edwin Lankester, introduced Mill as someone 'known wherever the interests of humanity lay deep in the hearts of men, wherever progress and civilization formed an element in the thoughts of men'. Lankester listed the clergymen supporting Mill, all of whom were standing against the 'wickedness' of attempts to disparage him on religious grounds. With a nod towards Mill's original promise not to campaign, he told the audience that 'they saw before them the great philosopher of the day, and he should have been still better pleased if they could have elected him without seeing him'. When Mill rose, the audience rose with him, waving their hats and cheering repeatedly. Only when silence was restored could Mill speak.[29] This address, widely reported, covered all the major themes of his campaign.

He opened by insisting that, for his own sake, he did not want to be an MP. 'I have no personal object to be promoted by it,' he said. 'It is a great sacrifice of my personal tastes and pursuits, and of that liberty which I value the more highly because I have only recently acquired it' – and then slid deftly into self-promotion – 'after a life spent in the restraints and refinements of a public office ... it is a fact that I have passed many hours every day for thirty-five years in the actual business of government'. In a subsequent meeting, he quoted the doctrine of an unnamed 'great writer' – in fact Plato - that 'those who wanted to be well-governed should look out for those who did not want to be governors'.[30]

Mill then made a virtue of necessity, using his declaration of political views as evidence that he 'would rather be honest than elected (*loud cheers – which continued for several minutes*)'. These views had, of course, been in the public domain long before his candidacy. His refusal to spend money on his own campaign stemmed not from meanness but from his disdain for the tendency towards bribery, and its corrosive implications for democracy. 'What shall we gain, what will it profit us, to weaken aristocratic ascendancy if seats in Parliament are to be put up to auction? (*Hear, hear.*) What is it but putting them up to auction if they are to be knocked down to the man with the longest purse, and who is willing to spend his money? (*Cheers.*)'[31] Accusing the Tories of trying to buy the constituency, Mill raised the stakes of the current contest:

It is no exaggeration to say that all eyes are upon you. Every friend of freedom and purity of election in the county is looking to you with anxious feelings ... If this great constituency should so degrade itself it will not only be the deepest mortification to all who put faith in popular institutions, but Westminster will have fallen from her glory.[32]

Mill declared himself as 'the candidate of advanced Liberalism'. His 'political creed' had two essential articles – first, that improvements in government lay 'not in the direction of some new form of dependence, but in the emancipation of the dependent classes – more freedom, more equality, and more responsibility of each person for himself.' This was what it meant, to Mill, to be a Liberal. Second, being 'advanced' required a belief that 'there are truths which the time has now arrived for proclaiming, although the time may not yet have arrived for carrying them into effect'. This was not

the same, however, as a doctrinaire insistence on immediate resolution: 'I would not object to any reasonable compromise which
would give me even a little of that of which I hope in time to be able
to obtain the whole. (*Cheers.*)'[33]

At the nomination meeting, a rumbustious affair in Covent
Garden, with plenty of noise from 'bands of ruffianly lads', Mill,
like the other candidates, spoke briefly and mostly for the benefit of
the reporters. On one of the presumably non-ruffianly lads in the
crowd – Thomas Hardy – he made quite an impression:

The appearance of the author of *On Liberty* (which we students of that
time knew almost by heart), was so different from the look of persons who
usually address crowds in the open air that it held the attention of people
for whom such a gathering in itself had little interest ... He stood
bareheaded, and his vast pale brow, so thin-skinned as to show the blue
veins, sloped back like a stretching upland, and conveyed to the observer
a curious sense of perilous exposure ... the cameo clearness of his face
chanced to be in relief against the blue shadow of a church, which, on its
transcendental side, his doctrines antagonized.[34]

The regular election meetings usually ended with a question-
and-answer session, during which several of Mill's opinions were
put to the test. In the most famous exchange, he was asked to
explain his statement that 'the lower classes – the working classes –
were habitual liars'. Mill retorted that the 'most intelligent of the
working classes' agreed, and pointed out that 'lying was the vice of
slaves': 'If they were educated and became free citizens, then he
should not be afraid of them.' According to Mill's recollection, this
statement was met by applause from the predominantly working-
class audience, and George Odger, a leader of the working-class
movement for suffrage, stood and declared that 'my class has no
desire not to be told its faults; we want friends, not flatterers'.[35]

Asked about the link between Church and state, Mill declared
himself to be against the existence of a 'State Church', but 'did not
think the time had yet arrived when it would be any use to try and

abolish it'.[36] Asked to justify his view 'that the working classes had not the right to have large families as well as the higher classes', he replied – perhaps not entirely convincingly – that he 'never said that the working classes had not as much right as the higher classes, but that they had no more right. Neither had the right to more children than they could support and educate.' How then, he was asked in a jocular supplementary question, could his views be squared with 'the Scriptural injunction, that we are to increase and multiply'? Mill replied: 'It says we are to eat and drink, but not over-eat and over-drink ourselves. (*Cheers and laughter*.)'[37]

In response to a number of questions, Mill declared himself to be in favour of Sunday trading in principle, and specifically supported the Sunday opening of Crystal Palace. He was guarded, however, when asked for his views on opening the theatres on the Lord's Day. According to a paraphrased report, he said that although he supported liberalization, 'he would not vote for [it] at present, as he thought it would be considered an affront to the religious opinions of a large and highly respectable portion of the public.'[38] He was fortunate that a letter he had written nine years earlier to the Sunday League did not surface. In it, he had dismissed Sunday prohibitions as the result of Christian 'superstition', and ridiculed the whole idea of a single day of devotion: 'Any devotion which is not felt equally at all times does not deserve the name.'[39] Mill's tone was also much more moderate than in the text of *On Liberty* when he turned to the temperance issue, declaring his pain at being opposed to the views of 'persons for whom he had a sincere respect and sympathy'. He nevertheless disagreed with those who said that 'because some persons abused the liberty now given to use intoxicating liquors, others should be deprived of the power of using them temperately'.[40]

In response to a demand for a description of the benefits which would flow from a broader suffrage, Mill urged his audience to look west. 'Let them look at America now. Look at the grand display of patriotism. Was it not the wonder of the world?. . .Did they not think that had something to do with everybody having a vote?

(*Hear, hear.*)'[41] In fact, the Civil War had considerably brightened Mill's outlook towards American democracy. 'If Tocqueville had lived', he told one correspondent, 'to know what those [New England] states have become, thirty years after he saw them, he would, I think, have acknowledged that much of the unfavourable part of his anticipations had not been realized. Democracy has been no leveller there, as to intellect and education, or respect for true personal superiority.'[42] The only time Mill stumbled during the campaign was in response to a question from a Mr Harrow, who asked 'What were Mr Mill's views with respect to marriage with a deceased wife's sister?' Mill was forced into the rare admission that he had not considered the matter, but could not see any reason why not, which seemed to please Mr Harrow.[43]

On 12 July, Mill joined Grosvenor again on the platform in Covent Garden for the formal announcement of the election results. Smith did not turn up. The crowd was so hot and excited that a watering cart was used to hose them down. The High Bailiff declared the poll: Grosvenor (4,534), Mill (4,525) and Smith (3,824). Topping the poll, Grosvenor spoke first. But when Mill rose, 'the vast mass of persons present set up a cheer of the most hearty, thrilling character, which was kept up for some minutes.' Looking out at the crowd, he tried to maintain his celebrated composure, but in the end his face cracked into a broad smile.[44] 'The Tories have done their worst,' he declared when it was quiet enough to speak. 'They have exercised all the powers that they could, particularly the force of money power – (*hear*) – but they have received a lesson they will not soon forget, and possibly they will think twice before they repeat it amongst the electors of Westminster. (*Loud cheers*.)'[45]

Actually, the Tories would repeat it, with more money and more success, just three years later. For now, though, Mill could enjoy his victory laps – *Punch* announced 'Logic's in Parliament with Mill. Hurrah!' – and ponder how best to make use of his new opportunities. He told Lord Russell that 'it remains to be seen if it [his election] is of any advantage either to myself or to anyone else.'[46] But he had some allies, at least, and he wrote to Henry Fawcett, who had just been elected for Brighton, that he looked forward to meeting 'on our common field of battle'.[47] Gladstone also won in South Lancashire, having lost his Oxford University seat, as expected, over his proposal to disestablish the Irish Church. Overall, the Liberals had slightly increased their majority.

On the other hand, the leader of the Liberal party was still Lord Palmerston, a sprightly eighty-one-year-old: not for nothing was he nicknamed 'Lord Evergreen'. He was the kind of Liberal most Conservatives could live with. Mill saw him as an incubus, a man who had blocked the cause of progress for decades, and in his earlier years he had denounced 'Pam' as a 'shallow and senseless coxcomb', someone he would be willing to walk 'twenty miles to see . . . hanged'. When Palmerston became Prime Minister in 1859, Mill had warned Hare to expect nothing but 'the well worn useless shibboleths of Whig mitigated democracy'.[48] During the 1865 election campaign, *Blackwood's Magazine* had fairly described Palmerston as 'looking forward to the future with an alarm which he scarcely takes the trouble to disguise'.[49]

But in October 1865, before the new Parliament had met, Palmerston died. 'Our quiet days are over,' said Charles Wood, Secretary of State for India, as he walked away from his leader's grave, 'no more peace for us.' Benjamin Disraeli, with more relish, agreed. 'The truce of parties is over,' he declared. 'I foresee tempestuous times, and great vicissitudes in public life' – an accurate prediction, although many of the tempests would be of Disraeli's own making.[50] Mill's reaction to Palmerston's death was not recorded, but is not hard to imagine. The new leaders of the Liberals, Lord Russell and Gladstone were publicly committed to parliamentary reform and Mill hoped that Gladstone could become the leader of the advanced Liberal party he wanted to help create.

By the end of August, Mill was bound for the Continent again, settling back into Avignon life after a month-long tour of Germany. With the new Parliament not due to meet until the following February, Mill spent his time replying to correspondence, climbing Mont Ventoux and preparing his review of Grote's book on Plato. 'The chief occupation of this year has been with Plato, Sokrates [*sic*], and you,' he wrote to Grote, 'and there could not have been, to me, a pleasanter one'.[51] Like the politicians of ancient Rome and revolutionary America, Mill would spend a good deal of time unfavourably contrasting metropolitan political life with a rural, literary one; one of his closest friends in Avignon was Jean Henri Fabre, later a celebrated entomologist, with whom he would embark on ambitious botanizing expeditions, usually in silence, with Fabre in front and Mill following. Even before his election, Mill had written to Hare that 'it is an infinitely pleasanter mode of spending May to read the *Gorgias* and *Theaetetus* under the avenue of mulberries which you know of, surrounded by roses and nightingales, than it would be to listen to tiresome speaking for half the night in the House of Commons.'[52] .

The parliamentary colleagues with whom Mill would spend his evenings were hardly kindred spirits. Even with the Liberals in the ascendancy, a 'cousinhood' of aristocratic members accounted for at least half the MPs. For them, and of course for the majority of the House of Lords, the interests of landowners remained dominant. Moreover, the city populations were woefully under-represented: Birmingham, with a population of 300,000, contained just 10,000 voters. The leading lights of the newly-rich commercial classes, rather than wanting to replace the aristocracy, generally wanted to ape them. Bagehot, as ever, was the most acute observer of the way social snobbery slowed the decline of the gentry, pointing out that 'every businessman had his eye already on a neightbouring park . . . and dreams of a coroneted descendant'.[53]

But if MPs were mostly 'gentlemen' – actual or aspirant – their leaders were becoming professional. Disraeli dismissed the 'hocus pocus' of non-party politics, and tightened the reins on the Conservatives. Gladstone, likewise, wanted to turn the Liberal party into a vehicle for change rather than a label for restraint. And outside Parliament, the clamour for reform was rising. Cholera, which so often seemed to prefigure electoral reform, had reappeared, and, sparked by a visit by Garibaldi – who addressed 20,000 people in

Crystal Palace – a Reform League had been created to press for universal male suffrage and the secret ballot.

When MPs were sworn in on 1 February 1866, the atmosphere was one of expectation. Mill took the oath which he had derided three decades earlier as among the many 'worthless formalities which do no good whatsoever, and much harm'.[54] Explaining his acquiescence years later to the atheist campaigner Jacob Holyoake, Mill said that unless a person had made it 'the special and peculiar work of his life' to argue against such laws, it was a reasonable compromise in order to get into Parliament. In a deleted passage he added: 'Perhaps however your question refers to the words which I think are in the parliamentary oath "on the true faith of a Christian". On this point my answer would be that I am as much entitled to call my own opinion about Christ the true faith of a Christian, as any other person is entitled to call his so.'[55] Maybe it was fear of publication which caused him to strike out these revealing sentences. He did, however, very politely refuse a much sought-after invitation to a Speaker's dinner, on the grounds that the compulsory dress code of either uniform or court dress was no longer appropriate, a requirement against which John Bright had already publicly protested.[56]

The public opening of Mill's parliamentary career was inauspicious. Not that the House was unwelcoming: indeed, Trevelyan told Kate Amberley that 'a sensation seemed to thrill through the house which filled rapidly when Mill rose'. Disraeli, brilliantly caustic as ever, turned to his neighbour and murmured: 'Ah, the Finishing Governess.'[57] Mill spoke 'rather inaudibly' and apparently without any forethought on the Cattle Diseases Bill, which provided compensation to landowners whose diseased cows had been destroyed. Given that the price of beef had already soared, he argued that this amounted to paying them twice. The landowning aristocracy ought instead 'to be willing to bear the first brunt of the inconveniences and evils which fell on the country generally'. He may have been right – Bagehot said the hurried passage of the Bill 'savoured of despotism' – but it was not the way to win over the House; and he was forced to clarify his views two days later.[58]

Having put his first foot wrong, Mill proceeded to stumble further with his second. Against the background of rising Fenian violence, the Home Secretary George Grey wanted to give the Irish authorities powers to hold suspects without trial for a year. Mill did not want to vote against the Russell–Gladstone government on the measure (or rather he did, but refrained), but he did want to give the House a lecture. The Bill, he averred, 'was a cause of shame and humiliation to this country'. While the current ministry were the inheritors rather than creators of the Irish problem, their proposal would mean that 'every foreigner, every continental writer, would believe for many years to come that Ireland was a country constantly on the brink of revolution, held down by an alien nationality, and kept in subjection by brute force.' He was answered with cries of 'No, no!'[59] Mill may have had justice on his side, but his timing and tone, for a newly elected member, were injudicious.

Mill's first month was in fact universally considered a failure. Although he stood by his views, he had, by his own later admission, 'lost the ear of the house'.[60] And there were of course plenty who wished him ill: William White, the Doorkeeper of the Commons, recorded that many members thought 'this big giant, whom we were all so afraid of, is after all, no giant at all, but a mere pigmy . . . these writing fellows never show well in the House.'[61] One of Mill's problems was his superior tone. As a great thinker, he perhaps thought the respect of the Commons would come automatically – and of course during the election campaign he had only had to stand up to win applause. After his intervention on the Cattle Plague bill, Robert Lowe complained that 'The hon-member for Westminster is a great deal too clever for us in this house.' Kate Amberley regretfully recorded the consensus: 'Mill's speaking seems to bore the house, they say he has spoken often – much, and cannot be heard. I am very sorry his first speech was not a good one and well prepared.' The *Pall Mall Gazette* lamented the errors of the 'lost philosopher'.[62]

Mill had failed to realize that renown gained outside the House provided no assurances on the inside. Indeed, fame could work against a newcomer, as the Conservative MP William Fraser explained: 'Not only was a man entering the House with a reputation out of doors looked at with the keenest severity; but he soon learnt, if he were capable of learning ... that your reputation must be made within its walls: there you must be born again.' The house would not 'brook a lecture' from a newcomer, warned Henry Lucy, no matter how famous.[63]

Fortunately, aided by some sound advice from Roebuck – transmitted via Chadwick – Mill was capable of learning his lesson. He did not speak again until the House was debating Gladstone's Reform Bill, and gave the address which Roebuck rightly thought 'ought to have been his debut'. This was territory where no one could doubt Mill's expert knowledge. It was also a critical moment for the fragile Gladstone administration, and Mill had to play his hand carefully. Gladstone had introduced a Bill to lower the electoral franchise requirements in the cities, lowering the value of property required to be owned from £10 to £7, and to add both country tenants paying more than £14 a year and those with savings of £50 or more to the electoral roll. Russell and Gladstone were delaying any move to redistribute seats until this Franchise Bill had passed. It was a gentle enough reform, which would have added some 400,000 voters to the existing electorate of one million and given the working class at best a quarter of the votes.[64]

Opposition to the Bill was led not by Disraeli but Robert Lowe, one of the most Whiggish of the Liberals and a brilliant parliamentary debater. Lowe and his band of followers were dubbed 'Adullamites' by Bright, a biblical reference to David's sheltering in the 'cave Adullam', along with all the discontented and distressed. Lowe was no admirer of the working classes, who were 'impulsive, unreflecting and violent people' with qualities including 'venality, ignorance, drunkenness, and facility for being intimidated.' He drew on his eight years' experience in New South Wales and Victoria, states which had introduced manhood suffrage and then a one-shilling registration charge – a change which had caused the number of electors to drop by half. 'A franchise which in the estimation of those who have it is literally not worth a shilling cannot,' he decided, 'be an elevation of the working classes.'[65]

The Adullamites fought an impressive rearguard action. One of the leading cave-dwellers, Lord Grosvenor (uncle to Mill's fellow Westminster MP), introduced an amendment calling for a postponement of the second reading of the Franchise Bill until after the presentation of the imminent one on redistribution. With Russell and Gladstone's majority slipping with each passing vote, the amendment was crafted to delay and kill the Bill. Mill's response was hard to predict. The Bill clearly fell a very long way short of the scale of reform he believed necessary. At the beginning of the previous year he had been doubtful that any reform bill 'which we are likely to see for some time to come, will be worth moving hand or foot for'.[66] In January 1866 he had expressed deep misgivings about separating a change in the franchise from other necessary changes, such as a redistribution of seats and proportional representation, believing that 'when *any* reform has been passed the whole subject of changes in the representation will be tabooed for years to come'.[67]

Now that Gladstone was leading the Commons, and was in trouble, Mill threw his weight behind him, while making it clear at the same time that the Bill was merely a down-payment on the reforms which must surely follow. It was to be Mill's finest parliamentary hour, at least in party political terms. His argument was strong and his tone confident but conciliatory, and he managed to support a weak Bill without diluting his standing as a radical reformer. He made the case for greater working-class representation, on the grounds that the voices of all classes, and all sides of any argument, needed to be heard in the Commons. 'Is there, I wonder, a single member of this House who thoroughly knows the working men's views of trades unions, or of strikes' he wondered. 'Are there many of us who so perfectly understand the subject of apprenticeships, let us say, or of the hours of labour, as to have nothing to learn from intelligent operatives?' Here he was echoing *Representative Government*, in which he had seen Parliament as the nation's 'Committee of Grievances, and its Congress of Opinions'. A diversity of opinions was also necessary for the pursuit of truth: 'Sir, we all of us know that we hold many erroneous opinions, but we do not know which of our opinions these are, for if we did, they would not be our opinions. (*Hear, hear.*)'[68]

There was nothing to fear from the Bill, which Mill said was 'not a democratic measure. It deserves neither that praise, nor if honourable members will have it so, that reproach.' A House of Commons dominated by working-class representatives would indeed be a cause for concern, Mill conceded, but this was not on the cards: 'What is asked for is a sufficient representation to ensure that their opinions are fairly placed before the House, and are met by real arguments.'[69] Lowe had argued that there should be no reform unless it could be proved that a broader franchise would lead to better government; his attitude was that unless Parliament could be shown to be broken, there was no need to fix it. Mill squared up to one of the best debaters in the House, and landed his punches:

If I understand my right honourable friend correctly, he thinks we ought to come to the House with a bill of indictment against itself (*a laugh*) – an inventory of the wrong things which the House does, and right things which it cannot be induced to do (*hear, hear*) – and when, convinced by our arguments, the House pleads guilty and cries *peccavi*, we have his permission to bring in a Reform Bill. (*Hear, hear, and laughter.*)[70]

Mill admitted that the Bill was 'far more moderate than is desired by the majority of reformers' who want 'a large and liberal representation of the working classes'. But, he said, with a nod to the disappointed radicals, and in contrast to his earlier private views, it was 'highly valuable even if nothing else were to follow'. Next, with the Whigs and Liberal Conservatives in his sights, he praised 'the good sense and good feeling which have made the governing classes of this country (unlike those of some other countries) capable of thus far advancing with the times'.[71] Up to this point in history, this advance had mainly consisted of the removal of obstacles to progress, such as the Corn Laws or religious discrimination. Mill now issued a more demanding to-do list to the government, one which would be more quickly ticked off by a reformed Parliament:

Is this all that the Legislature of a country can offer to its people? Is there nothing for us to do but only to undo the mischief that we or our predecessors have done? Are there not all the miseries of an old and crowded society waiting to be dealt with (*hear, hear*) – the curse of ignorance, the curse of pauperism, the curse of disease, the curse of a whole population born and nurtured into crime? (*Cheers.*) All these things we are just beginning to look at – just touching with the tips of our fingers; and, by the time two or three more generations are dead and gone, we may perhaps have discovered to keep them alive, and how to make their lives worth having.[72]

Liberal MPs stopped to shake Mill's hand after his triumphant speech; this was the Mill they had hoped to hear. Grosvenor's amendment was defeated, and Gladstone's administration survived to fight another day – although not for much longer. Kate Amberley, watching from the gallery was delighted. 'He was very much cheered when he spoke and when he sat down,' she recorded, 'and every time his name was mentioned later in the evg.' Roebuck described it as 'an outpouring of a great, honest, yet modest mind; the vigorous expression of well-considered & accurate thought'.[73] Gladstone noted in his diary: 'Reform Debate. Mill admirable.' Of course these were biased judgements. More store should perhaps be set by Disraeli's opinion: 'Mill has quite recovered himself politically now & is listened to as every first-rate man must be listened to in the House.'[74] The speech was reproduced as a 'penny pamphlet' and widely circulated.

Mill's had salvaged his parliamentary standing, in part by managing to conceal his condescension, which privately remained undiminished. 'I am indeed reduced to wonder,' he wrote to Gomperz a few months later, 'whether I shall ever be able to resume those quiet studies which are so prodigiously better for the mind itself than the tiresome labour of chipping off little bits of one's thoughts, of a size to be swallowed by a set of diminutive practical politicians incapable of digesting them.'[75] Although Mill continued to speak with his hands behind his back, 'like a schoolboy saying his lesson' according to Roebuck, it was still him doing the preaching. Gladstone described his 'conduct and language' in Parliament as a 'sermon'. Mill himself, just a month later, summarized the pros and cons of his new life: 'I have a taller pulpit now, but one in which it is impossible to use my best materials.'[76] He must have sometimes tried his colleagues' patience: on at least one occasion towards the end of the term, the Commons, by now used to his lengthy, densely-argued perorations, erupted into yells of 'Divide!' (a call to end the vote) the instant Mill got to his feet.[77]

While he never managed to drop his preachiness altogether, Mill was increasingly aware of the need to play the parliamentary game. He began to develop his skills in repartee. During one debate in which passages from *Representative Government* were quoted, he rose and declared that it was 'a flattering thing to find one's work so much referred to and quoted; but any vanity I might have felt in consequence has been considerably dashed, by observing that honourable Gentlemen's knowledge of my writings is strictly limited to the particular passages which they quote. (*Hear, hear, and laughter.*) I suppose they found my books too dull to read any further.'[78] On this occasion, his description in a footnote in *Representative Government* of the Conservatives as 'the stupidest party' had been cited. Given that the quote had 'some appearance of being less polite than I should wish always to be in speaking of a great party', Mill clarified the matter for the House's benefit and enjoyment:

What I stated was, that the Conservative party was, by the law of its constitution, necessarily the stupidest party. (*Laughter.*) Now, I do not retract this assertion; but I did not mean that Conservatives are generally stupid; I meant, that stupid persons are generally Conservative. (*Laughter and cheers.*) . . . And I do not see why honourable Gentlemen should feel that position at all offensive to them; for it ensures their always being an extremely powerful party. (*Hear, hear.*) . . . there is a dense solid force in sheer stupidity – such, that a few able men, with that force pressing behind them, are assured of victory in many a struggle; and many a victory the Conservative party have owed to that force. (*Laughter.*)[79]

Mill also spent some time on what would now be called public relations. For years he had refused to have his photograph taken – in 1863 he had told Chapman that 'I have not adopted that fashion, and am not likely to adopt it' – but in the run-up to his election, he relented.[80] He conscientiously answered his correspondence with a 'vast amount of letter-writing': Helen undertook much of the secretarial work, drafting and dictating letters, as well as acting generally as an editorial assistant and adviser in place of her mother. Mill was asked for his opinion on a whole range of subjects, more or less interesting to him, and for comment on a growing pile of books. He swapped useful thoughts on logic with John Venn, a young lecturer in moral science at Cambridge, later to be famous for his diagrams.[81] He was invited to join, chair or endorse a widening range of organizations, and mostly refused; the principal exception was to accept the Rectorship of St Andrews, where he delivered a three-hour inaugural address in February 1867. There was the odd glimpse into his frustration at the unreasonableness of some of the requests: to an unknown vicar who sent him a memoir of his equally unknown father, Mill offered thanks for the volume, which, he added, 'I am quite prepared to find very interesting' but only if he found the 'leisure' to read it.[82]

As a former editor and successful journalist, Mill was acutely aware of the power of the press. One of Mill's contemporaries wrote: 'It is *The Times* which leads the Government and the House of Commons. Ministers and Parliaments fear *The Times*, and *The Times* is not the least afraid of either.'[83] He was extremely courteous to Charles Ross, chief of *The Times*'s political staff, who had requested paper copies of his speeches to assist with their reporting.

'It is of much more importance to be well reported in the Times than elsewhere,' Mill wrote, explaining his refusal, 'but one is so much more certain of being so, that if one has to choose between sending one's note to the Times or to the other papers one would rather do it to the others.' To a friend he offered a rather different explanation: 'It would be a great piece of servility to give anything that depends on me to the Times alone; denying it to the papers with whose politics I agree, and which have acted in the most friendly manner to me throughout'.[84] Mill was willing to take up unpopular causes, and withstand an onslaught of opprobrium for doing so, but there was no need to make enemies unnecessarily.

During the first half of 1866, Mill also had political reasons for restraint. Given the precariousness of the Russell–Gladstone administration, he had mostly kept his counsel on the suspension of habeas corpus in Ireland and been conciliatory on parliamentary reform. He had avoided altogether any public comment on sensitive topics such as the brutal handling of a Jamaican uprising by the island's Governor, Edward John Eyre, and the convoluted argument over the relationship between the Queen's Colleges and Catholic Church in Ireland.[85] His political behaviour during this period gives a little credence to Leslie Stephen's claim that Mill was a 'thorough party man': in March 1866, Mill 'praised this [Gladstone's] Government very much' to the Amberleys, and 'hoped nothing would turn it out'.[86]

There was a strong mutual admiration between Mill and Gladstone, both of whom had a Scottish father, and passionate interests in classical history, political economy and Ireland. Their paths had crossed a few times since their first meeting over Guizot's dinner table in 1840. Both were in the Political Economy Club, and Gladstone, as Chancellor, had been part of the committee which cross-examined Mill, in his role as the nation's leading economist, on his views on property and taxation in 1861. Mill also attended one of Gladstone's political breakfasts in 1864. Bain wrote that at the time of Mill's entry to Parliament, 'for a number of years his [Mill's] relations with Mr Gladstone had been far more cordial and intimate than the outer world was aware of'.[87] At the height of the battle over the 1866 Reform Bill, Mill had publicly praised Gladstone as 'the first statesman who has come up to the idea of a modern statesman: a Minister should be the leader of a free people – not employing his mind only to do that which the people wished, but pointing out to them that which was for their benefit.' Toasting his leader at the inaugural meeting of the Cobden Club, Mill described him as a leader 'in whom the spirit of improvement is incarnate.'[88]

Gladstone, in turn, was heavily influenced by Mill's thinking. In his copy of *On Liberty*, the passage on religious toleration was twice-underscored and a '+' sign was placed in the margin – the Grand Old Man's highest approval rating. Like Mill, Gladstone had a 'mental crisis', and in his copy of the *Autobiography*, this period of Mill's life is the most heavily annotated. All his copies of Mill's books were in fact heavily underlined and scribbled on, and his reading diary demonstrates that he would typically consult Mill's work before making economic policy decisions.[89] When he was drafting his great free-trade budget in 1853, the *Principles* were being taken off the shelves on a daily basis. Nevertheless the personal relationship between the two men does not seem to have been as 'intimate' as Bain suggested. In any event, Mill was far from being a sycophant – during his MP years, he twice turned down a highly sought-after invitation to a dinner in the Gladstone household.[90]

In June 1866, the tottering Russell–Gladstone ministry was finally felled – by an Adullamite motion – and Lord Derby and Disraeli returned to power as leaders of a minority government. From the opposition benches, Mill enjoyed a new freedom, frequently voting against the 'party line'. On issues such as parliamentary reform, Ireland and Jamaica, he could now speak his mind without any risk of damaging a Liberal government. Indeed, it is one of the paradoxes of Mill's political career that it took the fall of his political lodestar, Gladstone, to create the conditions for his own rise. With Gladstone off the government benches, Mill himself was 'unmuzzled'.[91]

He wasted little time. Within a couple of weeks of the ministry's fall, Mill had labelled Eyre, the Governor of Jamaica, a murderer and pledged to bring him to justice. Following an uprising in Morant Bay – which resulted in the death of an English magistrate – the Governor had declared martial law the previous October. The disturbances were over within a week, but Eyre kept martial law in force for two months. During this time his troops burnt a thousand houses, executed 439 Jamaicans and flogged at least 600 more. There were no casualties among the soldiers. The most prominent hanging was of George William Gordon, a popular local politician, who was found guilty of high treason by a dubiously constituted court martial, on tendentious grounds.[92]

Eyre had been suspended by Russell, and a three-member Royal Commission dispatched to the island. In June 1866 the Commission reported, praising Eyre's initial response, but criticizing the continuance of martial law, the 'excessive' punishments meted out, and the unsound conviction of Gordon. In one of their last executive acts of the Parliament, Russell and Gladstone accepted the Commission's report and relieved Eyre of his post.

This was not enough for Mill. He was already a member of the Jamaica Committee, which had been formed the previous year to agitate for justice. John Bright, Herbert Spencer and Thomas Huxley, 'Darwin's Bulldog', were also members: later, Darwin himself would offer his support. The committee had been quiet while the Commission was still at work, but in July the majority of its members decided that Eyre should face trial and began to campaign towards this end. Charles Buxton, the chairman, believed this to be a mistake. While he agreed that the Jamaican events 'must cover the name of Mr. Eyre with infamy', he predicted that a legal case would be unsuccessful and have the perverse effect of giving Eyre a reputation 'as a martyr who had been vindictively and cruelly assailed; and his escape from danger would be hailed as a glorious triumph for himself and his partisans'.[93] As it turned out, Buxton was right on both counts – but he could not carry the committee, and was forced to relinquish the chairmanship. At the end of a dramatic meeting on 9 July, during which Bright loudly assailed Buxton for his weakness, Mill, who had remained silent throughout, was unanimously voted in as his successor. He spoke tersely: 'The objects of this committee are simply to ascertain whether there exist in this country any means for making a British functionary responsible for blood unlawfully shed – (*applause*) – and whether that be murder or not. I believe it to be murder.'[94]

The furious public row which erupted revealed some deep fault-lines in British society and opinion. As Mill's biographer, Leonard Courtney, put it: 'Two parties were formed in England on the issue'.[95] Although Mill had been publicly silent on the subject while Gladstone was clinging to office, his anger about Jamaica had in fact been simmering for months. The previous December, discussing the agenda for the upcoming Parliament, he had written that 'there is no part of it all, not even the Reform Bill, more important than the duty of dealing justly with the abomination committed in Jamaica'. In March 1866 'he spoke warmly and feelingly about Jamaica', said Kate Amberley, 'as if he felt it very deeply'.[96] Once he was free to act, Mill became the most vociferous and energetic member of the anti-Eyre, or pro-justice, camp – and sustained significant political damage as a result as the press proceeded relentlessly to disparage the 'Prosecuting Philosopher' for Westminster.[97] Mill posed the Eyre case as another test of the nation's moral health – following its failure during both the Indian Mutiny and American Civil War. He was, however, under no illusions about the unpopularity of the cause, telling a correspondent that 'from the first day I knew of it ... I determined to bring the [authors] to justice if there was not another man in Parlt to stand by me.' During the course of the argument, Mill received a stream of abusive mail – 'all anonymous, and as ineffably stupid as one might expect', including, according to Helen, 'incessant threats against his life', which worried her much more than him.[98]

Mill raised the Eyre case in Parliament, but was rebuffed by Disraeli. The committee then turned its attention to raising money, hiring lawyers and searching for a judge who might be willing to put Eyre in the dock. The former Governor arrived home at Southampton in August 1866, with more publicity than any colonial governor since Durham almost three decades earlier. While Durham had been feted by the radicals, however, Eyre was a poster-boy for conservative intellectuals. At a dinner in his honour, Eyre was toasted by Lord Cardigan, the man responsible for the Charge of the Light Brigade. Outside, a crowd protested against this 'Banquet of Death'. Charles Kingsley, to the disgust of his old Christian socialist friends, also toasted Eyre and made the ludicrous suggestion that he be given a peerage. Following an onslaught from the radical press Kingsley then kept his head down for the rest of the affair, prompting even his admirer John Ruskin to remark: 'I never thought much of muscular Christianity after that.'[99]

An Eyre Defence and Aid Fund Committee quickly signed up Thomas Carlyle. To the Scottish sage, Eyre was a 'just, humane, and valiant man, faithful to his trusts everywhere' who should receive 'honour and thanks, and wise *imitation* ... should similar emergencies rise.' Dickens, opposing 'that platform-sympathy with the black – or the Native, or the Devil', also sent a subscription.[100] So did Tennyson. Ruskin joined his hero Carlyle on the Eyre committee, a fact which his later Labour admirers have tended to gloss over. Ruskin stressed Eyre's personal qualities, too: 'From all I have heard of Mr Eyre's career, I believe that his humanity and kindness of heart, his love of justice and mercy, and his eminently Christian principles, qualified him in a very high degree for the discharge of his arduous and painful duties.'[101]

For Mill and his allies, the issue was not Eyre's character or motivation, but the rule of law. Huxley, in the *Pall Mall Gazette*, put forward the committee's view. 'I do not presume to speak with authority on a legal question;' he wrote, 'but, unless I am misinformed, English law does not permit good persons, as such, to strangle bad persons, as such.'[102] For the next two years, Mill pursued Eyre relentlessly, even when Gordon's wife backed away from a private prosecution for her husband's murder. In the Commons, he compared Eyre to Robespierre, and argued that the issue at hand was whether 'martial law indeed is what it is asserted to be, arbitrary power – the rule of force, subject to no legal limits'.[103]

With Eyre beyond the geographical reach of the lower London courts, a magistrate in Shropshire was persuaded to bring him to court in March 1867. James Fitzjames Stephen, acting for the Jamaica Committee, could not convince the court that there was sufficient evidence for a full trial, and the former Governor immediately walked free. The committee then applied to the Attorney-General, the Tory John Rolt, to order a trial – an application which, to nobody's surprise, was unsuccessful. By January 1868, Eyre felt confident enough to return to London, and brazenly informed the Jamaica Committee of his presence. Stephen advised against any further legal challenge, so Mill fired him and got another lawyer. After a series of increasingly desperate legal manoeuvres, the committee finally ran out of options. In July 1868 it was forced to disband.

Mill paid a high price for his zeal: the Eyre pursuit contributed to his defeat in the general election of 1868 and was the principal contribution to his reputation for recklessness. By the end of the struggle, 'Jamaica Committee' had become shorthand for blind, narrow partisanship. The satirical magazine *Judy* pictured Mill as the strongest-armed member of 'The Hanging Committee', acting against general wisdom, in the person of John Bull. The magazine *Will-o-the-Wisp*, no friend of radical causes, was even more acerbic, suggesting to Gladstone that, having 'changed his principles' he 'should also change his name – say to Mill-stone. No offence to poor Mill – he's a "gone coon".' Even the relatively liberal magazine *Fun*, in its preview of the 1868 candidates, listed 'Mill who's such nuts upon niggers'.[104] In Parliament, the Colonial Secretary, Charles Adderley, savaged the Jamaica Committee generally, and Mill especially, for 'seeing but one side of the question', a direct dig at the author of *On Liberty*. All the members, Adderley said, had 'forfeited for ever any title to be heard on any question that demands judicial calmness and impartiality for its consideration'.[105] Adderley was hardly unbiased, though; Eyre, during his lengthy Shropshire sojourn, was comfortably barracked at Adderley Hall.

Mill was unrepentant. By demonstrating that there was at least some opposition to Eyre, the committee, he claimed, had 'redeemed the character of the country' – although, it was equally arguable that by provoking such a strong defence of Eyre, it had done the opposite, as Buxton had warned. Writing to one of his supporters in his constituency, Mill showed that even failure had not diminished his fervour:

I have never in the whole course of my life felt myself called upon to take practical action on any matter on which I felt more clear as to the course indicated by the principles which I hold & have always endeavoured to promulgate. If the majority of any nation were willing to allow such events to pass unquestioned I have no hesitation in saying that all the ties of civil society would in that nation be at the mercy of accident...That the real or supposed crimes of men in authority should be subject to judicial examination, is the most important guarantee of English liberty.[106]

By twenty-first-century standards, Mill's stance requires no justification. Indeed, it adds to his stature as a courageous, principled and forward-looking public intellectual. Given the mood of the age, however, the likely damage to his reputation threatened the achievement of his other goals, and the charge of recklessness cannot be dismissed. For Mill, though, the rule of law was the very building block of a civilized society: a dimension of his Benthamism which never weakened. Anybody looking for an early warning of Mill's viewpoint would have found it in the chapter on justice in *Utilitarianism*, in which he declared that 'it is inconsistent with justice to be *partial*; to show favour or preference to one person over another'.[107]

'I am not on this occasion standing up for the negroes, or for liberty, deeply as both are interested in the subject,' he told Chadwick '– but for the first necessity of human society, law.'[108] Still, this was not sufficient explanation for his tenacity. The fact was that the Eyre case pushed simultaneously most of Mill's buttons: the rule of law, liberty in thought and action, the responsibilities of authority, progressive colonialism, and unthinking racism. From his perspective, black people in Morant Bay were entitled to the same protection from the state as whites in Manchester, but this was a view at least a century ahead of its time. Eyre's stock steadily rose until, in 1871, Gladstone's government agreed to pay his legal expenses. 'After this,' raged Mill, 'I shall henceforth wish for Tory government.'[109] He should have been more careful in his wishes: a few years later Disraeli's administration also reinstated Eyre's pension.

Shortly after seizing the reins of the Jamaica Committee in the summer of 1866, Mill had been presented with another opportunity to activate his principles: this time on the right to free speech – and to free protest. The Reform League, anxious to show their muscle to the new administration, announced a public demonstration in Hyde Park on 23 July. The Home Secretary, Spencer Walpole, declared that the Royal Parks were an inappropriate venue for such a gathering and ordered the Metropolitan Police to lock the gates and keep the protestors out. After a brief stand-off, the President of the League, Edmund Beales – another Jamaica Committee member – led the bulk of the marchers off to Trafalgar Square. A handful decided to tear down the railings to the Park instead, and a few days of unrest ensued. When Beales led a delegation to Walpole to try and resuscitate their plans for a demonstration, the Home Secretary burst into tears, a response which the working men struggled to decode.[110] Meanwhile, ever-fearful of revolution, MPs gathered in Westminster.

Mill launched a biting attack on the government, sarcastically dismissing their arguments against the use of the Royal Parks for mass meetings. He asked whether an occasional public meeting would 'cause a thousandth part of the interruption that an ordinary meeting of Volunteers in the Park does?' He then turned on the 'newspaper scribes of the Government', i.e. *The Times*'s leader-writers, who were 'already declaring that no open air meeting ought to be tolerated in the metropolis. I advise them to try that [banning outdoor meetings]. I promise them that they will have to encounter an opposition of a very different kind, and from different persons, to any they have yet encountered.' Mill concluded, with a twist, by laying the blame for the unrest firmly at the door of the government, rather than the mob: 'We know that there is a kind of people who can do more mischief in an hour than can be repaired in a lifetime. (*Ministerial cheers.*) I am afraid that the Members of the present Government are animated by the noble ambition of inscribing their names on the illustrious list of those persons.' (*Hear.*)[111]

This was the kind of speech – unyielding, sarcastic and pointed – which contributed to Mill's radical reputation. It was the one that prompted Matthew Arnold to accuse him of Jacobinism, and the conservative *Saturday Review* to deride the 'inflammatory harangue' of a 'violent and even acrimonious partisan'.[112] Disraeli, knowing that most of the House was against Mill, saw it as an opportunity. He rose as Mill finished, and declared the speech to be a specimen of the kind of rhetoric that could be expected at Hyde Park gatherings, and effectively contrasted the Government's cool even-handedness with Mill's rabid partiality. The ban stood.

But Mill wasn't done yet. He took up a self-appointed role as middleman between Parliament and the League, lambasting the former, and both supporting and restraining the latter. He fired off a cheque to the defence fund of those arrested in the disturbances, but when the League announced another meeting in Hyde Park, in defiance of the ban, Mill helped persuade them to back off, and meet in the Agricultural Hall in Islington instead. Following a meeting with Beales, Mill then communicated this decision to the House. In the *Autobiography*, he wrote that he 'would never forget the depth of his [Walpole's] relief or the warmth of his expressions of gratitude'.[113]

Mill now felt under an obligation to speak at the Islington meeting, where he was a fish out of water. The rowdy crowd, numbering tens of thousands, were mostly unsure of his identity, one voice calling out 'Bravo, Mills!', his voice did not carry in the Hall, and great 'surges of the crowd' prevented him from completing his remarks. What he did manage was a defence of the right to demonstrate in the Royal Parks combined with praise for the League's wisdom in backing off from another confrontation until the matter could be settled through the courts, where the judges would indeed later rule against the government. Beales tried to get Mill to stand on a table to speak, like the rest of the platform, an offer he 'politely declined'; he had a difficult enough balancing act as it was.[114] He believed that in helping to persuade the League to back down, he had single-handedly prevented a major riot. This was a considerable over-statement of his own role, though he was justified in feeling that the press, who he said accused him of being 'intemperate and passion-ate' were even less fair than usual.[115]

But Disraeli wasn't finished either: a year later, having lost the legal case, he introduced a Bill to formally ban public meetings in the Royal Parks. By this point, Mill had refused the League a writ-ten statement of support because of the increasingly revolutionary flavour of its rhetoric – at a time, as he firmly told them, when there was no justification for violence whatsoever.[116] None the less, of the principle he remained an emphatic supporter of free demonstra-tion. On the eve of the anniversary of the Hyde Park hiatus, Mill rose in the House again. This time he was focused on principle rather than provocation. The parks, he repeated, were public prop-erty and as such should be open to public meetings. It was certain-ly true that large meetings were not often conducive to discussion, but this was not their only purpose: 'They are a public manifesta-tion of the strength of those who are of a certain opinion.'[117] A restriction on using large open spaces for meetings was a simply a dishonest way of discouraging such meetings.

Most dangerously of all, on 29 July 1867, Mill invited a deputa-tion from the Reform League into the Houses of Parliament for a cup of tea. This – while hardly the gunpowder plot implied by gov-ernment ministers – was a breach of parliamentary etiquette, for which he subsequently had to make a public apology.[118] By mid-August the government benches were hot and tired: Mill and a group of allies filibustered the Bill until eventually, defeated, Disraeli dropped it for good. To this day, the north-east corner of Hyde Park is a voluble testament to Mill's victory.

By this point, the Commons probably needed a rest. The spring and summer had been months of high political drama, culminating in the passage of the 1867 Second Reform Bill, a radical measure compared to the insipid offering from Russell and Gladstone the previous year. In a chaotic and factional Commons, strange alliances had formed – for example, between the radicals (not including Mill) and the Adullamites against Gladstone – while Disraeli, Chancellor of the Exchequer, but effectively Tory leader in the Commons, tacked, plotted and compromised in order to keep the upper hand. In May, he performed a stunning parliamentary volte-face, accepting, without Cabinet consent, an amendment which had the effect of introducing household suffrage across the cities of England and Wales. He was attempting not only to out-flank Gladstone in the short term but to 'realize the dream of my life, re-establishing Toryism on a national foundation'. On top of the widening of the franchise – which had the effect of adding a million voters, doubling the size of the electorate – the final Bill contained a good dose of seat redistribution; eleven constituencies disappeared altogether and thirty-five lost one of their two MPs. The big cities and most populous counties saw their representation enhanced. Lord Derby admitted the Bill was 'a leap in the dark', while for Carlyle it was 'shooting Niagara' and 'the end of our poor old England'.[119] Both the Whig *Edinburgh* and Conservative *Quarterly* thought the move precipitate and dangerous: Disraeli compared them to the staff of rival coaching inns, 'condoling together in the street, over their common enemy the railroad'. *Fraser's Magazine* reported the story of a cheeky message boy who popped his head around the door of the Carlton Club to ask 'is this the Reform Club?', only to receive the disgruntled reply: 'No, you rascal, the Revolution Club'.[120]

Mill himself had some fun at Disraeli's expense, comparing him to the Irishman who walks his pig backwards into town, explaining to a quizzical observer: 'Hush! The pig must not suspect where I'm taking it to; walking this way it does not see where I'm taking it to; the pig thinks it's going home; I couldn't get it into Limerick otherwise.' The difference, Mill added, was that 'Mr. Disraeli made his own party believe they were going backward when they were really going forward.'[121]

During the heady, topsy-turvy politics of 1867, Mill seized the opportunity to impress his own reforming agenda on the public mind. The fact that the Reform Bill was being taken through the House by a Conservative government meant he had room to introduce his 'crotchets', namely women's suffrage and proportional representation. 'There will, in all probability, be a Tory Reform Bill,' he wrote to Hare at the end of 1866, 'and whatever may be its quality, no moving of amendments or raising of new points will in the case of a Tory bill be regarded by Liberals as obstructiveness, or damaging the cause.'[122] Mill had already presented a petition in support of women's votes; now he could press the point. On his sixty-first birthday, he proposed a tiny editorial alteration to the Reform Bill which, if accepted, would have triggered a social revolution: the amendment simply substituted the word 'person' for 'man' in the legislation. For the first time, women's suffrage was put before the House of Commons. Mill would later describe the move as 'perhaps the only really important public service I performed in the capacity as a Member of Parliament'.[123]

The start of his opening speech was inauspicious, as Kate Amberley recorded from the gallery: 'The house was very thin, but he was listened to with the utmost attention and respect. He came to a most painful pause at one time nr. the beginning of his speech and stood silent for near 2 minutes or more; he seemed quite lost, only his eyebrows worked fearfully.' [124] The enormity of the occasion had emptied Mill's mind and triggered his old nervous tic, but eventually his pre-prepared speech came back into his mind. As he began, the forensic force of his argument earned the attention of his colleagues. The speech was essentially a summary of the main arguments of *The Subjection of Women* – lying finished on his desk, but not published until 1869 – diluted a little to allow for the Commons' sensitive political palate. The question before the House, he said, was not one 'to excite ... party or class interest' but was 'whether there is any adequate justification for continuing to exclude an entire half of the community ... from the capability of ever being admitted within the pale of the Constitution'.[125] After this Gladstonian echo, Mill diagnosed opposition to the move as based on outdated customs and opinions about a 'hard and fast line of separation between women's occupations and men's' which belonged 'to a gone-by state of society ... receding further into the past'.[126] While the tone of his speech was mostly serious, he risked the odd foray into parliamentary playfulness. Dismissing arguments about women's inexperience of political and economic matters, he jibed:

It is thought perhaps ... that those whose chief daily business is the judicious laying-out of money, so as to produce the greatest results with the smallest means, cannot possibly give any lessons to right honourable gentlemen on the other side of the House or this, who contrive to produce such singularly small results with such vast means.[127]

Mill's measure was defeated, but it attracted seventy-three votes, including that of John Bright, who had previously been in the men-only camp. For the next few years, Mill's hopes of success on this issue would rise – only, as so often in his political life, to fall again. It is clear that his reputation was critical in getting the issue a hearing: even the *Saturday Review* admitted that 'when Mr. Mill makes a legislative proposal, something may probably be said in its defence'. For the *Review*, however, the clinching counter-argument to the amendment was the 'unfitness and impropriety of allowing women an active share in public affairs'. That this was the correct view was proved by the very eccentricity of the proposal: 'If an arrangement strikes ninety-nine out of a hundred persons as supremely ludicrous, there is probably some real incongruity in the plan itself'.[128] The leader-writer was clearly no fan of the arguments of *On Liberty,* either.

It is equally clear, however, that Mill's feminist stance took its toll on his reputation, although just how much is difficult to gauge from this historical distance. The serious press gave the debate a mostly thoughtful airing, but the magazines now latched on to their richest vein of anti-Mill humour. In cartoons, he frequently appeared dressed as a woman, regardless of the subject-matter. *Punch*, in its usual search for puns, managed 'The Ladies' Favourite Scent.-Mill-fleurs'. The magazine also reported a fictional debate between 'Professor Podgers' and 'Dr Harriet Brown' – her first name surely no accident – at the 'Progressive Institute'. Podger asks Brown a question: 'Why is Mr. Mill like a tongue?' She has no idea, but he helpfully provides the answer: 'Because he is the Ladies' Member.'[129]

Even if he had been a *Punch* reader, Mill would probably not have been more than mildly irritated. He was delighted with the debate, and threw himself fully into the campaign for women's votes for the last years of his life. Five days after the vote on his amendment, he addressed a reform meeting with the greeting 'Brother and Sister Reformers!' provoking laughter and cheers. By the middle of 1868 – when he introduced another petition, containing 21,757 signatures, which he persuaded the scientist Mary Somerville to head – he declared that 'the cause is prospering beyond all hope'.[130]

Ten days after moving his historic amendment for women's suffrage, Mill rose in the House to make the case for proportional representation. He had arranged for Thomas Hare and his family to watch from the gallery, which may have been a mistake: Mr. Hare's daughters 'were much disgusted at the stupidity of the M.P.s for they laughed very much and were very inattentive'.[131] Mill's speech was a rerun of his arguments in *Representative Government*, with just a few political modifications. He insisted that 'personal representation' along the lines suggested by Hare was 'neither democratic nor aristocratic – neither Tory, Whig, nor Radical ... it is a principle of fair play to all parties and all opinions without distinction'. Under the current system, those holding minority opinions were 'blotted out ... as if they had been legally disqualified.'[132] PR would help to break the grip of the party system. Describing the position of those elected under PR who held unorthodox views, he drifted into an autobiographical tone: 'What more inspiring position can there be for any man, than to be selected to fight the uphill battle of unpopular opinions, in a public arena, against superior numbers?'.[133] Having made his case, and in exchange for a fair hearing from the Government, he did not press for a division.

Mill also supported an amendment of Robert Lowe's which would have given voters in the proposed three-member constituencies the chance to cast more than one vote for the same candidate. Lowe hoped that this 'cumulative' voting would hold back the tide of working-class MPs – indeed, he saw it as 'the last and only chance' to do so – while Mill supported it on the grounds that it provided some possibility of minority representation. It was the only time that Mill was in the 'anti-reform' camp with regard to electoral reform, but from his perspective it was Bright, who violently opposed the measure, who was the 'conservative' in this case.[134] Anyone doubting Mill's determination to stick to his principles, rather than a party line, had only to watch him enter the 'Aye' lobby with the hated Adullamites. (The amendment was defeated none the less.) Mill was also anxious to deflect the credit for reform towards Gladstone and away from Disraeli, who he accused, in his unprincipled shifts of position, 'if not of tricks', then certainly of 'trying it on'. Gladstone's principles, Mill said, meant that he would support Conservative-sponsored measures if they promoted reform. 'Every good thing we have got in this bill', Mill told a St James's Hall crowd in May 1867, 'even that which seems to be more than Mr. Gladstone was prepared to give, has only been given for the sake of outbidding Mr. Gladstone.' [135]

Mill's multifarious political activities, both inside and outside Parliament, were largely intended to put into practice the social and political theories enunciated in his most famous works. He was an active member, for example, of the Select Committee on Metropolitan Government, attending twenty-three sessions between 9 March and 29 July 1866. He introduced three Bills to reorganize the government of London – none with any chance of success – simply in order to keep the issue alive. He was the first to introduce a Bill for a single metropolitan authority, as well as one for a Mayor for the whole city.[136] Despite some of his misgivings about the union movement, he also played a small part in the beginnings of the activities which would over the next eight years, 'with remarkably little fuss', as Eric Hobsbawm noted, give British unions a virtually complete system of legal recognition. He turned down a seat on the Royal Commission on Trade Unions, which sat from February 1867 to December 1869, but led a deputation to Spencer Walpole requesting that a working man be appointed instead.[137]

Mill also bolstered his green credentials, supporting a tax on coal to reduce waste, launching a parliamentary protest against deforestation in Hainault Forest and lending his support to the Commons Preservation Society, formed in 1865 to lobby for the maintenance of publicly accessible spaces of natural land. A forerunner to the Ramblers' Association, the Society was not above direct action, such as organized fence-breaks. Mill later became a member of his local branch, and then of the Executive Committee.[138] He also spoke in favour of the introduction of non-smoking carriages on trains, responding to a fellow MP's suggestion that the matter 'be left to public opinion' with a phrase lifted almost verbatim from *On Liberty*, that 'public opinion in this instance was swayed by the majority of smokers. It was a case of oppression by a majority of a minority.'[139]

As all this suggests, Mill was an industrious parliamentarian. But it wasn't all work: he escaped for a week in Somerset, taking 'a holiday in the only form in which a holiday does me any good, by long walks through beautiful scenery'.[140] And he continued to host his Wednesday and Sunday dinner parties in Blackheath, with the guest lists containing, as usual, a preponderance of political and intellectual allies. He enticed Anthony Trollope to Sunday lunch, and one soirée, in June 1866, included the Amberleys, William Thornton, Herbert Spencer and Elizabeth Garrett, as well as Frank Harrison Hill, Assistant Editor of the *Daily News*.[141] The conversation ranged over Comte, cosmology, feminism and George Eliot's new novel, *Felix Holt, the Radical*. Other evenings must have been lighter affairs, such as the one which included Mary Morris Hamilton, granddaughter of the US founding father, Alexander Hamilton, her two young nieces and their father, Colonel George Schuyler, who had fought for the North in the Civil War and as a keen yachtsman had just helped to establish the America's Cup race.[142] Whenever Parliament rose, Mill packed his trunk and headed south. He never stayed in London for the winter, and in 1867, with Gladstone's blessing, skipped the three-week autumn parliamentary session. He did offer to dash back if necessary, and it is an indication of the transforming impact of the growth of the French railway network that a telegram before noon was sufficient notice for him to be voting in the Commons the following night.[143]

Mill's politics between 1865 and 1868 lived up to his self-description as an 'advanced liberal'; in many areas he was much more advanced than most people had expected. His years in Parliament, far from showing a tempering of his radical spirit, were marked by an increase in his degree of outspokenness and moral indignation. But if his overall radicalism was in no doubt, nor was his independence. He had no hesitation voting with the 'conservative' side on some issues – such as capital punishment, one of the few issues on which Mill became more conservative over time. Having been opposed to the death penalty – Caroline Fox recorded his view in 1840 as being for 'entire' objection – his view had gradually hardened. In 1864, the year before he was elected to Parliament, he told another correspondent that he was of 'a very strong opinion against its total abolition' on the grounds that it acted as an effective deterrent against crimes of brutality.[144]

He therefore voted for the retention of the death penalty, to the disappointment of radical friends both at home and abroad. To a dismayed Louis Blanc he explained that on the issue they simply 'came to different conclusions from the same principles'.[145] The penalty should be retained only for crimes of aggravated murder, he insisted, and carried out in a dignified fashion: he was grateful for moves away from the public spectacle of hangings. The mid-century hangman William Calcraft, who according to Dickens conducted his work with tasteless jokes and brandy on his breath, was not Mill's kind of executioner. Dickens had vividly described the hanging of Marie and Frederick Manning in 1849, for which Mrs Manning wore black satin. While her husband's form was soon crumpled, her body was 'a fine shape so elaborately corseted and artfully dressed that it was quite unchanged in its trim appearance as it slowly swung from side to side.'[146]

In April 1868 Mill told the House of Commons that he himself recalled rows of people hanging outside Newgate prison – a sight he had no wish to return to. Still, for hardened murderers, the best solution was no 'solemnly blot him out from the fellowship of mankind and from the catalogue of the living'.[147] He accused the abolitionists of being faint-hearted about death. In a mode of speech which, if liberal at all, can only be described as of the muscular variety, he declared: 'What else than effeminacy is it to be so much more shocked by taking a man's life than by depriving him of all that makes life valuable?...Is it, indeed, so dreadful a thing to die? Has it not been from of old one chief part of a manly education to make us despise death?'[148] Palmerston would have been proud of him.

Similarly, Mill was no dove when it came to defence and military matters – although here there was more to his apparent conservatism than met the eye. He was a firm believer in the importance of a strong navy, seeing it as a vital defensive bulwark between English liberty and continental despotism. 'Naval power is as essentially defensive as military is aggressive,' he said. 'It is by armies, not fleets, that wars of conquest can be carried on; and naval Powers, both in ancient and modern times, have been the cradle and the home of liberty.'[149] For Mill, it seems, England was a modern Athens. On the same grounds, he supported the right for the British Navy to seize goods in international waters: a stance that put him at odds not only with the bulk of the radicals and Liberals, but with the Conservative Foreign Secretary, Lord Stanley. While Mill wanted a powerful, professional navy, he sought an amateur, citizen army. A standing, professional army was potentially an 'apt instrument of despotism'; a threat to liberty not only at home but abroad. Citing the American example of a citizen army, he declared to a Manchester reform meeting: 'That is the defensive army which we require – (*loud cheers*) – it is the defensive force we seek – (*cheers*) – and we ought with the utmost vigour to oppose any attempt to increase it so as to give us an aggressive force.'[150] Mill became a strong supporter of compulsory national service – giving every young man six months of military training – as well as of the introduction of military drill into schools.[151]

On the face of it, these were not liberal measures, but they tell us something about the nature of Mill's liberalism. He took a broad, historical view of freedom, and was willing to trade some liberties in the defence of the greater cause. England needed an army in case of foreign threat; but a professional one could be misused by the state. The best model was a citizenry ready to fight when necessary, but content like their American cousins to return 'to their ploughs and to their looms' once the war was over.[152] This was only a feasible approach if the citizens had some military skills, so national service was a necessity. This was an example of coercion in support of a liberal objective. It is also likely that Mill saw national service as containing a valuable educative role, boosting national pride, co-operation and character. In his essays on Comte, he had unfavourably contrasted civilian working life with a superior military culture: 'Until labourers and employers perform the work of industry in the spirit in which soldiers perform that of any army, industry will never be moralized, and military life will remain, what, in spite of the anti-social character of its direct object, it has hitherto been – the chief school of moral cooperation'.[153]

If some of these stances were more pleasing to those sitting opposite him than his interventions on the Hyde Park riots or Jamaica, there still remained one subject, just as dear to his heart, on which his radicalism had merely been in hiding. Since his early, poorly-received speech on Ireland, he had remained almost silent on the issue which loomed over late nineteenth-century politics. The only exception was his support for a woefully inadequate Bill from Gladstone's government in May 1866, which proposed to give tenants the right to claim compensation for improvements they had made to the land, in the event of being evicted by the landlord. Mill subsequently described his speech as 'one of my most careful' and 'calculated less to stimulate friends, than to conciliate and convince opponents'.[154] The fact that he felt the need to justify the speech suggests a degree of embarrassment – which in the circumstances was entirely appropriate. By this time, any reader of the sixth edition of Mill's *Principles*, published the year he entered Parliament, would have known that he believed the Irish crisis to require much more dramatic remedies.

Heavily influenced by John Cairnes, his Irish economist friend, Mill had come to appreciate the depth of Irish woes for the first time since the 1840s. In particular, he had been forced to acknowledge the pace of depopulation, with hundreds of thousands fleeing every year to the New World. In contrast to his position in the 1840s, Mill now saw the human necessity driving emigration, but he continued to view the westward exodus along 'the bridge to America' as a source of national shame.[155] 'The loss, and the disgrace, are England's', he wrote, 'and it is the English people and government whom it chiefly concerns to ask themselves, how far it will be to their honour and advantage to retain the mere soil of Ireland, but lose its inhabitants.' Given current conditions and attitudes, England faced a choice between the 'depopulation of Ireland, and the conversion of a part of the population into peasant proprietors'.[156]

Mill's sympathetic understanding of the Irish situation stirred him to a spirited defence of Fenian prisoners threatened with execution. In May 1867, he led a deputation urging the prime minister, Lord Derby, to commute the sentence of death passed on Thomas 'General' Burke for his role in the uprising in Tipperary that March. 'Sensibly moved by the affecting nature of the task,' according to a press report, Mill told Derby that the group had 'come here with as deep and earnest a feeling as it is possible for human beings to have, to implore your lordship not to erect the scaffold in this country for political offences.' More practically, he warned that the result would be to make Burke a martyr.[157] After some courteous exchanges, Derby allowed the group to use his drawing-room table to sign their petition, after which they thanked the Prime Minister for his reception, and quietly left.

Later that evening, in front of a packed crowd of 3,000 reformers in St James's Hall, Mill was not interested in courtesy. His frustration at decades of English complacency towards Ireland boiled over. After discussing Gladstone and the Reform Bill, he turned to the matter weighing most heavily on his mind. 'I should like to elicit a little feeling from you,' he announced. 'I should like to know, first, whether you think that we have any right to hold Ireland in subjection unless we can make Ireland contented with our government. (*Cries of No, no.*) That expression of sentiment will resound through Ireland, and win the hearts of her people to you. (*Cheers.*) Let me ask you now: do you think the Irish people are contented with our government? (*Cries of No, no.*) Is that your fault? (*No, no.*)'[158] It was against this backdrop, he said, that the actions of the Fenians had to be understood:

Their patience is worn out, and in most desperate circumstances they endeavour to get rid of what they think misgovernment at the risk of their lives – do you think, I say, that those men are not fit to live for that reason? (*Cries of No, no.*) ... It is necessary to punish these people, but it is not necessary to hang them. (*Cheers.*) It is important that the world should know that you, the people of England, abhor the idea of staining the soil with the blood of political offenders. (*Loud cheers, and a cry of Hang the Government.*)[159]

When he took his seat, the audience rose to their feet and gave the firebrand philosopher 'a vigorous three cheers'. Burke's sentence was commuted, although when the Fenians moved their campaign to the mainland later in the year – including a deadly bomb attack on Clerkenwell prison – the Government line hardened and captured Irish nationalist operatives were sent to the gallows. The rising tide of Fenian violence, however, did not deter Mill. Indeed, he decided that it was time to spell out his agenda, in the form of his own forty-four page explosion, *England and Ireland*, published in February 1868. In the *Autobiography*, Mill recalled that the work 'was not popular'. This was an understatement. 'Mr. Mill has in his time written and said a good many startling and unpopular things,' commented Thornton, 'but nothing that he ever before said or wrote gave such general offence.'[160]

The polemic described centuries of English misrule and analysed Fenianism as the dangerous symptom of legitimate grievances. The union could only survive – and only deserved to survive – if there was a transformation in the economics of Irish land: 'When ... the land is farmed by the very hands that till it, the social economy resulting is intolerable unless either by law or custom the tenant is protected against arbitrary eviction, or arbitrary increase of rent.' There was no longer any time for an 'amicable mediation ... between landlord and tenant': the state needed to act forcefully.[161] Mill's solution was to give fixity of tenure to the Irish tenant peasantry. Each tenant would make an annual rent payment, based on an official valuation to the landlord, and the state would underwrite this payment. In exchange, the tenant would receive a guarantee of the 'permanent holding' of their portion of the land.

Landlords would be given the option to 'sever altogether their connexion with the Irish soil' and derive their income, at the same level as the calculated rent payments, from Consols – imperishable, guaranteed government bonds. The Treasury would then receive the rent payments from the farmer. Mill thought that 'those landlords who are the least useful in Ireland, and on the worst terms with their tenantry, would probably accept this opportunity'.[162] It was clear that Mill thought this meant the majority: just a few pages earlier he had described the landlords of Ireland as having 'less to do with tilling' the land and having 'less connection with it of any useful kind – or indeed of any kind, for a large proportion did not even reside on it – than the landowners of any other known country'.[163] Mill's plan, given his assumption about the landlords, amounted to the wholesale replacement of the Irish landowning classes by the state. His later protests against critics who described his scheme as nationalization therefore rang somewhat hollow. 'Is it not curious' he complained to Cairnes, 'that the plan in my pamphlet is almost always spoken of as a simple proposal to buy out the landlords and hold all the land as a property of the State?'[164] While it was not exactly a 'simple proposal', Mill's scheme was in fact aimed at precisely this end. The *Saturday Review* was being no more mischievous than usual when it suggested the essay would give succour to the 'anarchists of Europe' who should now 'crown [Mill] the most thoroughgoing apostle of Communism in the next convention in Geneva'.[165]

Mill would continue to develop his ideas on land ownership in his last few years, but his correspondence shows that his views on the subject, heavily influenced by his Indian expertise, were already as radical as his opponents feared. 'I often think that it would be much better if a new country retained all its lands as state property, giving, as we do in India, leases renewable for ever at rents guaranteed against any augmentation except by a *general* measure,' he wrote to a American politician in May 1868. 'According to my own notions, absolute property in land, even when owned by the cultivators, is a prejudice and an abuse.'[166] His time in Parliament hardened his views on Ireland, as on other issues. As Bruce Kinzer, an expert on Mill's political life, has written: 'Theory generally blunted Mill's radical edge; practice sharpened it.'[167]

The reaction to the pamphlet was, as Thornton suggested, overwhelmingly hostile. Only the *Spectator* offered full-throated support. Thornton himself, in the *Fortnightly*, suggested that 'the author's reputation has availed little to bear down upon the pamphlet; rather the pamphlet seems calculated to bear down the author.'[168] Even supportive papers like the *Telegraph* and *Daily News* warned against adoption of Mill's plan. Bagehot, in the *Economist*, accused Mill of wielding a 'sort of intellectual terror' and argued that implementation of the plan would worsen Irish unrest. But he was more interested in what it said about Mill than what it proposed for Ireland, and offered a characteristically acute analysis of Mill's zeal when pursuing one of his moral crusades, whether on Ireland, Governor Eyre, the Hyde Park riots or the American Civil War:

An honester or a more simple-minded man than Mr. Mill – a man more ready, in season and out of season, to maintain an unpopular doctrine – does not live. But the fact is, he is easily excitable and susceptible; the evil that is in his mind at the moment seems to him the greatest evil, – for the time nearly the only evil, the evil which must be cured at all hazards.[169]

More straightforwardly, *The Times* dubbed *England and Ireland* 'the most ill-conditioned political essay which has yet appeared on the subject'. The *Pall Mall Gazette* lamented the 'crudity' of the scheme, doubting (reasonably enough) Mill's assumed connection between land economics and nationalist sentiment and lamenting the tone of 'a somewhat excited partisan'.[170] *The Morning Post* dismissed the central argument as 'unsound', adding for good measure that if Mill's name had not been on the cover, 'public opinion would have pronounced that a more absurd, because violent and exaggerated, pamphlet was never written upon such a serious subject'.[171]

As so often, *Punch* summarized the prevailing consensus, at least on the tone Mill had adopted: 'Try Mill's Territorial Peasant Proprietary Panacea, the Sole Specific for Irish Disorders. No others are genuine. N.B. Observe the Signature "John Stuart Mill". All opponents are Fools.'[172] After this torrent, Mill wrote to Cairnes that 'on the whole I have met with more approbation, and not more abuse, than I expected'. What Mill did not know was that Cairnes himself was privately among the abusers. 'I have been much mortified by this last pamphlet by Mill,' he wrote to a friend. 'It will neither add to his influence nor help the settlement of Ireland. In fact ... the crudity of the scheme is, after all, that which most impresses one.'[173]

For Mill, the issue at stake was nothing less than the future of the union itself. Unless the land question was fixed, 'Fenianism, or something equivalent to it' would be 'the standing torment of the

English government and people'. He admitted that giving Irish tenants 'permanent possession of the land' was 'revolutionary' but insisted that 'revolutionary measures are the thing now required'.[174] To Cairnes he declared that 'nothing short of what I propose would now tranquillise Ireland'. The only alternative to decisive, radical action on Irish land was 'total separation' of the two nations.[175]

When the issue of Ireland came before the House of Commons in March 1868, *England and Ireland* hovered over the debate from its outset. The most sustained attacks on Mill's stance were delivered by Charles Neate, MP for Oxford City and, perhaps inevitably, Robert Lowe. Neate claimed that the greatest obstacle to peace in Ireland was the proposal of 'extravagant and impossible remedies', to which Mill retorted that 'the real obstacle ... is the unwillingness of the House to look at any remedy which they have pre-judged to be extravagant and impossible ... Great and obstinate evils require great remedies.'[176] Mill then tested the patience of the House with a long defence of his scheme. He denied that his scheme included a proposal for the state to buy up the land or that it would be compulsorily enforced on tenants. He also expressed the hope, in contrast to his views in *England and Ireland*, that 'many landlords' would come to private, amicable arrangements with their tenants without coercion. While he did not contradict directly any of the specific statements from his pamphlet, his speech presented it in the most conservative light possible, and adopted a much more conciliatory tone. He ended with the hope that over time the difficulties associated with the plan would 'in a great measure, disappear, and the House will be more inclined to view it with more favour than at present'.[177] Significantly, the warmest reception was from Gladstone, who, while he 'had not daring sufficient' to follow Mill in his proposal 'for what seemed to me to be the dismissal of the landlords of Ireland', did lament that the 'false legislation, and the miserable system of ascendancy which has prevailed in Ireland [which] have so distorted and disfigured the relations of class to class within that country'.[178]

With the benefit of hindsight, Mill later recast his role in the debate over Irish land. By taking such a radical stance he had, he said, helped to 'stimulate and prepare' public opinion, and therefore create political space for other measures. Moving away from his all-or-nothing position of the time, by 1869 he was claiming that his intervention on Ireland had enjoyed 'some success' against this benchmark, on the grounds that his proposals, 'while they were almost universally decried as violent & extreme have had the effect of making other proposals, up to that time considered extreme, to be considered comparatively moderate & practicable'.[179] It was in this light that Mill, in the *Autobiography*, helped himself to a large share of the credit for Gladstone's 1870 Irish Land Act, which introduced a modest range of rights for tenants, including compensation for improvements which they carried out on the land and a degree of protection against arbitrary eviction:

It is most improbable that a measure conceding so much to the tenantry ... would have been proposed ... unless the British public has been led to perceive that a case might be made, and perhaps a party formed, for a measure considerably stronger ... the British people ... think every proposal extreme and violent unless they hear of some other proposal going still farther, upon which their antipathy to extreme views may discharge itself. So it proved in the present instance; my proposal was condemned, but any scheme of land reform, short of mine, came to be thought moderate by comparison.[180]

While Mill's direct influence on the 1870 Act was minimal – George Campbell's *The Irish Land*, published in 1869, had a much greater impact on policy – it was certainly true that he had altered the politics of the question. Had Mill been alive in 1881, the year of the second Irish Land Act, he could have felt even more satisfied: after years of violence, this Act established the Irish Land Commission, which set rents and gave tenants fixity of tenure. It did little, however, to dampen Irish nationalism.

Mill adopted a similar strategy of self-justification towards his principal parliamentary activity of 1868, the drive to toughen electoral anti-fraud measures. 'The great question of the next session will be the promised bill against electoral corruption,' he predicted at the end of 1867. Disraeli had promised some legislation, but 'the advanced Liberals must have *their* rival bill'.[181] Influenced by the work of William Dougal Christie, a former ambassador to Brazil and campaigner against political bribery, Mill pushed for amendments to appoint a public official in each constituency to oversee elections and keep them 'pure'; the opportunity to appeal through the courts, and a post-election investigation after parliamentary and municipal contests. This was 'no party measure,' he insisted, 'and no party were interested in passing it, except the party of honesty. Disraeli declined, however, Mill's entreaty to apply 'his ingenious and contriving mind' to the broader problem, restricting his Bill to a shift in responsibility for adjudicating complaints from a committee of MPs to a judicial tribunal.[182] This came as no surprise to Mill, whose anger was reserved for his own side. Gladstone, who did not engage with the issue, was surely in Mill's mind when he wrote, in the *Autobiography,* that 'the Liberal party in the House was greatly dishonoured by the conduct of many of its members in giving no help whatever to this attempt to secure the honest representation of the people'.[183] None the less Mill was as usual able to convince himself that his efforts were not in vain. 'Good however has been done by the discussion,' he told Christie in July, 'and a foundation laid for future success.'[184]

With the general election approaching, Mill was looking to the future with great optimism. He was convinced at the end of the 1860s, just as he had been at the end of the 1830s and 1840s, that an era of radicalism was dawning. In June 1868 he declared that 'the prejudices which beset every form of society . . . are rapidly melting away', and in September he wrote to Charles Norton that 'the old fetters of prejudice and routine seem to be giving way on all sides'.[185] Reform was clearly in the air, and – thanks to Disraeli – apparently on the agenda of both parties. Half the electors were newly enfranchised, and most of these first-time voters were working class, albeit from the artisan end of the labouring spectrum. The expected political gains of the working classes and 'advanced liberals' in the upcoming election would, he believed, 'transfer a large share of power to classes who are not under the influence of landed or Church prejudices'. In these changed circumstances, Parliament required 'an infusion' of 'new men', those with 'clear and well considered positive opinions'.[186] The next Parliament would have, Mill said, a historic role:

We are looking to it for a general revision of our institutions & for making a commencement of effort against the many remediable evils which infest the existing state of society ... We want, in the first place, representatives of the classes, now first admitted to the representation. And in the next place we want men of understanding whose minds can admit ideas not included in the conventional creed of Liberals or Radicals, & men also of ardent zeal.[187]

Solutions to the problems now confronting society required 'long and patient thought'. Encouraging Edwin Chadwick to stand – not that he needed much encouragement – he wrote: 'the time requires men who are not merely willing to adopt, but able to originate and prepare, important improvements'.[188]

Mill's hopes that the political complexion of England was changing would, once again, be dashed – but in the meantime they fuelled a one-man recruitment drive. It was time for the radicals to take the Liberal party away from the Whigs, and Mill actively campaigned on behalf of Henry Fawcett in Brighton and Chadwick in Kilmarnock, and gave financial support to the radical atheist Charles Bradlaugh in Northampton and the trade unionist George Odger in Chelsea. All but Fawcett were running in constituencies with sitting Liberal MPs. Edward Bouverie, the incumbent in Kilmarnock, was furious, and traded some sharp letters with Mill, which he then published – without Mill's permission – in *The Times*. Mill was no fan of Bouverie's, having already dismissed him privately as 'a very doubtful liberal' who 'was reckoned an Adullamite' and the author of an anti-Gladstone speech in 1866. In his first letter, though, Mill was reasonably restrained, suggesting merely that Chadwick was 'an altogether exceptional man, to whom it would be an honour to any other man to give way'.[189] When Bouverie went public with the dispute, however, Mill took the row right up the Richter scale. After some perfunctory niceties about Bouverie's twenty-five years' service, Mill put the knife in:

... 5 & 20 years & a new Reform Act make a great change in men & in politics ... The urgency of an infusion of new blood is as good a reason for making a new choice, as dissatisfaction with an existing candidate ... no untried man can be looked upon as less a member of the liberal party than the man who at the beginning of the present year, called the liberal party a rabble & declared that their leader was incapable of leading ... we are not now in ordinary times. There are not only new electors to be represented, but new questions to be decided, requiring men deeply impressed with the wants of the country, & who have exercised their minds on the means of remedying the most pressing existing evils ... We do not want men who cast reluctant looks back to the old order of things, nor men whose liberalism consists in a warm adherence to the liberal measures already passed, but men whose heart & soul are in the cause of progress, & who are animated by that ardour which in politics as in war kindles the commander to his highest achievements & makes the army at his command worth twice its numbers; men whose zeal will encourage their leader to attempt what their fidelity will give him strength to do.[190]

Needless to say, the conservative press made much of this dissension in the liberal ranks, and of Mill's meddling. He clearly believed, according to *The Times*, that it was his duty 'to interfere with every election but his own': true to form, he spent August, September and October in Avignon. *Will-o-the-Wisp* magazine described Mill as the 'Examiner-General and Issuer of Certificates to Liberal candidates'.[191] His certificate of support for Fawcett was reasonably uncontroversial, because he was already in the seat. Odger – to Mill's public disappointment – withdrew in Chelsea, in order to avoid splitting the Liberal vote and letting in the Tories.[192]

Most damaging to Mill was his embroilment with Charles Brad-laugh, the nation's best-known atheist, co-founder of the National Secular Society and editor of the *Reformer*. He was a controversial figure – far too much so for John Bright to endorse him – being prosecuted for blasphemy even as he ran his campaign. When he did finally succeeded in being elected for Northampton, in 1880, he refused to take the oath of office but still attempted to take his seat, for which he was arrested and briefly imprisoned in the clock tower of the Palace of Westminster. In 1868, Mill oscillated between insisting the Bradlaugh connection had no impact on his re-election chances and accepting that some collateral damage had been caused to his own candidacy.[193] Others were in no doubt of the damage. George Holyoake, whose sympathy for both Mill and Bradlaugh was beyond question – his brother was running 'Mr. B's' campaign – estimated that Mill's £10 donation 'was worth £10,000 to his Tory opponents'.[194] In an intrusive letter to one of the two Northampton MPs, Charles Gilpin, who was an ally from the Jamaica Committee, Mill made it clear that Bradlaugh was hoping to unseat the other sitting Liberal, Lord Henley. In a similar vein to his argument with Bouverie, he added that while Henley was 'hon-est & honourable' and 'a faithful supporter of our own party', his claim, 'ought [not] to be allowed to prevail against the claims of exceptional men'.[195] Even the loyal Kate Amberley was disappoint-ed. 'How very badly Mill is behaving about the Elections,' she wrote to her mother. 'I think he is much too meddlesome & Lord Henley is not a man to be turned out for a Bradlaugh'.[196]

To one of his own supporters, Mill insisted that 'in giving this aid to Mr B. I did not take at all into consideration his religious opin-ions, with which as practical politicians we have nothing whatever to do; and he repeated the biblical injunction about knowing a per-son 'by their fruits'.[197] However, given that the promotion of secu-larism was Bradlaugh's principal political objective, the committee can be forgiven for being unmoved by Mill's explanations and, in an uncanny repeat of the 1865 experience, ordering him back from France to face charges of advocating, or at least funding, atheist views. But at his public meetings Mill was not faced with the most damning charges against him. He implored his opponents to stand up 'like men and Englishmen, and tell what was the cause of complaint'. When this failed to flush out the enemy, he offered to attend a meeting packed with Conservatives 'and answer every question they might choose to bring forward'.[198]

But the Tories, represented once again by W. H. Smith, were quite content to let the press continue to keep Mill in the spotlight, and allow their canvassers to spread the news of his shady secularism to the few voters who remained ignorant of it. Smith's public attacks on Mill – who was clearly his principal target – were restricted to the general comment that the nation had 'gone far enough in the way of headlong progress' and a hope that the voters of Westminster would 'no longer advocate the policy of those who desired rapid and violent changes'.[199] At one meeting, Mill displayed some rare public irritation, telling one elector in answer to a question about the House of Lords that his views 'could be obtained by any elector for 18*d*. in the form of a book', i.e. *Representative Government*.[200]

Mill's role on the Jamaica Committee received plenty of attention, of course, and in June 1868 he had poured some fuel on the flames by presenting a petition from the Home and Foreign Affairs Association of Macclesfield, which condemned the 'injustice of the Abyssinian war' and called on the House to 'withhold its thanks' from General Sir Robert Napier who had successfully commanded a force ordered to rescue some British citizens being held prisoner by King Theodore III of Abyssinia. (Theodore committed suicide; Napier picked up a baronetcy.) *The Times*, in its now ceaseless quest for anti-Mill ammunition, paraded the petition as further evidence of his lack of patriotism. Mill patiently explained that he saw it as an important function of MPs to present petitions, especially from unrepresented groups, even if – as in this case – he did not agree with them.[201]

Any fair-minded observer would have conceded Mill's absolute integrity on this issue: as an MP, he presented dozens of petitions with which he would obviously disagree, including those calling for a secret ballot, universal male suffrage, and restrictions on Sunday trading. He even presented directly opposing petitions, such as one to restrict the sale of alcohol on Sundays and another to remove such restrictions.[202] But such subtle constitutional distinctions were unlikely to get much purchase during an election in which Smith and his supporters – gladly picking up the gauntlet laid down by Mill in 1865 – were pouring money and men into the constituency. The contest was anything but the 'pure' one for which Mill had urged legislation. Smith's agent retained the services of a 'Mr. Edwards', who had already spent eighteen months in jail for the electoral corruption which had led to the disenfranchisement of St Albans.[203]

At the public meeting for the official announcement of the election results, held on 18 November, the returning officer was delayed by two hours – even though the outcome was already known. Perhaps recalling Smith's failure to turn up three years previously, Mill, pleading a cold, rose to make his remarks before the formal results. (His cold was recovered by the following day.) A boy aged between ten and fourteen years, according to various newspaper reports, was providing an expert running commentary on events, and called for 'cheers for Mr. Mill', to which the crowd responded warmly, adding 'Don't mind, Mr. Mill, we'll pop you in for Greenwich'.[204] Mill regretted that the Tories had topped the poll (Smith received 7,648 votes, Grosvenor 6,584 and Mill 6,284), thanked his supporters, defended his independence of action in the Commons, and then walked the short distance to the Liberal committee rooms in Cockspur Street.[205] His parliamentary adventure was at an end.

Mill's committee apparently had enough fight in them for another round, however, and brought a petition against Smith for corruption. The resulting judicial enquiry, made possible by the Bill of Disraeli's that had so disappointed Mill, discovered that Smith had spent £8,908 during the campaign (equivalent to half a million pound today), compared to a joint total of just £2,296 for Grosvenor and Mill.[206] Enough evidence of bribery and dubious accounting was uncovered to put Smith's claim to the seat in real doubt; even

Smith's sympathetic biographer agreed that the election expenditure was 'lavish'. The judge concluded that the Tory spending was 'not creditable, and its extent was almost beyond belief', but could not find hard evidence of sufficient wrongdoing to declare Smith's election void.[207]

Under the strain of the inquiry, which ended in February 1869, Smith fell ill, his skin flaring with the red wounds of erysipelas – the same infectious disease which would kill his opponent five years later. During the post-election scrutiny, Smith's strong business connections and a general sense that he was a good chap helped to tip the balance of opinion in his favour. This, at any rate, was the view of *The Times*. 'A good character has, to Mr Smith at any rate, proved better than riches' concluded its leader-writer. 'It may be a question whether the latter won the seat for him, but there can be no question that the former saved it.'[208] From France, Mill observed the judicial review with detachment, although to Amberley he wrote that 'the result of the elections seems to justify the opinion of those who said that these elections would go by money'.[209]

The election results across the nation were in fact a mixed blessing. Gladstone was in with a sizeable majority, but in a replay of 1837, the 'advanced liberals' had received a pounding from the new electors. Chadwick, Bradlaugh and Amberley were unsuccessful in their attempts to gain a seat; Roebuck lost his again. Mill's response to a mailbag of condolences was a mixture of personal pleasure and political disappointment. His defeat was 'personally a great relief', he told Charles Eliot Norton, which was why he had declined 'the invitations I have received to stand elsewhere.'[210] In fact the only seats Mill appears to have turned down after his defeat were the politically unappealing ones of West Cornwall and Buckinghamshire, although it seems that he might indeed have stood for Greenwich, as the boy-pundit suggested, if the opportunity had arisen.[211] As it turned out, Gladstone needed his back-up seat after being defeated in Lancashire. Instead, Mill declared to Cairnes that he was enjoying 'great and fresh ... feeling of freedom'.[212]

Mill's hopes for an infusion of radical blood had been

disappointed. The election saw, he variously told his correspondents, 'the defeat of the radical party throughout the country'; a 'general rejection by the constituencies of candidates whose claims were either those of culture or democracy,' the complete failure of 'the new candidates of advanced opinions'; and a 'general rout of men of brains or of strong opinions'.[213] He warned presciently that the Liberal party would come to regret its failure to bring on 'the best leaders of the working men and help them to seats', although it would be some decades before the Labour party finally eclipsed the Liberals.[214]

The moderate make-up of the Commons made Mill even more glad to be out of it, as he told George Howell, the unsuccessful Liberal candidate for Aylesbury: 'The defeat of all the working class candidates & of most of those of any other class in whom the working classes took special interest, would have made my presence in the H of C of far less use than it might perhaps have been if I had been one of a phalanx of men of advanced opinions.'[215]

In fact it is hard to see what more Mill could have achieved after 1868, given the complexion of the House – bitter proof of which was the identity of Gladstone's first Chancellor, the arch-Adullamite, Robert Lowe. But while Mill was insightful about the general political result, his reflections on his own defeat were muddled. He was apparently unable to decide whether to take the line that his defeat was a price worth paying for sticking to his principles, or that his principles were not the cause of his defeat. To one of his committee members, he insisted: 'I can sincerely say ... that I acted in all things as I shd have done had my career been dependent upon my success', but it is hard to square this statement with the Bradlaugh donation, or indeed with Mill's own admission in his *Autobiography* that 'in subscribing ... to his [Bradlaugh's] election, I did what would have been highly imprudent if I had been at liberty to consider only the interests of my own reelection.'[216]

Mill seemed to realize, if only in retrospect, that his defeat was at least partially self-inflicted. But he would not have countenanced any compromise of his own principles simply to gain re-election:

for him, politics was always a means for communicating and acting on those principles. If that cost him a seat, so be it. A topical cartoon told the story of Mill's defeat. Smith is pictured putting a torch to 'The Westminster Guy' – Mill – who is holding two small monkeys: Odger, who represents 'ruffianism', and Bradlaugh who stands for 'atheism'. Going up in flames with Mill are his 'radicalism', 'female suffrage', as well as 'crotchets', 'whims' and 'dreams'. The torch bears the title 'Common Sense'.[217]

The politics were more complex than this, of course. Westminster was well on the way towards becoming a safe Tory seat – in 1874 two Conservatives would be returned. But the assessment would have pleased Mill. It was in order to fight complacent 'common sense' that he entered Parliament in the first place. The tyranny of public opinion which saw votes for women or Irish land reform as eccentricities or fancies was the evil identified in *On Liberty*; to be politically martyred for them at the hands of 'common sense' was a worthy achievement for its author.

John Morley was disdainful of the new Parliament, dubbing it in a *Fortnightly* article 'The Chamber of Mediocrity', although he was not an unbiased observer, having stood unsuccessfully in Preston.[218] Morley compared Mill's defeat to the dismissal of Turgot, Baron de Laune by Louis XVI in 1776, a year after the monarch had praised him as the only other man who truly cared for the French people. Mill was delighted by the comparison, telling Morley: 'it is indeed an honour to me that such an assimilation should have occurred to you.' It had not just occurred to him, though. Morley knew – because Mill had told him – that Turgot was a lifelong inspiration.[219] In any case, a careful reader of Mill's works would have known that Turgot represented Mill's ideal philosopher-statesman, 'the wonder not only of his age, but of history' for his 'astonishing combination' of 'the spirit of philosophy with the pursuits of an active life'.[220] In a youthful debating speech on 'The Use of History', unpublished until 1929, Mill had described Turgot's journey from his study into public service and back again:

That sublime character, whose whole soul was so strictly under the dominion of principle that he had not one wish which did not centre in the happiness of mankind – for whose elevated, comprehensive and searching intellect no speculation was too vast, no details too minute, provided they did but conduce to his great and generous purposes – who called from a private station to the councils of his sovereign, sacrificed every personal object in order to free his countrymen from the oppressions under which they groaned ... bearing the bitter and undissembled hatred of the privileged classes, and what is yet more difficult to bear, the clamours of a misguided people ... hunted down by one of the most worthless aristocracies that ever existed, as a visionary and a theorist – those epithets by which presumptuous and besotted ignorance never fails to stigmatize those who are wiser than itself.[221]

It is no wonder that Mill, licking his wounds in Avignon following his defeat, was so pleased with Morley's analogy. He saw the need for political tacticians like Gladstone; but the politicians who inspired him were the men who took progressive ideas and principles into the public domain. As Sterling suggested, Mill was 'a private in the army of Truth'.[222] At a breakfast held in honour of William Lloyd Garrison, the American anti-slavery campaigner, in 1867, Mill gave a speech which was as much a personal manifesto as a eulogy. The lessons from Garrison, he suggested, were these:

Aim at something great; aim at things which are difficult; and there is no great thing which is not difficult. Do not pare down your undertaking to what you hope to see successful in the next few years, or in the years of your own life. Fear not the reproach of Quixotism and impracticality, or to be pointed at as the knights-errant of an idea. After you have weighed what you undertake ... go forward, even though you, like Mr. Garrison, do it at the risk of being torn to pieces by the very men through whose changed hearts your purpose will one day be accomplished.'[223]

Mill's career in Parliament was marked by a few immediate successes: he played a significant role in securing the right to demonstrate in public parks and a lesser one in saving the life of the Fenian leader Thomas Burke. On some issues, such as the secret ballot, history would quickly show him to be on the wrong side of the argument. But he prepared the ground for Irish land reform, brilliantly articulated the argument for greater working-class electoral representation, and advanced the cause of better urban government. On topics such as colonial responsibility, racism and women's suffrage he was many decades ahead of his time, and on at least one issue, proportional representation, his version of the truth is still 'waiting for justice'. Gladstone later said of Mill's performance as an MP that 'he did us all good'.[224]

The loss of two letters after his name quenched none of the fire in Mill's belly, however. 'I hope to be quite as active for my opinions out of the House as I was in it', he told Cairnes in December 1868.[225] On at least one issue he was to prove even better than his word during the remaining four and a half years of his life. Mill was the finest nineteenth-century advocate for women's rights and a cornerstone of the suffrage movement; he was the father of British feminism.

CHAPTER FOURTEEN

The Father of Feminism

Mill's grave in Avignon, a stone's throw from the avenue bearing his name, has no dedication. In 1980, however, a small plaque was placed nearby, which reads: 'En hommage de John Stuart Mill, Defenseur des Femmes.' Mill would not approve, and not only because he was opposed to any epitaph for himself. In 1855, he had fiercely criticized a description of William Molesworth's life which focused almost exclusively on his work for the colonies. 'It . . . gives the idea of him as a man who devoted his life to that one object, and sacrificed his life to it,' he wrote to the unfortunate author, 'which, besides not being a true notion of him, is in reality a notion inferior to the truth.'[1]

The breadth of Mill's life and work is similarly obscured by the well-meaning twentieth-century addition to his tomb. But perhaps the gesture might be forgiven. There was, after all, no cause which Mill championed with greater consistency, tenacity or energy than equality for women. Having raised the banner for women in Parliament, Mill spent the last years of his life throwing his full intellectual, political, polemical and administrative energies into their fight for justice. There was no other area of his life in which his thoughts and actions were more closely entwined – Mill's status as a public intellectual is most powerfully demonstrated through his feminism. For him, the stakes were high. 'The emancipation of women, &

co-operative production, are, I fully believe, the two great changes that will regenerate society', he wrote on New Year's Day, 1869, to the American writer Parke Godwin, 'but though the latter of these may grow up without much help from the action of Parliaments and Congresses, the former cannot.'[2] Two and half years later, he insisted that 'the most vitally important political & social question of the future, [is] that of the equality between men and women'.[3] In terms of economic reform, his mature focus would be on the inter-related issues of cooperation, socialism and land reform, but politically he was now focused almost exclusively on women's rights.

In 1869, Mill told Alexander Bain, 'with much warmth', that 'the day of a temporizing policy was past'.[4] The time was finally ripe both for spelling out the full argument for equality, and agitating publicly for reform. *The Subjection of Women*, published in 1869, brilliantly, if controversially, achieved the first objective. It was a founding document of modern feminism and remains one of the finest polemics in the English language. The modern scholar Martha Nussbaum cites the work to support her description of Mill as 'the first great radical feminist in the Western philosophical tradition'.[5] Mill summarized his case in the first paragraph. It was, simply,

that the principle which regulates the existing social relations between the two sexes – the legal subordination of one sex to the other – is wrong in itself, and now one of the chief hindrances to human improvement; and that it ought to be replaced by a principle of perfect equality, admitting no power or privilege on the one side, nor disability on the other.[6]

In the elaboration of his argument, Mill was brutally direct. 'Marriage is the only actual bondage known to our law. There remain no legal slaves, except the mistress of every house,' he wrote, and: 'The family is a school of despotism, in which the virtues of despotism, but also its vices, are largely nourished.'[7] Given the peppering of the essay with such statements, Mill expected *Subjection* to be 'bitterly attacked' – and he was not disappointed: critics queued up to savage his advocacy of his 'fanciful rights of women'.[8] But in his older, bolder years, Mill used the ferocity of his critics as a gauge of his polemical accuracy, and was well pleased with the results.

Although Mill was in his sixties before he unveiled the full extent of his feminism, his support for women's rights was almost as old as he was. Even as a teenager he had passionately disagreed with his father's view that women did not need the vote, and Harriet had later infused him with additional zeal, highlighting the 'great moral and social interests of the [women's] cause'.[9] The space devoted to the question of women's suffrage expanded steadily with each of Mill's successive political tracts, from a footnote in his 1835 'Rationale of Representation', through a paragraph in *Thoughts on Parliamentary Reform* in 1859 to a robust, three-page treatment in his 1861 *Representative Government*. In the latter volume he insisted that gender was 'as entirely irrelevant to political rights, as difference in height, or in the colour of hair' and predicted that within a generation, 'the accident of sex, no more than the accident of skin' would have ceased to be 'sufficient justification for depriving its possessor of the equal protection and just privileges of a citizen'.[10]

Then, after his passionate pleas for women's votes in the House of Commons, came *The Subjection of Women* in 1869, which, according to the social historian Jose Harris, 'burst like a time bomb into the sexual arena' and remained a 'bible of the women's movement' until the First World War.[11] Three editions sold out within the first year of publication and translations into French, Danish, German, Italian, Polish and Russian followed almost immediately.[12] The book found its way into some unlikely hands. Visiting a Russian aristocratic household in the summer of 1869, two of Mill's American friends, Moncure Conway and George Schuyler (by now the US chargé d'affaires in Moscow), were warmly received by the four daughters of the house when they mentioned their association with Mill. According to Conway, they declared that the *Subjection* was their bible. 'Yes,' said the eldest, 'I sleep with that book under my pillow.'[13] *Subjection* was a declaration of Mill's deepest convictions about gender equality, the issue which, Bain judged, was the one 'which of all others most engaged his feelings'.[14] It was also a distillation of the major currents of Mill's thinking: the innate equality of all human beings, the corrosive power of dependency, the triumph of reason over custom; the intrinsic value of individual liberty, and the role of institutions and social customs in shaping character.

One of the obstacles to gender equality that Mill tackled head-on in *Subjection* was the mainstream Victorian view that women were simply not up to it. Their weakness, ignorance and lack of interest were all apparently reasonable grounds for their political disenfranchisement and legal inferiority. Mill did not, in general, deny that women were less well equipped for public life than men, but he insisted that this was the result of their subjection, rather than its cause:

What is now called the nature of women is an eminently artificial thing – the result of forced repression in some directions, unnatural stimulation in others ... It may be asserted without scruple, that no other class of dependents have had their character so entirely distorted from its natural proportions by their relation with their masters.[15]

For Mill, no arguments based on the supposed inferior 'nature' of women had any force in a society where women were taught from the day of their birth to act and think in particular, approved ways. 'Conventionalities have smothered nature still more in women than in men,' he wrote to John Nichol in 1869, so 'the greater is the necessity for getting rid of the conventionalities before the nature can be manifested'.[16] Women might appear to be focused solely on getting a husband, but this was only to be expected, given the current state of affairs. Back in 1834 Mill had noted that women were taught to be 'under a kind of moral necessity of allying themselves to some man': indeed 'it would be a miracle', Mill declared in *Subjection*, 'if the object of being attractive to men had not become the polar star of feminine education and formation of character.'[17] It may also have been the case that only a few women were crying out for political rights – although Mill disputed this – but if so, this was hardly surprising given that they had been 'strenuously taught to repress them ["such ambitions"] as contrary to the proprieties of their sex'. 'It would only prove', he told the Commons in the debate on his amendment to the 1867 Reform Bill, that 'all women are still under this deadening influence; that the opiate still benumbs their mind and conscience.'[18] He was being a bit cavalier here: even women like Beatrice Potter, later Mrs Beatrice Webb and founder of the Fabian Society, were opposing women's suffrage two decades after Mill introduced his motion, although she subsequently reversed her position.

It was also undeniable that women did not feature on the list of pioneering artists or scholars, but it was eminently deniable that this was a consequence of inherent inferiority. Only 'when women have had the preparation which all men now require to be eminently original' would it be 'time . . . to begin judging by experience of their capacity for originality'. The typical woman might lack individual spirit, but, then, Mill asked, 'how should she appreciate the value of self-dependence? She is not self-dependent; she is not taught self-dependence; her destiny is to receive everything from others.'[19] When one of Mill's female critics, Anne Mozley, wrote that 'woman, as she is, is his enemy', she was half-right.[20] Women did need to change – but no less so than men.

John Morley correctly saw *Subjection* as 'the capital illustration' of Mill's arguments about human nature and character formation in the *Logic*. 'Institutions, books, education, society,' wrote Mill, 'all go on training human beings for the old, long after the new has come.'[21] One of his deepest convictions was that there were no innate differences along gender lines – or at least that no conclusions could be drawn about such differences until the cultural, legal, social and economic playing fields had been levelled:

No one can safely pronounce that if women's nature were left to choose its direction as freely as men's, and if no artificial bent were attempted to be given to it except that required by the conditions of human society, and given to both sexes alike, there would be any material difference, or perhaps any difference at all, in the character and capacities which would unfold themselves.[22]

Only a successful elucidation of 'the most important department of psychology, the laws of the influence of circumstances on character' (in other words, his own, long-abandoned science of 'ethology') would 'entitle any one to affirm even that there is any difference, much more what the difference is, between the two sexes considered as moral and rational beings.' Nobody had yet earned that right, not least because – and here Mill could be scolding himself – 'there is hardly any subject which, in proportion to its importance, has been so little studied'.[23]

The view that women were simply 'naturally' inferior was, for Mill, an especially dangerous outcrop of the intuitionism with which he had already battled in the *Logic* and *Hamilton*, and in dozens of essays. He attacked it again in *Subjection* as an 'idolatry ... and the most pernicious of the false worships of the present day.'[24] Perversely, the irrational basis of the arguments against equality made them harder to overturn. 'So long as an opinion is strongly rooted in the feelings, it gains rather than loses in stability by having a pre-ponderating weight of argument against it,' he complained: 'When it rests solely on feeling, the worse it fares in argumentative contest, the more persuaded its adherents are that their feeling must have some deeper ground, which the arguments do not reach.' [25]

Mill's most dangerous opponents were not the open misogynists, but the men and women who romanticized women's delicate, domestic nature, seeing them, as in the title of Coventry Patmore's 1854 poem, as 'Angels in the House'. Inspired by the example of his wife Emily, Patmore had perfectly captured the nineteenth-century view of women as loving, submissive and devoted, whatever their lot:

Man must be pleased; but him to please
　　Is woman's pleasure; . . .
At any time, she's still his wife,
　　Dearly devoted to his arms;
She loves with love that cannot tire;
　　And when, ah woe, she loves alone,
Through passionate duty love springs higher,
　　As grass grows taller round a stone.[26]

Such was the enduring popularity of this poem that seventy-five years later, Virginia Woolf, Leslie Stephen's daughter, would maintain that 'Killing the Angel in the House was part of the occupation of a woman writer'.[27] Yet Patmore was speaking with the authentic voice of his generation; even Charles Dickens had earned Mill's opprobrium by pillorying women's rights in *Bleak House*. Mrs Beeton's feminine ideal, described in her *Book of Household Management*, was also in stark contrast with the sort of women with whom Mill spent his time. 'The modest virgin, the prudent wife, and the careful matron,' she advised, 'are much more serviceable in life than petticoated philosophers, blustering heroines, or virago queens'.[28] This idealization of women as fundamentally kind-hearted but dim infuriated Mill: 'I do not know a more signal instance of the blindness with which the world, including the herd of studious men, ignore and pass over all the influences of social circumstances, than their silly depreciation of the intellectual, and silly panegyrics on the moral, nature of women.'[29]

William Gladstone was still demonstrating these attitudes in 1892, basing his opposition to women's suffrage on his 'fear . . . lest he should invite her (woman) unwittingly to trespass upon the delicacy, the purity, the refinement, the elevation of her own nature, which are the present sources of its power'.[30] Such attitudes towards women were the real cause of their oppression, Mill believed: the prevailing symptoms of sexism described in *Subjection* were caused by the disease of 'despotic custom' diagnosed in *On Liberty*. 'The subjection of women to men being a universal custom,' he notes, 'any departure from it quite naturally appears unnatural'. Echoing the argument of *On Liberty* that opinion is capable of 'enslaving the soul itself', Mill said that in order to make 'willing slaves' of their wives, men have 'put everything in practice to enslave their minds'.[31]

The second-class status of women, Mill observed, was 'not felt to jar with modern civilization, any more than domestic slavery among the Greeks had jarred with their notion of themselves as a free people.' But, then, dominance always felt natural 'to those who possess it'. At a given point in time, the existing traditions of a nation tended to feel quite normal. So while foreigners were 'astonished' to be told that England had a queen, 'to Englishmen this does not seem in the least degree unnatural, because they are used to it; but they do feel it unnatural that women should be soldiers or members of Parliament.'[32]

Mill's critics, needless to say, departed unanimously from his view that the true equality between men and women was being hidden and distorted by a sexist society. For James Fitzjames Stephen, Mill's thesis was nothing more than 'a pet opinion', unsupported by the historical and contemporary evidence that 'men were stronger than women in every shape. They have greater muscular and nervous force, greater intellectual force, greater vigour of character.' These, to Stephen, were simply 'facts' and women's second-class status was therefore rational, just and beneficial. Even Bain accused Mill of 'postulating a degree of equality that does not chime with the experience of the least biassed [*sic*] observers'.[33]

To Mill, these observers were blindly trapped in their social and historical context and unable to see that the men and women around them – and indeed their own characters – were the product of the society in which they were born and raised. 'Men, with that inability to recognize their own work which distinguishes the unanalytic mind,' he wrote, 'indolently believe that the tree grows of itself in the way they have made it grow, and that it would die if one half of it were not kept in a vapour bath and the other half in the snow.[34]

One of the ways women were kept out in the cold was through

their exclusion from higher education. In his 1867 Commons speech, Mill applauded Elizabeth Garrett for finding a 'narrow entrance' into the medical profession, via the Society of Apothecaries, and then berated the Society for closing the door behind her so that 'no second Miss Garrett will be allowed to pass through it'.[35] (In fact three more had squeaked through.) He consistently supported moves to open up education to women, although his 1862 optimism that the question of women's admission to degrees was 'une cause gagnée' proved unfounded. In 1869, he set and marked the political economy examination for a new women's college in Hitchin established by Emily Davies, which later became Girton College, Cambridge.[36] In his will he bequeathed about half of his estate to the cause of women in higher education: £3,000 for a women's fellowship at whichever university became the first to admit women for degrees, and a further £3,000 to endow two women's scholarships at the same institution. However, it does not seem that these bequests were ever made.[37]

Even if girls did receive an education, albeit at a younger age, the nature of the lessons tended to reinforce gender roles, and Mill's call for 'perfect equality' in this as in other areas provoked the particular ire of J. F. Stephen. 'Are girls and boys to be educated indiscriminately, and to be instructed in the same things?' he demanded of Mill. 'Are boys to learn to sew, to keep house, and to cook, and girls to play at cricket, to row, and be drilled like boys?' he spluttered, before going on to prove Mill's point about irrational prejudices: 'I cannot argue with a person who says yes.'[38]

If attitudes to education were a significant barrier to women's advancement in England, the customary mechanisms of oppression in other cultures might be founded on religion or dress. In his 1835 essay on Adam Sedgwick, the Cambridge professor, Mill pointed to the 'absurdist' custom among Turks of seeing 'it as the height of indecency for women to be seen in the streets unveiled'. Fifteen years later, in a newspaper article, he had only slightly softened in this regard: 'A Turk thinks, or used to think (for even Turks are wiser now-a-days), that society would be on a sandbank if women were suffered to walk about the streets with their faces uncovered.'[39] In his work for the East India Company, Mill demonstrated a similarly 'liberal imperialist' view, citing among the achievements of the firm the stamping out of various 'barbarous usages of the natives' such as suttee – the voluntary burning of widows on their husband's funeral pyre – and female infanticide. Another 'great inroad into Hindoo prejudices' was the legalizing of remarriage for widows.[40]

In fact, Mill believed, the tide of history was on women's side and as all societies became wiser, equality would follow. All through the 'progressive' (i.e. modern) period of history, he argued, women had been catching up with men.[41] Women's position was, he went on, 'a single relic of an old world of thought and practice exploded in everything else, but retained in the one thing of most universal interest, as if a gigantic dolmen, or a vast temple of Jupiter Olympus, occupied the site of St. Paul's and received daily worship, while the surrounding Christian churches were only resorted to on fasts and festivals.'[42] The liberation of women would, in turn, help to keep the engine of progress running, because of the 'fresh social power that would be acquired by giving freedom to one-half of the whole sum of human intellect.'[43] In *Subjection*, Mill traced the broad social and cultural contours of women's oppression, but in terms of political objectives, he was convinced that getting the vote was the key which would unlock all the other doors to women, and his campaigning was focused primarily on the suffrage issue.

Naturally enough, his speech to the Commons highlighted the arguments for women's representation. There was no such thing as an abstract 'right' to vote, Mill declared: but there was a 'branch of expediency called justice'. It was on this basis that the suffrage should be opened to women. For one thing, women paid tax. Having argued in *Representative Government* that paying tax should be a requirement for suffrage, Mill now insisted that it should also be a sufficient justification for gaining the vote. It was, he said, 'one of the oldest and most cherished of our constitutional maxims ... that taxation and representation should be co-extensive'.[44]

It was also necessary for women to be granted the vote in order that they could protect their own welfare, just like every other group in society. Their interests could not, as the anti-reformers insisted, be seen as safe in their hands of their fathers, husbands and brothers. Dramatic demonstration of this was provided by the fact that these men were themselves all too often the brutal abusers of women, and were often lightly punished. In a passage which vividly captures the combination of sinewy logic and controlled anger employed in Mill's best pieces of oratory, he said:

I should like to have a return laid annually before the House of the number of women who are annually beaten to death, kicked to death, or trampled to death by their male protectors: and in an opposite column, the amount of sentences passed, in those cases in which the dastardly criminals did not get off altogether. I should also like to have, in a third column, the amount of property, the unlawful taking of which was . . . by the same judge, thought worthy of the same amount of punishment. We should then have an arithmetical estimate of the value set by a male legislature and male tribunals on the murder of a woman, often by torture continued through years, which, if there is any shame in us, would make us hang our heads.[45]

If female suffrage would be good for women, it would also, Mill suggested, be good for men – although obviously not for the ones he had in mind in the previous passage. Because wives were now, as a result of a 'silent domestic revolution', a man's 'chief associate, his most confidential friend, and often his most trusted adviser', her knowledge of and engagement in politics was a key ingredient in his own outlook. The woman could either be a source of stimulation and support, or frivolity and apathy; 'the two sexes must sink or swim together'.[46] Men were short-changing themselves by lowering the quality of their life companions; under current arrangements, all they got was 'an upper servant, a nurse, or a mistress'.[47] (The trouble, of course, was that for many men, this sounded like a pretty good deal.) For Mill, being around a passive, meekly subservient creature was not good for the soul. 'We see, according-ly, that young men of the greatest promise generally cease to improve as soon as they marry, and, not improving, inevitably degenerate,' he noted in *Subjection*. 'If the wife does not push the husband forward, she always holds him back.'[48]

He also argued that the power held by men over women was cor-rupting: 'It is wholesomer for the moral nature to be restrained,' he said, 'even by arbitrary power, than to be allowed to exercise arbi-trary power without restraint.' The result of being enthroned as the head of the household, Mill argued, was narcissism and indolence with 'the relation of superiors to dependents the nursery of these vices of character'.[49] His 1862 essay on 'Centralisation' contained the clearest exposition of this strand of his thinking:

If there be an ethical doctrine which more than all others requires to be taught ... it is that the love of power is the most evil passion of human nature; that power over others, power of coercion and compulsion, any power other than that of moral and intellectual influence, even in cases where it is indispensable, is a snare, and in all others a curse, both to the possessor and to those over whom it is possessed.[50]

For Mill, then, equality was a necessary condition for liberty, because 'the true virtue of human beings is fitness to live together as equals; claiming nothing for themselves but what they freely concede to everyone else'.[51]

Having made his principal case before the Commons, Mill then proceeded to demolish the specious arguments of his opponents. Politics, it was said, 'were not women's business, and would distract them from their proper duties'. No more so, Mill argued, than the typical man would be distracted from his own occupation: 'I have never understood that those who have votes are worse merchants, or worse lawyers, or worse physicians, or even worse clergymen than other people'.[52] Women, it was also claimed by the anti-reformers, already had enough influence, brought to bear indirect-ly through their male connections. He dispatched this argument

...les Kingsley (1819–75), the founder of ...he Christian Socialist Movement.

Thomas Hare (1806–91), the political theorist who developed a scheme for a form of proportional representation.

...enry Fawcett (1833–84) and ...illicent Fawcett, née Garrett ...47–1929). A Victorian power ...couple, both allies of Mill. ...nry Fawcett was Professor of ...Economics at Cambridge; ...Millicent was a leader of the ...omen's suffrage movement.

The nomination meeting in Covent Garden for the Westminster Election in 186
'This election affair is a better propaganda for all my political opinions than I mig
have obtained for many years,' wrote Mill.

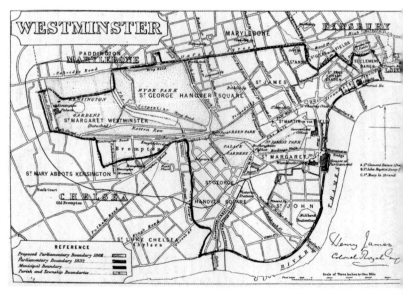

The Westminster Parliamentary Constituency. A flagship Liberal seat before 18
Westminster was becoming steadily more conservative even before Mill's radical te
in 1874 the constituency returned two Conservative MPs.

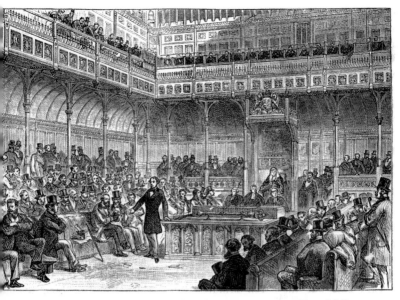

enjamin Disraeli (1804–81) addressing the Commons in 1867. When Mill rose to ver his maiden speech in 1866, the Tory leader said: 'Ah, the Finishing Governess.'

Reform League Demonstration, Hyde Park, July 1866.
Mill led the successful parliamentary battle to secure the legal right to protest in the Royal Parks after these disturbances.

MISS MILL JOINS THE LADIES.

Mill was ridiculed in the comic press for his support of the 'fanciful' rights of women. Cartoonists frequently dressed him in women's clothes, and referred to him as the 'women's member'.

ll's defeat at the polls in 1868 was the
lt of his partisan advocacy of 'radical'
causes such as women's suffrage,
iamentary representation for workers
nd freedom of religious expression.
mmon sense' is the torch that lights
effigy in this poster. Mill is holding
two small monkeys: Odger, who
resents 'ruffianism', and Bradlaugh
who stands for 'atheism'.

THE WESTMINSTER GUY

is caricature of Mill, which appeared
n *Vanity Fair* in 1873, captures his
aking posture, with his hands always
bed behind his back, 'like a schoolboy
saying his lesson'.

VANITY FAIR. March 29, 1873.

No. 130. STATESMEN, No. 141.
"A Feminine Philosopher."

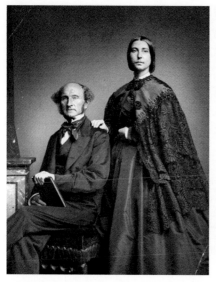

Mill with his step-daughter Helen Taylor (1831–1907), who succeeded her mother as Mill's editor, household manager and secretary.

Charles Wentworth Dilke (1843–1911) radical politician, and his wife, Em Francis Dilke, née Strong (1840–19c Dilke received delivery of Watts' fine portrait of Mill just a few hou after he had died.

John Morley (1838–1923), 'Mill's representative on earth', Liberal politician, editor and biographer, w described his hero as 'a man of extre sensibility and vital heat in thing worth waxing hot about'.

ill is buried next to Harriet in the cemetery at St Veran. The tomb, made from the same marble as the Pantheon, is inscribed with his eulogy to her.

omen finally won equal voting rights in February 1928, and Millicent Fawcett led a delegation to lay a wreath beside Mill's statue.

Mill aged fifty-nine, shortly after being elected as MP for Westminster.
He had previously eschewed the 'fashion' for photography.

swiftly: 'I should like to carry this argument a little further. Rich people have a great deal of indirect influence. Is this a reason for refusing them votes? Does anyone propose a rating qualification the wrong way, or bring in a Reform Bill to disenfranchise all who live in a £500 house, or pay £100 a year in direct taxes?'[53]

For the first three years after leaving Parliament, Mill was convinced the pace of change was quickening. 'The movement . . . is advancing very rapidly in England,' he wrote to Charles Eliot Norton in 1869, just after the publication of *Subjection*. 'We live in times when broad principles of justice, perseveringly proclaimed, end by carrying the world with them.' Walter Bagehot was somewhat more sanguine: 'No party, and scarcely any individual politician except himself, holds this theory, and it will be long before it becomes a practical question.'[54]

If Mill's hopes were optimistic, they were not utopian. A Bill giving women the right to vote in municipal elections passed through the Commons unopposed in June 1869. The Married Women's Property Act, introduced in 1870 – and which Mill clearly helped to bring about – gave women the right to hold property in their own name after matrimony. Women were able to vote and stand in the elections to the new school boards, established by the 1870 Education Act. 'The right of women to a voice in the management of education has been asserted by the triumphant return of two ladies as members of the London School Board & of several others in different parts of the country,' Mill wrote after the first poll.[55] The two were Emily Davies and Elizabeth Garrett, who pushed her former teacher, T. Huxley, into second place in the ward of Marylebone.[56] Davies was an old friend of Elizabeth's and her younger sister Millicent, who was now married to Henry Fawcett. Louisa Garrett, their mother, would later relish telling a story about the trio:

Before the bedroom fire, the girls were brushing their hair. Emily was twenty-nine, Elizabeth twenty-three and Millicent thirteen. As they brushed, they debated. 'Women can get nowhere', said Emily, 'unless they are as well educated as men. I shall open the universities.' 'Yes,' agreed

Elizabeth. 'We need education but we need an income too and we can't earn that without training and a profession. I shall start women in medicine. But what shall we do with Milly?' They agreed that she should get the parliamentary vote for women.[57]

Like many parental recollections, this sounds rather too good to be true: but there does seem to have been something in the water in the Garrett household. The third sister, Louise, was a successful sculptor and had taken Millicent to one of Mill's election speeches on women, which fired 'Milly's' enthusiasm for women's rights, or perhaps reminded her of her bedroom instruction from five years earlier.

While Mill held up the Garrett-Fawcetts as living examples of women's capabilities, he also delved back into history to dismiss arguments against women's suitability for public responsibilities, judging that 'a far larger proportion' of English queens had 'shown talents for rule' compared to their male counterparts, and good-naturedly debating the merits of Elizabeth I with John Nichol.[58] Drawing on his knowledge of Indian affairs, Mill also argued that women had been better provincial governors. 'If a Hindoo principality is strongly, vigilantly, and economically governed; if order is preserved without oppression; if cultivation is extending, and the people prosperous,' he wrote, 'in three cases out of four that principality is under a woman's rule.' Given the social and religious disadvantages faced by these princesses, 'the example they afford of the natural capacity of women for government is very striking'.[59] In correspondence, he highlighted the Muslim leader Sikandar Begum, ruler of Bhopal from 1844 to 1868, who had proved to be an 'energetic, prudent & just ruler'. She was an anomaly – Muslim law usually forbade women from ruling – but such was her popularity that on her death, her daughter succeeded her.[60]

Mill went on to describe a range of feminine attributes which might in fact make them better suited to politics and public office than men, including 'a general bent of their talents towards the practical', a 'sensibility to the present' and 'great quickness of apprehension'.[61] Although he did preface the laudatory list with the reminder that they 'may very well have been produced merely by circumstance', he was here running the risk of double standards, invoking feminine qualities when they suited his argument but dismissing them as 'artificial' when they did not. Bain reasonably suggested that in these sections Mill fell into 'the fallacy of proving too much'.[62]

Overall, Mill believed that whether or not equality was good for government, the economy, intellectual advance – or even men – it was certainly good for women, bringing the 'unspeakable gain in private happiness' which followed in the wake of 'a life of rational freedom'. In a passage of *Subjection* which brings to mind Mill's own liberation from his upbringing, he wrote:

Whatever has been said or written, from the time of Herodotus to the present, of the ennobling influence of free government – the nerve and spring which it gives to all the faculties, the larger and higher objects which it presents to the intellect and feelings, the more unselfish public spirit, and calmer and broader views of duty, that it engenders, and the generally loftier platform on which it elevates the individual as a moral, spiritual, and social being – is every particle as true of women as of men. Are these things no important part of individual happiness? Let any man call to mind what he himself felt on emerging from boyhood – from the tutelage and control of even loved and affectionate elders – and entering upon the responsibilities of manhood. Was it not like the physical effect of taking off a heavy weight, or releasing him from obstructive, even if not otherwise painful, bonds? Did he not feel twice as much alive, twice as much a human being, as before? And does he imagine that women have none of these feelings?[63]

Mill's call for women's equality was a cry for women's freedom, for the 'liberty of each' woman to guide her actions according to her 'own feelings of duty', and the 'laws and social restraints' of her own conscience. Liberation would give women the gift of 'the consciousness of working out their own destiny under their own moral responsibility'.[64]

At this stage, of course, most women were restricted by much more practical matters, such as lack of money. Even successful women such as Elizabeth Gaskell, whose biography of Charlotte Brontë had so upset the grieving Mill, were not supposed to dirty their hands with cash. When she received her first royalty cheque, for £100, her husband William, by all accounts a decent man, 'composedly buttoned it up in his pocket'.[65] When Elizabeth Garrett married James Anderson, she struck out the ceremonial vows on obedience, and was as good as her word: despite his protests, she insisted on controlling her own earnings. This was not a model of womanhood which found favour with many, however. The twentieth-century psychoanalyst Sigmund Freud was certain that whatever women really did want, Mill's *Subjection* was not where they should look for it. 'It really is a stillborn thought to send women into the struggle for existence exactly as men', he wrote to his fiancée after translating the book into German. 'If for instance, I imagined my gentle sweet girl as a competitor it would only end in my telling her, as I did seventeen months ago, that I am fond of her and that I implore her to withdraw from the strife into the calm uncompetitive activity of my home.'[66]

By contrast Mill wanted to both support and provoke women towards higher things. He told the House of Commons in 1867 that he wanted 'to awaken in [women] the political point of honour', and insisted to Bain that 'the most important thing we now have to do, is to stir up the zeal of women themselves. We have to stimulate their aspiration.'[67] Not content to be the 'mere thinker' of the movement – a trait for which he criticized men in *Subjection* – Mill, along with Helen, was deeply involved in the practicalities of the suffrage campaign, raising money, gathering petitions, giving speeches and using his position as one of the globe's most sought-after correspondents to propagandize for the cause. Half of all the letters from the last four years of his life related directly or indirectly to women's issues.

Both Mill and Helen were the moving spirits behind the establishment of the London National Society for Women's Suffrage, a branch of the existing organization which had strong sections in Manchester and Birmingham. At the first open meeting of the Society in 1869, Mill spoke alongside old allies like Thomas Hare, Henry Fawcett and John Morley, as well as the sometime foe Charles Kingsley. Introducing the meeting, the chairwoman, Clementia Taylor, attributed the success of the National Society to Mill's 'fearless and eloquent advocacy' and said that 'every woman in Great Britain' owed him a 'deep debt of gratitude'.[68] The secretary, Caroline Biggs, gave a brief report, and then Mill spoke. After a hero's welcome from the meeting, he reassured them that 'the spirit of the age is on our side', but he also had a hard political message to deliver. 'Our business is to strive for the suffrage, and for the suffrage only. The suffrage, while it is the road to other progress, commits no one as to what other things progress consists of. Let us but gain the suffrage, and whatever is desirable for women must ultimately follow.'[69] At the second AGM of the London Committee, in March 1870, the women on the platform outnumbered the men. Mill, Cairnes and Amberley spoke – as did Helen Taylor, Katherine Hare, Harriet Grote and Millicent Fawcett; although Kate Amberley's mother congratulated her daughter-in-law on keeping her silence.[70] Five weeks later, a parliamentary Bill to remove the political restrictions on women, introduced by John Bright's younger brother Jacob, passed its second reading by 124 votes to 91, rousing the whips to prevent it passing into committee, by 220 votes to 94.[71]

'I am in great spirits about our prospects, and think we are almost within as many years of victory as I formerly thought decades,' wrote an excited Mill to his new friend, the radical politician Charles Dilke, from Avignon later that month. The next day he took out his pen again, this time to enthuse to Hare: 'What immense progress the cause of Women's Suffrage has made since 1867: the number of votes rendered for it at one or other of the divisions 162, double the number of three years ago. As soon as a sufficient number of women can be sufficiently roused, success is certain.' He disagreed with Kingsley that the second lost vote was a 'check', calculating that 'within nine years, by a very simple process of arithmetic, we should have the measure passed by unanimity through the House of Commons, and then we might defy the Lords!'[72]

In fact 1870 was to prove the high point for Mill's hopes and the dynamism of the nineteenth-century women's movement. As so often in progressive movements, more energy was soon being spent on internal squabbling than on broader objectives. Mill, while maintaining a public stance of non-involvement, and an official line that his role as President made him only the 'nominal head', was in the thick of it. Through his man on the committee, George Croom Robertson (the young philosopher who Mill had helped to a professorship at UCL), Mill manoeuvred to 'weed' the Society of the opposing group led by Caroline Biggs, which he described as the 'obnoxious set' and, later, as 'the seceders'.[73] At the height of the row he was dispatching weekly letters to Robertson.

The *casus belli* was a sharp disagreement about the stance of the Society with regard to other issues affecting women. In particular, Caroline Biggs and others, including Jacob Bright, wanted to link the campaign for the suffrage to the one against the Contagious Diseases Acts (CDA), passed between 1864 and 1869. This legislation, born of official anxiety about rates of venereal disease in the armed forces, had granted legal powers to the police to seize any woman near a military base suspected of being a prostitute and submit her to a compulsory medical inspection. If diseased, she was kept in jail; otherwise she was required to return for regular re-examinations. The examinations were often brutal: the woman's legs were usually clamped open and her ankles tied down. Miscarriages among pregnant women were common, and cleaning of the crude surgical equipment between insertions into different victims was at best sporadic.

A campaign for the repeal of the Acts had been started in 1869, with the brilliant orator Josephine Butler at its head. Opinion was divided, though, even among progressive women: Elizabeth Garrett, for example, supported the Acts as the only way to protect the wives and children of men who might be exposed the risk of infec-

tion. Mill was opposed to the Acts, and voted against their extension in 1866. In private, he lambasted the CDA as 'utterly deprav-
ing' and a 'gross inequality between men and women', a 'monstrous
artificial cure for a monstrous artificial evil', whose repeal he would
'highly approve of'.[74] To John Nichol, who was in favour of the
Acts, he wrote: 'The law, being one-sided, inflicted on women by
men, and delivering over a large body of women intentionally, and
many other women unintentionally, to insulting indignity at the
pleasure of the police, has the genuine characteristics of a tyranny.'[75]

Mill's opposition was not surprising, given that the acts were as
illiberal as they were sexist, but in public he trod warily. No fiery
speeches were delivered on the issue, and his public comments were
restricted to a single mention of the CDA – 'under which the wives
and daughters of the poor are exposed to insufferable indignities on
the suspicion of a police officer' – as an example of the bad legislation which would be prevented if women had the votes.[76] This
caution was clearly not because Mill himself was afraid of the
controversy – there is enough evidence that, if anything, such
mêlées had a magnetic appeal for him.

Mill knew that Butler's campaign was controversial, and that in
the mistaken public mind, the Acts were a good way of combating
vice and immorality. He told Butler herself that while he supported
her campaign, 'political enfranchisement [was] ... both the foundation and safeguard of human worth and happiness'. His overriding concern was not to tar the respectable movement for suffrage
with what the general public saw as the grubby brush of the anti-
CDA campaign. 'To the mass of the English people,' he told
Robertson, 'the union of the CDA agitation with that for the
suffrage, condemns the latter utterly, because they look upon it as
indelicate and unfeminine.'[77]

He did agree, however, to appear before a Royal Commission
examining the workings of the Act. For the benefit of the members
– including Frederick Maurice, his old London Debating Society
colleague – Mill forensically and calmly pointed out the injustice of
the assumptions underlying the CDA. His replies focused on the

guilt of the man visiting the prostitute, rather than of the prostitute herself. Asked if he would look more favourably on the Acts if it could be shown they protected 'innocent wives and ... innocent children', Mill replied:

A woman cannot communicate the disease but to a person who seeks it, and who knowingly places himself in the way of it. A woman can communicate it only through a man; it must be the man who communicates it to innocent women and children afterwards. It seems to me, therefore, if the object is to protect those who are not unchaste, the way to do that is to bring motives to bear on the man and not on the woman, who cannot have anything to do directly with the communication of it to persons entirely innocent, whereas the man can and does.[78]

His solution to the problem was thus to lay 'severe penalties' on the man. If the concern was the health of the army and navy, why not run compulsory checks on the troops and sailors, and make it a 'ground for military penalties' to be found with an infection?[79] Needless to say, these arguments had little impact. Men's uncontainable lust was seen as an unalterable fact of life: the challenge was to prevent their randiness lowering combat readiness. As Butler told the same Commission, the principal, though undeclared, objective of the Acts was the 'providing of clean women for the army and navy'.

Caroline Biggs, who Mill saw as 'dangerous', and Lydia Becker, Secretary of the Manchester branch of the National Society, wanted to go much further, and campaign for both the granting of the suffrage and the repeal of the CDA. The battle raged throughout 1871, with the Biggs camp eventually setting up a rival 'Central Committee' to Mill's 'London Committee'. During the fight, Mill displayed some tendencies that would have served him well in the Soviet Communist party sixty years later. He told Robertson that 'no opportunity should be lost of getting rid of the different members whose votes are objectionable'. When the Central Committee was formed, Mill insisted that if '*any of the members of the London*

Committee consent to join it in their private capacity, they should be requested to retire from the London Committee'.[80] At one point, like an MP marshalling a Bill through Parliament, he drew up for Robertson a list of where he thought committee members stood on the issue, under the headings 'Certain', 'Uncertain' and 'Perhaps hostile'. Millicent Fawcett fell under his last heading: as Mill explained, she was a 'recent convert to the CDA movement' as well as being, like her husband, 'a little doctrinaire ... Hence she may at any time fancy that consistency demands what I might think foolish conduct'.[81]

The 'I' in this last sentence reveals Mill's proprietorial attitude to the committee; at a later date he threatened to resign if it went ahead with a proposed delegation to Gladstone, which he strongly opposed.[82] His view of Fawcett was that 'she is quite as detrimental as useful ... an excellent woman, with plenty of sense and energy but no experience, and a great deal of self confidence: a person, therefore, admirably calculated to fall headlong into mistakes'. He added: 'She has neither a speculative nor an organizing intelligence, and therefore, even supposing that she were twice her age, she is quite unfit to be a leader, though an excellent guerrilla partisan.'[83] It was an assessment which was fortunately not borne out by history – Fawcett become one of the most successful feminist campaigners of all time.

At the height of his hysteria – the word does not seem too strong – Mill ordered Robertson to refuse admission to the Society of anybody in favour of CDA repeal, 'unless well known personally'. Of the potential member William Christie (who had collaborated with Mill on electoral corruption), Mill said: 'I hardly know [him] well enough to answer for him'.[84] Yet Christie was a man with whom Mill had exchanged more letters than with Bain, and for whom he had written a published letter of recommendation in support of his bid for a Scottish parliamentary seat, declaring that his skills and experience would be of 'great value in Parliament'.[85] Mill's response to this crisis was certainly heavy-handed, and although he always acted by proxy, few were ignorant of the reality of the situation. It is surely no coincidence that the two Committees reunited a few years after his death.

Mill also paid a good deal of attention to the nuances of presentation, timing and tactics, in other words, to politics in its broader sense. He genuinely believed that the brand of the women's movement would be damaged by association with sex, disease and prostitution, and subsequent history suggested he might have been right. He was also constantly calibrating the timing of his interventions. The intention with *Subjection*, written eight years before it was published, had always been to 'publish it at a time when it should seem likely to be most useful'. Before publication, he had some 'misgivings' the book might still be a few years early – but was subsequently convinced that it came out 'at the right time'.[86] He had similarly delayed his article on the American Civil War until there was a 'chance of getting a hearing for the northern side of the question', and his revaluation of François Guizot as a politician was prompted in part by a growing appreciation of the Frenchman's tactical skills: 'I confounded the prudence of a wise man who lets some of his maxims go to sleep while the time is unpropitious for asserting them, with the laxity of principle which resigns them for personal advancement'.[87]

Mill himself had learned to let some of his maxims 'sleep' until the 'propitious' moment. There were also some occasions when it simply was not worth the fight: he was increasingly opposed to blood sports, for example, but 'having so many unpopular causes already on [his] hands', declined to make any public comment in order 'not to provoke fresh hostility', His own 'murderous propensities' were, meanwhile, 'confined to the vegetable world' and exercised through his botanizing excursions.[88] John Morley recalled that 'what Mill cared for in his own plans of work was that the aim should at least be definite and in season'.[89] The difficulty, of course, was in judging the weather.

There was no doubt in Mill's mind that the season for women's rights had arrived; but he was also aware that it was an issue that had to be handled with great care. He showed a high degree of sensitivity, for example, to the public image of the women's movement. For one thing, he recognized the value of the campaign being led visibly by women: once the movement had acquired sufficient momentum, men should not be in forefront. On more than one occasion Mill downplayed his own role, and refused a request to give a letter of support to a conference for women in New York, solely on the grounds that 'the cause, in America, has advanced beyond the stage at which it could need a recommendation from me, or from any man'.[90] Mill also thought it would help if the women were of the right sort. Winning the argument was one thing, but persuasive arts were not limited to logic. 'You seem to ... underrate the value of "a pretty face" in a lecturer on women's rights,' he told Robertson. Not, he hastened to add, 'for the sake of the effect on men ... but for the influence on the younger women: it shews them that the championship of women's cause is not confined to women who have no qualifications for success in the more beaten track, and that they would not, by joining in the movement, forfeit their chance of the ordinary objects of women's ambition.'[91] It was vital, in other words, that the movement was not seen as a magnet for unattractive women who had failed to snag a husband: 'Cannot we associate the cause with quiet, upright, and ladylike women, *as well* as with vulgar, questionable, and pushing ones?'[92]

Mill was attentive to his own PR, too. Those 'maxims' which could distract from the central aim of winning the vote – for example, his views on divorce, legal rights to children, sex and of course the CDA – were kept mostly under wraps. Likewise, his attitude to prostitution was one where his private pronouncements were stronger than any made in his publications. His views on this topic were in fact both highly liberal and highly moralistic.

In his evidence to the CDA Commission, Mill highlighted the tendency of the Acts to do 'moral injury' by effectively encouraging the market for bought sex. He had made it clear in *On Liberty* that prostitution could not be outlawed, but if the state should not ban prostitution, nor should it encourage it – and for Mill, state regulation of the sex industry amounted to official endorsement. 'I do not think that prostitution should be classed and recognized as such by the State,' he told the Commission. Even if women were to submit to the CDA medical inspections voluntarily – removing the principal liberal argument against the Acts – Mill would still be opposed to them, because it was not 'part of the business of the Government to provide securities beforehand against the consequences of immoralities of any kind'. Similarly, he was opposed to any system of licensing brothels, which would have 'the character of toleration of that kind of vicious indulgence'.[93] In a letter to John Nichol he was even more trenchant, arguing that

legal precautions taken expressly to make that kind of indulgence safe, are a license to it. There is no parallel case of an indulgence or pursuit avowedly disgraceful and immoral for which the government provides safeguards. A parallel case would be the supplying of stomach pumps to drunkards, or arrangements for lending money to gamblers.[94]

Prostitution was not considered by Mill a permanent feature of social life, and his optimism about the future stretched to the belief that improving standards of morality and better marriages would eventually kill the sex industry. In the meantime, the law should remain entirely neutral. His views regarding prostitution were strongly related to his thoughts on sexuality and marriage, which were on clearest display in an exchange of letters with Lord Amberley in early 1870, prompted by the pro-prostitution views of Amberley's friend William Lecky in his *History of European Morals*. Lecky had described the prostitute as 'the most efficient guardian of virtue' who acted as a release valve for 'the passion that would have filled the world with shame . . . She remains, while creeds and civilizations fall, the eternal priestess of humanity.'[95]

Lecky's argument – and Amberley agreed with him – was based on the assumption that men's sexual desire was greater, or was at least less easily checked, than women's. Monogamous marriage could not be expected to contain it. They believed it was better, in these circumstances, for men to seek an additional outlet in the form of an anonymous prostitute than, say, in a neighbour's wife. Mill questioned each of these claims. 'I see no proof of the difference of physical constitution you suppose to exist between men and women as to the point in question,' he wrote. On the contrary:

From all I have read or heard I believe there are no signs of it among savages: and the Hindoo books talk perpetually of the unrestrainable voluptuousness of women. I rather think the difference is merely that the masters, being more accustomed to indulge all their propensities than the subjected, find them more imperative and uncontrollable.[96]

Women, on the other hand, had learned to control their sexual desire because of a social climate which made chastity 'the condition upon which women hoped to obtain the strongest love and admiration of men'. But rather than sweeping these social customs away, Mill wanted to apply them to men. Given the 'same conditions', he thought it 'most probable that this particular passion will become with men, as it already is with a large number of women, completely under the control of the reason.'[97] Once men and women were entering into marriage on equal terms, he argued, male morality on matters of sex would rise to feminine levels. 'Marriage has not had a fair trial,' he pointed out. 'It has yet to be seen what marriage will do, with equality of rights on both sides.' Prostitution, meanwhile, acted as an obstacle to the achievement of these partnerships of 'perfect equality' by 'cutting at the heart of happiness in a marriage' and preventing the couple from 'having a frank confidence in one another'.[98] Perhaps monogamy would prove to be an unrealistic goal, but it was far too early to tell. Even if it did prove unrealistic, prostitution – the 'most degrading and the most mischievous' form of infidelity – was surely not the next best thing. 'When marriage under these conditions [of equality] shall have been tried and failed, it will be time to look out for something else,' he conceded. 'But that this something else, whatever it may be, will be better than prostitution, is my confirmed conviction.'[99] Sadly, Mill does not even speculate about what this 'something else' might look like: it would have made interesting reading. Perhaps some form of sexual cooperative?

Mill's argument here was certainly utopian, but it demonstrates that his views about the essential equality of men and women's natures extended as far as their sexuality; an eccentric view for the era, to say the least. It also demonstrated just how much store he set by the reinvention of marriage. The marital relationship is in fact at the heart of Mill's analysis of power in *The Subjection of Women*. For him, liberty for women, as well as moral regeneration for men, would come not from a rejection of marriage, but out of its rejuvenation. As things stood, Mill believed, the marriage contract was little better than the one between a pre-war Louisiana plantation-owner and his black slave. Indeed, because of the social climate repressing women, it was in some ways worse: 'I am far from pretending that wives are in general no better treated than slaves,' he wrote, 'but no slave is a slave to the same lengths, and in so full a sense of the word, as a wife is.'[100]

For Mill, marriage was 'the citadel of the enemy', the principal site of women's subjection, and an institution which repressed wives, disfigured the character of men and provided a daily lesson in despotism to children. The oppressive potential of marriage lay precisely in its intimate nature: 'Every one of the subjects lives under the very eye, and almost, it may be said, in the hands, of one of the masters.'[101] Here Mill was following the perilous path cut eight decades earlier by Mary Wollstonecraft, who in her *Vindication of the Rights of Woman*, had derided marriage as 'legal prostitution' in which women were 'convenient slaves'. But little had changed in the intervening period to render such views more respectable and the anti-feminist backlash against Mill's views included, as always, its fair share of women. Margaret Oliphant, writing in the *Edinburgh*, insisted that once they were married, a man and woman '*are* one person ... they are two halves of a complete being'. Political or economic independence for women thus 'ran counter to the whole theory of married life'.[102]

Such a theory was simply a cloak for tyranny according to Mill. A husband, he pointed out, could 'claim from her [his wife] and enforce the lowest degradation of a human being, that of being made the instrument of an animal function contrary to her inclinations.'[103] For Mill there was no better proof of the despotic nature of existing marriage law than the inability of wives to refuse their husbands 'the last intimacy'; that it would be 122 years before marital rape was criminalized demonstrates that the 'uphill fight' for women's rights has proved more arduous than Mill could possibly have imagined.

In contrast, his vision of marriage was one between mutually respectful partners. A spouse ought to be an intellectual equal, a motivator, critic, collaborator and friend: in short, Harriet. Her presence can be felt on almost every page of *Subjection*, in part because it clearly draws upon her contributions to their joint 'fund of thought' on women's issues, but mostly because of the model of womanhood and wifeliness she provided. He elsewhere described Harriet's 'intellectual department' as containing 'a vigour and truth of imagination, a delicacy of perception, an accuracy and nicety of observation, only equalled by her profundity of speculative thought, and by a practical judgment and discernment next to infallible.'[104]

These paeons are almost as embarrassing to read now as they must have been then; but the point is that if Harriet was one-tenth of the woman Mill described, she would indeed have been a good person to face over the dinner table each night. Reasonably enough, given Mill's apparently endless eulogizing of her, Harriet took her share of the blame for his unorthodox views on women and marriage. Herbert Cowell, writing in *Blackwood's Magazine* after Mill's death, described Mill's relationship with Harriet as 'the great blot on his career' which had also disfigured his philosophy. 'The social theories he elaborated with her, as a weapon of defence against adverse social opinion' – above all, the 'reduction of marriage to the state of partnership at will, with equal rights' – were, said Cowell, 'a stain upon his philosophic system'.[105]

Cowell was right to suggest that Mill's thinking on marriage and women was heavily influenced by his own life. It is inconceivable that his own experience of being in love with an extraordinary woman, initially trapped in a hollow marriage, but then finding union with her after her husband's death, did not impact on his attitudes to love and marriage. Nevertheless, Mill would have been led to support gender equality by the logical extension of his liberalism, regardless of his own experience. What his relationship with Harriet provided was an ideal model of marital friendship. He took the classical model of male friendship, derived from Aristotle and 'the free republics of antiquity', and transformed it into the foundation of modern marriage. More than thirty years earlier, he had lauded the notion of 'reciprocal superiority' in his male friendships and the same ideal of reciprocity resurfaces in *Subjection*, but with a feminine twist. Between wife and husband there should be 'that best kind of equality, similarity of powers and capacities with reciprocal superiority in them – so that each can enjoy the luxury of looking up to the other, and can have alternately the pleasure of leading and being led in the path of development'.[106]

Mill declared, surely with Harriet in mind, that he would not attempt to describe such a marriage, because 'to those can conceive it, there is no need: to those who cannot, it would appear the dream of an enthusiast', but dismissed any alternative conceptions of marriage as 'relics of primitive barbarism'.[107] By modern standards, the idea of a marriage based on mutual respect, shared leadership and long-term friendship is uncontroversial, but to many of his peers it was less appealing. 'To him marriage was a union of philosophers in the pursuit of truth,' was the judgement of Goldwin Smith, one of Mill's colleagues from the Jamaica Committee. While he gave a good deal of thought to marriage, he paid less attention to the obvious corollaries. 'Not only does he scarcely think of children,' added Smith, 'but sex and its influences hardly seem to be present to his mind.'[108] However, sex and children are not entirely absent. Sex, it is true, did not feature strongly in Mill's list of marital priorities, or indeed in his overall world-view, but *Subjection* contained perhaps his most positive – and even slightly playful – statement about sex:

Many a man thinks he perfectly understands women, because he has had amatory relations with several, perhaps with many of them. If he is a good observer, and his experience extends to quality as well as quantity, he may have learnt something of one narrow department of their nature – an important department, no doubt.[109]

More time was allocated to the subject of children, who appeared in *Subjection* in two guises: as legal charges, and as the citizens and parents of tomorrow. Mill points to the injustice of fathers having almost all the legal rights over children – a point he had made in earlier newspaper articles – but he held back from any further discussion about reform of the law on this point.[110] Privately, he thought that mothers should get greater legal rights than fathers, and that unmarried fathers should get no rights at all. He agreed with the American feminist Isabella Hooker that there was an 'infinitely closer relationship of a child to its mother than to its father', and added that this fact was 'full of important consequences with respect to the future legal position of parents & children'. His excuse for not addressing the issue in *Subjection* was, as so often, one of timing: 'This . . . is a portion of the truth for which the human mind will not, for some time, be sufficiently prepared to make its discussion useful'.[111] Mill was wrong about that – in 1873 an Act allowed the courts to grant custody of children under the age of sixteen to the mother.

Mill may also have been somewhat veiled in his comments on divorce. His published opinions favoured reform of the divorce laws from as early as 1834, and the treatment of the topic in both *On Liberty* and *Auguste Comte and Positivism* showed that while he did not believe marriages should be instantly dissolvable at the whim of either party, nor did he believe the marriage union should be permanently binding. Divorce was addressed only fleetingly in *Subjection*, however, despite its obvious pertinence to his argument; the most detailed discussion remains in *On Liberty*. In part, this lacuna may be explained by that fact that some improvements were taking place. In 1857 the law on divorce had been substantially improved –

over and above Gladstone's objections – and a formal legal procedure established to allow couples to divorce through the courts, rather than having to apply to Parliament. The new law, however, was a long way from treating men and women equally: to be granted a divorce, a husband had only to prove that his wife had been unfaithful, while she was required to prove not only spousal infidelity but, in addition, incest, buggery, bestiality, cruelty or rape.[112]

A comparison of *Subjection* and Mill's private note to Harriet, written in the early 1830s at the outset of their relationship, suggests at first glance that Mill was more radical in private than in public on the divorce issue. In this letter he had castigated the 'lottery' of existing marriage relations, pointing out that 'the chances . . . are many to one that a person who requires, or is capable of great happiness, will find that happiness in the first choice' and that 'the indissolubility of marriage' was 'the keystone of women's lot.'[113] In *Subjection*, by contrast, his view was that political and legal equality should come first. Once women had the vote, they could then exert the necessary pressure to reform divorce, if it still proved necessary. Mill had no reason to cloud his real opinion in an 1869 letter to Amberley:

I do not think the that the conditions of the dissolubility of marriage can be properly determined until women have an equal voice in determining them, nor until there has been experience of the marriage relation as it would exist between equals. Until then I should not like to commit myself to more than the general principle of relief from the contract in extreme cases.[114]

As far as divorce reform was concerned, Mill's view was that equal marriage first needs a 'fair trial': he was a long way from Shelley's libertarian view that 'any law which should bind [a husband and wife] to cohabitation for one moment after the decay of their affection would be a most intolerable tyranny ... Love is free; to promise for ever to love the same woman is not less absurd than to promise to believe the same creed.'[115] But while Mill had certainly come to place more emphasis on political than marital emancipation, his view on divorce was otherwise fairly consistent throughout his life: marriage should be dissolvable but not disposable.

The addition of children to the mix made a wholly laissez-faire approach to marriage even more dangerous. Children, after all, he had written to Harriet in the 1830s, were 'beings who are wholly dependent both for happiness and for excellence upon their parents: & who in all but the extreme causes of actual profligacy, or perpetual bickering and discussion, *must* be better cared for in both points if their parents remain together.'[116] Considering Mill was writing this to a married mother with whom he was falling deeply in love, it demonstrated considerable restraint and thoughtfulness. For Mill, domestic life was the primary ground for 'moral training', the place where morality and character were principally cultivated. As things stood, the patriarchal family was a 'nursery' of 'vices of character', a 'school of despotism'; a 'school of wilfulness, overbearingness, unbounded self-indulgence, and a double-dyed and idealized selfishness'. To Mill's mind, only a family built around the equality of the parents could make 'the daily life of mankind, in any high sense, a school of moral cultivation'.[117] The importance of this reform could hardly be overstated: 'The moral regeneration of mankind will only really commence, when the most fundamental of the social relations is placed under the rule of equal justice, and when human beings learn to cultivate their strongest sympathy with an equal in rights and cultivation.'[118]

While Mill can be celebrated wholeheartedly as a founder of the British feminist movement, not all of his views would pass muster with today's feminists. In the early letter to Harriet he took the line of male trade unionists – then and often subsequently – that women should not, in general, earn their own wages, because this would 'burthen the labour market with a double number of competitors'. Their role, he said, was to 'adorn & beautify' life, goals which they would accomplish 'rather by *being* than by *doing*'.[119] However by 1848, in the *Principles*, Mill more forcefully insisted that women should have equal access to the labour market rather than be allocated by 'the accident of sex' to the role of wife and mother. Years later he attacked men's hypocrisy in this area, point-ing out that 'nursing the sick is a privilege which men have seldom denied to women'.[120] He also pointed in the *Principles* to the huge 'moral and social benefits' that would flow from women being granted 'the same rights of citizenship as men' – although without listing them. By the time he came to write *Subjection*, Mill had taken a further step forward, and concluded that 'the *power* of earn-ing' was 'essential to the dignity of a woman'.[121]

None the less, even in *Subjection*, Mill's view remained that 'the common arrangement, by which the man earns the income and the wife superintends the domestic expenditure [is] ... in general the most suitable division of labour between the two persons'.[122] The rationale was no longer an economic one, however, because by now he had largely abandoned the 'wage fund' view of the labour mar-ket which suggested that a limited pool of money was available for salaries. His concern now was that women who attempted to do paid work and raise children would end up failing in the latter task. The fact that they were in the labour market 'seldom relieved' women from being expected to perform in full 'the ordinary func-tions of mistress of a family', but it would probably 'prevent her from performing [them] properly'.[123] Moreover, domestic labour would restrict women's ability to participate in public life. Mill quoted Florence Nightingale's insight that 'everything a woman does is done at odd times' and suggested that women's 'time and faculties' were sorely diminished by the fact that 'she must always be at the beck and call of somebody, generally of everybody'.[124] He recognized that this division of labour meant that having children inhibited women's opportunities: 'No alteration ... in the degrada-tion & slavery of women can be hoped for while their whole lives are devoted to the function of producing and rearing children.' But his response was to argue for smaller families, rather than a fairer distribution of caring responsibilities: house-husbands were simply not part of Mill's mental universe.[125]

It seems that Mill cannot be adequately defended from the accu-sations of some modern feminist scholars, such as Susan Moller

Okin or Julia Annas, that he 'never questioned or objected to the maintenance of traditional sex roles'.[126] He was blinkered himself when it came to one element of the sexist social customs which he so brilliantly dissected elsewhere, and never challenged the gendered division of labour when it came to childcare. Yet he was insistent that the division of labour within the family should be entirely the result of choice and opinion, not law.[127] It must also be acknowledged, even by Mill's critics, that his more 'traditional' views on this issue continue to be held by the majority of people today, even by women, and even in advanced nations such as the UK.

If Mill's views on the domestic division of labour were not up to twenty-first-century feminist standards, in other ways he was an energetic advocate for women taking on more public roles. As well as lauding Elizabeth Garrett in *Subjection*, he celebrated the achievements of the French feminist writer 'George Sand' (actually Amandine-Aurore Lucile Dupin, Baronne Dudevant), whose prose he said 'acts upon the nervous system like a symphony of Haydn or Mozart', and the Scottish-born scientist Mary Somerville.[128] Somerville had established her house in Chelsea as London's premier scientific salon as early as the 1820s and had been paid what Mill saw as the ultimate scholarly tribute when her *Physical Geography* caused an outburst from the pulpit of York Cathedral. As an MP Mill persuaded Somerville to head a petition for women's suffrage, so it is fitting that many of Mill's books have ended up in the library of the Oxford college which is named after her.

Mill also engaged in a spirited correspondence with Florence Nightingale, who initially described herself as 'brutally indifferent to the wrongs or the rights of my sex': in her 1860 *Notes on Nursing*, she had urged women to 'keep clear of the jargon ... about the "rights of women", which urges women to do all that men do, including in the medical and other professions, merely because men do it, and without regard to whether this *is* the best that women can do.'[129] He tried to persuade Nightingale that such sentiments inhibited women, and that it was impossible to know what women could do until they tried. She, in return, tried to open Mill's eyes to the truths of Christianity. He thanked her for a copy of her *Suggestions for Thought to the Searchers after Truth among the Artisans of England*, since 'I probably stand as much in need of conversion as those to whom it is addressed.'[130] However, Mill's attempt to convert her to feminism met with more success and she eventually joined the suffrage movement. Whatever his concerns about Millicent Fawcett's strategic strengths, he supported her suggested candidacy for the Political Economy Club (which sadly came to nothing).[131] He also backed both Harriet and Helen Taylor in their professional pursuits, particularly literary and political ones, mentoring Helen's efforts to edit the works of Henry Buckle and persuading Longman to publish the results: *Miscellaneous and Posthumous Works of Henry Thomas Buckle*, which appeared in 1872. He lavished praise on Helen's leadership of the suffrage movement in the late 1860s, and especially her success at keeping it 'disconnected from anything vulgar, fussy, pushing'.[132]

Following the breach within the London Committee in 1871, the Millian moderates had lost ground to the angrier branch of the movement led by Caroline Biggs and Jacob Bright, who continued to campaign for CDA repeal as well suffrage, the linking together of which was evidence, to Mill, of a 'total want equally of good taste and good sense'.[133] Bright also insisted on placing a Bill on women's suffrage before Parliament on an annual basis (echoing Grote's annual motion on the ballot three decades earlier), which Mill thought a tactical blunder, especially when the favourable vote began to drop, from 151 in 1871 to 143 in 1872. His view by this stage was that 'the public are tired of the subject, and their interest cannot be revived during the present session'.[134] He admitted to Cairnes that the movement had now suffered 'a check' – placing the blame firmly at the door of the opposing faction, and complaining that the Biggs–Bright–Becker triumvirate had 'thrown back the question into that refrain of feminine contempt & ridicule out of which it was raised a few years ago'.[135]

The right strategy now, Mill declared, was to 'go on propagandising in a quiet way, by lectures and otherwise', to 'quietly to let the fruit ripen' and wait for the Bright brigade to 'let the reins drop'.[136] Once the battle for public opinion was won, the contest in Parliament would be a foregone conclusion. For one brief, thrilling moment this strategy of political abstinence was altered by a rumour that Disraeli was considering putting his party behind women's right to vote. Given Disraeli's positive outlook on the question – at least when he was not prime minister – and his recent bout of democratic tendencies, this was not such a far-fetched idea. Mill saw that such a move would transform the question and, already disillusioned with Gladstone's government, declared:

The time, moreover, is, I think come when, at parliamentary elections, a Conservative who will vote for women's suffrage should be, in general, preferred to a professed Liberal who will not ... the bare fact of supporting Mr Gladstone in office ... does not now give a man a claim to preference over one who will vote for the most important of all political improvements now under public discussion.[137]

The 'Toryism of sex' was now, for Mill, a greater enemy than the Toryism of the Conservative Party. Sadly, Disraeli's rumoured feminization failed to materialize and women's suffrage was increasingly marginalized as a major political issue until after the turn of the century, when Emmeline Pankhurst led another breakaway from the National Union, then being led by Millicent Fawcett, and the First World War changed the political, economic and demographic landscape.[138]

In the meantime, the legal, economic and educational status of women was being steadily improved, but on the central question of the parliamentary vote, progress was very much slower than Mill could have envisaged. According to Bain, his most sanguine hopes were of 'slow progress in all things' – 'with the sole exception, perhaps, of the equality-of-women question.' Michael Packe suggests that if Mill had lived 'a few years longer', he would have 'got it through' Parliament. This is an over-statement; but there is no question that Mill was the mainspring of the movement for his last five years. Before his interventions, the question of women's votes 'had no political existence in this country', according to Millicent Fawcett. Mill was, she said, the 'principal originator' of the movement for women's suffrage, to which he gave 'the best powers of his mind, and the best years of his life.'[139] Perhaps an even greater tribute to his work was the fact that the anti-suffragists were forced to organize a response to the women's movement, in the form of a committee for 'Maintaining the Integrity of the Franchise'. Appropriately enough, it was led by Edward Bouverie, the 'Liberal' that Mill had wanted Chadwick to unseat in 1868.

In 1928, sixty-one years after Mill introduced his historic parliamentary amendment on women's suffrage, MPs passed a Bill giving women the same voting rights as men. An elderly Millicent Garrett Fawcett, who watched the vote from the Commons gallery, led a delegation of women to the statue of John Stuart Mill to lay a wreath in his memory. Within a year, 'Milly' herself was dead. The memorial in St George's Chapel, Westminster Abbey, describes her as 'a wise, constant and courageous Englishwoman (who) won citizenship for women'. Women's rights campaigners, still inspired by her example, gather there each year to pay their respects. Millicent would surely have been pleased. But she might have suggested that they also go to the statue of Mill on the Embankment, and pay homage to the man with whom she shares the victory.

CHAPTER FIFTEEN

Final Years (1868–73)

Two months after his ejection from Parliament, Mill wrote to update William Thornton on some home improvements to his Provençal idyll, which appear to have been of Benthamite inspiration:

Helen has carried out her long cherished scheme ... of a 'vibratory' for me, & has made a pleasant covered walk some 30 feet long where I can vibrate in cold or rainy weather. The terrace, you must know, as it goes round two sides of the house, has got itself dubbed the 'semi-circumgyratory.' In addition to this, Helen has built me a herbarium – a little room fitted up with closets for my plants, shelves for my botanical books, & a great table about which to manipulate them all. Thus you see with my herbarium, my vibratory, & my semi-circumgyratory I am in clover & you may imagine with what scorn I think of the H. of C., which, comfortable club as it is said to be, could offer me none of these comforts, or more properly speaking these necessaries of life.[1]

By the sound of it, Monloisir was beginning to live up to its name and, perhaps not surprisingly, Mill spent the majority of the last four and half years of his life in Avignon. With the exception of a long, mostly involuntary, stint in England between the summers of 1870 and 1871 – the fault of Bismarck and Napoleon III – France was now Mill's principal home. His much-underpinned house in Blackheath was finally given up in favour of a more convenient pied-à-terre in Albert Mansions, Victoria Street, just around the corner from his second childhood home. It was a modest flat, but with a fashionable address: Mill's new neighbours included Arthur Sullivan, who was putting the final touches to the music for *Thespis*, a new collaboration with a librettist named W. S. Gilbert, and Oscar Rejlander, busy with the photographs for Darwin's latest book, *The Expression of the Emotions in Man and Animals*.[2] None the less, Mill's centre of gravity was seven-and-a-half degrees south. 'I am no admirer of the English climate, which I think', he told a German friend, 'deserves the worst that I have ever heard said of it'.[3]

Mill was entitled to something resembling a retirement, after his long and productive multiple careers as public servant, journalist, editor, philosopher, campaigner and politician, and there was in fact a slight slackening of his pace during his final years. His piano was shipped to Avignon, and he also allowed himself to indulge in his favourite hobby. 'You are right in thinking that my absence from Parliament will give me more time for botany,' he told a fellow enthusiast in January, 1869. 'I am now looking through my herbarium for the first time since the winter of 1864/5'.[4]

Mill also mellowed towards friends and family. Warm letters were exchanged with old companions, including the two other members of the youthful 'Trijackia', John Roebuck and John Graham, and with some old foes, too: 'any communication from you' Mill wrote to Thomas Carlyle in 1869, 'not to mention your bodily presence – would always be most welcome'.[5] Mill came to the rescue of his estranged sister Mary, or more precisely to that of her son Henry, who had been fired for stealing from his employer, and paid for him to be articled to a London surveyor 'in order that he may have another opportunity of a fair start in life'.[6] With his usual probity, he made it a condition of the payment that the new employer was informed of Henry's crime. Both Mill and Helen took great pleasure in the household cat and dog. The latter, a

Pomeranian and a gift from the Amberleys, was called 'Kalos' – Greek for both beautiful and good – while the cat was named Phidias, a tribute to the great fifth-century Greek sculptor. Mill's pride in the latter animal extended to a belief that she would have won a prize at a 'pussical' show he saw advertised.[7]

During his last few years, then, Mill spent some time pottering with his plants, reminiscing with friends and catching up with some reading, the household pets curled up at his feet. A year before his death he even found time to go through his old letters and, to the dismay of any biographer, 'make a clearance of those which are no longer worth keeping'.[8] However, he certainly hadn't shut up shop, and his primary activities were still political and intellectual. He was heavily engaged on a number of political fronts, most intensively on women's rights, of course, but also on the struggle to increase working-class representation in the Commons, loosen the stranglehold of the Church over education, and break up the aristocratic monopoly of land. These causes were now best served, Mill thought, from an extra-parliamentary vantage point and he turned down a seat in Dudley, 'being of the opinion that I can promote my opinions more effectively at this time in the capacity of a writer, than in that of a member of the House of Commons'. He also turned down an entreaty to stand for the Southwark School Board.[9]

At the same time, he was busy recording his mature reflections on some enduring intellectual concerns, particularly the role of religion and the future of socialism. His publication record for the years 1869 to 1873 was, by his standards, fairly slim, but this is a misleading indicator of his output, since the most important intellectual fruits of his final years would be published posthumously. Mill was fond of quoting Carlyle's warning that 'the night cometh when no man can work' and he was focused on getting his thoughts down on paper, rather than into print. He also turned down one of the staple income sources for retired members of the British great and good, a lucrative lecture tour of America, on the grounds of 'the shortness of life & the numerous unexecuted literary projects ...

which require all the leisure of my remaining years'. In the summer of 1870 Mill and Helen shortened a planned holiday from ten days to four, 'such are the calls on our time and the quantity of work we have to do'.[10]

Politically, Mill continued to cut a radical figure. His youthful suggestion in 1835 that 'age is naturally conservative' was certainly not borne out by his own life.[11] He had become steadily more partisan after his entry to Parliament and the trend continued after his exit. His activism for women's rights was ceaseless and the growing conservatism of Parliament on this issue and others deepened his dissatisfaction with the Liberal party in general, and Gladstone in particular. 'The whole state of Europe inspires sadness enough,' he lamented to Cairnes, 'but that of England contempt.'[12] As always with Mill, the aftermath of a bout of political engagement was a hangover of cynicism. And, as usual, the contempt was only half-justified: after all, in 1869 the Irish Church was disestablished; in 1870 the principle of universal education was established, and the right of Irish tenants improved; in 1871 the requirement to subscribe to the Thirty-Nine Articles of faith in order to attend Oxford or Cambridge was abolished; and in 1872 the secret ballot was introduced.

None of this cut very much ice with Mill, though. 'It is plain that the Whigs intend to monopolise political power as long as they can without coalescing in any degree with the Radicals,' he fumed to George Odger. 'The working men are quite right in allowing Tories to get into the House to defeat this exclusive feeling of the Whigs, and *may* do it without sacrificing any principle.'[13] Mill supported organisations and publications committed to 'advanced liberal' aims, including a wider suffrage, investment in education and economic redistribution. George Snell, one of Odger's supporters in his aborted bid for the Chelsea candidacy, drew a group together for the purposes of promoting working-class candidates: Mill attended every meeting. The republican radical Charles Dilke, along with Fawcett and Mill, formed a Radical Club in 1869 to push the progressive agenda through both formal political channels and the press. Helen joined, too: the first rule of the club was that women would be admitted as equals. In 1869 Mill also subscribed to the Labour Representation League, a forerunner of the Labour party. He continued to give generous financial support to the *Westminster Review*, and moral support to Henry Chapman, its editor. When John Morley fell ill, Mill even offered to take over the editorship of the *Fortnightly Review* during his convalescence. Morley, perhaps fearing that he would not get the editorship back, declined.[14]

At the same time, Mill was adopting a more positive stance towards the trade union movement, as a stepping stone towards cooperative enterprises. This shift in position had a theoretical rather than political explanation. In 1869, Mill dramatically reversed his earlier support for the 'wage fund' theory found in classical Ricardian economics, which stated that the economic resources available to workers at any given time were essentially static, and that collective action to raise wages would therefore be self-defeating. William Thornton's, book, *On Labour*, convinced Mill that the amount available for wages was a product of the division between the capitalist's personal profit and the claims of his workers, rather than of any 'inexorable limits of the wages-fund'.[15]

In a review of the volume, Mill was open about his conversion. Thornton had 'destroyed a prevailing and mischievous error', he said, which meant that 'the doctrine hitherto taught by all or most economists (including myself) … is deprived of its scientific foundation, and must be thrown aside'.[16] Mill's volte-face generated delight and dissent in roughly equal measures. Fawcett, for one, did not follow his master's lead and Mill's recantation was somewhat unsatisfactory: the consensus among economists since has been that he threw the baby out with the bath-water. Wages are not fixed, but nor can the returns to the capitalist be easily reduced, since he or she will simply take their money elsewhere.[17] Mill himself might actually have been somewhat less convinced than the confessional language of his review suggested. For the final edition of his *Principles*, prepared in 1871, he made virtually no change to the text, instead using the preface to point readers to the 'instructive discussion' in Thornton's book and his own review, the results of which were 'not yet ripe for incorporation in a general treatise on political economy'.[18]

His public conversion was nonetheless an important fillip for the growing trade union movement, already in the process of acquiring – under both Gladstone and Disraeli – system of legal recognition, 'so favourable', according to Eric Hobsbawm, 'that periodic attempts have been made ever since to whittle away the freedom they were then granted.' Mill's view of the moral role of trade unions had also brightened; he now saw them as a 'means of educating the *élite* of the working classes for a future "universal Union".'[19]

Although he was more positive about the potential of trade unions, Mill remained sceptical about many of their current goals and methods. The general secretaries of the burgeoning unions – the group later dubbed 'The Junta' by Sidney and Beatrice Webb – must have been less pleased with some of the remainder of Mill's argument in 'On Labour'. He savaged union practices such as injunctions that 'no one shall move bricks in a wheelbarrow, but only in a hod' or that 'plasterers shall not do the work of plasterers' labourers, nor labourers that of plasterers, but a plasterer and a labourer must both be employed when one would suffice.' These 'vexatious' and 'ridiculous' approaches were, Mill warned, 'grave violations of the moral rule, that disputes should not be so conducted as to make the world a worse place for both together, and ultimately for the whole of the community'.[20] In the long run, Mill hoped that cooperatively owned companies would supersede the conflict between labour and capital. A transformation of 'the whole body of workpeople' into a group with 'a direct interest in the profits of the enterprise' would be 'the true euthanasia of Trades' Unionism'.[21] His support for the unions was thus conditional and short-term; if society improved beyond its current state, they should disappear. In this sense, he was a foul-weather friend of trade unionism.

Mill's attitude to one of the other great political issues of the first

Gladstone government – the funding of elementary schools – is also hard to position against modern political benchmarks. He refused to join the National Education League, which was campaigning for elementary education to be universal, compulsory, secular and free – because he disagreed with the last aim. He thought that parents who could afford it should pay something towards their children's education; for him it was part of the moral compact of parenthood. He did, however, support moves towards the secularization of schooling.[22] If had still been an MP, he would have voted against the 1870 Educational Bill – now seen as the first step to a national education system – because it allowed local school boards to use taxpayers' money to fund new denominational schools. In a speech to the League, he described the Bill as a device for 'enabling the clergy of the Church of England to educate the children of the greater part of England and Wales in their own religion at the expense of the public'. In private he went further, believing that it would have been better to have no Bill at all than one based on the 'denominational principle'.[23] He was unimpressed by arguments that Dissenters could also establish schools in those few areas where they were strong enough to gain representation on school boards. 'As if an injustice in one place were cured by an injustice in the other,' he said.

Mill was not opposed to religious teaching, but he was opposed to any of it being funded by the state: 'All we demand is, that those who make use of the religious teaching shall pay for it themselves instead of taxing others to do it'.[24] One of the reasons Mill was so concerned about faith schools was that he saw educational institutions as important sites for the cultivation of 'moral excellence'. 'Early religious teaching', he pointed out, 'has owed its power over mankind rather to its being early than to its being religious'.[25] It was not that Mill objected to moral education – quite the reverse – but he thought that Church-dominated schools were teaching bad morals: passivity, blind faith, fatalism, complacency and prejudice against other religions. This was true at all levels of society. 'You seem to me to regard Eton as a favourable specimen of what a school can do in the way of moral & religious training,' he railed against an Etonian master, 'an opinion from which all that I know of the kind of article turned out annually from Eton into the highest walks of life in this country leads me strongly to dissent.'[26]

Of course, moral education did not – or should not – begin and end at school, according to Mill: indeed other institutions, especially the family, typically played a more important role. During the course of his Rectoral address to the students of St Andrews, he insisted that 'no one can dispense with an education directed expressly to the moral as well as the intellectual part of his being', and that 'moral and religious training consist in training the feelings and the daily habits ... It is the home, the family which gives us the moral and religious education we really receive; and this is completed, and modified, sometime for the better, often for the worse, by society, and the opinions and feelings with which we are there surrounded.'[27] This was the message at the heart of *Subjection*, of course. Still, if universities had a limited 'direct' role in terms of moral education, Mill saw that they did have some influence via 'the prevailing tone of the place', which he believed should be one of duty and the honest seeking of truth. 'There is not one of us,' he declared, 'who may not qualify himself so to improve the average amount of opportunities, as to leave his fellow creatures some little the better for the use he has known how to make of his intellect.'[28] Amberley spent a Sunday afternoon reading this three-hour speech out loud to Kate, who found it 'very interesting': a sign both of the extent of their devotion to Mill and the kind of weekend amusements preferred by the more earnest classes of the Victorian era.[29]

Although he did look forward to a 'national' education system, Mill's views on educational role of government remained cautious. He certainly thought that educational districts, much larger than those covered by the proposed school boards, needed to be established. He was strongly in favour of a centrally based inspectorate to monitor standards, agreeing with the Bishop of Manchester's assessment that with regard to existing schools, 'the teaching in one third was tolerable, the teaching in another third was indifferent, and the teaching in the remaining third worthless.' Mill also gave an early endorsement to the idea of a community school, providing elementary, secondary and adult education. But he continued to argue strongly against the centralisation and standardization of educational provision.[30] In an 1869 essay on educational endowments, he wrote:

It is desirable that every particular enterprise for education or other public objects should be organised; that is, its conductors should act together for a known object, on a definite plan ... But it is far from desirable that all such enterprises should be organised exactly alike; that they all should use the same means for the attainment of exactly the same ends.[31]

This was a fair summary of his general approach to the role of government in the provision of public services. Some scholars detect a more favourable attitude towards state intervention in Mill's last years, and there is some evidence for this; in his correspondence, he made more positive noises about employment regulations, including the various Factory Acts and restrictions on hours of work, than in his most heated anti-philanthropic phases. In 1869, for example, he affirmed that 'legislative limitations of the hours of labour ... are properly within the competence of governments', but still insisted that their application would depend on the circumstances – a statement which is perhaps a notch or two more interventionist than his treatment of the same point in the *Principles*.[32] Once again, however, he did not alter the text of his main economic treatise when he was revising it two years later. Mill also endorsed in 1871 'the right of the State to take possession (with a view to their preservation) of all natural objects or artificial constructions which are of historical or artistic interest'.[33] This, however, was a fairly modest extension of his earlier support for state ownership of public parks and wilderness lands, and subsidies for artistic activities.

Mill's overall view on the role of government remained essentially unaltered, even through his radical old age. He believed that the state had a right to encourage people to lead good lives, but could not force them to do so; and that the government should be as much a moral persuader as a legal enforcer. In his own era, he saw the prejudice against state action as a greater obstacle to progress than excessive state control – but he was anxious that the scales might end up tipping the other way, once politicians got used to the idea of running the show from SW1. In the course of an 1870 speech on women's suffrage, he answered those who saw all state intervention as 'meddling':

There is wise as well as unwise meddling; well-directed as well as ill-directed benevolence; and there is a tendency in the present day to confound the two ... The time has passed away when Governments, generally speaking, were actively tyrannical; their favourite sins in the present time are indolence and indifference.[34]

These were not sins to which Mill succumbed, needless to say – and a testament to his continued energy and radicalism came in the form of a leading article in the *Deux Mondes*, in 1872, headed: 'Le Parti Radical en Angleterre: un manifeste de M. Stuart Mill.'[35] Of course there was no such party, but to the extent that there was a radical movement, Mill was seen by many as its natural leader. The 'manifeste' referred to by the French paper was in fact that of the Land Tenure Reform Association, formed in 1871, of which Mill was the Chairman and moving spirit. The transformation of the economics of land was, in fact, Mill's last radical campaign. In a series of articles, letters, speeches and reviews in the last three years of his life, he argued for the removal of the 'remains of feudality', which allowed a handful of landowners to get richer and richer as a result of historical accident.[36]

The land question drew together some of Mill's deepest political and economic convictions: a lifelong contempt for 'landlordism' and the English aristocracy; an economic philosophy in which the only properly 'private' property was the fruit of a person's labour; a deep interest in and knowledge of India and Ireland; disdain for the stubbornly Whiggish tendencies of English liberalism; and a powerful, bourgeois disapproval of 'unearned' material wealth. In his work on land economics, Mill further developed the distinction he had made in the *Principles* between the absolute right of individuals to the 'produce of [their] labour' and the conditional one to 'the ownership ... of things not made by themselves, nor made at all'.[37] The most important example of the latter kind of property was land, which Mill saw as 'a monopoly, not by the act of man, but of nature; it exists in limited quantity, not susceptible of increase'. The land was a 'bequest', an 'original inheritance of all mankind', and a 'gift of nature to the whole human race'.[38] This meant that the rights to ownership in land were subject to a tougher test than other forms of property: they had to be seen to foster 'the proper application of the land to the wants of the human race'. The beneficiary of the land ought to be 'the nation as a whole'.[39]

Mill believed that existing conditions fell a long way short of this ideal. Legal and economic structures meant that 'the land has been prevented, to a large extent from passing out of the hands of the idle into those of the industrious, and its ownership has been retained as the privilege of a small and decreasing number of families'.[40] The vast and growing wealth of these families, Mill wrote (recycling one of his favourite images), simply 'falls into their mouths as they sleep'.[41] Nor did he believe that the existing arrangements were fixed by the laws of economics. He used a review of a series of lectures on the history of village communities by Henry Maine, Oxford professor of jurisprudence, to argue that 'absolute ownership, which constitutes the idea of landed property as commonly conceived in England, is both modern as to time and partial as to place.' Maine had traced the gradual replacement of a patchwork of overlapping, collectively-based land ownership structures with aristocratic proprietorship. Mill's view was that 'the principle ... of the older institutions is fitter to be chosen that that of the more modern, as the basis of a better and more advanced constitution of society'.[42]

The typically subterranean influence of Indian affairs on Mill's thought broke through the surface here. He used Maine's discussion of property arrangements in India as a starting point for a spirited assault on the English management of the sub-continent.

Bengali villages had originally resembled the pre-feudal English ones, with ownership shared between an array of what Mill called 'co-proprietors', holding rights which were 'often extremely different in different places'. The difficulty, for the colonialists, was that 'there was nobody who could be called a proprietor in the absolute sense of English law'. Undeterred, the English had given the rent-collectors – who, being hereditary, looked a bit like the home-grown aristocracy – complete rights over the land. As a result of this blind application of an economic system from one country at a specific point in its history to another, the rights of the Bengali peasants had, Mill said, 'passed away *sub silentio*.' In the false names of civilization and political economy, 'one of the greatest social revolutions ever effected in a country' had turned a class of peasant proprietors into 'tenants-at-will'.[43]

Mill maintained his historical sensitivity when he turned his eye on England. His preference in theory was for state ownership of all the land, with the exception of homes and small gardens. But this policy was not feasible given the country's previous path of development. Nations in which the land had not been permitted to become the 'permanent property of individuals' were indeed 'fortunate', but the clock could not simply be turned back. The nationalization of land – called for by Odger's competing Land and Labour League – was, Mill thought, simply not a realistic policy. To Fawcett he criticized the 'the furious and declamatory violence of their [the League's] resolutions'. Here Mill was showing an awareness of existing social conditions which he had always believed the Benthamites (and the French), to lack. In private, Mill wrote that

I myself agree in principle with Mr. Odger and his friends; but if the [Land Tenure Reform] Assn. [the LTRA] were to adopt as its purpose the resumption of all the land from its proprietors, it could not hope for any support except from a portion of the working classes. The proposal is entirely new & startling to all other classes & a great deal of preparation will be required to induce them to listen to it patiently.[44]

To another correspondent he wrote: 'I agree with you that the land ought to belong to the nation at large, but I think it will be a generation or two before the progress of public intelligence and morality will permit so great a concern to be entrusted to the public authorities.'[45] In public, he focused on the incapacity of government for such a task, and frequently milked the argument for some entertainment value, telling one crowd: 'I have [too] poor an opinion of State management (*cheers*) or municipal management either (*hear, and laughter*) ... It requires, I fear, a greater degree of public virtue and public intelligence than has yet been attained (*laughter*) to administer all the land of the country like this on the public account.'[46]

Mill argued for 'not the abolition of landed property, but its reform'. He supported short-term moves to ensure that land was tradable like other goods, as Cobden had urged, but he did not think this would be sufficient to break the hold of the landlords. More radical steps were required. The peculiar property of land meant that it was 'subject to the will of the State'.[47] What this signalled was that even if nationalization was not 'expedient', an interception of future gains from landed property in the form of a land tax was both possible and necessary:

Though the State cannot replace itself in the fortunate condition in which it would now have been if it had reserved to itself from the beginning the whole rent of the land, this is no reason why it should go on committing the same mistake, and deprive itself of that natural increase of the rent which the possessors derive from the mere progress of wealth and population, without any exertion or sacrifice of their own. If the Grosvenor, Portman and Portland estates belonged to the municipality of London, the gigantic incomes of those estates would probably suffice for the whole expense of the local government of the capital.[48]

Apart from showing Mill's willingness to recommence his jabs at the family of his former Westminster colleague, this passage made the case for taxing rent increases. Mill did not 'propose to disturb the landowners in the past acquisitions': there was no question of a windfall tax. But any increases in rental income – which Mill, acutely aware of the power of language, always described as an 'unearned increment' – should be subject to 'special taxation'. This would mean that the 'wealth which now flows into the coffers of private persons ... will be gradually, and in an increasing proportion, diverted from them to the nation as a whole'.[49] By 1871 he was also supporting, in private correspondence at least, a 'heavy graduated succession duty on all inheritances exceeding that moderate amount, which is sufficient to aid but not to supersede personal exertion', and in the very last article published before his death, Mill contemplated a direct tax on capital.[50]

Through the vehicle of the Land Tenure Reform Association, Mill pushed his views on to a mostly unwelcoming public. By this stage, he was conscious of his growing reputation as a rabble-rouser, and seemed to be enjoying it. 'I shall be accused, I suppose, of exciting your passions', he told the very last audience he ever addressed, at Exeter Hall on the 18 March 1873, provoking loud laughter:

I am not ashamed of the charge. I want to excite your passions. (*Cheers.*) Without passion we shall never get this great iniquity put an end to. (*Hear, hear.*) Our Liberal Government is as bad on this subject as the Tories (*Hear, hear*) – perhaps even worse. (*Loud cheers.*) The passion of the many is needed to conquer the self-interest of the few. (*Cheers.*)[51]

Elsewhere, however, his arguments fell on stony ground. The Association may have been adopting what Mill considered a conciliatory and cautious approach, but that was not how others saw it. *The Times* bracketed Mill's tendency to 'propound some impracticable reform or revolutionary change in the laws relating to the land' with his support for women's rights as evidence of his elderly eccentricity.[52] Attacks from such quarters would of course have pleased Mill. But he was also, just two months before his death, ejected from the free-market Cobden Club – at which he had given one of the inaugural speeches in 1866, and been loudly cheered in

1869 – on the grounds that by supporting the Association he had 'publicly identified himself with principles radically opposed to those of the Club'. [53]

As so often, Mill was urging reform in order to stave off revolution. On 15 May 1871, the inaugural meeting of the Association, he described his proposals as 'very moderate and timid' adding that 'it is easy to foresee that this country, and all Europe, are entering upon an era in which they will have to discuss novelties far more alarming, and which will kindle much fiercer passions that these.'[54] Even as he was speaking, the Paris Commune was coming to its tragic denouement, with 25,000 lives lost during the 'Bloody Week' of 21-28 May. Like Marx, Mill did not take the side of either the Commune or the French government, and merely lamented the desperate consequences of an 'unfortunate civil war'.[55] But he sniffed socialism in the air. He watched the proceedings of the International Working Men's Association – the embryo of Marxism – with informed interest and he was sanguine about the 'First International' (as it later became known), especially in its home-grown incarnation. 'It is my opinion that this organisation pulls together a mass of widely differing representatives of all branches of socialism, both moderate and militant,' he told a correspondent in 1872:

The English branches, many of whose leaders are personally known to me, give me the impression, on the whole, of being made up of reasonable men, whose aim is, above all, to bring practical improvements to the lives of the working population, who are capable of sizing up the obstacles in their path, and who bear few grudges against those classes (in society) whose domination they wish to bring to an end.[56]

His assessment of the essentially reformist nature of the British labour movement – on which Marx initially placed high revolutionary hopes – was correct: one of the first members of the English branch was a Tory. Mill was also 'highly pleased' with a speech on the Franco-Prussian war given to the Council of the

International, writing to inform the Council that 'there was not one word of it that ought not to be there; it could not have been done with fewer words'.[57] The speech had been given by Karl Marx. Not too much should be read into Mill's endorsement, however, as the speech was essentially a long rant against Napoleon III's 'ferocious farce of the Restored Empire', along with an insistence that for the Germans the war was 'defensive' only. Mill agreed on both counts, seeing the war as 'one of the wickedest acts of aggression in history'.[58] According to Morley, when news of the war reached him as he sat in his garden in Blackheath, he 'violently struck his chair and broke out in a passionate exclamation, "What a pity the bombs of Orsini missed their mark, and left the crime-stained usurper alive!"'[59]

Mill's hatred of Napoleon III had blinded him to the deviousness of Bismarck and he attacked Gladstone (entirely unfairly) for his inactivity which, according to Mill, was partly the cause of the bitter war. 'If Gladstone had been a great man, this war would never have broken out,' he told Charles Dilke.[60] The Prime Minister, Mill believed, should have threatened to put the British Navy at the service of whichever country was attacked first, an approach to foreign policy – an unusual one, it must be said – which Mill saw as the potential beginning of an 'international police'. He was in fact increasingly convinced that international conflict could only be avoided by 'the creation of a police & an impartial umpire to settle quarrels.'[61]

If Mill and Marx shared an erroneous analysis of the Franco-Prussian war, there was little else to unite them. Mill never read, or appears to have heard of, the book published in 1867 which so transformed the world half a century later. Of course, *Das Kapital* was then unknown to all but a tiny circle of followers; but it would have been fortuitous for posterity if Mill had come across the work and subjected it to his balanced, forensic analysis. It is pretty clear, though, that while Mill might have appreciated parts of Marx, he would have had no time whatever for Marxism. For Mill, the chief value of the emerging movement for international socialism was to scare parliaments into faster reform by dangling 'alarm-ing novelties' before them. Even then, the scare-tactics had to be nationally and historically sensitive: he took one of the English socialist leaders to task for his use of revolutionary rhetoric. '"The Revolution" as a name for any set of principles or opinions, is not English,' he insisted. 'A Revolution is a change of government effected by force,' and for Mill, revolution would only be justified by much more extreme circumstances than the ones prevailing in England.[62]

These debates were in Mill's mind when he came to decide, on the focus of his next book. Its subject was to be socialism, and according to Helen he 'was occupied to the last' on the volume, which he believed would rival *Representative Government* in impor-tance.[63] Given subsequent history, it seems certain that had he lived to finish it, *Socialism* might in fact have rivalled *On Liberty* as his most famous work. As it was, all we have are the three 'Chapters on Socialism', published in the *Fortnightly Review* six years after Mill's death. In an editorial preface, Helen described them as 'rough drafts thrown down towards the foundation' of a work in which her stepfather intended to 'go exhaustively through the whole subject, point by point'.[64]

Scholars have fretted that because Mill's manuscript of the 'Chapters' has gone astray, Helen's editorial influence cannot be his-torically assessed. They worry too much. The 'Chapters' are vintage Mill. Far from being 'thrown down', they approach the subject of socialism in an orderly and disciplined fashion – certainly com-pared to the rather piecemeal treatment in the *Principles*. The prose is as taut as ever, and the arguments are entirely consistent with his earlier analysis. He agreed with the socialist critique of the current 'evils' of capitalism: 'great poverty ... very little connected with desert' and 'human misconduct; crime, vice, and folly', but he denied that market competition was depressing wages, insisting that wages were in fact rising across the board. 'Socialists', he said, 'forget that competition is a cause of high prices and values as well as of low'.[65] He was dismissive, too, of the relentless Jeremiad of much socialist thinking: 'The present system is not, as many Socialists believe, hurtling us into a state of general indigence and slavery from which only Socialism can save us. The evils and injustices under the present system are great, but they are not increasing; on the contrary, the general tendency is towards their slow diminution.'[66]

All around him, Mill could see the benefits of capitalism flowing, albeit it unevenly, to the whole of society; he would have largely endorsed Henry Buckle's description of national history as 'the living scroll of human progress'. In the previous decade, average real wages had risen by around 25 per cent and between 1850 and 1873, real incomes per head rose by 46 per cent.[67] The museums and theatres of London were multiplying and filling, with the 'penny gaffs' being gradually supplanted by more upmarket venues such as the Royal Victoria Theatre (now the Old Vic), where gallery seats cost 4d and for which, if there was a play 'with a good murder in it', the queues would begin forming hours before curtain-up. Shorter working hours had created new opportunities for leisure: in 1863, the Football Association had been formed and within five years thirty-eight clubs had joined. Another spectator sport, horse-racing, also took off with a hundred new track events added to the annual calendar during the 1860s.[68]

Rising incomes during the 'long Victorian boom' may have slightly influenced Mill's stance on the relative merits of socialist and laissez-faire economics: the tone of his 'Chapters' was more sceptical toward socialism than his *Principles* after its revisions during the 1850s. But his essential position was unchanged: in 1852 he had insisted that any preference for one system over the other was 'a mere question of comparative advantages.' In the 'Chapters', he likewise insisted that 'what is incumbent on us is a calm comparison between two different systems of society, with a view of determining the inevitable difficulties of life.'[69] Mill was content to be classed 'under the general designation of socialists' but for him, socialism meant a reformation of capitalism rather than its overthrow. His vision was of cooperatively owned firms competing in a market economy, not a recasting of the basis of human society. The improvement in the conditions of the working classes would come, he said, from them 'becoming their own capitalists'.[70] More radical change was possible, he admitted, but only over a long period of time:

An entire renovation of the social fabric, such as is contemplated by Socialism, establishing the economic constitution of society upon an entirely new basis, other than that of private property and competition, however valuable as an ideal, and even as a prophecy of ultimate possibilities, is not available as a present resource, since it requires from those who are to carry on the new order of things qualities both moral and intellectual, which require to be tested in all, and created in most; and this cannot be done by an Act of Parliament, but must be, on the most favourable supposition, a work of considerable time.[71]

Mill believed that full-blown communism would stunt the opportunities for 'the development of individual character' – his abiding concern – and that, at least for the foreseeable future, 'personal interest' would be the 'most effective stimulus to the most vigorous and careful conduct of the industrial business of society'.[72] What he did support was a move towards giving 'the whole body of labourers . . . a participation in the profits, by distributing among all who share in the work, in the form of a percentage of their earnings, the whole of a fixed portion of the gains after' – and the next ten words are crucial – 'a certain remuneration has been allowed to the capitalist'.[73] Mill suggested that when a company owner died, the firm may pass wholly into the hands of the workers – but this was a long way from suggesting that his death should therefore be brought about. He believed that the only way to test the viability of 'socialist' companies was by trying them out in the competitive marketplace. Ten years earlier, he had told Fawcett that in response to doubts about the viability of cooperative models of business, 'one can only say *Solvitur* (or *Solvetur*) *ambulando*. The thing is practicable or not, according to the intellectual and moral qualities of those who attempt it.'[74]

The literal interpretation of the Latin phrase is 'the solution comes through walking', which could have been an epitaph for Mill himself. Not only was he a strong proponent of trial and error in his philosophy and economics, he was consistently ambulant in his own life. 'I attribute the good health I am fortunate enough to have, very much to my great love of exercise,' he told Herbert Spencer, 'and for what I think the most healthy form of it, walking.'[75] From his Avignon base he and Helen climbed Mont Ventoux a 'score' of times. Often they would be trapped by sudden thunderstorms, and seek refuge in mountain farms. Helen described the Provençal hospitality:

Coffee, wine, milk, or the best of whatever the house afforded was always pressed upon us. Blazing fires lit, in spite of our protests, on bare mountain sides where wood is scarce; and guides offered for miles if we would accept them: and on the few occasions when we ventured to offer any gift in return, it was always refused, although with perfect courtesy, even by little children.[76]

Mill also undertook frequent botanizing trips with Henri Fabre, with whom he had planned a study of the flora of the Vaucluse. Fabre had become a good friend, especially after he had lost his teaching post for the crime of teaching biology to girls, and Mill had given him some financial support. When Mill died, he bequeathed the bulk of his herbarium to the Avignon museum of natural history, where it remains; Fabre then accepted the post of curator, 'out of respect' he said, 'for the memory of ... Stuart Mill'.[77] During his forced exile from France, Mill resorted to a summer botanizing trip to the north-east of Scotland, with an old botanical buddy, Alexander Irvine. Being July, and Scotland, it rained and Mill was disappointed with his haul. But he might have had better luck in Cornwall and Yorkshire, which he also visited that summer with Irvine.[78] In the summer of 1871, after a slow trip through Switzerland – Mill and Helen hired a boat and spent six days exploring Lake Lucerne – Mill was delighted to regain his perch at Monloisir in mid-August. 'Our irrigated meadows give the full freshness and greenness of Switzerland', he told Cairnes, 'the Ventoux gives the perceptions and feelings of mountain scenery, and all the effects of our glorious skies and lights come in addition.'[79]

By now, Mill also had a growing circle of friends to welcome him back to his French home. Pastor Rey, for whom, according to Helen, Mill had 'as much friendship as esteem', remained a close friend throughout his last years. He was also on good terms with the former mayor, Dr Chauffard, and it seems likely that he knew Charles Renouvier, the Kantian philosopher who was resident in Avignon during the same period: he certainly knew his work.[80] Mill had thus fashioned for his final years an agreeable combination of activism and pleasure. James Mill used to say 'that he had never known a happy old man, except those who were able to live over again the pleasures of the young', but his eldest son appeared to disprove the claim.[81] Mill's enjoyment in his work, the natural world and conversation were undiminished to his very last days. Not that he opened his door to just anybody. Queen Victoria's eldest daughter, the Princess Royal of Prussia, and her husband Prince Frederick William were refused an audience at Monloisier – Mill claiming ill-health as the reason for the rebuff.[82]

For the limited time that they spent in England, Mill and Helen continued to enjoy the company of the Amberleys. There is some evidence that they were considering renting a nearby property in order to see more of the couple.[83] Kate Amberley recalled a long, hot weekend in late September 1870, during which the quartet walked in the Forest of Dean and visited Raglan Castle and Tintern Abbey. 'After dinner Mr. Mill read us Shelley's *Ode to Liberty*,' Kate noted in her diary, '& he got quite excited & moved over it rocking backwards and forwards & nearly choking with emotion; he said himself: "it is almost too much for one."'[84] Shelley was Harriet's favourite poet, and the subject of the poem was, of course, close to Mill's heart, too:

He who taught man to vanquish whatsoever
　　Can be between the cradle and the grave.
Crowned him the King of Life. O vain endeavour! –
　　If on his own high will, a willing slave,
He has enthroned the oppression and the oppressor.[85]

The same day brought news of the breakdown of public order in France: Mill and Helen went to Geneva, where Mill waited, and Helen dashed to Avignon to collect the manuscript of her edition of Henry Buckle's work. She did not want him to go with her for 'fear he shd be taken for a Prussian spy', which, given his views on the war, might not have been such an absurd thought.[86]

The following summer, 1871, Mill lost his last intimate link to his youthful Benthamism, when George Grote died at the age of seventy-six. To Mill's displeasure, Grote's funeral service was held in Westminster Abbey. He was a reluctant pallbearer. Leaving the Abbey, he turned to Bain: 'In no very long time,' he said, 'I shall be laid in the ground with a very different ceremonial than that.' He confessed that Grote's death left 'a great blank' in his life, and turned a review of Grote's unfinished *Aristotle* into a eulogy.[87] But he was inspired by the example of his old friend who continued to work until the last moment, and told Pasquale Villari that his own hope was to 'help to train the thinkers of the time to come ... My own work lies rather among anticipations of the future than explanations of the past.'[88] Grote left Mill £100 in his will, a symbol of his affection, which was almost certainly passed on immediately to one of the many good causes to which Mill contributed. These included the Blackheath Volunteer Band, the Drinking Fountain Association, the Life Boat Fund and the Parsee Girls' School – the latter an example, it seems, of Mill's feminism overriding his strictures on religious education.[89]

Mill's visit to Westminster Abbey, and Tintern Abbey the previous year, contradict the claim by the historian David Newsome that Mill 'had never even entered a church'.[90] His correspondence and journals, as well as the letters and diaries of contemporaries, show that during the course of his life he visited no fewer than fifty churches, and almost certainly very many more. In a number of these he also attended services. At the age of sixteen he went to mass in Toulouse, 'but could not see much'; twenty-five years later he went to a sung mass in St Peter's, Rome, conducted by Pope Pius IX, but did not enjoy the music. He was annoyed to miss Mass at Palermo Cathedral. Closer to home, he admired the internal architecture of the Chiltern churches during his walking tours of 1827 and 1828 and caught part of a Sunday evening service in Peterborough cathedral, which he described to Harriet as 'one of the finest I know (in England)'.[91]

Of course, none of this should be seen as evidence of any personal faith on Mill's part. His motivation for visiting churches was aesthetic or sociological curiosity, rather than piety, but Newsome's error reflects an aspect of the 'received version' of Mill, adding atheism to his alleged asceticism and dry-as-a-bone personality. It would be more accurate to describe Mill – as both Bain and Rey did – as a 'sceptic' on religious matters, or, perhaps even better, using the label coined by Huxley in 1870, as an 'agnostic'. Mill himself rebuffed the charge of atheism during the 1868 election. 'If any one again tells you that I am an atheist,' he wrote to his committee, in a letter which was published in the *Daily News*, 'I would advise you to ask him, how he knows and in what page of my numerous writings he finds anything to bear out the assertion.'[92] Helen was furious about this move, which she saw as evidence that electioneering had forced him to yield to popular prejudice: 'I cannot tell you how ashamed I feel.'[93]

Helen was perhaps too harsh. Mill may have been under political pressure, but he was quite right to claim that there was no trace of atheism in his writings; nor indeed in his thinking. Mill saw that for his father, a former preacher, and Bentham, who signed the Thirty-Nine Articles to go to Oxford, opposition to religion was a vital source of their radicalism – but this was not the case for him. Two months before his death, Mill visited John Morley at his home in Guildford, and remarked during their conversation on the difference in the feeling of modern refusers of Christianity as compared to men like his father, impassioned deniers, who believed that if only you broke up the power of the priests and checked superstition, all would go well – a dream from which they were partially awakened by seeing that the French Revolution which overthrew the Church still did not bring the millennium.[94]

For Mill, with no religious teaching to unburden and a distinctly unBenthamite appreciation of poetry, history, beauty and idealism, 'impassioned denial' was not necessary. On a personal level, he apparently had no faith; Mill frequently wrote letters on Christmas Day, without any mention of the date. But at least during one period of his life – the peak of his Carlylean-Coleridgean phase – he saw this as a weakness rather than a strength. 'I have . . . a merely probable God,' he told Carlyle in 1834:

By *probable* . . . I mean that the existence of a Creator is not to me a matter of faith, or of intuition. . .it is but a hypothesis, the proofs of which as you I know agree with me, do not amount to absolute certainty. As this is my condition in spite of the strongest wish to believe, I fear it is hopeless . . . there is wanting something positive in me, which exists in others.[95]

It is impossible to imagine James Mill, Bentham, Grote or Roebuck writing in a similar vein. Nor was this theological position a passing fad. In 1861 he wrote to a correspondent: 'That . . . the world was made, in whole or part, by a powerful Being who cared for man, appears to me, though not yet proved, yet a very probable hypothesis.'[96]

Such sentiments were not on public display during Mill's lifetime. Although he had tackled some theological issues in his *Logic* and *Hamilton,* and embraced some aspects of Comte's 'Religion of Humanity', Mill did not publish an examination of religion – but he was writing on the subject. In 1874, a year after his death, the *Three Essays on Religion* appeared. 'To some the book came as a disappointment, to others as a relief, to all as a surprise,' recorded

Leonard Courtney in his 1889 biography.[97] Morley and Bain were displeased with, and a little ashamed of, their master. The first two essays – 'Nature' and 'Utility of Religion' – were not the source of the shame. These had been written in the mid-1850s, under Harriet's watchful, heathen eye. She was particularly keen on the latter essay, urging him in 1854 to make it his top priority:

About the Essays, dear, would not Religion, the Utility of Religion be one of the subjects you would have most to say on – there is to account for the existence nearly universal of some religion (superstition) by the instincts of fear hope and mystery etc., and throwing over all doctrines and theories, called religion, as devices for power, to show how religion & poetry will the same want, the craving after higher objects . . . how all this must be superseded by morality deriving its power from sympathies and benevolence and its rewards from the approbation of those we respect.[98]

Mill headed in the direction signalled by Harriet, but was more cautious than her about 'throwing over' religious doctrines. He outlined the moral role of religion:

What vast efficacy belongs naturally to any received doctrine received with tolerable unanimity as true, and impressed on the mind from the earliest childhood as duty. A little reflection will, I think, lead us to the conclusion that it is this which is the great moral power in human affairs, and that religion only seems so powerful because this mighty power has been under its command.[99]

However, it did not have to be a supernatural religion exerting this moral pressure. 'It is perfectly conceivable' he wrote 'that religion may be morally useful without being intellectually sustainable.' Mill argued that any good religion could be of value in helping with the important goals of 'overcoming ordinary temptations, and regulating the course of daily life' in acting 'as a supplement to human laws, a more cunning sort of policeman, an auxiliary to the thief-catcher and the hangman.'[100]

Following Harriet, Mill also gave a more 'exalted' case for religious belief. 'Religion and poetry address themselves to the same part of the human constitution', he said: 'they both supply the same want, that of ideal conceptions grander and more beautiful than we see realized in the prose of human life.' Religion was 'the strong and earnest direction of the emotions and desires towards an ideal object, recognized as of the highest excellence, and as rightfully paramount over all selfish objects of desire'.[101] In correspondence, Mill even saw prayer as a potential source of 'the elevating influence of an endeavour to commune & to become in harmony with the highest spiritual ideal', and in *Hamilton* he had insisted on the value of 'wonder' at the beauty of the natural world.[102] Prayer, wonder, devotion: not themes generally associated with the 'Saint of Rationalism', but the human value of striving for an ideal was in fact a recurrent theme in Mill's writing, whether dealing explicitly with religion or not.

In its ideal versions, then, Mill saw religion as 'a source of personal satisfaction and of elevated feelings'; his question was whether it was possible to retain these attributes without the supernatural element of existing religions, for which he had no time: 'There is not a single miracle in either the Old or New Testament the particular existence of which is worth a farthing,' he told one correspondent. They were simply, he told another, 'part of the halo which popular enthusiasm throws around its heroes' – from Christ to the Roman Emperor Vespasian.[103] He believed morals did not need miracles: 'It was not religion which formed the strength of the Spartan institutions,' he pointed out, 'the root of the system was devotion to Sparta, to the ideal of the country or State: which transformed into ideal devotion to a greater country, the world, would be equal to that and far nobler achievements.'[104] Here, in essence, was Comte's 'Religion of Humanity' reborn:

A morality grounded on large and wise views of the good of the whole, neither sacrificing the individual to the aggregate nor the aggregate to the individual, but giving to duty on the one hand and to freedom and spontaneity on the other their proper province, would derive its power in the superior natures from sympathy and benevolence and the passion for ideal excellence: in the inferior, from the same feelings cultivated up to the measure of their capacity, with the superadded force of shame.[105]

Mill was not out to demolish Christianity, however. For all its faults, it did perform some of these useful moral functions, including the one which led Voltaire to ban discussions of atheism in front of his servants: 'I want my lawyer, tailor, valets, even my wife, to believe in God,' the Frenchman said, 'I think that if they do I shall be robbed less and cheated less.'[106] Anybody setting out to 'subvert or weaken the belief of mankind in Christianity . . . misunderstands the wants & tendencies of his age,' Mill told Sterling. The effects of such exertions would 'probably be to make men worse instead of better by shaking the only firm convictions & feelings of duty which they have, without having even a remote chance of furnishing them with any effectual substitute.' His goal, as far as the bulk of the population was concerned was rather to 'try to improve their religion than to destroy it'.[107]

These reflections on the moral value of religion – actual and potential – startled no one. It was the third essay, that Mill wrote after Harriet's death, 'Theism', which upset his admirers. Although it was completed between 1868 and 1870, he appears to have made no moves towards publication. Helen was clear in her editorial preface that Mill never intended to publish the three essays together, but that he did consider the opinions within them to be 'fundamentally consistent'.[108] But in fact the difference in tone is quite startling. In 'Theism' Mill sided strongly with those seeing evidence for the existence of God in 'intelligent design'. While he accepted that Darwin's 'remarkable speculation' may come to be proven, he concluded that 'in the present state of our knowledge, the adaptations in Nature afford a large balance of probability in favour of creation by intelligence'. Worse – or better, depending on your point of view – was to come. Mill went on to claim that belief in life after death, while clearly only a hope, was 'legitimate and philosophically defensible'.[109] Finally, he issued a description of Christ that is close to a Hallelujah:

When [his] pre-eminent genius is combined with the qualities of probably the greatest moral reformer, and martyr to that mission, who ever existed on earth, religion cannot be said to have made a bad choice in pitching on this man as the ideal representative and guide of humanity; nor even now, would it be easy, even for an unbeliever, to find a better translation of the rule of virtue from the abstract to the concrete, than to endeavour so to live that Christ would approve of our life . . . it remains a possibility that Christ actually was what he supposed himself to be . . . a man charged with a special, express and unique commission from God to lead mankind to truth and virtue.[110]

Mill had always expressed an admiration for Christ as a historical figure; but this 'twilight land of semi-faith', in Courtney's words, seemed like something different.[111] Perhaps Pastor Rey had more influence than he knew. In any case, many of Mill's followers were understandably unhappy. 'It made a sort of intellectual scandal,' recalled Morley of the essay. In the *Fortnightly Review* he pointed to what he saw as the 'incongruity in the author's final appeal to a mystic sentiment', which he feared would support 'a new and mischevious reaction towards supernaturalism'.[112] Alexander Bain confessed that he was 'unprepared' for the last essay, and agreed with Morley that it gave succour to the wrong side of the argument. Mill had made 'concessions to the existing Theology; and, as usual in such cases, the inch has been stretched to an ell'. Having chided Mill for making such sweeping statements on the basis of thin theological knowledge, Bain partially excused him on the grounds that the piece was surely only a 'rough note' – which it was not. Bain also correctly suggested that Mill was trying to have it both ways – to keep the good bits of God without the need for faith in his existence. But, Bain insisted, 'a Deity dethroned should retire altogether from playing a part in human affairs, and remain simply as an historic name.'[113]

For most modern readers, Mill's somewhat amateur theological attempts to salvage the positive aspects of Christianity are largely antique curiosities. The most striking feature of the essays, however, was his unrelenting focus on individual character. Mill's near-resurrection of Christ was motivated not by a hope of a seat in heaven – there is no evidence Mill ever entertained such a wish – but by the desire for general moral improvement:

We may well conclude that the influences of religion on the character which will remain after rational criticism has done its utmost against the evidences of religion, are well worth preserving, and that what they lack in direct strength as compared to those of a firmer belief, is more than compensated for by the greater truth of the morality they sanction.[114]

Mill's attitude to the supernatural claims of religion did not change, but he did come to have more faith in the capacity of a renovated Christianity to act as a force for moral good; Mill's ideal God was a moral motivator. Old-style Christianity bred passivity, fatalism and prejudice, but a reformed version held out the prospect of an 'an increased inducement to cultivate the improvement of character'.[115] Just as Mill judged socialism and capitalism by their impact on individual character and autonomy, so religion could be measured against the same benchmarks. When Mill discussed the 'utility' of a religion, or the efficacy of an economic system, or the justice of a marriage law, his yardstick was not their capacity to make people happy, but first, to make them free, and second, to make them good. In his essay on 'Nature', Mill argued that goodness, virtue and justice were not 'natural', but the achievements of civilization and of mankind's cultivation of his own character: 'the duty of man is the same in respect of his own nature as in respect to the nature of all other things, namely not to follow but to amend it.'[116]

In the course of one of his 1846 newspaper articles on the Irish famine, Mill had written a sentence which better captured this deep conviction than any other: 'What shapes the character is not what is purposely taught, so much as the unintentional teaching of institutions and social relations.'[117] For Mill, the institutions of marriage, family, workplace, trade union, army, university, civic association and democracy were 'schools' within which individual character was formed, for good or ill. Public opinion, social custom, religious belief, and attitudes to race and gender were also vital components in the crucible of character formation. Mill battled in the *Logic* to show that individuals were not trapped in the character created by their circumstances – that they could escape their conditioning – but he also highlighted how difficult such an escape could be. In *On Liberty* he sketched an inspiring vision of a society of individuals striving for self-improvement, and in the *Principles* and *Subjection*, he described the kind of economic and familial institutions most conducive to its creation. In *Representative Government* he likewise insisted that 'the *spirit* of an institution, the impression it makes on the mind of the citizen, is one of the most important parts of its operation.'[118]

With 'Theism' complete, Mill and Helen further indulged their love of European travel. They spent a week in Hyères and St Tropez in the spring of 1872 and returned to the Alps, this time on the Austrian side, for two of the summer months of the same year. It was, Mill reported to Cairnes (the chief recipient of Mill's travel bulletins), 'quite as beautiful and enjoyable as we expected.' During the Austrian trip, Helen discussed with Mill a request to them both from the Amberleys, and from Hieflau they sent their response: 'I should like to be godmother to your little boy', Helen declared, adding that Mill did 'not think that it would conflict with his opinions to enter into that relation.' Kate was delighted, declaring that 'there is no one in whose steps I wd. rather see a boy of mine following in ever such a humble way, than in Mr Mill's.'[119] Kate died just two years later, and Amberley twenty months after that, but their son fulfilled their wish. The only British philosopher of the twentieth century who rivalled Mill's status as a public intellectual in the nineteenth century, was his godson, Bertrand Russell.

After another tour in early 1873, this time around Burgundy, Mill and Helen returned to England for a few weeks in March and

April. Mill was on good form. During a Surrey ramble, he 'chatted', Morley recalled, 'with something of the amiableness of a child, about the wild flowers, the ways of the insects, and notes of bird. He was impatient for the song of the nightingale.' Four days later, Mill, unusually, agreed to sit for a portrait by George Frederic Watts, which had been commissioned by Charles Dilke.[120] He also engaged in an energetic burst of entertaining, hosting three dinner parties during the week beginning 26 March, for Morley, Fawcett, Spencer, Maine and other friends and attending at least one more. He squeezed in a day's botanizing with Alexander Irvine in Wimbledon, and then headed south to France. As soon as he arrived in Avignon, Mill arranged another plant-hunting expedition, with Fabre, around Orange. Bain reports that the pair covered fifteen miles. This may have been an exaggeration, given that Mill was only in Orange for six hours, and that they broke off their botanizing for lunch at Fabre's new house. But Mill was clearly full of energy.

Two days later, however, at home in Avignon, he developed a fever. Dr Chauffard was called, and immediately sent a telegram to Dr Cecil Gurney in Nice. By the time he arrived the following day, Mill had developed an 'enormous swelling ... over his face and neck'. Gurney diagnosed him with the bacterial infection erysipelas – and told Mill that the attack was fatal. The patient received the news 'with calmness and resignation'. Mill had expected to die many years earlier, and was grateful that his intellect had not failed him in his last years.

There is, as Mill himself wrote twenty years before his death, 'a tinge of melancholy in all biographies; the more interested we are in the hero, the sadder is our foreknowledge of the inevitable fifth act.' As Mill waited for death, Gurney walked the tree-lined avenue leading to the house. The garden was filled with nightingales, 'so tame', he recalled, 'that when I paced up and down between my visits to his bedside, they followed me from tree to tree.' Early the next morning, Mill offered a final reassurance to the vigilant Helen: 'you know that I have done my work'. Then, with a chorus of nightingales in his ears, he turned away and died. A few hours later, Charles Dilke – unaware of the death – received delivery of Watts's fine portrait. The following day, in a light rain, Mill's body was carried the short distance to the graveyard. The funeral party consisted of Helen, Pastor and Madame Rey, and the two doctors, proof of Dickens' claim that 'the more truly great the man, the more truly little the ceremony'.[121] A knot of locals waited respectfully at the cemetery gate. Rey offered a prayer, an act for which he would later have to publicly apologize. The tomb, fashioned from the same marble as the Pantheon, was opened, and Mill was laid beside his wife.

Epilogue

><

'I cannot go on –' wrote Henry Sidgwick, 'Mill is dead!' Kate Amberley likewise told her mother: 'We are both very miserable at the loss to us of the warmest & truest friend we have known & one who will make a great blank in our lives.'[1] The blank was in the life of the nation, too. Mill's increasingly partisan activities had dented his image in the view of many, and polished it in the eyes of others, but there was no dispute about the fact that in 1873 Mill towered over the nation's intellectual and political scene. As news of his death reached the English shores, obituarists for every newspaper and journal took out their pens and, in many cases, sharpened them.

Mill had repeatedly demolished Abraham Hayward in the London Debating Society half a century previously, and Hayward's obituary of him in *The Times*, of course, was a vengeful piece of character assassination. Alongside some perfunctory praise for the *Logic* and *Principles*, Hayward drew attention to Mill's youthful, 'foolish scheme for carrying out the Malthusian principle', and went on to lament Mill's 'unceasing feuds' in philosophy, his 'reckless' selection of causes in politics and his advocacy of 'the fanciful rights of women'.[2]

The following day, the liberal cleric Stopford Brooke denounced *The Times* from the pulpit of St James's Church on York Street,

London. Lord John Russell then received a letter from a priest, 'complaining of Mr Stopford Brooke for having spoken highly of Mr Mill in the pulpit,' recalled Russell's wife: 'how nasty clergymen can be!'[3] Not as nasty as Hayward, however. In response to Brooke's sermon, he printed and circulated widely a letter which laid out an even fuller case against Mill. His achievements as a thinker were belittled – 'to class him with Locke, Bentham, Adam Smith or Malthus is preposterous', Hayward, declared; his teenage brush with the law in 1823 was described in greater detail – Mill had supposedly circulated literature on contraception 'for the edification of the maid-servants' – and his relationship with Harriet was described in terms which stopped just an inch short of openly labelling the couple adulterers. William Christie, Mill's collaborator on anti-corruption initiatives in the 1860s, who received a copy of the letter, was incensed. He and Hayward engaged in an increasingly hostile exchange of letters, leading to an incident in the whist room of the Athenaeum, with Christie walking out rather than play in a 'four' with his antagonist.[4] These scuffles in the liberal chattering-class were of course gleefully reported in the conservative press, and one of the results of the row was the withdrawal of Gladstone's support for the construction of a memorial to Mill. His letter to the fund-raising Committee was a perfect specimen of political cowardice:

In my view this painful controversy still exists. I feel it is not possible for me, situated as I am at the present time, to decide it or to examine it with a view to decision. The only course open to me is to do no act involving a judgement either way, and, therefore, while I desire to avoid any public step whatever, I withdraw from co-operation, and request that my name be no further mentioned.[5]

John Morley, who admired Gladstone at least as much as Mill, was ashamed. The Duke of Argyll, he pointed out, 'had manfully brushed wasps aside' and sent a subscription for the memorial, as well as 'men as orthodox' as Lord Salisbury and Lord Derby. Other supporters included the Fawcetts and Dilkes as well as Bain,

Spencer and Bagehot. The Political Economy Club chipped in £50. However, two of the remaining subscribers would have pleased Mill most: one was described simply as 'A Lady', and the other, 'The Workmen of Britannia Works, Bedford'.[6] The product of the contributors' collective generosity was a fine bronze statue by Thomas Woolner, raised on the Thames Embankment in 1879. With £333 of funds left over, the committee decided to endow a scholarship at UCL for 'distinction in the study of Philosophy of Mind and Logic', which is awarded to the present day.[7]

Hayward was the most bitter obituarist, but there were plenty of others ready to join the assault. The *Saturday Review* accused Mill of being, on subjects such as slavery, 'an obstinate fanatic' and said his 'delusion' about the equality of the sexes, cast doubt on his authority. The piece concluded by recycling the old slurs about Mill's masculinity: 'There was in truth something feminine in his mental constitution, which disturbed the calm balance of his judgement'. The *Illustrated London News* considered that Mill's attitude towards 'several important questions ... was at variance with the soundest and best-informed English minds'.[8] These were not the obituary notices of a national treasure, but of a controversial activist.

Cooler voices emphasized his intellectual and literary qualities. Bagehot, in the *Economist*, admitted that Mill was not the most original thinker of his generation, but that 'his great merit was ... of intellectual combination'; or the 'art of piecing together'. Henry Sidgwick, in *Academy*, described him as 'the best philosophical writer – if not the best philosopher – England has produced since Hume'. Mill still had his outright fans, too. The *Athenaeum* lamented 'the death of a master' and the *Spectator* defended him against the charge of reclusiveness: 'no recluse was ever before so honestly devoted as he to the cause of the people, and no popular reformer was ever before so honestly devoted as he to the cause of abstract truth.'[9]

The dust had barely settled from the first round of posthumous hostilities, when Helen rang the bell for a second, publishing the

Autobiography in October 1873. Mill and Harriet had wanted it to 'stop the mouths of enemies hereafter', but it was to prove a vain hope.[10] Henry Reeve used forty pages of his *Edinburgh Review* for an extended demolition of Mill and his works, placing great emphasis on Mill's suspicious relationship with Harriet and likening him at length to Rousseau, a man of similarly doubtful morals and doctrinaire politics. Hayward continued his obsessive attacks, this time from the pages of *Fraser's Magazine*, accusing Mill of 'unconscious egotism'; *The Times* added foreignness to its charge of femininity, dubbing him an 'un-English ... outsider'. Even friendlier reviewers were forced to admit that the book portrayed a life of 'monotonous joylessness', which slightly missed the point of Mill's exercise. The conservative *Daily News*, ironically, had a better grasp of it, describing the book as 'not so much the history of a life as of a mind'. Carlyle was typically unrestrained, describing it as 'the life of a logic-chopping engine, little more of human in it than if it had been done by a thing of mechanized iron'.[11]

In such cases, it was usually the job of a sympathetic biographer to level the score, but nobody rose to the challenge. It was widely assumed that Morley – to whom Mill had granted the copyright on all his published works – would produce the definitive 'Life and Letters' expected of every eminent Victorian, and it seems, on the basis of second-hand evidence, that he intended to.[12] For whatever reason, though, it never appeared, and Morley made no mention of it in his *Recollections*. Two short assessments – by Alexander Bain and Leonard Courtney – were published in 1882 and 1889; Mill's early letters appeared in 1910; and an attempt was made at a full biography only in 1954, by Michael St John Packe. Courtney's conclusion that 'longer study may perhaps lessen our admiration of him as a thinker, but increase our affection for him, as a man', neatly prefaced a century during which Mill's intellectual stock fell, and his radicalism was covered over with dust. Friedrich Hayek would follow in a similar vein in 1951, describing Mill as 'a great moral figure perhaps rather than a great thinker'. Mill would not have been troubled by Nietzsche's dismissal of him as 'flathead', but would have been justifiably incensed at being labelled by him as 'respectable'.[13]

The serious work of attacking Mill's philosophy began in his own century, with some gentle but relentless unpicking of his so-called utilitarianism by Sidgwick, and full-frontal assaults by James Fitzjames Stephen, F. H. Bradley and William Stanley Jevons – who described Mill's theoretical work as an 'incubus of bad logic and bad philosophy'.[14] However, his posthumous decline was not caused by scholarly erosion. Larger forces were at work. Mill's subtle and nuanced discussions of the nature of liberty, democracy and socialism were eclipsed by the emerging, titanic struggle between collectivism and individualism, and he was retrospectively recruited as a leading advocate of the ultra-liberal school of thought. As Stefan Collini has persuasively shown, two turn-of-the century works – Albert V. Dicey's *Law and Public Opinion in the Nineteenth Century* and Leslie Stephen's *The English Utilitarians* – were instrumental in this repackaging of Mill's position. For Dicey, *On Liberty* was 'the final and conclusive demonstration of the absolute truth of individualism' and Stephen concluded that 'the general disparagement of so-called "individualism" has led for some time to a lower estimate of Mill's services to liberal principles'. By 1947, Ernest Barker's influential history of nineteenth-century political thought was positioning Mill as 'the prophet of an empty liberty and an abstract individual'.[15] Despite, Mill's 'liberty' being full to the brim, and his 'individual' described in graphic, realistic detail – the label as an 'extreme' libertarian stuck to Mill's reputation.

The late twentieth century saw a flowering of Mill studies, however, and a renewed interest in the application of his thought to modern dilemmas. The completion of the first *Collected Edition* of his works in 1991 – accurately described by one scholar as 'an outstanding monument of editorial scholarship' – provides some explanation for the revival. For the first time, the whole of his published thought was in print. Mill once pointed to the paradox that the generations immediately following Aristotle did not have access to some of his most important treatises, which lay in an underground hiding place in Skepsis, Asia Minor, for a century and a half; later scholars were therefore able to make a better fist of appraising his work.[16] Something similar can be said of Mill: much of the content of the *Collected Works* was buried in archives and attics for a similar period.

John Morley reflected that Mill's 'true ambition . . . was to affect the course of events in his time by affecting the course of thought'.[17] In fact, Mill came to believe that much of his writing would have more value in the future than in his own time. He was right. It is hard to think of a point in our history where his words could be more useful, more needed, than today. Stefan Collini suggests that if Mill 'is to have a claim on the attention of any but scholarly specialists in the twenty-first century it will be on account of the continued vitality of a political theory calling itself "liberal".'[18] There is a good deal of truth in this remark; but the resuscitation of just such a theory may itself require a rediscovery of John Stuart Mill.

With the exception of the odd plaque, the Watts portrait and the Embankment statue, there is no shrine to which Mill admirers can make their pilgrimage. His house in Avignon was bulldozed in 1961 to make way for an ugly block of flats, although the row of trees, along which the nightingales hopped, remain. In a side-room of the Palais du Roure in Avignon sits his Broadwood piano, badly out of tune. In a nearby corner, unlabelled and out of sight, is a medium-sized bust of his head. Mill himself would have been utterly indifferent to this treatment. His books are pored over, and argued over, across the world. His causes – for liberty, for women, for justice – have advanced and are fought for still. And his questions are our questions once again. Goethe said that one of the measures of genius was posthumous productivity; in which case Mill's claim is unanswerable.

Mill's legacy rests not only in the power of his thought, however, but also in the inspiring conduct of his life – the finest example of thought in action of the last two centuries. He is unquestionably the greatest public intellectual in the history of Britain – and perhaps even the world. One of his rivals for the global title, Benjamin

Franklin (who Mill, unsurprisingly, greatly admired), gave some advice to anyone who wished to be remembered: 'Either write things worth reading, or do things worth the writing.' Mill is among the very few who managed both. One of the results of reading history, according to Mill, is to see a long succession of historical characters who have 'strutted and fretted their hour upon the stage' and he recorded his 'unbounded contempt for all those lives which make a great noise in their day, and leave the state of mankind in no respect better than they found it'.[19] Mill himself was hardly quiet, but his gifts to the cause of human progress were generous indeed. The world he left was unquestionably better for his efforts. It still is.

Notes

><

Unless otherwise stated, all references to Mill's work are to the complete edition, *Collected Works of John Stuart Mill*, 33 volumes, in the following form: *CW*, XXV, p. 1107. A full list of the volumes appears at the beginning of the Bibliography. The following abbreviations of Mill's principal works are used in the notes:

Autobiography (*AB*)
Auguste Comte and Positivism (*Comte*)
An Examination of Sir William Hamilton's Philosophy (*Hamilton*)
A System of Logic: Ratiocinative and Inductive (*Logic*)
On Liberty (*OL*)
The Principles of Political Economy (*POPE*)
Considerations on Representative Government (*Rep. Gov.*)
The Subjection of Women (*Subjection*)
Utilitarianism (*Util.*)

Prologue

1. Richard Carlile, 'What is Love?', in M. L. Bush (ed.), *The Republican*, 6 May 1825, p. 73.
2. For historical analyses of this incident, see Norman Himes, 'John Stuart Mill's attitude towards neo-Malthusianism', *Economic Journal* (Economic History Series no.4, Supplement), January 1929, especially pp. 462–74, and Francis Mineka in the *Mill News Letter*, vol. VIII, no 1. (Fall 1972). There is also a letter from John Robertson to Lord Amberley written on 23 May 1873, which refers to it; Robertson suggested that Mill had been incarcerated for '3 or 4

days': see *The Amberley Papers*, ed. Bertrand Russell and Patricia Russell, 2 vols, London: Allen and Unwin, 1937, vol. 2, p. 248.

3. Thomas Moore, 'Ode to the Goddess Ceres', lines 21–4 (1826), published in *The Times* on 21 February 1826. The single verse was reprinted in *The Times* in Mill's obituary on 10 May 1873, p. 5.

4. William Christie, *John Stuart Mill and Mr. Abraham Hayward Q.C. A reply about Mill to a letter to the Rev. Stopford Brooke, privately circulated and actually published*, London: Henry S. King and Co., 1873. p. 10.

5. John Morley, *Recollections*, 2 vols, London: Macmillan, 1917, vol. 1, p. 55.

6. Henry Trimen, 'His Botanical Studies', in H. R. Fox Bourne (ed.), *John Stuart Mill: Notices of His Life and Works*, London: Dallow, 1873, p. 30.

7. The first quote is from 'Mr Mill as a Politician', *Saturday Review* (22), 11 August 1866, pp. 167–9; and the second is from Leslie Stephen, 'The Late John Stuart Mill', *The Nation*, 5 June 1873, pp. 382–3.

8. John Morley, 'John Stuart Mill: An Anniversary', *Times Literary Supplement*, 18 May 1906, p. 1735; reprinted in *Morley's Critical Miscellanies*, Fourth Series, London: Macmillan, 1908.

9. John Stuart Mill, *The Subjection of Women*, London: Longmans, 1870. *CW*, XXI, p. 307.

10. Journal, 25 February 1854, *CW*, XXVII, pp. 657–8. (Mill kept a journal in 1854 when his life was threatened.)

11. Speech to Parliament on 'Representation of the People', 31 May 1866. *CW*, XXVIII, pp. 85–6.

12. 'Coleridge', *London and Westminster Review*, March 1840. *CW*, X, p. 155.

13. 'The Negro Question', *Fraser's Magazine*, January 1850. *CW*, XXI, p. 95.

14. In a letter to Harriet Taylor Mill (HTM), 17 February 1855. *CW*, XIV, p. 332.

15. R. H. Hutton, 'Mr John Stuart Mill's *Autobiography*', *Spectator*, 46 (1873), quoted in Stefan Collini, *Public Moralists: Political Thought and Intellectual Life in Great Britain 1850–1930*, Oxford: Clarendon Press, 1991, p. 322. In a similar vein, Hayek wrote almost eighty years later that it was 'one of the most impersonal accounts of a mental development ever attempted', Friedrich Hayek, *John Stuart Mill and Harriet Taylor – Their Correspondence and Subsequent Marriage*, London: Routledge and Kegan Paul, 1951, p. 17.

16. Hugh Brogan, *Alexis de Tocqueville – Prophet of Democracy in the Age of Revolution*, London: Profile, 2006, p. 371.

17. Quoted in Asa Briggs, *Victorian People – A Reassessment of Persons and Themes 1851–67*, London: Penguin, 1965, p. 22.

18. The term 'public moralists' is Stefan Collini's: see his volume of that name and also his 'Introduction' to *CW*, XXI, pp. viii–xix.

19. *Subjection*, *CW*, XXI, p. 323.

20. Millicent Garrett Fawcett, 'His Influence as a Practical Politician', in Fox Bourne (ed.), *John Stuart Mill: Life and Works*, p. 61.

21. John Stuart Mill, *On Liberty*, London: Longmans, 1869. *CW*, XVIII, p. 310.

1. An Unusual and Remarkable Education (1806–20)

1. James Mill to William Forbes, a relative of his patron John Stuart, on 7 July 1806, quoted by Anna J. Mill, 'The Education of John Stuart Mill – Some Further Evidence', *Mill News Letter*, XI, no.1 (Winter 1976), pp. 10–11.

2. Quoted in the introduction to *The Letters of John Stuart Mill*, ed. Hugh S. R. Elliot, London: Longmans, 1910, p. xv.

3. Alexander Bain, *James Mill, a Biography*, London: Longmans, Green and Company, 1882, p. 119.

4. Isaiah Berlin, 'John Stuart Mill and the Ends of Life' in *Four Essays on Liberty*, Oxford: Oxford University Press, 1969, p. 175.

5. John Stuart Mill, *Autobiography*, *CW*, I, p. 13.

6. *AB*, *CW*, I, p. 21.

7. Michael Packe, *The Life of John Stuart Mill*, New York: Macmillan, 1954, p. 4.

8. Bain, *James Mill*, p. 110.

9. *AB*, *CW*, I, p. 57. Mill also wrote in a letter to James M. Barnard, 28 October 1869: 'I can trace a great influence in my own development to the accident of having passed several years of my boyhood in one of the few old abbeys which are still inhabited.' *CW*, XVII, pp. 1661–2.

10. Letter from James Mill to Frances Place, 7 December 1814, quoted in Graham Wallas, *Life of Francis Place 1771–1854*, London: Longmans, 1898, p. 70.

11. Paul Johnson, *The Birth of the Modern: World Society 1815–1830*, London: Weidenfeld and Nicolson, 1991, p. 725.

12. *AB*, *CW*, I, p. 39.

13. *AB*, Early Draft Rejected Leaves, *CW*, I, p. 612. (Mill drafted various sections of the *Autobiography* which were not used in the final version.)

14. Henry Solly in 1832: Henry Solly, 'These Eighty Years', or, *The Story of an Unfinished Life*, 2 vols, London: Simpkin, Marshall, 1893, vol. 1, pp. 147–8, quoted in Packe, *Mill*, p. 105.

15. *AB*, Early Draft Rejected Leaves, *CW*, I, pp. 612–13.

16. Mill's third sister Harriet, in a letter to the Revd J. Crompton (26 October 1873), quoted in Packe, *Mill*, p. 33n.

17. Harriet Grote in conversation with Kate Amberley, 4 December 1865, *The Amberley Papers*, vol. 1, p. 412.

18. *The Works of Jeremy Bentham*, 10

vols, ed. John Bowring, New York: Russell and Russell, 1838–1962, vol. X, p. 567.

19. Letter from Francis Place to his wife, 17 and 20 August 1817, quoted in Wallas, *Francis Place*, p. 76.

20. *Romilly–Edgeworth Letters, 1813–1818*, ed. Samuel Henry Romilly, London: John Murray, 1936, pp. 177–9.

21. *AB, CW*, I, p. 35.

22. Ibid., p. 23.

23. Ibid., p. 25.

24. Leslie Stephen, *The English Utilitarians*, 3 vols, London: Duckworth and Co., 1900, vol. III, pp. 8–9, quoted in Jack Stillinger, 'Mill's Education – Fact, Fiction and Myth', in Michael Laine (ed.), *A Cultivated Mind: Essays on J. S. Mill Presented to John M. Robson*, Toronto: University of Toronto Press, 1961, p. 38.

25. The Bagshot story was recounted by James Mill in a letter to David Ricardo. See *The Works and Correspondence of David Ricardo*, ed. Piero Sraffa, 11 vols, Cambridge: Cambridge University Press, 1952, vol. VII, pp. 313–14.

26. *AB, CW*, I, p. 49.

27. Alexander Bain, after visiting Forde Abbey, wrote: 'In summer, when heating was required, they might easily have had a room apiece.' Bain, *James Mill*, p. 135.

28. For 'companionship' see Harriet Mill in her letter to the Revd J.

Crompton 26 October, 1873, quoted in Packe, *Mill*, p. 47.

29. *AB, CW*, I, p. 49.

30. *AB*, Early Draft Rejected Leaves, *CW*, I, p. 613.

31. Quoted in G. Karl Galinsky, *The Herakles Theme : the adaptations of the hero in literature from Homer to the twentieth century*, Oxford: Blackwell, 1972, p. 215.

32. *AB, CW*, I, p. 39.

33. Bain, *James Mill*, p. 333.

34. Caroline Fox, *Memories of Old Friends*, London: Smith, Elder and Co, 1883, journal entry for 10 April 1833, p. 107.

35. *AB, CW*, I, p. 51.

36. Quoted in Nicholas Capaldi, *John Stuart Mill: A Biography*, Cambridge: Cambridge University Press, 2004, p. 26.

37. Letter from Harriet Grote to Alexander Bain, 24 October 1873, reprinted in the *Mill News Letter*, vol. XIII, no. 2, Summer 1978, p. 18.

38. 'Wordsworth and Bryon', 30 January 1829, *CW*, XXVI, p. 434.

39. Letter to John Lalor, 27 June 1852, *CW*, XIV, p. 91.

40. *AB, CW*, I, p. 115.

41. Ibid., p. 17.

42. Alexander Bain, *John Stuart Mill: A Criticism with Personal Recollections*, London: Longmans, 1882, p. 191.

43. *AB*, Early Draft Rejected Leaves, *CW*, I, pp. 609, 612.

44. *AB, CW*, I, p. 53.

45. Letter to James Mill, almost certainly dating from autumn 1822,

written, according to Bain, during a visit to Norwich. Bain, *John Stuart Mill*, pp. 37–8. *CW*, XII, p. 14.

46. *AB*, *CW*, I, p. 17.

47. Letter to Sir Samuel Bentham, 30 July 1819, *CW*, XII, p. 7: 'The Greek which I read in the year 1815 was, I think, Homer's Odyssey ... In Latin I read the first six books, I believe, of Ovid's metamorphoses ...'

48. Johnson, *Birth of the Modern*, pp. xviii–xix.

49. *AB*, *CW*, I, p. 20.

50. Ibid., p. 23.

51. Ibid., p. 27.

52. *AB*, Early Draft Rejected Leaves, *CW*, I, p. 609.

53. *AB*, *CW*, I, p. 31.

54. Johnson, *Birth of the Modern*, p. 370.

55. *AB*, *CW*, I, p. 33.

56. Ibid., p. 55.

57. Capaldi, *Mill*, p. 36.

58. *AB*, *CW*, I, p. 33.

59. Ibid.

60. William Wordsworth, *The Prelude*, 1850, Book V, lines 341–4.

2. A Man Among Men (1820–16)

1. *Works of Jeremy Bentham*, vol. IX, pp. 380–1, quoted by John Robson in his 'Introduction' to Mill's *Journals and Debating Speeches*, *CW*, XXVI, p. xii.

2. *AB*, *CW*, I, p. 37.

3. *Works of Jeremy Bentham*, vol. IX, p. 386, quoted by John Robson in his 'Introduction' to Mill's

Journals and Debating Speeches, *CW*, XXVI, p. xii.

4. Journal entry, 28 May 1820, *CW*, XXVI, p. 15.

5. Journal entry, 31 May 1820, *CW*, XXVI, p. 17.

6. The earlier meeting is described by Mill in a later letter to Sir Samuel Bentham, 30 July 1819, *CW*, XII, p. 6.

7. *AB*, *CW*, I, p. 59.

8. *AB*, Early Draft Rejected Leaves, *CW*, I, p. 612.

9. Journal entry, 21 June 1820, *CW*, XXVI, p. 28.

10. Letter to James Mill, 24 June 1820, *CW*, XXVI, p. 25.

11. Johnson, *Birth of the Modern*, p. 537.

12. Quoted in Johnson, *Birth of the Modern*, p. 531.

13. Journal entry, 2 July 1820, *CW*, XXVI, p. 36.

14. Letter from Lady Bentham to James Mill, 14 September 1820, quoted in Bain, *John Stuart Mill*, p. 22.

15. For bookselves. see journal entry, 25 June 1820, *CW*, XXVI, p. 32.

16. Journal entry, 22 June 1820, *CW*, XXVI, p. 28.

17. Journal entries, 4, 5, 6, 7, 8 July 1820, *CW*, XXVI, pp. 38–41.

18. Journal entry, 8 July 1820, *CW*, XXVI, p. 41.

19. Journal entry, 28 July 1820, *CW*, XXVI, p. 58.

20. Mill reports that he 'understood a good deal' of Molière's play *L'estourdy, ou Les contretemps*, which he saw in Toulouse on 3

June 1820. Journal entry, *CW*, XXVI, p. 58. In the same month George Bentham recorded in his own journal that Mill had 'conversed a good deal in French about crops, the country he has passed etc.' and that he had made 'rapid progress in French'. See John Robson's 'Introduction' to Mill's *Journals and Debating Speeches*, *CW*, XXVI, p. xv.

21. Letter to Harriet Mill, 19 July 1820, *CW*, XXVI, p. 52.

22. *AB*, *CW*, I, p. 59.

23. Letter to Auguste Comte, 12 August 1842, *CW*, XIV, p. 540. Translation from *The Correspondence of John Stuart Mill and Auguste Comte*, ed. and trans. Oscar Haac, New Brunswick and London: Transaction, 1995, p. 93.

24. *AB*, *CW*, I, p. 59.

25. *AB*, *CW*, I, p. 63.

26. 'Inaugural delivered to the University of St. Andrews on February 1st 1867', *CW*, XXI, p. 226.

27. Letter from James Mill to David Ricardo, 23 August 1821, in Sraffa (ed.), *Works of David Ricardo*, vol. IX, p. 43.

28. *AB*, *CW*, I, p. 67.

29. Jeremy Bentham, *An Introduction to the Principles of Morals and Legislation* (first published in 1781 and included in the French translation of Bentham's work by Pierre Etienne Louis Dumont, Paris: Bossange, Masson & Besson, 1802), edited by Alan Ryan, London: Penguin, 1987, p. 65.

30. Bentham, *Introduction*, pp. 86–7.

31. Francis Hutcheson, *An Inquiry into the Original of Our Ideas of Beauty, Order, Harmony, Design*, Section iii, quoted in Roy Porter, *Enlightenment – Britain and the Creation of the Modern World*, London: Penguin, 2000, p. 168.

32. See Alan Ryan's 'Introduction' to John Stuart Mill and Jeremy Bentham, *Utilitarianism and Other Essays*, London: Penguin, 1987, p. 16.

33. See Alan Ryan, *J. S. Mill*, London: Routledge and Kegan Paul, 1974, p. 114.

34. Quoted by Martha Nussbaum in 'Mill's Feminism: Liberal, Radical and Queer', presented to the Mill Bicentennial Conference (MBC), University College London, 7 April 2006.

35. *AB*, *CW*, I, p. 69.

36. Ibid., p. 68.

37. Ibid., p. 73.

38. Johnson, *Birth of the Modern*, pp. 865–8 and p. 903.

39. Packe, *Mill*, p. 69.

40. Mary Mack, *Jeremy Bentham, An Odyssey of Ideas, 1748–1792*, New York: Columbia University Press, 1963, p. 336, quoted in Porter, *Enlightenment*, p. 422.

41. The passages are one third of three essays in which Macaulay attacked utilitarianism in general and James Mill's *Essay on Government* in particular: 'Utilitarian Theory of Government, and the "Greatest Happiness Principle"', *Edinburgh Review*, October 1829,

quoted in *Life and Letters of Lord Macaulay*, ed. George Otto Trevelyan, 2 vols, London & New York: Thomas Nelson & Sons, 1876, vol. 1, pp. 160–1.

42. Thomas Babington Macaulay, *Critical and Historical Essays, Contributed to the Edinburgh Review*, London: Longmans, 1867, vol. I, p. viii, quoted in Jane Millgate, *Macaulay*, London: Routledge, 1973, p. 25.

43. *AB, CW*, I, p. 123.

44. Ibid., p. 127.

45. Ibid.

46. Letter to John Bowring, 10 March 1828, *CW*, XII, p. 23.

47. Both quotes from *AB, CW*, I, p. 79.

48. *Life and Letters of Lord Macaulay*, vol. 1, p. 96.

49. For a description of the intersection between Mill's views on friendship, as influenced by the 'Trijackia' and his evolving views on character, see 'The Formation of Character: Mill's "Ethology" Reconsidered', Terence Ball, *Polity*, vol. 33, No. 1 (Autumn 2000), pp. 25–48.

50. *Autobiography and Letters of John Arthur Roebuck*, ed. Robert Eaden Leader, London: E. Arnold, 1897, cited in Packe, *Mill*, pp. 67–8.

51. Bain, *John Stuart Mill*, pp. 39–40.

52. On 29 March 1823, Townshend wrote to James Mill: 'I again entreat you to permit me to write to the tutor at Trinity to enter your son's name at that noble college. Whatever you may wish his eventual destiny to be, his prosperity in life cannot be retarded, but must on the contrary be increased, by making an acquaintance at an English University with his Patrician contemporaries'; quoted in Bain, *John Stuart Mill*, p. 29.

53. Quoted in Packe, *Mill*, p. 19.

54. Both quotes from *AB, CW*, I, p. 85.

55. *AB, CW*, I, p. 67.

56. 'The Influence of Lawyers', 30 March 1827 [?], *CW*, XXVI, p. 389.

57. *AB, CW*, I, p. 85.

58. See Briggs, *Victorian People*, p. 108.

59. William Thornton, 'His Career in the India House', in Fox Bourne (ed.), *John Stuart Mill: Life and Works*, p. 22.

60. Quoted in Alan Ryan's 'Introduction' to *J. S. Mill's Encounter with India*, Martin Moir, Douglas Peers and Lynn Zastoupil (eds), Toronto, Buffalo and London: Toronto University Press, 1999, p. 14.

61. The calculation of the value of Mill's £2,000 salary (which he received from 1856 until his retirement in 1858) is based on the data series created by Lawrence H. Officer, Professor of Economics at the University of Illinois at Chicago, and Samuel H. Williamson, Professor of Economics Emeritus, at Miami University, which is

available at www.measuring
worth.com. I have used the GDP
deflator series rather than Retail
Price Index (RPI), but the estimate is still likely to be on the
conservative side. All subsequent
financial comparisons in this volume are made on the same basis,
unless otherwise stated.

62. *AB*, Early Draft Cancelled Text,
CW, I, p. 84n.

63. Comment made by JSM in 1832,
recorded in Henry Solly, *These
Eighty Years*, London: Simpkin,
Marshall, 1893, vol. 1. p. 204.

64. Trevor Lloyd, 'Mill and the East
India Company', in Laine (ed.),
A Cultivated Mind, pp. 72–3.

65. *AB*, *CW*, I, p. 67.

66. Ibid., p. 129.

67. 'Population: Reply to Thirlwall',
1825, *CW*, XXVI, p. 305.

68. *AB*, *CW*, I, p. 129.

69. *AB*, *CW*, I, p. 73.

70. Speech on 'Parliamentary
Reform' to the Mutual Improve-
ment Society, August 1824, *CW*,
XXVI, p. 262, and on 'Population'
at the Co-operative Society, 1825,
CW, XXVI, p. 286.

71. 'John Arthur Roebuck', *British
Ladies' Newspaper*, 27 January
1838, p. 56, quoted by John Robson in his 'Introduction', *CW*,
XXVI, p. xxviii.

72. Letters from Henry Taylor (no
relation to Harriet) to his mother
in December 1825, and to his
father (undated), *Correspondence
of Henry Taylor*, ed. Edward
Dowden, London: Longmans,

1888, pp. 6–7, quoted by Robson
in his 'Introduction', *CW* XXVI,
p. xxvi.

73. Stefan Collini, 'Introduction' to
*Essays on Equality, Law and
Education*, *CW*, XXI, p. xxv.

74. 'The British Constitution', May
1826, *CW*, XXVI, p. 379.

75. 'The Universities', 7 April 1826,
CW, XXVI, p. 355.

76. 'Parliamentary Reform' [2]
August 1824, *CW*, XXVI, p. 277.

77. 'Population: Reply to Thirlwall',
1825, *CW*, XXVI, p. 298.

78. 'Parliamentary Reform', August
1824, *CW*, XXVI, pp. 269–70.

79. See Packe, *Mill*, p. 72.

80. *AB*, *CW*, I, p. 73.

81. François Emmanuel Toulongeon,
*Histoire de France, depuis la
révolution de 1789*, 4 vols, Paris;
Treuttel and Würtz, 1801 –10. In
a letter to Charles Comte on 25
January 1828, Mill said that he
had read Toulongeon's and
Mignet's histories of the revolution, *CW*, XII, p. 23. As Mignet's
book was not published until
1824, it seems likely that he was
referring to Toulongeon. Mill
reviewed Mignet's history in the
Westminster Review in April 1826,
CW, XX, pp. 3–14.

82. *AB*, *CW*, I, p. 65.

83. As part of his education, Mill
wrote 'a defence of Pericles on a
supposed impeachment for not
marching out to fight the
Lacedaemonians on their invasion of Attica', *AB*, *CW*, I, p. 75.

84. *AB*, *CW*, I, p. 67.

85. Ibid., p. 119.
86. 'Exchangeable Value', *Traveller*, 6 December 1822, *CW*, XXII, pp. 3–5.
87. Mill's first article in the *Morning Chronicle* was published under the title 'Religious Persecution' on 1 January 1823, *CW*, XXII, pp. 6–7. His first piece in the *Westminster Review* was 'Periodical Literature: *Edinburgh Review*', April 1824. *CW*, I, pp. 291–325.
88. Packe, *Mill*, p. 61.
89. An outstanding public speaker, Henry Hunt (1773–1835) in August 1819 addressed the crowd at the great meeting at St Peter's Fields, which led to the 'Peterloo Massacre', for which he spent two years in jail. From 1830 to 1833 he was Radical Member of Parliament for Preston.
90. Johnson, *Birth of the Modern*, p. 367.
91. Ibid., pp. 534–5.
92. Ibid., p. 537.
93. Porter, *Enlightenment*, p. 201. At the same time, after the bloodshed of Peterloo, the radical movement became a bit more bookish. As Johnson puts it, 'the agitators turned from violence, arms and drilling to education, propaganda, and doctrine', *Birth of the Modern*, p. 870.
94. James Mill's article was 'Periodical Literature: *Edinburgh Review*', January 1824, *Westminster Review*. See *AB, CW*, pp. 93–6. Mill wrote the next instalment of the attack for the April 1824 issue; *CW*, I, pp. 291–325.
95. *AB, CW*, I, p. 95.
96. Ibid., p. 97.
97. Immanuel Kant, 'Answering the Question: What is Enlightenment?' *Berlin Monthly*, December 1784.
98. *AB, CW*, I, p. 111.
99. Ibid., p. 101.
100. Ibid., p. 103.
101. Ibid., p. 105.
102. Ibid., pp. 122–3.
103. Leader (ed.), *Roebuck*, p. 28, quoted in Capaldi, *Mill*, p. 43.
104. In the letter to his father; see note 10 above
105. 'Blessings of Equal Justice', *Morning Chronicle*, 20 August 1823, *CW*, XXII, pp. 43–6.
106. 'Population: Reply to Thirlwall', 1825, *CW*, XXVI, p. 298. Mill may have had some support, though: as Professor William Stafford points out in a personal communication, the cooperative movement contained its own feminist strand.
107. *AB, CW*, I, p. 107.
108. Marie Jean Antoine Nicolas Caritat de Condorcet, *Vie de Monsieur Turgot*, London, 1786, pp. 28–9. *AB, CW*, I, p. 117.
109. *AB, CW*, I, p. 117.
110. The unpublished essays are not extant.
111. 'Free Discussion' [1st letter], *Morning Chronicle*, 28 January 1828, *CW*, XXII, p. 11. The next two letters were published on the

8 and 12 February. *CW*, XXII, pp. 12–15.

112. 'Ireland./The ADDRESS – Catholic Association – Catholic Claims – Elective Franchise – Provision for Catholic Clergy – Church Establishment, &c.', *Parliamentary History and Review, Containing Reports of the Proceedings of the Two Houses of Parliament during the Session of 1825*, 2 vols, London: Longmans, 1826, vol. 2 pp. 603–26. *CW*, VI, pp. 59–98.

113. *Life and Letters of Macaulay*, vol. 1, p. 184.

114. William Hazlitt, *The Spirit of the Age* (1825), Oxford: Oxford University Press, 1935, pp. 14–15. The volume can now be downloaded as an e-book for free at www.gutenberg.org/etext/11068.

115. *AB*, *CW*, I, p. 117.

116. Letter to Jeremy Bentham, April 1827, *CW*, XII, p. 18.

117. Letter from Bentham to Mill, 24 April 1827, reprinted in *CW*, XII, p. 18, n1.

118. *AB*, *CW*, I, p. 119.

119. Letter to William Johnson Fox, 3 April 1832, *CW*, XII, p. 97.

120. 'Brodie's History of the British Empire', *Westminster Review*, October 1824, *CW*, VI, p. 5.

121. Hazlitt, *Spirit of the Age*, p. 223.

122. 'Population: Reply to Thirlwall', 1825, *CW*, XXVI, p. 303.

123. 'Parliamentary Reform' [1] August 1824, *CW*, XXVI, p. 263. Mill's objections to the staus quo were not based on a particular constitutional theory, but on the pernicious effects of the current structure on the quality of government. In a speech given in May 1826 on 'The British Constitution', he said: 'I care ... little about the theory of the Constitution. I care not by what machinery my pocket is picked: picked or not is the essential point.' *CW*, XXVI, p. 358.

124. 'Parliamentary Reform' [2], August 1824, *CW*, XXVI, p. 273.

125. 'Parliamentary Reform' [1], August 1824, *CW*, XXVI, p. 264.

126. 'The British Constitution', May 1826, *CW*, XXVI, p. 373.

127. 'Influence of the Aristocracy', 9 December 1825, *CW*, XXVI, p. 334.

128. Ibid., pp. 327–8.

129. 'Parliamentary Reform' [1], August 1824, *CW*, XXVI, p. 265.

130. 'The British Constitution', May 1826, *CW*, XXVI, pp. 380–81.

131. 'Primogeniture', 20 January 1826, *CW*, XXVI, p. 336.

132. Ibid.

133. *AB*, *CW*, I, p. 113.

134. Ibid., p. 111.

135. I am grateful to Andrew Saunders for reminding me of this song.

136. 'Population: Reply to Thirlwall', 1825, *CW*, XXVI, p. 307.

3. Strange Confusion (1826–30)

1. *AB*, *CW*, I, p. 69.

2. Collini, *Public Moralists*, p. 122.

3. *AB*, *CW*, I, p. 139.

4. See Kathleen Thomas, *The Crisis*

and Analysis of John Stuart Mill's Life, Durham: Pentland Press, 1994, pp. 7–9; Packe, *Mill*, p. 74; Gertrude Himmelfarb, 'Clio and Oedipus', *Times Literary Supplement*, 23 May 1975, pp. 565–6, quoted in Alan Ryan, 'Sense and Sensibility in Mill's Political Thought', in Laine (ed.), *A Cultivated Mind*, p. 137; and Capaldi, *Mill*, p. 57.

5. *AB, CW*, I, p. 143.

6. Ibid., p. 149.

7. Ibid., p. 139.

8. Macbeth, Act V, scene iii, ll. 40–5; *AB, CW*, I, p. 139.

9. *AB, CW*, I, p. 145. Jean François Marmontel, *Mémoires d'un père*, 4 vols, London: Peltier, 1805, vol. I, pp. 87–8.

10. William Wordsworth, 'Ode: Intimations of Immortality from Recollections in Early Child-hood', 1815, ll. 23–7. (First published in 1807 as 'Ode: There Was a Time'.)

11. Wordsworth, 'Ode', ll. 108–12.

12. *AB, CW*, I, p. 151.

13. Morley, *Recollections*, vol. I, p. 67.

14. Robert Browning was similarly provoked by Wordsworth's perceived treachery to pen his poem 'The Lost Leader'. Johnson, *Birth of the Modern*, p. 431.

15. Morley, *Recollections*, vol. 1, p. 67.

16. Porter, *Enlightenment*, pp. 89–90.

17. Fox, *Memories of Old Friends* p. 141.

18. *AB, CW*, I, p. 147.

19. 'Perfectability', 2 May 1828, *CW* CW,, XXVI, p. 432.

20. Robson, 'Introduction' to *Journals and Debating Speeches, CW*, XXVI, p. xli.

21. Most recently, the philosopher Martha Nussbaum has argued that 'emotions are not just the fuel that powers the psycho-logical mechanism of a reasoning creature, they are parts, highly complex and messy parts, of this creature's reasoning itself'. *Upheavals of Thought – The Intelligence of Emotions*, Cambridge and New York: Cambridge University Press, 1991, p. 3.

22. 'It is not every one who has either the physical power or the inclination to speak for two hours', Mill said in 'Cooperation: Closing Speech', 1825, *CW*, XXVI, p. 319. Henry Cole reported that Mill spoke for two hours in the poetry debate; see *CW*, XXVI, p. 434.

23. 'Wordsworth and Byron', 30 January 1829, *CW*, XXVI, p. 435.

24. 'The Present State of Literature', 16 November 1827, *CW*, XXVI, p. 410.

25. 'Wordsworth and Byron', 30 January 1829, *CW*, XXVI, p. 441.

26. *AB, CW*, I, p. 139.

27. Wordsworth gave the poem to Coleridge because, at that point, he had no answer to the question with which these stanzas end: 'Whither is fled the visionary gleam? / Where is it now, the

glory and the dream?' Coleridge published 'Dejection' in 1802, after which Wordsworth completed the poem.

28. *AB*, *CW*, I, p. 163.

29. Letter to John Sterling, 15 April 1829, *CW*, XII, p. 30.

30. The quote is from Macaulay's 1829 attack on utilitarianism; see Trevelyan, *Life and Letters of Macaulay*, vol. 1, p. 161 and p. 38 in Chapter 2 of this volume.

31. 'The Use of History', 1827, *CW*, XXVI, p. 397. This is almost a paraphrase of some lines in Wordsworth's 'Lines Left Upon a Seat in a Yew Tree', 1798: '. . . he, who feels contempt / For any living thing, hath faculties / Which he has never used . . . O, be wiser thou! / Instructed that true knowledge lead to love . . .'

32. Harriet Grote in conversation with Kate Amberley, 4 December 1865: 'J. S. Mill wrote an essay (never printed it) when he was young against all sentiment & feeling etc. He was much ashamed of it later in life & got Mrs. Grote's copy fr. her and destroyed it.' *The Amberley Papers*, vol. 1, p. 421.

33. William Wordsworth, 'Preface to the *Lyrical Ballads*' (1802), *Wordsworth: The Major Works*, Oxford: Oxford University Press, 2000, p. 605.

34. Letter to Carlyle, 5 July 1833, *CW*, XII, p. 163.

35. 'What is Poetry', *Monthly Repository*, January and October 1833. *CW*, I, p. 363.

36. Peregrine Bingham, 'Moore's *Fables for the Holy Alliance*', p. 21, quoted in *AB*, *CW*, I, p. 115.

37. Wordsworth, *The Prelude*, Book X, ll. 818–23.

38. In the early nineteenth century, this was not such an idiosyncratic view as it would be today. Poets and political philosophers were not yet mutually exclusive categories, and most leading poets – Wordsworth, Tennyson, Coleridge, Southey – were politically active, generally as youthful radicals maturing into thoughtful conservatives.

39. 'What is Poetry', *Monthly Repository*, January and October 1833. *CW*, I, pp. 343–65.

40. For the quote 'poetry is overhead', see *CW*, I, p. 348.

41. Mill wrote in the *Autobiography* that while he 'had several relapses, some of which lasted many months, I never again was as miserable as I had been', *AB*, *CW*, I, p. 145. Bain writes that the 1820 'crisis' was a harbinger of the 'maladies that oppressed the second half of his life'; Bain, *John Stuart Mill*, p. 38. In a letter to Thomas Carlyle, 11 and 12 April 1833, Mill wrote: 'At all events I will not if I can help it give way to gloom and morbid despondency, of which I have had a large share in my short life . . . I will and must . . . master it,

or it will surely master me.' *CW*, XII, p. 149.

42. William Minto, 'His Miscellaneous Criticisms', in Fox Bourne (ed.), *John Stuart Mill: Life and Works*, p. 33.

43. 'What is Poetry?', January 1833, *CW*, I, p. 356. In the same article, Mill described poetry as 'impassioned truth' and 'man's thoughts tinged by feelings', *CW*, I, p. 348.

44. 'Tennyson's Poems', *London Review*, July 1835, *CW*, I, pp. 399, 414.

45. William Griffin and Harry Minchin, *The Life of Robert Browning*, London: Methuen, 1911, pp. 58–60.

46. Letter to Thomas Carlyle, 22 October 1821, *CW*, XII, p. 128.

47. *AB*, *CW*, I, p. 133.

48. Letter to Charles Maurice (Frederick Maurice's son), 19 May 1872, *CW*, XVII, p. 1898.

49. *AB*, *CW*, I, p. 161.

50. 'Long and rambling', according to Henry Cole, whose diaries recorded the activities of the Society and are held at the Victoria and Albert Museum, London; quoted in Robson's 'Introduction', *CW*, XXVI, p. xxxi. Mill, however, later described Sterling's speech as 'brilliant', *AB*, *CW*, I, p. 153.

51. John Sterling, *The Election, a Poem, in Seven Books*, London: John Murray, 1841, ll. 9–11. Mill warmly reviewed the poem: 'Sterling's The Election',

Morning Chronicle, 29 July 1841, *CW*, XXIV, pp. 806–11, and cited these lines, p. 807.

52. Anne Kimball Tuell, *John Sterling, a Representative Victorian*, London: Macmillan, 1941, p. 69, quoted in Packe, *Mill*, p. 86.

53. Letter to John Sterling, 15 April 1829, *CW*, XII, p. 29.

54. Adams was also a husband to Mary Place, Francis Place's daughter, and, after Mary's death, to Sarah Flower.

55. Letter to William Bridges Adams, 20 October 1832, *CW*, XII, pp.123–4.

56. Quoted in Newsome, *Victorian World Picture*, p. 57.

57. 'The Old Cumberland Beggar'(1800), *Major Works*, p. 605, ll. 66–70.

58. *CW*, XXVII, pp. 482, 491, 480, 493.

59. Ibid., p. 493.

60. John Ruskin similarly lamented Cole's advocacy of 'mechanical standards of excellence'. Roger Ellis, *Who's Who in Victorian Britain*, London: Shepheard-Walwyn, 1997, p. 124.

61. See especially *CW*, XXVII, pp. 522–9.

62. Letter to John Sterling, 20–22 October 1831, *CW*, XII, p. 81.

63. 'The Present State of Literature', 16 November 1827, *CW*, XXVI, p. 413.

64. Bain, *James Mill*, p. 285.

65. See 'Mill's Essay on Government, Utilitarian Logic and Politics' (March 1829);

'Bentham's Defence of Mill.
Utilitarian System of Philosophy'
(June 1829); 'Utilitarian Theory
of Government, and the
"Greatest Happiness Principle"'
(October 1829), all in the
Edinburgh Review; this passage is
also quoted in Packe, *Mill*, p. 88.

66. Quoted in Eugene August, *John
Stuart Mill – A Mind at Large*,
London: Vision Press, 1976, p. 37.

67. For evidence of Mill's interest
during this period, see letters to
Gustave d'Eichthal, 15 May 1829,
CW, XII, pp. 30–34; 8 October
1829, *CW*, XII, pp. 34–8, and 7
November 1829, *CW*, XII, pp.
38–43. Mill discussed one of
Saint-Simon's most important
works, *Nouveau christianisme,
dialogues entre un conservateur et
un novateur* in 'Fontana and
Prati's St. Simonism in London'
in the *Examiner*, 2 February 1834,
CW, XIII, pp. 674–80.

68. 'The Spirit of the Age I', 9
January 1831, *Examiner*, *CW*,
XXII, p. 228.

69. Packe, *Mill*, p. 101.

70. 'The Spirit of the Age I', *CW*,
XXII, p. 230.

71. 'The Spirit of the Age III', 6
February 1831, *Examiner*, *CW*,
XXII, pp. 257–8.

72. *AB*, *CW*, I, p. 169.

73. Ibid., pp. 181 and 181n; see also
Richard Sanders et al., *The
Collected Letters of Thomas and
Jane Welsh Carlyle*, Durham, NC:
Duke University Press, 1970, vol.
V, pp. 235n and 398.

74. Henry Cole, *Diary*, 23 November
1831, quoted in Joseph
Hamburger, *Intellectuals in
Politics: John Stuart Mill and the
Philosophic Radicals*, New Haven,
CT: Yale University Press, 1961,
p. 76.

75. Letter to Gustave d'Eichthal, 7
November 1829, *CW*, XII, p. 38.

76. Letter to John Sterling, 20–22
October 1831, *CW*, XII, p. 84.

77. *AB*, *CW*, I, p. 179.

78. According to Roebuck; see
Leader (ed.), *Roebuck*, p. 28,
quoted in John Cairns,
'Introduction', *Essays on French
History and Historians*, *CW*, XX,
p. lvii.

79. Letter to James Mill, 13 August
1830, *CW*, XII, p. 54.

80. 'French News' [73], *Examiner*,
2 December 1832, *CW*, XXIII,
p. 531.

81. *AB*, *CW*, I, p. 169.

82. 'The Coalition Ministry', 29 June
1827, *CW*, XXVI, p. 402.

83. Ibid., p. 399.

84. Letter to Thomas Carlyle, 5
October 1833, *CW*, XII, p. 181.

85. Letter to Thomas Carlyle, 12
January 1834, *CW*, XII, p. 205.

86. Basil Willey, *Nineteenth Century
Studies: Coleridge to Matthew
Arnold*, New York: Columbia
University Press, 1949, chapter
VI, quoted in Thomas Woods,
*Poetry and Philosophy, A Study in
the Thought of John Stuart Mill*,
London: Hutchinson, 1961, p. 46.

4. This Imperfect Companionship (1830–6)

1. Brougham was elected in 1830 as MP for Yorkshire, 'or rather one should say the Member for Leeds, Huddersfield and Sheffield', all then towns without their own representation, according to the Whig MP for Newcastle, William Orde, quoted in Johnson, *Birth of the Modern*, p. 991.

2. It was Henry Solly's sister. Mill's quote is from a letter to Gustave d'Eichthal, 9 February 1830, *CW*, XII, p. 44.

3. *Memoir of the Reverend Sydney Smith by his daughter Lady Holland*, 2 vols, London: Longmans, 1855, vol. 1, p. 320; quoted in *CW*, XIV, p. 431, n10.

4. Leader (ed.), *Roebuck*, p. 38.

5. The only evidence for this is in Moncure D. Conway, *Centenary History of the South Place Society*, London: Williams and Norgate, 1894, p. 89, quoted in Hayek, *Mill and Taylor*, p. 29.

6. James Anthony Froude, *Thomas Carlyle: A History of the First Forty Years of Life, 1795–1835*, 2 vols, London: Longmans, 1882, vol. 2, p. 190.

7. Fox, *Memories of Old Friends*, p. 85.

8. Thomas Carlyle, *Reminiscences*, ed. James Anthony Froude, 2 vols, London: Longmans, 1881, vol. 1, p. 11, quoted in Capaldi, *Mill*, p. 82.

9. In conversation with Kate Amberley, 19 February 1865, *Amberley Papers*, vol. 1, pp. 371–2.

10. Letter from Thomas Carlyle to Dr John Carlyle, 22 July 1834, quoted in Froude, *Carlyle*, vol. 2, p. 441.

11. Richard Garnett, *The Life of W. J. Fox, public teacher & social reformer, 1786–1864*, London: J. Lane, 1910, p. 66. Fox's daughter would have been about seven at the time.

12. Quoted in Newsome, *Victorian World Picture*, p. 57.

13. 'Blue-Stocking Revels; or, The Feast of the Violets', first published in July 1837 in the *Monthly Repository*, of which Hunt had become editor; reprinted in *The Poetical Works of Leigh Hunt*, Oxford: Oxford University Press, 1832/1923, p. 176, Canto I, ll. 8, 11–12.

14. Letter to Thomas Carlyle, 17 September 1832, *CW*, XII, p. 118.

15. *AB*, *CW*, I, p. 193.

16. Letter from Eliza Flower to Harriet Taylor, undated but which Hayek argues, I think correctly, is continued in another letter which is dated 30 June 1831, *Mill–Taylor Collection* in the British Library of Political and Economic Science, XXVII/32 and XXVII/37, ff. 17–70. The review of Byron appeared in the *Edinburgh Review* in June 1831; in fact neither of them wrote it.

17. Letter from B. E. Desainteville to John Taylor, also undated but

mentioning a dinner which included not only Mill but also Alexandre Bontemps, a Saint-Simonian who visited London in the early months of 1831, *Mill–Taylor Collection*, XXIX/257, ff. 25–6. Harriet's invitation to Mill, dated 28 January, refers to dinner with 'some friends of M. Desainteville', Jo Ellen Jacobs, Paula Harms Payne (eds), *The Complete Works of Harriet Taylor Mill*, Bloomington, Ind.: Indiana University Press, 1998, p. 323. Mill referred to his meeting with Bontemps in a letter to Gustave d'Eichthal, 1 March 1831, *CW*, XII p. 71.

18. Letter to Harriet Taylor, August 1832, *CW*, XII, p. 114. The letter is in French, translation in Packe, *Mill*, p. 139.

19. Heinrich Gomperz, *Theodor Gomperz, Briefe und Aufzeichnungen*, 2 vols, Vienna: Griechische Denker, 1936, vol. 1, p. 233, quoted in Hayek, *Mill and Taylor*, p. 56.

20. Letter from Thomas Carlyle to Dr John Carlyle, 15 August 1834, quoted in Froude, *Carlyle*, vol. 2, p. 448.

21. *Complete Works of HTM* pp. 323–4. The note is undated.

22. 'Flower's Mignon's Song and When Thou Wert Here', *Examiner*, 21 April 1833, *CW*, XXIII, pp. 562–3.

23. 'On Genius', *Monthly Repository*, VI, October 1832, *CW*, I, pp. 330, 335.

24. 'On Genius', *CW*, I, p. 332.

25. Wordsworth, 'Essay, Supplementary to the Preface', *Poems* (1815), *Wordsworth: The Major Works*, p. 659.

26. 'On Genius', *CW*, I, p. 33.

27. [Untitled], *Complete Works of HTM*, pp. 137–8.

28. *Monthly Repository*, November 1832, *Complete Works of HTM*, pp. 198–204.

29. 'The Seasons', *Monthly Repository*, VI, 1832, pp. 825–8, *Complete Works of HTM*, p. 207. The passage in question reads: 'Flowers are utilitarians in the largest sense. Their very life is supported by administering to the needs of others – producers and distributors, but consumers only [*sic*] what, unused, would be noxious. Ornaments in happiness, companions in solitude, soothing "the unrest of the soul".'

30. David Thomson, *England in the Nineteenth Century*, London: Penguin, 1950, p. 42.

31. Johnson, *Birth of the Modern*, p. 993.

32. Ibid., p. 987.

33. Ibid., p. 986.

34. Juliet Barker, *Wordsworth, A Life*, London: Penguin Viking, 2000, p. 587.

35. Hazlitt, *Spirit of the Age*, p. 4.

36. Alfred Tennyson, *Maud* (1855), Part I (I) l. 21.

37. The Trevelyan quote is from George Macaulay Trevelyan, *British History in the Nineteenth Century*, London: Longmans,

Green and Co., 1922, p. 244, quoted in Hamburger, *Intellectuals in Politics*, p. 144. Mill saw it as 'one of the greatest steps in improvement made by peacable legislation in the internal government of a country'. *CW*, VI, p. 308.

38. The quote is from Lord Greville, at the time Secretary to the Privy Council, recorded in his diary on 20 November 1830 and printed in his *Memoirs*, vol. 2, pp. 64–5, quoted in Johnson, *Birth of the Modern*, p. 996.

39. *The Letters of Charles and Mary Lamb*, ed. E. V. Lucas, 3 vols, London: Methuen, 1935, vol. 3, pp. 298–9, 20 December 1830, quoted in Johnson, *Birth of the Modern*, p. 1000.

40. Letter to Thomas Carlyle, 5 July 1833, *CW*, XII, p. 162.

41. Letter to Thomas Carlyle, 11 and 12 April 1833, *CW*, XII, p. 149.

42. Letter to William J. Fox, 20 May 1833, *CW*, XII, p. 158.

43. HTM to Mill, 6 September 1833, *Complete Works of HTM*, pp. 326–7.

44. Letter from Jane Welsh Carlyle to Dr John Carlyle, May 1834, quoted in Froude, *Carlyle*, vol. 2, p. 441.

45. Leader, *Roebuck*, p. 38.

46. Letter to William Tait, 13 February 1834, *CW*, XII, p. 212.

47. Letter to William J. Fox, 7 September 1833, *CW*, XII, p. 178.

48. Letter to Thomas Carlyle, 2 February *CW*, XII, p. 141.

49. *Complete Works of HTM*, p. 325. The letter is not dated, but it seems almost certain that the 'next month' refers to the Paris trip.

50. Letter from HTM to William J. Fox and Eliza Flower, 5/6 November 1833, *Complete Works of HTM*, p. 328.

51. Letter to William J. Fox, 5/6 November 1833, *CW*, XII, p. 186.

52. Ibid., p. 187.

53. Letter to William J. Fox, 22 November 1833, *CW*, XII, p. 189.

54. In either 1832 or 1833; see John Robson, 'Textual Introduction' to *Essays on Equality, Law and Education, CW*, XXI, pp. lviii–lx.

55. 'On Marriage', 1832 or 1833, first published in Hayek, *Mill and Taylor*, pp. 58–75, *CW*, XXI, p. 42.

56. 'On Marriage', *CW*, XXI, p. 49.

57. Harriet's article, also titled 'On Marriage', is in *Complete Works of HTM*, pp. 21–5 (along with some notes which appear to be preparatory to the main piece).

58. 'On Marriage', *CW*, XXI, p. 44.

59. 'On Marriage', *Complete Works of HTM*, p. 23.

60. 'On Marriage', *CW*, XXI, p. 45.

61. 'On Marriage', *Complete Works of HTM*, p. 23.

62. Sarah Ellis, *The Wives of England, Their Relative Duties, Domestic Influence, and Social Obligations*, London: Fisher, Son & Co., 1843, quoted in Johnson, *Birth of the Modern*, p. 495.

63. Johnson, *Birth of the Modern*, p. 540.

64. See Roebuck's reply, *Mill–Taylor Collection*, XXVII/121–2, ff. 253–6.

65. The 'empty mouthing' comment is in a letter to John Nichol, 18 December 1834, *CW*, XII, p. 245.

66. Millicent Fawcett, *Life of the Rt. Hon. Sir William Molesworth*, London: Macmillan, 1901, p. 63.

67. Letter to Edward Lytton Bulwer, 23 November 1836, *CW*, XII, p. 312.

68. Fawcett, *Molesworth*, p. 63, quoted in Packe, *Mill*, p. 197.

69. Hamburger, *Intellectuals in Politics*, pp. 128–9.

70. 'Professor Sedgwick's Discourse – State of Philosophy in England', *London Review*, April 1835, *CW*, X, p. 71.

71. *AB*, *CW*, I, p. 209.

72. Letter to John Nichol, 14 October 1834, *CW*, XII, p. 236.

73. Letter to Thomas Carlyle, 12 January 1834, *CW*, XII, pp. 207–8.

74. Charles Buller's niece, see Packe, *Mill*, p. 197.

75. Porter, *Enlightenment*, p. 425.

76. Letter from Thomas Carlyle to Dr John Carlyle, 15 August 1834, quoted in Froude, *Carlyle*, vol. 2, p. 448: 'We dined with Mrs. (Platonica) Taylor and the Unitarian Fox (of the Repository if you know it) one day: Mill was also of the party, and the husband, an obtuse, most joyous natured man, the pink of social hospitality.' Quoted in Hayek, *Mill and Taylor*, p. 81.

77. 'In January 1836, John Graham wrote to her [HTM] about two casks of wine he had brought over at John Mill's request for the stocking of the Kent Terrace cellar', Packe, *Mill*, p. 205

78. Letter to William J. Fox, 14[?] February 1834, *CW*, XII, pp. 213–14.

79. Letter to William J. Fox, 26 June 1834, *CW*, XII, p. 227.

80. HTM to Mill, 20 February 1834 [?], *Complete Works of HTM*, p. 329. The letter is undated but it is attached to an envelope with a typed date. Jacobs speculates that this was added by Mary Taylor, HTM's niece, in the early twentieth century, so the dating may not be reliable – but it fits with the tone of the correspondence for that period.

81. Letter to HTM, summer 1834[?], *CW*, XII, pp. 227–8. The letter is not dated.

82. *Complete Works of HTM*, p. 324. The letter is not dated.

83. Ibid., p. 335. The letter is not dated, but must pre-date late 1838, since it mentions meeting Arthur Hardy, HTM's youngest brother, who emigrated to Australia at the end of that year.

84. Letter from Thomas Carlyle to Dr John Carlyle, 28 October 1834, quoted in Hayek, *Mill and Taylor*, p. 82.

85. Mill's letter has not survived, but its content can be surmised from Harriet's two replies, which are dated only 'Tuesday eveng.' and 'Wednesday', but which are on paper with an 1835

watermark; *Complete Works of HTM*, p. 332.

86. Ibid., p. 332.

87. Oriental and India Office Collections (OIOC), draft despatch, 5 October 1836, Home Misc. 723, quoted in Penelope Carson, 'Golden Casket or Pebbles and Trash? J.S. Mill and the Anglicist/Orientalist Controversy', in Moir, Peers and Zastoupil (eds), *J. S. Mill's Encounter with India*, 1999, p. 165.

88. Letter to Henry Taylor [a friend – no relation to Harriet], 1837, *CW*, XVII, p. 1970. Undated but on paper watermarked 1837.

89. Bain, *James Mill*, p. 391.

90. Letter to William Johnson Fox, 23 February 1835, *CW*, XII, p. 298.

91. 'Civilization', *London and Westminster Review*, April 1836, *CW*, XVIII, p. 119.

92. 'Guizot's Lectures on European Civilisation', *London and Westminster Review*, XXXI, January 1836, *CW*, XX, p. 374.

93. 'Sedgwick', *CW*, X, p. 34.

94. 'Guizot's Lectures', *CW*, XX, p. 374.

95. 'Civilization', *CW*, XVIII, p. 122.

96. Quoted in Christopher Turk, *Coleridge and Mill*, Aldershot: Averbury, 1988, p. 172.

97. 'I am now, however, inclined to think that my father was not so much opposed as he seemed, to the modes of thought in which I believed myself to differ from him …' *AB*, *CW*, pp. 209–11.

98. Letter to Edward Lytton Bulwer, 23 November 1836, *CW*, XII, p. 312.

99. William Leonard Courtney, *Life of John Stuart Mill*, London: Walter Scott, 1889, p. 69.

100. James Anthony Froude, *Thomas Carlyle: A History of his Life in London*, 2 vols, London: Longmans, 1884, vol. 1, p. 74, quoted in Packe, *Mill*, p. 206.

101. Letter to John Sterling, 20–22 October 1831, *CW*, XII, p. 85.

102. Letter to Thomas Carlyle, 12 January 1834, *CW*, XII, p. 205.

5. Laid Hold of by Wolves

1. Richard Holmes, *Coleridge: Darker Reflections*, Flamingo, 1998 pp. 442, 439.

2. For 'dunghill', see letter from Thomas Carlyle to Dr John Carlyle, Froude, *Carlyle*, vol 1, p. 303, quoted in Christopher Turk, *Coleridge and Mill*, Aldershot: Averbury, 1988, p. 3. For 'moonshine' see Packe, *Mill*, p. 84.

3. James Mill (1773–1836); Samuel Taylor Coleridge (1772–1834).

4. Samuel Taylor Coleridge, *Collected Letters*, ed. Earl Leslie Griggs, 6 vols, Oxford: Clarendon Press, 1956–90, vol. 4, p. 768, quoted in Turk, *Coleridge and Mill*, p. 117; and Samuel Taylor Coleridge, *Table Talk and Omniana*, ed. T. Ashe, London: Bell and Sons, 1923, 20 August 1831, quoted in Newsome, *Victorian World Picture*, p. 57.

5. Holmes, *Coleridge*, p. 14.

6. *AB*, *CW*, I, pp. 169–70.

7. Letter to John Nichol, 15 April 1834, *CW*, XII, p. 221.

8. Richard Armour and Raymond Howes, *Coleridge the Talker, A Series of Contemporary Descriptions and Comments*, New York: Cornell University Press, 1940, p. 182, quoted in Turk, *Coleridge and Mill*, p. 23.

9. 'Civilization', *London and Westminster Review*, XXV, April 1836, pp. 1–28, *CW*, XVIII, pp. 119–47; 'Coleridge', *London and Westminster Review*, XXXIII, March 1840, pp. 257–302, *CW*, X, pp. 119–63; 'De Tocqueville on Democracy in America' [I], *London Review*, October 1835, *CW*, XVIII, pp. 49–90; 'De Tocqueville on Democracy in America' [II], *Edinburgh Review*, October 1840, *CW*, XVIII, pp. 155–204.

10. 'Coleridge', *CW*, X, p. 155.

11. Coleridge, *Table Talk*, p. 183, quoted in Turk, *Coleridge and Mill*, p. 213.

12. Coleridge, *Table Talk*, p. 62, quoted in Turk, *Coleridge and Mill*, p. 216.

13. 'The Works of Jeremy Bentham', *London and Westminster Review*, August 1838. *CW*, X, p. 114.

14. Johann Daniel Falk, *Characteristics of Goethe*, trans. Sarah Austin, London, 1833. Mill mentions the work in a letter to Thomas Carlyle, 17 September 1832, *CW*, XII, p. 119.

15. *AB*, *CW*, I, p. 171.

16. Letter to Thomas Carlyle, 17 July 1832, *CW*, XII, p. 111. Mill also told Carlyle that he was in a state, 'in which one feels *quite sure* of scarcely anything respecting Truth, except that she is many-sided', 5 October 1833, *CW*, XII, p. 181.

17. Cf. Turk, *Coleridge and Mill*, pp. 221–3.

18. 'Spirit of the Age', *CW*, XXII, p. 234.

19. *AB*, *CW*, p. 171.

20. Letter to John Sterling, 4 November 1839, *CW*, XIII, p. 411.

21. 'Coleridge', *CW*, X, p. 122.

22. 'Civilization', *CW*, XVIII, pp. 131–2.

23. *AB*, *CW*, I, p. 169.

24. 'Auguste Comte and Positivism', [Part II], *Westminster and Foreign Quarterly Review*, July 1865. *CW*, X, p. 359.

25. *AB*, *CW*, I, p. 177.

26. Mill also thought a wider suffrage would force education improvements: 'if the democracy obtained a large, and perhaps the principal share in the governing power, it would become the interest of the opulent classes to promote [the people's] education, in order to ward off really mischievous errors'. *AB*, *CW*, I, p. 179.

27. *AB*, *CW*, I, p. 239.

28. Letter to John Nichol, 21 December 1837, *CW*, XII, p. 365.

29. Letter to J. F. Mollett, December 1847, *CW*, XIII, p. 727: 'I have much pleasure in enclosing a

30. Letter to William Lovett, 27 July 1842, *CW*, XIII, pp. 533–4.

31. John Dunn, *Setting the People Free – The Story of Democracy*, London: Atlantic Books, 2005, p. 153.

32. 'Pledges' [I], *Examiner*, 1 July 1832. *CW*, XXIII, p. 488.

33. 'Tocqueville' [II], *CW*, XVIII, p. 158.

34. Letter to Alexis de Tocqueville, September 1835, *CW*, XII, p. 272.

35. 'Tocqueville' [II], *CW*, XVIII, p. 198.

36. Letter to John Nichol, 10 July 1833, *CW*, XII, p. 166.

37. *Considerations on Representative Government*, London: Longmans, 1861. *CW*, XIX, p. 390.

38. Brogan, *Tocqueville*, p. 371.

39. Ibid., p. 303.

40. Letter to Alexis de Tocqueville, 9 August 1842, *CW*, XIII, p. 537.

41. Twice, in fact: 'Bentham', *CW*, X, p. 109 and 'Tocqueville' [II], *CW*, XVIII, p. 57.

42. Letter to Alexis de Tocqueville, 15 December 1856, *CW*, XV, p. 518. Tocqueville to Mill, 19 December 1856, quoted in Brogan, *Tocqueville*, pp. 595–6.

43. Tocqueville to Mill, 12 September 1836, quoted in Bernard Semmel, *John Stuart Mill and the Pursuit of Virtue*, New Haven: Yale University Press, 1984, p. 132.

44. Quoted in Dunn, *Setting the People Free*, p. 27.

45. 'Guizot's Lectures', *CW*, XX, p. 268.

46. 'Pledges' [I], *CW*, XXIII, p. 489.

47. 'Pledges' [II], *Examiner*, 15 July 1832. *CW*, XXIII, p. 502. On a similar theme, see Mill's letter to Gustave d'Eichthal, 11 March 1829, *CW*, XII, pp. 27–8: 'The intelligent classes lead the government, & the government leads the stupid classes'; and 'Rationale of Representation', *London Review*, July 1835, *CW*, XVIII, p. 23, in which Mill cited as one of the conditions of good government that 'political questions be not decided by an appeal, either direct or indirect, to the judgement or will of an uninstructed mass, whether of gentlemen or of clowns, but by the deliberately-formed opinions of a comparatively few, specially educated for the task'.

48. Letter to John Nichol, 15 April 1834, *CW*, XII, p. 221.

49. *On the Constitution of the Church and State, according to the Idea of Each*, London, 1829, Chapter V, reprinted in Samuel Taylor Coleridge, *The Major Works*, ed. H. J. Jackson, Oxford: Oxford University Press, 1985, p. 694.

50. *Church and State*, quoted in Turk, *Coleridge and Mill*, p. 174.

51. 'Coleridge', *CW*, X, p. 147.

52. Ibid., p. 151.

53. 'Corporation and Church Property', *The Jurist, or Quarterly Journal of Jurisprudence and*

Legislation, February 1833, *CW*, IV, pp. 209–20.

54. 'Tocqueville' [I], *CW*, XVIII, p. 85.

55. 'Civilization', *CW*, XVIII, p. 127.

56. Letter to John Sterling, 20–22 October 1831, *CW*, XII, pp. 84–5.

57. Letter to Gustave d'Eichthal, 9 February 1830, *CW*, XII, p. 48.

58. Mill had in fact been using the term to warn about the potential for conservatism in such an endowed class if it were given political authority: 'The majority of an educated class may well be less disposed than any other to be led by the most advanced minds in its midst; and since this majority would doubtless be composed, not of great thinkers, but simply of scholars or of scientists lacking true originality, there could result only what one finds in China, a *pedant-ocracy*.' Letter to Auguste Comte, 25 February 1842, *CW*, XIII, p. 502, translation from *The Correspondence of John Stuart Mill and Auguste Comte*, ed. and trans. Oscar Haac, New Brunswick and London: Transaction, 1995, p. 52. For Mill's permission for Comte to use the term, see his letter to Comte, 9 June 1842, *CW*, XIII, p. 524, translation from Haac (ed.), *Mill and Comte*, p. 74.

59. 'Tocqueville' [II], *CW*, XVIII, p. 198.

60. *Comte*, *CW*, X, p. 314. See also: 'Reason itself will teach most men that they must, in the last resort, fall back upon the authority of still more cultivated minds, as the ultimate sanction of the convictions of their reason itself', 'Spirit of the Age' [II], *CW*, XXII, p. 244.

61. Letter to John Austin, 13 April 1847, *CW*, XIII, p. 713.

62. 'Coleridge', *CW*, X, pp. 134–5.

63. 'Bentham', *CW*, X, p. 99.

64. According to Alison Winter, *Mesmerized: Powers of Mind in Victorian Britain*, Chicago: University of Chicago Press, 1998, p. 308.

65. 'Coleridge', *CW*, X, p. 135.

66. Ibid., p. 134.

67. *A System of Logic Ratiocinative and Inductive*, London, 1843. *CW*, VIII, p. 922.

68. Gertrude Himmelfarb, *On Liberty and Liberalism: The Case of John Stuart Mill*, New York: Knopf, 1974, esp. pp. 46–7.

69. *Logic*, *CW*, VIII, p. 922n.

70. 'Bentham', *CW*, X, p. 114.

71. 'Coleridge', *CW*, X, p. 134.

72. Plato was also a shared influence on both Coleridge and Mill. See Holmes, *Coleridge*, pp. 492–3 and Terence H. Irwin, 'Mill and the Classical World', in John Skorupski (ed.), *The Cambridge Companion to Mill*, Cambridge: Cambridge University Press, 1998, pp. 439–45.

73. 'Coleridge', *CW*, X, p. 138.

74. Footnote to 'Thoughts on Poetry and its Varieties' (1833), *CW*, I, p. 365. Mill was quoting from Wordsworth's 'Essay, Supple-

mentary to the Preface', *Poems* (1815), *Major Works*, p. 661.

75. Coleridge', *CW*, X, p. 138.

76. 'Parliamentary Reform', August 1824, *CW*, XXVI, pp. 269–70.

77. 'The Word "Destructive"', *Globe and Traveller*, 6 January 1835. *CW*, XXIV, p. 762.

78. Peter Levi, *Tennyson*, London: Macmillan, 1993, p. 152.

79. Thomas Carlyle, 'Sartor Resartus' first published in *Fraser's Magazine*, 1833–4, reprinted in Thomas Carlyle, *Selected Writings*, London: Penguin, 1971, p. 103.

80. Carlyle, *Sartor Resartus*, quoted in Newsome, *Victorian World Picture*, p. 57.

81. 'Sartor Resartus', *Selected Writings*, p. 103.

82. Letter to John Sterling, 20–22 October 1831, *CW*, XII, p. 85.

83. Letter to John Sterling, 24 May 1832, *CW*, XII, p. 101.

84. Letter to Thomas Carlyle, 17 July 1832, *CW*, XII p. 113.

85. Thomas Carlyle, 'On History', *Fraser's Magazine*, November 1830, *Selected Writings*, p. 53.

86. Thomas Carlyle, 'Signs of the Times', *Edinburgh Review*, June 1829, *Selected Writings*, p. 81.

87. In his 1847 essay, 'Thomas Carlyle and His Works', Henry David Thoreau judged *On Heroes, Hero-Worship, and the Heroic in History* to be Carlyle's crowning achievement.

88. 'Civilization', *CW*, XVIII, pp. 131–2.

89. Letter to Thomas Carlyle, 18 May 1833, *CW*, XII p. 153.

90. Coleridge supported a scheme of 'national education' – at the time a radical doctrine – but insisted that it had to go far beyond the acquisition of basic skills. True education, he wrote, 'consists in educing the faculties, and forming the habits' of the 'whole man', Holmes, *Coleridge*, p. 441. Mill agreed that liberal societies had to enforce moral codes via the education system but, unschooled himself, saw this as primarily a parental, or in fact, maternal, duty. In his private note on marriage for Harriet, he wrote that 'the education which it does belong to mothers to give, and which if not imbibed from them is seldom obtained in any perfection at all, is the training of the affections: & through the affections, of the conscience, & the whole moral being', 'On Marriage', *CW*, XXI, p. 44.

91. 'Civilization', *CW*, XVIII, pp. 132.

92. Letter to Thomas Carlyle, 2 February 1833, *CW*, XII, p. 141.

93. 'The whiff of grapeshot' occurs in Carlyle's description of the scene during the 13 Vendémiaire, the battle between French Revolutionaries and Royalists on 5 October 1795 in Paris; the Republicans were led by General Napoleon Bonaparte. Carlyle used a similar phrase earlier in his *History*, in his description of

the storming of the Bastille on 14 July 1789, in which the revolutionaries were 'a rabble to be whiffed with grapeshot'. See vol. 1, Ch. 5, Book 6, *Selected Writings*, p. 81. 'Sea-green incorruptible' was Carlyle's assessment of Robespierre.

94. In a letter to Thomas Carlyle in 1873, Mill's younger sister Harriet wrote: 'I can, perfectly well, remember our search, and my dear brother's extreme distress.' She also suggested that the blame may not rest on the maid's shoulders: 'As far as my recollection goes, the misfortune arose from my brother's own inadvertence in having given your papers among waste paper for kitchen use.' *Letters of Thomas Carlyle to John Stuart Mill, John Sterling and Robert Browning*, ed. Alexander Carlyle, London: T. Fisher Unwin, 1923, p. 107.

95. 'Gracious Providence, he has gone off with Mrs. Taylor', was supposed to be Jane Welsh Carlyle's response: see Charles Gavan Duffy, *Conversations and Correspondence with Thomas Carlyle, The Contemporary Review*, 61, 1892, p. 169.

96. 'Carlyle's French Revolution', *London and Westminster Review*, July 1837, pp. 17–53, *CW*, XXI, pp. 133–66.

97. Letter from Thomas Carlyle to Dr John Carlyle, 27 November 1835, *Collected Letters*, vol. 8, p. 263, quoted in Rosemary Ashton,

142 Strand, A Radical Address in Victorian London, London: Chatto & Windus, 2006, pp. 106–7.

98. Jane Welsh Carlyle to Thomas Carlyle, 2 August 1836, quoted in Hayek, *Mill and Taylor*, p. 85.

99. Thomas Carlyle to John Sterling, 17 January 1837, in Froude, *Carlyle: A History of his Life in London*, vol. 1, p. 108.

100. David Alec Wilson, *Life of Carlyle*, 6 vols, London: K. Paul, Trench, Trubner, 1923–34, vol. 3, p. 85, quoted in Packe, *Mill*, p. 265.

101. Letter to William Thornton, 23 October 1869, *CW*, XVII, p. 1657.

102. 'Coleridge', *CW*, X, p. 129.

103. See, for example, letters to Thomas Carlyle on 29 May 1832, *CW*, XII, p. 102; 17 September 1832, *CW*, XII, p. 116; 22 October 1832, *CW*, XII, p. 125; 27 December 1832, *CW*, XII, p. 132; and 9 March 1833, *CW*, XII, p. 143.

104. Letter from Thomas Carlyle to Dr John Carlyle, 15 August 1834, Froude, *Carlyle*, vol. 2, p. 448.

105. 'Perfectability', 2 May 1828, *CW*, XXVI, pp. 428–9.

106. Letter to John Sterling, 4 November 1839, *CW*, XIII, p. 411.

107. Fox, *Memories*, 7 August 1840, p. 141.

108. Fox, *Memories*, 6 June 1842, p. 201.

6. Independence (1836–42)

1. 'John Mill, as perhaps you know, is home again, in better health,

still not in good. I saw him the day before yesterday, sitting desolate under an Influenza we all have.' Letter from Thomas Carlyle to Dr John Carlyle, 17 January 1837, quoted in Hayek, *Mill and Taylor*, p. 86.

2. Letter to Alexis de Tocqueville, 7 January 1837, *CW*, XIII, p. 317.

3. Letter from John Roebuck to Arthur Place, 4 January 1837, quoted in Hamburger, *Intellectuals in Politics*, p. 170.

4. Quoted in A. N. Wilson, *The Victorians*, London: Hutchinson, 2002, p. 28. (Wilson says Melbourne was quoting Walter Scott.)

5. 'Parliamentary Proceedings of the Session', *London Review*, July 1835, *CW*, VI, p. 300.

6. Henry George Ward, cited in *Fraser's Magazine*, January 1838, quoted in Hamburger, *Intellectuals in Politics*, p. 69.

7. Letter to Alexis de Tocqueville, 7 January 1837, *CW*, XIII, p. 317.

8. Edward Lytton Bulwer in *England and the English*, 1833, vol. 2, p. 268, quoted in Hamburger, *Intellectuals in Politics*, p. 117.

9. Letter to John Nichol, 29 January 1837, *CW* XII, p. 324

10. 'Fonblanque's England under Seven Administrations', *London and Westminster Review*, April 1837, pp. 65–98, *CW*, VI, p. 380.

11. 'Armand Carrel', *London and Westminster Review*, October 1837, *CW*, XX, p. 171.

12. For the quotes on 'hack' journalists, see 'The Present State of Literature', 16 November 1827, *CW*, XXVI, pp. 416–17. 'Slaves of the day' is a quote from Goethe's 'Zeit und Zeitung', 1815, vol. 2, p. 309.

13. 'Carrel', *CW*, XX, p. 172.

14. Joseph Parkes to Lord Durham, 24 August 1837, quoted in Hamburger, *Intellectuals in Politics*, p. 127.

15. 'Locksley Hall' (1837–8), l. 182.

16. Martin Tupper, *Proverbial Philosophy*, London, 1838, quoted in Asa Briggs, *The Age of Improvement 1783–1867*, London: Longman, 1959, p. 395.

17. John Ruskin, quoted in Newsome, *Victorian World Picture*, p. 31.

18. 'Soiled and darkened' from *Taine's Notes on England*, ed. and trans. Edward Hymans, London, 1957, quoted in Liza Picard, *Victorian London, The Life of a City 1840–1870*, London: Weidenfeld & Nicolson, 2005, p. 9.

19. 'Parliamentary Proceedings of the Session', July 1835, *CW*, VI, p. 297.

20. 'Terms of Alliance Between Radicals and Whigs', *London and Westminster Review*, January 1837, quoted in Hamburger, *Intellectuals in Politics*, p. 179. For evidence of Mill's editorial involvement, see letter to William Molesworth, 3 December 1836, *CW*, XII, p. 315.

21. Melbourne reportedly said he

'was not sorry that Burdett had got in; . . . [as] the Ultras were already hard to manage, and if Leader had won, there would be no doing anything with them'. See William T. Torrens, *Memoirs of the Right Honourable William, Second Viscount Melbourne, 2 vols, London, 1878, vol. 2, p. 228*, quoted in Hamburger, *Intellectuals in Politics*, p. 179.

22. For Cobden, see Solly, *These Eighty Years*, vol.1, p. 149; for Smith, see *The Letters of Sydney Smith*, ed. Nowell Smith, Oxford: Clarendon, 1953, 2 vols, 1952, vol. 2, p. 704, and Packe, *Mill*, p. 68; for Place, see Hamburger, *Intellectuals in Politics*, p. 13.

23. 'Fonblanque's England', *CW*, VI, p. 353.

24. Joseph Parkes to E. J. Stanley, 9 September 1835, quoted in Hamburger, *Intellectuals in Politics*, p. 188.

25. Harriet Grote to Francis Place, 16 August 1837, quoted in Hamburger, *Intellectuals in Politics*, p. 107.

26. Letter to Francis Place, 10 February 1837, *CW*, XII, p. 326.

27. *Spectator*, 9 December 1837, pp. 1164–66.

28. Joseph Parkes to Charles Sumner, 2 June 1840, quoted in Hamburger, *Intellectuals in Politics*, p. 181.

29. R. P. Anschutz, 'J. S. Mill: Philosopher of Victorianism' in Arthur Sewell (ed.), *1840 and*

After, Auckland: Auckland University Press, 1940, p. 131.

30. *AB, CW*, I, p. 205.

31. 'Mr E. Bulwer and Mr Grote', *Examiner*, 28 January 1838, p. 50, quoted in *CW*, XIII, p. 37.

32. Letter to Albany Fonblanque, 23 January 1838, *CW*, XIII, p. 370.

33. *Examiner*, 28 January 1838, p. 50, quoted in Hamburger, *Intellectuals in Politics*, p. 207.

34. Letter to Albany Fonblanque, 23 January 1838, *CW*, XIII, p. 370.

35. Letter to Albany Fonblanque, 7 February 1838, *CW*, XIII, p. 377.

36. 'Carlyle's Works', *London and Westminster Review*, October 1839, pp. 1–68.

37. 'Carlyle's French Revolution', *CW*, XXI, p. 133.

38. Sarah Austin to Mill, 3 March 1837, quoted in Packe, *Mill*, p. 214.

39. Tuell, *Sterling*, p. 76.

40. 'Bentham', *CW*, X, pp. 77, 100.

41. Ibid., pp. 90–91.

42. Ibid., p. 95.

43. Quoted in Alan Ryan, 'Introduction' to Mill and Bentham, *Utilitarianism and Other Essays*, p. 33, and in Alan Ryan, 'A New Vision of Liberty', *The New York Review of Books*, 5 July 2001, pp. 42–5.

44. 'Bentham', *CW*, X, p. 110.

45. 'Blakey's History of Moral Science', *Monthly Repository*, October 1833, pp. 691–9, *CW*, X, p. 29: Mill's 'least utilitarian' work, according to Alan Ryan.

46. Jeremy Bentham, *Rationale of*

Reward, in *Works of Jeremy Bentham*, vol. II, p. 253, quoted by Mill in 'Bentham', *CW*, X, p. 113.

47. 'Bentham', *CW*, X, p. 96.

48. *AB*, *CW*, I, p. 227.

49. Francis Place to Thomas Falconer, 2 September 1838, quoted in Hamburger *Intellectuals in Politics*, p. 108.

50. *AB*, *CW*, I, p. 215.

51. Letter to Edward Lytton Bulwer, 5 March 1838, *CW*, XIII, p. 383.

52. Plato made great play of Aspasia's supposed authorship in his *Menexenus*.

53. Jane Welsh Carlyle recalled Cavaignac's comment in a letter to John Sterling, January–February 1842, in *Letters and Memorials of Jane Welsh Carlyle*, ed. James Froude, London, 1893, vol. 1, p. 138. Armida was an enchantress in Tasso's *Gerusalemme Liberata* who lured crusading knights away from their duty. She had become popular through operas by Gluck and Rossini.

54. Mill suggested that Cavaignac's writing would 'not suit England'. Letter to Aristide Guilbert, 19 March 1835, *CW*, XII, p. 256.

55. See *CW*, XII, p. 307 n1.

56. Thomas Carlyle to John Sterling, 3 October 1836, reprinted in *Letters of Thomas Carlyle*, pp. 197–8.

57. Letter to Sarah Austin, 28 January 1837, *CW*, XII, p. 321.

58. See letters to John Robertson from Leamington, Ross, Brecon and Farnborough, September–October 1837, *CW*, XII, pp. 349, 351, 354–5.

59. Thomas Carlyle to John Carlyle, 17 January 1837, reprinted in Froude, *Carlyle: History of his Life in London*, vol. 1, p. 108.

60. HTM to Mill, 1837, *Complete Works of HTM*, pp. 334–5. The letter is not dated but the paper has an 1837 watermark.

61. The calculation of the value of Mill's £1,200 salary (which he received from 1836) was made using the data series at www.measuringworth.com: see Chapter 2, note 61, for more details. For the other figures, see Harold Perkin, *The Origins of Modern English Society 1780–1880*, London: Routledge & Kegan Paul, Toronto: University of Toronto Press, 1969, p. 135. Perkin quotes Farr's 1848 analysis, which suggests that 1.18 per cent of the population earned over £200. As late as 1867, only 0.5 per cent of families had an income above £1,000 a year, p. 420.

62. Perkin, *Origins*, p. 256.

63. Letter to John Robertson, April 1839, *CW*, XIII, p. 396; Croker was also author of a famous attack on Keats's poem *Endymion: A Poetic Romance* in the April 1818 issue of the *Quarterly Review*, which gives a good flavour of his style: 'We confess that we have not read [the poem]. Not that we have been wanting in our duty – far from it – indeed, we have

made efforts almost as super-human as the story itself appears to be, to get through it; but with the fullest stretch of our perseverance, we are forced to confess that we have not been able to struggle beyond the first of the four books of which this Poetic Romance consists . . . [Mr Keats] is a copyist of Mr Hunt; but he is more unintelligible, almost as rugged, twice as diffuse, and ten times more tiresome and absurd than his prototype.'

64. Letters to Edward Lytton Bulwer, 3 March 1838, *CW*, XIII, p. 381; and to John Robertson, June or July [?] 1839. *CW*, XIII, p. 385.

65. Letter to Robert Barclay Fox, 16 April 1840, *CW*, XIII, pp. 42–7.

66. Letter to Edward Lytton Bulwer, 3 March 1838, *CW*, XIII, p. 380.

67. *AB*, *CW*, I, p. 205.

68. Letter to John Nichol, 26 November 1834, *CW*, XII, p. 239.

69. J. S. Morison, 'The Mission of the Earl of Durham', *Cambridge History of the British Empire*, vol. 6, pp. 288–9, quoted in Packe, *Mill*, p. 230.

70. Letter to Albany Fonblanque, 3 February 1838, *CW*, XIII, p. 374.

71. Letter to William Molesworth, 19 October 1838, *CW*, XIII, p. 390.

72. Letter to Molesworth, 14 November 1838, *CW*, XIII, p. 391.

73. Edward Ellice to Lord Durham, [December 1838?], quoted in Hamburger, *Intellectuals in Politics*, p. 234.

74. 'Lord Durham's Return', *London and Westminster Review*, October 1839, pp. 241–60, 464.

75. John Roebuck to Lord Brougham, *Intellectuals in Politics*, quoted in Hamburger, *Intellectuals in Politics*, p. 237.

76. Letter to Robert Barclay Fox, 16 April 1840, *CW*, XIII, p. 234.

77. *AB*, *CW*, I, p. 223.

78. Ibid., p. 225.

79. Letter to William Molesworth, 14 November 1838, *CW*, XIII, p. 391.

80. Briggs, *Age of Improvement*, p. 338.

81. Francis Place to Harriet Grote, 2 January 1839, quoted in Hamburger, *Intellectuals in Politics*, p. 240.

82. Lord Durham to Joseph Parkes, 16 December 1833, quoted in Hamburger, *Intellectuals in Politics*, p. 41.

83. Letter to John Robertson, 6 April 1839, *CW*, XIII, pp. 396–7.

84. Letter to Albany Fonblanque, 13[?] February 1837, *CW*, XII, p. 327.

85. Letter to Robert Barclay Fox, 16 April 1840, *CW*, XIII, p. 426.

86. *AB*, *CW*, I, p. 223.

87. Letter to Albany Fonblanque, 3 February 1838, *CW*, XIII, p. 374; and 'Parties and the Ministry', *London and Westminster Review*, October 1837, *CW*, VI, p. 389.

88. *AB* Early Draft, *CW*, I, p. 202.

89. *AB, CW*, I, pp. 203, 205.

90. Peel is quoted by Briggs, *Age of Improvement*, p. 190; see also Perkin, *Origins*, p. 171.

91. 'Parties and the Ministry', *CW*, VI, p. 404.

92. *Rep. Gov., CW*, XIX, p. 438.

93. 'Reorganization of the Reform Party', *London and Westminster* Review, April 1839, *CW*, VI, p. 468. Although published in 1839, the piece had been drafted at least a year earlier, so the views expressed within it are not an accurate reflection of Mill's views at the time of publication. Mill in fact regretted its appearance in 'a posture of affairs so unsuitable to it': letter to John Robertson, 6 April 1839, *CW*, XIII, p. 397; letter to Macvey Napier, 30 July 1841, *CW*, XIII, p. 483.

94. Bruce Kinzer, Ann Robson and John Robson, *A Moralist In and Out of Parliament, John Stuart Mill at Westminster 1865–1868*, Toronto: University of Toronto Press, 1992, p. 17. Joseph Hamburger also suggests a degree of wasted effort during this period: 'For more than a decade the Philosophic Radicals channelled into parliamentary politics the energies of the largest group of Bentham's disciples, thereby narrowing the focus and scope of Benthamite political thought.' *Intellectuals in Politics*, p. 2.

95. This section draws heavily on my paper, 'Partisan Mill', presented at the Mill Bicentennial Conference, UCL, 6 April 2006.

96. Hamburger, *Intellectuals in Politics*, p. 110.

97. John Taylor to Messrs. G. H. Gower [who were business associates], 19 December 1838. 'I am on the point of leaving London with Mrs. Taylor who is very seriously unwell . . .She intends to proceed to Pisa where she has relations and I hope and trust she will derive benefit from passing the winter in a warm and genial air.' Quoted in Packe, *Mill*, p. 237.

98. Mill was walking for four weeks from mid-September. 'I shall be out of town for the next four weeks': letter to an unidentified correspondent, 12 September 1838, p. 387. He wrote to John Robertson from Axminster on 2 October, and mentions his next destination of Weymouth: *CW*, XIII, p. 388. See also Packe, *Mill*, p. 238, for evidence that Edward Gibbon Wakefield, founder of the National Colonization Society, was surprised by the gap between Mill's reported condition and his productivity.

99. Letter to HTM, 12 Feb 1855, *CW*, XIV, p. 326.

100. Tuell, *Sterling*, pp. 52–3.

101. There is a hint that Harriet was jealous of Sterling, which may also have been a factor. In a letter to Mill concerning a request to publish some of his letters to Sterling she described him as

Mill's '*evident* inferior' and wondered how Mill could 'ever see with complacency or even with indifference such a quantity of misapprehension of your character to be published'. 8 July [?] 1849, *Complete Works of HTM*, p. 323.

102. Duffy, *Conversations with Carlyle*, p. 167.

103. Thomas Carlyle to John Sterling, 29 September 1838, *Letters of Thomas Carlyle*, pp. 225–6, quoted in Hayek, *Mill and Taylor*, pp. 86–7.

104. Tuell, *Sterling*, pp. 52–3.

105. Letters to HTM, 17 February 1857, *CW*, XV, pp. 523–4; and 23 April 1855, *CW*, XIV, pp. 429–30.

106. Letter to HTM, 10 February 1854, *CW*, XIV, p. 154.

107. HTM to Mill, 14–15 February 1854, *Complete Works of HTM*, p. 373.

108. *AB*, *CW*, I, p. 237.

109. Letter to HTM, 13 July 1852, *CW*, XIV, pp. 96–7.

110. Personal communication from Jo Ellen Jacobs, editor of HTM's works: 'It is clear she guarded her letters carefully and had them locked and mentions the location of the key the night she died. It is also clear that many letters are missing or "edited" by way of scissors. The missing ones can be deduced because both she and John regularly numbered their letters when apart so that they would be alerted to any that went astray and because he refers to many letters that no longer survive. They may have been destroyed not by John but by the executors of Helen's estate.'

111. *AB*, *CW*, I, p. 237; and journal, entry for 26 March, 1854, *CW*, XXVII, p. 664.

112. 'Enlightened Infidelity', unpublished letter to *The Reasoner*, after 2 June 1857, *CW*, XXIV, pp. 1082–4.

113. *AB*, *CW*, I, p. 237.

114. Ibid., p. 247.

115. Bain, *John Stuart Mill*, p. 149.

116. Letter to HTM, 1850, *CW*, XIV pp. 42–3.

117. Quoted in the *Mill News Letter*, vol. XIX, no.1, Winter 1984, p. 1.

118. Packe, *Mill*, p. 317; Jo Ellen Jacobs, *The Voice of Harriet Taylor Mill*, Bloomington & Indianapolis: Indiana University Press, 2002, p. 144.

119. Capaldi, *Mill*, p. 230.

120. Jacobs, *Voice of HTM*, pp. 136–46.

121. Letter to Helen Taylor, 7 February 1860, *CW*, XV, p. 673.

122. 'Utilitarianism', *Fraser's Magazine*, October–December 1861, *CW*, X, pp. 210–11.

123. I am grateful to Gregory Claeys for this thought, passed on in conversation at the Mill Bicentennial Conference, UCL, April 2006.

124. *AB*, *CW*, I, p. 195.

125. Letter to HTM, 1850[?], *CW*, XIV pp. 42–3.

126. Letter to George Henry Lewes, 1 March 1841, *CW*, XIII, p. 467.

127. Letter to Macvey Napier, 22 April 1840, *CW*, XIII, p. 430.

128. Fox, *Memories*, 27 March 1840, p. 97.

129. Ibid., 28 March 1840, p. 99.

130. Ibid., 22 March 1840, p. 94; and 20 March 1840, p. 87.

131. Ibid., 6 April 1840, p. 103.

132. Letter to Robert Barclay Fox, 16 April 1840, *CW*, XIII, p. 425.

133. In conversation with Caroline Fox, *Memories*, 7 April 1840, p. 105.

134. Packe estimates his total personal expenditure at £1500: Packe, *Mill*, p. 247.

135. Letter to Macvey Napier, 27 April 1840, *CW*, XIII, p. 431. Mill was not alone: Roebuck and Buller also began contributing to the *Edinburgh* and expressed similarly conciliatory sentiments; see. Hamburger, *Intellectuals in Politics,* p. 108.

136. Letter to Macvey Napier, 21 September 1840, *CW*, XIII, p. 445, which Mill concluded with 'much satisfaction at the new connexion which is now formed between us'.

137. For 'timid' and 'octogenarian' jibes, see letter to Sarah Austin, 18 January 1845, *CW*, XIII, p. 655. For examples of Mill's resentment on editorial interventions, see *CW*, XIII, pp. 661, 683, 701.

138. Letter to Macvey Napier, 15 October 1842, *CW*, XIII, p. 551.

139. Letter to Albany Fonblanque, 17 June 1841, *CW*, XIII, pp. 478–9.

140. The debate on trade, 'According to what principle is the benefit of the Trade between two nations shared between those two nations?', took place on 6 May 1841. For a full list of subjects addressed by Mill at the PEC, see *CW*, XXXI, pp. 407–10.

141. Edwin Chadwick, *Report on the Sanitary Condition of the Labouring Population of Great Britain*, 1842. (Chadwick was quoting figures from the Manchester Statistical Society.) Cited in Perkin, *Origins*, p. 171.

142. 'Moral and Educational Statistics of England and Wales', *Statistical Journal*, 1847, vol. X, p. 193, quoted in Perkin, *Origins*, p. 161.

143. Picard, *Victorian London*, pp. 37–8.

144. Letter to Robert Barclay Fox, 19 December 1842, *CW*, XIII, pp. 563–4.

145. Letter to Robert Barclay Fox, 6 May 1841, *CW*, XIII, p. 474.

146. Letter to John Murray, 20 December 1841, *CW*, XIII, p. 494.

147. Letter to John Sterling, 28 September 1839, *CW*, XIII, p. 406; letter to Robert Barclay Fox, 6 May 1841, *CW*, XIII, p. 474.

7. Eminence (1843–7)

1. Letter from HTM to Mill, June 1841 [?], *Complete Works of HTM*, p. 336.

2. Fox, *Memories*, 31 May 1841, p. 195.

3. Letter to Henry Cole, 14 November 1843, *CW*, XIII, p. 614.

4. Letters to John Murray, 31 January 1842, *CW*, XIII, p. 497, and 24 February 1842, *CW*, XIII, p. 500.

5. Letter to Sarah Austin, 11 March 1842, *CW*, XIII, p. 506.

6. *AB*, *CW*, I, p. 231.

7. Bain, *John Stuart Mill*, p. 146.

8. Letter to Alexander Bain, 3 October 1842, *CW*, XIII, p. 549.

9. Fox, *Memories*, 16 June 1842, p. 206.

10. Tuell, *Sterling*, p. 74.

11. Arthur James Balfour, *Theism and Humanism*, London: Hodder and Stoughton, 1915, p. 138.

12. *AB*, *CW*, I, p. 231.

13. HTM to Arthur Hardy [her brother], 7 September 1856, *Complete Works of HTM*, p. 423.

14. See Chapter 5 of this volume and letter to Thomas Carlyle, 5 July 1833, *CW*, XII, p. 163: 'I conceive that most of the highest truths are, to persons endowed by nature in certain ways which I think I could state, intuitive; that is, they need neither explanation nor proof, but if not known before are assented to as soon as stated.'

15. *AB*, *CW*, I, p. 233.

16. Ibid.

17. Letter to Theodor Gomperz, 19 August 1854, *CW*, XIV, p. 239.

18. *AB*, *CW*, I, p. 235.

19. Letter to Thomas Carlyle, 5 July 1833, *CW*, XII, p. 347.

20. 'Liberalism as Free Thought', Paper to Mill Bicentennial conference, UCL, April 2006.

21. *Logic*, *CW*, VII, p. 163.

22. Such was Mill's anti-intuitionist zeal that he even suggested, implausibly, that mathematical rules might prove not to be applicable in some remote corner of the universe. See Ryan, *J. S. Mill*, pp. 66–70.

23. Quoted in 'Mill on induction and scientific method', Geoffrey Scarre, in Skorupski, (ed.), *Cambridge Companion to Mill*, p. 115; and by Caroline Fox, *Memories*, 4 September 1859, p. 391.

24. *AB*, *CW*, I, p. 231: 'What hopes I had of exciting any immediate attention were mainly grounded on the polemical propensities of Dr Whewell; who, I thought, from observation of his conduct in other cases, would probably do something to bring the book into notice, by replying, and that promptly, to the attack on his opinions.'

25. *AB*, *CW*, I, p. 233.

26. *An Examination of Sir William Hamilton's Philosophy*, London 1865, *CW*, IX, pp. 45–6.

27. Letter to William Hickson, 15 October 1851, *CW*, XIV, p. 78.

28. Wilson, *The Victorians*, p. 105, and also Winter, *Mesmerized*. For a readable account of Snow's efforts, see Steven Johnson, *The Ghost Map – A street, an epidemic and the two men who battled to*

save Victorian London, London: Allen Lane, 2006, esp. chapter 3.

29. The article appeared in the *British Critic*, October 1843, and is quoted in Bain, *John Stuart Mill*, p. 69. Mill described it as a 'lofty panegyric' in a letter to Caroline and Anna Maria Fox, 23 October 1843, *CW*, XIII, pp. 603–4.

30. Letter to Robert Barclay Fox, 14 February 1843, *CW*, XIII, p. 569.

31. Letter to Caroline and Anna Maria Fox, 23 October 1843, *CW*, XIII, p. 603.

32. *Logic*, *CW*, VIII, pp. 839–40. This was 'commonly called the doctrine of Necessity, as asserting human volitions and actions to be necessary and inevitable', *Logic*, *CW*, VIII, p. 836. Elsewhere Mill refers to the 'doctrine commonly called Philosophic Necessity' (*Logic*, *CW*, VIII, p. 836) and to the 'necessitarian doctrine' (*Logic*, *CW*, VIII, p. 840).

33. *Logic*, *CW*, VIII, p. 840.

34. Ibid.

35. Letter to William Ward (the *British Critic* reviewer), Spring 1849, *CW*, XIV, p. 25.

36. *Hamilton*, *CW*, IX, p. 558.

37. *Logic*, *CW*, VIII, pp. 864–5.

38. Ibid., p. 869; ibid., pp. 873–4.

39. Ibid., p. 841.

40. Ibid., p. 842.

41. Alan Ryan, *The Philosophy of John Stuart Mill*, London: Macmillan, 1970, 2nd edn, New York: Macmillan, 1988, p. 117.

42. *Logic*, *CW*, VIII, p. 869.

43. 'Intolerable mass . . .' from letter to Sarah Austin, 18 January 1845, *CW*, XIII, p. 655; 'wild notions' from letter to John Austin, 13 April 1847, *CW*, XIII, p. 715.

44. Letter to Henry Chapman, 8 November 1844, *CW*, XIII, p. 640. The Peel legislation regulated working hours for children.

45. Letter to Macvey Napier, 9 November 1844, *CW*, XIII, p. 643.

46. Letter to Henry Chapman, 8 November 1844, *CW*, XIII, p. 642.

47. Lord Ashley in his diary, 29 June 1841, quoted in Wilson, *Victorians*, p. 60.

48. Cobden is quoted in Wilson, *Victorians*, p. 60.

49. Letter to John Austin, 13 April 1847, *CW*, XIII, p. 713.

50. Macaulay quoted in Briggs, *Age of Improvement*, p. 289.

51. 'The labouring classes . . .' in 'The Claims of Labour', *Edinburgh Review*, April 1845, *CW*, IV, pp. 365–6; 'to politics what', *CW*, IV, p. 369.

52. See 'The Claims of Labour' for 'resume their place', *CW*, IV, p. 372; 'Who were these?', *CW*, IV, p. 374; and 'With paternal care', *CW*, IV, pp. 374, 375.

53. 'The Claims of Labour' for 'schools in which', *CW*, IV, p. 378; become their own employers', *CW*, IV, p. 385; '*Aide-toi*', *CW*, IV,

p. 381; and 'make themselves capitalists' *CW*, IV, p. 385.

54. Letter to Macvey Napier, 20 November 1844, *CW*, XIII, p. 645.

55. 'The Westminster Election of 1865' [4], 8 July 1865, *CW*, XXVIII, p. 32.

56. Letter to Edward Lytton Bulwer, 27 March 1843, *CW*, XIII, p. 579.

57. Letter to Edwin Chadwick, April 1842, *CW*, XIII, p. 516.

58. Benjamin Disraeli, in a speech at Free Trade Hall in Manchester, 3 April 1872. ('Health, health, nothing but health'.)

59. Helen Taylor, Diary, 16 August 1844, quoted in Packe, *Mill*, p. 292.

60. Letter from John Sterling to John Murray, 16 December 1841, quoted in Tuell, *Sterling*, pp. 74–5.

61. Letter to John Sterling, 29 May 1844, *CW*, XIII, p. 629.

62. Letter to John Sterling, 16 August 1844, *CW*, XIII, p. 635.

63. Letter to Henry Chapman, 8 November 1844, *CW*, XIII, p. 640.

64. *AB*, *CW*, I, p. 235.

65. Ibid., p. 197.

66. *Logic*, *CW*, VIII, p. 944.

67. Ibid., p. 949.

68. Letter to John Sterling, 29 May 1844, *CW*, XIII, p. 630.

69. 'On the Definition of Political Economy; and on the Method of Investigation Proper to It', *London and Westminster Review*, October 1836, *CW*, IV, p. 312.

70. Letter to William Hickson, 16 June 1847, *CW*, XIII, p. 719.

71. 'Connop Thirlwall: Historian and Theologian' in James Westfall Thompson, *A History of Historical Writing*, 2 vols, London: Society for Promoting Christian Knowledge, 1936, vol. I, p. 97.

72. 'Tory perverters' in 'The Phædrus', *Monthly Repository*, June and September 1834, *CW*, XI, p. 79n.

73. Bain, *John Stuart Mill*, p. 85; 'Grote's History of Greece' [I], *Edinburgh Review*, October 1846, *CW*, XI, p. 294. See Terence Irwin's assessment in 'Mill and the Classical world' in Skorupski (ed.), *Mill*, p. 432.

74. 'Grote's History of Greece' [II], *Edinburgh Review*, October 1853, *CW*, XI, p. 324.

75. *Thoughts on Parliamentary Reform*, London: Parker and Son, 1859, *CW*, XIX, p. 314.

76. Letter to Robert Barclay Fox, 6 May 1841, *CW*, XIII, p. 473.

77. Letter to Sarah Austin, 28 February 1843, *CW*, XIII p. 572; letter to Macvey Napier, 20 October 1845, *CW*, XIII, p. 683: 'I do not know how a writer can be more usefully employed than in telling his countrymen their faults, & if that is considered anti-national I am not desirous to avoid the charge.'

78. Letter to Macvey Napier, 17

February 1845, *CW*, XIII, p. 661.

79. For the 'idea' scolding, see *AB*, *CW*, I, p. 35.

80. *Works of Jeremy Bentham*, vol. 10, p. 482, quoted in Hamburger, *Intellectuals in Politics*, p. 41.

81. Letter to Macvey Napier, 22 October 1843, *CW*, XIII, p. 601.

82. Letter to Macvey Napier, 14 October 1843, *CW*, XIII, p. 598. Mill's public reply was printed as 'Letter from John S. Mill, Esq., to the Editor', *Edinburgh Review*, January 1844, *CW*, I, pp. 535–8.

83. Letter to John Austin, 13 April 1847, *CW*, XIII, pp. 711–12. See also a letter to Sarah Austin, 18 January 1845, *CW*, XIII, p. 655: 'The time for writing books seems to have come again, though unhappily not for living by doing it.'

84. 'The Condition of Ireland' [1], *Morning Chronicle*, 5 October 1846, *CW*, XXIV, p. 880.

85. 'The Condition of Ireland' [10], *Morning Chronicle*, 23 October 1846, *CW*, XXIV p. 912.

86. 'The Condition of Ireland' [20], *Morning Chronicle*, 19 November 1846, *CW*, XXIV, p. 955.

87. 'The General Fast', *Morning Chronicle*, 23 March 1847, *CW*, XXIV, p. 1074.

88. 'The Condition of Ireland' [13], *Morning Chronicle*, 2 November 1846, *CW*, XXIV, p. 929.

89. Bain, *John Stuart Mill*, p. 86.

90. 'What is to be done with Ireland?', unpublished manuscript, *CW*, VI, pp. 502–3.

91. *England and Ireland*, London: Longmans, 1868, *CW*, VI, pp. 507–32.

92. Letter to Alexander Bain, 28 December 1846, *CW*, XIII, p. 705.

93. Letter to Thomas Hare, 27 January 1864, *CW*, XV, p. 919; *AB*, *CW*, I, p. 243.

94. 'The Condition of Ireland' [27], 7 December 1846, *CW*, XXIV, p. 979.

95. Wilson, *Victorians*, p. 76

96. P. Gray, 'Potatoes and Providence: British Government Responses to the Great Famine', *Bullán: An Irish Studies Journal*, no. 1, 1994, quoted in Wilson, *Victorians*, p. 77.

97. 'The Condition of Ireland' [27], 7 December 1846, *CW*, XXIV, p. 979.

98. 'The Condition of Ireland' [11], 23 October 1846, *CW*, XXIV, p. 915.

99. Letter to Henry Chapman, 9 March 1847, *CW*, XIII, pp. 709–10.

100. Letters to William Hickson, 15 November 1847, *CW*, XIII, p. 724 and Edwin Chadwick, 19 November 1847, *CW*, XIII, p. 724.

101. Quoted in Eric Hobsbawm, *The Age of Capital*, New York: Charles Scribner's Sons, 1975, p. 9.

8. French Revolutionary (1848)

1. Letter to Henry Chapman, 29 February 1848, *CW*, XIII, p. 731.
2. Ibid., pp. 731–2.
3. Bain, *John Stuart Mill* p. 90.
4. 'French Affairs', *Daily News*, 9 August 1848, *CW*, XXV, p. 1112.
5. Letter to Gustave d'Eichthal, 17 June 1840, *CW*, XIII, p. 438.
6. 'Scott's Life of Napoleon', *Westminster Review*, April 1828, *CW*, XX, pp. 55–110.
7. Letter to Alexis de Tocqueville, 9 August 1842, *CW*, XIII, p. 536.
8. Letter to HTM, 30 December 1854, *CW*, XIV, pp. 269–70.
9. *AB*, *CW*, I, p. 61.
10. Letter to John Austin, 13 April 1847, *CW*, XIII, p. 713.
11. Letter to Macvey Napier, 20 October 1845, *CW*, XIII, p. 683.
12. Lord Henry Brougham, *Letter to the Marquess of Lansdowne. K.G., Lord President of the Council, on the late Revolution in France*, London: Ridgway, 1848, pp. 4, 5, 15.
13. 'A singular incident . . .', see 'Vindication of the French Revolution of February 1848', *Westminster Review*, April 1849, *CW*, XX, p. 322; 'cash-box', *CW*, XX, p. 325; 'No government', *CW*, XX, p. 325.
14. Letter to John Nichol, 30 September 1848, *CW*, XIII, p. 739.
15. 'Vindication', *CW*, XX, p. 349.
16. Trevelyan (ed.), *Life and Letters of Macaulay*, vol. 2, p. 171.
17. Letter to Sarah Austin, 7 March 1848, *CW*, XIII, p. 734.
18. Letter to Sarah Austin, March [?] 1848, *CW*, XIII, p. 734.
19. Edmund Burke used the phrase in his 1790 *Reflections on the Revolution in France*, in *The Works of Edmund Burke*, Boston: Charles C. Little and James Brown, 9 vols, 1839, vol. 3, p. 114.
20. Letter to Gustave d'Eichthal, 17 June 1840, *CW*, XIII, p. 439.
21. 'The Reform Debate', *Daily News*, 8 July 1848, *CW*, XXV, p. 1102.
22. *The Letters of Queen Victoria*, London: John Murray, 1908, vol. 2, p. 194, quoted in Briggs, *Age of Improvement*, p. 296.
23. *The Princess*, Alfred Lord Tennyson (1847), 'Conclusion', ll. 51–2 and 70–71.
24. *Our Mutual Friend*, Book 1, ch. 11, pp. 138–9, quoted in Walter E. Houghton, *The Victorian Frame of Mind*, New Haven and London: Yale University Press, 1957, p. 47.
25. 'Inaugural Address to the University of St Andrews', delivered on 1 February 1867 and published in the same year by Longmans, 8 July 1848 *CW*, XXI, p. 226.
26. 'The Reform Debate', *Daily News*, *CW*, XXV, p. 1103.
27. Ibid. pp. 1105–6.
28. Ibid., p. 1105.
29. 'On Reform', *Daily News*, 19 July 1848, *CW*, XXV, p. 1106.
30. Ibid., pp. 1005–6.

31. Letter to Henry Chapman, 29 May 1849, *CW*, XIV, p. 34.

32. Letter to Sarah Austin, 18 January 1845, *CW*, XIII, p. 654.

33. Assessments of Guizot in letters to James Mill, 21 August 1830, *CW*, XII, p. 61; to Robert Barclay Fox, 23 December 1840, *CW*, XIII, p. 454; and to John Austin, 13 April 1847, *CW*, XIII, p. 714.

34. Trevelyan (ed.), *Life and Letters of Macaulay*, vol. 2, p. 172.

35. Letter to Robert Barclay Fox, 3 August 1840, *CW*, XIII, p. 442.

36. 'Michelet's History of France', *Edinburgh Review*, January 1844, *CW*, XX, p. 228.

37. 'Guizot's Essays and Lectures on History', *Edinburgh Review*, October 1845. Mill quotes the following passage from Guizot describing contemporary Europe: 'There is none of that imperturbable hardness, that blindness of logic, which we find in the ancient world. In the feelings of mankind, the same contrasts, the same contrasts, the same multiplicity: a most energetic love of independence, along with a great facility of submission.' *CW*, XX, p. 268.

38. 'Guizot's Essays', *CW*, XX, p. 269.

39. Ibid., p. 274.

40. Mill labelled this approach the 'Inverse Deductive Method', and borrowed from it for parts of his *Logic*, e.g. Book III, Chapter V, 'Of the Law of Universal Causation', and Chapter XIV,

'Of the Limits to the Explanation of Laws of Nature', *CW*, VII, pp. 341 and 495–7.

41. For 'avidity', see *AB*, *CW*, I, p. 217; 'grandest work', letter to Alexander Bain, autumn 1841, *CW*, XIII, p. 487; 'most profound books', letter to John Nichol, 21 December 1837, *CW*, XIII, p. 363.

42. Letter to HTM, 27 January 1849, *CW*, XIV, p. 6.

43. For Napier's and Bain's comments, see Bain, *John Stuart Mill*, pp. 84, 174.

44. Letter to HTM, 27 January 1849, *CW*, XIV, p. 6.

45. *Speeches by Lord Macaulay*, ed. G. M. Young, Oxford: Oxford University Press, 1935, p. 31, quoted in Hamburger, *Intellectuals in Politics*, p. 286.

46. Henry Brougham, 'Letter on the Revolution', pp. 41–2, quoted by Mill in his 'Vindication', *CW*, XX, p. 356.

47. 'Guizot's Essays and Lectures on History', *CW*, XX, p. 332.

48. Letter to Henry Chapman, 28 May 1849, *CW*, XIV, p. 34.

49. 'Modern French Historical Works', *Westminster Review*, July 1826, *CW*, XX, p. 17.

50. James Fitzjames Stephen, 'Mr Mill's Essays (Second Notice)', *Saturday Review*, 16 July 1859, quoted by Georgios Varouxakis, to whom I am indebted for this insight, *Victorian Political Thought on France and the French*, Basingstoke: Palgrave, 2002, pp. 18–19.

51. Letter to Auguste Comte, 22 March 184, *CW*, XIII, p. 508. The translation provided by Varouxakis, *Victorian Political Thought on France*, p. 14, is more faithful than the one given in Haac, *Mill and Comte*, p. 60.

52. Stefan Collini, *English Pasts*, Oxford: Oxford University Press, 1999, p. 136.

53. For the 'glasses' passage, see 'Inaugural to St. Andrews', *CW*, XXI, p. 226.

54. Letter from Comte to Mill, 25 March 1843, Haac, *Mill and Comte*, p. 144; letter to Comte, 20 April 1843, *CW*, XIII, p. 582.

55. Letter to John Nichol, 30 September 1848, *CW*, XIII, p. 739.

56. Comte quoted in John Skorupski, *Why Read Mill Today?*, London: Routledge, 2006, p. 75.

57. *Logic*, *CW*, VIII, p. 879.

58. Mill read, for example, the six volumes of Franz Joseph Gall's *Sur les function de cerveau et sur celles de chacune de ses parties*, Paris, 1825, with 'une attention sérieuse'; letter to Auguste Comte, 9 June, 1842, *CW*, XIII, p. 525.

59. Letter to Auguste Comte, 9 June, 1842, *CW*, XIII, p. 525, translation from Haac, *Mill and Comte*, p. 75.

60. Letter from Auguste Comte to Mill, 24 August 1841 in Haac, *Mill and Comte*, p. 98. Bernard Semmel provides a slightly different translation: 'educated under vicious principles, and pursuing a false conception of the necessary status of her sex . . .', in *John Stuart Mill and the Pursuit of Virtue*, New Haven: Yale University Press, 1984, p. 71.

61. Letter from Auguste Comte to Mill, 5 October 1843, in Haac, *Mill and Comte*, p. 192.

62. *Système de Politique Positive, ou Traité de sociologie*, 4 vols, Paris: Mathias, 1851–4.

63. For 'ridiculousness', see letter to John Nichol, 30 September 1848, *CW*, XIII, p. 739; 'Catholicism . . .', see Huxley's article on Comte, *Fortnightly Review*, February, 1869, pp. 141–2; 'melancholy decadence', Comte, *CW*, X, p. 367; 'mania', Comte, *CW*, X, p. 343.

64. Letter from HTM to Mill, 1844 [?], *Complete Works of HTM*, p. 337.

65. 'Preface' to *Système de Politique Positive*, quoted in Packe, *Mill*, p. 280.

66. 'Vindication', *CW*, XX, p. 362.

67. Letter to Henry Chapman, 28 May 1849, *CW*, XIV, p. 33.

68. 'Downhearted', in letter to Alexander Bain, summer 1851, *CW*, XIV, p. 76; 'whole problem', letter to Henry Chapman, 28 May 1849, *CW*, XIV; after 1848 he wrote 'nothing of substance', in Collini's accurate assessment, *English Pasts*, p. 134.

69. 'The Californian Constitution',

Daily News, 2 January 1850, *CW*, XXV, pp. 1147–50.

70. Letter to Gustave d'Eichthal, 25 December 1840, *CW*, XIII, p. 457.

71. Bain, *John Stuart Mill*, p. 78.

72. Mark Pattison, *Memoirs*, London: Macmillan, 1885, quoted in Newsome, *Victorian World Picture*, p. 49.

9. A Dismal Science? (1848–52)

1. HTM to John Taylor, 12 January 1849, *Complete Works of HTM*, pp. 492–3.

2. HTM to John Taylor, 30 March 1849, *Complete Works of HTM*, p. 501.

3. Letter to HTM, 21 February 1849, *CW*, XIV, p. 12.

4. Letters from HTM to Mill, early June 1849, *Complete Works of HTM*, p. 360; and 8 [?] July 1849, *Complete Works of HTM*, p. 501.

5. Letter from HTM to Mill, 19 [?] July 1849, *Complete Works of HTM*, p. 371.

6. Letter from HTM to John Taylor, 31 March 1848, *Complete Works of HTM*, p. 472; John Taylor's reply reproduced in *Complete Works of HTM*, pp. 472–3, and in Hayek, *Mill and Taylor*, p. 121.

7. This is the dedication Harriet was clearly referring to in her anxious letter to Mill above.

8. Letter from HTM to William J. Fox, 12 May 1848, *Complete Works of HTM*, p. 392.

9. *AB*, *CW*, I, p. 257.

10. Reproduced in Hayek, *Mill and Taylor*, p. 122 and Capaldi, *Mill*, p. 202.

11. Letter to John Austin, 22 February 1848, *CW*, XIII, p. 731.

12. For Bagehot's description of Mill as 'monarchical' in economics, see 'The Late Mr Mill', *The Economist*, 17 May 1873, pp. 588–9; for evidence of 'popular' sales, see John Robson's 'Textual Introduction', CW, II, p. lxvi, n.8.

13. Dicey is quoted in Collini, *Public Moralists*, p. 326.

14. *Principles of Political Economy*, London: Parker, 1848, *CW*, III, p. 456.

15. *Logic*, *CW*, VIII, p. 807; the reference is to Coleridge's *Second Lay Sermon*.

16. *POPE*, *CW*, III, p. 593.

17. *POPE*, *CW*, III, p. 594.

18. Letter to Edward Herford, 22 January 1850, *CW*, XIV, p. 45.

19. Letter to Max Kyllman, 24 December 1862, *CW*, XV, p. 813.

20. Letter to Karl Heinrich Rau, 20 March 1852, *CW*, XIV, p. 87.

21. 'Cooperation: Closing Speech', 1825, *CW*, XXVI, p. 325.

22. *AB*, *CW*, I, p. 243.

23. Letter to Henry Chapman, 8 November 1844, *CW*, XIII, p. 642.

24. *POPE*, *CW*, II, p. 21; in the fifth, sixth and seventh edition, Mill used 'obtaining' rather than 'prevalent'.

25. *POPE*, *CW*, III, p. 456.

26. *POPE*, *CW*, II, p. 200.

27. Letter to Thornton, 19 October 1867, *CW*, XVI, p. 1320.

28. In the 'Preface' to the 1873 edition of *Capital*: quoted in Semmel, *Mill and Virtue*, p. 95.

29. *POPE, CW*, III, pp. 819–20.

30. Ibid., p. 821: 'tax . . . imposed, as it so justly might, upon the very large portion of this income which was unearned . . .' Mill used the 'permanent' versus 'life' income terminology in his 'Evidence to the Select Committee on Income and Property Tax', 18 June 1861, *CW*, V, p. 554; in later years, especially with regard to land taxes, he reverted to the term 'unearned' – see, for example, 'Land Tenure Reform', *CW*, V, p. 691.

31. *POPE, CW*, II, pp. 225–6.

32. *POPE, CW*, III, p. 809.

33. Ibid., pp. 810–11

34. Letter to William Thornton, 23 October 1863, *CW*, XV, p. 892.

35. Letter to Thomas Acland, 1 December 1868, *CW*, XVI, p. 1498. Four years earlier, however, he had admitted the difficulty of distinguishing between 'comforts and luxuries', in a letter to John Elliott Cairnes, 12 December 1864, *CW*, XV, p. 976. I am grateful to William Stafford for pointing out this passage. For alcohol taxation, see *On Liberty*, *CW*, XVIII, p. 298.

36. Letter to Henry Chapman, 9 March 1847, *CW*, XIII, p. 709.

37. Thomas Carlyle, 'An Occasional discourse on the Negro Question', *Fraser's Magazine*, December 1849: 'Not a "gay science," I should say, like some we have heard of; no, a dreary, desolate and, indeed, quite abject and distressing one; what we might call, by way of eminence, the *dismal science*'. Carlyle's principal objection was Mill's insistence that all people, regardless of race or gender, were equal. John Ruskin's *Unto this Last* was first published as a series of essays in *Cornhill Magazine* in 1860, in which he argued that conventional economics was incapable of measuring true human progress.

38. Letter to John Jay, November 1848, *CW*, XIII, p. 741.

39. Letter to Adolf Soetbeer, 18 March 1852, *CW*, XIV, p. 85.

40. Letter from HTM to Mill, 22 July 1849: 'As there is no one there but old Mrs. Delarne it wd not do for any one to sleep there but me & Lily as she is too old to do anything – but even a day would be much after such an interval.'

41. Letter to Gustave d'Eichthal, 23 February 1841, *CW*, XIII, p. 464.

42. Letter to Anna Mill Ferraboschi, 11 April 1851, *CW*, XIV, p. 60.

43. Journal, 'Walking Tour of Cornwall', 3–9 October 1832, *CW*, XXVII, p. 634.

44. 'Statement on Marriage', 6 March 1851, *CW*, XXI, p. 99.

45. *AB, CW*, I, p. 247.

46. Letter to Clara Esther Mill, 5 March 1852, *CW*, XIV, p. 82.

47. Letter to Mrs. James Mill', 5 March 1852, *CW*, XIV, p. 83.

48. George Grote Mill to HTM, 20 May 1851, reprinted in Hayek, *Mill and Taylor*, p. 176.

49. HTM to George Grote Mill to HTM, 5 July 1851, *Complete Works of HTM*, pp. 433–4; letter from Mill to George Grote Mill, 4 August 1851, *CW*, XIV, pp. 73–4.

50. Letter to George Grote Mill, 8 April 1851, *CW*, XIV, pp. 59–60.

51. Letter to Mrs. James Mill', 5 April 1854, *CW*, XIV, p. 197.

52. Letter to Mary Mill Colman, 20 February 1858, *CW*, XV, p. 547.

53. Francis Mineka and Dwight Lindley, 'Introduction' to the *Later Letters*, *CW*, XIV, p. xxvi.

54. Letter to Mrs. James Mill', 9 June 1854, *CW*, XIV, p. 207.

55. Letter to HTM, 26 June 1854, *CW*, XIV, p. 220.

56. Letter to HTM, 24 July 1854, *CW*, XIV, p. 223.

57. Mineka and Lindley, 'Introduction', *CW*, XIV, p. xxvii.

58. Letters to HTM, 1850 [?], *CW*, XIV pp. 42–3; and (after 29 October 29) 1850, *CW*, XIV, p. 49.

59. Letter to HTM, 27 January 1849, *CW*, XIV pp. 4–5.

60. Collini, 'Introduction', *CW*, XXI, p. xxx.

61. See, for example, *POPE*, *CW*, II, pp. 218–19: in these two pages alone, Mill makes nine changes to neutralize gender.

62. Letter to Sir George Grey, 5 May 1852, *CW*, XIV, p. 63.

63. In a footnote to 'Rationale of Representation', *CW*, XVIII, p. 29.

64. 'Papers on Women's Rights', 1847–1850 [?], *CW*, XXI, p. 390.

65. Letter to William Hickson, 19 March 1850, *CW*, XIV, p. 48.

66. 'The Enfranchisement of Women', *Westminster and Foreign Quarterly Review*, July 1851, *CW*, XXI, Appendix C, pp. 399–400.

67. 'Enfranchisement', *CW*, XXI, p. 402.

68. See letters to Anna Blackwell, 16 August 1851, *CW*, XIV, p. 75; and George Jacob Holyoake, 21 September 1856, *CW*, XVII, p. 509.

69. Thomas Carlyle, 'Occasional Discourse on the Negro Question', *Fraser's Magazine*, December 1849.

70. 'The Negro Question', *Fraser's Magazine*, January 1850, *CW*, XXI, pp. 95 and 92–3.

71. Carlyle's journal entry for 7 February 1850, quoted by Collini, 'Introduction', *CW*, XXI, p. xxi.

72. Letter to HTM, 15 May 1855, *CW*, XIV, p. 451.

73. Journal entry, 9 March 1854, *CW*, XXVII, p. 660.

74. Bain, *John Stuart Mill*, p. 146.

75. *Subjection*, *CW*, XXI, p. 274.

76. Bain, *John Stuart Mill*, p. 131.

77. William Stafford 'How can a paradigmatic liberal call himself a socialist? The case of John Stuart Mill', *Journal of Political Ideologies*, 3(3), p. 326.

78. *AB*, *CW*, I, p. 241.

79. Letter to Walter Coulson, 22 November 1850, *CW*, XIV, p. 53; letter to HTM, 31 March 1849, *CW*, XIV, p. 21. In 1851 he also inveighed against the 'nonsense of the *Economist*' opposing the state public management of the water supply, letter to Edwin Chadwick, January 1851, *CW*, XIV, p. 55.

80. *POPE, CW*, III, p. 793; p. 792; pp. 895–7.

81. *POPE, CW*, II, pp. 204–5.

82. Ibid., p. 205.

83. Letter to Adolf Soetbeer, 18 March 1852, *CW*, XIV, p. 85.

84. Letter to HTM, 14 March 1852, *CW*, XIV, p. 186: 'One of the most discreditable indications of a low moral condition, given of late by the English working classes, is the opposition to piece work.'

85. *POPE, CW*, III, p. 767.

86. Letter to William Carr, 7 January 1852, *CW*, XIV, p. 81.

87. 'The Negro Question', *CW*, XXI, pp. 90–91.

88. *POPE, CW*, III, p. 792.

89. Ibid., p. 793.

90. *POPE, CW*, II, p. 111; and in letters to Henry Chapman, 12 November 1845, *CW*, XIII, p. 687; and Auguste Comte (who recommended Dunoyer's work), 26 April 1845, *CW*, XIII, p. 664.

91. Letter to Karl Heinrich Rau, 20 March 1852, *CW*, XIV, p. 87.

92. *POPE, CW*, III, p. 754.

93. Letter to Gustave d'Eichthal, 15 May 1829, *CW*, XII, p. 31; letter to Sarah Austin, 26 February 1844, *CW*, XIII, p. 622.

94. *POPE, CW*, II, p. 207.

95. Ibid., p. 208, 207.

96. Ibid., pp. 207–8.

97. Ibid., p. 208.

98. Karl Marx and Friedrich Engels, *The Communist Manifesto* (1848), London: Penguin, 1985.

99. Letter to Frederick Sinnett, 22 October 1857, *CW*, XV, p. 541.

100. Marx and Engels, *Communist Manifesto*, Chapter 2.7, p. 105.

101. 'Vindication', *CW*, XX, pp. 351–2

102. *POPE, CW*, II, p. 208. In an article written in the midst of the revisions to *POPE*, Mill had already set out his basic position in somewhat starker terms. The 'bondage' he feared 'in the cooperative communities' was that 'the yoke of conformity would be made heavier rather than lighter; that people would be compelled to live as it pleased others, not as it pleased themselves; that their lives would be placed under rules, the same for all, prescribed by the majority; and that there would be no escape, no independence of action left to any one, since all must be members of one or another community'. 'Constraints of Communism', *The Leader*, 27 July 1850, *CW*, XXV, pp. 1179–80.

103. *POPE, CW*, II, p. 208.

104. Ibid., p. 209.

105. *POPE, CW*, III, p. 938.

106. Ibid.

107. Capaldi, *Mill*, p. xiv; Jacobs, *Voice of HTM*, p. 196; Packe, *Mill*, p. 315.

108. Packe, *Mill*, p. 371.

109. Letter to HTM, 30 August 1853, *CW*, XIV, p. 112.

110. Letter to Louis Blanc, 4 March 1859, *CW*, XV, p. 601.

111. Bain, *John Stuart Mill*, p. 171.

112. Letter to HTM, 17 March 1849, *CW*, XIV, p. 17: 'The bargain with Parker is a good one & that it is so is entirely your doing.'

113. Letter to HTM, 21 February 1849, *CW*, XIV, p. 11.

114. Letter to HTM, 21 March 1849, *CW*, XIV, p. 19. For evidence of Mill's gradualism see his speech on 'Cooperation', 28 March 1864, *CW*, XXVIII, p. 7: 'it is necessary to state that this [movement towards a co-operative economy] is a gradual process.'

115. HTM to Mill, 28 July 1849, *Complete Works of HTM*, p. 341. For Mill's view, see letter to John Austin, 13 April 1847, *CW*, XIII, p. 713.

116. 'Glittering roof' quoted in Wilson, *Victorians*, p. 144; 'sacred place' quoted in Walter Ralls, 'The Papal Aggression of 1850: A Study in Victorian Anti-Catholicism', *Church History*, vol. 43, no. 2, June 1974, pp. 242–56; for the membership of the Working Classes Central Committee, see Jerry White, *London in the Nineteenth Century*, London: Jonathan Cape, 2007, p. 269.

117. 'England's Danger through the Suppression of Her Maritime Power', 5 August 1867, *CW*, XXVIII, p. 222.

118. W. L. Burn, *The Age of Equipoise. A Study of the Mid-Victorian Generation*, London: Allen and Unwin, 1964; for 'plateau', see Briggs, *Victorian People*, p. 9; 'great boom' quoted in Briggs, *Victorian People*, p. 16; 'Wall Street crash', Hobsbawm, *Age of Capital*, pp. 5, 46.

119. Hobsbawm, *Age of Capital*, p. 4.

120. Brown's description is from the catalogue that accompanied the first exhibition of *Work* in 1865, *The Exhibition of "Work," and other Paintings by Ford Madox Brown, at the Gallery, 191 Piccadilly*, London, 1865.

121. 'Electoral Districts', *Daily News*, 25 July 1848, *CW*, XXV, p. 1109.

122. *POPE, CW*, III, p. 756.

123. Ibid.

124. *Comte, CW*, X, pp. 357–8.

125. Bain, *John Stuart Mill*, pp. 153–4. Lord Lincoln was Commissioner between 1841 and 1846, but Mill's letters have apparently not survived.

126. 'Notes on the Newspapers', *Monthly Repository*, 6 June 1834, *CW*, VI, pp. 249–50.

127. *Comte, CW*, X, p. 420.

128. *POPE, CW*, III, p. 755.

129. John Maynard Keynes, 'Economic Possibilities for our Grandchildren', *The Nation and Athenaeum*, 11 and 18 October 1830, reprinted in *Essays In*

Persuasion, New York: Norton, 1963, p. 368.

130. *POPE, CW*, III, p. 756.

131. *POPE, CW*, III, pp. 755, 754.

132. Mill was still considering the subject in 1859. See letter to Alexander Bain, 14 November 1859, *CW*, XV, p. 645: 'I may hereafter write on Ethology – a subject I have long wish to take up, at least in the form of Essays, but have never yet felt myself sufficiently prepared.' The weakness of Mill's ideas on progress was the subject of Glyn Morgan's paper 'J. S. Mill, Progress, and Liberal Reform', presented to the Mill Bicentennial Conference, UCL, 7 April 2006.

133. Letter to HTM, 15 January 1855, *CW*, XIV, p. 294.

134. Michel de Montaigne, *Essays*, Paris, 1575. Mill's annotated copy of the 1739 edition is in the library of Somerville College, Oxford; see his markings on p. 268.

10. A Seven-Year Blessing (1852–8)

1. Letter to Edward Herford, 22 January 1850, *CW*, XIV, p. 45.

2. 'Hibernation', in Hobsbawm, *Age of Capital*, p. 31; for growth rates, see Hobsbawm, *Age of Capital*, p. 30; 'popular agitation', Sir J. Walsh, *The Practical Results of the Reform Act of 1832*, London, 1860, p. 7, quoted in Briggs, *Age of Improvement*, p. 361; 'electric

impulse' from *The Times*, quoted in Briggs, *Victorian People*, p. 30; 'calm desire', Francis Hutcheson quoted in Porter, *Enlightenment*, p. 388.

3. For examples of Mill's 'swamping' fears, see letters to Lord Monteagle, 20 March 1853, *CW*, XIV, p. 102, in which his reform proposals were also spelled out most fully; and to an unidentified correspondent, 11 December 1857, *CW*, XV, p. 543, where the 'educated text is also mentioned.

4. Letters to HTM, 15 February 1854, *CW*, XIV p. 160; and 30 June 1854, *CW*, XIV, p. 221; to Lord Monteagle, 20 March 1853, *CW*, XIV, p. 103.

5. *AB, CW*, p. 245.

6. Letters to HTM, 15 February 1854, *CW*, XIV, p. 164; 10 February 1854, *CW*, XIV, p. 153; and 17 May 1855, *CW*, XIV, p. 453.

7. Stefan Collini makes this point in *English Pasts*, p. 140.

8. Letters to William Hickson, *CW*, XIV, p. 56; and letters to John Chapman, 9 June 1851, *CW*, XIV, pp. 68–9; 17 October 1851, *CW*, XIV, pp. 68–9.

9. 'Whewell on Moral Philosophy', *Westminster Review*, October 1852, *CW*, X, pp. 167–201.

10. Letter to Arthur Hardy, 29 September 1856, *CW*, XV, p. 511.

11. Letter to HTM, 18 April 1854, *CW*, XIV, p. 421.

12. 'Quiet corner' is Mill's description, in a letter to Thoma

Carlyle, 8 July 1858, *CW*, XV, p. 557; letter to Giuseppe Mazzini, 21 February 1858, *CW*, XV, p. 548.

13. Algernon Taylor, *Memories of a Student*, London, 1895, quoted in Packe, *Mill*, p. 359; letters to HTM, 24 August 1853, *CW*, XIV, pp. 108–9; 27 August 1853, *CW*, XIV p. 110; and 7 February 1854, *CW*, XIV, p. 151.

14. Letters to HTM, 30 December 1853, *CW*, XIV, p. 118; and 24 August 1853, *CW*, XIV, pp. 108–9; and 29 August 1853, *CW*, XIV, p. 110; and 20 December 1854, *CW*, XIV, pp. 259, 262.

15. Letters to HTM, 22 December 1854, *CW*, XIV, p. 263; 23 December 1854, *CW*, XIV, p. 264; and 27 December 1854, *CW*, XIV, p. 268.

16. Letter to HTM, 7 June 1855, *CW*, XIV, p. 476.

17. Letter to HTM, 18 February 1854, *CW*, XIV, p. 164.

18. 'Considerable bulk', *AB*, *CW*, p. 245; letter to Edward Herford, 1 February 1850, *CW*, XIV, p. 45; letter to the Secretary of the Neophyte Writers' Society, 23 April 1854, *CW*, XIV, p. 205.

19. Letter to Herbert Fry, 14 November 1856, *CW*, XV p. 513. Mill changed his mind about having his photo taken in 1865: see letter to John Plummer, *CW*, XVI, p. 1078.

20. Letter to Frederick Lucas, 28 March 1851, *CW*, XIV, p. 58.

21. *POPE*, *CW*, III, p.754n; 'servitude', letter to John Jay, November 1848, *CW*, XIII, p. 741.

22. 'Great experiment', see Collini, 'Introduction', *CW*, XXI, p. xxii; 'outspoken like America', letter to HTM, (after October 29) 1850, *CW*, XIV, p. 49; 'eclipse' quoted in Briggs, *Age of Improvement*, p. 347; letter to the Chairman of the Library Committee, South Carolina, 3 March 1854, *CW*, XIV, p. 173; 'a public for ... speculations', letter to Asa Gray, 19 January 1857, *CW*, XV, p. 520.

23. Letter to Thomas Hare, 2 February 1860, *CW*, XV, p. 665, n9.

24. Letter to HTM, 1853, 30 December 1853, *CW*, XIV, p. 117.

25. 'General impression', letter to HTM, 6 January 1854, *CW*, XIV, p. 122; Fox, *Memories of Old Friends*, p. 98; Mill's journal, 3 April 1854, *CW*, XXVII, p. 665.

26. Journal, 19 January 1854, *CW*, XXVII, p. 644; Journal, 30 March 1854, *CW*, XXVII, p. 665; letter to HTM, 30 August 1853, *CW*, XIV, p. 111.

27. Letters to HTM, 18 February 1854, *CW*, XIV, p. 171; and 10 April 1854, *CW*, XIV, p. 202; and 9 January 1854, *CW*, XIV, p. 125.

28. Peter Ackroyd, *Dickens*, London & New York: Guild Publishing, 1990, pp. 746–7; letters to Sir Charles Trevelyan, (after 8 March) 1854, *CW*, XIV, p. 178; and 6 June 1854, *CW*, XIV, p. 207; Bentham on 'maximising

aptitude', quoted in Perkin, *Origins*, p. 258.

29. Letters to HTM, 23 January 1854, *CW*, XIV, p. 137; 7 February 1854, *CW*, XIV, p. 152; and 5 April 1854, *CW*, XIV, p. 197.

30. 'pemican' in letter to HTM, 29 January 1855, *CW*, XIV, pp. 141–2; Journal, 23 March 1854, *CW*, XXVII, p. 663.

31. In *Utilitarianism*, Mill compared Socrates to a fool rather than a pig, *Util.*, *CW*, X, p. 212; Berlin in his *Four Essays on Liberty*, p. 182. Newsome also writes that Mill 'never acquired a sense of humour', *Victorian World Picture*, p. 60; 'laughing philosopher', Journal, 16 January 1854, *CW*, XXVII, p. 643.

32. Fox, *Memories of Old Friends*, p. 94; Bain, *John Stuart Mill*, p. 190.

33. Letters to HTM, 12 July 1854, *CW*, XIV, p. 228; 15 July 1854, *CW*, XIV, p. 229.

34. The article on domestic violence was 'A Recent Magisterial Decision', *Morning Post*, 8 November 1854, *CW*, XXV, pp. 1196–7; for details of the sick leave, see letter to HTM, 11 April 1855, *CW*, XIV, p. 417.

35. For seasickness, see letter to HTM, 9 December 1854, *CW*, XIV, p. 249; for Avignon description, see letter to HTM, 25 December 1854, *CW*, XIV, p. 264.

36. 'The more I think', letter to HTM, 15 January 1854, *CW*, XIV, p. 294; *AB*, *CW*, I, p. 249; for

evidence of the timings of his visits in Rome in relation to his plans for *On Liberty* , see letters to HTM, 15 January 1854, *CW*, XIV, pp. 293–4; and 22 January 1854, *CW*, XIV, p. 303.

37. Letters to HTM: 'nervous state', 7 February 1855, *CW*, XIV, p. 322; 'If these things', 3 February 1855, *CW*, XIV, p. 317; 'bathed in art', 8 June 1855, *CW*, XIV, p. 480; Titian's *Assumption*, 12 June 1855, *CW*, XIV, p. 487; 'earth earthy', 26 January 1855, *CW*, XIV, pp. 311–12; Mantegna's frescoes, 12 June 1855, *CW*, XIV, p. 487; 'peculiar glow', 25 January 1855, *CW*, XIV, p. 310; preference for viewing art in church, 8 January 1855, *CW*, XIV, p. 283; St Agnes and St Antony's services, 21 January 1855, *CW*, XIV, pp. 301, 302; 'comic opera', 28 January 1855, *CW*, XIV, p. 314; and Messina cathedral, 1 April 1855, *CW*, XIV, p. 401.

38. Letters to HTM: 'admired exceedingly', 14 June 1855, *CW*, XIV, p. 489; *La Sirena*, 12 February 1855, *CW*, XIV, p. 326; Pnyx, 20 April 1855, *CW*, XIV, p. 427; frogs in Attica, 2 May 1855, *CW*, XIV, p. 437; 'What light it throws', 20 April 1855, *CW*, XIV, p. 427; butter at Syracuse, 25 March 1855, *CW*, XIV, p. 390.

39. 'Logic by heart', letter to HTM, 7 April 1855, *CW*, XIV, p. 409; offer of Residentship, letter to HTM, 14 April 1855, *CW*, XIV, p. 420; 'dread the heat', HTM to

Arthur Hardy, March 1855, *Complete Works of HTM*, p. 415.

40. Letters to HTM: 'It is curious', 5 March 1855, *CW*, XIV, p. 361; 'danced a saraband', 26 and 27 March 1855, *CW*, XIV, pp. 463, 466; Greek fleas, 25 March 1855, *CW*, XIV, p. 461; 'early in the morning', 16 March 1855, *CW*, XIV, p. 377.

41. Letters to HTM: description of Villari, 9 June 1855, *CW*, XIV, p. 483; Alps crossing, 18 June 1855, *CW*, XIV, p. 493; weight at the end of the trip, 9 June 1855, *CW*, XIV, p. 483.

42. Harriet was away from January to mid-April in 1854; Mill was away for June and July 1854, and between December 1854 and June 1855; 'let us make', letter to HTM, 30 December 1854, *CW*, XIV, p. 272.

43. Letter to HTM, 7 February 1854, *CW*, XIV, p. 151.

44. Letter to HTM, 29 January 1854, *CW*, XIV, p. 142.

45. Letter to HTM, 24 February 1855, *CW*, XIV, p. 346.

46. Ley refused to relinquish the role unless instructed by Herbert, Harriet's eldest son, who now managed the portfolio. He in turn refused, according to Harriet purely out of spite; he was the child who was most loyal to his father. For evidence that Harriet saw her mother only once a year, see letter to Arthur Hardy, March 1855, *Complete Works of HTM*, p. 414. For a fuller account of the contretemps, see Packe, *Mill*, p. 383, where the letter to Harriet from her mother, dated 31 August 1858, is also reproduced.

47. Theodor Gomperz is quoted in Capaldi, *Mill*, p. 241.

48. Letter from HTM to Helen Taylor, 24 November 1856, *Complete Works of HTM*, p. 514.

49. Mill's promotion followed the retirement of his superior, Thomas Love Peacock. The estimate of the quantity of Mill's dispatches was given by William Thornton, 'His Career in the India House', in Fox Bourne, *John Stuart Mill: Life and Works*, p. 20.

50. Wilson, *Victorians*, p. 214.

51. *The Petition of the East-India Company*, London: Cox and Wyman, 1858. *CW*, XXX, p. 75.

52. Thornton, 'Career at India House', p. 21.

53. 'A thing to be scrambled for', *AB*, *CW*, I, p. 249; Johnson, *Birth of the Modern*, p. 351.

54. 'Given enough', *AB*, *CW*, I, p. 249; in fact, the original title for *School of Athens* was *Causarum Cognitio* (Knowledge of Causes), which would not have made the gift any less apposite for Mill; he viewed it on 18 January 1855, see letter to HTM, *CW*, XIV, p. 297.

55. Thornton, 'Career at India House', p. 23.

56. Letter to Helen Taylor, 21 October 1858, *CW*, XV, p. 571; letter to Dr Cecil Gurney, 28

October 1858, *CW*, XV, p. 571;
Cable to Helen Taylor, 1
November 1858, *CW*, XV, p. 573.

57. 'Seven years', *AB*, *CW*, I, p. 24,
letter to William Thornton, 9
November 1858, *CW*, XV, p. 574;
'The Notice' (enclosed with the
letter to Thornton), *CW*, XV, p.
575; the dedication in *On Liberty*,
CW, XVIII. p. 216.

11. *On Liberty* (1859)

1. Kingsley Amis, *Jake's Thing*,
London: Penguin, 1978, pp. 82–3,
84.

2. 'Ten Most Harmful Books of the
19th and 20th Centuries',
www.humanevents.com, posted
31 May 2005.

3. 'education or development', *OL*,
CW, XVIII, p. 262; letter to
Theodor Gomperz, 4 December
1858, *CW*, XV, p. 581.

4. Mill quoted from a letter sent to
him by Kingsley in a letter to
Alexander Bain, 6 August 1859,
CW, XV, p. 632; evidence for
Hardy's interest is in Evelyn
Hardy, *Thomas Hardy: A Critical
Biography*, New York: Russell
and Russell, 1954, p. 68, quoted
by Mary G. McBride in 'The
Influence of *On Liberty* on
Thomas Hardy's *The Mayor of
Casterbridge*', *Mill News Letter*,
vol. XIX, Winter 1984, p. 12; the
Russian edition is mentioned in
a letter to Theodor Gomperz, 21
August 1861, *CW*, XV, p. 740;
Frederic Harrison is quoted in
Himmelfarb, *On Liberty and*

Liberalism, p. 295; the American
admirer was Adam Gurowski,
and the quote is from his diary, 8
February 1864, quoted in *CW*,
XVI, p. 1113 n1.

5. *OL*, *CW*, XVIII, p. 223.

6. Joel Feinberg, *Harm To Others:
Moral Limits of Criminal Law*, 4
vols, New York: Oxford
University Press, 1984.

7. *OL*, *CW*, XVIII, p. 223.

8. Ibid., p. 276.

9. 'No person is', *OL*, *CW*, XVIII,
p. 280; 'taken out of', *OL*, *CW*,
XVIII, p. 281; 'simply for being
drunk', *OL*, *CW*, XVIII,
p. 282.

10. *OL*, *CW*, XVIII, p. 295.

11. 'More liable to', *OL*, *CW*, XVIII,
p. 294; 'innocent', *OL*, *CW*,
XVIII, p. 294; 'no material
impediment', *OL*, *CW*, XVIII, p.
295; John Tavell's case is
described in Picard, *Victorian
London*, pp. 272–3.

12. 'Inconvenience', *OL*, *CW*, XVIII,
p. 282; 'gambling, or
drunkenness', *OL*, *CW*, XVIII,
p. 280.

13. *OL*, *CW*, XVIII, pp. 282–3.

14. *AB*, *CW*, I, p. 259; for
Himmelfarb's error see *On
Liberty and Liberalism*, p. 3.

15. 'Coleridge', *CW*, X, p. 144; *OL*,
CW, XVIII, p. 230.

16. 'Clearer perception', *OL*, *CW*,
XVIII, p. 229; Devil's Advocate
discussion, *OL*, *CW*, XVIII, p.
232; 'indispensable to imagine',
OL, *CW*, XVIII, p. 245; 'to sleep
at their post', *OL*, *CW*, XVIII, p.

250 (on the same page Mill also cited with approval an aphorism, lamenting 'the deep slumber of a decided opinion', from Sir Arthur Helps' *Thoughts for the Cloister and Crowd*, London, 1835, p. 21); 'dead dogma', *OL, CW*, XVIII, p. 243.

17. *OL, CW*, XVIII, p. 253.

18. Ibid., pp. 258, 260.

19. 'No wise man' and 'The steady habit', *OL, CW*, XVIII, p. 232; 'Aphorisms: Thoughts in the Cloister and the Crowd', *London and Westminster Review*, January 1837, *CW*, I, p. 427; Podsnap quoted in Briggs, *Age of Improvement*, p. 411.

20. See discussion of Neophyte Writer's Society on p. 243 of this volume; letter to James Martineau, 6 July 1866, *CW*, XVI, p. 1181; Elizabeth Gaskell, *The Life of Charlotte Brontë*, New York, 1857, quoted in Himmelfarb, *On Liberty and Liberalism*, pp. 49–50; see also letter to Elizabeth Gaskell, July 1859, *CW*, XV, p. 629.

21. For assistance to Bain, see letter to John William Parker, 6 December 1858, *CW*, XV, pp. 582–3 and Bain, *John Stuart Mill*, p. 156; Spencer's comments are in 'His Moral Character', in Fox Bourne (ed.), *John Stuart Mill: Life and Works*, p.26; letter to Herbert Spencer, 29 May 1865, *CW*, XVI, p. 1061.

22. William James Ward, *On Nature and Grace. A Theological Treatise.*

Book I. Philosophical Introduction, London, 1860, p. xliii, quoted at *CW*, XV, p. 647 n4; Gladstone was quoted by Todd Campbell, in 'Gladstone and John Stuart Mill: an intellectual history of Mill's influence on Gladstone's political and economic philosophy', paper to Mill Bicentennial Conference, April 2006, University College London; Spencer's comments are in 'His Moral Character', letter to E. T. Carne, 25 November 1859, p. 26.

23. Fox, *Memories of Old Friends*, p.393.

24. *AB, CW*, I, pp. 264–5; 'chère fille', letter to Louis Ménard, 1 December 1858, *CW*, XV, p. 580; 'one person beside myself', letter to William Thornton, 9 November 1858, *CW*, XV, p. 574.

25. Marie Bonafous, *John Stuart Mill à Avignon, La Dépêche de Provence*, in the *Mill–Taylor Collection* in the British Library of Political and Economic Science, Add. 311. Pastor Louis Rey, in his paper *John Stuart Mill en Avignon*, presented at a conference in Avignon, 25 April 1921 (copies held at the Archives Muncipales, 6, rue Saluces), described it as 'small, basic, humid, but near the cemetery' (p. 2); for evidence of previous ownership, see Alain Maureau, 'Stuart Mill à Avignon', paper presented to a conference at the Palais du Roure, Avignon, 22

May 1987, p. 5 (copies available from the Palais).

26. Pastor Louis Rey, *Le Roman de John Stuart Mill*, Paris: E. Monzein, 1913, p. 35 (copies held at the Archives Muncipales, 6, rue Saluces, Avignon), translation by Simon Burton; *AB*, *CW*, I, p. 251. The reviewer of the *Autobiography* in the *British Quarterly Review*, concluded: 'Mill had no great faith in a God. He had unbounded confidence in a goddess', quoted by Mineka and Lindley, 'Introduction', *CW*, XIV, p. xxiii.

27. Mill's sketches for the tomb are now in the possession of Raphaël Mérindol of Avignon, along with two unpublished letters from Mill to Pascal, dated 27 December 1858 and 28 December 1858, which are short notes concerned with practical issues regarding the construction of the tomb. The sketches were sent with the second note; for descriptions of their planting schemes, see letter from Helen Taylor to Algernon Taylor, 23 October 1859, in the *Mill–Taylor Collection*, quoted in Packe, *Mill*, p. 411. Packe mistakenly believed the planting was in the cemetery, but in a later letter from Helen – intended to squash some myths about Mill's time in Avignon – she wrote that they 'never planted, or planned the planting of anything in the cemetery':

Mill–Taylor Collection, vol. VIII, letter 122; the record of labour on the tomb is in Pascal's personal papers, held in the Bibliothèque Municipales, Avignon, MS 3796 and MS 3798.

28. Packe, *Mill*, p. 412, for his estimate of the cost of the tomb; the conversion into today's value is made using the Retail Price Index and the data set at www.measuringworth.com; letter from Helen Taylor to Algernon Taylor, 23 October 1859, in the *Mill–Taylor Collection*, quoted in Packe, *Mill*, p. 412.

29. For details of the black stationery, produced by Hugh Curry Hann of Gray's Inn Road London, see *CW*, XV, p. 662, n11.; the translation of the inscription is in Pascal's papers in the Avignon Bibliothèque, MS 3796; *OL*, *CW*, XVIII, p. 226. See also the following later passage: 'If a person possesses any tolerable amount of common sense and experience, his own mode of laying out his existence is the best, not because it is the best in itself, but because it is his own mode', *OL*, *CW*, XVIII, p. 270.

30. *The Prelude*, Book XIII, ll. 120–23, *Wordsworth: The Major Works*, p. 581.

31. 'Ach Gott in Himmel!', letter from Thomas Carlyle to Dr John Carlyle, 4 May 1859, *Letters of Thomas Carlyle*, vol. 2, p. 196; 'volunteers', Ryan, *Mill*, p. 148;

'He who lets', *OL*, *CW*, XVIII, p. 262.

32. 'Originality does not', letter to E. R. Edger, 13 September 1862, *CW*, XV, p. 793; 'less capable', *OL*, *CW*, XVIII, pp. 267–8; 'l'autonomie', letter to Emile Acollas, 20 September 1871, *CW*, XVIII, pp. 1831–2.

33. 'Nearer to', *OL*, *CW*, XVIII, p. 267; described as a 'motto' in *AB*, *CW*, I, p. 261; 'The grand', *OL*, *CW*, XVIII, p. 215; 'the end of man', *OL*, *CW*, XVIII, p. 261.

34. *OL*, *CW*, XVIII, p. 263.

35. 'Pollards', *OL*, *CW*, XVIII, p. 265; 'compressed', *OL*, *CW*, XVIII, pp. 267, 271; 'cramped', *OL*, *CW*, XVIII, pp. 242, 265; 'pinched', *OL*, *CW*, XVIII, p. 265; 'dwarfed', *OL*, *CW*, XVIII, p. 265, 310; 'starved', *OL*, *CW*, XVIII, pp. 262, 265; 'withered', *CW*, XVIII, p. 265; Ryan, *Philosophy of Mill*, p. 255.

36. 'As it is useful', *OL*, *CW*, XVIII, pp. 260–61; 'rounded off', Journal, 6 February 1854, *CW*, XXVII, pp. 651–2; the letter with the list was to HTM, 7 February 1854, *CW*, XIV, p. 152; 'what do I prefer?', *OL*, *CW*, XVIII, p. 264; in the interests of social experimentation, Mill also wanted more 'spontaneity' – see *OL*, *CW*, XVIII, pp. 224, 261, 277 – and more 'eccentricity', *OL*, *CW*, XVIII, pp. 265, 269.

37. James Fitzjames Stephen, *Liberty, Equality, Fraternity*, 2nd edn, London: Smith, Elder, 1874,

quoted in Himmelfarb, *Liberty and Liberalism*, p. 286.

38. Mill was not teetotal, but was 'exceedingly temperate as regarded the table', with his 'simple breakfast' at the India House typically followed later by a 'plain dinner' at home, Bain, *John Stuart Mill*, p. 149; the American prohibitive moves were enacted in the Main Liquor Law of 1815.

39. For *On Liberty* discussion, see *OL*, *CW*, XVIII, p. 298; in 'Notes on the Newspapers', *Monthly Repository*, 24 April 1834, *CW*, VI, p. 215: 'Make it in the labourer's interests to be frugal and temperate, and you will not need to make his cottage a prison, in order to keep him from wasting his wages and getting drunk'.

40. '*Deorum injuriae*', *OL*, *CW*, XVIII, p. 298; 'rather trivial', *OL*, *CW*, XVIII, p. 284; 'suppose now', *OL*, *CW*, XVIII, pp. 284–5 (Mussulmans = Muslims); 'with the personal tastes', *OL*, *CW*, XVIII, p. 285.

41. Police figures and Dostoyesky quote in Picard, *Victorian London*, pp. 255, 257.

42. *OL*, *CW*, XVIII, p. 296; Stephen, *Liberty, Equality,* quoted in Packe, *Mill*, p. 404.

43. *OL*, *CW*, XVIII, pp. 296–7; for later views, see letter to Lord Amberley, 2 February 1870, *CW*, XVII, p. 1693.

44. For 'animal appetites', see *OL*, *CW*, XVIII, p. 278 and *Util. CW*,

X, pp. 210–11; and in his preface to 'Grote's Aristotle' he laments that his old friend's 'merely animal and nutritive organs of his bodily frame' did not last as long as 'the properly human organ, the reasoning and thinking brain', *CW*, XI, p. 475.

45. Jeremy Bentham, 'Offences Against One's Self', ed. Louis Crompton, *Journal of Homosexuality*, vol. 3, no. 4, 1978, pp. 389–405.

46. See the *Principles* for Mill's suggestion that the pursuit of money, while inferior to a struggle for 'better things', was more desirable than leaving people to 'rust and stagnate', *POPE*, *CW*, III, pp. 754, 127; 'vigorous impulse' is in 'Property and Taxation', *Fortnightly Review*, March 1873, *CW*, V, p. 699; Stephen's description of Fawcett appeared in his 'Thoughts of an outsider: public schools', *Cornhill Magazine*, 27, 1873, quoted in Collini, *Public Moralists*, p. 193; 'Strong impulses', *OL*, *CW*, XVIII, p. 263.

47. 'Passive rather than active' *OL*, *CW*, XVIII, p. 255; Florence Nightingale, *Cassandra*, 1852, quoted in J. M. Golby (ed.), *Culture and Society in Britain 1850–1890*, Oxford: Oxford University Press, 1986, p. 248.

48. Thomas Hardy, *Jude the Obscure* (1895), London: Macmillan, 1971, p. 233, quoted in the *Mill News Letter*, Summer 1975, vol. X, no. 2.

49. 'One whose desires', *OL*, *CW*, XVIII, p. 264; 'independent centres', *OL*, *CW*, XVIII, p. 272; 'moral obligation', *Hamilton*, *CW*, IX, p. 466; 'really is of importance', *OL*, *CW*, XVIII, p. 263.

50. 'Starved specimens', *OL*, *CW*, XVIII, p. 263; 'Spencer so good', letter to Alexander Bain, 18 March 1864, *CW*, XV, p. 927; 'indefinite progressiveness' in 'Spirit of the Age', *CW*, XXII, p. 234; Himmelfarb, *On Liberty and Liberalism*, p. 321.

51. *Logic*, *CW*, VIII, p. 842; 'Civilization', *CW*, XVIII, p. 136; for a discussion of the prevailing views on the issue of forming habits see Collini, *Public Moralists*, pp. 98–9.

52. Letter to Theodor Gomperz, 5 October 1857, *CW*, XV, p. 539; *Rep. Gov.*, *CW*, XIX, p. 392. In 1829, he had argued to Gustave d'Eichthal that 'government exists for all purposes whatever that are for man's good: and the highest & most important of these purposes is the improvement of man himself as a moral and intelligent being', 8 October 1829, *CW*, XII, p. 36.

53. Letter to John Austin, 13 April 1847, *CW*, XIII, p. 712.

54. *POPE*, *CW*, III, p. 799 (*in limine* = in the gut); *OL*, *CW*, XVIII, p. 223.

55. 'Centralisation', *Edinburgh*

Review, April 1862. *CW*, XIX,
p. 609.

56. *OL*, *CW*, XVIII, p. 306.
57. 'Certain evil', *POPE*, *CW*, III, p.
945; conditional support for Plate
Lock Manufactory, see letter to
Thomas Jones, 22 March 1865,
CW, XVI, p. 1020; for evidence
of support for state ownership of
parks, see letter to Herbert
Spencer, 27 March 1859, *CW*, XV,
p. 609.
58. Alan Ryan, 'Mill in a Liberal
Landscape', in Skorupski (ed.),
Mill, p. 525: 'Mill treats
governments as if they were
individuals writ large; individuals
can advocate moral visions
without imposing them on
others, and in Mill's eyes
governments can do so, too.'
Quote from 'Coleridge', *CW*, X,
p. 156.
59. *POPE*, *CW*, III, pp. 947–50, for
the discussion of education and
all quotes in this paragraph.
60. *OL*, *CW*, XVIII, p. 302, for the
quotes on education in this
paragraph, and the following
passage: 'Hardly anyone will
deny that it is one of the most
sacred duties of the parents (or,
as law and usage now stand, the
father), after summoning a
human being into the world, to
give to that being an education
fitting him to perform his part
well in life towards others and
towards himself.' In 1868, his last
year as an MP, he took the same
line: 'I entertain the strongest

objections to any plan which
would give a practical monopoly
to schools under government
control'. Letter to Leopold John
Bernays, 8 January 1868, *CW*,
XVI, p. 1347; 'All that has been
said', *OL*, *CW*, XVIII, p. 302.
61. *POPE*, *CW*, III, p. 947.
62. *Util.*, *CW*, X, p. 216.
63. 'Weber & Beethoven', letter to
James Barnard, 28 October 1869,
CW, XVII, p. 1661; *Util.*, *CW*, X,
p. 212.
64. Letter to Herbert Spencer, 27
March 1859, *CW*, XV p. 609;
'Claims of Labour', *CW*, IV,
pp. 387, 388; 'better house
accommodation' in letter to John
Campbell, 4 April 1866, *CW*,
XVI, p. 1155; 'foster high art' in
'The Right of Property in Land',
The Examiner, 19 July 1873, *CW*,
XXV, p. 1240.
65. *POPE*, *CW*, III, p. 968; for
'public spirit', see 'Centralisation',
CW, XIX, p. 603; 'rare and
precious', *POPE*, *CW*, III,
p. 968.
66. For the discussion of 'learned
class', see *POPE*, *CW*, III,
pp. 968–9. In *Representative
Government*, Mill suggested that
if the UK needed a second
chamber – which he doubted – it
should be composed of former
chief justices, cabinet ministers,
military chiefs, senior civil
servants and perhaps some
professors, but that 'mere
scientific and literary eminence'
was 'too indefinite and

67. *POPE, CW*, III, pp. 957–8.

68. Ibid., pp. 960–62.

69. 'Notes on the Newspapers', *Monthly Repository*, 18 April 1834, *CW*, VI, p. 203.

70. *POPE, CW*, III, pp. 961, 962.

71. 'Centralisation', *CW*, XIX, pp. 582, 601–2. But the growth of legislation did not necessarily unbalance the relationship between state and individual, according to Mill. Progress meant more law, but it also implied a strengthening in the capacities of individuals, communities and enterprises; the role for the state was, in fact, much greater when 'civilization was at the lowest' and little could be expected of the people. With social and economic advancement came not only new laws but also more capable citizens: 'though the progress of civilization is constantly requiring new things to be done, it also multiplies the cases in which individuals or associations are able and willing to do them gratuitously': *CW*, XIX, p. 603.

72. 'Worth of a State', *OL, CW*, XVIII, p. 310; 'the individuals may not', *OL, CW*, XVIII, p. 305; 'mental education', *OL, CW*, XVIII, p. 305; 'principal . . . recommendation', *OL, CW*, XVIII, p. 305; 'peculiar training', *OL, CW*, XVIII, p. 302; 'Government operations', *OL,*

CW, XVIII, p. 306; 'special duty', *OL, CW*, XVIII, p. 309.

73. Thomas Hobbes, *Leviathan* (1651), quoted in Quentin Skinner, *Liberty Before Liberalism*, Cambridge: Cambridge University Press, 1998, p. 9; 'tyranny of the majority', *OL, CW*, XVIII, pp. 219–20. Mill's review of Tocqueville's first volume anticipated this element of *On Liberty*: 'M. de Tocqueville's fears, however, are not so much for the security and the ordinary worldly interests of individuals, as for the moral dignity and progressiveness of the race. It is a tyranny exercised over opinions, more than over persons, which he is apprehensive of. He dreads lest all individuality of character, and independence of thought and assessment, should be prostrated under the despotic yoke of public opinion.' 'Tocqueville' [I], *CW*, XVIII, p. 81; 'social tyranny', *OL, CW*, XVIII, p. 220.

74. 'So natural', *OL, CW*, XVIII, p. 222; Spanish anti-Protestantism, *OL, CW*, XVIII, p. 285; Mormon polygamy, *OL, CW*, XVIII, pp. 290–91; 'offensive words', *OL, CW*, XVIII, p. 239; 'yoke of opinion', *OL, CW*, XVIII, p. 241; 'Who can compute', *OL, CW*, XVIII, p. 242.

75. Darwin is quoted in Joseph Hamburger, 'Religion and 'On Liberty', in Michael Laine (ed.),

A Cultivated Mind, p.143; 'chief danger of the time', *OL*, *CW*, XVIII, p. 269.

76. 'Civilisation', *CW*, XVIII, p. 125.

77. Stephen and Hutton are both quoted by H. S. Jones in his excellent 'John Stuart Mill as Moralist', *Journal of the History of Ideas*, 53, 1992, pp. 301, 305; 'bohemian nonsense' is the accusation of R. P. Anschutz in *The Philosophy of John Stuart Mill*, Oxford: Oxford University Press, London, 1953, p. 25, quoted in C. L. Ten, *Mill On Liberty*, Oxford: Oxford University Press, 1980, p. 70.

78. 'Well directed', speech on 'Perfectability', London Debating Society, 2 May 1828, *CW*, XXVI, p. 433; 'great efficacy' in 'On Marriage', *CW*, XXI, p. 48; 'Acts injurious', *OL*, *CW*, XVIII, p. 279; 'moral disapprobation', *OL*, *CW*, XVIII, p. 281.

79. 'It would be absurd', *OL*, *CW*, XVIII, p. 262; 'He who does anything', *OL*, *CW*, XVIII, p. 262; 'Different persons', *OL*, *CW*, XVIII, p. 270; 'plan of life', *OL*, *CW*, XVIII, p. 262.

80. 'Opinions of masses', *OL*, *CW*, XVIII, p. 269; 'general average', *OL*, *CW*, XVIII, p. 271; ; 'honour and glory', *OL*, *CW*, XVIII, p. 269.

81. *OL*, *CW*, XVIII, pp. 269–70.

82. Herbert Cowell, 'Liberty, Equality, Fraternity: Mr John Stuart Mill', *Blackwood's Edinburgh Magazine*, quoted in Jones, 'John Stuart Mill as Moralist', p. 301; *OL*, *CW*, XVIII, p. 277. Years later, giving evidence to a Royal Commission on Contagious Diseases, Mill said: 'If we were never to interfere with the evil consequences which persons have brought upon themselves, we should help one another very little.' *CW*, XXI, p. 358 (Mill gave evidence on 13 May 1871).

83. *OL*, *CW*, XVIII, pp. 302, 304.

84. Ibid., p. 300.

85. Ibid., pp. 300–301.

86. Trevelyan, *Macaulay*, vol. 2, pp. 469–70.

87. Stephen's quote is from his piece in the *Saturday Review*, 12 and 19 February 1873, quoted by Peter Nicholson, 'The Reception and Early Reputation of Mill's Political Thought', in Skorupski (ed.), *Mill*, p. 468; Henry Buckle, 'Mill on Liberty', *Fraser's Magazine*, also quoted by Nicholson, p. 468. Mill may have anticipated some of these reactions, protesting – perhaps a little too much – 'I am not endeavouring to erect a barrier against imaginary evils.' *OL*, *CW*, XVIII, p. 284.

88. For the codes in *The Times*, see Matthew Sweet, *Inventing the Victorians*, London: Faber and Faber, 2001, p. 42; for 'The Baboon Lady', see ibid., pp. 142–3.

89. 'Semi-heathenism', from

Ecclesiastical Returns, 1851, quoted in Briggs, *Age of Improvement*, p. 405; Shaftesbury is quoted in Gertrude Himmelfarb, *The Roads to Modernity – The British, French and American Enlightenments*, New York: Vintage, 2004, p. 39.

90. For 'brightest ornaments', see *AB* Early Draft, *CW*, I, p. 46; for Froude's *travails*, see Herbert Paul, *The Life of Froude*, New York: Scribner's, 1905, pp. 47–52.

91. 'Consecrated', *AB*, *CW*, I, p. 261; 'Nothing can better shew', *AB*, *CW*, I, p. 259.

92. *AB*, *CW*, I, pp. 259, 260.

93. See, for example, Nicholson, 'The Reception and Early Reputation of Mill's Political Thought' in Skorupski (ed.), *Mill*, p. 470: 'to that extent, the verdict of his contemporaries was irrelevant'.

94. 'Lost in the crowd', in 'Civilization', *CW*, XVIII, p. 132, and *OL*, *CW*, XVIII, p. 268; 'stretch unduly', *OL*, *CW*, XVIII, p. 227; 'got the better of', *OL*, *CW*, XVIII, p. 264; 'already begins', *OL*, *CW*, XVIII, p. 274; 'every day diminishing', *OL*, *CW*, XVIII, p. 274; 'dreaded censorship', *OL*, *CW*, XVIII, p. 264.

95. 'Still more the woman', *OL*, *CW*, XVIII, p. 270; 'Spartans and Helots', *OL*, *CW*, XVIII, p. 221; 'despotic power', *OL*, *CW*, XVIII, p. 307.

96. The Willis Rooms meeting took place on 6 June 1859; among those present were Russell, Palmerston, Bright and Roebuck. For Mill's comment on Darwin, see letter to Herbert Spencer, 2 December 1858, *CW*, XVI, p. 1505. Two years later he described Darwin's work as being 'as great a triumph as knowledge and ingenuity could possibly achieve on such a question', letter to Alexander Bain, 11 April 1860, *CW*, XV, p. 695.

97. Letter to Alexander Bain, 15 October 1859, *CW*, XV, p. 640; Morley, *Recollections*, vol. 1, p. 61.

12. To Hell I Will Go (1859–65)

1. Letter to William Thornton, November 1861, *CW*, XV, p. 747.

2. 'Wallflower Growing on the Living Rock', May 1860, *Phytologist. CW*, XXXI, p. 283; 'Spring Flowers of the South of Europe', October 1860, *Phytologist. CW*, XXXI, p. 283.

3. 'Ceases to be a philosopher', in 'J. S. Mill on the American Contest', *The Economist*, 8 February 1862, p. 144, quoted in Collini, *Public Moralists*, p. 137; 'satanic school' in the *Record*, 2 June 1865, p. 3, quoted in Kinzer et al., *A Moralist In and Out of Parliament*, p. 50; letter to Helen Taylor, 11 February 1860, *CW*, XV, p. 675.

4. Letter to Harriet Grote, 2 September 1863, *CW*, XV, p. 880. Why a male dog was apparently called Daisy is not known.

5. *AB* Early Draft, *CW*, I, pp. 202, 204; *AB*, *CW*, I, p. 203; letter to George Grote, 4 February 1866, *CW*, XVI, p. 1144.

6. Letter to HTM, 22 February 1855, *CW*, XIV, p. 338.

7. 'Tocqueville' [I], *CW*, XVIII, pp. 72–3.

8. *Rep. Gov.*, *CW*, XIX, pp. 457, 473.

9. Macaulay is quoted in Briggs, *Age of Improvement*, p. 267; letter from Harriet Grote to Kate Amberley, 11 December 1866, *Amberley Papers*, vol. 1, p. 545; Bagehot's *The English Constitution* was first published in 1865 and 1867 in the *Fortnightly*; the passages quoted are cited in Briggs, *Age of Improvement*, pp. 358, 391.

10. Letter to John Cairnes, 2 March 1859, *CW*, XV, p. 597; letter to Thomas Hare, 3 March 1859, *CW*, XV, p. 599.

11. 'Great discovery', letter to Thomas Hare, 19 December 1859, *CW*, XV, p. 653; 'effectual and practicable', letter to Lord Overstone, 25 March 1860, *CW*, XV, p. 690; 'well-dressed friends', letter to Thomas Hare, 4 February 1865, *CW*, XVI, p. 991; 'justice to all', from Mill's speech on 'Hare's Plan for the Metropolis' to the National Association for the Promotion of Social Science, 10 April 1865, *CW*, XXVIII, p. 13.

12. 'Mob-government', in 'Pledges' [2], *Examiner*, 15 July 1832, *CW*, XXIII, p. 504; 'numerical majority', letter to Thomas Hare, 4 February 1860, *CW*, XV, p. 668; 'every or any section', *Rep. Gov.*, *CW*, XIX, p. 419; 'fair representation', letter to Henry Chapman, 12 January 1862, *CW*, XV p. 765: 'Fair representation of minorities. I look upon ... as the sheet anchor of the democracy of the future. If it is not adopted, there is no knowing that society may not be barbarized down into not only a dead level of narrow minded stupidity, but into lawlessness.'; 'a democratic people would', *Rep. Gov.*, *CW*, XIX, p. 460.

13. 'Recent Writers on Reform', *Fraser's Magazine*, April 1859, *CW*, XIX, p. 364.

14. Letter to Moncure Conway, 23 October 1865, *CW*, XVI, p. 1106; *Rep. Gov.*, *CW*, XIX, p. 452.

15. 'Point to be decided', letter to Alexander Bain, 17 March 1859, *CW*, XV p. 606; 'relax their despotism', letter to Henry Fawcett, *CW*, XV p. 672; 'mere demagogue', letter to Edwin Chadwick, 20 December 1859, *CW*, XV, pp. 654–5.

16. 'Millions of voters', *Thoughts on Parliamentary Reform*, London: Parker, 1859. *CW*, XIX p. 327; letter to Helen Taylor, 23 Feb 1860, *CW*, XV p. 686.

17. *Rep. Gov.*, *CW*, XIX, p. 470; 'exclude nobody', letter to Thomas Potter, 16 March 1865, *CW*, XVI, p. 1013: the full quote reads: 'after a few years, exclude

none but those who cared for so little for the privilege that their vote, if given would not in general be an indication of any real political opinion'.

18. *Rep. Gov.*, *CW*, XIX, pp. 472–3.

19. 'When all have votes' and 'unskilled labourer', *Thoughts on Parliamentary Reform*, *CW*, XIX p. 324; in *Representative Government*, Mill stopped short of prescribing the specific numbers of votes to be allocated, but he did suggest that 'two or more' be given to a 'banker, merchant of manufacturer' as well as university graduates and members of a recognized profession, *Rep. Gov.*, *CW*, XIX, p. 475.

20. *Thoughts on Parliamentary Reform*, *CW*, XIX p. 323.

21. 'Render unnecessary', *AB*, *CW*, I, p. 261; *Rep. Gov.*, *CW*, XIX, pp. 477–8.

22. In a letter to an unidentified correspondent, 10 May 1867, *CW*, XVI, p. 1269, Mill wrote: 'My letter did not amount to a promise that I would support the proposal to omit the word "certificated" in the clause giving the franchise to attornies, though it expressed a willingness to entertain the question.'

23. Letter to Earl Grey, 13 May 1864, *CW*, XV, p. 941.

24. Reported in a letter from John Bowring to Edwin Chadwick, 23 December 1868, in the Chadwick Papers at UCL, quoted in Hamburger, *Intellectuals in Politics*, p. 274.

25. *Thoughts on Parliamentary Reform*, *CW*, XIX, p. 332.

26. Letter to George Cornewall Lewis, 20 March 1859, *CW*, XV, p. 608; letter to Mary Carpenter, 29 December 1867, *CW*, XVI, p. 1340.

27. *Thoughts on Parliamentary Reform*, *CW*, XIX, p. 333; the comments on shopkeepers were made during election meetings on 6 July 1865, reported in the *Daily News* and *Daily Telegraph*, *CW*, XXVIII, p. 31, and 8 July 1865, which was additionally reported by *The Times CW*, XXVIII, p. 40.

28. John Adams is quoted in Stephen Breyer, *Active Liberty, Interpreting Our Democratic Constitution*, New York: Vintage Books, 2005, p. 135; 'A man who does not care', *Thoughts on Parliamentary Reform*, *CW*, XIX, pp. 338–9.

29. Romilly's pamphlet *Public Responsibility and Vote by Ballot*, p. 42, quoted by Mill in his 'Romilly's Responsibility and the Ballot', *The Reader*, 29 April 1865; the passage from Mill in response to Romilly is at *CW*, XXV, p. 1215; for the Calhoun dream, see letter to HTM, 12 January 1855, *CW*, XIV, p. 289; For evidence for continued bribery and coercion, see H. J. Hanham, *Elections and Party Management: Politics in the Time*

of Disraeli and Gladstone, London: Longmans, 1958.

30. Canvassing as a 'degrading practice', see letter to Henry Chapman, 8 July 1858, *CW*, XV, pp. 558–9; for 'property qualification', see *Thoughts on Parliamentary Reform*, *CW*, XIX, p. 320; 'access to Parliament to rich men', *Rep. Gov.*, *CW*, XIX, p. 498.

31. 'Adventurers', letter to Henry Chapman, 8 July 1858, *CW*, XV, p. 558; '658 prizes', *Rep. Gov.*, *CW*, XIX, p. 419.

32. *Rep. Gov.*, *CW*, XIX, p. 507.

33. Ibid., p. 432.

34. Carlyle, 'Downing Street', *Latter Day Pamphlets*, No. 3, reprinted in Thomas Carlyle, *Selected Writings*, London: Penguin, 1971, p. 300; Bentham, quoted by Dr Peter Niesen in 'Bentham and J. S. Mill on Parliamentary Deliberation', a paper presented to the Mill Bicentennial Conference, April 2006, UCL; *Rep. Gov.*, *CW*, XIX, pp. 432–3.

35. 'The House of Lords', *Globe and Traveller*, 16 October 1835, *CW*, XXIV, p. 783; 'Vindication of the French Revolution of February 1848', *CW*, XX, p. 539; *Rep. Gov.*, *CW*, XIX, p. 516; letter to Edwin Chadwick, 2 May 1869, *CW*, XVII, p. 1595.

36. 'Armand Carrel', *CW*, XX, p. 199; Bentham is quoted by Mill in *AB*, *CW*, I, p. 109; 'Vindication', *CW*, XX, p. 331.

37. 'Identity of political antecedents',

38. Ibid., p. 549.

39. 'Least centralized', *Rep. Gov.*, *CW*, XIX, p. 534; 'One God', 'Centralisation', *CW*, XIX, p. 613.

40. 'Most aristocratic', *Rep. Gov.*, *CW*, XIX, p. 537; 'oligarchy', *AB*, *CW*, I, p. 201; 'fantastical trappings', *Rep. Gov.*, *CW*, XIX, p. 538.

41. 'Centralisation', *CW*, XIX, p. 581.

42. *AB*, *CW*, I, p. 203.

43. 'Fine fellow', letter to Helen Taylor, 4 February 1860, *CW*, XIV, p. 671; 'Puritan knows Bible' is quoted by Collini, *Public Moralists*, p. 179; for details of Fawcett's accident and 'shan't make any difference', see Edward Carpenter's memoir, *My Days and Dreams*, London: George Allen & Unwin, 1916; for Disraeli's quote, see William Flavelle Monypenny and George Earle Buckle, *The Life of Benjamin Disraeli, Earl of Beaconsfield*, 6 vols, London: John Murray, 1910–20, vol. 5, p. 501.

44. Monypenny and Buckle, *Benjamin Disraeli*, vol. 4, p. 331.

45. Wilson, *The Victorians*, p. 262.

46. 'Gathering the health and spirits', letter to Theodor Gomperz, 23 April 1863, *CW*, XV, p. 855; for evidence of his 'catch-up' reading, see letter to Thomas Hare, 11 January 1866, *CW*, XVI, pp. 1138–40; letter to William Longman, *CW*, XV,

p. 922; 'I propose giving up all pecuniary benefits to myself from the popular editions, to enable them to be sold cheaper', for details of sales of the popular edition of the *Principles*, see John Robson's 'Textual Introduction, *CW*, II, p. lxvi, n.8.

47. 'Popular influence', letter to Charles Cummings, 23 February 1863, *CW*, XV, p. 843; for evidence of Mill's support for the *Westminster*, see Ashton, *142 Strand, A Radical Address in Victorian London*, pp. 288–9.

48. For Mill's list of subjects at the Political Economy Club, see *CW*, XXXI, pp. 407–10; for Gladstone, see letter to John Cairnes, 5 March 1865, *CW*, XVI, p. 1002; for Cairnes, see his letter to William Nesbitt, 9 May 1859, in *Mill–Taylor Collection*, vol. 23, f. 51.

49. 'Brotherhood in arms', letter to John Cairnes, 24 June 1862, *CW*, XVI, p. 785; speech on 'Hare's Plan for the Metropolis' to the National Association for the Promotion of Social Science, 10 April 1865, *CW*, XXVIII, pp. 11–13.

50. For 'little treatise' description, see letter to Alexander Bain, 15 October 1859, *CW*, XV, p. 640 and letter to William Ward, 28 November 1859, *CW*, XV, p. 640; Alan Ryan in his 'Introduction' to the 1987 Penguin edition of Mill and Bentham, *Utilitarianism and Other Essays*,

p. 12; and for 'exasperating', see his *Philosophy of Mill*, p. 96.

51. Letter to Theodor Gomperz , 30 August 1858, *CW*, XV, p. 570; letter to Charles Dupont-White, 10 October 1861, *CW*, XV, p. 745.

52. For Mill's revisions to the essay, see *CW*, X, p. cxxv – the textual editor John Robson estimates that only eight are of any substance; *AB*, *CW*, I, pp. 265–6; for Mill's contemplation of a 'popular' edition of the *Logic*, see letter to William Longman, 22 December 1867, *CW*, XVI, p. 1336 (he decided against, see letter 9 January 1868, *CW*, XVI, p. 1351); for the Durham Cooperative Institute gift, see letter to William Longman, 18 February 1866, *CW*, XXXII, p. 163.

53. 'Only as much depth' refers to Samuel Bailey, whose work Mill reviewed in 'Rationale of representation', *London Review*, July 1835, *CW*, XVIII, p. 17; 'All action', *Util.*, *CW*, X, p. 206.

54. 'Whewell', *CW*, X, p. 191.

55. *Util.*, *CW*, X, p. 234; ibid., p. 209.

56. 'Not amenable', *Util.*, *CW*, X, p. 134; 'the only proof', *Util.*, *CW*, X, p. 234.

57. 'The Gorgias', *Monthly Repository*, October, November, December 1834, *CW*, XI, p. 150; for a discussion of Mill's approach to approximation, see Ryan, *Philosophy of Mill*, pp. 40–41.

58. Letter to Theodor Gomperz, 23 April 1868, *CW*, XVI, p. 1391, in

reply to a letter from Gomperz to Mill on 26 March 1868, quoted in *CW*, X, p. cxxvi.

59. For the passage, see *Util.*, *CW*, X, p. 234; letter to Henry Jones, 13 June 1868, *CW*, XVI, p. 1414.

60. *Util.*, *CW*, X, pp. 227, 228.

61. Ibid., pp. 250–51.

62. Letter to Charles Norton, 24 September 1868, *CW*, XVI, p. 1443.

63. 'Healthy growth', *Util.*, *CW*, X, p. 231; 'the complete spirit', ibid., p. 218; 'Religion of Humanity', ibid., p. 232; 'small number of moulds', *OL*, *CW*, XVIII, pp. 267–8.

64. *Util.*, *CW*, X, p. 215.

65. Ibid., p. 211.

66. Ibid., pp. 210–11.

67. Ibid., p. 211.

68. Ibid., p. 212.

69. For Grote's doubts about Mill's 'persistence in the true faith', see Bain, *John Stuart Mill*, p. 83; for Grote's tempered praise for utilitarianism, see his letter to Mill, January 1862, partially reprinted in Harriet Grote, *The Personal Life of George Grote*, London: Murray, 1873, pp. 257–8 and Mill's reply, 10 January 1862, *CW*, XVI, p. 763; for Jevons's criticism, see 'Mill's Philosophy Tested', in W. Stanley Jevons, *Pure Logic and Other Minor Works*, London: Macmillan, 1890, pp. 200–201, quoted in Capaldi, *Mill*, p. 262; for 'considerably embarrassed', Courtney, *Mill*, p. 168.

70. *Logic*, *CW*, VIII, p. 952.

71. *Util.*, *CW*, X, p. 213.

72. 'The Death of Mr Mill', *Spectator*, May 1873; 'utility in the largest sense', *OL*, *CW*, XVIII, p. 224; 'where, not the person's own character', ibid., p. 261.

73. *AB*, *CW*, I, pp. 145, 147.

74. Letter to John Cairnes, 18 August 1861, *CW*, XV, p. 738.

75. Letter to Samuel Wood, 2 June 1867, *CW*, XVI, p. 1278.

76. 'Free and slaveholding', in 'The Slave Power', *Westminster Review*, October 1862, *CW*, XXI, p. 157; 'destined to give instruction', see letter to the Chairmen of the Library Committees, South Carolina, 3 March 1854, *CW*, XIV, p. 173.

77. Commager is paraphrased by Porter, *Enlightenment*, p. xx; letter to John Motley, 17 September 1862, *CW*, XV, p. 797: 'If you come well and honourably through one of the severest trials which a nation has even undergone, the whole futurity of mankind will assume a brighter aspect. If not, it will for some time to come be very much darkened.'; and 'present gigantic struggle', letter to unidentified correspondent, 2 July 1864, *CW*, XV, p. 946.

78. 'More exultation', letter to John Motley, 31 October 1862, *CW*, XV, p. 800; for discussion of the impact of the Civil War on northern England, see Briggs,

Age of Improvement, p. 431 and Hobsbawm, *Age of Capital*, p. 345.

79. 'For the sake of cotton', in 'The Contest in America', *Fraser's Magazine*, February 1862, *CW*, XXI, p. 128; 'moral feeling', ibid., p. 140; for details of US publication, see John Robson's 'Textual Introduction' to *CW*, XXI, p. lxiv.

80. Radical support for secession is discussed by Collini, *Public Moralists*, p. 141; Mill's 'slaveholders' rebellion' line was in a speech, 'Goldwin Smith', 4 February 1867, *CW*, XXVIII, p. 130.

81. From the report of Gladstone's speech in *The Times*, 9 October 1862, quoted in Roy Jenkins, *Gladstone*, London: Macmillan, 1995, p. 237.

82. 'Magnificent moral spectacle', quoted in Collini, *Public Moralists*, p. 112; letter from William Gladstone to the Duchess of Sutherland, 7 November 1862, quoted in John Morley, *Life of Gladstone*, 3 vols, London: Macmillan, 1908, vol. 2, pp. 71–2.

83. 'The Slave Power', *CW*, XXI, p. 157.

84. 'Room for his elbow', Bain, *John Stuart Mill*, p. 118; 'sad aberration . . . ashamed and grieved', letter to John Cairnes, 25 November 1861, *CW*, XV, pp. 750–52; letter to William Whewell, 24 May 1865, *CW*, XVI, p. 1056.

85. 'Event of our age', quoted in Briggs, *Age of Improvement*, p. 432; for the Gomperz description, see Adelaide Weinberg, *Theodor Gomperz and John Stuart Mill*, Geneva: Librairie Droz, 1963, quoted in Capaldi, *Mill*, p. 307. For Mill's plans to attend the Bright meeting, see letter to John Cairnes, 25 March 1863, *CW*, XV, p. 851.

86. Bain, *John Stuart Mill*, p. 119; Harriet Grote, *Life of Grote*, p. 264; 'J. S. Mill on the American Contest', *The Economist*, 8 February 1862, p. 144; 'burn people alive', 'The Contest in America', *CW*, XXI, p. 136.

87. 'The Contest in America', *CW*, XXI, p. 137.

88. 'Full equality to negroes', letter to Parke Godwin, 15 May 1865, *CW*, XVI, p. 1052; 'aristocracy of skin', 'Tocqueville' [I], *CW*, XVIII, p. 55; for discussion of Cairnes's position, see 'The Slave Power', *CW*, XXI, pp. 163–4; for his change of mind, see Adelaide Weinberg, *John Elliott Cairnes and the American Civil War*, London: Kingwood Press, 1970, p. 42.

89. 'I cannot join', 'The Contest in America', *CW*, XXI, p. 141; 'infinitely less evil', letter to J. F. Mollett, 30 December 1847, *CW*, XIII, p. 729.

90. 'True principles', *AB*, *CW*, I, p. 263; 'A Few Words on Non-Intervention', *Fraser's Magazine*,

December 1958, *CW*, XXI, pp. 116–17.

91. 'A Few Words on Non-Intervention', *CW*, XXI, p. 118.

92. Ibid., p. 122.

93. Ibid., pp. 122, 123.

94. Ibid., pp. 118–19.

95. *OL*, *CW*, XVIII, p. 224.

96. Letter to John Cairnes, 15 June 1862, *CW*, XV, p. 784; p. 1758, letter to Henry Kilgour, 15 August 1870, *CW*, XVII, p. 1758.

97. 'Government of leading-strings' walk alone', *Rep. Gov.*, *CW*, XIX, p. 396; Alan Ryan in his 'Introduction' to Moir et al. (eds), *Mill's Encounter with India*, p. 15.

98. Letter from Charles Kingsley, 1866, quoted in Bernard Semmel, *The Governor Eyre Controversy*, London: MacGibbon & Kee, 1962, p. 100.

99. Letter to George Grote, 11 June 1862, *CW*, XV, p. 778; letter to Henry Fawcett, 6 March 1862, *CW*, XV, p. 780.

100. 'Greece-intoxicated', Bain, *John Stuart Mill*, p. 94; letter inviting the Grotes, 10 January 1862, and extract from George Grote's reply, *CW*, XV, p. 761; for a full weather report, see letter to Henry Fawcett, 6 March 1862, *CW*, XV, p. 777.

101. Letter from Helen Taylor to Fanny Stirling, 6 July 1862, quoted in Packe, *Mill*, p. 428.

102. Letter to George Grote, 11 June 1862, *CW*, XV, pp. 779–80.

103. Letter to Theodor Gomperz,

23 April 1863, *CW*, XV, pp. 854–5.

104. For evidence of Hare's visit when Mill was busy, see letters to John Cairnes, 3 October 1864, *CW*, XV, p. 959; and to Thomas Hare, 1 December 1964, *CW*, XV, p. 970; letter to Theodor Gomperz, 16 June 1863, *CW*, XV, p. 863.

105. Letters to Theodor Gomperz, 5 July 1863, *CW*, XV, p. 866; and 29 July 1863, *CW*, XV, pp. 874–5.

106. Letter to Helen Taylor, 7 July 1863, *CW*, XV, p. 867.

107. *AB*, *CW*, I, p. 270.

108. Tennyson, 'Niggers are tigers', quoted in Wilson, *Victorians*, p. 272; 'at root' *AB*, *CW*, I, p. 270.

109. Ryan, *Mill*, p. 220; letter from George Grote to Mill, June 1865, in Harriet Grote, *Life of Grote*, p. 257.

110. For Mill's view of Mansel's 'detestable' book, see letter to Alexander Bain, 7 January 1863, *CW*, XV, p. 817, for Mansel's reciprocal view, see *CW*, XV, p. 817; n.7; Mill quoted the passage from Mansel, 'A God understood', in *An Examination of Sir William Hamilton's Philosophy*, *CW*, IX, pp. 34–5.

111. *Hamilton*, *CW*, IX, pp. 102–3.

112. *Record*, 2 June 1865, p. 3, and *Morning Advertiser*, 3 June 1865, p.3, both quoted in Kinzer et al., *A Moralist In and Out of Parliament*, pp. 50–51.

113. *Spectator*, 27 May 1865, p. 585 and 10 June 1865, p. 631, quoted in Kinzer et al., *A Moralist In and Out of Parliament*, p. 50.

114. F. D. Maurice quoted in Packe, *Mill*, p. 444; Connop Thirlwall, letter to the editor, *Spectator*, 17 June 1865, p. 668; letter from Mill to George Grote, 18 June 1865, *CW*, XVI, p. 1068.

115. *Hamilton*, *CW*, IX, p. 179.

116. Ibid., p. 189.

117. Ibid., p. 194; See Ryan, *Mill*, pp. 223-4 for a helpful discussion.

118. Bain, *John Stuart Mill*, p. 121; for Mill's note on Mansel, see *Hamilton*, *CW*, IX, p. 195; 'finding of bad reasons' is quoted (without attribution) by R. P. Anschutz in Arthur Sewell (ed.), *1840 and After*, Auckland: Auckland University College, 1940, pp. 125-6.

119. Lord Neaves is quoted in Packe, *Mill*, p. 445.

120. David Wilson, *Life of Carlyle*, vol. 6, pp. 59-60.

121. Letter to Thomas Carlyle, 11 April 1866, *CW*, XVI, p. 1157. There is some confusion about this letter. The only copy in existence is a draft in Mill's hand, to which a typed copy has been added along with this note: 'The lost letter of Mill's to Carlyle, which gave some offence to JWC. This copy is from Mill's rough draft which was, and I suppose is, among Carlyle's letters to Mill, now in the Carlyle house in Chelsea.' In Mill's draft, the last paragraph has been crossed out. But since everything else in the letter is unexceptional, it must have been in the version opened by Jane for it to have upset her. Perhaps Mill sent the draft, rather than the fair copy, by mistake.

122. For Mill's thank-you note, see letter to Harriet Grote, 22 February 1865, *CW*, XVI, p. 1000.

123. Letter from Harriet Grote to Helen Taylor, 11 November 1867, quoted in Packe, *Mill*, p. 435.

124. Mill and Amberley had met briefly a couple of times previously; 'opponents as allies', in Kate Amberley's journal, 20 February 1865, *Amberley Papers*, vol. 1, p. 373; letter to John Chapman, 28 February 1865, *CW*, XVI, p. 1000; Russell on 'Millenium', Kate Amberley's journal, 21 February 1865, *Amberley Papers*, vol. 1, p. 375.

125. The dates in question were 17, 18 and 19 June 1866, see *Amberley Papers*, vol. 1, pp. 513-14.

126. Thornton's letter to Fawcett, October 1862, is partially reprinted in Elliot (ed.), *The Letters of John Stuart Mill*, vol. 1, p. 262.

127. Thornton's letter to Gomperz is reprinted in Weinberg, *Gomperz and Mill*, pp. 32-3; *The Letters of Charles Eliot Norton*, vol. 1, p. 330, quoted in Packe, *Mill*, p. 430; for Mill's subscription to the *American Review*, see letter to Edwin Godkin, 24 May 1865, *CW*, XVI, p. 1056; Moncure Conway's comments are in his *Autobiography*, 2 vols, Boston and New York, 1904, vol. 2, p. 14.

128. Letter to Jane Mill Ferraboschi, 18 July 1865, *CW*, XVI, p.1079; for evidence that Mill usually passed quickly through Paris, see letter to Gustave d'Eichthal, 18 July 1863, *CW*, XV, p. 869: 'Ordinairement je ne traverse Paris qu'en courant, et sans m'y arrêter même une seule nuit.' But on at least two occasions he planned to see D'Eichthal on his way through Paris – see letters of 5 May 1865, *CW*, XVI, p. 1046, and 17 January 1867, *CW*, XVI, p. 1229; letter to Harriet Grote, from the Hotel Windsor, Rue de Rivoli, Paris, 2 September 1863, *CW*, XV, pp. 869–70.

129. Kate Amberley's Journal, 20 February 1865, *Amberley Papers*, vol. 1, pp. 372–4.

130. For examples of alterations to the *Logic*, see *CW*, VII, p. 495, where for the second edition (1846) Mill removed the following reference to Comte: 'who of all the philosophers seems to me to have approached the nearest to a sound view of this important subject'. Also see *CW*, VIII, p. 859, where Mill added, also for the second edition, a criticism of Comte for assuming human attributes to be 'ultimate facts' rather than the result of 'ultimate causes' – a reference to Comte's phrenology – and concluded: 'no writer, either of early or of recent date, is chargeable in higher degree with this aberration from the true scientific spirit, than M.

Comte.' For the footnote in *Hamilton*, see *CW*, IX, pp. 216–17n.

131. *AB*, *CW*, I, p. 271.

132. 'Source within themselves', Journal entry 21 January 1854, *CW*, XXVII, p. 645; letter to HTM, 16 September 1857, *CW*, XV, p. 537; 'great powers', *Logic*, *CW*, VII, p. 342; *Comte*, *CW*, X, pp. 367 –8.

133. *Comte*, *CW*, X, pp. 322–3.

134. 'Man in the story', *Comte*, *CW*, X, p. 302; 'ludicrous side', ibid., p. 341; 'ever laughed', ibid., p. 343.

135. 'Entire dissent', ibid., p. 352; Clotilde', ibid., p. 345.

136. Ibid., pp. 364, 368.

137. Letter to Richard Congreve, 8 August 1865, *CW*, XVI, p. 1085.

138. For details of the positivist movement, see Walter M. Simon, *Positivism in the Nineteenth Century*, Ithaca, New York: Cornell University Press, 1963, chapters 7 and 8, and also John Edwin McGee, 'A Crusade for Humanity: The History of Organized Positivism in England', *The Journal of Philosophy*, vol. 29, no. 8, 14 April 1932, pp. 220–22; for Mill's concerns, see letter to John Morley, 6 January 1871, *CW*, XVII, p. 1795. In fact, the nation most deeply penetrated by positivism was Brazil, whose motto is still the Comtean 'Ordem e Progresso' (Order and Progress), emblazoned on the flag raised after the republican

revolution of 1889; see
Hobsbawm, *Age of Capital*,
p. 120.

139. 'Purely literary life', *AB*, *CW*, I, p.
264; Morley's epithet is in his *On Compromise*, London, 1874, 2nd
edn, 1886, p. 126, quoted in
Collini, *Public Moralists*, p. 33;
'long slumbering idea', Bain, *John Stuart Mill*, p. 124; 'Girondist',
AB, *CW*, I, p. 67; 'really advanced
liberal party', letter to Theodor
Gomperz, 22 August 1866, *CW*,
XVI, p. 1197.

140. Speech to the House of
Commons, 11 May 1864, cited in
Jenkins, *Gladstone*, pp. 247–8 and
Briggs, *Age of Improvement*,
p. 429.

141. 'Selling my cheap editions', letter
to Thomas Hare, 29 May 1865,
CW, XVI, pp. 1060 –61; 'ear of
England', letter to Max
Kyllmann, 30 May 1865, *CW*,
XVI, p. 1063: only the
manuscript draft of this letter has
survived, and this passage has
been struck out; perhaps Mill
thought it came across as
immodest.

13. A Short, Bad Parliament (1865–8)

1. *The Times*, 23 December 1868,
quoted in Kinzer et al., *A Moralist in Parliament*, pp.
270–71.

2. Bain, *John Stuart Mill*, p. 125.

3. Leslie Stephen is quoted in
Collini, *Public Moralists*, p. 156.

4. John Morley, 'John Stuart Mill:

an anniversary', *Times Literary Supplement*, 18 May 1906,
pp. 173–5.

5. 'Elevated Tribune or Chair',
letter to Arnold Ruge, 7 February
1867, *CW*, XVI, p. 1234; 'vantage
ground', letter to Parke Godwin,
1 January 1869, *CW*, XVII, p. 1535.
In the *Autobiography* Mill
similarly described Parliament as
a 'rostra or teacher's chair for
instructing and impelling the
public mind', *AB*, *CW*, I, p. 205.

6. Walter Bagehot, *The English Constitution*, quoted by Bruce
Kinzer in his 'Introduction' to
Mill's *Public and Parliamentary Speeches*, *CW*, XXVIII, p. xxiv.

7. Letter to George Smalley, 6
January 1869, *CW*, XVII, p. 1541.

8. The passage from *Fun* appears in
'The Ballad of the Beaten', 5
December 1868, p. 247.

9. Letter to James Beal, 7 March
1865, *CW*, XVI, pp. 1005–6. In his
address to the electors of Bristol
on 3 November 1774, Edmund
Burke said: 'You choose a
member indeed; but when you
have chosen him, he is not
member of Bristol, but he is a
member of *parliament*.' Edmund
Burke, *Works*, vol. I, pp. 446–8.

10. Letter to James Beal, 17 April
1865, *CW*, XVI, pp. 1031–3; for
confirmation of the 50 per cent
aspiration, see 'The Westminster
Election of 1865' [6], 10 July 1865,
CW, XXVIII, p. 43.

11. Walter Bagehot, 'Mr. Mill's
Address to the Electors of

Westminster', *The Economist*, 29 April 1865, quoted in Kinzer, 'Introduction', *CW*, XXVIII, p. xxv.

12. The meeting was reported in a number of papers, including the *Morning Star*, 7 April 1865, p. 2, quoted in Kinzer et al., *A Moralist in Parliament*, pp. 34–5.

13. Kate Amberley's Journal, 19 February 1865, *Amberley Papers*, vol. 1, p. 369.

14. 'Newman's Political Economy', *Westminster Review*, October 1851, *CW*, V, p. 453.

15. Report from the *Daily Telegraph*, 18 February 1865, p. 3, quoted in Kinzer et al., *A Moralist in Parliament*, p. 27.

16. According to a report in *Mr J. S. Mill and Westminster: The Story of the Westminster Election*, a pamphlet issued by Mill's supporters after his victory, quoted in Kinzer et al., *A Moralist in Parliament*, pp. 28–9.

17. Leading articles in the *Daily Telegraph*, 24 March 1865, p. 6; and the *Morning Star*, 25 March 1865, p. 6.

18. For Mill's acquiescence, see letter to Edwin Chadwick, 6 July 1865, *CW*, XVI, p. 1075; for doubts about Smith see a letter from his friend Robert Cheese on 7 April 1865: 'I fear tho' you will make a good fight you will not get in', quoted in Kinzer et al., *A Moralist in Parliament*, p. 39.

19. Herbert Maxwell, *Life and Times of the Right Honourable William Henry Smith, M.P.*, 2 vols, London and Edinburgh: William Blackwood and Sons, 1893, vol. 1, p. 116; Smith's first speech was made in Willis's Rooms, St James's on 13 June 1865; for evidence of support from Fortnum and Mason and Debenhams, see Mill's letter to John Cairnes, 6 April 1865, *CW*, XVI, p. 1027.

20. Letter to Max Kyllmann, 30 May 1865, *CW*, XVI, p. 1063.

21. For Mill's pessimism, see letter to Edwin Chadwick, 22 June 1865, *CW*, XVI, p. 1072; for Helen's, see her letter to Kate Amberley, 1 June 1865, *Amberley Papers*, vol. 1, p. 434; the attack in the *Standard* was printed on 10 July 1865, see *CW*, XVI, p. 1075, n4.

22. Letter to Henry Chapman, 5 October 1863, *CW*, XV, p. 889.

23. For Mill's itinerary, see letter to Thomas Hare, 29 May 1865, *CW*, XVI, p. 1061.

24. Letter to Edwin Chadwick, 26 June 1865, *CW*, XVI, p. 1072. (One of the volunteers Mill did not want to let down was the father of Sidney Webb, one of the founding figures of the Labour party.)

25. The *Daily News* estimated that there were 300 and 400 in attendance; the description of the meeting is from *Mr J. S. Mill and Westminster*, p. 14.

26. 'The Westminster Election of 1865' [1], 3 July 1865, *CW*, XXVIII, p. 15.

27. Ibid., p. 16.

28. Ibid., pp. 16–17.

29. 'Feature not common', and Lankester's opening comments are taken from the full report of the meeting in the *Morning Star*, 6 July 1865, *CW*, XXVIII, pp. 18–19.

30. 'The Westminster Election of 1865' [4], 8 July 1865, *CW*, XXVIII, p. 34.

31. 'The Westminster Election of 1865' [2], 5 July 1865, *CW*, XXVIII, pp. 22, 24.

32. Ibid. p. 26.

33. Ibid., p. 23.

34. Hardy's description was in a letter to *The Times*, 20 May 1906, quoted in Claire Tomalin, *Thomas Hardy, The Time-Torn Man*, London: Viking, 2006, pp. 75–6. (Tomalin speculates that Hardy may have been working from an old diary entry.)

35. 'The Westminster Election of 1865' [4], 8 July 1865, *CW*, XXVIII, p. 35; *AB*, *CW*, I, pp. 274–5.

36. Ibid., p. 38.

37. Ibid., pp. 36–7.

38. 'The Westminster Election of 1865' [6], 10 July 1865, *CW*, XXVIII, p. 43.

39. Letter to the Secretary of the Sunday League, November 1856, *CW*, XV, pp. 512–13.

40. 'The Westminster Election of 1865' [2], 5 July 1865, *CW*, XXVIII, pp. 26–7.

41. 'The Westminster Election of 1865' [4], 8 July 1865, *CW*, XXVIII, p. 39.

42. Letter to Edwin Godkin, 24 May 1865, *CW*, XVI, p. 1055.

43. 'The Westminster Election of 1865' [2], 5 July 1865, *CW*, XXVIII, p. 26.

44. Report in the *Morning Star*, 13 July 1865, p. 2, quoted in part in *CW*, XXVIII, pp. 43–4. The report included a description of Mill's 'pleasing smile which his intellectual features could not conceal, however desirous their owner may have been to do so'.

45. 'The Westminster Election of 1865' [7], 12 July 1865, *CW*, XXVIII, p. 44. Mill used the same phrase 'money power' – an adaptation, presumably, of Cairnes's 'Slave Power' – in a letter to James Marshall, 26 October 1867, *CW*, XVI, p. 1322.

46. Mill's comment to Russell was recorded by Kate Amberley in her Journal for 27 July 1865, *Amberley Papers*, vol. 1, p. 401.

47. Mill's letter to Henry Fawcett, 1 January 1866, *CW*, XVI, p. 1131.

48. 'Coxcomb', letter to Gustave d'Eichthal, 25 December 1840, *CW*, XIII, p. 456; 'twenty miles', letter to Alexis de Tocqueville, 30 December 1840, *CW*, XIII, p. 460; 'useless shibboleths', letter to Thomas Hare, 17 June 1859, *CW*, XV, p. 626.

49. *Blackwood's Magazine*, June 1865, p. 754.

50. 'Our quiet days', quoted in

Robert Blake, *Disraeli*, London: Eyre & Spottiswoode, 1966; 'tempestuous times', in Monypenny and Buckle, *Disraeli*, vol. 2, p. 158.

51. Letter to George Grote, 26 November 1865, *CW*, XVI, p. 1121.

52. Letter to Thomas Hare, 29 May 1865, *CW*, XVI, p. 1060.

53. Bagehot, 'The Spirit of Whiggism', 1836, quoted in Briggs, *Age of Improvement*, p. 354.

54. 'Notes on the Newspapers', *Monthly Repository*, 12 March 1834, *CW*, VI, pp. 186–8.

55. Letter to George Jacob Holyoake, 8 August 1869, *CW*, XVII, p. 1630.

56. Letter to the Speaker's Secretary, 22 February 1866, *CW*, XVI, p. 1149.

57. For Trevelyan's description of Mill's speech, see Kate Amberley's Journal entry for 14 February 1865, *Amberley Papers*, vol. 1, p. 468; Disraeli's comment is recorded by John Morley, *Recollections*, vol. 1, p. 55.

58. For evidence of Mill's lack of preparation, see his letter to Edwin Chadwick, 10 February 1865, *CW*, XVI, p. 1147: 'as the debate being on the Cattle Plague, I shall not feel bound to pay any special attention to it'; the passage from Mill's speech, 'The Cattle Diseases Bill' [I], 14 February 1865, *CW*, XXVIII, p. 49, speech; Bagehot's assessment is in *The English Constitution*, p. 144.

59. 'Suspension of Habeas Corpus in Ireland', 17 February 1866, *CW*, XVIII, p. 53.

60. *AB*, *CW*, I, pp. 276 –7.

61. William White, *The Inner Life of the House of Commons*, London: T. F. Unwin, 1897, vol. 2, pp. 31–3, quoted in Kinzer et al., *A Moralist in Parliament*, p. 9.

62. Robert Lowe is quoted in Packe, *Mill*, p. 451; Kate Amberley's reflection is in her Journal, 21 February 1866, *Amberley Papers*, vol. 1, p. 470; *Pall Mall Gazette*, 28 July 1866, p.11, quoted in Collini, *Public Moralists*, p. 156.

63. William Fraser, *Disraeli and His Day*, 2nd edn, London: Kegan, Paul, 1891, pp. 286–7; Henry Lucy, *Men and Manners in Parliament*, London: Fisher Unwin, 1919, p. 140 – both quoted in Kinzer et al., *A Moralist in Parliament*, pp. 9, 83.

64. Eric J. Evans, *The Forging of the Modern State, Early Industrial Britain, 1783–1870*, London and New York: Longman, 1983/1996, p. 400.

65. Lowe is quoted in Briggs, *Age of Improvement*, p. 435–6.

66. Letter to Max Kyllman, 15 February 1865, *CW*, XVI, p. 997.

67. Letter to Thomas Hare, 11 January 1866, *CW*, XVI, p. 1138.

68. 'Representation of the People' [2], 13 April 1866, *CW*, XXVIII, pp. 64–5.

69. Ibid., p. 65.

70. Ibid., p. 63 (*peccavi* – 'I have sinned').

71. Ibid., p. 61.

72. Ibid., p. 67.

73. Kate Amberley's Journal, 13 April 1866, *Amberley Papers*, vol. 1, pp. 483–4; Roebuck in a letter to Edwin Chadwick, 14 April 1866, in the J. S. Mill papers in Yale Library, quoted in Kinzer et al., *A Moralist in Parliament*, p. 10.

74. Gladstone's comment recorded in his diary on 13 April 1866, *The Gladstone Diaries*, ed. H. Colin Matthew, 14 vols, Oxford: Clarendon Press, vol. 6, p. 430; Disraeli's assessment in Monypenny and Buckle, *Disraeli*, vol. 5, p. 501.

75. Letter to Theodor Gomperz, 22 August 1866, *CW*, XVI, pp. 1196–7.

76. Gladstone on 'sermon', in Courtney, *Life of Mill*, pp. 141–2; 'taller pulpit', letter to John Lothrop Motley, 6 May 1866, *CW*, XVI, p. 1165.

77. For an example of MPs calling 'Divide!', see 'Capital Punishment', 21 April 1868, *CW*, XXVIII, p. 266.

78. 'Representation of the People' [5], 31 May 1866, *CW*, XVIII, p. 84.

79. Ibid., pp. 85–6. (The reference to the 'stupid party' was made in *Rep. Gov.*, *CW*, XIX p. 452n.)

80. Letter to Henry Chapman, 24 February 1863, *CW*, XV, p. 845; for his agreement to a photo, see letters to John Plummer, 14 July 1865, *CW*, XVI, p. 1078 and 11 August 1865, *CW*, XVI, p. 1089.

81. 'Vast amount', see letter to Rowland Hazard, 15 November 1865, *CW*, XVI, p. 1117; for Helen's assistance, see letter to Mary Carpenter, 3 February 1868, *CW*, XVI, p. 1359: 'Without this help it would be impossible for me to carry on so very voluminous a correspondence as I am at present able to do.' See also Helen's letter of 11 September 1869 to Kate Amberley describing her editorial assistance: 'Mr. Mill's writings which I go over five or six times, putting in words here, stops there; scratching through whole paragraphs; asking him to write whole new pages in particular places where I think the meaning is not clear; condensing, enlarging, polishing &c.', *Amberley Papers*, vol. 2, p. 312; letter from Mill to John Venn, 4 February 1868, *CW*, XVI, pp. 1360–61.

82. Letter to Robert Herbert Story, 9 February 1867, *CW*, XVI, pp. 1237–8.

83. Sir John Benn Walsh, *The Practical Results of the Reform Act of 1832*, London, 1860, p. 112, quoted in Briggs, *Age of Improvement*, p. 371.

84. Letter to Charles Ross, June 1866, *CW*, XVI, p. 1173; letter to William Fraser Rae, 2 June 1866, *CW*, XVI, p. 1174.

85. John Cairnes was pressing him

to act on this issue: for the best account, see Bruce Kinzer, *England's Disgrace? J. S. Mill and the Irish Question*, Toronto: University of Toronto Press, 2001, pp. 120–63. See also Mill's letter to Cairnes, 15 July 1866, *CW*, XVI, p. 1184: 'I would rather not be *the* prominent person in a move which is very likely to break up the alliance between the Irish Catholics and the English Liberals, and perhaps keep the Tories in office for years.'

86. Stephen, *English Utilitarians*, vol. 3, pp. 66–7; conversation with Kate Amberley recorded in her Journal on 9 March 1866, *Amberley Papers*, vol. 1, p. 477.

87. 'Evidence to the Select Committee on Income and Property Tax', 18 June 1861, *CW*, V, pp. 553–98; for a lengthy exchange with Gladstone, see pp. 562–75; Bain, *John Stuart Mill*, p. 125.

88. 'The first statesman', in 'Representation of the People' [1], 12 April 1866, *CW*, XXVIII, p. 58; speech to Cobden Club, 21 July 1866, *CW*, XXVIII, pp. 97–8.

89. For evidence of Gladstone's annotations, see Todd Campbell, 'Gladstone and John Stuart Mill: an intellectual history of Mill's influence on Gladstone's political and economic philosophy', paper to the Mill Bicentennial Conference, April 2006, UCL.

90. For Mill's refusals to attend , see his letters to William Gladstone of 6 March 1866, *CW*, XVI, p. 1152: 'I find it absolutely necessary, just at present, to avoid all engagements on the evenings which attendance in the House leaves me for other indispensable purposes', and 21 April 1866, again *CW*, XVI, p. 1159: 'I still find so much need of repose on the evenings on which the House does not sit.'

91. In a speech to the electors of South Lancashire, 18 July 1865, Gladstone famously declared that 'I come among you unmuzzled'.

92. The best account of the events and ensuing controversy is in Bernard Semmel, *The Governor Eyre Controversy*, London: MacGibbon and Kee, 1962.

93. Buxton's position was set out in a letter to *The Times*, 30 June 1866, p. 12.

94. 'The Jamaica Committee', 9 July 1966, *CW*, XXVIII, p. 91.

95. Courtney, *Life of Mill*, p. 149.

96. 'The abomination', letter to William Fraser Rae, 14 December 1865, *CW*, XVI, p. 1126; Kate Amberley's Journal, entry for 4 March 1866, *Amberley Papers*, vol. 1, p. 475.

97. Prosecuting Philosopher,' *Will-o'-the-Wisp*, 12 September 1868, p. 2.

98. For evidence of Mill's three 'moral tests', see his letter to Thomas Perronet Thompson, 4 October 1866, *CW*, XVI,

pp. 1203–4; 'from the first day', letter to David Urquhart, 4 October 1866, *CW*, XVI, p. 1206; for Mill's description of abusive and threatening letters, see his letter to Goldwin Smith, 28 May 1868 *CW*, XVI, p. 1405; for Helen's fears about these threats, see her letter to Kate Amberley, 29 May 1870, *Amberley Papers*, vol. 2, p. 346.

99. For the exchange with Disraeli, see 'The Disturbances in Jamaica' [1], 19 July 1866, *CW*, XXVIII, p. 95; Ruskin's remark is quoted in Semmel, *The Governor Eyre Controversy*, p. 113.

100. Caryle's comments are from his letter to *The Times*, 12 September 1866, quoted in Kinzer et al., *A Moralist in Parliament*, pp. 206–7; Dickens is quoted in Ackroyd, *Dickens*, p. 971.

101. Ruskin quoted in Semmel, *The Governor Eyre Controversy*, p. 112.

102. Thomas Huxley, 31 October 1865, *Pall Mall Gazette*, quoted in Semmel, *The Governor Eyre Controversy*, pp. 121–2.

103. 'The Disturbances in Jamaica' [2], 31 July 1866, *CW*, XXVIII, p. 111.

104. 'The Hanging Committee', *Judy*, 10 June 1868; *Will-o-the-Wisp*, 25 December 1868; *Fun*, 22 February 1868.

105. Charles Adderley spoke in response to a motion from Charles Buxton, 31 July 1866, quoted in Kinzer et al., *A Moralist in Parliament*, p. 202.

106. Letter to William Sims Pratten, 9 June 1868, *CW*, XVI, p. 1410.

107. *Util.*, *CW*, X, p. 243.

108. Letter to Edwin Chadwick, 4 April 1865, *CW*, XVI p. 1025.

109. Letter to Cairnes, 21 August 1871, *CW*, XVII, pp. 1828–9.

110. Briggs, *Age of Improvement*, p. 439.

111. 'The Reform Meeting in Hyde Park' [2], 24 July 1866, *CW*, XXVIII, pp. 99–100.

112. See Matthew Arnold, *Culture and Anarchy*, quoted by Bruce Kinzer in his 'Introduction' to Mill's *Public and Parliamentary Speeches*, *CW*, XXVIII, p. xxxii; 'Mr Mill as a Politician', *Saturday Review*, (22) 11 August 1866, pp. 167–9, quoted by Janice Carlisle, *John Stuart Mill and the Writing of Character*, Athens, GA: University of Georgia Press, 1991, p. 288.

113. For the £5 donation to the Defence Fund, see letter to Edmund Beales, 26 July 1866, *CW*, XVI, p. 1186; Mill's statement to the House of Commons, 'The Reform Meeting in Hyde Park' [3], 26 July 1866, *CW*, XXVIII, pp. 101–2; *AB*, *CW*, I, p. 278.

114. Details from the report in the *Daily News*, 31 July 1866, partially reproduced in *CW*, XXVIII, pp. 102–3.

115. *AB*, *CW*, I, pp. 278–9.

116. See letter to William Cremer, 1 March 1867, *CW*, XVI, p. 1248, in which Mill said that only two things could justify revolution: 'personal oppression & tyranny' or a situation in which 'the system of government does not permit the redress of grievances to be sought by peaceable & legal means'.

117. 'Meetings in Royal Parks', 22 July 1867, *CW*, XXVIII, p. 216.

118. 'Meeting in the Tea-Room of the House of Commons', 2 August 1867, *CW*, XXVIII, p. 219. See Hansard, *Parliamentary Debates*, vol. 189, 13 August 1867, cols. 1462–13.

119. Derby made his famous 'leap in the dark' comment during the third reading of the Reform Bill in the House of Lords in August 1867; Carlyle's comments were in his article 'Shooting Niagara – And After?', *Macmillan's Magazine*, April 1867.

120. Disraeli's comments on the *Edinburgh* and *Quarterly* are quoted in Briggs, *Victorian People*, p. 273, as is the story from *Fraser's Magazine*, p. 300.

121. 'The Westminster Election of 1868' [5], 6 November 1868, *CW*, XXVIII, p. 346.

122. Letter to Thomas Hare, 18 November 1866, *CW*, XVI, p. 1215.

123. Mill presented his first petition for women's suffrage on 7 June 1866, see letter to Caroline Liddell, 6 May 1866, p. 1164 n2;

'really important public service', *AB*, *CW*, I, p. 285.

124. Kate Amberley's Journal, 20 May 1867, *Amberley Papers*, vol. 2, pp. 36–7.

125. 'The Admission of Women to the Electoral Franchise', 20 May 1867, *CW*, XXVIII, p. 151.

126. Ibid., p. 155.

127. Ibid., p. 154.

128. 'Female Suffrage', 30 March 1867 and 25 May 1867, *The Saturday Review*, quoted in Peter Nicholson, 'The Reception and Early Reputation of Mill's Political Thought', in Skorupski (ed.), *Mill*, p. 472.

129. *Punch*, 30 March 1867, p. 128.

130. For Mill's upbeat assessment of the debate, see letter to John Cairnes, 26 May 1867, *CW*, XVI, p. 1272. The vote, he reported, 'would have been nearer 100 if the division had not taken place unexpectedly at a bad time of the evening . . . the greatest triumph of all is getting Bright's vote: ten days before, he was decidedly against us.' 'Brother and Sister Reformers!' was his opening to 'Reform of Parliament', 25 May 1867, *CW*, XXVIII, p. 167; for his persuasion of Mary Somerville, see his letter to her of 31 March 1868, *CW*, XVI, p. 1382. The petition was presented on 14 May 1868; 'cause is prospering', letter to William Wood, 28 July 1868, *CW*, XVI, p. 1427.

131. See Mill's letter to Thomas Hare, 26 May 1867, *CW*, XVI,

p. 1273; Hare's daughters' reactions were recorded by Kate Amberley in her Journal for 30 May 1867, *Amberley Papers*, vol. 2, p. 39.

132. 'Personal Representation', 30 May 1867, *CW*, XXVIII, pp. 177–8.

133. Ibid., p. 183. For three among many other uses of the 'uphill fight' image see *AB*, *CW*, p. 131; letter to Pasqule Villari, 16 February 1871, *CW*, XVII, p. 1806; and letter to Cairnes, 13 February 1867, *CW*, XVI p. 1239.

134. 'The Reform Bill', 5 July 1867, *CW*, XXVIII, p. 208.

135. 'Reform of Parliament', 25 May 1867, *CW*, XXVIII, pp. 169, 171.

136. The proceedings of the Select Committee are in *CW*, XXI, pp. 389–406; Mill introduced bills on the reform of municipal government on 21 May 1867 and 5 May 1868; 'The Municipal Corporations (Metropolis) Bill', 5 May 1868, *CW*, XXVIII, pp. 273–6.

137. Hobsbawm, *Age of Capital*, pp. 37, 109, 113; letter to Spencer Walpole, 29 January 1867, *CW*, XVI, p. 1231, in which Mill stated that the invitation to join the Royal Commission on Trades Unions was 'proof of your desire that it should be so conducted as to do complete justice to the artisans' side of the question'; for details of the deputation, see letter to George Jacob Holyoake,

16 February 1867, *CW*, XVI, pp. 1242–3.

138. For coal tax, see letter to Charles Hayes, 15 February 1868, *CW*, XVI, p. 1362; 'Inclosure of Hainault Forest', 25 April 1866, *CW*, XXVIII, p. 74; for Commons Preservation Society, see letter to Arthur Lankester, *CW*, XVI, p. 1140 and to Edward Fithian, 6 April 1869, *CW*, XVII, p. 1584.

139. 'Smoking in Railways Carriages' [1], 24 July 1868, *CW*, XXVIII, p. 328.

140. Letter to Thomas Beggs, 25 May 1866, *CW*, XVI, p. 1170.

141. The June 1866 dinner was described by Kate Amberley in her Journal, 17 June 1866, *Amberley Papers*, vol. 1, p. 513.

142. This dinner took place on 20 June 1866; see letter to John Cairnes, 13 June 1866, *CW*, XVI, pp. 1175–6.

143. Letter to William Gladstone, 19 November 1867, *CW*, XVI, p. 1330.

144. Fox, *Memories*, 10 April 1840, p. 109; letter to Caroline's father, Robert Barclay Fox, 6 May 1841, *CW*, XIII, p. 474; see also letter to William Tallack, 18 January 1865, *CW*, XVI, p. 987.

145. Letter to Louis Blanc, 20 June 1868, *CW*, XVI, p. 1417.

146. Picard, *Victorian London*, p. 281.

147. 'Capital Punishment', 21 April 1868, *CW*, XXVIII, p. 267.

148. Ibid., pp. 269–70.

149. 'England's Maritime Power', 5 August 1867, *CW*, XXVIII, p. 223.

150. 'Apt instrument', in letter to Edwin Chadwick, 2 January 1871, *CW*, XVII p. 1792; 'Political Progress', speech at the opening of the Manchester Reform Club, 4 August 1867, *CW*, XXVIII, p. 129. For more on Mill's support for a purely 'defensive force', see letter to T. E. Cliffe Leslie, 5 February 1871, *CW*, XVII, p. 1806.

151. Letters to Edwin Chadwick, 2 January 1871, *CW*, XVII p. 1792, and 29 December 1866, *CW*, XVI, p. 1224.

152. 'Political Progress', *CW*, XXVIII, p. 129.

153. *Comte*, *CW*, X, p. 341.

154. *AB*, *CW*, I, p. 279.

155. *England and Ireland*, London: Longmans, 1868, *CW*, VI, p. 529.

156. *POPE*, *CW*, II, p. 334 – this section having been added for the 1865 (6th edition).For more detail see Bruce Kinzer's excellent study, *England's Disgrace? J. S. Mill and the Irish Question*.

157. 'The Fenian Convicts', 25 May 1867, *CW*, XXVIII, pp. 165–6.

158. 'Reform of Parliament', 25 May 1867, *CW*, XXVIII, p. 172.

159. Ibid., pp. 172–3.

160. *AB*, *CW*, I, p. 280; Willliam Thornton in his 'Notice' of *England and Ireland*, in the *Fortnightly Review*, April 1868, p. 472, quoted in Kinzer, *England's Disgrace?*, p. 185, to which this section is also is heavily indebted.

161. *England and Ireland*, *CW*, VI, pp. 517, 527.

162. Ibid., p. 527.

163. Ibid., p. 513.

164. Letter to John Cairnes, 16 November 1869, *CW*, XVII, p. 1666.

165. *Saturday Review*, 29 February 1868, p. 282, quoted in Carlisle, *Mill and the Writing of Character*, p. 273.

166. Letter from Mill to George Julian, (a US Congressman), 29 May 1868, *CW*, XVI, p. 1407.

167. Bruce Kinzer, 'John Stuart Mill and the Experience of Political Engagement', in Laine (ed.) *A Cultivated Mind*, p. 209.

168. William Thornton, 'Notice' in the *Fortnightly*, p. 472.

169. Walter Bagehot in *The Economist*, 22 February 1868, p. 203, quoted in Kinzer, *England's Disgrace?*, pp. 191, 189.

170. 'Mr. Mill on Ireland', *The Times*, 20 February 1868, pp. 10–11; 'Mr. Mill and Ireland', *Pall Mall Gazette*, 24 February 1868, pp. 1–2.

171. *Morning Post*, 21 February 1868, p. 4. All quoted in Kinzer, *England's Disgrace?*, pp. 186–7.

172. *Punch*, 29 February 1868, p. 97.

173. Letter from Mill to John Cairnes, 1 March 1868, *CW*, XVI, p. 1369; letter from John Cairnes to Leonard Courtney, 5 March 1868, quoted in Kinzer, *England's Disgrace?*, p. 192.

174. *England and Ireland*, *CW*, VI, pp. 532, 518.

175. Letter to John Cairnes, 10 March 1868, *CW*, XVI, p. 1369; for the alternative of 'total separation', see letters to John Henry Bridges, 16 November 1867, *CW*, XVI, p. 1329: 'total separation is what I think we must make up our minds to if after having done full justice to the Irish in church & land matters & done all we can do for their educational & economical interests we find that their aversion to union with us remains unabated.' He made the same point to Lord Hobart, 23 February 1868, *CW*, XVI, p. 1366.

176. 'The State of Ireland', 12 March 1868, *CW*, XXVIII, p. 248. Halfway through Mill's speech, according to the record in Hansard, 'the honourable member was here interrupted by expressions of impatience from several members', and the *Pall Mall Gazette*, 13 March 1868, p. 1, reported that the honourable members 'took pains to show him that they did not want to hear him at all'.

177. Ibid., pp. 255, 261.

178. Gladstone's contributions to the debate on 12 March 1868 is quoted in Kinzer, *England's Disgrace?*, pp. 198–9.

179. Letter to Philip Rathbone, 9 January 1869, *CW*, XVII, p. 1545.

180. *AB*, *CW*, I, p. 280.

181. Letter to Edwin Chadwick, 4 November 1867, *CW*, XVI, p. 1325.

182. *AB*, *CW*, I, p. 280.

183. Ibid., p. 283.

184. Letter to William Christie, 27 July 1868, *CW*, XVI, p. 1425.

185. 'William Lloyd Garrison', 29 June 1867, *CW*, XXVIII, p. 202; letter to Charles Eliot Norton, 11 September 1868, *CW*, XVI, p. 1434.

186. 'Transfer a large share', letter to an unidentified correspondent, before 3 September 1867, *CW*, XVI, p. 1316; 'infusion of more useful elements', letter to John Cairnes, 29 October 1868, *CW*, XVI, p. 1465; 'positive opinions', letter to Charles Eliot Norton, 11 September 1868, *CW*, XVI, p. 1434.

187. Letter to Thomas Beggs, 27 September 1868, *CW*, XVI, p. 1449.

188. 'Patient thought', in 'The Westminster Election of 1868' [1], 22 July 1868, *CW*, XXVIII, p. 322; letter to Edwin Chadwick, 20 August 1867, *CW*, XVI, p. 1311.

189. 'Very doubtful liberal', letter to John Nichol, 16 July 1868, *CW*, XVI, p. 1423; letter to Edward Bouverie, 4 October 1868, *CW*, XVI, p. 1453.

190. Letter to Edward Bouverie, 19 October 1868, *CW*, XVI, pp. 1461–3.

191. *The Times*, 16 October 1868, p. 6, quoted in Carlisle, *Mill and the Writing of Character*, p. 268; *Will-*

o-the-Wisp, 7 November 1868, p. 96.

192. Mill on Odger: 'I applaud Mr. Odger. I highly regard his conduct, and I deeply regret that he is the candidate who has had to retire.' 'The Westminster Election of 1868' [3], 2 November 1868, *CW*, XXVIII, p. 335.

193. Mill suggested that compared to the Bouverie row, the Bradlaugh affair was the 'more likely of the two to alienate voters in Westminster': letter to John Cairnes, 29 October 1868, *CW*, XVI, p. 1465. On the other hand, in a letter to George Grote, 1 December 1868, *CW*, XVI, p. 1502, he wrote: 'As a matter of fact, I greatly doubt whether Bradlaugh, Bouverie, &c. are at all accountable for my defeat.' And he wrote to Edwin Chadwick, 9 October 1868, *CW*, XVI, p. 1458: 'I think it is a mistake to suppose that my support of Bradlaugh at all diminished my weight. The sort of people with whom it does so have had to put up with my Women's Suffrage, Jamaica Committee, representation of minorities, and other "crotchets", and probably have long ago given me up, or more properly speaking, have never taken me up at all.'

194. Letter to Austin Holyoake, 28 August 1868, *CW*, XVI, p. 1433, with which Mill enclosed his £10 donation; George Holyoake's

appraisal is quoted in Carlisle, *Mill and the Writing Character*, p. 273.

195. Letter to Charles Gilpin, 12 September 1868, *CW*, XVI, p. 1435.

196. Letter from Kate Amberley to Lady Russell, 16 October 1868, *Amberley Papers*, vol. 2, p. 139.

197. Letter to Thomas Beggs, 27 September 1868, *CW*, XVI, p. 1449: 'atheists as well as the professors of any, even the worst, religions, may be & often are, good men, estimable and valuable in all the relations of life., & are entitled like all other persons to be judged by their actions ("By their fruits ye shall know them" are the words of Christ).'

198. 'The Westminster Election of 1868' [6], 9 November 1868, *CW*, XXVIII, pp. 347–8.

199. 'Election Intelligence', 27 October 1868, quoted in Kinzer et al., *A Moralist in Parliament*, p. 244.

200. 'The Westminster Election of 1868' [2], 24 July 1868, *CW*, XXVIII, p. 331.

201. The petition was presented on 5 June 1868, and is reprinted in *CW*, XXIX, p. 592; see report in *The Times*, 6 June 1868; for Mill's defence, see his letter to William Sims Pratten, 9 June 1868, *CW*, XVI, p. 1412.

202. For a petition to restrict alcohol sales on Sunday presented on behalf of Trinity Independent

Church on 15 February 1867, see *CW*, XXIX, p. 577; for one against any restrictions, presented on 16 March 1868 on behalf of 530 signatories, see *CW*, XXIX, p. 588.

203. Maxwell, *Life of W. H. Smith*, vol. 1, p. 146.

204. *Daily Telegraph*, 19 November 1868, p. 8.

205. 'The Westminster Election of 1868' [10], 18 November 1868, *CW*, XXVIII, p. 369.

206. This calculation uses the Retail Price Index, see www.measuringworth.com, and Chapter 2, note 61.

207. Maxwell, *Life of W. H. Smith*, vol. 1, pp. 148–50.

208. *The Times* leader comment, 20 February 1868, quoted in Maxwell, *Life of W. H. Smith*, vol. 1, p. 150.

209. Letter to Lord Amberley, 30 November 1868, *CW*, XVI, pp. 1494–5.

210. Letter to Charles Eliot Norton, 29 November 1868, *CW*, XVI, p. 1483.

211. Letter to Edwin Chadwick, 19 November 1868, p. 1488, in which Mill discusses the Cornwall and Buckinghamshire offers, and speculates about the Greenwich seat.

212. Letter to John Cairnes, 4 December 1868, *CW*, XVI, p. 1506.

213. 'Defeat of the radical party', letter to Charles Eliot Norton, 28 November 1868, *CW*, XVI, p.

1493; 'general rejection', letter to John Cairnes, 4 December 1868, *CW*, XVI, p. 1506; 'the new candidates', letter to Edwin Chadwick, 19 November 1868, *CW*, XVI, p. 1488; 'general rout', letter to George Grote, 1 December 1868, *CW*, XVI, p. 1502.

214. 'Best leaders', letter to John Plummer, 5 November 1868, *CW*, XVI, p. 1479.

215. Letter to George Howell, 27 December 1868, *CW*, XVI, p. 1534.

216. 'I can sincerely say', letter to Thomas Beggs, 11 December 1868. *CW*, XVI, p. 1518; *AB*, *CW*, I, p. 289.

217. Reprinted in Kinzer et al., *A Moralist in Parliament*, p. 290, and in the plates of this volume.

218. 'The Chamber of Mediocrity', 1 December 1868, *Fortnightly Review*, pp. 681–94.

219. Letter to John Morley, December 1868, *CW*, XVI, p. 1497; see John Morley's, *Recollections*, vol. 1, p. 57 for his description of Mill's admiration for Turgot: 'he told me that in his younger days, when he was inclined to fall into low spirits, he turned to Condorcet's Life of Turgot'.

220. 'On the Definition of Political Economy', October 1836, *London and Westminster Review*, *CW*, IV, p. 335.

221. 'The Use of History', 1827, *CW*, XXVI, pp. 396–7.

222. Courtney, *Life of Mill*, p. 73.

223. 'William Lloyd Garrison', 29 June 1867, *CW*, XXVIII, p. 202.

224. Courtney, *Life of Mill*, p. 142.

225. Letter to John Cairnes, 4 December 1868, *CW*, XVI, p. 1506.

14. The Father of Feminism

1. Letter to an unidentified correspondent, 5 November 1855, *CW*, XIV, pp. 498–9.

2. Letter to Parke Godwin, 1 January 1869, *CW*, XVII, p. 1535.

3. Letter to Joseph Giles, 24 August 1871, *CW*, XVII, p. 1830.

4. Bain, *John Stuart Mill*, p. 131. See also Mill's letter to Bain, 14 July 1869, *CW*, XVII, p. 1623.

5. Martha Nussbaum, in 'Mill's Feminism: Liberal, Radical and Queer', paper presented to the Mill Bicentennial Conference, UCL, 7 April 2006.

6. *The Subjection of Women*, London: Longmans, 1869, *CW*, XXI, p. 261.

7. Ibid., pp. 323, 294–5.

8. Letter to John Cairnes, 9 April 1869, *CW*, XVII, p. 1587; 'fanciful rights', *The Times*, 10 May 1873, p. 5.

9. Letter to Paulina Wright Davis, 11 December 1869, *CW*, XVII, pp. 1670–1.

10. 'Rationale of Representation', 1835, *CW*, XVIII, p. 29n; *Thoughts on Parliamentary Reform*, 1859, *CW*, XIX, p. 334; *Representative Government*, 1861, *CW*, XIX, pp. 479–81.

11. Jose Harris, *Private Lives, Public Spirit: Britain 1870–1914*, London: Penguin, 1993, p. 28.

12. Each of the English editions had a print run of 1,500 and there were also two American editions in the same year. See John Robson's 'Textual Introduction' to *Essays on Equality, Law and Education*, *CW*, XXI, p. lxx. This contradicts Alan Ryan's claim that *Subjection* was the 'only book on which Mill's publisher lost money', Ryan, *Mill*, p. 125. (Perhaps Ryan was thinking of the 1868 pamphlet containing Mill's 1867 speech to parliament, along with Harriet's *Enfranchisement of Women* and a piece by Helen, which was in fact published at a loss, by Trubner.)

13. Moncure Conway, *Autobiography*, Boston and New York: Houghton, Mifflin & Co., 2 vols, 1904, vol. 2, p. 165.

14. Bain, *John Stuart Mill*, p. 130.

15. *Subjection*, *CW*, XXI, p. 276.

16. Letter to John Nichol, 18 August 1869, *CW*, XVII, p. 1633.

17. 'St. Simonism in London', 1834, *CW*, XIII, p. 680; *Subjection*, *CW*, XXI, p. 272.

18. *Subjection*, *CW*, XXI, p. 271; 'The Admission of Women to the Electoral Franchise', 20 May 1867, *CW*, XXVIII, p. 156.

19. *Subjection*, *CW*, XXI, pp. 316, 330. Also: 'All women are brought up from the very earliest years in the belief that their ideal of character is the very opposite to that of

men; not self-will, and government by self-control, but submission, and yielding to the control of others', ibid., p. 486.

20. Anne Mozley, 'Mr Mill on the Subjection of Women', *Blackwood's Magazine*, 106, 1995, quoted in Peter Nicholson, 'The Reception and Early Reputation of Mill's Politcal Thought', in Skorupski (ed.), *Mill*, p. 474.

21. John Morley, 'Mr Mill's Autobiography', *Fortnightly Review*, 1973, quoted in Nicholson, 'Reception and Early Reputation of Mill's Political Thought', p. 482; *Subjection, CW*, XXI, p. 294.

22. *Subjection, CW*, XXI, p. 305.

23. Ibid., p. 277.

24. Ibid., p. 263.

25. Ibid., p. 261.

26. *The Angel in the House*, Book I, Canto IX, 'Sahara', I. 'The Wife's Tragedy'.

27. In her paper 'Professions for Women', a speech Virginia Woolf made to the National Society for Women's Service, 21 January 1931, and published posthumously in *The Death of the Moth and Other Essays*, London: The Hogarth Press, 1942.

28. For Mill's disapproval of Dickens, see letter to HTM, 20 March 1854, *CW*, XIV, p. 190. (The offending section of *Bleak House* is in Chapter VIII.) For the passage from Mrs Beeton, see Golby (ed.), *Culture and Society in Britain 1850–1890*,

Oxford: Oxford University Press, 1986, p. 190.

29. *Subjection, CW*, XXI, p. 321.

30. *Female Suffrage. A Letter from the Rt. Hon. W. E. Gladstone, M.P., to Samuel Smith, M.P.*, pamphlet, London: John Murray, 1892, quoted in Constance Rover, *Women's Suffrage and Party Politics in Britain 1866–1914*, London: Routledge & Kegan Paul, 1967, p. 120.

31. *Subjection, CW*, XXI, pp. 270, 271.

32. 'Not felt to jar', ibid., p. 265; 'to Englishmen', ibid., p. 270.

33. J. F. Stephen, *Liberty, Equality, Fraternity* (1873), p. 185; Bain, *John Stuart Mill*, p. 131.

34. *Subjection, CW*, XXI, p. 277.

35. 'The Admission of Women to the Electoral Franchise', *CW*, XXVIII, p. 159–60.

36. 'Une cause gagnée', letter to Henry Fawcett, 21 July 1862, *CW*, XV, p. 787; letter to Emily Davies, 6 May 1872, *CW*, XVII, p. 1891.

37. For Mill's bequest, see the codicil to his will, signed on 14 February 1872, *CW*, XXXI, p. 333. The University of London should have received the money – although Bristol University have made a claim to have been first to admit women, I have been able to find no evidence that the money was ever paid.

38. Stephen, *Liberty, Equality, Fraternity*, p. 194.

39. 'Sedgwick's Discourse', 1835, *CW*, X, p. 66; 'Stability of Society',

Leader, 17 August 1850, *CW,* XXV, p. 1181.

40. *Memorandum of the Improvements in the Administration of India During the Last Thirty Years,* London: Cox and Wyman, 1858, and presented to Parliament, *CW,* XXX, pp. 122, 123, 125.

41. *Subjection, CW,* XXI, p. 276: 'Through all the progressive period of human history, the condition of women has been approaching nearer to equality with men.'

42. Ibid., p. 491.

43. Ibid., p. 326.

44. 'The Admission of Women to the Electoral Franchise', *CW,* XXVIII, p. 152.

45. Ibid., pp. 158–9.

46. Ibid., pp. 155–6.

47. *Subjection, CW,* XXI, p. 334.

48. Ibid., p. 335.

49. Ibid., pp. 321, 288.

50. 'Centralisation', *CW,* XIX, p. 610.

51. *Subjection, CW,* XXI, p. 294.

52. 'The Admission of Women to the Electoral Franchise', *CW,* XXVIII, p. 154.

53. Ibid., p. 157.

54. Letter from Mill to Charles Norton, 23 June 1869, *CW,* XVII, p. 1618; Walter Bagehot, 'Mr. Mill's Address to the Electors of Westminster', *The Economist,* 29 April 1865, pp. 542–3.

55. Letter to Charles Loring Brace, 19 January 1871, *CW,* XVII, p. 1799.

56. Adrian Desmond, *Huxley, Evolution's High Priest,* London: Michael Joseph, 1997, p. 20.

57. Louisa Garrett recounted this scene she reportedly witnessed at the family home, Alde House, Aldeburgh, Suffolk, according to the historian John Simkin, in an article on Fawcett available at www.spartacus.schoolnet.co.uk.

58. *Subjection, CW,* XXI, p. 302; letter to John Nichol, 18 August 1869, *CW,* XVII, p. 1633.

59. *Subjection, CW,* XXI, p. 303.

60. Letter to Charlotte Speir Manning, 14 January 1870, *CW,* XVII, p. 1687. (Mill used the alternative spelling 'Sekunder'.)

61. *Subjection, CW,* XXI, pp. 305, 307.

62. Bain, *John Stuart Mill,* p. 131.

63. *Subjection, CW,* XXI, pp. 336–7.

64. Ibid., pp. 336–7. (Mill actually used male pronouns in these sentences, which Harriet would surely have banished.)

65. See Johnson, *Birth of the Modern,* p. 474.

66. Letter from Sigmund Freud to Martha Bernays, 5 November 1883, Ernest Jones (ed.), *The Life and Works of Sigmund Freud,* vol. I, pp. 175–7, quoted in the *Mill News Letter,* vol. VII, no. 1, Fall 1971, pp. 1–2.

67. 'The Admission of Women to the Electoral Franchise', *CW,* XXVIII, p. 157; letter to Alexander Bain, 14 July 1869 *CW,* XVII, p. 1623.

68. 'Meeting of the London National Society for Women's

Suffrage' [1], 17 July 1869, *CW*,
XXIX, p. 373.

69. Ibid., p. 379.

70. Lady Russell to Amberley, after
26 March 1870: 'Goodbye dear
Boy I congrat yr wife on not
hang made a speech.' *Amberley
Papers*, vol. 2, p. 325.

71. The Women's Disabilities Bill
passed its second reading on 4
May 1870, by 124 votes to 91; at
the next division on 12 May 1870
it was defeated.

72. Letters to Charles Dilke, 28 May
1870, *CW*, XVII, p. 1728; Thomas
Hare, 29 May 1870, *CW*, XVII, p.
1744; Charles Kingsley, 9 July
1870, *CW*, XVII, p. 1744.

73. 'Obnoxious set', letter to George
Croom Robertson, 31 October
1871, *CW*, XVII, p. 1849;
'seceders', letter to George
Croom Robertson, 18 January
1872, *CW*, XVII, p. 1866.

74. 'Monstrous evil', letter to
William Malleson, 18 January
1870, *CW*, XVII, p. 1688; 'highly
approve' repeal, letter to an
unidentified correspondent, 11
January 1870, *CW*, XVII, p. 1681.

75. Letter to John Nichol, 29
December 1870, *CW*, XVII,
p. 1790.

76. 'Women's Suffrage' [2], 26
March 1870, *CW*, XXIX, p. 388.

77. Letter to Josephine Butler, 22
March 1869, *CW*, XXXII, p. 204;
letter to George Croom
Robertson, 15 November 1871,
CW, XVII, p. 1854.

78. 'The Contagious Diseases Acts',

Mill's evidence to the Royal
Commission of 1870, given on
13 May 1871, *CW*, XXI,
p. 354.

79. Ibid., p. 361.

80. Letter to George Croom
Robertson, 20 September 1871,
CW, XVII, p. 1836.

81. Letter to George Croom
Robertson, 6 November 1871,
CW, XVII, p. 1850.

82. Letter to George Croom
Robertson, 12 December 1872,
CW, XVII, p. 1850. Mill also sent
a shorter version of the threat by
telegram (he was in Avignon) to
make sure it got there in time.

83. Letter to George Croom
Robertson, 21 November 1972,
CW, XVII, p. 1921.

84. Letter to George Croom
Robertson, 25 October 1871, *CW*,
XVII, p. 1845.

85. Letter to William Christie, 8
March 1868, *CW*, XVI, p. 1371.

86. *AB*, *CW*, I, p. 265; letter to
Alexander Bain, 14 July 1869,
CW, XVII, p. 1624.

87. Letter to Robert Barclay Fox, 23
December 1840, *CW*, XIII,
pp. 454–5.

88. Letter to John Morley, 20
December 1869, *CW*, XVII, pp.
1673–4: 'I honour him [Edward
Freeman] for having broken
ground against field sports, a
thing I have been often tempted
to do myself, but having so many
unpopular causes already on my
hands, thought it wiser not to
provoke fresh hostility'; letter to

Herbert Spencer, 6 July 1869, *CW*, XVII, p. 1620: 'My murderous propensities are confined to the vegetable world.' (Spencer had apparently invited Mill on a fishing trip.)

89. Morley, *Recollections*, vol. 1, p. 57.

90. Letter to Elizabeth Cady Stanton, 25 April 1869, *CW*, XVII, p. 1594. As it turned out, he was over-optimistic; although America did move more quickly than the UK on female suffrage, granting women the vote state by state: Colorado (1893), Idaho (1896), Washington (1910), California (1911), Arizona (1912), Kansas (1912), Oregon (1912), Illinois (1913), Nevada (1914) and Montana (1914).

91. Letter to George Croom Robertson, 5 November 1872, *CW*, XVII, p. 1918.

92. Letter to Charles Kingsley, 9 July 1870, *CW*, XVII, p. 1743.

93. Mill's evidence to the Royal Commission on the CDA, May 1871, *CW*, XXI, pp. 359, 353, 356.

94. Letter to John Nichol, 29 December 1871, *CW*, XVII, p. 1791.

95. William Edward Lecky, *History of European Morals from Augustus to Charlemagne*, 2 vols, London: Longmans Green, 1869, vol. 2, p. 300, quoted in *CW*, XVII, p. 1692 n3.

96. Letter to Lord Amberley, 12 February 1870, *CW*, XVII, p. 1695.

97. Letter to Lord Amberley, 2 February 1870, *CW*, XVII, p. 1693.

98. Ibid.

99. Ibid., p. 1694.

100. *Subjection*, *CW*, XXI, p. 284. Likewise, he wrote: 'The relation between husband and wife is very like that between lord and vassal, except that the wife is held to more unlimited obedience than the vassal was,' ibid., p. 325.

101. 'Citadel of the enemy', ibid., p. 325; 'under the very eye', ibid., p. 268.

102. Margaret Oliphant, 'Mill on the Subjection of Women', *Edinburgh Review*, 1869, quoted in Nicholson, 'The Reception and Early Reputation of Mill's Political Thought' in Skorupski (ed.), *Mill*, p. 474.

103. *Subjection*, *CW*, XXI, p. 285.

104. In an introductory note to Harriet's 'Enfranchisement of Women', published in Mill's *Dissertations and Discussions*, vol. 2, a selection of his own writings, in 1859, reprinted in *CW*, XXI, p. 393.

105. Herbert Cowell, 'Sex in Mind and Education: A Commentary', *Blackwood's Magazine*, June 1874, pp. 738–9.

106. 'Free republics', *Subjection*, *CW*, XXI, p. 294; 'best kind of equality', ibid., p. 336.

107. Ibid., p. 336.

108. Goldwin Smith, 'Female Suffrage', *Macmillan's Magazine*, June 1874, quoted in Collini's

'Introduction' to *CW*, XXI,
p. xxxv.

109. *Subjection*, *CW*, XXI, p. 278.

110. Ibid., p. 285; for earlier instances,
see 'The Suicide of Sarah
Brown', *Morning Chronicle*, 28
October 1846, *CW*, XXIV, p. 918,
and 'The Case of the North
Family', *Morning Chronicle*,
29 December 1846, *CW*, XXIV,
p. 1020.

111. Letter to Isabella Beecher
Hooker, 13 September 1869, *CW*,
XVII, p. 1640.

112. For evidence of Mill's earlier
views on liberalizing divorce, see
'Notes on the Newspapers',
Monthly Repository, 6 June 1834,
CW, VI, pp. 248–9; for discussion
of the 1857 reform, see Briggs,
Age of Improvement, p. 379, and
Picard, *London*, p. 266.

113. 'On Marriage', *CW*, XXI, pp. 42,
45.

114. Letter to Lord Amberley, 18
August 1869, *CW*, XVII, p. 1634.

115. See Shelley's note on free love in
Queen Mab (1813), quoted in
Walter Houghton, *The Victorian
Frame of Mind*, New Haven and
London: Yale University Press,
1957, p. 361.

116. 'On Marriage', *CW*, XXI, p. 47.

117. *Subjection*, *CW*, XXI, pp. 288–9.

118. Ibid., p. 336.

119. 'On Marriage', *CW*, XXI, p. 43.

120. *POPE*, *CW*, III, p. 765; for the
comment about nursing, see
'Women's Suffrage' [2], 26
March 1870, *CW*, XXVIII,
p. 377.

121. *POPE*, *CW*, II, pp. 372–3;
Subjection, *CW*, XXI, p. 298.

122. *Subjection*, *CW*, XXI, p. 297.

123. Ibid.

124. Ibid., p. 319.

125. 'No alteration', letter to Professor
[Henry?] Green, 8 April 1852,
CW, XIV, p. 88. For Mill's
support for smaller families, see
POPE, *CW*, III, p. 372.

126. Susan Okin, *Women in Western
Political Philosophy*, Princeton:
Princeton University Press, 1979,
p. 237: 'Mill never questioned or
objected to the maintenance of
traditional sex roles within the
family, but expressly considered
them to be suitable and
desirable.' Julia Annas, 'Mill and
the Subjection of Women',
Philosophy, 52, 1977, p. 189: Mill's
proposals, she writes, are 'timid
and reformist at best. He
assumes that most women will in
fact want only to be wives and
mothers.'

127. *Subjection*, *CW*, XXI, p. 298:
'These things, if once opinion
were rightly directed on the
subject, might with perfect safety
be left to be regulated by
opinion, without any interference
of law.'

128. For Mill's comments on George
Sand, see *Subjection*, *CW*, XXI,
p. 315.

129. 'Brutally indifferent', letter from
Florence Nightingale to Harriet
Martineau, 1858, quoted in
Perkin, *Origins of Modern English
Society*, p. 160; the passage from

Notes on Nursing: What Nursing Is, What Nursing is Not, 1860, p. 135, quoted in part in *CW*, XV, p. 707, n3.

130. Letter to Florence Nightingale, 10 September 1860, *CW*, XV, pp. 706–7.

131. Letter to Charles Wentworth Dilke, 17 January 1871, *CW*, XVII, p. 1797, supporting Millicent Fawcett for the PEC.

132. Letter to John Cairnes, 15 May 1872, *CW*, XVII, p. 1895.

133. Ibid.

134. Letter to George Croom Robertson, 23 May 1872, *CW*, XVII, p. 1900.

135. Letter to John Cairnes, 15 May 1872, *CW*, XVII, p. 1895.

136. Letter to George Croom Robertson, 23 May 1872, *CW*, XVII, p. 1900.

137. Letter to George Croom Robertson, 5 November 1872, *CW*, XVII, p. 1917; see Rover, *Women's Suffrage and Party Politics in Britain*, p. 103 for details of Disraeli's politically qualified support.

138. For the phrase 'Toryism of sex' in relation to women's suffrage, see letter to Henry Chapman, 8 July 1858, *CW*, XV, p. 557; a half-hearted attempt was made to re-open the question in 1884, when the male franchise was extended still further, the failure of which led even John Morley to give up the ghost – see Nicholson, 'The Reception and Early Reputation of Mill's Political Thought', in

Skorupski (ed.), *Mill*, p. 483.

139. Bain, *John Stuart Mill*, p. 132; Packe, *Mill*, p. 501; Fawcett, in Fox Bourne, *John Stuart Mill: Life and Works*, pp. 60–61.

15. Final Years (1868–73)

1. Letter to William Thornton, 16 January 1869, *CW*, XVII, pp. 1548–9.

2. The full address was 10 Albert Mansions, Victoria Street, London. See letter to Franz Bretano, 16 January 1869, *CW*, XVII, p. 1876.

3. Letter to Franz Bretano, 22 June 1869, *CW*, XVII, p. 1902.

4. Letter to Hewett Watson, 30 January 1869, *CW*, XVII, p. 1553.

5. Letter to Thomas Carlyle, 12 April 1869, *CW*, XVII, p. 1590.

6. Letter to Stuart Colman, 6 February 1873, *CW*, XVII, p. 1936.

7. Letter to Helen Taylor, 13 July 1871, *CW*, XVII, p. 1827.

8. Letter to John Cairnes, 6 April 1872, *CW*, XVII, p. 1879.

9. For the Dudley seat, see letter to William Henry Duignan, 20 October 1869, *CW*, XVII, p. 1649; for the School Board, see letter to the Secretary, Southwark Radical Association, 30 September 1870, *CW*, XVII, p. 1768.

10. 'The night cometh', see letter to Alexander Bain, 4 November 1867, *CW*, XVI, p. 1324. For details of the US trip, see letter to Henry Villard, 19 January

1869, *CW*, XVII, p. 1550. (He was being offered £300 a lecture, around £27,000 in today's terms; – see www.measuringworth.com.) See also letter to Paulina Wright Davis, 11 December 1860, *CW*, XVII, p. 1670, in which he writes, 'I have received many kind and cordial invitations to visit the United States' and pleads 'want of time. I have many things to do yet, before I die.' He did, however, accept honorary membership of the New York Liberal Club in 1871 – see letter to the Club, 20 January 1871, *CW*, XVII, p. 1801. For the shortening of the 1870 holiday, see letter to Charles Eliot Norton, 26 June 1870, *CW*, XVII, p. 1740.

11. 'Rationale of Representation', 1835, *CW*, XVIII, p. 38.

12. Letter to John Cairnes, 21 August 1871, *CW*, XVII, p. 1828.

13. Letter to George Odger, 19 February 1870, *CW*, XVII, p. 1697.

14. For George Snell's group, see letter to Charles Wentworth Dilke, 10 May 1870, *CW*, XVII, p. 1716 n3; for the Radical Club, see letter to Charles Wentworth Dilke, 23 May 1870, *CW*, XVII, p. 1698; in 1867 Mill lent John Chapman £600 to keep the *Westminster Review* afloat – see Ashton, *142 Strand, A Radical Address in Victorian London*, p. 106; for Mill's support of Chapman, and praise for his 'devotion of time and energy', see

letter to John Chapman, 27 December 1868, *CW*, XXXII, p. 202; for the offer to Morley, see Mill's letter to him of 28 November 1870, *CW*, XVII, p. 1785.

15. 'Thornton on Labour and Its Claims', *Fortnightly Review*, May 1869, *CW*, V, p. 645.

16. Ibid., p. 646.

17. See, for example, Henry Sidgwick, 'The Wages Fund Theory', *The Fortnightly Review*, July–December 1879, pp. 401–413; and Lord Robbins' 'Introduction' to Mill's *Essays on Economics and Society*, *CW*, IV, pp. xxix–xxx.

18. For the relevant text, see *POPE*, *CW*, III, p. 930; for the preface, see *POPE*, *CW*, II, p. xciv.

19. Hobsbawm, *Age of Capital*, pp. 109, 113; 'educating the *élite*', 'Labour and Its Claims', *CW*, V, p. 663.

20. 'Labour and Its Claims', *CW*, V, p. 665.

21. Ibid., p. 666.

22. See letter to Henry Fawcett, 24 October 1869, *CW*, XVII, p. 1658, and *OL*, *CW* XVIII, p. 302.

23. 'The Education Bill' [1], 25 March 1870, *CW*, XXIX, p. 382; letter to Charles Wentworth Dilke, 28 February 1870, *CW*, XVII, p. 1703.

24. 'The Education Bill' [1], 25 March 1870, *CW*, XXIX, pp. 383–4.

25. 'Nature' in *Three Essays on Religion*, London: Longmans, 1874, *CW*, X, p. 410.

26. Letter to Revd Stephen Hawtrey, 10 August 1867, *CW*, XVI, p. 1305.

27. 'Inaugural Address to the University of St. Andrews', *CW*, XXI, p. 348.

28. Ibid., pp. 248, 256.

29. Kate Amberley's Journal, 3 February 1867, *Amberley Papers*, vol. 2, p. 15.

30. 'The Education Bill' [1], 25 March 1870, *CW*, XXIX, pp. 382–3; for his support for schools including 'a national school, a middle-class or commercial school, and an evening school for adults', see 'Inaugural Address to the University of St. Andrews', *CW*, XXI, pp. 212–13.

31. 'Endowments', *Fortnightly Review*, April 1869, *CW*, V, p.617.

32. For a nuanced version of the view that Mill became more favourably disposed towards state action in his last years, see Collini, *Public Moralists*, pp. 167–8; for evidence of a more positive tone on regulation, see Mill's letter to William Wood, 24 February 1869, in which Mill dismisses Wood's claim that tighter regulation of children's working hours was patronizing, *CW*, XVII, p. 1568; for 'legislative limitations', see letter to Henry Villard, 26 July 1869, *CW*, XVII, p. 1626.

33. See 'Land Tenure Reform', Mill's statement published with the *Programme of the Land Tenure Reform Association*, London,

Longmans, 1871, *CW*, V, p. 695; and Mill's letter to Alfred Russel Wallace, July 1870, *CW*, XVII, p. 1741.

34. 'Meeting of the London National Society for Women's Suffrage' [1], 17 July 1869, *CW*, XXIX, p. 387.

35. René Millet, 'Le Parti Radical en Angleterre: un manifeste de M. Stuart Mill', *Revue des Deux Mondes*, 15 February 1872, pp. 932–59.

36. After two years of recruiting and organization by Mill and allies, including Thomas Hare and Jacob Bright, the Land Tenure Reform Association held its first public meeting on 15 May 1871. For evidence of Mill's involvement from the earliest stages, see letter to Thomas Hare, 4 August 1868, *CW*, XVII, p. 1628; for 'remains of feudality', see 'Land Tenure Reform', *CW*, V, p. 689.

37. *POPE*, *CW*, II, p. 208; see also 'Right of Property in Land', *Examiner*, 19 July 1873, *CW*, XXV, p. 1236.

38. 'Monopoly', in 'Leslie on the Land Question', *Fortnightly Review*, June 1870, *CW*, V p. 672; 'bequest', in 'Land Tenure Reform' [2], speech to the Association, 18 March 1873, *CW*, XXIX, p. 425; 'gift of nature', in 'Land Tenure Reform' [1], speech to the Association, 15 May 1873, *CW*, XXIX, p. 418; 'original inheritance', 'Land

Tenure Reform', *CW*, V, p. 691.

39. 'Proper application', in 'Land Tenure Reform' [1], 15 May 1873, *CW*, XXIX, p. 417; 'nation as a whole', in 'Land Tenure Reform', *CW*, V, p. 691.

40. 'Land Tenure Reform', *CW*, V, p. 689.

41. 'Right of Property in Land', *CW*, XXV, p. 1234; for previous use see *POPE*, *CW*, III, pp. 819–20.

42. 'Maine on Village Communities', *Fortnightly Review*, 1 May 1871, *CW*, XXX, p. 216.

43. Ibid., pp. 223, 225.

44. Letter to Henry Fawcett, 24 October 1868, *CW*, XVII, p. 1659; 'I myself agree', letter to Andrew Reid, 5 October 1869, *CW*, XVII, p. 1644.

45. Letter to Alex Campbell, 28 February 1870, *CW*, XVII, p. 1702.

46. 'Land Tenure Reform' [1], *CW*, XXIX, p. 419. See also letter to John Stapleton, 25 October 1871, *CW*, XVII, p. 1848: 'In the present low state both of our political morality & of our administrative habits, I shd expect that the land department would become a mass of corrupt jobbing.'

47. 'Not abolition', in 'Land Tenure Reform', *CW*, V, p. 690; 'will of the State' in 'Land Tenure Reform' [1], *CW*, XXIX, p. 418.

48. 'Should public bodies be required to sell their lands?' *Examiner*, 11

January 1873, *CW*, XXV, p. 1233.

49. 'Land Tenure Reform', *CW*, V, p. 691; he had made the same argument, somewhat less polemically, in *POPE*, *CW*, III, pp. 819–21.

50. Letter to John Stapleton, 25 October 1871, *CW*, XVII, p. 1848; 'Property and Taxation', *Fortnightly Review*, *CW*, V, pp. 701–2. Mill discussed this article in a letter to John Cairnes 9 December 1872, *CW*, XVII, pp. 1925–6.

51. 'Land Tenure Reform' [2], 18 March 1873, *CW*, XXIX, p. 428.

52. *The Times*, 10 May 1873, p. 5.

53. For details of Mill's expulsion, see Clive Dewey, 'The rehabilitation of the peasant proprietor in nineteenth-century economic thought', *History of Political Economy*, 6, 1974, pp. 17–47. The phrase 'publicly identified himself' is from a letter by Sir Louis Mallet, quoted in Collini, *Public Moralists*, p. 323. For Mill's earlier speeches to the Cobden Club, see *CW*, XXVIII, pp. 96–8 and *CW*, XXIX, pp. 371–3.

54. 'Land Tenure Reform' [2], 18 March 1873, *CW*, XXIX, p. 424.

55. Letter to Gustave d'Eichthal, 21 May 1871, *CW*, XVII, p. 1821.

56. Letter to Gustave d'Eichthal, 4 March 1872, pp. 1874–5: 'Je crois que cette Association renferme une foule très diverse de représentants de toutes les écoles

socialistes, tant modérées que violentes. Les members anglais dont je connais personnellement plusieurs des chefs, me paraissent en général des hommes raisonnables, visant surtout aux améliorations pratiques dans le sort des travailleurs, capables d'apprécier les obstacles, et peu haineux envers les classes dont ils veulent faire cesser la domination.' Translation in the text provided by Fred Austin.

57. Letter to the General Council of the International Working Men's Association, after 23 July 1870, *CW*, XXXII, p. 220.

58. Letter to Charles Wentworth Dilke, 30 September 1870, *CW*, XVII, p. 1767.

59. Morley, *Recollections*, vol. 1, p. 55.

60. Letter to Charles Wentworth Dilke, 30 September 1870, *CW*, XVII, p. 1767.

61. Letter to Patrick Hennessey, after 25 August 1870, *CW*, XVII, p. 1761.

62. Letter to Thomas Smith, 4 October 1872, *CW*, XVII, p. 1911.

63. Helen Taylor's Continuation of the *Autobiography*, *CW*, I, p. 625. (This was never published.)

64. Helen Taylor's Preface to 'Chapters on Socialism', *Fortnightly Review*, February 1879, *CW*, V, p. 705.

65. 'Chapters on Socialism', *CW*, V, pp. 715, 729.

66. Ibid., p. 736.

67. Henry Buckle, *Edinburgh Review*, October 1851, quoted in Briggs, *Age of Improvement*, p. 347; for the rise in wages, see R. A. Church, *The Great Victorian Boom 1850–1873*, London: Macmillan, 1975, p. 72; for the increase in real incomes, see Harold Perkin, *Origins of Modern Society*, p. 413.

68. For the growth in the popularity of the theatre, see Picard, *London*, p. 198; for football and horse-racing, see Wilson, *Victorians*, p. 409.

69. *POPE*, *CW*, II, p. 208; 'Chapters on Socialism', *CW*, V, p. 736.

70. 'General designation', *AB*, *CW*, I, p. 239; 'becoming capitalists', letter to J. R. Ware, 13 September 1868, *CW*, XVI, pp. 1439–40.

71. Chapters on Socialism', *CW*, V, p. 740.

72. Ibid., pp. 746, 740.

73. Ibid., p. 743.

74. Letter to Henry Fawcett, 17 May 1863, *CW*, XV, p. 859.

75. Letter to Herbert Spencer, 6 July 1868, *CW*, XVII, p. 1620.

76. Draft letter in *Mill–Taylor Collection* in British Library of Political and Economic Science, quoted in Packe, *Mill*, p. 485.

77. Henri Fabre's letter to the Mayor of Avignon, accepting the post, is in the archives of the Palais de Roure, Avignon: it is undated, but must have been written in 1873.

78. Letter to Helen Taylor, 13 July 1871, *CW*, XVII, pp. 1826–7; Helen Taylor also recalled the

trips in her Continuation of the *Autobiography*, *CW*, I, p. 627.

79. Letter to John Cairnes, 21 August 1871, *CW*, XVII p. 1828.

80. Mill discussed Renouvier's work in a letter to Dr Emile Cazelles, 23 October 1869, *CW*, XVII, p. 1652.

81. *AB*, *CW*, I, p. 56.

82. Letter to the Princess Royal of Prussia, 26 December 1869, *CW*, XVII, p. 1675.

83. Letter to Kate Amberley from her sister, Blanche Airlie (she was married to the Earl of Airlie), 14 May 1873, *Amberley Papers*, vol. 2, p. 541: 'What a great bit of wisdom & sunshine has gone out of yr life with him & I hear that he meant to take a place this summer in yr neighbourhood for the sake of yr company . . .'

84. Kate Amberley's Journal, 28 September 1870, *Amberley Papers*, vol. 2, pp. 374–5.

85. Percy Bysshe Shelley, 'Ode to Liberty', published with *Prometheus Unbound*, 1820, ll. 240–45.

86. Kate Amberley's Journal, 27 September 1870, *Amberley Papers*, vol. 2, p. 375.

87. Bain, *John Stuart Mill*, p. 133; 'great blank' in letter to Pasquale Villari, 28 February 1872, *CW*, XVII, p. 1872; 'Grote's Aristotle', *Fortnightly Review*, January 1873, *CW*, XI, p. 475. As Grote would have wished, however, Mill felt as free as ever to note his disagreements, on, for example, the history of Realism and its links with Aristotelian thought (pp. 489–90).

88. Letter to Pasquale Villari, 28 February 1872, *CW*, XVII, p. 187

89. Mill's account book for 1866–70 is in Box IX/2 in the *Mill–Taylor Collection* at the London School of Economics; see also Packe, *Mill*, p. 484.

90. Newsome, *Victorian World Picture*, p. 58.

91. For Toulouse, see Mill's French Journal, 2 August 1820, *CW*, XXVI, p. 53; St Peter's, Rome, letters to HTM, 25 February 185 18 January 1855, *CW*, XIV, p. 297; Palermo, letter to HTM, 25 February 1855, *CW*, XIV, p. 34 for a couple of examples of Mill' interest in Chiltern churches, se his Journal for 6 July 1828, *CW*, XXVII, p. 484 and 8 July 1828, *CW*, XXVII, p. 487; for Peterborough, letter to HTM, 1 February 1857, *CW*, XV, p. 522.

92. Letter to Frederick Bates, 9 November 1868, *CW*, XVI, p. 1483.

93. Letter from Helen Taylor to Mill, 12 November 1868, in the *Mill–Taylor Collection*, quoted ir Packe, *Mill*, p. 474.

94. Morley, *Recollections*, vol. 1, p. 67

95. Letter to Thomas Carlyle, 12 January 1834, *CW*, XII, p. 206.

96. Letter to Arthur W. Greene, 16 December 1861, *CW*, XV, p. 754.

97. Courtney, *Life of Mill*, p. 165.

98. Letter from HTM to Mill, 14 &

15 February 1854, *Complete Works of HTM*, p. 374.

99. 'Utility of Religion', in *Three Essays on Religion*, *CW*, X, p. 407.

00. Ibid., pp. 405, 415.

01. Ibid., pp. 419, 422.

02. 'The elevating influence', letter to Henry Jones, 13 June 1868, *CW*, XVI, p. 1414; 'wonder' in *Hamilton*, *CW*, IX, p. 487.

03. 'Source of personal satisfaction', in 'Utility of Religion', *CW*, X, p. 420; 'no miracle . . .worth a farthing', letter to Henry Chenevix, 4 November 1863, *CW*, XV, p. 895; 'part of the halo', letter to William George Ward, spring 1849, *CW*, XIV, pp. 27–8.

04. 'Utility of Religion', *CW*, X, p. 409.

05. Ibid., p. 421.

06. Voltaire is quoted in Owen Chadwick, *The Secularization of the European Mind in the Nineteenth Century*, Cambridge: Cambridge University Press, 1975, p. 10.

07. Letter to John Sterling, 20–22 October 1831, *CW*, XII, p. 76; 'improve their religion', letter to Alexander Bain, 6 August 1859, *CW*, XV, p. 631. Far from urging an exodus from the Church, Mill encouraged clergymen and potential clergymen with a liberal outlook to remain inside, on the grounds that a 'church is far more easily improved from within than from without', in 'Inaugural Address', *CW*, XXI, p. 251.

08. Helen Taylor's 'Introductory Notice' to *Three Essays on Religion*, *CW*, X, p. 371.

09. 'Theism', *Three Essays on Religion*, *CW*, X, pp. 450, 485.

10. Ibid., p. 488.

11. For examples of Mill's respect for Christ, see letters to Thomas Carlyle, 5 October 1833, *CW*, XII, p. 182, and to Arthur W. Greene, 16 December 1861, *CW*, XV, p. 754: 'Nor would I willingly weaken in any person the reverence for Christ, in which I myself very strongly participate.'

12. John Morley, 'Mr. Mill's Three Essays on Religion', *Fortnightly Review*, 1 November 1874 and 1 January 1875, quoted in Semmel, *Mill and the Pursuit of Virtue*, p. 174.

13. Bain, *John Stuart Mill*, p. 138. An ell is an old measurement, mostly used in the textile industry, equivalent to six hand breadths, or roughly 45 inches.

14. 'Theism', *CW*, X, p. 488.

15. Ibid., p. 485.

16. 'Theism', *Three Essays on Religion*, *CW*, X, p. 397.

17. 'The Condition of Ireland', *Morning Chronicle*, 19 November 1846, *CW*, XXIV, p. 955.

18. *Rep. Gov.*, *CW*, XIX, p. 488

19. Letter to John Cairnes, 1 July 1872, *CW*, XVII, p. 1902; letter from Helen Taylor to Kate Amberley, 1 July 1872, *Amberley Papers*, vol. 2, p. 495; letter from Kate Amberley to Helen Taylor, quoted in Packe, *Mill*, p. 439.

120. Morley, *Recollections*, vol. 1, p. 67, where he referred to his journal for 5 March 1873; Dilke paid £315 for the portrait of Mill, see *CW*, XVII, p. 1940 n.2. It now hangs in the National Portrait Gallery, London. A detail from the painting is reproduced on the cover of this volume.

121. Journal entry, 1 February 1854, *CW*, XXVII, p. 649; 'so tame', letter from Dr H. Cecil Gurney to Helen Taylor, 12 May 1873, *Mill–Taylor Collection* at the LSE, vol. 8., no. 70. ff. 137–8, see also Packe, *Mill*, p. 507; 'you know I have done my work', Pastor Louis Rey, *John Stuart Mill en Avignon*, April 1921, p. 10 (Helen did not in fact know how to interpret these final words); 'more truly great', Ackroyd, *Dickens*, p. xiii.

Epilogue

1. Letter from Henry Sidgwick to C. H. Pearson, 10/15 May 1873, quoted in Collini, *Public Moralists*, p. 178; letter from Kate Amberley, 12 May 1873 to Lady Russell, *Amberley Papers*, vol. 2, p. 541.

2. *The Times*, 10 May 1873, p. 5.

3. Letter from Lady Russell to Kate Amberley, 20 May 1873, vol. 2, p. 542.

4. See William Christie, *John Stuart Mill and Mr Abraham Hayward Q.C.*, London: Henry S. King, 1873, p. 37.

5. Gladsone's letter is partially published in John Morley, *Life of Gladstone*, vol. 2, p. 544.

6. The Committee met on 3 July 1873; the list of contributors is in the *Mill–Taylor Collection* at the LSE.

7. Minutes of the Council, University College London, 15 June 1878. I am grateful to Wendy Butler of the UCL Records Office for providing this information.

8. 'Mr Mill', *Saturday Review*, 35, 1873, pp. 638–9; 'John Stuart Mill', *Illustrated London News*, 17 May 1873, p. 456.

9. Bagehot, 'The Late Mr Mill', *The Economist*, 17 May 1873, pp. 588–9; Sidgwick, 'John Stuart Mill', *Academy*, 15 May 1873, p. 193; May 1873 issues of both the *Athenaeum* and the *Spectator*.

10. Letter to HTM, 23 January 1854, *CW*, XIV, p. 138.

11. Henry Reeve, 'The Autobiography of John Stuart Mill', *Edinburgh Review*, 139, 1874, pp. 91–129; Abraham Hayward, 'John Stuart Mill', *Fraser's Magazine*, 8, 1873, pp. 663–81; 'The Autobiography of John Stuart Mill', *The Times*, 4 and 10 November 1873; 'monotonous joylessness' is from R. H. Hutton in the 'Mr John Stuart Mill's *Autobiography*', *Spectator*, 46, 1873, pp. 1337–9; *Daily News*, 18 October 1873; Thomas Carlyle quoted in Basil Willey, *Nineteenth-Century Studies, Coleridge to Matthew*

Arnold, London: Chatto & Windus, London, 1964 (first published 1949), p. 152.

12. Comments made by Frederick Harrison and Henry Sidgwick, in 1896 and 1885, suggest that Morley was generally supposed to be working on a biography, quoted by Collini, *Public Moralists*, p. 333.

13. Courtney, *Life of Mill*, p.174; Hayek, *Mill and Taylor*, p 16; Nietzsche described Mill as a 'flathead' in *Will to Power*, p. 30 and 'respectable' in *Beyond Good and Evil*, p. 253, and is quoted in Martha Nussbaum, *Upheavals of Thought – The Intelligence of Emotions*, Cambridge, New York: Cambridge University Press, 1991, p. 385. The 'flathead' quote is also in the *Mill News Letter*, vol. 17, no. 1, winter 1982, p. 1.

14. William Stanley Jevons, *Pure Logic and Other Minor Works*, New York: Burt Franklin (first published 1890), 1971, p. 201.

15. Albert V. Dicey, *Lectures on the Relation between Law & Public Opinion in England during the Nineteenth Century*, London: Macmillan, 1905, p. 183; Leslie Stephen, *The English Utilitarians*, 3 vols, London and New York, G. P. Putnam's Sons, 1900, vol. 3, pp. 65–71; Ernest Barker, *Political Thought in England 1848–1914*, London and Oxford: Oxford University Press, (first ed. 1915), 1947, p. 4. See Collini, *Public Moralists*, pp. 327–8 for discussion.

16. 'Outstanding monument' was the assessment of Prof. J. H. Burn in his introductory comments to the Mill Bicentennial Conference, UCL, April 2006; Mill's observation about Aristotle is in 'Grote's Aristotle', *CW*, XI, p. 510.

17. John Morley, 'John Stuart Mill: an anniversary', *Times Literary Supplement*, 18 May 1906, p. 174.

18. Collini, *Public Moralists*, p. 341.

19. Journal entry, 1 February 1854, *CW*, XXVII, p. 649.

Bibliography

➤⭠

1. Works by John Stuart Mill

Collected Works of John Stuart Mill, ed. John Robson and others, 33 vols, Toronto and London: Toronto University Press, 1965–91. These are the volumes:

I	*Autobiography and Literary Essays* (1981)
II, III	*Principles of Political Economy* (1965)
IV, V	*Essays on Economics and Society* (1967)
VI	*Essays on England, Ireland and the Empire* (1982)
VII, VIII	*System of Logic: Ratiocinative and Inductive* (1973)
IX	*An Examination of Sir William Hamilton's Philosophy* (1979)
X	*Essays on Ethics, Religion and Society* (1969)
XI	*Essays on Philosophy and the Classics* (1978)
XII, XIII	*Earlier Letters* (1963)
XIV, XV, XVI, XVII	*Later Letters* (1972)
XVIII, XIX	*Essays on Politics and Society* (1977)
XX	*Essays on French History and Historians* (1985)
XXI	*Essays on Equality, Law and Education* (1984)
XXII, XXIII, XXIV, XXV	*Newspaper Writings* (1986)
XXVI, XXVII	*Journals and Debating Speeches* (1988)
XXVIII, XXIX	*Public and Parliamentary Speeches* (1988)
XXX	*Writings in India* (1990)
XXXI	*Miscellaneous Writings* (1989)
XXXII	*Additional Letters* (1991)
XXXIII	*Indexes* (1991)

2. Collections, Letters and Memoirs

The Amberley Papers: Bertrand Russell's Family Background, ed. Bertrand Russell and Patricia Russell, 2 vols, London: Allen and Unwin, 1966

The Collected Works of Walter Bagehot, ed. Norman St John-Stevas, 15 vols, London: *The Economist*, 1965–86, vol. 3, 1968

The Works of Jeremy Bentham, ed. John Bowring, 11 vols, Edinburgh: W. Tait, 1859

Letters of Thomas Carlyle to John Stuart Mill, John Sterling and Robert Browning, ed. Alexander Carlyle, London: T. Fisher Unwin, 1923

Carlyle, Thomas, *Reminiscences*, ed. James Anthony Froude, 2 vols, London: Longmans, Green, 1881

Christie, William, *John Stuart Mill and Mr. Abraham Hayward Q.C. A reply about Mill to a letter to the Rev. Stopford Brooke, privately circulated and actually published*, London: Henry S. King and Co, 1873

Collected Letters of Coleridge, Samuel Taylor, ed. Earl Leslie Griggs, 6 vols, Oxford: Clarendon Press, 1956–71

Conway, Moncure D., *Centenary History of the South Place Society*, London: Williams and Norgate, 1894

Fawcett, Millicent, *Life of the Rt. Hon. Sir William Molesworth*, London: Macmillan, 1901

Fox, Caroline, *Memories of Old Friends*, London: Smith, Elder & Co., revised edn, 1883

Froude, James Anthony, *Thomas Carlyle: A History of His Life in London*, 1834–1881, 2 vols, London: Longmans, Green, and Co., 1884

Froude, James Anthony, *Thomas Carlyle: A History of the First Forty Years of Life*, 1795–1835, 2 vols, London: Longmans, Green, and Co., 1882

Garnett, Richard, *The Life of W. J. Fox, public teacher & social reformer, 1786–1864*, London: J. Lane, 1910

Gomperz, Heinrich, *Theodor Gomperz, Briefe und Aufzeichnungen*, 2 vols, Vienna: Griechische Denker, 1936

Griffin, William and Harry Minchin, Harry, *The Life of Robert Browning*, London: Methuen, 1911

Grote, Harriet, *The Personal Life of George Grote*, London: Murray, 1873

Hazlitt, William, *The Spirit of the Age*, Oxford: Oxford University Press, 1825/1935

The Correspondence of John Stuart Mill and Auguste Comte, ed. and trans. Oscar Haac, New Brunswick and London: Transaction, 1995

Life and Letters of Lord Macaulay, ed. George Otto Trevelyan, 2 vols, London & New York: Thomas Nelson & Sons, 1876

Maxwell, Sir Herbert, *Life and Times of the Right Honourable William Henry Smith, M.P.*, 2 vols, London and Edinburgh, William Blackwood and Sons, 1893

The Complete Works of Harriet Taylor Mill, ed. Jo Ellen Jacobs, Bloomington and Indianapolis: Indiana University Press, 1998

Monypenny, William Flavelle and George Earle Buckle, *The Life of Benjamin Disraeli, Earl of Beaconsfield*, 6 vols, London: John Murray, 1910–20

Morley, John, *Life of Gladstone*, 3 vols, London: Macmillan, 1908

Morley, *Recollections*, 2 vols, London: Macmillan, 1917

The Works and Correspondence of David Ricardo, ed. Piero Sraffa, 11 vols, Cambridge: Cambridge University Press, 1952

Rey, Pastor Louis, *John Stuart Mill en Avignon*, unpublished paper presented to conference in Avignon, France, 25 April 1921

Rey, Pastor Louis, *Le Roman de John Stuart Mill*, Paris: E. Monzein, 1913

Autobiography and Letters of John Arthur Roebuck, ed. Robert Eaden Leader, London: E. Arnold, 1897

Romilly–Edgeworth Letters, 1813–1818, ed. Samuel Henry Romilly, London: John Murray, 1936

Works of John Ruskin, eds E. T. Cook and A. D. C. Wedderburn, 39 vols, London: George Allen, 1902–12

Richard Sanders et al., *The Collected Letters of Thomas and Jane Welsh Carlyle*, Durham, N.C.: Duke University Press, 1970

Solly, Henry, *These Eighty Years*, 2 vols, London, 1893

Memoir of the Reverend Sydney Smith by his daughter Lady Holland, 2 vols, London: Longmans, 1855

Stephen, Leslie, *Life of Henry Fawcett*, London: Smith, Elder, 1885

Correspondence of Henry Taylor, ed. Edward Dowden, London: Longmans, 1888

Wallas, Graham, *Life of Francis Place 1771–1854*. London: Longmans, 1898

3. Principal Works on Mill

Bain, Alexander, *John Stuart Mill: a Criticism with Personal Recollections*, London: Longmans, 1882

Bain, Alexander, *James Mill, a Biography*, London: Longmans, Green and Co., 1882

Berger, Fred, *Happiness, Justice, and Freedom: The Moral and Political Philosophy of John Stuart Mill*, Berkeley: University of California Press, 1984

Britton, Karl, *John Stuart Mill*, London: Penguin, 1953, reprinted New York: Dover, 1969

Capaldi, Nicholas, *John Stuart Mill: A Biography*, Cambridge: Cambridge University Press, 2004

Carlisle, Janice, *John Stuart Mill and the Writing of Character*, Athens, Georgia: University of Georgia Press, 1991

Collini, Stefan, *Public Moralists: Political Thought and Intellectual Life in Great Britain 1850–1930*, Oxford: Clarendon Press, 1991

Courtney, William Leonard, *Life of John Stuart Mill*, London: Walter Scott, 1889

Cowling, Maurice, *Mill and Liberalism*, Cambridge: Cambridge University Press, 1963

Donner, Wendy, *The Liberal Self: John Stuart Mill's Moral and Political Philosophy*, Ithaca: Cornell University Press, 1991

Fox Bourne, H.R. (ed.), J*ohn Stuart Mill: Notices of His Life and Works*, London: Dallow, 1873

Hamburger, Joseph, *Intellectuals in Politics: John Stuart Mill and the Philosophic Radicals*, New Haven: Yale University Press, 1961

Hayek, Friedrich von, *John Stuart Mill and Harriet Taylor – Their Correspondence and Subsequent Marriage*, London: Routledge & Kegan Paul, 1951

Himmelfarb, Gertrude, *On Liberty and Liberalism: The Case of John Stuart Mill*, New York: Knopf, 1974

Hollander, Samuel, *The Economics of J. S. Mill*, 2 vols, Toronto: University of Toronto Press, 1985

Hollander, Samuel, *The Economics of John Stuart Mill*, Toronto: UTP and Oxford: Blackwell, Volume I, *Theory and Method*, Volume II, Political Economy, 1985

Kinzer, Bruce L., Ann P. Robson, and John M. Robson, *A Moralist In and Out of Parliament, John Stuart Mill at Westminster 1865–1868*, Toronto: University of Toronto Press, 1992

Kinzer, Bruce L., *England's Disgrace? J. S. Mill and the Irish Question*, Toronto: University of Toronto Press, 2001

Laine, M. (ed.), *A Cultivated Mind. Essays on J. S. Mill Presented to John M. Robson*, Toronto: University of Toronto Press, 1991

Moir, Martin, Douglas Peers and Lynn Zastoupil (eds), *J. S. Mill's Encounter with India*, Toronto, Buffalo and London: Toronto University Press, 1999

Packe, Michael St John, *The Life of John Stuart Mill*, London: Secker and Warburg, 1954

Radcliff, Peter (ed.), *Limits of Liberty: Studies of Mill's On Liberty*, Belmont, Calif.: Wadsworth, 1966

Robson, John M., *The Improvement of Mankind: The Social and Political Thought of John Stuart Mill*, Toronto: University of Toronto Press; London: Routledge & Kegan Paul, 1968

Robson, John M., and Michael Laine (eds), *James and John Stuart Mill: Papers of the Centenary Conference*, Toronto: University of Toronto Press, 1976

Ryan, Alan, *The Philosophy of John Stuart Mill*, London: Macmillan, 1970, 2nd edn, New York: Macmillan, 1988

Ryan, Alan, *J. S. Mill*, London: Routledge & Kegan Paul, 1974

Schneewind, J. B. (ed.), *Mill: A Collection of Critical Essays*, Garden City, NY: Doubleday; London: Macmillan, 1968

Semmel, Bernard, *John Stuart Mill and the Pursuit of Virtue*, New Haven: Yale University Press, 1984

Skorupski, John, *John Stuart Mill*, London: Routledge, 1989

Skorupski, John (ed.), *The Cambridge Companion to Mill*, Cambridge: Cambridge University Press, 1998

Skorupski, John, *Why Read Mill Today?* Routledge, London, 2006

Stafford, William, *John Stuart Mill*, London: Macmillan, 1998

Ten, C. L., *Mill on Liberty*, Oxford: Oxford University Press, 1980

Zastoupil, Lynn, *John Stuart Mill and India*, Stanford: Stanford University Press, 1994

4. Other Works

Ackroyd, Peter, *Dickens*, London & New York: Guild Publishing, 1990

Amis, Kingsley, *Jake's Thing*, London: Penguin, 1978

Annan, Noel, *Leslie Stephen: The Godless Victorian*, Chicago: University of Chicago Press, 1984

Annas, Julia, 'Mill and the Subjection of Women', *Philosophy*, 52, 1977

Arnold, Matthew, *Culture and Anarchy and Other Writings*, Cambridge: Cambridge University Press, 1993

Ashton, Rosemary, *142 Strand, A Radical Address in Victorian London*, London: Chatto & Windus, 2006

August, Eugene, *John Stuart Mill – A Mind at Large*, London: Vision Press, 1976

Bagehot, Walter, 'Mr. Mill's Address to the Electors of Westminster', *The Economist* (29 April), 1865, reprinted in Norman St John-Stevas (ed.), *The Collected Works of Walter Bagehot*, vol. 3, London: *The Economist*, 1968

Balfour, Arthur James, *Theism and Humanism*, London: Hodder and Stoughton, 1915

Barker, Ernest, *Political Thought in England 1848–1914*, London and Oxford: Oxford University Press (1st edn, 1915), 1947

Barker, Juliet, *Wordsworth, A Life*, London: Penguin Viking, 2000

Bebbington, David, *The Mind of Gladstone, Religion, Homer, and Politics*, Oxford: Oxford University Press, 2004

Becker, Lydia E., 'Liberty, Equality, Fraternity. A Reply to Mr. Fitzjames Stephen's Strictures on Mr. J. S. Mill's *Subjection of Women*', *Women's Suffrage Journal*, 1874, reprinted in Lewis (ed.), *Before the Vote was Won: Arguments For and Against Women's Suffrage* (1987)

Berlin, Isaiah, *Four Essays on Liberty*, Oxford: Oxford University Press, 1969

Breyer, Stephen, *Active Liberty, Interpreting Our Democratic Constitution*, New York: Vintage Books, 2005

Briggs, Asa, *The Age of Improvement 1783–1867*, London: Longman, 1959

Briggs, Asa, *Victorian Cities*, London: Penguin, 1963, 1968

Briggs, Asa, *Victorian People – A Reassessment of Persons and Themes 1851–67*, London: Penguin, 1965

Britton, Karl, 'John Stuart Mill on Christianity', in Robson and Laine (eds), *James and John Stuart Mill: Papers of the Centenary Conference* (1976)

Brogan, Hugh. *Alexis de Tocqueville – Prophet of Democracy in the Age of Revolution*, London: Profile, 2006

Buckle, Henry Thomas, 'Mill on Liberty', *Fraser's Magazine*, 1859, reprinted in Andrew Pyle (ed.), *Liberty: Contemporary Responses to John Stuart Mill* (1994)

Burn, W. L., *The Age of Equipoise. A Study of the Mid-Victorian Generation*, London: Allen and Unwin, 1964

Burns, J. H., 'J. S. Mill and Democracy, 1829–1861', in J. B. Schneewind (ed.), *Mill: A Collection of Critical Essays* (1968)

Burrow, J. W., *Whigs and Liberals: Continuity and Change in English Political Thought*, Oxford: Clarendon, 1988

Carlile, Richard, 'What is Love?' *The Republican*, XI, 18 (6 May 1825), reprinted in M. L. Bush, *What is Love? Richard Carlile's Philosophy of Sex*, London and New York: Verso, 1998, pp. 55–80

Chadwick, Owen, *The Secularization of the European Mind in the Nineteenth Century*, Cambridge: Cambridge University Press, 1975

Church, R. A., *The Great Victorian Boom 1850–1873*, London: Macmillan, 1975

Clarke, M. L., *George Grote*, London: Athlone Press, 1962

Coleridge, Samuel Taylor, *The Major Works*, Oxford: Oxford University Press, 1985

Collini, Stefan, 'Liberalism and the Legacy of Mill', *Historical Journal*, 20, 1977

Collini, Stefan, 'The Idea of "Character" in Victorian Political Thought', *Transactions of the Royal Historical Society*, 5th series, 35, 1985

Collini, Stefan, Donald Winch, and John Burrow, *That Noble Science of Politics: A Study in Nineteenth-century Intellectual History*, Cambridge: Cambridge University Press, 1983

Collini, Stefan, *English Pasts*, Oxford: Oxford University Press, 1999

Cowell, Herbert, 'Liberty, Equality, Fraternity: Mr John Stuart Mill', *Blackwood's Edinburgh Magazine*, 1873, reprinted in Pyle (ed.), *Liberty: Contemporary Responses to John Stuart Mill* (1994)

Desmond, Adrian, *Huxley, Evolution's High Priest*, London: Michael Joseph, 1997

Dicey, Albert V., *Lectures on the Relation between Law & Public Opinion in England during the Nineteenth Century*, London: Macmillan, 1905

Donner, Wendy, 'John Stuart Mill's Liberal Feminism', *Philosophical Studies*, 69, 1993

Dunn, John, *Setting the People Free – The Story of Democracy*, London: Atlantic Books, 2005

Ellis, Roger, *Who's Who in Victorian Britain*, London: Shepheard-Walwyn, 1997

Ellis, Sarah, *The Wives of England, Their Relative Duties, Domestic Influence, and Social Obligations*, London: Fisher, Son, & Co., 1843

Evans, Eric J., *The Forging of the Modern State, Early Industrial Britain, 1783–1870*, London and New York: Longman, 1983, 1996

Fawcett, Henry, 'His Influence at the Universities', in H. R. Fox Bourne (ed.), *John Stuart Mill: Notices of His Life and Works*

Feinberg, Joel, *Harm to Others: Moral Limits of Criminal Law*, New York: Oxford University Press, 1984, vol. 1

Filipiuk, Marion, 'John Stuart Mill and France', in Laine (ed.), *A Cultivated Mind. Essays on J. S. Mill Presented to John M. Robson* (1991)

Golby, J. M. (ed.), *Culture and Society in Britain 1850–1890*, Oxford: Oxford University Press, 1986

Gray, John, and G. W. Smith (eds), *J. S. Mill's 'On Liberty' in Focus*, New York: Routledge, 1991

Gray, John, *Liberalisms: Essays in Political Philosophy*, London: Routledge, 1989

Gray, John, *Mill on Liberty: A Defence*, London: Routledge & Kegan Paul, 1983 (revised edn, 1996)

Green, Thomas Hill, *The Logic of J. S. Mill*, in R. L. Nettleship (ed.), *Works of Thomas Hill Green*, London: Longmans, 1890

Grote, G., *A History of Greece*, 12 vols, London: John Murray, 1846–56

Grote, G., *Plato and the other Companions of Socrates*, 4 vols, London: John Murray, 1888 (new edn)

Hamburger, J., 'Religion and "On Liberty"', in Laine (ed.), *A Cultivated Mind: Essays on J. S. Mill Presented to John M. Robson* (1991)

Hanham, H. J., *Elections and Party Management: Politics in the Time of Disraeli and Gladstone*, London: Longmans, 1958

Harris, Jose, *Private Lives, Public Spirit: Britain 1870–1914*, London: Penguin, 1993

Harrison, Ross, *Bentham*, London: Routledge, 1983

Hayward, Abraham, 'John Stuart Mill', *Fraser's Magazine*, n.s. 8, 1873

Hazlitt, William, *Table Talk*, London: J. M. Dent & Sons Ltd, 1959

Himes, Norman, 'John Stuart Mill's attitude towards neo-Malthusianism', *Economic Journal* (Economic History Series No.4, Supplement), January 1929

Himmelfarb, Gertrude, *The Roads to Modernity – The British, French and American Enlightenments*, New York: Vintage, 2004

Himmelfarb, Gertrude, *Victorian Minds*, London: Weidenfeld & Nicolson, 1968

Hitchens, Christopher, *Thomas Paine's Rights of Man, A Biography*, London: Atlantic Books, 2006

Hobsbawm, Eric, *The Age of Capital*, New York: Charles Scribner's Sons, 1975

Hollander, Samuel, 'Ricardianism, J. S. Mill, and the Neo-classical Challenge', in Robson and Michael Laine (eds), *James and John Stuart Mill: Papers of the Centenary Conference* (1976)

Holmes, Richard, *Coleridge: Darker Reflections*, London: Flamingo, 1998

Holmes, Richard, *Coleridge: Early Visions*, Sevenoaks: Hodder and Stoughton, 1989

Houghton, Walter E., *The Victorian Frame of Mind*, New Haven and London: Yale University Press, 1957

Humboldt, Wilhelm von, *The Sphere and Duties of Government*, trans. Joseph Coulthard, Bristol: Thoemmes Press, 1996

Irwin, Terence H., 'Mill and the Classical World', in *The Cambridge Companion to Mill*, ed. John Skorupski (1998)

Jacobs, Jo Ellen, *The Voice of Harriet Taylor Mill*, Bloomington & Indianapolis: Indiana University Press, 2002

Jenkins, Roy, *Gladstone*, London: Macmillan, 1995

Jenks, Edward, *Thomas Carlyle and John Stuart Mill*, Bristol: Thoemmes Antiquarian Books Ltd., 1990, a reprint of the 1888 edition

Jevons, William Stanley, *Pure Logic and Other Minor Works* (1890), New York: Burt Franklin, 1971

Johnson, Paul, *The Birth of the Modern: World Society 1815–1830*, London: Weidenfeld and Nicolson, 1991

Johnson, Steven, *The Ghost Map – A street, an epidemic and the two men who battled to save Victorian London*, London: Allen Lane, 2006

Jones, H. S., 'John Stuart Mill as Moralist', *Journal of the History of Ideas*, 53, 1992

Keynes, John Maynard, *Essays in Persuasion*, New York: W. W. Norton & Company Inc., 1963

Kinzer, Bruce, 'John Stuart Mill and the Experience of Political Engagement', in Laine (ed.), *A Cultivated Mind* (1991)

Larg, David, *John Ruskin*, London: Peter Davies Ltd, 1932

Levi, Peter, *Tennyson*, London: Macmillan, 1993

Lively, J. and J. Rees (eds), *Utilitarian Logic and Politics*, London: Oxford University Press, 1978

Lloyd, Trevor, 'Mill and the East India Company', in Laine (ed.), *A Cultivated Mind* (1991)

Locke, John, *Two Treatises of Government* (1690), ed. Peter Laslett, New York: Mentor Books, 1988

Macaulay, T. B., 'Mill's Essay on Government: Utilitarian Logic and Politics', reprinted in Lively and Rees, *Utilitarian Logic and Politics* (1978)

Mandler, Peter, *The English National Character*, New Haven and London: Yale University Press, 2006

Marx, Karl and Friedrich Engels, *The Communist Manifesto*, trans. Samuel Moore (1888), Introduction and Notes by A. J. P. Taylor, London: Penguin Books, 1967

Maureau, Alain, 'Stuart Mill à Avignon', paper presented to a conference at the Palais du Roure, Avignon, 22 May 1987

McCloskey, H. J., *John Stuart Mill: A Critical Study*, London: Macmillan, 1971

Millar, Alan, 'Mill on Religion', in Skorupski (ed.), *The Cambridge Companion to Mill* (1998)

Millgate, Jane, *Macaulay*, London: Routledge, 1973

Minto, W., 'His Miscellaneous Criticisms', in Fox Bourne (ed.), *John Stuart Mill: Notices of His Life and Works* (1873)

Moir, Martin, 'Introduction' to *Writings on India*, in J. S. Mill, *CW*, XXX, 1990

Morley, John, 'John Stuart Mill: An Anniversary', *Times Literary Supplement*, 18 May 1906

Mozley, Anne, 'Mr. Mill on the Subjection of Women', *Blackwood's Magazine*, 106, 1869, reprinted in Pyle (ed.), *Liberty: Contemporary Responses to John Stuart Mill* (1994)

Newsome, David, *The Victorian World Picture*, London: John Murray, 1997

Nicholson, Peter, 'The Reception and Early Reputation of Mill's Political Thought', in Skorupski (ed.), *The Cambridge Companion to Mill* (1998)

Nussbaum, Martha, *Upheavals of Thought – The Intelligence of Emotions,* Cambridge, New York: Cambridge University Press, 1991

Okin, Susan M., *Women in Western Political Philosophy*, Princeton: Princeton University Press, 1979

Oliphant, Margaret, 'Mill on "The Subjection of Women"', *Edinburgh Review*, 130, 1869, reprinted in Pyle, *Liberty: Contemporary Responses to John Stuart Mill* (1995)

Oliphant, Margaret, 'The Great Unrepresented', *Fraser's Magazine*, 100, 1866

Perkin, Harold, *The Origins of Modern English Society 1780–1880*, London: Routledge & Kegan Paul; Toronto: University of Toronto Press, 1969

Picard, Liza, *Victorian London: The Life of a City 1840–1870*, London: Weidenfeld & Nicolson, 2005

Porter, Roy, *Enlightenment – Britain and the Creation of the Modern World*, London: Penguin, 2000

Porter, Roy, *Flesh in the Age of Reason*, London: Penguin Allen Lane, 2003

Pyle, Andrew (ed.), *Liberty: Contemporary Responses to John Stuart Mill*, Bristol: Thoemmes Press, 1994

Pyle, Andrew (ed.), *The Subjection of Women: Contemporary Responses to John Stuart Mill*, Bristol: Thoemmes Press, 1995

Rawls, John, *A Theory of Justice*, Oxford: Oxford University Press, 1971

Rees, John C., 'A Re-Reading of Mill on Liberty', *Political Studies*, 8, 1960, reprinted with a new postscript in Radcliff (ed.), *Limits of Liberty: Studies of Mill's* On Liberty (1966)

Roazen, Paul, *Political Theory and the Psychology of the Unconscious*, London: Open Gate Press, 2000

Robson, Ann P., 'Mill's Second Prize in the Lottery of Life', in Laine (ed.), *A Cultivated Mind* (1991)

Robson, John M., 'Harriet Taylor and John Stuart Mill: Artist and Scientist', *Queen's Quarterly*, 73, 1966

Robson, John, 'J. S. Mill's Theory of Poetry', in J. B. Schneewind (ed.), *Mill: A Collection of Critical Essays*, London: Macmillan, 1968

Rosen, Fred, *Jeremy Bentham and Representative Democracy*, Oxford: Clarendon Press, 1983

Rover, Constance, *Women's Suffrage and Party Politics in Britain 1866–1914*, London: Routledge & Kegan Paul, 1967

Ryan, Alan (ed.), *The Idea of Freedom, Essays in Honour of Isaiah Berlin*, Oxford: Oxford University Press, 1979

Semmel, Bernard, *The Governor Eyre Controversy*, London: MacGibbon & Kee, 1962

Sen, Amartya, and Bernard Williams (eds), *Utilitarianism and Beyond*, Cambridge: Cambridge University Press, 1982

Sewell, Arthur (ed.), *1840 and After*, Auckland: Auckland University College, 1940

Sidgwick, Henry, 'John Stuart Mill', *The Academy* 4 (15 May), 1973

Skinner, Quentin, *Liberty Before Liberalism*, Cambridge: Cambridge University Press, 1998

Skorupski, John, 'The Parts of Happiness', *Philosophical Books*, 26, 1985

Smith, Adam, *The Wealth of Nations*, ed. Edwin Cannan, New York: Random House, 1904

Smith, K. J. M., *James Fitzjames Stephen: Portrait of a Victorian Rationalist*, Cambridge: Cambridge University Press, 1988

Smith, V. R., 'John Stuart Mill's Famous Distinction Between Production and Distribution', *Economics and Philosophy*, 1, 1985

Snyder, Laura J., *Reforming Philosophy*, Chicago and London: University of Chicago Press, 2006

Stafford, William, 'How can a paradigmatic liberal call himself a socialist? The case of John Stuart Mill', *Journal of Political Ideologies*, 3 (3), 1998

Stafford, William, 'Is Mill's "liberal" feminism "masculinist"?', *Journal of Political Ideologies*, 9 (2), 2004

Stafford, William, 'John Stuart Mill on War', in Keith Dockray and Keith Laybourn (eds), *The Representation and Reality of War*, Sutton Publishing, 1999

Stephen, James Fitzjames, 'Mr. Mill on Political Liberty', *Saturday Review*, 1859, reprinted in Pyle, (ed.), *Liberty: Contemporary Responses to John Stuart Mill* (1994)

Stephen, James Fitzjames, *Liberty, Equality, Fraternity*, 2nd edn, London: Smith, Elder, 1874, reprinted, R. J. White (ed.), Cambridge: Cambridge University Press, 1967

Stephen, Leslie, 'The Late Stuart Mill', *The Nation*, 414, 1873

Stephen, Leslie, *The English Utilitarians*, 3 vols, London and New York, G. P. Putnam's Sons, 1900

Stillinger, Jack, 'Mill's Education – Fact, Fiction and Myth', in Laine (ed.), *A Cultivated Mind* (1961)

Sumner, L. W., 'Welfare, Happiness, and Pleasure', *Utilitas*, 4, 1992

Sweet, Matthew, *Inventing the Victorians*, London: Faber and Faber, 2001

Taylor, M. W., *Men versus the State: Herbert Spencer and Late Victorian Individualism*, Oxford: Clarendon Press, 1992

Thomas, Kathleen, *The Crisis and Analysis of John Stuart Mill's Life*, Durham: Pentland Press, 1994

Thomas, William, *The Philosophic Radicals: Nine Studies in Theory and Practice 1817–1841*, Oxford: Clarendon Press, 1979

Thompson, E. P., *The Making of the English Working Class* (1963), London: Penguin, 1968

Thomson, David, *England in the Nineteenth Century*, London: Penguin, 1950

Thornton, William, 'His Career in the India House', in Fox Bourne (ed.), *John Stuart Mill: Life and Works* (1873)

Tocqueville, Alexis de, *Democracy in America*, London: Dent (Everyman Library), 1994

Tomalin, Claire, *Thomas Hardy, The Time-Torn Man*, London: Penguin Viking, 2006

Toulongeon, François Emmanuel, *Histoire de France, depuis la révolution de 1789*, 4 vols, Paris; Treuttel and Würtz, 1801–10

Trimen, Henry, 'His Botanical Studies', in Fox Bourne (ed.), *John Stuart Mill: Life and Works* (1873)

Tuell, Anne Kimball, *John Sterling, a Representative Victorian*, London: Macmillan, 1941

Turk, Christopher, *Coleridge and Mill*, Aldershot: Averbury, 1988

Urbanati, Nadia, 'John Stuart Mill on Androgyny and Ideal Marriage', *Political Theory*, 19, 1991

Varouxakis, Georgios, *Victorian Political Thought on France and The French*, London: Palgrave, 2002

Weinberg, Adelaide, *John Elliot Cairnes and the American Civil War*, London: Kingwood Press, 1970

Whewell, William, *The Elements of Morality, including Polity*, New York: Harper, 1845

Whewell, William, *The Philosophy of the Inductive Sciences*, new edn, 2 vols, London: John W. Parker, 1847

White, Jerry, *London in the Nineteenth Century*, London: Jonathan Cape, 2007

Willey, Basil, *Nineteenth-Century Studies, Coleridge to Matthew Arnold* (1949), London: Chatto & Windus, 1964

Williams, Bernard, 'A Critique of Utilitarianism', in J. J. C. Smart and B. Williams (eds), *Utilitarianism: For and Against*, Cambridge: Cambridge University Press, 1982

Williams, Raymond, *Culture and Society 1780–1950*, New York: Columbia University Press, 1983

Wilson, A. N., *The Victorians*, London: Hutchinson, 2002

Wilson, David Alec, *Life of Carlyle*, 6 vols, London: K. Paul, Trench, Trubner, 1923–34

Winter, Alison, *Mesmerized: Powers of Mind in Victorian Britain*, Chicago: University of Chicago Press, 1998

Wittgenstein, Ludwig, *Philosophical Investigations*, trans. and ed. E. Anscombe and R. Rhees, Oxford: Blackwell, 1953

Woods, T., *Poetry and Philosophy: A Study in the Thought of John Stuart Mill*, London: Hutchinson, 1961

Woods, Thomas, *Poetry and Philosophy, A Study in the Thought of John Stuart Mill*, London: Hutchinson, 1961

Wordsworth, William, *The Major Works*, edited with an Introduction and Notes by Stephen Gill, Oxford: Oxford University Press, 2000

Index

Note: The following abbreviations are used in sub-headings: JM for James Mill; JSM for John Stuart Mill, and HTM for Harriet Taylor, subsequently Harriet Taylor Mill.

Adams, John 316
Adams, William Bridges 72–3
Adderley, Charles 381
Adullamites 370–1, 377, 386, 390, 403, 409
Amberley, John Russell, Viscount
    friendship with JSM 347, 391, 451, 456,
        469, 478
    and Parliament 347, 357, 408
    and suffrage 310
    and women's rights 429, 436, 442
Amberley, Kate Stanley Russell, Lady
    and death of JSM 481
    and female suffrage 429
    friendship with JSM 347, 349, 391, 451,
        456, 469, 478
    and Jamaica Committee 379
    and JSM in Parliament 357, 368, 369,
        373, 387, 405
Amis, Kingsley 262
Annas, Julia 445
Anning, Mary 52
aristocracy
    and Liberal government 367
    and local government 321

as obstacle to progress 76, 458
    radical attacks on 50, 53, 56–8, 130,
        145–6, 164
Arnold, Matthew 5, 291, 384
art, and science 176–7
associationism 39, 51, 69
atheism 344, 471
    of Bradlaugh 403, 405–6, 410
    of Carlile 54, 272
    of Darwin 295
    of Holyoake 368
Athenaeum 80, 296, 482
Austin, Charles 38, 40, 50, 136
Austin, John 42, 145, 180, 187, 188–9, 207
Austin, Sarah 80, 109, 136, 139–40, 188–9
Autobiography 241
    on Bradlaugh 409
    on Coleridge 107
    on Comte 349–50
    on democracy 110
    on East India Company 43
    on education 4, 13, 14, 26
    on France 29, 30, 33, 186
    on Goethe 109

on Grote 308–9
on happiness 333
on Helen Taylor 274
and HTM 26, 82–3, 150–3, 176, 206, 229, 247, 484
impact 484
on intuitionism 164
on Ireland 182, 397, 401
on Liberal party 402
on *On Liberty* 251, 268, 302–4
on London Debating Society 66–7
on *London and Westminster Review* 144
on mental crisis 66, 377
on moral reform 239
on mother 30
on *Principles* 221
on radicalism 146
on reformist writings 52
on *System of Logic* 162, 349
on utilitarianism 59–60, 77, 96–7, 138
autonomy 70, 84–5, 168–71, 263, 276–8, 416
and democracy 114
and education 84–5, 171, 284
and happiness 97
and social reform 171–4
Avignon
HTM's death in 260, 274
JSM's grave 413, 480
JSM's home in 274–5, 306, 307, 323, 341, 347–8, 354, 366–7, 404, 449–50, 486
memorial to HTM 275–6
and pets 450–1

Bagehot, Walter 249, 291, 367, 483
English Constitution 310, 356
on JSM 26, 207, 356–7, 398–9
and Parliament 42, 356, 368
as public moralist 5
and rights of women 425
Bailey, Samuel 38
Bain, Alexander 200, 202, 285, 308, 340, 346
and American Civil War 336
as biographer of JSM 20, 376–7, 479, 484
The Emotions and the Will 273
and JSM as MP 354

and JSM's health 186
and JSM's marriage 152–3, 217, 229, 243
and JSM's religious views 471, 473, 476–7
and JSM's sense of humour 249
and JSM's writing style 196
and rights of women 221, 414, 416, 420, 427, 447
and memorial to JSM 482
and *System of Logic* 162–3
Balard, Antoine Jérôme 33
Baldwin, Robert 50
Balfour, Arthur 163
ballot, secret 130, 191, 368, 452
and Chartism 111
and Grote 94, 130
and JM 146, 315
and JSM 7, 111, 142, 239, 315–17, 357, 412
Barker, Ernest 485
Barton, Susan 71
Beal, James 357
Beales, Edmund 383–5
Beattie, James 20
Beauchamp, Philip *see* Grote, George
Beccaria, Cesare 75
Becker, Lydia 432, 446
Beeton, Isabella 419
Bentham, George 30, 33, 40
Bentham, Jeremy
and debating societies 44
and France 30
and health 246
and history 75
and homosexuality 282
and JM 11–13, 179
and JSM 5–6, 12, 15, 18, 28, 55, 62, 117, 119, 136–8
and Parliament 87, 318
and poetry 20, 137
on Southey 74
and utilitarianism 34–6, 37–8, 40, 96–7, 103, 137–8, 308, 324, 326, 330–3
and *Westminster Review* 50–1
works
Introduction to the Principles of Morals and Legislation 34
Rationale of Judicial Evidence 55

Bentham, Jeremy (*cont.*)
    Traité de Législation Civile et Penale
    34, 36
Bentham, Lady Mary Sophia 30, 31
Bentham, Sir Samuel 28, 30
Berlin, Isaiah 12, 248
bicameralism 318–19
Biggs, Caroline 429, 430, 432, 446
Bildung (self-creation) 70, 79
Bingham, Peregrine 68
Black, John 48, 94
Blackheath home 241, 256, 324, 450
  dinner parties 309, 322, 347, 391, 479
Blackwood's Magazine 366, 439
Blakey, Robert 137, 324
Blanc, Louis 229, 241, 309, 392
Bouverie, Edward 403–4, 448
Bowen, George 252–3
Bowring, John 50, 65, 94, 127, 179
Boyd, Robert 71–2
Bradlaugh, Charles 403, 405, 408, 409–10
Bradley, F. H. 485
Briggs, Asa 146, 232
Bright, Jacob 429, 430, 446–7
Bright, John
  and Adullamites 370
  and American Civil War 336
  and Jamaica Committee 378
  JSM on 313, 359
  and radicalism 359, 368, 405
  and suffrage 388, 390
British Critic 167–8, 273
British North America Bill 144
Brodie, George 56
Brooke, Stopford 481–2
Brougham, Henry 49, 64, 80, 88, 93, 196
  and French Revolution of 1848 186, 187
Brown, Ford Madox, *Work* 233
Browning, Robert 5, 69–70
Buckle, Henry Thomas 301, 350, 446, 466, 470
Buller, Charles 141, 142–3
Buller, Mrs Charles 80, 90
Burdett, Francis 133
Burke, Edmund 189, 195, 356
Burke, Thomas 395–6, 412
Burn, W. L. 232

Burns, Robert 20
Butler, Josephine 430–2
Buxton, Charles 378–9, 382
Byron, Lord George Gordon 64, 66
Cairnes, John Elliot 323–4, 333–6, 395, 399–400, 429, 446
Calcraft, William 392–3
Cambridge Apostles 71
Cambridge Union 2, 40
Campbell, George 401
Canada, and Lord Durham 142–4, 157, 339
Canning, George 78
Capaldi, Nicholas 153, 228
capital punishment 392–3, 395–6
capitalism
  and co-operatives 173, 222–4, 454, 467
  and socialism 8, 222, 227, 230–1, 465–7
Carlile, Richard 1, 54, 272
Carlyle, Jane 90, 104, 121, 125
Carlyle, Thomas
  on Coleridge 106
  and conservatism 121–6, 271
  on economics 4, 121–2, 212
  and Eyre affair 380
  friendship with JSM 5, 67–8, 70, 78–9, 89, 97, 104, 121–6, 450
  on *Hamilton* 344
  on HTM 81, 84, 139, 140, 149–50
  influence 108, 109
  as intuitionist 166
  on JM 122
  on JSM 4, 52, 77, 81, 276–7, 346–7, 484
  and *London Review* 95, 136, 157
  on Parliament 318, 386
  on race 4, 123, 220
  on utilitarianism 121–2, 126, 325, 330
  works
    Frederick the Great 123
    The French Revolution 5, 125, 126, 136, 157
    On Heroes 123
    Past and Present 163, 173
    Sartor resartus 157
Caroline, Queen 31, 49
Carrel, Armand 131, 193, 319
Cavaignac, Godefroy 139, 149, 201

Chadwick, Edwin 77, 232–3, 243, 357, 370
  and Parliament 356, 403–4, 408
  and Poor Law Amendment Act 73
  *Sanitary Conditions of the Labouring
    Population* 146, 174–5
change, economic 159
change, social 131–3, 176, 236
Chapman, Henry 175, 185, 193, 210,
    212
Chapman, John 240, 323, 349, 453
character
  and custom 416
  and families 443
  in *On Liberty* 277–8, 284–5
  and religion 477–8
  and self-creation 70, 79, 85, 114, 168–71,
    180, 268
  and women 416–18, 420
Charles X of France 77
Chartism 111–12, 172, 189–91, 238
Chauffard, Dr 479–80
children
  and ability to learn 26
  and rights of women 7, 92, 441, 443,
    445
Christian Socialism 71, 221–2
Christianity *see* Church of England;
    religion; theology
Christie, William Douglas 2, 402, 433,
    482
Church of England
  and Coleridge 114–15
  and education 455
  and JM 97–8
  as obstacle to progress 76, 164
  as state Church 363–4
civil service, reforms 241, 247
civilization 102–3
Clark, Sir James 246, 250
clerisy
  in Coleridge 115
  in Mill 116–17, 290–1
co-operation, economic 285, 287, 414
  and civilization 103
  in France 188
  and gradualism 230
  and Holyoake 222

  and labour and capitalism 173, 222–4,
    454, 467–8
  and Malthusianism 209
Cobbett, William 31, 48–9, 56, 94
Cobden Club 3, 377, 463
Cobden, Richard 133, 172, 323, 461
coercion, in *On Liberty* 265, 268, 276–7,
    287
Cole, Henry 74, 77, 83, 157, 162, 231, 232–3
Coleridge, Samuel Taylor 4
  and conservatism 106–9, 114–15, 117–21,
    126, 184, 271
  and cultivation 103, 147–8
  influence on JSM 20–1, 66, 69, 71, 104,
    147–8, 269, 319
  Lay Sermon 106
  and nationalism 117–21, 126
  On the Constitution of Church and State
    114–15
Collini, Stefan 46, 62, 196–7, 217, 485,
    486
Colman, Charles 216
colonies/colonialism 43–4, 142–4, 339–40,
    412
Commager, Henry 334
communism *see* socialism
competition, economic 224–5
Comte, Auguste 116, 236, 349–52
  and conservatism 108, 114
  and history 193, 195, 197, 350
  and politics 199–200
  and religion 198, 200, 329, 472–5
  and sociology 198–9
  and women 199
Congreve, Richard 351–2
conservatism
  and Carlyle 121–6, 271
  and Coleridge 106–9, 114–15, 117–21,
    126, 184, 271
  and fear of working class 191–2
  and intuitionism 68, 126, 164–7
  and JSM 8–9, 68, 103, 104–5, 106–28,
    157, 167
  and nationalism 117–21
  and *System of Logic* 164–5
  see also elitism
constitution, British 56, 57–8

Contagious Diseases Acts 430–4, 435–6, 446

contraception 1–2, 51, 482

conversation 80–2

Conway, Moncure Daniel 312, 324, 348, 415

Cook, Thomas 159

Corn Laws, repeal 37, 178

Courtney, William Leonard 332, 379, 473, 476, 484

Cowell, Herbert 298–9, 439

Cowper, William 20

crime and punishment
    and fatalism 168–9
    and harm principle 266–8, 278–82
    and utilitarianism 36–7

Crimean War 231–2, 239–40

Croker, John Wilson 141

cultivation
    in Coleridge 103, 147–8
    in JSM 289–90, 331, 443, 477

custom
    and liberty 6, 227–8, 294–7, 303, 316
    and status of women 219, 305, 416, 419–20

Daily News 186, 191, 391, 398, 471, 484

Darwin, Charles 269, 295, 302, 306, 378, 475

Davies, Emily 421, 425

Davies, J. L. 344

democracy 7, 8, 23, 24, 110–16, 130
    and ancient Greece 177–8, 310
    and France 47, 201, 313
    and the individual 111, 124
    and liberty 178, 316
    and philanthropy 172
    and proportional representation 311–13
    and secret ballot 130, 191, 239, 315–17
    and Tocqueville 7, 108, 110–13, 136
    and tyranny of the majority 7, 58, 108, 148, 178, 239, 312–13, 316
    and United States 7, 111, 202, 244, 365
    see also society

demonstration, rights of 3, 272, 383–5, 411–12

Derby, Edward Geoffrey Smith Stanley, 14th Earl 239, 377, 386, 395–6, 482

Desainteville, B. E. 83

Dicey, Albert V. 207, 485

Dickens, Charles 157, 220, 380, 392–3, 480
    Bleak House 419
    A Christmas Carol 163
    Hard Times 74
    Little Dorrit 247
    Our Mutual Friend 190
    Pickwick Papers 141

Dilke, Charles 429, 452, 464, 479, 480

Disraeli, Benjamin 322, 366, 377
    and Chadwick 73, 175
    and electoral reform 402, 407
    and Eyre affair 379, 383
    and female suffrage 447
    and JSM 5, 368, 373, 384–7
    and party politics 366–7
    and representative government 312, 314, 386–7, 390
    and utilitarianism 73, 82

dissenters, and radicalism 82

divorce 92–3, 199, 297, 299, 441–3

Doane, Richard 28, 37

Dryden, John 20

Dumont, Pierre 34

Dunn, John 112

Dunoyer, Charles 224

Dupont-White, Charles 293, 325

Durham, Lord 'Radical Jack' 142–6, 155, 157

East India Company
    abolition 257–9
    and Indian Mutiny 3, 257
    and JM 24, 41, 101
    and JSM 2, 3, 22, 41–4, 63, 95, 131, 224, 244, 422
        as Chief Examiner 257
        retirement 249, 254–5, 259, 306
        salary 43, 77, 101, 140, 249, 257
        sick leave 139–40, 245, 249–54

eccentricity 6, 227, 269, 295–6, 300–1

economics
    Carlyle on 4, 121–2, 212
    and competition 224–5, 287

economic growth 231–5, 239, 322–3
egalitarian 59
and environment 233–5, 391
free-market 112, 222, 286–7
and Gladstone 5
in JSM's education 24–5
laissez-faire 39, 51, 207–8, 466
as lifelong interest of JSM 25–6, 159
and prices 207–8
and Ricardo 24–5, 26, 45, 48, 70,
207–10, 235, 453
wage fund theory 208, 444, 453
see also co-operation
The Economist 244, 336, 398, 483
Edinburgh Review 1, 323
and Carlyle 132
and JM 50, 179
and JSM 157–8, 484
JSM's articles 17, 24, 158, 172–3, 177, 196,
241, 273
as Whiggish 24, 48, 50, 158, 386
education
and autonomy 84–5, 171, 284
and democracy 110, 112–13, 192
and faith schools 455–6, 470
in India 101
moral 224, 236, 238, 455–6
and national character 285
and the state 288–9, 455–7
universal 85, 94, 108, 173, 192, 452, 455
for women 92, 416, 421
Education Act (1870) 455
egalitarianism, economic 59
Eichthal, Gustave d' 75, 213, 225, 348
electoral reform
anti-fraud measures 402, 407
equal electoral areas 233, 239
redistribution of seats 386
Eliot, George (Marian Evans) 240, 352,
391
elitism 9, 85, 101, 108, 114–17
Ellice, Edward 143
Ellis, Sarah 93
Ellis, William 37–8
Emerson, Ralph Waldo 123
emotion
and education of JSM 18–20, 21

and JSM 63–5, 69
and thought 63–4, 66, 69
and utilitarianism 59–60, 63, 95–6
empiricism 166–7, 344–5
England, and revolution 186–7, 189–90,
465
Enlightenment 51
environment, and economics 233–5, 391
ethology 169–70, 199, 236, 329, 418
*An Examination of Sir William Hamilton's
Philosophy* see *Hamilton*
The Examiner 48, 76, 84, 135, 158, 175
experience, and knowledge 165–6
experiments in living 6, 278, 282, 296–8
Eyre, Gov. Edward John 126, 202, 376,
377–83

Fabre, Henri 367, 468, 479
Factory Acts 88, 457
Falconer, Thomas 102
Falk, Johann Daniel 109
fatalism 168–70
Fawcett, Henry
friendship with JSM 321–2, 404, 467–8,
479
in Parliament 365–6, 403–4
as public moralist 5, 283
and Radical Club 452–3
and women's suffrage 429
Fawcett, Millicent 5, 7, 322
and women's suffrage 425–6, 429, 433,
447–8
feelings *see* emotion
Feinberg, Joel 265
feminism 52–3
of HTM 217–18
of JSM 7–8, 52, 73, 94, 217–18, 304–6,
387–9, 413–48
Fenianism 369, 395–7, 399–400
Fletcher, Joseph 159
Flower, Eliza 'Lizzie' 70, 81, 82–4, 89,
98–9, 175
Flower, Sarah 82
Fonblanque, Albany William 135–6, 158
Forde Abbey (Somerset) 13, 15, 18, 316
Fortnightly Review 158, 323, 398, 410, 453,
465, 476

Fox, Anna Maria 167–8
Fox, Caroline 65, 81, 99, 156, 167–8, 246,
    249, 392
  and *On Liberty* 274
  and *System of Logic* 161, 163, 167
Fox, Robert Barclay 145, 156–7, 160
Fox, William Johnson 69–70, 81–2, 89–91,
    206, 241
  and Lizzie Flower 70, 81, 89, 98–9
  and *Monthly Repository* 28, 69, 84, 91,
    100
France
  JSM's early year in 27, 28–34
  JSM's love of 28, 31, 33–4, 47–8, 53, 60,
    184, 186–203
  and Paris Commune 463
  revolution of 1830 77–8
  Revolution of 1848 184, 185–203, 226
franchise *see* suffrage
Franchise Bill 370–3, 377, 386
Franco-Prussian war 464, 470
Fraser, William 370
Fraser's Magazine 220, 311, 323, 386, 484
free trade 51, 148, 202, 208, 232, 323, 377
free will 168–71, 248
freedom of belief 54, 294–5
freedom of speech 3, 6, 51, 54, 148, 202, 383
  in *On Liberty* 124, 263, 268–72
French Revolution 23, 47, 120
Freud, Sigmund 428
Froude, James Anthony 302

Galt, John, *Annals of the Parish* 37
Garibaldi, Guiseppe 367–8
Garrett, Elizabeth 391, 421, 425, 428,
    430–1, 445
Garrett, Louisa 425–6
Garrett, Louise 426
Garrison, William Lloyd 411
Gaskell, Elizabeth 271–2, 428
gender equality 6–7, 92–4, 221, 244, 285,
    437–47, 483
  HTM's views 92–3, 200, 439–40
  in *On Liberty* 304–5
  and *Subjection* 413–27
George IV, and Queen Caroline 31, 49
Gibbon, Edward 41, 302

Gilpin, Charles 405
Gladstone, William Ewart
  and American Civil War 335
  and electoral reform 402
  and Eyre affair 378–9, 381, 383
  Franchise Bill 370–3, 377, 386
  and Franco-Prussian war 464
  and free trade 323, 377
  and Ireland 395, 400, 401
  and JSM 2, 5, 193, 273, 344, 370, 373–4,
    376–7, 392, 411–12
  and liberalism 94, 352, 366, 367, 408
  and memorial to Mill 482
  and parliamentary reform 317, 390
  and women's suffrage 419, 452
Globe and Traveller 120–1
Godwin, Parke 414
Godwin, William 35
Goethe, Johann Wolfgang von 18, 70, 77,
    108, 109, 255, 279, 486
Goldsmith, Oliver 20, 48
Gomperz, Theodor 164, 241, 256, 309
  and American Civil War 336
  and Helen Taylor 341
  and HTM 84
  and *On Liberty* 263, 285
  and utilitarianism 325, 327
good life
  in *On Liberty* 268, 276–85, 296–8
  in *Utilitarianism* 85–6, 326–32
government, local 294, 320–1
Graham, George John 37–8, 40–1, 73, 81,
    450
Grant, Horace 73, 104
Gray, Thomas 20
Great Exhibition (1851) 74, 159, 231
Greece
  and democracy 177–8, 310, 340
  JSM's travels in 252–3, 340–1
Grey, Charles (later 2nd Earl Grey) 56–7,
    76, 88
Grey, Henry George, 3rd Earl 314–15
Grey, Sir George 217–18, 369
Grosvenor, Robert Wellesley 357–9, 365,
    407, 462
Grote, George 43, 48, 50, 291
  and American Civil War 336

death 470
friendship with JSM 5, 43, 177, 243, 308–9, 340, 343, 347, 366–7
History of Greece 5, 19, 37, 150, 177–8, 241, 347
and London Debating Society 58
in Parliament 94, 129–30, 133–5, 145, 309
and secret ballot 94, 130
and utilitarianism 40, 331
Grote, Harriet
and female suffrage 310, 429
friendship with JSM 67, 80–1, 308, 347
on JM 19
on HTM 81
on Lord Durham 145
and radicalism 133, 136
Guizot, François 102–3, 114, 141, 178, 187, 193–4, 376, 434
Gurney, Cecil 245, 260, 479–80
Gurney, Ellen 245

habit, and character 285
Hamburger, Joseph 147
Hamilton 308, 342–6
and Carlyle 346
and character 284
editions 343, 346, 349, 352
and free will 248
and intuitionism 166–7, 342, 346, 418
and metaphysics 344–6
reviews 273
and theology 343–4, 359–60, 472, 474
Hamilton, Mary Morris 392
Hamilton, Sir William 166–7, 245, 342–6
happiness
and autonomy 97
collective 328–30
and distribution 59
and freedom 6
in JSM 328–33, 427
and love of humankind 67
quality and quantity 248
in utilitarian theory 34–5, 37, 100, 106, 137, 326–7
Hardy, Thomas 264, 283–4, 363
Hare, Katherine 429

Hare, Thomas 367
and electoral fraud 324
and female suffrage 389, 429
friendship with JSM 309, 321, 341, 347
and proportional representation 309, 310–11, 314, 389
harm principle 228, 264–8, 279–81
Harris, Jose 415
Harrison, Frederic 264, 352
Hartley, David, *Theory of the Human Mind* 39
Hayek, Friedrich 263, 484
Hayward, Abraham 47, 141, 481–4
Hazlitt, William 55, 56, 76, 106, 249
Helps, Sir Arthur 271
heroism
and Carlyle 123
and JSM 102–3, 108, 122–3
Herschel, Sir John 174
Hickson, William 157, 167, 177, 183, 218–19, 240
Hill, Frank Harrison 391
Himmelfarb, Gertrude 118, 119, 268, 284
history
and Carlyle 123
and Comte 195, 197–8, 350
and Guizot 193–4
and JSM 76–7, 79, 113, 119–21, 194–8, 487
and Macaulay 75–6, 119, 194, 195–7
and utilitarianism 75
Whig 4, 195–7
Hobbes, Thomas 294
Hobsbawm, Eric 232, 238, 391, 454
Holyoake, George Jacob 212, 219, 368, 405
homosexuality 282
Hooker, Isabella 441
House of Lords, reform 8, 319, 406
housing, and the state 290
Howell, George 409
Humboldt, Wilhelm von 277–8, 299–300
Hume, David 56, 65, 302
Hume, Joseph 94, 129, 191
Hunt, Henry 'Orator' 48–9
Hunt, John 48
Hunt, Leigh 48, 82
Huskisson, William 87

Hutcheson, Francis 35, 238
Hutton, Richard 296
Huxley, Thomas Henry 200, 302, 378,
    380, 425, 471
Hyde Park Corner 3, 385

Illustrated London News 483
imagination 79, 82,100,108
India, and land ownership 460
Indian Mutiny 3, 257
individual
    and emotion 65
    in *On Liberty* 263, 276–9, 295–304, 485
    and society 6, 9, 84, 86, 102–3, 121,
        198–9, 262–8, 295–304
    see also autonomy
individualism III, 124, 298–9
individuality
    and education 84–5, 108
    HTM on 86
    and socialism 226–8, 467
Industrial and Provident Societies
    Partnership Act (1852) 222
industrialization 59, 76, 86–7, 116, 132, 159,
    202, 233
inference 165–6, 167
intellectuals, state support for 290–1
International Working Men's Association
    463–4
intuitionism 67–8, 126, 164–7, 241, 325,
    328–9, 349, 418
    and *Hamilton* 166–7, 342, 346
Ireland
    and democracy III
    disestablishment of Irish Church
        452
    and emigration 183
    and Fenianism 369, 395–7, 399–400
    land reform 3, 94, 180–3, 393–4,
        397–401, 412
Irvine, Alexander 468–9, 479
Italy, JSM's travels in 250–3

Jacobs, Jo Ellen 153, 228
Jamaica Committee 378–83, 405, 406, 440
Jevons, William Stanley 331, 485
Johnson, Paul 23, 49, 259

journalism
    and JM 12–13
    newspaper 180, 186, 240
    periodical 131, 157-8, 180, 240-1, 323, *see
        also Edinburgh Review; London
        Review; London and Westminster
        Review*
justice, and utility 329, 382

Kant, Immanuel 51, 164, 278
Keate, John 21
Keston Heath, Kent 84, 99
Keynes, John Maynard 235
Kingsley, Charles 219–20, 231, 264, 340,
    344, 380, 429
Kinzer, Bruce 398
Kinzer, Bruce, Robson, John and
    Robson, Ann 147
knowledge
    and intuitionism 164–7, 325
    as liberating 51, 268–9
    and *System of Logic* 165–6
Kyllmann, Max 359

labour market, wage fund theory 208,
    444, 453
Labour Representation League 453
Lafayette, Marie Joseph de 77, 185
Lamartine, Alphonse de 188, 193, 201
Lamb, Charles 88–9, 249
Lamb, William (later Lord Melbourne)
    53, 129–30, 133–4
land ownership, reform 458–63
Land Tenure Reform Association 458,
    462–3
language, and knowledge of a people
    33–4
Lankester, Edwin 361
Leader, John Temple 133
Lecky, William 436
Lewes, George Henry 155
Lewis, George Cornewall 315
Ley, Arthur 255
Liberal party 143, 306, 352–3, 356–62
    and Gladstone 352, 366, 367, 402,
        408
    and radicals 308, 403–5, 408–9

and Whigs 403, 459
and women's rights 452
see also Adullamites
liberalism
and dissent 118–19
and Gladstone 94
and JSM 6–8, 33, 79, 227–8, 236, 325, 354–62, 392–4, 486
and socialism 227–8, 230, 236
and Tocqueville 113
and utilitarianism 325–6, 332
see also On Liberty
liberty 6–7, 70
in ancient Greece 178
and autonomy 85, 169–70, 194, 236, 263, 416
and custom 6, 227–8, 294–8, 316, 416
and democracy 178, 316
and energy 283–4, 292–3
and happiness 6, 427
and women 427, 438
see also On Liberty
literary criticism 69–70, 73
Locke, John 39
Logic see *A System of Logic*
London, *salon* culture 80–1, 90
London Debating Society 45–7, 58, 63, 65–7, 70–1, 75, 141, 209, 481
London Review 100, 126, 127
and HTM 138–9
and JSM 95–8
and Molesworth 95–6, 98, 101
and radicalism 95–6
and *Westminster Review* 101–2
London and Westminster Review 126, 127
editors 95, 102, 126, 141
and HTM 138–9
and JSM 101–3, 131, 133, 135–44, 157
and Molesworth 133, 138
and radicalism 131, 133, 135–8, 142–5, 147, 157
Louis Napoleon of France *see* Napoleon III
Louis Philippe of France 77, 187, 193
Lovett, William 111–12
Lowe, Robert 369, 370–2, 390, 400, 409

Lucas, Frederick 244, 250
Lucy, Henry 370
Lytton Bulwer, Edward 97, 104, 138, 141

McAdam, John Loudon 59
Macaulay, Thomas Babington
on French Revolution of 1848 188, 193, 201
on history 75–6, 119, 194, 195
History of England 195–7
and India 38, 101
JSM on 4, 241
as MP 54
on *On Liberty* 300
on reform 67, 172
and religion 302
on suffrage 310
and utilitarianism 38, 40
as writer 14, 42
Maine, Henry 459–60, 479
Malthusianism 45, 208–9, 292, 359, 481
Mansel, Henry 343–4, 346
Marmontel, Jean-François, *Mémoires* 63
marriage 73, 92–3, 214, 282, 299–300, 414, 437–43
and division of labour 444–5
and reciprocal superiority 73, 92, 440
and rights of women 7, 92–3, 414
see also divorce
Married Women's Property Act (1870) 425
Martineau, Harriet 81, 90, 349, 352
Martineau, James 271–2
Marx, Karl 75, 110, 210, 224, 226, 322–3, 463–4
Das Kapital 464–5
Maudsley, Henry 285
Maurice, Frederick Denison 70–1, 107, 296, 344, 431
Mazzini, Giuseppe 241–2
Melbourne, William Lamb, 2nd Viscount 53, 129–30, 158
and Lord Durham 142–3
and radicals 133–4, 142
and reform 146
Michelet, Jules 195

middle class
  in Comte 199
  and fears of working class 58
  JSM on 13
  and radicalism 112, 190–1
  and reform 146
Mill, Anna (sister of JSM) 214
Mill, Clara (sister of JSM) 156, 214–15
Mill, George (brother of JSM) 139, 177,
    215–16
Mill, Harriet (mother of JSM) 11, 14, 30,
    41, 214–16
Mill, Harriet (sister of JSM) 14–15, 214–15
Mill, Harriet Taylor (HTM), *see* Taylor,
    Harriet
Mill, Henry (brother of JSM) 25, 139,
    155–7, 175
Mill, Henry (nephew of JSM) 450
Mill, James (brother of JSM) 101
Mill, James (father of JSM)
  attack on Whigs 50
  and Bentham 5, 12–13, 179
  and Carlyle 122
  and Church of England 97–8
  as East India Company examiner 24,
    41, 101
  education and early career 12
  and emotions 18–20, 21
  family life 14–15
  and HTM 89–90
  illness and death 101, 103–4, 175
  as journalist 12–13 50, 51, 96
  and JSM
    education 5, 11–21, 28–9, 169–70
    friendships 41
    year in France 31, 34
  marriage 19
  and poetry 20–1
  and political economy 37
  and rights of women 53
  and secret ballot 146
  and utilitarianism 38, 40, 96–7
  works
    *Analysis of the Phenomena of the
      Human Mind* 39
    Elements of Political Economy 25
    Essay on Government 5, 75–6

  The History of British India 13, 22
Mill, Jane (sister of JSM) 348
Mill, John Stuart
  appearance 81, 162, 243
  assessments of 481–7
  career
    in East India Company 2, 3, 22,
      41–4, 63, 95, 224
    and *London Review* 95–8, 101–3, 131,
      133
    as MP 5, 42, 46–7, 133, 159–60, 352–3,
      354–6, 368–412
    offered Residentship of Cephalonia
      252–3
    political campaigns 356–65, 369,
      405–10
    salary 43, 77, 101, 140, 249, 257
    as writer 42, 47–8, 50–5, 84
  character
    as bibliophile 31–2
    as Francophile 28, 31, 33–4, 47–8, 53,
      60, 184, 186–203
    generosity 273
    integrity 406–7, 409–10
    intellectual strengths 176–7
    morality 22
    open-mindedness 108–9, 198, 212,
      273–4
    pragmatism 44, 120, 226, 286
    pride and modesty 28–9, 55, 176, 256
    recklessness 381–2, 481
    sense of humour 248–9, 374
    work ethic 18, 27, 60–1, 140, 223
  early life
    birth 15
    education 2, 11–27, 28–9, 36, 70,
      169–70
    and emotion 19–20
    loneliness 14, 63
    and siblings 14, 15, 22
    and university 41
    and virtue 17–18
    year in France 28–34
  economics 4, 40, 59, 79, 103
  health
    and continental holidays 139, 148,
      204–5, 216

depression 89
erysipelas 479–80
injury 186
mental crisis 6, 21, 61, 62–70, 105, 377
physical problems 102, 104, 129, 161,
  249–50, 253–4
and sexuality 84, 150, 151–4, 262–3
tuberculosis 245–7
honours
and American Academy of Arts and
  Sciences 244
portrait and statue 479, 480, 486
Rectorship of St Andrews 33, 190,
  375, 456
interests
botany 3, 30, 33, 41, 42, 233, 241, 307,
  342, 367, 449–50, 468–9, 479
music 32, 63
walking 33, 43, 73–4, 102, 140, 148,
  162–3, 233, 246, 254, 391, 468
obituary 2, 47, 481–3
philosophy
and autonomy 70, 84
conservative influences 104–5,
  106–28
and emotion 63–8, 95–6
and intuitionism 67–8, 126, 164–7,
  241, 325, 328–9, 342
and nationalism 108, 117–18, 189
and sectarianism 109–10
see also utilitarianism
as polemicist
on American Civil War 333–7, 342
on Brougham 186
on Hume 56
on Irish land reform 3, 180–3, 393–4,
  397–401, 412
on paternalism 173–4
on Tories 4, 146, 312, 374–5
on Wellington 56, 117
see also The Subjection of Women
politics
as activist 3, 145–8, 483
and armed forces 393–4
and colonialism 43–4, 339–40, 412
and debating societies 45–7, 48, 63
and foreign intervention 337–9

and French Revolution of 1848
  185–203, 226, 333
as Girondist 48, 184, 185, 352–3
and land ownership 458–63
liberalism 6–8, 33, 79, 227–8, 236, 325,
  354–62, 392–4
and memorial 482–3
and socialism 7–8, 213, 221–7, 232,
  463–8
withdrawal from 129, 183, 238, 244
see also democracy; radicalism;
  Representative Government
private life
Blackheath home 241, 256, 309, 322,
  324, 347, 391, 450
death and burial 480, 481
family 214–17, 256, 348, 450
friendships 21, 33, 44, 66–7, 70–4,
  156, 217, 275, 308–9, 347, 450, 469;
  see also Bain, Alexander; Cairnes,
  John Elliot; Carlyle, Thomas;
  Fawcett, Henry; Graham, George
  John; Grote, George; Hare,
  Thomas; Roebuck, John A.;
  Sterling, John
grief at death of HTM 260–1
marriage 5, 151–2, 213–17, 439–40
memorial to HTM 275–6
pets 450–1
retirement 249, 254–6, 259–60, 306,
  449–51
royalties 255, 323
withdrawal from social life 175–6,
  238, 241–3
see also Taylor, Harriet
social attitudes
capital punishment 392–3, 395–6
contraception 1–2, 51, 482
as feminist 6–8, 52–3, 73, 92, 94,
  217–19, 305–6, 308, 387–9, 413–48,
  451–2
marriage 73, 92–3, 214, 282, 359, 414,
  437–43
race 219–21, 337, 340, 412
and social reform 171–4
travels
in England 73–4, 140, 148, 471

Mill, John Stuart (*cont.*)
> with Helen 250, 469, 478–9
> with HTM 139, 140, 148–50, 161–2, 175, 186, 204–5, 245
> in Italy and Greece 250–3, 340–1
> *see also* interests, walking *above*
> works 27, 60–1
>> *Auguste Comte and Positivism* 308, 349–52, 441
>> 'Centralisation' 285, 293, 424
>> 'Chapters on Socialism' 465–8
>> 'Civilization - Signs of the Times' 102, 108, 116, 123–4, 285, 296
>> 'The Claims of Labour' 172–3, 179, 290
>> 'Coleridge' 118–20, 126, 127, 157, 269, 287
>> *Collected Edition* 485–6
>> 'The Condition of Ireland' 180–1
>> 'The Contest in America' 334, 337
>> 'Corporation and Church Property' 115
>> *Dissertations and Discussions* 118
>> *England and Ireland* 181, 397–400
>> 'A Few Words on Non-Intervention' 338
>> literary criticism 69–70, 73
>> 'Nature' 477
>> 'On the Definition of Political Economy' 177
>> 'On Genius' 84–6, 277
>> 'Rationale of Representation' 415
>> 'Recent Writers on Reform' 311, 312
>> 'The Slave Power' 334, 341
>> 'The Spirit of the Age' 75–6, 77, 298
>> *Thoughts on Parliamentary Reform* 248, 313–14, 415
>> *Three Essays on Religion* 241, 473–8
>> 'The Use of History' 410–11
>> 'Vindication of the French Revolution of February 1848' 187
>> 'Wallflower Growing on the Living Rock' 307
>> 'What Is to be Done with Ireland?' 181
>> *see also Autobiography; Hamilton; On Liberty; Principles of Political Economy; Representative Government; The Subjection of Women; System of Logic; Utilitarianism*

Mill, Mary Elizabeth (sister of JSM) 177, 216, 450
Milton, John 20
Mineka, Francis E. and Lindley, Dwight N. 217
Mitford, William 50, 177–8
Molesworth, Sir William 104, 143, 145, 413
> and *London Review* 95–6, 98, 101, 133, 138
monarchy, constitutional 319–20
money
> and politics 317–18, 356, 362, 407–8
> and women 428
Monthly Repository 69, 82, 84, 91, 100, 109, 280
morality
> consequentialist 326
> international 337–9
> intuitionist 35, 68, 325, 328
> and religion 283, 473–7
> utilitarian *see* utilitarianism
Morley, John 2–3, 5, 64, 309, 352, 429, 434, 464, 479, 486
> illness 453
> on JSM in Parliament 355, 410–11
> and JSM's religious views 472, 473, 476
> and memorial to JSM 482
> on *On Liberty* 306
> on *Subjection* 417
> works, *Recollections* 484
Morning Chronicle 48, 53, 54, 180
Morning Post 250, 399
motherhood, and status of women 219
Mozley, Anne 417
Municipal Reform Act (1835) 88
Murray, John 160, 162
Mutual Improvement Society 44–5, 56

Napier, Gen. Sir Robert 406
Napier, Macvey 155, 157–8, 171, 172–3, 179, 187, 195–6
Napoleon III 189, 200–1, 232, 240, 313, 464

National Association for the Promotion of Social Science 324

National Society for Women's Suffrage 7, 428–34, 446

nationality 108, 117–21, 189, 319–20

Neate, Charles 400

Neophyte Writers' Society 243, 271, 272

Newsome, David 470

newspapers, and diffusion of ideas 180, 186

Nichol, John 97, 107, 114, 416, 426, 431, 436

Nietzsche, Friedrich 484–5

Nightingale, Florence 5, 283, 444, 445–6

North American Review 244, 348

Northcote, Sir Stafford 247

Norton, Charles Eliot 348, 402, 408, 425

Nussbaum, Martha 414

O'Connell, Daniel 94

O'Connor, Feargus 189

Odger, George 363, 403, 404, 410, 452, 460

Okin, Susan Moller 444–5

Oliphant, Margaret 438

On Liberty 4, 9, 262–306, 333
  and coercion 265, 268, 276–7, 287
  criticism of 298–306
  and divorce 297, 299, 441
  and drunkenness 269–80
  and economic systems 227
  and education 288–9
  and energy 283–4, 292–3
  and freedom of speech 124, 263, 268–72
  and gender equality 304–5
  and the good life 268, 276–85, 296–8
  and harm principle 228, 264–8, 279–81
  impact 262–4, 306, 323, 391
  and individuality 85, 171, 263, 276–9, 295–304, 410, 420, 478, 485
  and influence of HTM 228
  and marriage 299–300
  as memorial to HTM 261, 276, 302–3
  and nationalism 118–19, 339
  plans for 241, 251
  and poverty 292–3
  and prostitution 280–1, 435–6

and religious toleration 294–5, 300–1, 377

and the state 285–94

and *Utilitarianism* 329–30

opinion, as half-truth 109, 158, 170

oratory 23–4, 45–7, 55
  and journalism 131

Owen, Robert 45, 222

Owenites 45, 56, 60, 168, 209

Packe, Michael 94, 153, 228–9, 275, 447, 484

pain principle, in utilitarianism 34–5, 39, 96

Pall Mall Gazette 369, 380, 399

Palmerston, Henry John Temple, 3rd Viscount 87, 158, 337, 366, 394

Pankhurst, Emmeline 447

Papineau, Louis 142

Parker, William 162

Parkes, Joseph 132–4

Parliament
  aristocratic influence 56–8, 145–6, 367
  bicameralism 318–19
  deliberative function 318, 372
  JSM as MP 5, 42, 133, 159–60, 352–3, 354–412
  and party system 133–5
  and payment of MPs 317–18
  and property qualification 317
  and radicals 80, 88–9, 94, 128, 129–36, 141–7, 191, 322
  reform 50, 56–7, 78–9, 87–8, 103, 108, 178–9, 191–2, 239, 308, 367–8; *see also* ballot, secret; representation, proportional; suffrage
  and women's rights 94
  working-class representation 239, 308, 310–12, 356–7, 371–3, 390, 402–3, 409, 452–3

Parliamentary History and Review 51–2, 54

parliaments, triennial 142, 191

paternalism, and social reform 171–4

Patmore, Coventry 418–19

patriarchy 304, 443

Pattison, Mark 202

Paxton, Joseph 231

pedantocracy 116
Peel, Robert 94, 129, 130, 158, 193
    and Irish famine 182
    and social reform 37, 146, 171
Perkin, Harold 140
Philosophical Radicals 133, 135, 240
philosophy, and politics 133–5
phrenology 199
Pitt, William (younger) 23
Place, Francis 13, 15–16, 133, 134, 138, 145,
    315
pleasure principle, in utilitarianism 34–5,
    39, 96, 154, 326, 330–1
Plummer, John 322
Plumptre, John Pemberton 180
poetry
    and emotion 63–7
    and JM 20
    and JSM 63–9, 71
    and utilitarianism 20–1, 68, 95–6, 137
political economy see economics
Political Economy Club 158–9, 323–4, 376,
    446, 483
politics
    and canvassing for votes 317
    of Comte 199–200
    and economics 25
    and foreign intervention 337–9
    and money 317–18, 356, 362, 407–8
    participatory 110, 112, 178, 286
    and reformers 50–1, 78–9, 146
    and role of history 75, 79, 113, 119–21
    and systematic antagonism 194
    women in 426–7
    see also Parliament; radicalism
Pompignan, Jean-Louis Lefranc de
    29–30, 31
Poor Law Amendment Act (1834) 73, 88,
    148
Porter, Roy 50, 98
poverty
    and progress 25, 159
    and state welfare 292–3
Prescott, William 37–8
Principles of Political Economy 192, 478
    dedication 206–7
    and distribution 210, 235
    and earned/unearned income 211, 459
    and economic role of women 443–4
    editions 207, 212, 229, 291, 341, 352
    gender-neutral language 217
    and Gladstone 377
    and harm principle 265
    HTM's influence on 207, 213, 228–9
    and international trade 159, 208
    and Ireland 180, 183, 395
    and population 208–9
    and prices 207–8
    and private property 225–6
    revision 212–13, 228–30, 457
    and Ricardo 24, 26, 207–10
    and socialism 221, 223, 226–37, 465,
        466
    and the state 285–6, 291–2, 457
    success 207, 212, 244, 255, 323
    and taxation 210–11
    and United States 244
    and wage fund theory 453–4
Prisons Act (1835) 88
progress 5, 132, 232–3
    and democracy 112
    and economics 209, 238
    and gradualism 195
    and history 75–6, 79, 119–21, 194–5
    moral 278
    and poverty 25, 159
    and radicalism 65, 77, 98
    and social order 188
    and systematic antagonism 194
property
    and land 458–61
    and married women 7, 92, 425
    rights 45, 192, 210, 225–6, 458–9
prostitution 281–2, 435–7
Proudhon, Pierre Joseph 112
psychology
    associationist 39, 51, 69, 168
    empirical 344–5
    as science 168–71
    and sociology 198–9
    see also ethology
public opinion 54, 86, 115–16, 123, 259
    and liberty 6, 148, 294–8, 303, 316,
        410

and politics 31, 57
and socialism 226–7, 236
Punch 159–60, 365, 389, 399

Quarterly Review 48, 386

race 219–21, 337, 340, 412
Radical Club 452–3
radicalism
 and French Revolution of 1848 185–203
 of JM 50
 of JSM 3, 12, 32, 52–9, 65, 77, 92–6, 120,
  131, 133–8, 146–7, 191–2, 402–3,
  451–2, 457–8, 484
 leadership 193
 of *London Review* 95–6
 of *London and Westminster Review* 131,
  133, 135–8, 142–5, 147, 157
 and marriage 92–3
 parliamentary 80, 88–9, 94, 128, 129–36,
  141–7, 191, 322
 Philosophical Radicals 133, 135, 240
 and religious dissent 82
 and revolution 77
 and Whigs 129–30, 131–4, 141–5, 158, 452
 and Wordsworth 64
radicals, and Liberal party 403–5, 408–9
railways 87, 132, 159, 233, 392
Ramadge, Francis 246
rationalism, and emotion 65, 68
Rawls, John 263
The Reasoner 212
Reeve, Henry 241, 484
reform
 of civil service 241, 247
 moral 123–4
 parliamentary 50, 56–7, 78–9, 87–8, 103,
  108, 178–9, 367–8
 and poetry 68–9
 and radicalism 49–57, 78–9, 88–9, 94
 and revolution 463–5
 social 88, 171–4
 and Tories 146
 and Whigs 76, 88, 94, 101, 143, 146,
  232
 see also electoral reform
Reform Act (1832) 56, 87–8, 94–5, 114, 173

Reform Act (1867) 5, 111, 192, 314, 370,
  386–7, 417
Reform Club 101, 359
Reform League 368, 383–5
Regent's Park, Zoological Gardens 99
religion
 and Comte 198, 200, 329, 352, 472–5
 and freedom of speech 270
 and JSM 471–7
 and secularization 301–2
 and toleration 54–5, 294–5, 300–1, 377
 utilitarian view 37, 477
 see also Church of England; theology;
  Unitarianism
Renouvier, Charles 469
representation, proportional 239, 310–14,
  371, 387, 389–90, 412
Representative Government 248, 308, 374,
  478
 and bicameralism 318–19, 406
 and canvassing for votes 317
 and deliberative function of
  Parliament 318, 372
 editions 352
 and educational qualification 313
 and government apparatus 285
 and local government 320–1
 and money 317–18
 and nationalism 320
 and payment of MPs 317–18
 and plural votes 314
 and proportional representation 311–14,
  389
 and secret ballot 315–17
 and suffrage 192, 309–10, 415
 and taxation 313, 422
revolution 77
 and reform 463–5
Rey, Louis 274–5, 469, 471, 476, 480
Ricardo, David 24–6, 38, 42, 45, 48, 50, 79
 and Mill's *Principles* 24, 26, 207–10, 235
 and wage fund theory 208, 444, 453
Robertson, George Croom 271–2, 430,
  431, 432–3, 435
Robertson, John 141, 145
Robinson, Henry Crabb 109
Robson, John 65

Roebuck, John A.
  and American Civil War 335
  and Canada 144
  and democracy 114
  friendship with JSM 40–1, 52, 65–6, 70,
    81, 90, 357, 370, 450
  and HTM 90
  and JM 41
  and London Debating Society 65–6
  and Mutual Improvement Society
    44–6
  in Parliament 46, 94, 129–30, 134,
    373–4, 408
  and Tocqueville 113
  and utilitarianism 38–9
Rolt, John 381
Roman Catholics, and toleration 54
Romanticism
  English 106–7, 122–3
  German 70, 79, 109, 164
Romilly, Anne 16, 18
Romilly, Henry 316
Ross, Charles 375
Rostow, Walt Whitman 232
Royal Parks, as site for demonstrations
  383–5, 411–12
Ruskin, John 14, 132, 163, 212, 231, 233, 380
Russell, Bertrand 478
Russell, Lord John 182, 190, 365, 377–8,
  482
  and parliamentary reform 78, 134, 178,
    366, 370–1, 386
Ryan, Alan 170–1, 277, 287, 325, 339–40,
  343

Sabbatarianism 280
St Andrews University, JSM as Rector 33,
  190, 375, 456
Saint-Simon, Claude Henri de Rouvary
  de 75–6, 79, 104, 194
salon culture 80–1, 90
Sand, George (Amandine-Aurore Lucile
  Dupin) 99, 445
Sarrans, Bernard 86
Saturday Review 384, 388, 398, 483
Say, Jean-Baptiste 29
Schuyler, Col. George 392, 415

science, and art 176–7
Scott, Sir Walter 20, 186, 320
sectarianism, intellectual 53–4, 101, 107,
  109–10
secularization 301–2, 455
Sedgwick, Adam 96, 102, 324
Select Committee on Metropolitan
  Government 390
sexuality, and JSM 84, 150, 151–4, 262–3,
  282, 436–8, 440
Shaftesbury, Anthony Ashley Cooper,
  3rd Earl 301–2
Shaftesbury, Anthony Ashley Cooper,
  7th Earl 171–2
Shee, William 47
Shelley, Percy Bysshe 64, 66, 68–9, 154,
  344, 442, 469–70
Sidgwick, Henry 481, 483, 485
Skorupski, John 165
slavery 126, 173, 188, 333–7, 483
  and status of women 219, 244, 414, 438
Smith, Adam 24, 45, 208, 210, 286
Smith, Goldwin 440
Smith, Sydney 80, 133, 166
Smith, W. H. 359, 365, 406–8, 410
Snell, George 452
socialism 7–8, 213, 221–7, 232
  and capitalism 8, 222, 227, 230–1, 465–6
  and 'Chapters on Socialism' 465–8
  and HTM 221–2, 229–30
  and liberalism 227–8, 230, 236
  and Principles 221, 223, 226–37, 465
society
  and history 75–6, 119–20
  and individual 6, 9, 84, 86, 102–3, 121,
    198–9, 262–8, 295–304
  and the poor 292–3
  and tyranny of the majority 114, 148,
    294–8, 316
  see also democracy
Society of Students of Mental
  Philosophy 38–9
sociology, and psychology 198–9
Soetbeer, Adolf 213
Somerville, Mary 389, 445
South Place Unitarian Chapel 81, 99
Southey, Robert 74, 87

The Spectator 134, 186, 332, 344, 398, 483
Spencer, Herbert 273, 284–5, 290, 302, 378, 391, 479, 483
Spenser, Edmund 20
Stafford, William 221–2
state
    and Church 363–4
    and harm principle 266–7
    and intellectuals 290–1
    in *On Liberty* 285–94
    and provision of education 288–9, 455–7
    role 457–8
    and welfare 292–3
statue of JSM 448, 483, 486
Stephen, James Fitzjames 197, 279, 281, 291, 381, 484
    and *On Liberty* 296, 300–1
    and rights of women 420–1
Stephen, Leslie 16, 283, 321, 344, 355, 376, 485
Sterling, John 74
    and Carlyle 122
    death 175
    friendship with JSM 71, 107, 109, 116, 149, 156, 411
    and HTM 89, 149–50
    and London Debating Society 70–1
    and *London Review* 136
    and radicalism 71–2, 77
    and *System of Logic* 163
strike, right to 356–7
Stuart, Sir John 12, 41
The Subjection of Women 171, 304–5, 414–24, 428, 438–42, 444–5
    and children 441, 443, 444–5
    and divorce 441–3
    and domestic labour 219
    editions 415
    and female suffrage 387, 422–8
    and formation of character 416–18, 420, 478
    and HTM 219, 228–9, 439
    impact 4, 415
    and power 438
    publication 434
    and race 221

and reciprocal superiority 440
    and sex 440–1
    and sexism 305, 419–20
    and women in public life 425–6, 444–5
suffrage
    educational qualification 239, 313, 315
    extension 51, 57, 78, 87, 134, 148, 364–5, 402
    female 7, 94, 218, 306, 356, 387–9, 412, 415, 422–32, 446–8
    household 142, 191, 386
    municipal elections 425
    property qualification 370
    universal 111, 192, 309–14, 368
    working-class 58, 191–2, 239, 308, 309–14, 356, 370–1, 402–3, 412
Sunday trading 238, 304, 355, 364
superiority, reciprocal
    in friendship 72–3
    in marriage 73, 92, 440
A System of Logic 158, 198
    and Bain 162–3
    and Comte 349–50
    and conservatism 164–5
    and desire 326
    editions 163, 180, 207, 349, 352
    and knowledge 164–7
    and psychology 168–71, 199, 417–18, 478
    publication 161–2
    reviews 163
    and roles of science and art 176
    and society 117, 118–19, 199
    success 160, 163–4, 174–5, 255
    and theology 167–8, 472

taxation 210–11, 313, 356, 422, 462
Taylor, Algernon ('Haji') 214, 241–2, 245, 275
Taylor, Clementina 429
Taylor, Harriet (HTM) 18, 26, 79
    affair with JSM 4–5, 70, 82–4, 89–93, 98–9, 101
        continental trips together 139, 140, 148–50, 161–2, 175, 186, 204–5, 245
        first meeting 80–1
        and loss of friendships 70

Taylor, Harriet (HTM) (*cont.*)
    and physical intimacy 4–5, 84,
      149–55
    public comments on 482, 484
    rows 99
    rumour and gossip 90, 125, 140,
      149–50, 152, 176, 205–6, 213
    appearance 81–2
    and *Autobiography* 26, 82–3, 150–3, 176,
      206, 229, 484
    character
      intellectual strengths 176–7
      open-mindedness 79
      pleasantness 217
      strength of will 100
    correspondence with JSM 83
    death 260–1, 274
    health 139, 148, 161, 245, 249–50, 257, 260
      possible syphilis 153–4
    influence on JSM 86, 138–9, 155, 207, 213,
      217–18, 221, 228–30, 247–8, 473
    marriage to John Taylor 81, 90–3, 150,
      152–4, 203, 204–6
    marriage to JSM 4, 151–2, 213–14,
      242–3
      deification by JSM 207, 217, 242,
        275
      home 241
      and JSM's family 214–17
    private life
      children 139
      family 254–5
      memorial 275–6
    and *System of Logic* 163
    views
      gender equality 92–3, 200, 415
      on individuality 86
      on religion 473–4
    writing 86, 91, 138–9
      'Emancipation of Women' 218–19,
        271–2
Taylor, Helen (daughter of Harriet) 241,
    250, 260
    as actress 256–7
    and 'Chapters on Socialism' 465
    as a child 139, 149, 175
    as editor of Buckle 446, 470

    and female suffrage 428–9, 446
    and Gomperz 341
    as JSM's assistant 274, 308–9, 323,
      340–1, 348, 359, 375, 379, 449, 469,
      480
    on JSM's religious views 471, 474
    and marriage of JSM and HTM 214
    publication of *Autobiography* 483–4
    travels with JSM 250, 469, 478–9
Taylor, Henry 52
Taylor, John 80–1, 83–4, 90–3, 98, 150,
    152–4, 203
    estate 255
    illness and death 152, 204–6, 213, 214
Taylor, William (brother of Harriet) 156
Telegraph 358, 398
temperance movement 159, 279–80, 304,
    355, 364
Tennyson, Alfred, Lord 14, 20, 71, 121
    and industrialisation 132
    and JSM 5, 66, 69, 97
    'Locksley Hall' 132
    Maud 88
    The Princess 190
    and race 342, 380
theology
    and *Hamilton* 343–4, 359–60, 472,
      474
    and *System of Logic* 167–8, 472
Thiers, Louis 195, 196
Thirlwall, Connop 45, 177–8, 344
Thistlewood, Arthur 28
Thompson, Col. Thomas Perronet 94–5,
    101
Thoreau, Henry 123
Thornton, William 260, 309, 347–8, 391,
    449
    and East India Company 255, 258–9
    and Ireland 397–8
    and John Taylor 255
    On Labour 453–4
thought, and emotion 63–4, 66, 69, 96
The Times
    and American Civil War 336
    and Chadwick 73
    and Crimean War 240
    influence on politics 375–6, 383

and JSM 180, 183, 354, 357–8, 399,
    403–4, 406, 408, 462
  obituary of JSM 2, 47, 481–4
Tocqueville, Alexis de 104, 129, 136, 157–8,
    193, 321
  Ancien Régime 113
  De la démocratie en Amerique 5, 100,
    108, 113, 126, 244
  and democracy 7, 108, 110–13, 136
  and French Republic 201
  and liberalism 113, 294
  and revolution 183, 188
toleration, religious 54–5, 294–5, 300–1,
    377
Tooke, William Eyton 37, 80
Tories 94, 129
  and JSM 4, 56, 312, 374–5
  and nationalism 117
  and reform 146
Torrens, Col. Robert 48
Torrijos, Gen. 71–2
Toulongeon, François-Emmanuel 47
trade, free 51, 148, 202, 208, 232, 323, 377
trade unions 391, 453, 454
Trevelyan, George 40
Trevelyan, M. 88
Trevelyan, Sir Charles 247, 368
Trijackia 40–1, 63, 77–8, 81, 450
Trollope, Anthony 220, 391
truth, in JSM 109, 124, 158, 165–7, 268–70,
    273, 483
Tupper, Martin, *Proverbial Philosophy* 132
Turgot, Jacques, Baron de Laune 53,
    410–11
Tuson, Edward William 153

Unitarianism 82
United States 33
  Civil War 202, 245, 308, 324, 333–7, 342,
    358, 365, 392, 434
  and democracy 7, 111, 202, 244, 365
  JSM's love of 333–4
Utilitarian Society 37–8
utilitarianism 5–6, 34–40
  and Bentham 34–6, 37–8, 40, 96–7, 103,
    137–8, 324, 326, 330–3
  Carlyle on 121–2, 126, 325, 330

and crime and punishment 36–7
  and emotion 59–60, 63, 95–6
  and history 75
  JSM's loss of faith in 62–3, 70–5, 78–9,
    96–7, 103, 485
  and pleasure and pain 34–5, 39, 96, 154,
    326, 330–1
  and poetry 20–1, 68, 95–6, 137
  and religion 37, 96
  and rights 329
  and Unitarianism 82
Utilitarianism (Mill) 241, 248
  and Bentham 36, 308, 324–5
  and collective happiness 328–30
  criticism of 325
  and cultivation 289–90, 331
  editions 325, 328
  and ends 326–7, 332–3
  and good life 85–6, 326–32
  and higher and lower pleasures 138,
    330–1
  and justice 329, 382
  and *On Liberty* 329–30
utility principle 35–6, 59, 137, 326, 332

Varouxakis, Georgios 197
venereal diseases, and Contagious
    Diseases Acts 430–4, 435–6, 446
Venn, John 375
Victoria, Queen 134, 180, 190
Victorianism, and JSM 134
Villari, Pasquale 241, 253, 470

Wakley, Thomas 134
Walpole, Spencer 383–4, 391
Ward, Henry George 130
Ward, William George 273
Watts, George Frederic 479, 480, 486
Webb, Beatrice 417, 454
Webb, Sidney 454
Wellington, Arthur Wellesley, 1st Duke
    239
  and Chartism 189
  and JSM 56, 117
  as Prime Minister 42, 54, 80
  and Queen Caroline affair 49
Westminster Reform Association 143

Westminster Review 24, 38, 48, 50, 68, 94–5, 240
  and HTM 218–19
  and JSM 50–1, 157, 162, 163, 177, 183, 323, 335, 349, 453
  and radicalism 186, 335
  see also London and Westminster Review
Wheatstone, Charles 301
Whewell, William 166, 241, 326, 335–6
Whigs
  and history 4, 195–7
  and JM 50
  and JSM 56–7, 101, 158
  and radicals 129–30, 131–4, 141–5, 158, 191, 403, 452
  and reform 76, 88, 94, 101, 143, 146, 190, 232, 238
White, Henry 48
White, Joseph Blanco 102–3
White, William 369
Wilberforce, William 49
Will-o'-the-Wisp 381, 404
William IV 93, 134
Williams, Bernard 35–6
Wollstonecraft, Mary 438
women
  and Comte 199
  control of money 428
  and domestic violence 250, 423
  and domesticity 418–19
  and education 92, 416, 421
  in employment 443–4
  and motherhood 219
  in politics 426–7
  rights 6–7, 52–3, 92–4, 217–19, 229, 304, 308, 322, 413–48, 451–2
  and suffrage 7, 94, 218, 306, 356, 387–9, 412, 415, 422–32, 446–8
  as writers 141
  see also marriage
Wood, Charles 182, 366
Woolf, Virginia 419
Woolner, Thomas 483
Wordsworth, William 20–1, 71–2, 73–4, 103
  and emotion 63–8
  and genius 85
  and imagination 79
  and nature 234
  and politics 64, 88, 120
  The Prelude 27, 68, 276
workhouses 73, 88, 209
working class
  'as liars' 355, 363
  and capitalism 173, 222–4, 454, 467
  and Great Exhibition 231
  and life expectancy 159
  and moral education 224, 238
  and Parliament 239, 308, 310–12, 356–7, 371–3, 390, 402–3, 409, 452–3
  and social reform 171–4, 223
  and socialism 223
  and suffrage 58, 191–2, 239, 309–14, 356, 370–1, 402–3, 412
working hours, regulation 88, 171, 172, 230, 291, 457, 466
Wyatt, Digby 259

Young, Sir John 252–3

Acknowledgements

><

The usual form, I know, is to thank family last: but in this case my partner, Erica Hauver, and my three sons, George, Bryce and Cameron, really must come first. Erica, thank you for your love, faith and patience. I really couldn't have done it without you. Boys, thank you for bearing with both the absences and absent-mindedness of a father immersed for so much of your lives in a mystifying project.

Any Mill scholar is now enormously indebted to John Robson, the overall editor of Mill's *Collected Works*. The volumes have been produced with huge care and sensitivity, and edited flawlessly. This biography is possible only because of the work of Robson and his team at the University of Toronto. I have also relied heavily on the intellectual labours of a number of Mill scholars, most particularly Alan Ryan on Mill's philosophy, Stefan Collini on his place in intellectual history and Bruce Kinzer on his politics. Professor Kinzer has also given his unstinting support to my efforts. To Professor William Stafford I am doubly grateful. First, for his wonderful book on Mill which was one of the factors drawing me towards the writing of this biography and secondly, for reading the whole volume in manuscript and making a range of helpful comments and suggestions. Georgios Varouxakis, a fine analyst of Mill's nationalism and attitude to France, has been a wonderful guide to these areas, but also a steadfast ally and friend, supplying both ideas and inspiration. As the organiser of the Mill Bicentennial Conference in 2006 he provided the setting for a feast of ideas on Mill and an opportunity for me to try out some ideas. Throughout, Georgios has demonstrated, as Herbert Spencer wrote of Mill, 'a generosity that might almost be called romantic'.

Thanks, too, to my friend Simon Burton, who acted as a translator and companion during my research visit to Avignon and has supplied advice, ideas and wine ever since. And to John Knell, my friend and business partner, for understanding, support and diverting conversation. Fred Austin also helped with some translations, for which many thanks. My parents, Margaret and David Reeves, have provided moral support, emergency childcare and, at one crucial stage in the process, a place to work.

My thanks also to the archivists in the British Library of Political and Economic Science and to the librarians of Somerville College, Oxford. I am grateful to the following people in Avignon for their enthusiastic support and assistance: Sylvester Clap at the Archives Municipales; Sabine Barnicaud, the curator of the Palais du Roure – who allowed me to play Mill's piano; Pierre Moulet at the Musée Requien, who opened up Mill's botanical collection; and above all Raphaël Mérindol who acted as a guide and advocate in all matters relating to Mill's time in Avignon.

I am grateful for the keen eyes, thoughtful reading and considerable patience of Sarah Norman, my editor at Atlantic, and for the tenacity and professionalism of Jane Robertson, who copy-edited the book. Toby Mundy at Atlantic is the only publisher for whom one could wish to write such a book.

All the usual disclaimers apply. If you do find any errors, or disagree with any of my opinions, do let me know. I am grateful to all those readers who took the time to point out errors in the previous edition, especially Anthony Skelton and Hilary Spurling. As Mill said, 'we all of us know that we hold many erroneous opinions, but we do not know which of our opinions these are, for if we did, they would not be our opinions'.

4999308